THE
KEY TO
CHINESE
COOKING

THE
KEY TO
CHINESE
COOKING

IRENE KUO

DRAWINGS BY CAROLYN MOY

CALLIGRAPHIC SEALS DESIGNED BY C. C. KUO

Alfred · A · Knopf / New York

19 77

THIS IS A BORZOI BOOK

PUBLISHED BY

ALFRED A. KNOPF, INC.

Copyright © 1977 by Irene Kuo

All rights reserved under International and Pan-American Copyright Conventions. Published in the United States by Alfred A. Knopf, Inc., New York, and simultaneously in Canada by Random House of Canada Limited, Toronto. Distributed by Random House, Inc., New York.

Library of Congress Cataloging in Publication Data

Kuo, Irene. / The key to Chinese cooking.

Includes index.

1.   Cookery, Chinese. / I.   Title.

TX724.5.C5K78 / 641.5'951 / 77-4147

ISBN 0-394-49638-8

MANUFACTURED IN THE

UNITED STATES OF AMERICA

ACKNOWLEDGMENTS

I am sincerely grateful to Suzi Arensberg for her help on this book. Her limited exposure to Chinese cooking when she first started working with me was a great asset because she represented the kind of reader I wanted my book to reach. She tried many of the recipes, asked all the right questions, her responses and her enthusiasm encouraged me, and she edited my writing with superb sensitivity.

And I am forever thankful for my good fortune at having Judith Jones as my editor. By glancing at a few words at a time, she was able to inspire the direction and illuminate the shape and form of this outpouring of my knowledge, my experience, and my love for Chinese cuisine.

CONTENTS

THE
COOKING
TECHNIQUES

INTRODUCTION

Over the centuries, having been alternately buffeted by famine or warfare and blessed with the splendors of a great civilization at peace, the Chinese have had both the dire need to experiment on all things edible for sheer survival and the leisure of prosperity to perfect their cooking techniques for sensual enjoyment. They eat boiled bark, weeds, and roots when there is nothing else; they eat shallow-fried transparent prawns from preference, jasmine blossoms out of poetic sentiment, and wine-braised camel's hump from blatant extravagance. If there is anything the Chinese are perpetually serious about it is food. As the great sage Kwan Tze said in 700 B.C.: "To the ruler the people are Heaven; to the people food is Heaven."

Out of this realistic earthiness, the Chinese developed a healthy respect for food and concluded a long time ago that good eating is always a matter of good cooking, which means knowing the inherent qualities of the food itself and how different techniques can subtly alter flavor and texture. Let's take a boiled chicken as an example.

If we were to simmer a chicken over low heat and serve it sprinkled with a sauce of minced ginger, sherry, sugar, and soy sauce, it would be a soft-textured chicken with a subtle teasing flavor. If we were to simmer it over medium heat and then plunge it into ice water and serve it doused with a mixture of minced ginger and fresh coriander, sherry, sugar, soy sauce, and a touch of hot mustard, it would be a crisp-textured chicken with a stronger aroma and a sharper flavor. And if we were to boil a chicken in water strongly flavored with sherry, soy sauce, star anise, Szechuan peppercorns, and rock sugar, and then let it steep and soak in the sauce off the heat, tightly covered, for a few hours, it would be a firm-textured chicken with a rich, mellow, permeating flavor.

All these dishes are basically boiled chicken, but by applying slightly different seasonings and cooking techniques, the chicken instantly takes on a new personality and makes each dish quite a different one.

Basically, Chinese food is brought from the raw to the cooked stage through four mediums: water, oil, wet heat (steam), and dry heat (roasting). From these, the Chinese have developed an elaborate string of cooking techniques, ranging from the familiar procedures of boiling, simmering, stewing, braising, steeping, steaming, deep-frying, roasting, baking, grilling, barbecuing, curing, preserving, smoking, and the cold-stirring of salads to more specifically Chinese methods, such as stir-frying, red-cooking, pan-sticking, slithering, exploding, plunging, purifying, smothering, mating, nestling, capturing, choking, flavor-potting, light-footing, sizzling, rinsing, scorching, drowning, wine-pasting, and intoxicating.

Most of these terms apply to techniques only professional cooks need to learn. We will confront them only as they might apply to a specific recipe in this book. The major techniques, however, are the subject of the first part of the book.

Many people, while loving Chinese food, are hesitant about cooking it at home because of the prevailing impression that the cuisine is totally committed to tedious cutting and split-second timing. In reality, these are found in but one corner of Chinese cooking—the stir-frying technique. On the whole, preparing a Chinese meal is leisurely and free from tension. There are slow methods of cooking and many recipes use whole or chunky ingredients. Even seemingly complex dishes are fundamentally carefree, since they are based on simple preparational procedures, which can be done long in advance.

The key lies in understanding the basic techniques—how and why they are used, what they will do to food.

The first part of this book is devoted to explaining these techniques. I will show you method by method, using detailed and explicit recipes to illustrate both major points and those subtle fine points that create Chinese cooking. Once you understand them, you will find that Chinese cooking is much easier than you thought and fascinating as well—for you will discover that it is the continual play of these techniques that captures and creates the different flavors and textures.

UTENSILS
AND CUTTING

Before we proceed to discuss techniques and the recipes that demonstrate them, let's have a look at the utensils and cover some of the fine points of cutting.

Utensils

A well-equipped American kitchen is more than adequate to handle Chinese cooking. For years, before Chinese implements were widely obtainable here, I did very well with American cookware; I still do. The only frustration I encountered was when I cooked a large fish whole or tried to toss several pounds of leafy vegetables in a shallow skillet—they were hard to maneuver and tended to cook unevenly. But even these dilemmas can be easily overcome. A sea bass simmers or steams nicely in a Western fish poacher if you raise the level of the handled "plate" with spoons or small saucers and then make a foil receptacle to catch the juices of the fish. It can also deep-fry and steam beautifully in a roasting pan. And 2 to 3 pounds of spinach tumble to perfection in a large soup kettle. However, there are a few special Chinese utensils that are very useful. Once you come to know them, and have developed skill, rhythm, and rapport with them, you will find them versatile, convenient, and great fun to use.

Wok

The wok is a round-bottomed pan that is traditionally made from thin, tempered iron, for the fast conduction of even heat. The name is a romanization of the Cantonese pronunciation for "cooking vessel." Woks range in size from to 12 to 24 inches in diameter and are sold with an aluminum cover and rim collar. The 14-inch size is the most useful; it is large enough to be versatile—providing enough space for spirited stir-frying of a few small-cut ingredients as well as enough depth for the deep-frying, simmering, and steaming of bulky meats, large fowls, and fish—but it is not too large to interfere with the functioning of the other burners on the stove.

Although, today, woks are made in various metals, from thin iron to stainless steel, copper, brass, and aluminum, the first is the best to buy. A 14-inch size should not weigh less than 2¼ pounds, however, so that while the metal is thin enough for the fast spreading of heat it is thick enough so that the oil won't smoke immediately.

A new wok should be seasoned with oil before using it, to prevent food from sticking and the metal from rusting. It should be heated over very low heat, brushed lightly all over with oil, then tilted and rotated while resting on the rim collar so that the oil coats all of the interior. Wipe it clean with paper towels. Oil and wipe clean twice; then rinse it well and dry it thoroughly with a towel or over direct heat. A wok that is well seasoned by repeated use doesn't rust, but it should be oil-treated before storage if you don't use it often, especially when it is new and the metal is still "raw."

The rim collar should be sloping, not straight, and about 2½ inches high. The 9-inch top spreads to about 10½ inches on the bottom. There are holes along the sides for ventilation. Set your wok over the smaller opening when you want less heat, say for simmering, and over the larger one when you want it to be closer to and more engulfed by flames, as for stir-frying. Make certain the rim collar is anchored very securely over the burner, removing the regular burner grid if necessary.

The cover should be well fitting, so as to retain the heat so essential for Chinese cooking.

A wok should not be used on an electric stove. There simply isn't enough heat to engulf the pan for even cooking. If used with the rim collar the wok would be separated from the heat and if put directly on the burner it would perch dangerously, acting like a spinning top. For electric stoves, then, use instead a large, deep skillet to stir-fry neat, compact ingredients and a large soup kettle for bulky, leafy ingredients. And since stir-frying requires the instant raising and lowering of heat, which is impossible to achieve on an electric stove, preheat several units to different levels called for in a recipe; then move the pan swiftly accordingly.

There are electric woks on the market with dial-control heat. I have one and use it frequently for cooking demonstrations. They are satisfactory substitutes for the real thing if your stove is electric, particularly since they eliminate the inconvenience of tying up several burners for one stir-fried dish.

The long-handled Chinese spatula and ladle spoon are sometimes sold with the wok. They are the smaller models of the professional tools used by restaurant cooks. They are meant to be used as a pair, one for each hand, but they are clumsy unless you've been trained to use them. More maneuverable are chopsticks or a small Western spatula. Being light, chopsticks enable you to move your arm and wrist agilely when you are stir-

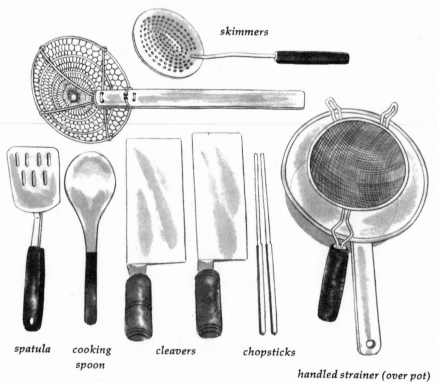

skimmers

spatula   cooking   cleavers   chopsticks
spoon

handled strainer (over pot)

frying in those turning, sweeping, tossing motions. If you are more comfortable with a cooking spoon, by all means stay with it. Cooking tools are extensions of your hands—you should have complete control over them in order for them to perform precisely as you wish.

The Chinese skimmer is made with copper-wire mesh in the shape of a shallow ladle. It is very effective in turning ingredients in hot oil and then scooping them out fast. It is also very useful in velveting or slippery-cooking ingredients, and you may substitute it for the regular-handled strainer in the draining process.

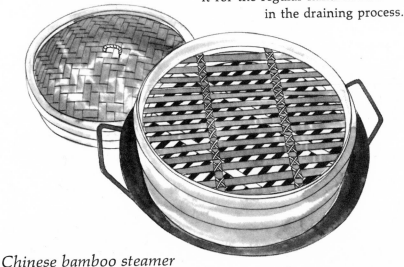

Chinese bamboo steamer

This steamer comes with stacking trays having bottoms made of woven bamboo. The heat then flows over the food. For details on Chinese steamers and making improvised ones, see *page 104* in the steaming section.

Chinese earthenware casserole

This is made of sand and clay and is known as the sandy-pot. It is creamy white outside, with a dark brown glaze inside and over the cover.

It is inexpensive, simmers like a dream, and looks wonderful on the table. It comes either with a long handle on the side or two squared-off ones on the rim. The two-handled one is better for purely aesthetic reasons—it looks as warm as its customary contents. A 2-quart casserole is a good one to buy for general use. You will come to love the sandy-pot as I do. It prevents dissipation of precious liquid during the cooking and it retains heat when on the table.

A sandy-pot is fragile. It should not be heated over intense heat suddenly or without liquid. When ingredients have to be seared first, do them in a skillet and then transfer them to the sandy-pot for the long simmering. The bottom may crack over the years, but as long as the glazed lining inside the pot is intact, it is still usable. On old-fashioned electric stoves that have few gradations of heat use an asbestos pad under the casserole when simmering.

Cutting, Chopping, Slicing

For a Chinese cook, cleavers are indispensable. This preference doesn't come just from sentiment or habit but from the demands of the cuisine itself. Since Chinese cooking involves far more hacking, chopping, mincing, and scraping than Western cooking, it would require an enormous number of different types of knives had the cleaver not been invented. Larger and heavier than regular cutting knives, Chinese cleavers provide both weight (crucial to rough cutting) and dexterity (essential to fine cutting). Once you are familiar with them, you will find they are indeed splendid, irreplaceable tools. But before you use a cleaver, you need something to chop or cut on.

The traditional matchmate for the cleaver is the Chinese chopping block, a cross-section of a hardwood tree trunk measuring about 15 inches in diameter and 6 inches in thickness. Unfortunately, it is rarely sold in Chinese stores anymore, but if you can get one at a wood specialty store or know a woodchopper who will saw you a section from a hardwood tree, you will find it marvelous to use. It is spacious, solid, and porous, qualities that not only make chopping safe but also lend this part of preparing a meal a special resonance.

If you do buy a raw wood cross-section, you must season it first, so that the wood doesn't split on the side. Spread ½ cup oil over the surface, cover with aluminum foil, and let it season for 2 days. Then turn the block over, oil the other surface, and let it sit another 2 days. Wipe the surfaces with paper towels, then lightly sponge them with soap and water. Dry the block thoroughly and it is now ready to use. After each use, scrape the surface with the blunt edge of the cleaver to remove any food residue and then sponge it with soap and hot water. Dry it. Properly cared for, such a chopping block will last a lifetime.

A good substitute for the Chinese chopping block is a large, thick wooden cutting board—at least 12 inches to a side and at least 2 inches thick. Anything smaller will slip away under pressure of heavy chopping. Or a solid butcher's block on legs is, of course, marvelous. Plastic cutting boards are not only rather dangerous but they have no ring to them, no style at all. Make your own choice, but if you do decide on plastic, get the largest, most solid piece you can find.

Chinese cleavers, measuring 3 to 4 inches wide and 8 to 9 inches long, have wooden handles and come in three weights: the light, weighing about ½ to ¾ pound, is for extremely fine and fancy cutting; the medium, weighing about ¾ to 1 pound, is for all standard cutting and for light mincing and chopping; the heavy, 1½ to 2 pounds, is for hard mincing and chopping through meat bones. They are made of stainless steel or tempered carbon steel; the latter is more useful, since it is harder and maintains a sharper cutting edge for a longer time. Contrary to common fears, the sharper the knife, the safer it is. Most accidents occur with the careless handling of dull knives, which tend to slip. A razor-edged cleaver sobers one's mind and sharpens vigilance.

The sharpening of cleavers was considered an advanced task in culinary training in China, the province of the seasoned apprentice. He would hone the tool of the master chef—in either home or restaurant—on a slab of stone that was divided into coarse and smooth surfaces. And for homes that did not have cooks, knife sharpening was generally left to the itinerant professional. It was a thriving trade often handed down for many generations from father to son. Governed by the unwritten laws of territorial propriety, as was the case for food vendors also, a professional sharpener would always work a particular area, sauntering down the streets pushing his wheelbarrow, which sported a pole bent over with a string of metal nuggets, the calling card of the trade. When people heard the "bell," they gathered around him with their cleavers, and he would sharpen them with his slab of abrasive stone attached to a pulley and a foot pedal.

If you will be sharpening your cleaver yourself, buy a small abrasive stone that has a rough and a smooth honing surface—the rough for dull and nicked edges, the smooth for polishing and maintaining knives already in good shape.

First rinse and dry the cleaver thoroughly and sprinkle a few drops of oil or water over the rough side of the stone. Hold the cleaver with the blunt edge right in front of you, almost flat to the surface of the stone. Grip the handle in a tight fist and rest your thumb against this blunt edge. Press the fingers of your other hand on the flat of the cleaver—this position makes the honing easier, the feel of the cleaver light. Rub the sharp edge of the cleaver gently away from you and then back several times, not lifting the cleaver; then grasp the cleaver in your other hand, turning it over as you do so, and rub that side of the edge back and forth a few times.

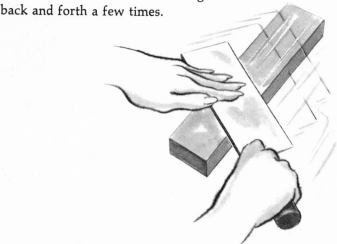

Rinse the cleaver to remove any metal particles and then rub it on the smooth surface of the stone a few times to polish the blade.

Every part of a cleaver is functional: besides cutting, the sharp edge and tip purée and sculpture; the broad side flattens, smashes, and scoops up ingredients like a spatula; the blunt edge tenderizes; and the wooden handle grinds and pulverizes.

Knowing how to hold this multifaceted instrument for different purposes is the deciding factor in whether it becomes a dexterous implement, as it's meant to be, or a clumsy one, as it appears to be.

There are three basic holds: the chopping hold, the mincing hold, and the cutting hold.

THE CHOPPING HOLD—In chopping, the motion occurs in the arm, not the wrist. It is imperative that you chop with firm, decisive strokes so the bones don't splinter. Slide your hand up the handle until your index finger falls naturally around the neck of the blade; curl it firmly as you rest your thumb against the side of the blade or the top—whatever feels steady and natural. The placement of the thumb creates the anchoring force.

THE MINCING HOLD—The motion is in the wrist and the force in the weight of the cleaver. Hold the end of the handle firmly in the palm of your hand; curl your fingers over and around the handle and grip as though in a tight fist. This hold creates a slight imbalance, so that as you tilt and lift the handle, the blade falls downward with its own weight, making mincing fast and easy with practically no exertion on your part. It is even faster if you wield two equal cleavers, working them up and down alternately.

THE CUTTING HOLD—Hold the cleaver as for chopping, but instead of curling your index finger over and around the neck, rest it against the side of the blade on one side as you rest your thumb against the blade on the other side, so that your index finger and thumb are in full control of the blade; then you will be able to tilt and turn the blade as you wish.

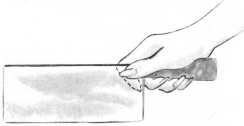

Leaving the specialized cuttings to individual recipes and the heavy chopping, such as cracking through pigs' knuckles, to the butcher, I will describe here the basic and most common cuts in Chinese cooking.

Chopping

Chopping consists of three methods: the straight chop, the mincing chop, and the tenderizing chop.

THE STRAIGHT CHOP—The straight chop is used for cutting ingredients with small and relatively soft bones, such as poultry, spareribs, and fish. Place the cleaver tentatively over the spot at which you want to chop; then, holding the ingredient firmly with one hand as far away from the cleaver as possible, lift the cleaver about 3 inches and bring it straight down, fast and decisively.

To chop poultry: 1) Disjoint the wings; the trick is to snap back the joint and expose the connecting bone. 2) Then slice through the connecting bone at the shoulders and thighs; snap back and cut through, removing leg and thigh on each side. 3) Now turn the body on its side and, with one strong whack with your cleaver at the base of the ribs, separate the breast from the back; you'll probably need to whack firmly a second time to chop through the lower part. Place the breast rib side down and make a guideline cut lengthwise almost down the center but a little to one side of the ridge. 4) Following that line whack the top of your knife with a wooden or rubber mallet to divide the breast into two sections. Then cut each half crosswise into three or four pieces. The work on the breast may look hard at first (and it *is* unusual cutting in Western cuisine), but with practice and convincing chops, you will soon find it easy. 5) Chop each wing and whole leg crosswise, always keeping the turns—the major joints where the upper wing meets the lower and the thigh meets the drumstick—intact. A wing should be cut into three pieces; the leg and thigh into five pieces. Not only are the

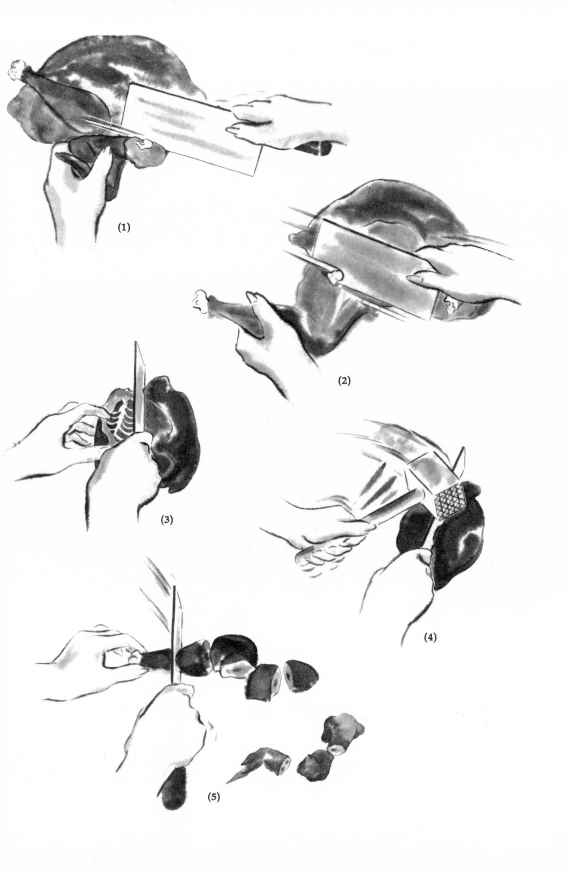

(1)

(2)

(3)

(4)

(5)

soft connecting bones rather nice to eat when intact, but if you're called on to reassemble a cut fowl into a symbolic whole, as many Chinese recipes specify, the result will look much better.

To reassemble a cut fowl: First, place the back pieces down the center of a platter. Place the wings, one on each side, near one end and the legs at the other. Then lay the breast pieces on top of the back pieces. You **may,** if you wish, bone the breasts first.

To chop spareribs: Laying the rack lean side down, cut it into individual ribs. Then, holding each rib firmly, chop it into the desired number of pieces.

For stir-frying, deep-frying, and steaming, spareribs should be chopped into about 1-inch pieces. For simmering, they should be about 1½ to 2 inches long.

To chop a large fish: There are also two ways to do this: either calculate the number and size of pieces you want and chop into crosswise strips or slice through the meat to the bone and then bang the top of the cleaver with a wooden or rubber mallet. Strong Chinese chefs always pound the blunt edges of cleavers with the base of their palms, but it's a risky, potentially bruising business. Do remember that a fish should not be cut in a sawing motion, which leaves the edges messy. Always chop it.

THE MINCING CHOP—The mincing chop is used for mincing meat, seafood, and vegetables from a coarse to a fine texture. As mentioned earlier in this section, mincing is much easier and faster when two equal cleavers are used. Wet them first so that the ingredients won't cake too much on the blades, and keep them clean by occasionally scraping one with the other. There is the basic mince, described below, and the *march-chop*, a polishing finish for refining hand-minced meats or loosening the tight formation of machine-ground meats. Gather minced or ground meat into a flat pile; march-chop straight up and down from one end of the pile to the other a few times. Then flip the pile over with the side of the cleaver and march-chop now at 90 degrees to the first row a few times. This method does wonders for ground meat.

To mince meat, poultry, or seafood: Cut the ingredient into coarse pieces and then place them in a neat pile. Holding either one or two cleavers,

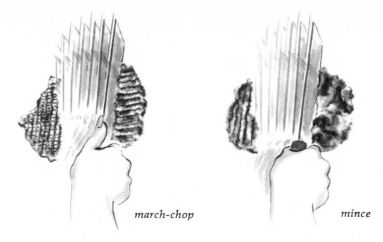

march-chop   *mince*

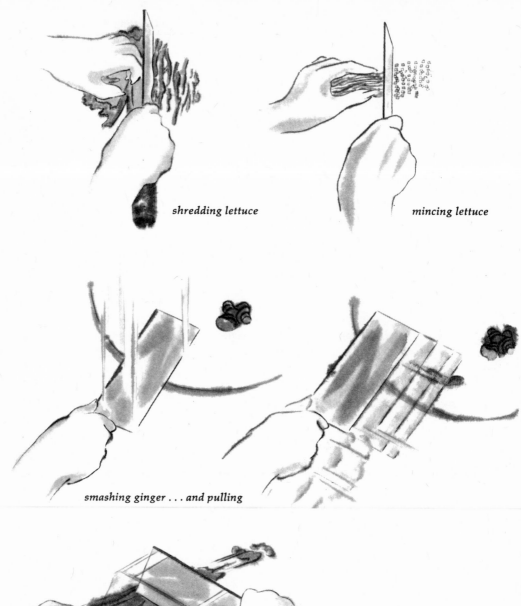

shredding lettuce

mincing lettuce

smashing ginger . . . and pulling

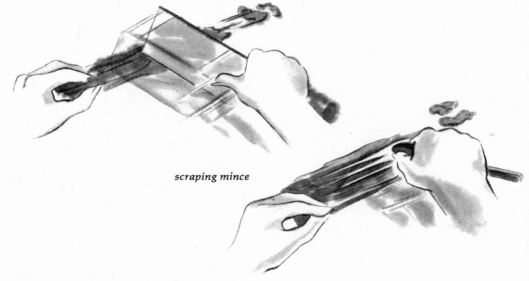

scraping mince

mince from one end of the pile to the other, repeating several times. Then flip the pile over with the side of the cleaver and repeat the mincing and flipping until the ingredient is of a very fine consistency. You may, of course, use a meat grinder to achieve this effect, putting the ingredient through the coarse blade and then march-chopping it to finish, or try a food processor, but if you practice the hand method, you'll find it almost as fast and much more fun.

To mince vegetables: It is much easier to mince vegetables if they're cut neatly before they are minced.

For *leafy vegetables,* such as spinach or parsley: Hold them in bunches and cut fine before mincing.

For *thin-leaved vegetables,* such as lettuce or cabbage: Stack several leaves together, cut in the center to flatten out the curves, and shred them lengthwise; then hold the shreds in bunches and cut fine crosswise before mincing.

For *solid vegetables,* such as carrots or turnips: Peel, slice, shred, and dice before mincing.

Ginger comes in odd knobs. To mince it, slice off a piece the size you need, then trim off the peel. With the broad side of the cleaver 1) smash the piece of ginger and 2) pull the cleaver away—with these motions you break down the fibers. Now mince it. For refined mincing, as called for in a dip sauce, slice the ginger thin, peel, then stack the slices and shred them. Hold the shreds and cut them very closely to yield a fine mince.

Scallions: Since the bulb ends are slippery and roll under pressure of the knife, always flatten them with the broad side of the cleaver before you gather some stalks or sections together and cut them thin. Then mince.

Garlic: The hard work of peeling very fresh garlic cloves is eliminated when you smash them lightly or press them first with the broad side of a cleaver. The skin breaks, and you lift out the meat. Then mince.

The scraping mince is used when you want to purée soft and fine-textured ingredients, such as breast of chicken or fillet of fish, for forming into balls or simmering in creamy soups. Place the whole, uncut ingredient on the chopping board with the membrane side down. Wet the cleaver and, holding it in the cutting position, using the tip end, scrape across the surface in short outward strokes so the meat shaves away. A final mincing will make a smooth paste. You can scrape-mince with a knife or sharp-edged spoon.

The rocking mince is excellent for mincing finely chopped firm-textured ingredients, such as smoked ham, walnuts, or sesame seeds. Its action prevents these tiny hard ingredients from scattering, which an ordinary mince will make them do. Hold the cleaver in the mincing position;

place the tip at the far edge of the piled ingredients and then anchor it down to the board through the ingredients, pressing the blunt edge with the palm of one hand as you lift the handle up and down.
Do this action in semicircles until the
ingredient is powdery.

THE TENDERIZING CHOP—The tenderizing chop is to pound slices of meat on both sides with the blunt edge of the cleaver in a crisscross pattern to break the meat fibers. Tough meats usually become quite tender after pounding and marinating.

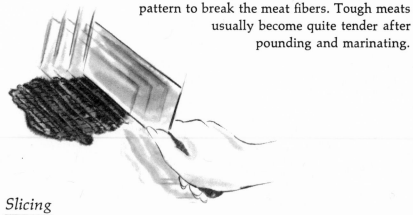

Slicing

Slicing also consists of three basic methods: the straight slice, the slanting cut, and the roll cut.

THE STRAIGHT SLICE—Used to cut meat or vegetables into the desired size, using the given thickness of the ingredient. Meats are easier to slice when they are frozen and much tenderer when they are cut across the grain. Put the ingredient on your chopping board and hold it with one hand, fingers tucked under, so that the middle knuckles of your index, middle, and fourth fingers form a protective shield as well as a cutting guide. The flat side of the cleaver will rest ever so slightly against your protruding knuckles as you cut straight down. Slide your fingers back evenly with each cutting so that the slices are uniform. When cutting meat, as you finish each

slice press it over onto the board with
the other side of the cleaver, so that in
the end you will have a slanting stack
of meat. This makes any further
shredding or dicing easier. "Paper-thin"
means the slices should be about
$\frac{1}{16}$ inch thick; "thin" about $\frac{1}{8}$ inch
thick; and "medium" about $\frac{1}{4}$ inch thick.

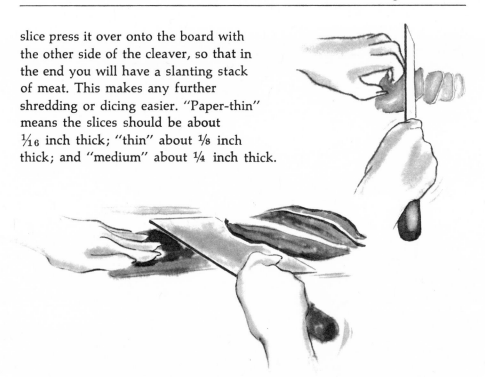

THE SLANTING CUT—Used when you want the slices to be
larger than the width and thickness of the ingredient by itself would allow—
such as those that can be created from a thin piece of flank steak or a stalk of
asparagus. Place the ingredient on the chopping board and make a diagonal
cut at the tip of the ingredient; then follow the slant and slice down to the
end for longer pieces or tilt the cleaver back slightly and almost shave from
the top so that the pieces are not only longer but wider as well.

THE ROLL CUT—Used when you wish to obtain many exposed
surfaces. When roll-cut, fibrous vegetables
such as carrots, turnips,
and asparagus

cook faster and absorb more flavor from the seasonings or sauce and meats release more flavor in a shorter time when simmered in stocks. Place the ingredient on the chopping board and make a diagonal cut at the end of it; then roll the ingredient a quarter turn and cut again; turn and cut in this fashion to the end. Instead of even slices, triangle-like pieces appear, with three exposed surfaces.

Shredding is cutting ingredients into uniform strips about the size of wooden matchsticks. The easiest way is to straight-slice the ingredient first (*see page 20*) and press or let each slice fall neatly into an overlapping stack like a flat staircase; then cut crosswise into shreds at even intervals. Shreds usually measure about ⅛ by ⅛ inch or ¼ by ¼ inch in width and about 1½ to 2 inches in length.

Dicing is cutting ingredients into small cubes. Slice and shred first; then hold the shreds together and cut them into dice. Dice range from ⅛ inch to ½ inch to a side. When dice are 1 inch to a side they are called cubes.

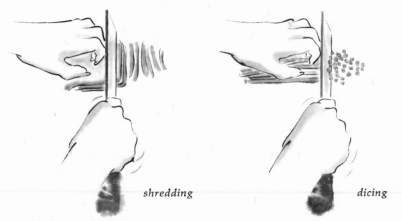

shredding   dicing

Freezing meat or chicken breast for three to four hours, until firm, makes cutting neater and much easier. But you do have to plan for the extra time this partial freezing involves; if you leave the meat in the freezer too long, until it is solid, then you have the frustrating problem of thawing it before you can cut it properly. So, for general purposes, don't bother with the partial freezing unless you can work it easily into your schedule. The one exception, when partial freezing is essential, is when "paper-thin slices" are required—as for the Chrysanthemum Pot.

Boning and skinning a whole fowl

These procedures, special to just a few recipes in this book, are described in the poultry chapter, *pages 283 and 303.*

How to Hold and Use Chopsticks

Chopsticks are not indispensable to Chinese dining or cooking except to those who have used them since childhood. But it's nice to know how to use them and they are not difficult to master once you get the knack of holding them correctly.

Chopsticks are made of gold, silver, ivory, ivory trimmed with gold, silver, or jade, polished bone, plastic, lacquered wood, and plain bamboo. The bamboo ones, though not elegant, are very practical. They are less "slippery" in hands that are not used to them, are easy to maintain, extremely inexpensive, and widely available; and they may be used for cooking as well as eating. They are about 10½ inches long—square on the top half for holding and round on the bottom half for eating or cooking.

The principle of chopsticks lies in holding two sticks in one hand but keeping one stick firm and stationary at the bottom and the other movable on top, so that the ends may be widened and tightened to slip over, pick up, and hold the food like a pair of tongs. For eating, they should be held three-quarters up from the tip ends, leaving about 4 inches of stick free and clear; for cooking, they should be held halfway down from the top, leaving about 6 inches.

The easiest way to form a correct basic hold is 1) to first stiffen out your hand with your fingers pointed straight forward. 2) Then curl back your fingers, except your thumb, and part them slightly into two units, with your curved index fingertip resting over the first joint of your curved middle finger as one unit, and your curved fourth fingertip resting over your curved little finger as another unit, leaving a small gap between the two.

3) Place the upper part of one chopstick within the crook of your thumb and rest the lower part over your fourth finger, keeping it firm by pressing *down* with the base of your thumb and pressing *up* with your fourth finger, reinforcing the pressure with your little finger acting as a supporter. 4) Then place the other chopstick over the first joint of your middle finger and bring your index finger over the stick and close your thumb tip over to form a triangle hold as if you were holding a pencil for writing. 5) Now, when you want to widen the space between the tips for grasping food, lift the top unit up by tilting up and stretching forward your

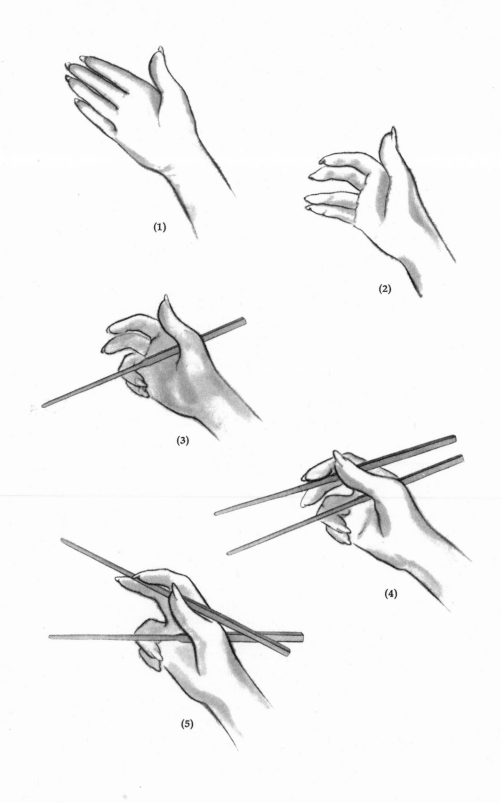

(1)

(2)

(3)

(4)

(5)

middle finger; and when you want to narrow the gap for holding the food, bring the top unit down by dropping your middle finger over the bottom stick. In each case your middle finger is the controlling factor. Your index finger and thumb tip are general stabilizers; they go along with the middle finger, helping to hold the movable stick in its place.

There are many individual ways of holding chopsticks, even among Chinese—subtle variations that seem to work for different people's hands, but the basic principle is the same: to keep the bottom chopstick firm, and the top one movable. Some people use the tip of the fourth finger to rest the bottom chopstick against, others may even use the third finger, as well, to give support to the bottom chopstick. But, in trying some of these variations, be sure that the points of the chopsticks are even. The important thing is that when you feel at ease and your hand is not straining, then that is the right way for you.

Chopsticks are capable of picking up any form of cut ingredients. For chunks, cubes, slices, and shreds: Make the basic hold; widen to appropriate width, slip over the piece or pieces, then tighten the ends to hold the food securely. For minced ingredients and rice: Make the basic hold; widen the space to about 2 inches, slip the chopsticks around the food, then tighten the gap slowly in a scraping motion to scoop up the food over the chopsticks. For whole meat or poultry: Make the basic hold; push the tips of the sticks through the meat and widen them to separate one piece partially from the main body; then slip your chopsticks over the separated piece, tighten the ends, and pull the piece off completely.

Light, smooth, and dainty, chopsticks are marvelous implements for stir-frying, shallow-frying, and deep-frying, since they may be used to slip around and under cuts of ingredients in fast tossing and turning motions. They are also wonderful for preparing food—they whip, beat, stir, and mix like a dream.

Don't despair if you can't get the knack of using chopsticks right away. Keep practicing.

COOKING
IN LIQUID

Chinese cooking that involves water consists of two types of stocks—the clear (chicken) and the rich (meat); three categories of soups—the simmered, the poached, and the "mixed" soups; and five types of main dishes—the clear-simmered, the white-cut, the salt-water-marinated and salt-cured, the red-cooked, and the flavor-potted. Let's take the stocks first.

•

Fukien, a southeast coastal province of China, is best known for its stocks, soups, and soupy dishes. Not until a Fukien cook came to work for my family in Shanghai when I was a little girl did I realize what an extraordinary amount of time and care went into the cooking of these exceptional broths.

Some of his secrets are too involved and elaborate for modern cooking, but, with modifications, they are invaluable and timeless.

To him, the minimal requirement of a kitchen was always having on hand one clear stock and one rich stock. I fully agree, for stocks are the foundations of good soups and enhance the flavors of food in general cooking, especially for vegetables. This book uses chicken stock more often than meat stock. Whether or not you do a lot of soup making, it is always a good idea to have some frozen stock on hand for that moment you need some but don't have the time to make it up fresh. The main point is that it should be homemade, not doctored from a can, since any canned product has some artificial flavorings.

In the grand old style, our Fukien cook used equal parts of ingredients and water, stating that even a slight increase of water would degenerate stocks into insipid "rinse water," which naturally is an exaggeration. Translating his measurements into ours, it would be 1 pound of meat or poultry to 2 cups of water, which made his stocks uncommonly rich. A nice modification is 1 pound of meat or poultry to about 3 cups of water.

He would bone the pork and chicken. The meat was then sliced into small diagonal pieces, so that a maximum amount of surface was exposed to release taste. The bones were chopped, smashed, or hacked for complete rendering of their hidden flavors. In principle, boning is sound, but we can also modify this by chopping the pork or chicken into very small pieces. After all, the meat will separate from the bones during the long process of cooking. When hard bones, such as ham bone, knuckles, or pigs' feet, are used, it definitely enhances the density and flavor of the rich (meat) stock if they are hacked or sawed into small pieces—if not by you then by your butcher.

He used only earthenware pots for the clear (chicken) stocks, so their clarity wouldn't be contaminated by metallic tastes, and heavy cast-iron pots for the rich (meat) stocks, so the precious brew wouldn't be dissipated because of the faster heating properties of thinner metals. One can't dispute the wisdom of using heavy, well-made pots and pans with good, tight-fitting covers. And the virtues of an earthenware pot are many.

To summarize all his other fine points of stock making: First, fat hens are the base for clear stock. A buxom hen, with plenty of fat underneath its skin, indeed makes the stock richer, mellower, and more flavorful. But since they are difficult to buy and rather costly, I have found roasting chickens to be excellent substitutes.

Pork and bones are the base for rich stocks.

Both stocks are cooked the same way: The ingredients are cooked in cold water to start, and then they simmer until the meat almost disintegrates, at which point they are strained through layers of cheesecloth to remove bone splinters, specks of fiber, and fat. The seasonings are added at two different times. Ginger and scallions are cooked with the ingredients from the beginning, acting as neutralizing agents to soften odor. Salt and sometimes sherry are added at the very end to bring the flavor to life.

When completed, the two stocks are treated a little differently. For chicken stock, a little fat is purposely left in, so that the broth will be silky. For meat stock, all excess fat is removed, so it won't be heavy.

Stocks

上 CHICKEN STOCK
湯

Since stock is basically a component ingredient, you can really cheat a little by removing some of the meat–say the breasts or legs–after the first 30 to 40 minutes of full simmering; thus you will have a tenderly cooked piece of chicken to use for a meal. If you plan to do this, keep whatever you want to remove whole or in large pieces and add that portion only after the water has come to a boil; that way the flesh will retain its flavor. Then bone this portion and return bones to stock. This act of impropriety would upset a purist, of course, but it doesn't really upset the stock and, of course, it makes the chicken go farther. *This recipe makes about 3 quarts.*

1 roasting chicken, about 4 pounds	1 whole scallion
4 quarter-sized slices peeled ginger, about ⅛ inch thick (*see below*)	3 quarts cold water
	2 teaspoons salt, or to taste

Remove the fat from the cavity and cut off the tail. Rinse the chicken in cold water and swish out the cavity to remove all attaching tissues and loose blood clots—they cloud the clarity of the broth.

Slice through the chicken at the wing and leg joints and chop the wings and legs into about 1-inch pieces, as described on *page 14*. Turn the chicken on its side and chop through it lengthwise to separate the breast from the back. Chop the breast and back sections in two lengthwise and then chop these sections crosswise into 1-inch pieces.

Slice off four ⅛-inch-thick pieces from a large knob of ginger, then trim off the peel. The pieces should approximate the size of an American quarter coin. Rinse the scallion, trim off the root, and leave it whole, including green part.

Place the chicken, ginger, and scallion in a large, heavy pot. Add the cold water and bring it to a brisk boil. Turn heat low and with a large spoon wrapped in cheesecloth skim off the foam with the motion of a bird gliding over a lake, darting and dipping in wherever this foam appears. When the liquid is clear, turn heat higher and bring to a boil again, then adjust the heat to maintain a very gentle simmer, with sporadic bubbles rising lazily to the surface. Cover and simmer 3 to 4 hours, stirring once in a while to give the chicken room to relax and expand. The simmering, after the initial stage, may be interrupted at any time; you may turn off the heat and resume at your convenience.

Let the broth cool a little. Line a large strainer or colander with 3 layers of cheesecloth and place it over a large pot. Pour in the broth and let it strain through. Remove the large bones and then dump in all the chicken. Pick up the cheesecloth by its corners, twirl them together, and wring out all the remaining juice. Discard the meat and bones. If the stock still contains some specks of impurities, rinse out the cheesecloth, wring it dry, and repeat the straining. Season the stock with salt to taste but with a restrained hand, since more seasonings will be added when the stock is used for soup bases and general cooking.

Now you have a delicious golden broth, very flavorful and chickeny. It is covered with a layer of shiny transparent fat. If you are bottling it for future use, leave the fat in as a seal, removing it only before reheating the stock. If you are using the stock immediately, skim off most, but not all, of the fat. A little is essential to the well-being of a good chicken stock; it is the oil that makes a stock smooth, mellow, and fragrant.

The stock keeps well for 4 to 5 days in the refrigerator and for months in the freezer.

VARIATIONS

A nice stock can also be made from the pieces of poultry that are accumulated in an active kitchen, such as the backs, bones, wings, skin, and trimmings. Freeze them until you have enough. If you do this, use only enough water to cover the bones, and don't use a very wide pot, lest the water reduce too much.

You could even use the carcass of a roasted turkey or duck, chopped and covered with water. The first stock, rather milky, may be used for soups as well as for general cooking, but the latter, strongly tasting of duck, can be used only for a soup base or for simmering vegetables like turnips or cabbage or vegetarian products like bean curd and transparent noodles—when you definitely want that duck taste.

濃
湯　MEAT STOCK

This is a thick, delicious, rich stock. *Makes about 2½ quarts.*

2 pounds boneless pork, shoulder
　　or butt
2 pounds pork bones, neck, ham
　　bone, or ribs (or assorted
　　trimmings)
8 slices ginger, unpeeled, each
　　about ⅛ inch thick

2 large whole scallions, or
　　4 small ones
3 quarts cold water
1 to 2 teaspoons salt, to taste
2 tablespoons dry sherry

Cut the boneless pork into 1½-inch-wide strips and then cut them into small diagonal pieces. Have your butcher hack or saw the bones into 1-inch pieces. If such service is unavailable, wrap the bones in a towel and crack them with a hammer into pieces. Remove all sharp splinters.

Slice the ginger. Peeling is not necessary in this stock; in fact, the peel will add a little stronger ginger flavor, which is desirable in a rich stock. Rinse the scallions and leave them whole.

Place the meat, bones, ginger, and scallions in a large, heavy pot that has a well-fitting cover. Pour in the 3 quarts cold water. Bring the liquid to a brisk boil over high heat and then adjust the heat to maintain a faint simmer. Skimming is not necessary, since clarity is not important to a rich stock. Cover and simmer for 4 to 5 hours, stirring once in a while to give the meat room to relax and expand. Just as with the chicken stock, the simmering may be interrupted and resumed at your convenience.

Let it cool a little. Line a strainer or colander with 3 layers of cheesecloth and place it over a large pot. Pour the broth into the strainer and let it filter through. Pick out and discard all the large bones but leave the meat. Lift up the four corners of the cheesecloth, twirl them together, and wring out to extract all the juice. Discard the remaining meat and bones.

There will be a great deal of transparent fat on top, which must be completely removed. If you make the stock a few hours before using it, you could refrigerate it and remove the fat when solid. If you want to use the stock at once, the most effective way to skim off fat is to tilt a large spoon against the edge of the pot at the fat line. When it is filled, remove and discard. Repeat until the stock is clear of fat. If there are specks of glistening grease, drop in a corner of dry cheesecloth and gently pull it over the surface until they are eliminated. Season the stock with a little salt and sherry to taste.

If you are bottling the stock, skimming is omitted at this time, since the fat will act as a seal. Lift off the solid fat just before reheating the stock for use. This rich stock keeps about the same length of time as the light stock, 4 or 5 days in the refrigerator and for months in the freezer. If you are going to store it for a long time, however, *do* remove the fat before freezing, or it will turn slightly rancid and spoil the stock.

This stock is rich and flavorful, an excellent base for hearty soups and for enriching bland dishes. Added in jellied form to fillings for steamed or shallow-fried dumplings, it melts into a luscious gravy.

VARIATION

The combination of 2 pounds pork bones—neck, knuckles, or feet— or gristly parts of spareribs and 2 pounds chicken backs will yield a good, milky stock. Chop them into manageable pieces. Heat the soup pot over high heat until hot; add 2 tablespoons oil, swirl, and heat until hot. Add the ingredients and stir rapidly until they are superficially whitened. Add the ginger and scallions, and 2 to 2½ quarts water. When it boils, turn heat low, cover, and simmer for 2 to 3 hours. Strain, add salt to taste, skim, and use or bottle.

Soups

Chinese soups have an entirely different status from Western soups. Not served as a prelude to the meal itself, they are an integral part of all informal meals, because the principle of Chinese dining, with the exception of banquets, is that all the dishes of a meal are served simultaneously for communal sharing. And, since water is never served and tea is presented only before or after a meal, the soup performs the dual role of being something good to eat as well as a delicious liquid to quench one's thirst. Always set in the center of the dining table, surrounded by the other dishes, the soup is taken by the diners at random throughout the meal. Of course, you have the option to serve soup either the Western or Chinese way.

Even though frugality is considered a virtue, few Chinese ever condone skimping on soups, for they regard them as sources of rich nourishment and seductions for dull appetites.

In spite of their scope, Chinese soups are fundamentally simple. They may be classified into three types—the simmered, the poached, and the "mixed" ones. In general, they consist of a stock or water base with main ingredients (usually meaning meats) and secondary ingredients (vegetables and vegetarian products). For simmered and poached soups, the secondary ingredients are proportionately fewer in quantity, acting as garnishes or providing variety of taste and texture. "Mixed" soups are made of whatever you have on hand, and there is no distinction between main and secondary ingredients.

Simmered soups

Simmered soups are what the Chinese call the "big affairs"; they are generally hearty, rich, and substantial, if not in density, at least in appearance. They are natural brews, with little or no seasonings other than ginger, scallions, salt, and sherry. The most popularly used main ingredients are pork and chicken. Lamb and innards are regional or personal choices. Beef, not a Chinese staple, is used sparingly. But a dense soup, similar to a rich bouillon, is occasionally made as a tonic, particularly for a convalescent. Exotic ingredients such as sharks' fins, birds' nests, or turtle are reserved for festive occasions and formal entertainment.

The cuttings for simmered soups are chunky; frequently meats and fowls are left whole, to preserve their impressive appearance as well as their essence. They are always put into boiling water rather than cold water, so that they don't give up all their flavor to the broth. They are simmered until tender, but never to the point of disintegration. The aim of a good simmered soup is to obtain delicious liquid as well as tasty morsels of food.

蘿蔔肉湯 PORK AND RADISH SOUP

This typical simmered soup is nourishing, delicious, and simple to make. The meat can be any pork cut, with or without bones. The vegetable can be white or red radishes, or icicle turnips. In spite of their light consistency, these vegetables are amazingly durable—they withstand long simmering and soaking without disintegrating. You may make this soup hours or even a day in advance and reheat it just before serving.

The meaty broth is light amber in color, the chunks of meat and radish or turnip tender and juicy. If you use turnips, they impart a faintly sweet taste to the soup. *Makes about 6 cups.*

1 pound pork shoulder or butt, cubed, or meaty spareribs, chopped
½ pound white or red radishes, or icicle turnips

4 cups water
4 quarter-sized slices peeled ginger
Salt to taste

Cut the meat into ½-inch cubes; if you use spareribs, cut between the ribs and then chop each rib into 2 or 3 pieces—it's easier, and the bones won't splinter, if you place the ribs curved side (bony side) up to chop them.

Trim, wash, and peel the radishes; cut the white ones crosswise in two; leave the red ones whole. If you use icicle turnips, peel and then roll-cut them into pieces approximately the size of the meat chunks. The roll cut is used for all firm or tubular vegetables to present more exposed surface, for deeper cooking and absorption of flavor. Lay the turnip across the cutting board; make a small slanting cut through the end and then roll the vegetable each time a quarter turn as you continue cutting it through on the slant (see illustration, *page 21*). This cutting will give you trianglelike pieces with 3 exposed surfaces.

Bring 4 cups water to a boil with the ginger. Add the meat, and when the water boils again, turn the heat low, skimming the surface until clear. Bring to a boil again and then adjust the heat to maintain a weak simmering. Cover and simmer for 1½ hours, stirring once in a while. Season with salt to taste.

Add the radishes or turnips and simmer another 30 minutes, covered. Remove the excess fat by spooning off the transparent layer; scoop out the ginger and discard. Adjust taste with salt. Pour the soup into a hot serving bowl.

VARIATION

You can use the more familiar white turnip, but to offset its heavier texture and stronger turnip taste add a small piece of ham bone, a little more meat, or a small smoked knuckle with a little more water to bring up the meat taste.

冬
菇
鷄
湯
CHICKEN WITH BLACK MUSHROOM SOUP

This simmered soup gives you a very well cooked whole chicken and a broth that has been lightened by the subtle taste and aroma of dried black mushrooms. The touch of ground Szechuan peppercorns in the dip sauce gives this essentially delicate chicken just the right amount of exotic spiciness.

The parboiling of the chicken not only seals in the flavor but also prevents an initial cloudy residue, thus making the broth very clear.

This is a substantial eating-soup. Serve the chicken whole in the soup, ensconced in a deep bowl or tureen. The dip sauce should be in individual saucers. The server can tear off pieces of meat with a fork or chopsticks to be put into soup bowls along with a little broth and a few mushrooms. *The recipe will serve 6 to 8* and any leftover chicken can be used for one of the cold salads.

1 small roasting chicken, about 4 pounds	*Individual dip sauce:*
9 to 10 cups water	1 tablespoon light soy sauce
2 quarter-sized slices peeled ginger, each ⅛ inch thick	1 teaspoon sesame seed oil
12 medium dried black Chinese mushrooms (presoaked)	Sprinkling roasted and crushed Szechuan peppercorns (*see below*)
1 tablespoon dry sherry	
Salt to taste	

Discard the fat from the cavity, cut off the tail, and rinse the chicken in cold water. Bring a large pot of water to a boil over high heat and plunge in the chicken; when the water comes to a boil again let the chicken cook for 1 minute to firm the skin. Then remove it and rinse it briefly with running warm water to rid it of foam.

Bring the 9 to 10 cups water to a boil with the ginger slices in a deep pot that fits the chicken snugly. Add the chicken, and when the water boils again turn the heat down to maintain a weak simmer. Cover, and simmer for 1½ hours, turning the chicken several times so that it cooks evenly.

While the chicken is simmering, cover the mushrooms with 1 cup hot water and soak for 30 minutes. Squeeze them lightly dry over the soaking bowl; then rinse them in cold water to remove sand. Cut off and discard the stems, add the caps to the soup, and strain in the soaking liquid without the sandy residue. Cover and simmer for another 30 minutes or a little longer. Add the sherry and season with salt to taste.

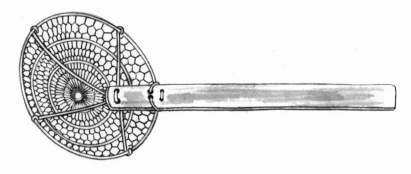

Roasting the peppercorns

While the soup is cooking, roast 1 tablespoon Szechuan peppercorns in a dry frying pan over very low heat for about 5 minutes, shaking the pan or raking the peppers occasionally, until you can smell the aroma and they are smoking faintly. Let them cool, then either roll them with a rolling pin or crush them with a mortar and pestle. This roasting and crushing bring out their flavor and they remain aromatic for a long time. Mix with other sauce ingredients.

VARIATIONS

A number of other ingredients in small quantities can be added as embellishment or extender when you wish to serve a larger soup. Add alone or in combination 8 to 12 slices of cooked Smithfield ham or substitution for it (*page 492*), each about 2 inches long, 1 inch wide, and ¼ inch thick, and ¾ to 1½ cups roll-cut spring or regular bamboo shoots.

Poached soups

While simmered soups emphasize drawing flavors from the main ingredients through long simmering and mixed soups from added seasonings, poached soups emphasize independent flavors. The intrinsic flavors of the ingredients and the broth are purposely left alone so that each can be tasted simultaneously.

Poached soups result from the fast cooking of pieces of meat, chicken, or seafood and leafy or crisp vegetables in a rich stock or seasoned water. The main ingredients are generally sliced, marinated, and coated with cornstarch or egg white and then parboiled before they are poached in the liquid very briefly, so that the meat is tender, the vegetables are crisp, and the broth is clear.

There are deviations—some poached soups are created right out of a frying pan. The ingredients are stir-fried with seasonings, or sometimes shallow-fried if a whole fish is involved, then stock or water is added and simmered into a soup. The broth in these cases is not clear; more often it is slightly thickened or milky.

PORK AND CUCUMBER SOUP

黄瓜肉片湯

This soup demonstrates the essence of poaching, offering a full-flavored meat, refreshingly crisp cucumbers, and a savory stock. It is clear and uncomplicated, each flavor coming through on its own. *Makes about 5 cups.*

2 center-cut loin chops (about ½ pound with the bone in)

Marinade:
1 tablespoon light soy sauce
1 tablespoon dry sherry
1 tablespoon cornstarch dissolved in 1 tablespoon water
2 teaspoons oil

1 medium-sized cucumber
4 cups chicken or meat stock
½ to 1 teaspoon salt, to taste
Chopped fresh coriander (optional)
Sesame oil (optional)

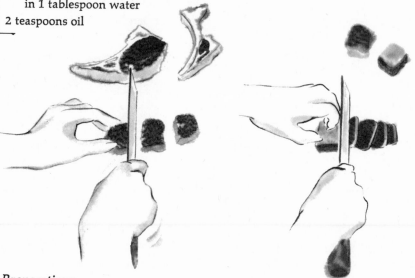

Preparations

Remove the bones and trim the fat from the pork chops. First cut each chop into 3 sections; then turn each section on its cut surface and cut lengthwise into ⅛-inch-thick slices. By turning the meat on its cut side to slice it, you are cutting against the grain, or the fibers, of the meat. Cutting meat against the grain cannot be overemphasized—it breaks the tough fibers, thereby making the meat tenderer and smoother when cooked.

Toss the meat into a bowl, separating the pieces if any are attached. Add the marinade, mix to coat evenly, and refrigerate the meat for 30 minutes or longer to set the coating.

Rinse the cucumber and cut off both ends. Peel and then cut it in half lengthwise; scrape out the seeds with a spoon. Slice the halves crosswise into pieces a little thicker than ⅛ inch. Set aside.

Bring 3 cups water to a boil in a small saucepan; turn the heat down to maintain a slow simmering. Give the meat a few gentle stirs to separate the slices, and then scatter these into the water. Stir them gently until the water comes to a boil again and the coating has firmed—this should take about 1 minute. Immediately pour through a colander to drain; then place the meat on a dish, covering and refrigerating until ready to use. This step may be done hours in advance.

Simmering the soup

Bring the stock to a gentle simmer in a pot. Add the meat; when the stock comes to a simmer again, turn heat low, cover, and simmer for 3 minutes. Add the cucumber; when the stock simmers again, cover and cook 1 more minute. Turn off the heat and add salt to taste. Pour the soup into a serving bowl. You may add a little chopped coriander and 1 teaspoon sesame oil for a stronger flavor and aroma.

VARIATIONS

Substitute ½ pound sliced chicken breast (*page 76*) for the pork, using ½ teaspoon salt instead of the light soy sauce in the marinade. Then proceed with the rest of the recipe. For further variation, you may enhance the color and flavor by floating in a few thin slices of cooked Smithfield ham or one of its substitutes (*page 492*) during the last 2 minutes of cooking.

西洋菜鷄片湯 CHICKEN AND WATERCRESS SOUP

Coated with egg white and cornstarch to make it white and velvety, the delicate chicken is contrasted with the crisp green watercress and flavorful red ham in this poached soup. *Makes about 5 cups.*

½ pound boneless and skinless chicken breast

Velvet coating:
½ teaspoon salt
1 egg white
2 teaspoons cornstarch
2 teaspoons oil

1 bunch watercress
¼ cup sliced cooked Smithfield ham (*page 492*) or a substitute
4 cups chicken stock
½ to 1 teaspoon salt to taste
1 tablespoon dry sherry (optional)

Preparations

Cut the meat crosswise, against the grain, into ⅛-inch-thick slices— if the chicken breast is very wide, cut it in half lengthwise before slicing.

Place the slices in a bowl and sprinkle with ½ teaspoon salt. Beat the egg white just enough to break the gel, add to the chicken, and then blend in the cornstarch and the oil, stirring until the mixture is smooth. Let the coating set in the refrigerator for at least 30 minutes. This may be done hours in advance.

Bring a small saucepan of water to a boil and then adjust the heat to maintain a slow simmering. Give the chicken a few gentle stirs with chopsticks or a wooden spoon and then scatter into the water, stirring gently to separate the pieces until they are firm and white—about 40 seconds. Pour both water and chicken into a colander to drain, then place the meat on a plate. This "velveting" may be done in advance; cover and refrigerate until ready to use. (A full discussion of velveting begins on *page 75*.)

Cut off the long stems of the watercress and rinse the leaf clusters in cold water. Cut the ham into slices about ⅛ inch thick and 1½ inches long.

When ready to serve, bring a saucepan of water to a rolling boil. Plunge in the watercress and stir to submerge the leaves, then pour water and watercress immediately into a colander. This scalding procedure is to prevent the vegetable from diluting the flavor of the stock. Scatter the drained watercress over the bottom of your serving bowl or tureen.

Final cooking

Bring the stock to a gentle boil in a heavy soup pot. Add the chicken and ham, lower heat to maintain a gentle simmering, cover, and simmer for 2 minutes. Add the salt and sherry to taste, and then pour the soup over the watercress and serve.

VARIATION

Two cups of small young spinach leaves may be substituted for the watercress. Rinse carefully to remove sand and scald them as done with the watercress.

榨菜粉絲湯 SPICY TRANSPARENT-NOODLE SOUP

This is an example of a stir-fried poached soup. The pork is stir-fried in oil with seasonings to acquire a deeper flavor with the spicy Szechuan preserved mustard stems. Then water is poured in to make a broth before the transparent noodles are added for a very brief simmering. Seasoned with sesame oil, black pepper, and minced coriander, it's a refreshingly spicy soup that takes no time at all to make. *Makes about 5 to 6 cups.*

¼ pound lean pork, loin or butt,
  shredded

Marinade:
1 teaspoon light soy sauce
1 teaspoon dry sherry

¼ cup shredded Szechuan preserved mustard greens
2 ounces transparent noodles,
  presoaked for 15 minutes

2 quarter-sized slices peeled ginger
1 tablespoon finely chopped fresh
  coriander or scallion greens
2 tablespoons oil
4 cups water or stock
¼ teaspoon salt
1 tablespoon light soy sauce
  to taste
2 teaspoons sesame oil
Black pepper to taste

Preparations

Slice the meat against the grain into shreds about 1½ inches long. Toss the shreds in a mixing bowl. Add the marinade, mix well, and let the meat marinate while you prepare the vegetables.

The preserved mustard greens come in a can and are very salty and spicy. They make a tasty seasoning agent—having a remarkable crisp texture and an unusual fresh aroma. The knobby stems are covered with a film of ground chili peppers and come in lumpy chunks. Select a piece with a tender head; rinse it in cold water, then cut it into shreds, comparable to the meat shreds.

Soak the transparent noodles in hot water; then drain and cut them into 3- to 4-inch lengths. The soaking of transparent noodles need not be a stumbling block to the spontaneity of your wish to use them—they can be soaked in warm water at any time until softened. Then cover with cold water and refrigerate for 2 to 3 days for instant use. The water should be changed every other day.

Shred the ginger, and set it and the finely chopped coriander or scallions on a small dish. Gather all the other seasoning ingredients and place within reach.

Stir-frying and making the soup

Heat a wok or large, heavy pot over high heat until very hot; add the oil, swirl, and heat 30 seconds. Scatter in the meat and stir in rapid shaking and turning motions to sear shreds in the hot oil for about 30 seconds—until they are no longer pink. Add the ginger and coriander or scallions and stir a few times. Then add the shredded mustard stems and stir in fast tossing and flipping motions to mingle them well. Add the water; when it comes to a boil, scatter in the transparent noodles, add the salt, even out the contents of the pan, turn heat low to maintain a gentle simmering, cover, and simmer for 2 to 3 minutes. Season with soy sauce to taste, add the sesame oil and pepper, and serve.

VARIATION

If you like the meat softer, add 2 teaspoons cornstarch and 2 teaspoons oil to the marinade and let meat set 30 minutes in the refrigerator before stir-frying as before. The soup is then very faintly thickened.

"Mixed" soups

The "mixed" soups are a conglomeration of diversified tastes and textures. They range from the mild and smooth to the sharp and textured, as exemplified by Egg-Drop Soup and Hot and Sour Soup.

In general, they are short-order soups of easily cooked or finely chopped ingredients. Some involve no more than the collision and fusing of hot liquid with seasonings or ingredients placed in the serving bowl.

The basic cooking techniques are simple, a matter of simmering mixtures of minced, shredded, or diced raw, precooked, or leftover meats, poultry, seafood, and vegetables in stock or water; thickening with beaten eggs, egg whites, or dissolved cornstarch; and seasoning with soy sauce, sesame oil, and one or all of the sharper seasonings, such as black pepper, vinegar, and chili oil.

蛋花湯 EGG-DROP SOUP

Fast and simple to make, this delicate, smooth soup can be superb or disastrous, depending on whether you carry out certain crucial points.

A beaten egg stirred into a rapidly boiling liquid forms stringy shreds and clusters of spongy mess. But when oil is added and the mixture is poured over the surface of thickened, still liquid, it congeals and floats into silky petals as soft as roses. Dissolved cornstarch dumped quickly into agitated liquid results in lumps. The heat, therefore, should always be turned to the lowest level while it is being stirred ever so slowly into the pot. Adding oil to the cornstarch mixture, and mixing it well, will not only give the consistency of the soup an added dimension of smoothness, but will also break down the "floury" element of the cornstarch itself, preventing it from forming into lumps and leaving a floury aftertaste. *Makes about 4 cups.*

1 large egg

1 teaspoon vegetable oil

4 teaspoons cornstarch dissolved
    in 2 tablespoons cold stock

1 teaspoon sesame oil

4 cups chicken stock, well seasoned

Beat egg well but not till frothy. Blend in the teaspoon of vegetable oil, mix well, and set aside. Remove 2 tablespoons of the cold stock and dissolve the cornstarch. Add the sesame oil and mix well. Set it aside.

Bring the stock to a gentle simmer. Turn heat to the lowest point; give the cornstarch a brisk stir and pour it in ever so slowly with your left hand while you stir the stock with chopsticks or a spoon with your right hand, circularly, for about 30 seconds, until the broth is lightly thickened. Turn off the heat. Pour the beaten egg over the surface in a wide circle. As it congeals into floating ribbons and large flakes, stir gently a few times so that the soup is covered evenly by dainty petals of chiffony eggs. Pour it into a soup bowl and serve.

VARIATION

One-half cup of slivered skinned and seeded tomato may be added just before the cornstarch.

紫菜湯 PURPLE SEAWEED SOUP

Purple seaweed is very popular with the Chinese. It is considered to have a cooling, cleansing property that is good for you, particularly in warm weather. This soup is clear, light, and simple, with no thickening. *Makes about 4 cups.*

4 sheets purple seaweed (each 5 by
    3 inches)

2 eggs

½ teaspoon salt

1 tablespoon sesame oil

4 cups chicken stock

1 teaspoon light soy sauce

Salt and pepper to taste

1 small scallion, including green
    part, minced

Tear the seaweed into small pieces, about 1-inch squares. Beat the eggs well, but not till frothy, with the salt, add the sesame oil, and blend until well mixed.

Bring the stock to a boil over high heat, turn heat to medium, and add the seaweed by scattering in a few pieces at a time, so they don't stick together. Stir, then cook for about 2 minutes. Turn off the heat, pour in the beaten egg slowly with one hand while you stir with a spoon in a circular fashion with the other hand until the eggs fluff out into soft clusters. Add the soy sauce and the salt and pepper to taste, scatter in the minced scallion, and serve.

VARIATION

To give the soup more substance, instead of using eggs make miniature meatballs from the recipe for Meatball and Transparent-noodle Soup and simmer them in the stock for 5 minutes. Skim off the foam, add the seaweed, and cook for 2 minutes. Add a sprinkling of black pepper and a little chopped coriander or parsley.

青豆鷄丁湯 DICED CHICKEN AND GREEN PEA SOUP

This recipe illustrates the convenience aspect of mixed soups—one can put leftover ingredients to good use. When odds and ends of boiled or roasted chicken, turkey, duck, pork, or beef are diced and combined with a few simple ingredients, they create a delicious and easy-to-make soup.

This soup has a wonderful contrast between the soft meat and the crisp peas, which should pop as you bite into them. The beaten egg and cornstarch mixtures make the soup creamy and therefore suitable for high seasonings if you want them; a thin broth with high seasonings would be harsh. *Makes about 4½ cups.*

1 cup cooked chicken, turkey,
    duck, or meat, in ¼-inch cubes
½ cup frozen or fresh green peas
1 egg
1 teaspoon vegetable oil
2 teaspoons cornstarch dissolved in
    2 teaspoons cold stock

1 teaspoon sesame oil
3 cups chicken or meat stock
2 teaspoons light soy sauce
Salt or light soy sauce to taste
Black pepper, vinegar, or chili-
    pepper oil (*page 489*), optional
    for hotness

Cut the meat into ¼-inch cubes, discarding any dry or burned parts.

Place the frozen peas in a strainer and dip it into rapidly boiling water for 30 seconds. Parboil fresh peas about 3 minutes. Set aside.

Beat the egg well, but not long enough to become frothy; then add the vegetable oil and mix well. Set aside. Add the sesame oil to the cornstarch dissolved in stock, and mingle well.

Bring the 3 cups stock to a gentle boil; then add the soy sauce and the chicken (or duck, turkey, or meat). Lower the heat, cover, and simmer for 2 minutes. Add the peas, and when the soup boils again, adjust the heat to very low and add the cornstarch mixture with one hand as you stir circularly with the other. Stir until the soup is smooth and very slightly thickened, about 30 seconds.

Turn off the heat (so the egg won't curdle) and gently stir in the beaten egg in a circular motion until egg flakes float to the top. Season with salt or light soy sauce, and if you like a hot and spicy soup, add a little black pepper, vinegar, or chili-pepper oil to taste.

VARIATION

As a substitute for frozen peas you could fold in some finely chopped lettuce or watercress (about ½ cup) just before the final seasoning.

Clear-simmering

The objective of clear-simmering is to capture the natural flavors of food by means of slow cooking in stock until the ingredients are tender and the liquid has either become clear and brothy or thickened naturally into a rich gravy.

The seasonings for clear-simmered dishes are generally light—salt, wine (sherry), and a rich stock—so that the flavor is pure. However, seasoning ingredients such as ham, dried shrimp and scallops, and dried mushrooms are used to add flavor and color to more delicate ingredients, such as squabs or vegetables. Stronger seasonings, such as soy sauce, garlic, and pepper, are used only with fish.

Traditionally, clear-simmering is synonymous with earthenware. A clay or porcelain casserole or urn prevents evaporation of the precious liquid as well as loss of the dish's fragrance, since it may be brought directly from stove to table, and it looks more dramatic. It is one thing to glance at a dish of cabbage and quite another to gaze with anticipation into a pot as it is being uncovered, billowing with steam. Certainly you can make clear-simmered dishes in a heavy metal casserole, but, like the famous French onion soup, they will be much more impressive if served in earthenware.

All meats and fowls, large fish, and firm vegetables and vegetarian products are suitable for clear-simmering. The first requirement is that they be fresh and of excellent quality, since there is no dissembling in this kind of cooking—the beauty of a good piece of meat will be brought out just as an inferior piece of fish will be shown up. For this reason, clear-simmering is considered by the Chinese as the foundation of haute cuisine. Rare delicacies, such as sharks' fins and mountain-creek turtles, are, without exception, clear-simmered.

For meats, fatty and sinewy cuts are preferred because they are more succulent after long simmering and they turn the liquid more readily into rich gravy. Any poultry may be used, from chicken or duck to the smaller domestic and wild birds, which can be clear-simmered whole, in large pieces, or boned and combined with a scattering of seasoning ingredients.

For fish, the Chinese look to the large, oil-rich kind, such as carp or shad, because they believe the thicker and oilier the skin, the richer the flavor. With carp, the big, fat head is coveted as much as the body, since to the Chinese gourmet it not only enhances the sauce but also offers some incomparable delicacies—the fine cheek meat, the melting, rich lips, and the luscious silky tongue. However, a number of other less oily fish bring equally good results, such as a big striped bass, mullet, or whitefish. The head can be simmered, then removed before serving if you are squeamish about it.

As for vegetables and vegetarian products, all those that keep their shape are fine—from the delicate celery cabbage, Chinese cabbage, and bean curd to the deep-flavored dried mushrooms. In clear-simmering vegetables, the aim is to produce a light clarity of the ingredient and a subtly rich broth.

清燉牛肉　CLEAR-SIMMERED BEEF

Perhaps the most representative clear-simmered dish would be this simple but rich beef. Shin beef is used because it is marbled with tendons, which enables the meat to withstand long cooking without breaking into small pieces. The large amount of sherry acts as an astringent, sealing in the flavor and purifying the broth. Wine is indispensable to clear-simmering meats, because the alcohol prevents the meat from clouding the rich broth.

The meat is meltingly succulent, the sauce rich, and the flavor pure essence of beef. Serve it as a main dish with two stir-fried vegetables such as Stir-fried Green Beans and Celery, plus rice, or, if making a Chinese meal, accompany it with light stir-fried seafood with vegetable dishes, such as Shrimp with Mo-er Mushrooms and Cucumbers.

This beef is never made in small quantities, for good reasons. The dish, being all meat, would appear meager if the amount were reduced, especially since it should be cooked and served in an earthenware casserole. And, since the meat is cooked with practically no seasonings, its density and flavor would be weakened if there were less. This is decidedly a party dish. Resting over a small flame or warmer on a buffet table, it is ideal when the occasion involves friends drifting in throughout an evening. *It serves 6 to 8 as a main course.*

4 pounds boneless shin beef in large pieces	2½ cups dry sherry
	1 cup boiling chicken or meat stock
4 quarter-sized slices peeled ginger	Salt to taste

Peel off the membrane and trim the meat of all fat. Cut it lengthwise with the grain into 1½-inch-wide strips, then crosswise into 1½-inch cubes. Put the meat and ginger slices in a casserole (earthenware, if possible), pour in the sherry and the hot stock, and bring to a boil over medium heat. Remove any foam. Adjust heat to very low to maintain a very gentle simmering, cover, and simmer for about 3½ to 4 hours, until the meat is tender and the sinews meltingly soft. Remove and discard the ginger. Extra seasonings are really superfluous, but you may add a little salt to taste if you like. Raise the heat to bring the broth to a gentle boil, then cover and take the casserole, bubbling, to the table. It is good with rice, steamed Chinese buns, or hot crusty Western rolls or bread.

清燉蹄膀 CLEAR-SIMMERED PORK

What clear-simmering does for a piece of fatty pork is beyond belief. Unlike beef fat, which really does not take to long simmering, pork fat becomes particularly tasty and smooth. You do not have to eat it, of course, but its mere presence enhances the flavor of the meat. The combination of a light salting, a brief blanching, and a long simmering with sherry cuts the grease and makes the meat extraordinarily light and flavorful.

This rich pork would go beautifully with Szechuan Eggplants and Red-cooked Chinese Black Mushrooms or Spicy Minced Watercress. *It serves 4 to 6 as a main course.*

1 small fresh ham or a shoulder, about 4½ pounds, with the skin on	*Individual dip sauce:*
	1 tablespoon light soy sauce
3 tablespoons salt	1 teaspoon Chenkong, red-wine, or cider vinegar
4 quarter-sized slices peeled ginger	½ teaspoon minced ginger
2 whole scallions	
2½ cups dry sherry	
1½ cups boiling chicken or meat stock	

The meat should weigh about 4½ pounds *before* the bone is removed. Either have your butcher bone the meat or do it yourself: cut along the center bone in short scraping motions to free the meat in 1 piece.

Stock

Use the bone for making stock if you don't already have some on hand for the recipe. Have the bone sawed into small pieces or, if at home, wrap it in a kitchen towel and crack it with a hammer. Put the bone in a heavy saucepan, add water to cover, bring to a boil, then cover and simmer over low heat until the broth is tasty—about 2 hours. Strain and defat the amount you need; bottle the rest.

Rub the meat with the salt, put it in a bowl, cover, and let it sit for 2 hours or so at room temperature. This step purifies the flavor, since some of the blood is removed. It also seasons the meat ever so subtly.

Bring a large pot of water to a boil, add the salted meat, and when the water boils again, let it boil vigorously over high heat for 2 minutes. Drain the meat in a colander and rinse it with warm water to remove all foam. This step seals in the flavor, eliminates unwanted residue, and removes the salt.

Put the meat in a snug, heavy casserole (earthenware if possible), skin side down. Add the ginger and scallions, the sherry, and the hot stock. When the liquid boils, turn the heat very low to maintain a faint simmering —bubbles coming lazily to the surface—and cover and simmer for 1 hour. Then turn the meat skin side up, slip an asbestos pad over the flame, cover, and let the meat simmer undisturbed for 4 to 5 hours.

When ready to serve, discard the ginger and scallions; skim off most of the fat, and then raise the heat to generate a gentle bubbling. Cover and bring the casserole to the table.

You do not need to cut this meat; it is so tender that you can tear off chunks with a fork or chopsticks. It is scrumptious as is or dipped in the refreshing ginger and vinegar sauce. Many Chinese passionately love the gelatinous skin and satiny fat, but if you don't like them, slide a knife underneath the fat and discard.

沙
鍋
魚

CASSEROLE OF FISH

Even though this dish isn't clear in the sense of purity, it falls into this category because it is simmered in a casserole and has the general characteristics of being substantial and brothy. The vinegar and brown sugar give the fish a tasty richness. The sea bass may be replaced by striped bass or whitefish or any thick-meated fish, as long as the meat is not coarse.

The fish is dark and gleaming, the bean curd light brown, and the whole dish is speckled with green coriander. It's a hearty-looking dish with a matching robust flavor and fragrance. The soft bean curd, plump with the sauce, bursts into a mouthful of tasty flavor upon eating. *It serves 4 for a main course, with rice for the lovely sauce.*

1 sea bass, about 2½ pounds
6 whole scallions, cut into 1½- to
    2-inch pieces
6 quarter-sized slices peeled ginger
3 large cloves garlic, lightly
    crushed and peeled
6 Szechuan peppercorns

1 tablespoon finely chopped
    fresh coriander
4 squares bean curd
4 tablespoons oil
Generous pinch black pepper or
    to taste
2 teaspoons sesame oil

Sauce:
5 tablespoons dark soy sauce
1 tablespoon dry sherry
5 tablespoons Chenkong or
    red-wine vinegar
1 tablespoon light brown sugar
1 teaspoon salt
2 cups chicken or meat stock

Preparations

Have the fish cleaned but leave the head and tail on. Rinse and dry it thoroughly. Cut it crosswise (chopping sharply through the backbone) into 2 or 3 sections to fit your casserole. If you don't like to serve the head and tail, cut them off, cook with the rest, and remove before serving.

Rinse and chop the scallions; peel and slice the ginger; crush and peel the garlic; and count out the Szechuan peppercorns. Place them on the working platter. Rinse and chop the coriander and place it on a small dish.

Combine the sauce seasonings and stir until the sugar is dissolved.

Cut each bean-curd square in half, then cut each half twice, crosswise, to make 6 small squares. Place them in a bowl or saucepan, cover with hot water, and let them soak until ready to use. Presoaking bean curd in hot water makes it extremely soft and smooth—something too many people neglect to do.

Cooking

Heat a wok or large, heavy skillet over high heat until very hot; add the 4 tablespoons oil, swirl, and heat for about 30 seconds to coat the bottom and sides. Lower in the fish pieces and shallow-fry (see *page 87*) for about 1½ minutes until they are firm and brown. Slide a spatula carefully under the pieces, flip them over, and shallow-fry another 1½ minutes. If your pan is small, fry them in 2 batches to avoid crowding.

Transfer the fish and oil to a casserole (earthenware preferred) and set it over medium heat. Scatter in the scallions, ginger, garlic, and Szechuan peppercorns. Give the sauce seasonings a big stir and pour over the fish, swirling the pot a few times to let the sauce wash over the fish. When it comes to a boil, turn heat low to maintain a very gentle simmer, cover, and simmer for 10 minutes. Pour the bean-curd cubes into a colander, shake gently to drain, and scatter them over the fish, using a spoon or chopsticks to even them out in the liquid. Cover and simmer for another 10 minutes. Add the black pepper to taste, sprinkle in the coriander, and then add the sesame oil. Turn and baste the bean curd with a spoon a few times. Cover and bring the pot to the table to serve.

VARIATIONS

Not having fresh bean curd on hand should not deter you from making this wonderful dish. Many dry vegetarian products, which can be kept for months, may be used with excellent results. The idea is to have some absorbing ingredients to soak up the tasty sauce and to add a different texture. Soak 4 to 6 pieces of dry bean sticks as described on *page 190*; cut each into 1½-inch-long pieces. Or soak ¼ pound dry bean sheets in hot water for 10 to 15 minutes and then cut the sheets in half. Or soak 2 to 3 ounces transparent noodles in hot water for 15 minutes; cut them in half to make shorter strands and add them to the pot.

White-cut

When a piece of pork or whole chicken is simmered without soy sauce, and served without the broth but accompanied by a sauce, either on the side or doused on top, it is known as a white-cut. It is always served cold.

The method of cooking involves more than simple boiling. The meat or poultry is first simply simmered, or simmered and then steeped, until just done. Then it is plunged into ice water; this instant chilling tightens the muscles and captures all the natural juices within the meat fibers and beneath the skin of poutry. It is this ice-water plunging that makes the meat of the white-cuts so firm and tasty.

Popular all over China, white-cuts are one of those marvelous basic items that are easy to prepare and lend themselves to endless variations.

They make excellent main dishes or appetizers, and the flavor may be varied with different sauces. White-cut chicken in particular is used as a base for a number of salads, combined with different kinds of vegetables and vegetarian products. And the liquid in which either pork or chicken is simmered makes an instant stock for soup or general cooking.

白
切
肉 WHITE-CUT FRESH HAM

Before China had refrigerators and manufactured ice, the congealing of the white-cut's juices was done by submerging the meat in a bucket of icy well water, itself lowered halfway down into the well. The meat is magnificent in texture and taste, the jelled juices acting as a network of concentrated flavor. The dip sauce and the seasonings, to be added by the individual, give the meat a piquant touch. This is a typical Chinese trait— whenever a main dish is plain and simple it is served with a fanfare of trappings, to make a presentation and generate a sense of excitement. *The ham will serve up to 8 as a main course, or more as a party dish.* It would go beautifully with any of the stir-fried cabbage dishes for a simple course.

1 fresh ham or shoulder, about
    5½ pounds
Boiling water to cover
5 to 6 trays ice cubes

Master dip sauce:
½ to 1 cup light soy sauce
¼ to ½ cup dry sherry
2 to 4 tablespoons sesame oil

Seasonings:
3 to 4 tablespoons finely chopped
    coriander
3 to 4 tablespoons finely chopped
    whole scallions
2 to 3 tablespoons minced peeled
    ginger
3 to 4 tablespoons Chenkong or
    cider vinegar
2 to 3 tablespoons chili-pepper oil
    (*page 489*)
2 to 3 tablespoons hot mustard
1 to 2 tablespoons roasted and
    crushed Szechuan peppercorns
    (*page 500*)
1 to 2 tablespoons puréed garlic
    (optional)

Preparing and cooking the meat
    Have the butcher bone the meat in 1 piece, with the skin on, or do it yourself: with a sharp knife cut through the skin and scrape around the bone all the way down, until it can be removed. Form the meat into a roll

and tie it up crosswise with 3 pieces of string to make it hold this shape, neither too loose nor too tight.

Place the ham and the bone in a deep, heavy pot that fits the meat snugly. Pour in enough boiling water to cover and set over high heat. When the water comes to a boil again, boil for 2 minutes. Then turn heat low and skim the surface until the water is more or less clear. Adjust heat to medium low to maintain a strong simmer, with bubbles shooting up rapidly. Cover and simmer for 2 hours, turning the meat every 30 minutes and adding boiling water to cover whenever necessary. The crucial point is to maintain a strong simmering, so that the meat is thoroughly cooked and its texture is firm.

Preparing the sauce and seasonings

While the meat is cooking, prepare the sauce. The quantity of master sauce depends on the number of people you are serving. Basically, allow 1 tablespoon soy sauce, ½ tablespoon dry sherry, and ½ teaspoon sesame oil for each person. You could either mix the sauce and divide it into individual saucers or serve it in a bowl and let each person pour out what he or she wants into individual saucers.

The seasonings should be presented in small saucers, cups, or bowls and set on attractive small trays for easy passing around.

Cut off the roots and the tough ends of the coriander. Rinse and shake dry. Hold the stalks together and chop leaves closely into fine pieces. Three stalks will give you about 1 tablespoon.

Rinse, shake dry, and cut off the root ends of the scallions; hold the stalks and chop closely into fine pieces. One small whole scallion will give you about 1 tablespoon finely chopped.

Peel 1 to 2 inches of ginger and cut it crosswise into ⅛-inch slices. Stack them, shred them, and then mince finely. Six quarter-sized slices will give you about 1 tablespoon minced.

Chenkong vinegar is made of rice and is mellower than cider vinegar, but the latter or red-wine vinegar may be used if you don't have the imported one on hand.

The recipes for making chili-pepper oil and hot mustard are on *pages 489 and 495*.

Roast and crush the Szechuan peppercorns (*page 500*).

The garlic is optional; it is very strong, but to many northern Chinese a white-cut fresh ham is incomplete without a dab or two of garlic in the sauce.

Ice-water plunging and serving the meat

When the meat is done, fill a large pot half full of cold water and the ice cubes. Remove the meat from the broth and plunge it immediately into the ice water; let it soak for 20 minutes. The water should cover the meat and the ice cubes should blanket it to stop the cooking and jell the juices.

Remove the ham and pat it dry with paper towels, wiping off any congealed fat on the surface. Cut and remove the strings. Place the ham in a bowl, skin side down, cover, and chill in the refrigerator for about 2 to 3 hours. While the ice-water plunging may look redundant if you are chilling the meat anyway, in reality it isn't: it performs the important task of instantly jelling the juices, which definitely makes the meat richer and tastier.

You may cook and chill the meat a day in advance if you like, but cover it well so that no part is dried or discolored.

There are two ways to serve the meat—with the skin and fat on and with them removed. While the Chinese generally eschew fatty dishes, they consider clear-simmered and white-cut pork skin and fat to be great delicacies. And, in truth, the skin is wonderfully resilient and the fat very smooth.

Cut the meat lengthwise into 2 strips if you prefer large slices or 3 if you want smaller ones. Then cut the strips crosswise into ⅛- to ¼-inch-thick slices and arrange them in a circular pattern or in rows. Garnish the platter with a few sprigs of coriander or parsley.

The sauce should be used sparingly, since it is supposed to subtly enhance the flavor of the meat, not mask it. The seasonings should be added to the sauce in small quantities, starting with the indispensable ginger, then either the coriander or the scallion; vinegar if you like a sour taste, then either mustard or chili-pepper oil for spiciness. Szechuan peppercorns are not peppery in the ordinary sense—they are exotically aromatic, numbing rather than burning.

The broth in which the meat has been simmered is already a good stock. Skim off the fat and bottle the broth for future use. I usually seize this opportunity to enrich it with bones and odds and ends of meat or poultry; simmer until very rich, then strain, skim, and bottle it.

白
切
鷄
WHITE-CUT CHICKEN

For the more delicate chicken, the white-cut procedure is slightly different. The chicken is simmered briefly and then steeped for a long time before it is plunged into the ice water. You will find it firm, flavorful, and extraordinarily succulent–between the meat and skin there is a marvelous layer of jelled juices.

The sauce and seasonings for the fresh ham may be used here, but omit the vinegar and garlic; they do not go well with chicken. Better still, make any one of the delicious sauces listed at the end of this recipe–they are especially good with poultry.

This recipe would serve 6 or more accompanied by a spirited stir-fried vegetable dish, such as Green Peas with Minced Pork or Mushrooms in Oyster Sauce.

1 roasting chicken, about 4 pounds	4 trays ice cubes
8 cups water	

Remove the fat from the cavity and cut off the tail; rinse the chicken well. Put a metal spoon inside the cavity to conduct the heat. Bring the 8 cups water to a boil in a deep, heavy pot that fits the chicken snugly. Slip the chicken in breast down. When the water comes to a boil again, skim it until more or less clear, turn heat to medium low to maintain a strong simmer (bubbles shooting rapidly to the surface), cover, and simmer for 25 minutes. Then turn off the heat and let the chicken steep for 45 minutes. Do not peep during the cooking and steeping time lest you dissipate the heat.

When the chicken is done, fill a large pot half full of water and scatter in the ice cubes. Drain the chicken, remove the spoon, and plunge the chicken immediately into the ice water. Let it soak for 15 minutes under the blanketing ice cubes.

Drain and place it in a bowl, cover, and chill for at least 2 hours; it could be made the day before. A boiled chicken loses some of its precious juice while being cooled and chilled—the juice seeps out under the weight of the bird, forming into a sheet of jelly. Instant chilling while hot prevents that; it also tightens the skin, making it extremely smooth and delicious.

When you are ready to serve, chop the chicken the Chinese way (*page 14*) and reassemble it into a symbolic whole chicken (*page 16*).

Make any one of the following sauces and pour over the chicken, garnishing with a little coriander or parsley.

The sauces
There are three sauces that go well with white-cut chicken: the mild Basic Sauce, the aromatic Scallion-Oil Sauce, and the spicy Odd-flavored Sauce from Szechuan.

BASIC SAUCE

1 teaspoon sugar	2 tablespoons finely chopped
3 tablespoons light soy sauce	coriander, leaves and stems
	1 tablespoon sesame oil

Dissolve the sugar in the soy sauce; add the coriander and sesame oil and stir well. Pour the sauce over the chicken. This is a light and unobtrusive sauce.

SCALLION-OIL SAUCE

4 large scallions, whites only
½-inch piece peeled ginger
3 tablespoons oil

3 tablespoons light soy sauce
1 tablespoon dry sherry
⅛ teaspoon salt

Trim off the root ends from the scallions and cut about 2 inches off the firm white ends, saving the greens for another use. Rinse and shake dry the scallion whites and then chop them finely. Peel about ½ inch off a large knob of ginger, then slice, shred, and mince.

Combine the scallions and ginger in a bowl. Heat the oil over low heat until very hot and pour it over them. As they sizzle with an enticing aroma, add the remaining seasonings, stir, and pour the sauce over the chicken. This is a wonderfully aromatic sauce.

ODD-FLAVORED SAUCE

Liquid seasonings:
2 teaspoons sesame paste
1 tablespoon boiling water
3 tablespoons light soy sauce
1 tablespoon Chenkong or
   red-wine vinegar
2 teaspoons sugar
¼ teaspoon salt
1 tablespoon sesame oil

Dry ingredients:
1 small scallion, finely chopped
2 quarter-sized slices peeled ginger,
   minced
1 large clove garlic, finely chopped
2 small fresh chili peppers, seeded
   and minced
¼ teaspoon roasted and crushed
   Szechuan peppercorns
   (*page 500*)

3 tablespoons oil

Chinese sesame paste comes in a bottle and has the consistency of soft clay. It must first be thinned, or what the Chinese call "opened," with hot water or oil before being blended with other seasonings. Scrape 2 teaspoons of the paste (without oil) into a bowl, add 1 tablespoon boiling water, mix by pressing with the back of a spoon until smooth. Add the other liquid seasonings and mix until the sugar is dissolved.

Prepare the dry ingredients. If fresh chili peppers are not available, presoak 2 or 3 dried red chili peppers in a little boiling water until softened. Cut each in half, seed, then mince. Place everything on a small plate.

Heat a small skillet until hot, add the oil, swirl, and heat for a few seconds. Scatter in the scallions, ginger, garlic, chili peppers, and crushed peppercorns; stir rapidly for 10 seconds until they are bright and aromatic. Pour the oil and the minced ingredients into the liquid seasonings, stirring until well blended.

Pour the sauce over the chicken and serve. This is hot and stimulating, a heady blend of flavors that is spicy but not harsh. It is a great sauce.

VARIATION
If you don't have sesame paste, substitute 1 tablespoon peanut butter.

Salt-watering and Salt-curing

When small ingredients such as livers, kidneys, gizzards, unshelled shrimp, or pieces of duck are simmered with salt and Szechuan peppercorns and chilled in the brine before serving, they are described as "salt-watered." Cooking, soaking, and chilling in the salted brine give these ingredients a clean, refreshing flavor and a firm texture.

When large pieces of meat or whole fowls are rubbed with a mixture of roasted salt and Szechuan peppercorns and salted away for hours or days, then simmered or steamed and chilled before serving, they are described as "salt-cured." Salting intensifies the flavor and makes the meat smooth and tight, the fowls firm and silky. A small turkey, salted and steamed, is unbelievably delicious.

Both these kinds of dishes are the Chinese equivalent of Western cold cuts, and, like them, are good as a main dish or appetizer. Except for the shrimp, they keep for up to a week refrigerated, and in fact their flavor improves on the second or third day.

臨水牛肝 PEPPER-SALT-WATER BEEF LIVER

This is a firm-textured liver with the clean taste of salt and the faint spiciness of Szechuan peppercorns.

Many people avoid liver because of its strong taste and troublesome texture. When undercooked, it is bloody and mushy; when medium-cooked, it is mealy; and when overcooked, it is dry. The parboiling procedure here eliminates the strong odor and draws out the thick residue. The long simmering firms the texture without drying out the meat. Finally, the marinating and chilling allow the flavor of the salt and peppercorns to soak in, giving the meat its refreshing taste. It combines beautifully with the white, tasty Spicy Cold Celery Cabbage. *It serves 4 as a cold supper, 6 to 8 as an appetizer.*

1 pound beef liver	2 tablespoons salt
4 cups water	Garnish: Fresh coriander or
1 teaspoon Szechuan peppercorns	parsley sprigs

Buy the pound of beef liver in 2 thick strips.

Bring 2 cups water to a boil in a small pot. Add the liver slices and boil over high heat for 10 minutes. Remove the slices and rinse them under running warm water until free of the residue. Set them aside.

Bring 2 cups water to a boil with the peppercorns and salt. Add the liver and when the water boils again adjust the heat to low, cover, and simmer gently for 1 hour.

Transfer the liver and brine to a small, deep bowl, one that will allow the brine to completely cover the liver. Cover the bowl and chill in the refrigerator for a few hours or overnight.

Cut the liver into thin slices for a main course, smaller pieces for an appetizer. Dribble a little of the brine over the meat, garnish with sprigs of coriander or parsley, and serve.

SALT-CURED BEEF BRISKET

Similar in taste and texture to corned beef, this is a delicious home-cured meat without chemical preservatives. It keeps well refrigerated. Slice only the amount you need for each serving as a main dish, an appetizer, or for sandwiches.

1 teaspoon Szechuan peppercorns	3 pounds beef brisket
4½ tablespoons salt	

Measure the peppercorns and salt into a dry skillet set over low heat. Let them roast, stirring or shaking the pan occasionally, until the salt turns slightly brown and the peppercorns are faintly smoky and aromatic. Pour the mixture into a dish to cool.

Place the beef on a large piece of aluminum foil or in a deep bowl. Rub it well on all sides with the pepper-salt mixture. Wrap the meat securely or cover the bowl. Let it cure in the refrigerator for 4 or 5 days, turning the meat over each day.

Unwrap and place the meat in a heavy pot that fits it snugly. Pour in enough boiling water to cover the meat by about 1 inch and turn the heat high. When the water boils again, adjust heat to medium low to maintain a strong simmer, with bubbles shooting up rapidly. Cover and simmer for 2½ to 3 hours, turning the meat a few times. The meat is ready when you feel just a little resistance as you spear it with a chopstick.

Transfer meat and broth to a container, cover, and refrigerate until chilled and firm. To serve, slice the meat thin against the grain; for an appetizer, cut the slices into smaller pieces. The brine, now thickened into a soft jelly, may be dabbed over the meat if you want this moistness. The meat is also very good for making sandwiches; combining with other meats, poultry, seafood, and vegetables, in small amounts, as an assorted appetizer; and, in larger amounts, as a cold platter for a buffet or light supper.

Red-cooking

Red-cooking is Chinese stewing. The seasonings that give a red-cooked dish its special character are dark soy sauce for a deep reddish color; light soy sauce and a pinch of salt for added saltiness; star anise or five-fragrance powder for the distinctive aroma; and sherry and rock sugar for an overall mellowness.

The method is to sear the ingredients in oil first and then to add the seasonings with a small amount of boiling water. The stew is then simmered until the ingredients are tender, richly colored, and glazed by the thick sauce. The cooking time can range from 45 minutes to 3 hours.

Any firm-textured ingredient can be red-cooked, from any cut of meat or poultry to certain fish and vegetables. With a few exceptions, most red-cooked dishes are cooked with a good number of secondary ingredients, not only to give the dishes variety but also to provide a taste contrast and ample bulk. Turnips, carrots, and pressed bean curd or transparent noodles are often added to chunky meats; roll-cut bamboo shoots and whole hard-boiled eggs are often used with a large piece of fresh ham or whole chicken; black mushrooms and blanched whole chestnuts are frequently cooked with cut-up chicken; and shredded bamboo shoots and black mushrooms are generally found with the more delicate fish.

Unlike the Western stew, which is often thought of as an economical, catch-all meal for family eating only, a Chinese red-cooked dish is considered both economical *and* lavish. Red-cooked dishes are extremely versatile: because of the rich seasonings, they are good made with equal parts of meat and vegetables or they can be extravagantly solid with meat. Red-cooked dishes keep very well; they are good both hot and cold and they often taste better upon reheating. The leftover broth and meat are also excellent as a flavoring in which to simmer noodles or vegetables.

Since a red-cooked dish is rich and chunky in appearance, you should serve with it dishes that are light, crisp, and finely chopped, to provide contrast in flavor and texture.

紅燒鴨 RED-COOKED WINE DUCK

Red-cooked Wine Duck is a magnificent dish of meat that is tender and flavorful, a sauce that is wine rich. It should be accompanied by plenty of steamed rice or steamed buns to soak up all the ambrosial sauce.

This duck is especially good for entertaining, since it may be done in advance and reheated just before serving. Combine it with one vegetable dish that can be precooked and reheated or served at room temperature, such as the Stir-fried Broccoli Stems or Stir-fried Cauliflower, and one fast stir-fried one, such as Celery Cabbage, and *you have an excellent dinner for 4.*

Rock sugar is crucial to red-cooking; its sweetness is subtler than granulated sugar's and it gives the ingredients and sauce a lovelier sheen. Since duck skin scorches easily, the duck must be cooked in a heavy pot. A perfectionist of the classic school, Ar-chang, our family cook in China, always used an earthen casserole with a fitted bamboo doily as a cushion to prevent the blemishing of the duck, which I've modified here by using scallions as a base.

5- to 6-pound duck
2 tablespoons oil
8 large whole scallions, each cut into 3 sections
6 slices peeled ginger, each ⅛ inch thick
3 whole star anise
5 tablespoons dark soy sauce

2 tablespoons light soy sauce
¼ teaspoon salt
2 cups dry sherry
1 cup boiling water
4 tablespoons crushed rock sugar or 3 tablespoons granulated sugar

Even though some Chinese gourmets claim that the duck tail is the best part of the duck, don't believe them; cut it off. Rinse out the cavity and dry the duck thoroughly.

Heat a large, heavy pot until hot; add 2 tablespoons oil, swirl, and heat until hot but not smoking. Lower the heat to medium, then sear the duck, breast and back, until the skin is taut and slightly brown. Sticking a pair of chopsticks or a wooden spoon through the cavity makes turning very easy, but care must be taken not to tear the opening. The searing does two things: it makes the duck taut so that it colors evenly and it eliminates some of the fat from the skin.

Remove the duck. If you have a large earthenware casserole, set it over medium heat and spread the scallions over the center. If you don't have one, drain off the oil from the original pot, scatter in the scallions, and place the duck, breast down, on top of the scallions. Add the ginger, star anise, dark and light soy sauces, salt, and sherry. Turn heat high and, when the sauce bubbles, add the boiling water. When it boils again, let it bubble for about 30 seconds as you stir the sauce and baste the duck a few times. Turn heat low to maintain a very weak simmer, cover, and simmer for 1½ hours. (It's deceptive when you turn high heat to low to adjust boiling to slow simmering, so you should always check a minute or two later after covering the pot to see if it is maintaining the right level of simmer.)

After 1½ hours, turn the duck over gently, and push the scallions back underneath it. Wrap the rock sugar in a kitchen towel and smash it with a hammer (or measure out the granulated sugar). Scatter the sugar into the sauce and stir to let it dissolve a bit. Cover and simmer for another hour, basting a few times.

Taste the sauce at this point, adding a little more sherry or soy sauce if you feel it is too sweet for you. The sauce should have a rich wine sweetness, with the underlying flavors of star anise and scallions.

Turn heat a little higher to bring the sauce to a gentle bubbling and baste the duck for a few minutes until it is glistening and the color deepens. Turn off the heat. Slip a large spatula carefully underneath the duck and anchor it down with chopsticks or a wooden spoon inside the cavity. Transfer it to a deep platter or large serving bowl; scoop out the scallions and discard. Tilt the pot and skim off the fat; then bring the sauce to a boil and pour it over the duck. (If you do the duck in advance to this point, either hours or even a day before, cover and refrigerate. Scrape off the congealed fat and reheat over low heat for 20 to 25 minutes until piping hot. Then serve.)

The Chinese traditionally serve this duck whole, the hostess pulling away the meat with chopsticks and serving each guest spoonfuls of the rich sauce. You may carve it, or chop it the Chinese way (*page 14*), however, before you pour the sauce over it.

Since there is a good deal of the sauce, you may have some left over. Bottle it, refrigerate, and use it for simmering noodles or vegetables such as turnips.

VARIATION

1½ cups of Golden Needles and 8 to 10 medium-sized Chinese black mushrooms may be substituted for the scallions. Place them in separate bowls and cover with hot water and soak for 30 minutes. Rinse them to remove sand; shake lightly to drain off the excess water. Remove the knobby ends of the Golden Needles by pinching or cutting them off. Cut off the hard stems of the mushrooms. Add the Golden Needles after searing the duck, spreading them out as a cushion, as with the scallions, to prevent the skin of the duck from scorching. Add the mushrooms after pouring in boiling water.

蘿蔔燒肉 RED-COOKED BEEF AND TURNIPS

This recipe demonstrates the red-cooking of cut-up meat. Fatty pork and sinewy beef are usually preferred by the Chinese because the meat comes out tenderer. But I have always had excellent results with round steak or top-grade chuck, as long as they are not completely lean. Turnips are popular in stewing; they are durable and absorbent, retaining a good shape as well as a deep flavor after long simmering with meat. If you don't care for them, substitute any of the other vegetables or vegetarian products listed in Variations. *Serves 3 or 4 with rice and a cold vegetable, for instance Hot and Sour Cucumbers.*

3 tablespoons oil
2 cloves garlic, lightly crushed
    and peeled
1 pound boneless round or chuck,
    cut in 1½-inch cubes

2 cups boiling water
1 pound peeled icicle turnips,
    roll-cut
½ teaspoon salt

Seasonings:
2 tablespoons dry sherry
4 tablespoons dark soy sauce
2 teaspoons sugar
1 star anise
1 medium whole scallion, cut into 4
2 quarter-sized slices peeled ginger

Heat a wok or large, heavy pot over high heat until hot; add the oil, swirl, and heat for 30 seconds. Toss in the garlic and press against the pan and smear around to season the oil; then add the meat and brown all sides quickly. Put in all the seasonings and stir to mix well. Then pour in the boiling water and even out the contents of the pan. When the liquid boils again, adjust heat to low to maintain a very gentle simmering, cover, and simmer for 1½ hours, turning the meat a few times.

Add the turnips and salt and simmer covered another 30 to 40 minutes, until the meat is tender and the turnips are plump and moist.

VARIATIONS
Instead of the turnips you could use ½ pound roll-cut carrots, 3 or 4 presoaked bean sticks (*page 190*), 10 to 12 presoaked black mushrooms (*page 494*) or 1½ cups cubed bamboo shoots. For variety, combine the vegetables in smaller quantities.

Flavor-potting

Called *lu* in Chinese, flavor-potting starts with the making of the sauce. Consisting primarily of soy sauce and water, but well seasoned with sugar, sherry, and spices, it is used as a base with which to cook and steep assorted ingredients individually or several kinds at the same time. Depending on what they are, the ingredients are first browned, deep-fried in oil, or scalded or boiled in water—to firm them for even coloring, extract excess fat, or remove strong odor—before they are simmered and steeped in the flavoring sauce. They are then removed to drain, cool, firm, and deepen in taste before they are cut and served. As a consequence, flavor-potted ingredients are generally served at room temperature or cold, making them ideal for serving as main dishes or as something to nibble with drinks or wine.

The sauce is then strained and used again and again, with more spices, seasonings, and liquid added to taste when necessary. As time goes on, the sauce gets richer and richer. Traditionally, once a flavor-pot is started, it should last "forever." Many restaurants in China, particularly in Peking, became famed for their flavor-pots, some of them claiming, hyperbolically, to be sure, that their sauces were twenty generations old. In realistic terms, a flavor-pot sauce will keep for months if it is frozen in between usings.

Any type or cut of meat, innards, fowls, and game birds may be flavor-potted. While meat and poultry may be cooked after one another in the sauce, a separate sauce should be maintained for such strong ingredients as lamb, liver, or kidneys.

While flavor-potted ingredients resemble red-cooked ones in color, they are much firmer in texture and herbier in aroma. The flavor is essentially superficial, since slightly higher heat and a shorter cooking time are deliberately used, so that they do not acquire the same rich and saucy characteristics as red-cooked "stews."

鹵汁 FLAVOR-POT SAUCE

Even though the sauce has an established flavor, it can vary slightly from cook to cook. It is primarily a soy sauce brine mellowed by wine and sugar and seasoned with star anise, fennel seeds, cinnamon stick, and dried tangerine peel. But some people make it richer by using stock instead of water or spicier by adding Szechuan peppercorns, dried licorice roots, and five-fragrance powder. The special sauce for mutton, prepared in the Muslim restaurants in Peking, called for no fewer than twenty different kinds of flavoring ingredients, involving strong agents such as bean paste, fermented black beans, garlic, onions, and so forth.

Besides this standard sauce, which is called the "red brine," there is a "white" one, in which the soy sauce is replaced by 1/3 cup salt. It is used when you want the flavor but not the color of flavor-potting.

The spices are usually tied up in cheesecloth for easy removal, but you may scatter them in the sauce and then strain them off before bottling the sauce for future use.

1 cup dark soy sauce	1 teaspoon fennel seeds
1/2 cup light soy sauce	1 stick cinnamon
1/3 cup dry sherry	1 piece dried tangerine peel, about
2 tablespoons sugar	2 inches square
2 whole star anise	5 cups water

Combine the seasonings with the water and bring to a boil. Turn heat low, cover, and simmer for 1 hour. The sauce is now ready for you to flavor-pot any ingredient you wish.

鹵鷄 FLAVOR-POTTED CHICKEN

This serves 4 to 6 as a main course and would go very well with Egg Shreds and Cold-stirred Vegetables. Since it is good hot or cold and it may be served as a main dish as well as an appetizer, carve or chop the amount you need for one meal and save the rest for an appetizer for another.

1 roasting chicken, about 4 pounds
Flavor-pot Sauce (preceding recipe)
4 slices peeled ginger, each ¼ inch
    thick

4 large scallions, white part only
1 tablespoon sesame oil

Bring a pot of water to a rolling boil. Submerge the chicken, and when the water boils again let the chicken boil vigorously for about 2 minutes. Drain and rinse it under warm water to remove all foam.

Bring the flavor-pot sauce to a boil with the ginger and scallions in a pot large enough to hold the chicken snugly. Add the chicken, breast down; when the sauce boils again, turn the heat to medium low to maintain a strong simmering, cover, and cook for 15 minutes. Turn the chicken breast up, cover, and cook another 10 minutes. Then turn the chicken breast down once more, adjust heat to low, cover, and cook for 20 minutes at this slow simmer. Turn off the heat and let the chicken steep in the sauce for 30 minutes—do not peek, or the heat will dissipate.

Drain the chicken and put it on a chopping board. Brush it all over with the sesame oil and let it cool and firm. Then either carve it the Western way or chop it the Chinese way (*page 14*).

Sprinkle a tablespoon or so of the sauce over the chicken, if you wish, and serve. It may be covered and refrigerated and served cold.

Skim off any fat from the flavor-pot sauce, strain it, and freeze it for future use.

COOKING
IN OIL

Cooking in oil consists of stir-frying, shallow-frying, and deep-frying. Each of these basic techniques has its own set of procedures that brings about distinctly different results.

There is one factor crucial to all three, however—the cooking oil itself. Chinese cooking demands that the oil be able to tolerate high heat without vaporizing into smoke. Liquid oils made from either corn, soybeans, cottonseeds, or peanuts have that strength, and are suitable to use for Chinese cooking. Butter and olive oil cannot be used: butter smokes easily and both have distinctive flavors that are foreign to Chinese tastes. Sesame oil, with its heavy density and strong aroma, is used primarily as a flavoring. As a cooking agent it not only smokes but also overpowers the ingredients and flavor of the dish. I never use lard, a favored cooking fat in China and preferred by most professional Chinese cooks here, because I find it too greasy. But it does enrich the flavor and gives food a beautiful sheen.

Stir-frying

Stir-frying is a dashing, flamboyant technique that produces a great variety of trim, textured dishes. It is the brisk cooking of small cuts of ingredients in hot oil over intense heat, calling for split-second timing and swift movements. It requires an uninterrupted rhythm in its pursuit of that vitality the Chinese call "wok-heat." The importance of capturing and retaining the heat of the pan and the energy of fast stirring within the dish cannot be overemphasized. As Ar-chang, our incomparable family cook, said to me in Shanghai: "Once you toss in the ingredients for a sizzling stir, even if the stove catches on fire and the fire is spreading with leaping flames, pick up the pan and let it ride the crest of the heat to completion before you put out the fire."

Three elements are crucial to stir-frying: (1) proper preparation, wherein the ingredients are conditioned through small cutting, marinating, and partial precooking to respond to the fast cooking; (2) thorough organizing, in the sense that everything needed is measured out and within reach so no interruption will disturb the cooking once it starts; and (3) vigilance from the cook—you must be ready to adjust timing and volume of heat instantly, not just by following recipe guidelines but intuitively by the smell, look, and feel of the food and the sound of the cooking.

Stir-frying may appear nerve-racking at first, but once you know what you are doing and why, you will find that it falls into a logical and orderly sequence. With a little practice, you will be able to approach it instinctively with a sense of concentration without stress, since the bulk of the work can be done at a leisurely pace in advance. In time, you will find it a delightful, freewheeling method that is easy, flexible, and great fun.

So let's start with the background preparations first.

Preparations

Preparations consist of matching compatible ingredients, cutting appropriately, marinating or tenderizing, and organizing.

A stir-fried dish is generally composed of one main ingredient—meat, poultry, or seafood—and one or several secondary ingredients, either fresh, dried, or preserved vegetables. There are many single-ingredient dishes, particularly in the realm of vegetables, and there are occasionally dishes where meat and seafood are combined. When made up of more than one ingredient, the dish either glorifies the main one by a light touch of the secondary or plays on variety and the contrast of textures by embellishing the main with an assortment of the secondary. The play on ingredients cannot be done without knowing the fundamentals of good matchmaking.

MATCHMAKING—Matchmaking is first of all sensible balance. The delicate shouldn't be overwhelmed by the strong, which would happen if you smothered tiny baby shrimp with strong onions. The strong should not be made grotesque by the dainty, which would be the result of embellishing thick slices of beef with a sprinkling of tiny bean sprouts. And the compact shouldn't be dwarfed by the extensive, the result of combining green peas and leafy spinach. Clashing personalities in food can be intriguing, but only as long as there is a basic compatibility.

Matchmaking is also balance without monotony of color as well as texture. Take chicken breast, for instance. When it is shredded and given a velvety coating of egg white and cornstarch, it is as light and fluffy as a cloud. In form and texture it pairs wonderfully with crisp, dainty bean sprouts, since they are also light but have a different texture. But without spot coloring, such as shredded scallions or peppers, or red ham or carrots, this combination would be dull. One needs accentuation by contrast.

CUTTING—In cutting, the emphasis is on small cuts, of even size. All ingredients involved in a dish must be cut uniformly, to facilitate even cooking and to give a trim look to the finished product. Therefore, everything is either sliced, shredded, cubed, diced, or minced. And meats must always be cut against the grain—the grain meaning those long tissue fibers that form the meat. This breaks up the stringy texture and makes the meat smoother and tenderer.

MARINATING—In Chinese cooking marinating consists of steeping meats or poultry in soy sauce, sherry, sugar, salt, and any other special seasonings a recipe may call for. The time required ranges from a few minutes to a few hours, depending on the ingredients and how deeply seasoned they should be. Marinating serves two purposes: it gives meats or poultry a flavor they could not otherwise acquire in the fast method of stir-frying, and it tenderizes them with an extra feeding of moisture, so they won't shrink and harden when they come into contact with the hot oil.

Besides marinating, there are the other protective methods that I have translated as "velveting" and "slippery-coating." These two remarkable procedures not only ensure tenderness but also impart either a velvety or satiny texture to meat, chicken, and seafood.

VELVETING—Velveting means coating an ingredient with egg white, cornstarch, and oil after it has been seasoned. It is usually done with such delicate ingredients as chicken, shelled shrimp, and fish fillets. The ingredient is given at least 30 minutes to sit in the refrigerator so the coating will adhere to it. It is then scattered into either warm oil or hot water to firm and partially cook. After being drained the ingredient is ready to be stir-fried. See the detailed master recipe for velveting on *page 75.*

SLIPPERY-COATING—Slippery-coating is almost identical to velveting, except that the egg white is omitted. The coating then becomes satiny and slippery rather than fluffy. Although the method is used to tenderize meat, poultry, and seafood, it is especially good for beef, making less expensive cuts, such as flank or prime shoulder, as tender as fillet.

Both slippery-coating and velveting can be done either in oil or water, and you must always use water if you're going to refrigerate or freeze the ingredient—the chilled oil would harden the ingredient. To slippery-coat,

I prefer to put chicken through water, since the moisture of the water makes it softer, whereas I put beef through oil, since water would weaken its beefy flavor. However, when slippery-coated beef is to be combined with vegetables that require liquid to steam-cook until tender, the coated meat may be spread over the vegetables for a brief steaming before the meat and vegetables are rapidly tossed together for final blending, as in the sample recipe, Beef in Black Bean Sauce, and others in the meat chapter.

VEGETABLE PREPARATION—Stir-frying does wonderful things to vegetables. The short cooking and intense heat not only preserve their freshness but also beautifully enhance their inherent qualities—for example, their colors become vivid, unmatched in any other cooking method.

If cooked by the stir-frying method, sometimes preceded by a dip in boiling water, macerating with salt, or deep-frying, your vegetables will never become limp or watery. As an object lesson, here is a brief description of how the Chinese would stir-fry carrots and frozen green peas to get a dish of brilliant colors, lovely textures, and delicious flavors:

First you sear the diced carrots in a little hot oil to give them a protective shield; then you sprinkle them with salt, sugar, and sherry to heighten their natural sweet taste and let them steam-cook vigorously with a little stock or water under cover very briefly so that they will cook but not wither. Meanwhile, put the defrosted peas in a strainer and dip them into a pot of boiling salted water for a few seconds to eliminate the raw taste and brighten the color. When the carrot pan crackles, an indication that the water is about to be completely evaporated, join the two vegetables for a grand tumble in the hot pan with the final seasonings—a little salt and sesame oil.

One general rule to remember in preparing vegetables for the hot oil is to wash them before the cutting, and shake them dry as much as possible before they go into the hot oil.

ORGANIZING—In stir-frying, when the timing involved is but a few minutes and the heat is volatile, each second counts, making organization mandatory.

The first step is to provide yourself with a working platter; put on it all the ingredients for a dish in the order of their descent into the pan. This platter should be light, so that it can be handled easily, and preferably without sides, so you can easily scrape the ingredients into the pan. An aluminum platter or cookie sheet would be good. The order is generally first the aromatic ingredients, such as ginger and garlic; then the vegetables; then the velveted or slippery-coated meat (except when soy sauce—marinated meat is used, in which case the meat precedes the vegetables). The

final touches—the garnishes—such as minced ham, scallions, or coriander should be placed on a separate dish.

The seasonings—premixed liquid flavorings and thick pastes, dissolved cornstarch, and beaten eggs—should be prepared and grouped within easy reach. So should any necessary utensils.

When numerous kinds of seasonings are involved and you are not yet at ease with last-minute measuring, by all means premeasure them into small dishes for instant adding. (In time, out of experience, you will instinctively gauge how much 3 tablespoons of oil is by pouring and 1¼ teaspoons of salt by pinching or pouring directly from the spout.) In short, have everything ready so you don't break the rhythm of the cooking once it starts.

Some recipes may appear formidable, involving long lists of ingredients. But once you group them, they fall into a logical pattern of component parts. Each component is done separately; then they meet at different stages until the dish comes to the grand finale. Until you are more familiar with them, you might try using a piece of cardboard or a sheet of Lucite and marking numbers of progressions and keynotes, over which you line up and group the different components. This guide will serve as a reminder, so you won't have to pause as much to check with the instructions of the recipe.

The stir-frying process

As for the cooking itself, stir-frying is composed of either three or four fast steps: (1) quick exploding, to bring out the aromas of any flavoring ingredients such as garlic, scallions, ginger, etc., in the oil; (2) rapid searing, to acquire a protective shield for the main ingredients; (3) vigorous steam-cooking under cover, when a little liquid is added to "blossom" the ingredients into a cooked state; and (4) fast blending with dissolved cornstarch and/or final seasonings to complete the character and consistency of the dish.

Let's look at each in detail.

(1) QUICK EXPLODING—You must start with a very hot pan before adding the oil. When oil is heated in a cold pan, it clings to the metal and makes the food stick to the pan. But if the pan is already hot, the oil flows free of the metal, letting the ingredients tumble over the surface with freedom and spirit.

The pan should be heated for about 30 seconds, but exact timing depends on the type of pan. You may use a wok, a large, deep skillet, or even a large, heavy pot—as long as there's enough space and depth for brisk stirring and the metal is not too thin, which causes scorching. To test for hotness, flip a drop of water into the pan; if it sizzles and evaporates instantly, the pan is hot enough. Or hold your hand 3 inches above the pan; if your palm feels hot, the heat is right.

After adding the oil, let it heat a second or so; then swirl the pan to cover the entire surface with oil. This is especially important for meats,

since they will stick to any dry metal during the stirring. Let the oil heat for about 30 seconds, but do not let it smoke. Then throw in the seasoning ingredients, such as garlic, scallions, or ginger, lowering the heat slightly. These ingredients should be tossed in flipping motions or pressed quickly against the pan with a spatula or slotted spoon and smeared around so that they flavor the oil.

(2) RAPID SEARING—Add the main ingredients in a scattering motion, not all at once, so the oil temperature doesn't drop too much. Then immediately start stirring, with a pair of chopsticks, a wooden fork, a spatula, or any implement you feel comfortable with. The crucial point to remember is that stir-frying is not the flat circular movement one usually associates with the word "stir." The ingredients are tossed, turned, flipped, swept, poked, and swished, according to how they are cut and how they are best moved rapidly around the pan. You want to give them surface exposure and coat them with oil, so that the natural juice and marinade are seared in. And you want to skid them over the oiled hot pan so that they spin, slither, dart, and tumble, giving the hot metal no time to scorch or pull out their juice and flavor. It is these brisk motions of your stirring hand that make a stir-fried dish spirited. This searing, or stir-frying, takes from a few seconds to several minutes, depending on the ingredients.

(3) VIGOROUS STEAMING—Here you first quickly add any seasonings, if called for, then the liquid. When it comes to a boil, you should quickly cover the pan, adjust the heat down a little to maintain a vigorous simmer, and then let the pan alone so the ingredients are "blossomed" into the cooked state. The time ranges from 1 minute to about 4 minutes, depending on the ingredients. Crackling noises from the pan will generally tell you that the liquid has evaporated.

(4) FINAL FAST BLENDING WITH SEASONINGS—You uncover the pan, add whatever should be added—dissolved cornstarch as a thickening or a few drops of sesame oil for an aromatic sheen, for example. Then you give the ingredients a few fast turns over high heat. This action shouldn't take more than a few seconds, since the purpose is to flavor and redistribute the moisture, not to cook further. But remember that a stir-fried dish is never watery, so do toss and turn long enough to glaze the ingredients. In general, there should be little or no liquid left in the pan, except for those dishes meant to be saucy.

Unlike Western cooking, where sauce making is often a separate procedure, most sauces in Chinese cuisine are created as the ingredients are being cooked. This is particularly true of stir-frying, where various seasonings are added during all steps, so that in spite of the short cooking time the ingredients have the benefit of being "marinade-cooked" and the sauce gets the added flavors of the ingredients. In shallow-frying and deep-frying, however, the sauce must be made separately.

A stir-fried dish should always be served immediately in a heated dish so that the "wok-heat" isn't dissipated.

•

I am using Stir-fried Green Beans as an initial recipe to illustrate the basic steps of the technique. The subsequent recipes, gradually becoming more complicated and involving a greater variety of ingredients, will cover key aspects of stir-frying. Practice them by using one recipe at a time to blend into your daily menu until you get the feel and rhythm of stir-frying.

清炒四季豆　STIR-FRIED GREEN BEANS

These brilliantly green beans are firm but tender and subtly aromatic of garlic. There is no ginger taste. The piece of ginger is not meant to season; it is used to eliminate the faint raw taste of grass often found with green beans when they are just lightly cooked and seasoned. *This will serve 3 to 4 as a vegetable dish.*

2 medium cloves garlic, lightly smashed and peeled	2 tablespoons oil
2 quarter-sized slices peeled ginger	1 to 1½ teaspoons salt, to taste
1 pound fresh green beans	¼ cup chicken stock or water
	2 teaspoons sesame oil (optional)

Preparations

Smash the garlic sharply with the flat of a cleaver or a wide, heavy knife; then slip off the peel. You'll find that this simple action makes peeling garlic very simple.

From a knob of ginger, slice off 2 pieces the size of an American quarter, then trim off the peel. Put both the ginger and garlic on your working platter.

Rinse the whole green beans in cold water and then pat them dry with paper towels. Then snip off the ends of the beans and break them in two. (All vegetables should be well drained or dry before being put into hot oil; excess water will splatter and will dilute the flavor in the initial searing step.) Place the beans on the working platter.

Assemble the oil, salt, and stock or water by the stove. Set a wok or large, heavy skillet on the burner and put its lid within reach. Take out a small spatula, chopsticks, slotted spoon, or whatever feels best. Have a hot serving dish ready.

Stir-frying

Heat the wok or large, deep skillet over high heat until hot, about 30 seconds. Add the 2 tablespoons oil, swirl, and heat about 30 seconds. Lower heat to medium and toss in the garlic and ginger; press them against the pan for a few seconds. Be careful not to let them burn; if you do, throw them out, along with the oil, and start over.

Turn the heat high and scatter in the green beans. Stir and toss them rapidly until every piece is covered with oil and the color has deepened to a bright green.

Then sprinkle in the salt, toss, and pour in the liquid. Turn heat to medium-low, even out the beans in the pan, cover, and let them steam-cook on medium-high heat for about 4 minutes. It is time to remove the cover when the even sound of boiling becomes almost a crackling sound, indicating that the liquid is almost evaporated.

Remove the cover and stir the beans in quick flipping motions until the liquid is completely gone. Taste and adjust with salt if necessary. If, for some reason, the beans are still a little too hard and grassy-tasting, add a spoonful of stock or water and continue to stir until it disappears, but remember, these beans should have some resilience. (This rule applies to any ingredient that hasn't quite "blossomed" during the steam-cooking step.) If adding sesame oil, dribble it over the beans, give a few stirs, and then turn the beans out into a hot serving dish. Remove the ginger and garlic if you wish.

•

Here is a recipe, using green beans as a base, to show how the approach changes when beans are combined with meat and seasonings. In this case, the beans are deep-fried as a preparational step.

乾燒四季豆 SPICY GREEN BEANS WITH MEAT

This is a typical spunky Szechuan dish, in which the aromatic hot flavor is beautifully complemented by the crisp and chewy texture of the deep-fried beans. Green beans have a firm consistency; they don't absorb seasonings unless they are well simmered in a sauce or glazed with a cornstarch thickening. Since both would result in a moist softness that is not desired here, the beans are deep-fried in hot oil until wilted and wrinkled (in China in the old days this was accomplished by drying them in the sunlight), so that seasonings will penetrate them while they also acquire that unique sinewy crispness that comes only from having the water content extracted through dry heat.

An absolutely scrumptious dish with superb texture. *It is ideal for a simple dinner for 2 to 3 if served with rice.*

1 pound green beans
1 teaspoon minced peeled ginger
1 medium whole scallion, finely
    chopped
1 medium clove garlic, minced
½ pound ground lean pork or beef

2 cups oil
¼ cup meat or chicken stock or
    water
1 teaspoon cider vinegar
1 teaspoon sesame oil

Sauce:
1 teaspoon sugar
¼ teaspoon salt
1 teaspoon hot bean paste
1 tablespoon light soy sauce
1 tablespoon dry sherry

Preparations

Rinse the beans and dry with paper towels; snip off the ends and break beans in two. Put them on your working platter.

A slice of ginger about ¼ inch thick and 1 inch in diameter will yield 1 teaspoon minced ginger. The easiest way is to peel it, then cut off the proper amount, and place it flat on the board. Smash it with the side of a cleaver or heavy knife, then pull the knife forcefully over the smashed surface in one fast continued motion so that the ginger fibers are thoroughly squashed. Gather up the pulp and chop it a few times; it will readily break up in fine minces. Put them on your working platter.

Rinse and trim off the root end of the scallion. Flatten the bulb with the side of your knife to prevent rolling; then cut the scallion crosswise into 3 sections, hold them in a bundle, and chop them closely into fine pieces. Smash and peel the garlic, then mince it. Place the garlic and scallions with the ginger on your platter.

Put the meat on your chopping board and press it into a flat pile. March-chop it following illustrations on *page 17:* chop with a cleaver or heavy knife in a straight line, up and down, from one end to the other, a few times; then flip the meat over with the flat of the blade and repeat the march-chopping until the meat is smooth. (Ground meat should always be march-chopped; once "polished" this way, it seasons more evenly and cooks to a better consistency.) Put the meat on the working platter.

Measure out the sauce ingredients into a small bowl and stir until the sugar and salt are dissolved. One teaspoon hot bean paste is moderately hot.

Assemble all the rest of the seasonings and liquid near the stove; put a strainer over a small pot for draining the beans.

Heat a wok or large, deep skillet over high heat until hot; then add the oil and heat until hot enough to foam a cube of bread or piece of scallion instantly, about 375 degrees. Scatter the beans into the oil gradually, so the oil temperature doesn't drop drastically. Deep-fry them, stirring constantly, for about 3 minutes, until they are wrinkled. Turn off the heat and pour the whole thing, oil and beans, into the strainer over the pot. When oil is cold, rebottle it for general cooking. This step may be done in advance; cover and refrigerate the beans, but bring them to room temperature before the final stir-frying.

Stir-frying

Heat the wok or skillet until hot; add 2 tablespoons oil, swirl to cover the entire surface, and heat until hot. Turn the heat to medium, scrape in the ginger, garlic, and scallions, and stir a few times. Then turn the heat high and scatter in the meat, stirring it rapidly in poking and swishing motions to break up the lumps. Turn and flip it with chopsticks or a small spatula until it's no longer pink, about 1 minute. Then quickly pour the seasoning sauce over the meat and stir a few times to flavor it evenly. Add the stock or water, even out the pile of meat, turn heat to medium, cover, and let it steam-cook vigorously for about 2 minutes.

Turn heat high, add the green beans, and stir, flipping and turning, until the sauce has been absorbed by the beans and the meat clings nicely to them. Scrape the contents to the center of the pan, dash in the vinegar on the side, and immediately give the meat and beans a few sweeping turns. Sprinkle in the sesame oil, give the contents a few fast turns, and pour immediately into a hot serving dish.

•

Now that we have done the basics of stir-frying and have stir-fried a pretreated vegetable, we shall go on to an ingredient that has been marinated.

葱 爆 羊 肉 SCALLION ''EXPLODED'' LAMB

Because of the marinating and the short cooking time, the lamb is very tender and full of flavor. The scallions are used as a secondary ingredient, so don't stint on them. The seasoning sauce and high heat will wilt them slightly, but don't overdo that part of the cooking—they should retain their sweet, sharp flavor while being coated in the tasty sauce. This is a wonderful robust northern specialty. Beef (flank steak) can be substituted for the lamb with equally good results. A good accompaniment would be the Stir-fried Green Peas or Cauliflower and rice. *As a main course it would serve 2 or 3 people.*

1 pound boneless leg of lamb or loin, trimmed of fat	½ pound whole medium scallions 4 large cloves garlic, lightly smashed and peeled

Marinade:
½ teaspoon salt
1 teaspoon roasted and crushed
    Szechuan peppercorns
    (*page 500*)
2 tablespoons dark soy sauce
1½ tablespoons dry sherry

Seasoning sauce:
1 teaspoon sugar
1 tablespoon dark soy sauce
1 tablespoon dry sherry
1 tablespoon cider vinegar
1 tablespoon sesame oil

5 tablespoons oil

Preparations

Cut the lamb across the grain into paper-thin slices about 2 inches long and 1½ inches wide. Place them in a deep bowl. Mix the marinade and pour it over the meat, stir to coat well, and let the lamb marinate for at least 30 minutes.

Trim off the root ends and then rinse and dry the scallions. Flatten the bulbs slightly with the side of a heavy knife, slit the white part in two lengthwise, and then cut the entire scallions crosswise into 1½-inch-long sections. Smash and peel the garlic. Mix the seasoning sauce in a bowl until the sugar is dissolved. Put all the ingredients on a working platter.

All the cutting preparations may be done in advance, but the seasoning sauce should not be mixed until you are ready to cook, lest the aroma of the vinegar dissipate. Any ingredients refrigerated should be brought to room temperature before stir-frying.

Stir-frying

Heat a wok or large, heavy skillet over high heat until hot, about 30 seconds; add the oil, swirl, and heat until hot. Lower the heat, add the garlic, and quickly stir and press the cloves in the hot oil for about 5 seconds. Turn up the heat again, scatter in the marinated meat, and stir and toss briskly for 10 seconds. Shower in the scallions; stir rapidly in tossing motions until their color deepens and each piece is gleaming with oil. Then quickly splash in the seasoning sauce and stir vigorously for about

1 minute in sweeping and flipping motions until the meat and vegetables have absorbed most of the seasonings.

Pour the meat and scallions into a hot serving dish and serve immediately.

•

The meat of chicken breast, with its white color and even texture, is ideal for velveting. Once velveted, it becomes snowy, fluffy, and extremely tender—its tendency to dryness being completely eliminated. Once treated, it lends itself to endless variety when mingled with various other ingredients or seasonings. Almost all chicken used in stir-fried dishes is velveted. Here is the master recipe.

MASTER RECIPE FOR VELVETING CHICKEN

1 pound boneless and skinless
    chicken breasts (about 2
    pounds with bone in)

Velvet-coating:
½ teaspoon salt
1 tablespoon dry sherry
1 large egg white
1 tablespoon cornstarch
1 tablespoon oil

2 cups oil

Boning and cutting the meat

If you have to bone the breast meat yourself, follow these steps: 1) Remove the skin, 2) cut through the meat along the breast ridge, then cut in scraping motions over the rib cage to free the meat as you pull it with your

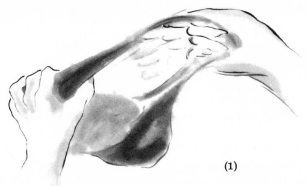

(1)

other hand. Trim off the fat and membrane, and separate the 2 tubular fillets from the breast meat. You now have 4 pieces.

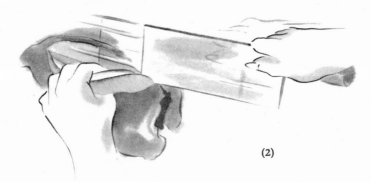

(2)

    Cutting is easier and neater if you wrap the meat in aluminum foil and freeze it for a few hours until firm but not hard. See discussion on *page 22.*

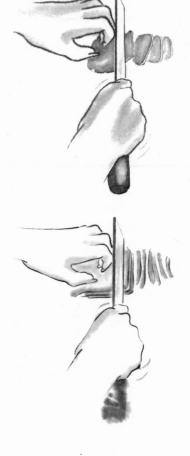

    FOR SLICES—Cut the large pieces of breast meat crosswise (against the grain) into ⅛-inch-thick slices, then cut the slices in half if they are very long. They should be 1½ to 2 inches long. The tubular fillets are formed over a tough tendon: score the meat along the tendon with the tip of your knife halfway to flatten the meat and expose the tendon; then pull and loosen it with the tip of your knife and discard. Then slice the meat on a slant crosswise to get wider slices, comparable to those made from the rest of the breast meat.

    FOR SHREDS—Slice the meat crosswise into ⅛-inch-thick slices, or a little thicker. Stack a few of these slices together or place them in a slanting stack, then cut them along their length into shreds. If they are very long, cut in half. Shreds should be about 1½ inches long, ⅛ inch in diameter.

FOR DICE—Cut the meat
lengthwise (*with* the grain) into
¼-inch-wide strips; gather them up
and cut them crosswise into ¼-inch
dice.

FOR CUBES—Cut the meat
lengthwise into ½-inch-wide strips;
gather them up and cut them crosswise into ½-inch cubes.

Coating

Put the cut meat into a bowl, add the salt and sherry, and stir. Beat
the egg white only until the gel is completely broken—it should not be
frothy, lest the coating puff and disintegrate upon cooking. Add this to the
chicken, sprinkle in the cornstarch, and mix well. Add the tablespoon of oil
and stir until smooth. Let the chicken sit in the refrigerator for at least
30 minutes so that the coating has time to adhere to the meat.

VELVETING IN OIL—Just before velveting the chicken, assemble everything you need: a wok or deep skillet on the stove, a strainer set
over a small pot, and a pair of chopsticks, wooden spoon, or spatula. Do
not use sharp implements such as a fork for turning the meat in the oil.

Heat the wok or skillet over high heat until very hot; then turn heat
to medium, add 2 cups oil, and heat for about 40 seconds until it is warm,
about 275 degrees, or until it foams a cube of bread or piece of scallion very
slowly. Give the coated chicken a big stir and scatter in the pieces; quickly
but gently stir them to separate them. The oil should cover every piece.
Lower the heat immediately if the chicken begins to sizzle; hot oil will make
velveted chicken hard and yellow.

When the meat turns white, which takes about 30 to 45 seconds only,
immediately pour both oil and chicken into the strainer, reserving the oil.
The chicken is now velveted, ready to be stir-fried. When the oil is cool,
strain and rebottle it.

Velveting can be done well before the stir-frying. If you are going
to use the chicken in an hour or so, do it in oil as above; do not refrigerate
the chicken, however, or it will harden. If you do want to refrigerate or
freeze velveted chicken, you must use water instead of oil.

VELVETING IN WATER—Bring 1 quart water to a boil, add 1
tablespoon oil to "grease the liquid," and then lower the heat to maintain
a very gentle simmer. Scatter in the chicken, stir to separate, and keep

stirring gently until the coating turns white. Then immediately pour into the strainer to drain.

As the name "velveting" implies, the coating is white and fluffy and the meat is as soft as velvet. While the oil method gives the meat a firmer texture, the water method produces a softer coating. In either case, the meat is on the verge of being fully cooked, which is ideal for the process of stir-frying.

• *The keys to velveting:* The oil in the coating makes it lustrous and prevents lumping; it also eliminates the mealiness of cornstarch. When velveting is done in oil, the wok or skillet must be very hot before the oil goes in, so that the coated chicken does not stick to the pan. The oil, however, should not be hot, or it will toughen the chicken.

•

Now that you have velveted chicken on hand, here are some recipes showing how to use it in stir-frying.

磨菇鷄片 CHICKEN WITH ASSORTED VEGETABLES

Better known as Moo Goo Gai Pan in Chinese restaurants, this recipe is very popular among people who love crisp Chinese vegetables. Characteristic of Cantonese cooking, this is a chunky, glazy dish; *it would serve 2 or 3 people as a main course with rice.*

1 pound velveted chicken breast in slices (*see preceding recipe*)

1 large clove garlic, lightly smashed and peeled

2 quarter-sized slices peeled ginger

Vegetables:
¾ cup Chinese or celery cabbage, cut into ½-inch pieces
¼ cup sliced bamboo shoots
4 water chestnuts, sliced
½ cup canned button mushrooms
8 to 10 fresh snow peas

3 tablespoons oil
½ teaspoon salt
¼ cup chicken stock or water

Sauce:
1 tablespoon light soy sauce
1 tablespoon oyster sauce
1 tablespoon dry sherry
½ teaspoon sugar
A dash white pepper
2 teaspoons cornstarch dissolved in 2 tablespoons water
2 teaspoons sesame oil

Preparations

Set out the velveted chicken; if you have done it in water and refrigerated or frozen it, let it come to room temperature.

Smash the garlic lightly and peel. Slice the ginger. Wash and shake dry 2 or 3 inner stalks of Chinese or celery cabbage; cut them crosswise into ½-inch pieces. Rinse and drain the sliced bamboo shoots. Turn the water chestnuts on their sides and cut them into slices. Drain the mushrooms. Rinse and string the snow peas; place them in a strainer, dip in boiling water for 15 seconds, spray with cold water, and drain. Put all the vegetables in separate piles on your working platter. Combine the sauce seasonings and stir until the sugar is dissolved. All these preparations may be done in advance.

Stir-frying

Heat a wok or large, heavy skillet over high heat until hot; add the 3 tablespoons oil, swirl, and heat until hot. Toss in the garlic and ginger and press them against the pan; scatter in the cabbage and bamboo shoots and stir-fry about 30 seconds. Then scrape in the water chestnuts and mushrooms. Stir them in rapid turning and tossing motions a few times; sprinkle in the salt and toss a few more times. Add the stock or water, even out the vegetables, spread the chicken on top, cover, and steam-cook vigorously over high heat for about 45 seconds.

Uncover, toss in the snow peas, add the sauce seasonings, and stir spiritedly in brisk turning, tossing, and flipping motions for about 30 seconds, until the sauce glazes the meat and vegetables. Sample the flavor and add a little more soy sauce if you find it necessary, especially if you use water instead of stock. Pour into a hot serving dish.

VARIATION

If you don't like oyster sauce, use more soy sauce instead.

薑
葱
茄
汁
鷄
球
CHICKEN IN GINGER-SCALLION TOMATO SAUCE

The dark meat of chicken legs is coarser than breast meat, but it's very tasty. It does not slice well, but it is good for dicing or cubing. First scored so that it may be cooked in a very short time, the meat is then cut into chunky cubes, velveted until done, then tumbled briefly with a rich sauce by the stir-frying technique. Fluffy, thick, and reddish in color, this pure meat dish makes *a delicious main course for 2 or 3 when accompanied by rice and two vegetable dishes,* either Spicy Minced Watercress plus Stir-fried Cauliflower or Stir-fried Lima Beans plus Celery.

2½-pound broiler or 1 pound
    boneless chicken meat, light
    and dark
2 large or 4 small scallions, finely
    chopped
4 quarter-sized slices peeled ginger,
    minced

Sauce:
2 tablespoons light soy sauce
2 tablespoons dry sherry
2 tablespoons catsup
1 teaspoon cider vinegar
¼ teaspoon salt
½ teaspoon sugar
Sprinkling black pepper

2 tablespoons oil
2 teaspoons sesame oil

Preparations

A 2½-pound broiler will yield about 1 pound of white and dark meat. It pays to bone a whole chicken yourself if you need the carcass to make a light stock or soup. If you buy chicken parts, get a breast and two whole legs (drumstick and second joint).

BONE THE BROILER—First disjoint the wings and the entire legs. Peel off the breast skin, and cut against the breast ridge and ribs to remove the meat. Pull the leg skin down; then, using the tip of a small knife, cut down the middle of the second joint and leg bones, then around the bones, and free the meat. Set aside the skin, bones, wings, and the carcass for making stock.

Score the smooth surface of both light and dark meat by cutting about halfway through in a crisscross fashion; your scoring should be about ½-inch apart. Cut the scored chicken into 1-inch cubes or as close as possible to that size.

Marinate, set, and velvet the meat in oil as in the master recipe (*page 75*), increasing the cooking time to about 2 minutes so that the meat is really fully cooked. Keep heat on and stir gently but rapidly in abrupt scooping, turning, swishing, and basting motions. Strain the meat, reserving the oil; when drained, pile meat on your working platter. You should not do this too much in advance; it is better for the meat to be still a little warm for the final brief cooking.

Rinse and shake dry the scallions; trim off the root ends, flatten bulbs with the side of a knife, and then chop the scallions into fine pieces. Peel and slice the ginger; smash lightly, then chop a few times to break them into fine minces. Place the scallions and ginger on the working platter. Combine the sauce ingredients and stir until the salt and sugar are dissolved. Put sauce and sesame oil near the stove.

Stir-frying

Heat a wok or large, heavy skillet over high heat until hot; add the 2 tablespoons oil, swirl, and heat until hot. Lower the heat and scatter in the scallions and ginger; toss them rapidly for about 15 seconds. Give the sauce a big stir and pour into the pan, getting every last bit with a spoon, then stir it quickly with the back of the spoon about 2 to 3 seconds to blend the sauce with the seasoning agents and the hot oil. Add the chicken cubes and turn the heat high; stir briskly in rapid folding and sweeping motions to roll and tumble them in the sauce. Sprinkle in the sesame oil, give the chicken a few final sweeping folds, and pour immediately into a hot serving dish, scraping in all the tiny scallion pieces.

•

Being so inherently tender and versatile, shrimp are beautiful candidates for stir-frying. They are stir-fried either shelled or with shells on. When shelled, they are often first velveted to preserve their fine texture and prevent them from acquiring a woodiness that comes from cooking them in liquid without protection. Sometimes the shrimp are briefly deep-fried, called "passing-through-oil" in Chinese, until they acquire a blistered surface as protection against woodiness. This method makes the shrimp firm and crisp instead of fluffy and soft.

Here, as basic practice, I am giving you three recipes: the master recipe for velveting shrimp; velveted shrimp combined with a vegetable; and shrimp stir-fried with the shells on. You will find the shrimp "passing-through-oil" in the seafood chapter (Shrimp in Lobster Sauce).

MASTER RECIPE FOR VELVETING SHRIMP

1 pound shelled medium-sized shrimp, about 25 to 30 shrimp to a pound	*Velvet-coating:*
	½ teaspoon salt
	2 teaspoons sherry
	1 large egg white
	1½ tablespoons cornstarch
	1½ tablespoons oil

2 cups oil

Preparations

The procedure is the same as that for velveting chicken except that there's a bit more cornstarch—shrimp need extra protection because of their fragile texture.

Place the shrimp in a deep bowl; sprinkle in the salt and sherry, and mix well gently. Beat the egg white just until the gel is completely broken and add to the shrimp. Sprinkle in the cornstarch and mix until smooth. Add the oil and stir well. Place the shrimp in the refrigerator for 30 minutes, so that the cornstarch will set and the coating adhere to the shrimp.

Velveting in oil

Heat a wok or large, deep skillet over high heat until very hot. Add the 2 cups oil and heat over medium heat until the oil is warm but not hot —about 275 degrees, or until it foams a cube of bread very slowly. Scatter in the shrimp and stir gently in a rocking motion so that they separate and are coated all over with oil. The moment they turn white with a pinkish undertone, pour both oil and shrimp into a strainer over a pot and let them drain; then put them on a plate. The shrimp are now ready to be stir-fried.

Velveting in water

Like chicken, shrimp can be velveted by water. Bring a small pot of water to a boil, add 1 tablespoon oil, and scatter in the coated shrimp. Stir gently to keep them in motion, and when they float to the top and have turned white, pour water and shrimp immediately into a strainer over a pot and drain.

Do not freeze velveted shrimp, even if done in water; they harden.

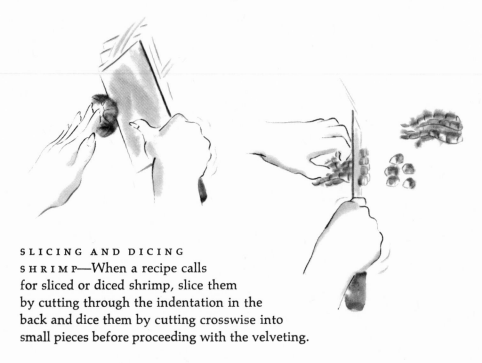

SLICING AND DICING
SHRIMP—When a recipe calls
for sliced or diced shrimp, slice them
by cutting through the indentation in the
back and dice them by cutting crosswise into
small pieces before proceeding with the velveting.

芥蘭炒蝦 VELVETED SHRIMP WITH BROCCOLI FLOWERETS

This is a lovely light dish, bright green broccoli contrasting with the fluffy pink-and-white shrimp. In a Chinese meal it would blend well with a red-cooked meat or fowl or any one of the spicy bean-paste-seasoned meat or poultry dishes. *It serves 2 or 3 as a main course.*

2 cups fresh broccoli flowerets
1 pound velveted medium-sized
    whole shrimp (*see preceding
    recipe*)

Sauce:
1 tablespoon light soy sauce
1 tablespoon dry sherry
½ teaspoon sugar
2 teaspoons sesame oil

3 tablespoons oil
4 thin slices peeled ginger
1 medium clove garlic, lightly
    smashed and peeled
½ teaspoon salt
1 tablespoon dry sherry
3 tablespoons chicken stock or
    water

Preparations

Rinse and shake dry a medium head of broccoli. Break off the individual flowerets; cut any large ones so that they are all uniform in size. (Save the broccoli stalks for another dish. See vegetable chapter. Sliced thin they are a lovely substitute for snow peas in any recipe calling for them.)

Bring a large pot of water to a boil with a dash of salt and cook the flowerets rapidly for about 1 minute. Drain into a colander. Spray with cold water to stop the cooking; cover and refrigerate. This step can be done in advance. Let them come to room temperature before stir-frying.

Velvet the shrimp. If done in advance, do not refrigerate.

Mix the sauce seasonings, stirring till sugar is dissolved.

Stir-frying

Heat a wok or large, heavy skillet over high heat until hot; add the 3 tablespoons oil, swirl, and heat for 30 seconds. Lower the heat and press the ginger and garlic around in the hot oil a few times. Then turn the heat up and scatter in the broccoli; stir and toss briskly for about 30 seconds. Sprinkle in the salt and sherry, add the stock, and stir a few times. Then add the shrimp, stir to mingle well—just long enough to heat through, and finally add the sauce seasonings. Stir in fast turning and folding motions until the liquid has evaporated. Pour into a hot serving dish and serve immediately.

葱爆蝦 SCALLION-OIL SHRIMP

A marvelous cold shrimp dish that I especially like because it can be done in advance and its flavor improves with standing. The crackling shells are left on, giving the meat protection and a richer flavor, as well as slowing down the eating so that you can enjoy the texture and aromatic sauce between sips of wine. A popular dish in the East on a cold buffet, here the pink-orange shrimp speckled with dark green scallions could be piled into a pyramid and surrounded by assorted meats, poultry, and vegetables. Also good hot, *it will serve 2 to 4 as a main course with vegetables and rice, and 6 to 8 as an appetizer.*

1 pound bay or very small shrimp
1 chubby knob peeled ginger,
    about 1 inch long, minced
4 medium-sized cloves garlic,
    lightly smashed and peeled
8 medium whole scallions, finely
    chopped

3 tablespoons oil
¼ cup light soy sauce
¼ cup dry sherry
4 teaspoons sugar

If you don't live in an area where bay shrimp are available (which number about 50 shrimp to a pound), buy the smallest shrimp you can. Remove the legs, leaving the shells on; rinse and pat them dry thoroughly. If you have to use larger shrimp, then cut in half crosswise. Be sure they are dry—excess water will make the oil splatter and dilute the flavor.

Peel the ginger, smash it hard with the flat of a knife in a pulling motion, and mince by chopping it a few times. Smash the garlic cloves and peel them. Cut off the root ends, rinse, and dry the scallions; flatten the bulbs with the flat of a knife and cut them into sections; hold them together and chop both the green and white parts fine. Put everything in order on the working platter.

Heat a wok or large, heavy skillet over high heat until hot; add the oil, swirl, and heat for 30 seconds. Lower the heat and press and stir the ginger and garlic in the hot oil about 10 seconds. Turn the heat high, add the shrimp, and stir rapidly until they turn a pink-orange (about 30 to 45 seconds). Then scatter in the scallions, stir and toss until their color deepens; then add the soy sauce, sherry, and sugar. Stir-fry, flipping briskly, for about 1 minute until the sauce is slightly condensed and cooked into the shrimp. Pour into a serving dish and serve, or let the shrimp cool slightly and then cover and refrigerate them to serve cold later. Bite into the shell and extract the meat, sucking the wonderful light sauce.

豆
豉
牛
肉

BEEF IN BLACK-BEAN SAUCE

This recipe is a good illustration of slippery-coating. Flank steak is coarse-grained and tough, but we shall see how the meat becomes extremely tender through cutting, marinating, coating, and fast cooking in hot oil over high heat.

Seasoned with fermented black beans, garlic, ginger, and oyster sauce, and embellished with onions and peppers, this is a hearty dish full of aroma and good flavor. *It serves 2 or 3 as a main course with rice to soak up the delicious sauce.*

1 pound flank steak, trimmed of fat

Slippery-coating:
1 tablespoon light soy sauce
1 tablespoon dry sherry
¼ teaspoon sugar
1½ tablespoons cornstarch
1 tablespoon oil

2 large cloves garlic
2 quarter-sized slices peeled ginger
1 tablespoon fermented black beans
1 large green pepper, sliced
    (about 1 cup)

1 large onion, sliced (about 2 cups)
⅓ cup chicken or meat stock or
    water

Sauce:
1 tablespoon oyster sauce
2 teaspoons dark soy sauce
1 tablespoon dry sherry
½ teaspoon sugar
2 teaspoons sesame oil

2 cups oil
¼ teaspoon salt

Preparations

Cut the meat lengthwise (with the grain) into 3 strips; then cut each strip crosswise (against the grain) into ⅛-inch-thick slices, snapping your knife outward with each cutting to break the attaching fibers so that each piece is separated and neat. Toss the slices into a bowl and add the slippery-coating ingredients in the order listed, sprinkling in the cornstarch and mixing it in before stirring in the oil. Let the meat marinate, refrigerated, for at least 30 minutes. This coating process may be done hours in advance. The chilling sets the cornstarch, making the coating adhere to the meat.

Smash the garlic cloves and peel them; then mince. Smash the ginger; then mince it. Rinse the fermented black beans in a strainer briefly to remove salt; drain and chop them coarsely. Put all these ingredients at one end of a working platter in separate piles.

Rinse and dry the pepper; cut it in half lengthwise; seed and derib it. Trim off the curved ends so that the pieces lie flat for even cooking. Slice the halves lengthwise into ¼-inch-wide pieces; if they are very long, cut in half crosswise first. Peel the onion; cut it in half lengthwise, then cut each half into wedges comparable in size to the pepper pieces. Place the peppers and onions at the other end of the working platter in separate piles.

Measure out the stock or water. Combine the sauce ingredients and stir until the sugar is dissolved. Place a strainer over a small pot for draining the slippery-coated meat.

Heat a wok or deep skillet over high heat until hot; add the 2 cups oil and heat until hot enough to foam a cube of bread or a piece of scallion instantly, about 375 degrees. Pour in the meat and immediately stir with chopsticks or a metal or wooden spoon in fast but gentle circular motions to separate the pieces and to swish them with the hot oil for about 30 seconds, until the coating is formed. Pour meat and oil immediately into the strainer over the pot. When the oil has drained off, turn the meat onto a plate.

You can do all these preparations and slippery-coating an hour or longer in advance, but the succulence of the meat will suffer if the slices sit around too long or are chilled.

Stir-frying

Heat a wok or large, heavy skillet over high heat until hot; add 2 tablespoons oil, swirl, and heat until hot. Lower the heat, scrape in the garlic and ginger, and stir a few times until the garlic is slightly browned.

Add the fermented black beans and press and toss them with a spoon or spatula for 30 seconds to release their flavor. Turn heat high, scatter in the peppers, and stir for 30 seconds in brisk flipping and turning motions to sear them well. Add the onions and the salt and stir rapidly for 1 minute until the onions are glistening. Pour in the stock, spread the beef over the vegetables, cover, and let them steam-cook vigorously over medium-high heat for 1½ minutes.

Uncover, turn heat high, pour in the sauce, and stir briskly in fast sweeping motions for about 30 seconds until the meat and vegetables are evenly flavored and the sauce is slightly glazy. Pour into a hot serving dish.

One of the common errors in making this beef is to use additional cornstarch in the sauce, which makes it far too starchy. The beef is already well coated with cornstarch, and during the steam-cooking a sufficient amount of it is drawn into the sauce. When the beef and vegetables are stirred together in the final stage, the seasonings and stock blend with the cornstarch to give a consistency that needs no further thickening.

VARIATIONS

You could use additional dark soy sauce instead of the oyster sauce.

You could also omit the vegetables and use the beef as a crowning meat over a separately stir-fried vegetable, such as spinach, Chinese or celery cabbage, or broccoli (see the vegetable chapter). In that case, after slippery-coating the meat in the oil, turn it out onto a plate and then stir-fry the vegetable you want; put it on a hot serving platter, in a neat flat mound. Then sear the garlic, ginger, and fermented black beans in hot oil as above, add the meat and stir a few times, then add the stock or water, cover, and steam-cook for 1 minute over high heat. Add the sauce; stir briskly until the meat is evenly seasoned and the sauce is slightly glazy. Pour the meat over the stir-fried vegetables. This "crowning" is characteristic of the Cantonese school of cooking—especially nice, and practical, when you have just a small amount of meat. When spread on top, it looks better and is not dwarfed by the vegetables.

Shallow-frying

Shallow-frying is the slow searing of thick slices or chunks of floured or battered ingredients in hot oil over moderate to low heat. They are spread evenly in the pan, browned on one side, and flipped over to brown on the other side until the center is cooked through. The method is very similar to sautéing. Since the ingredients cannot be disturbed, the sauce is cooked separately and either poured on after the dish is cooked or splashed on the ingredients toward the end of the cooking, over high heat. Sometimes the sauce is served as a dip on the side. The sauces accompanying these firm, crusty ingredients are either thin and spunky or creamy and rich.

Usually a shallow-fried dish is made up of only one ingredient, although sometimes different ingredients are sliced and stacked or minced and mixed together and formed into patties for shallow-frying.

In spite of its basic limitations, compared to the almost infinite range of stir-frying, shallow-frying is a much used technique, especially for cooking and reheating doughy dishes such as savory or sweet pastries and dumplings. When noodles are shallow-fried until crisp and crunchy, they are known as the "two-sides-brown"—unusual and delicious (*page 441*).

As simple as shallow-frying is, there are a few rules to keep in mind: (1) Use a heavy skillet, since food burns easily in thin metal. (2) Always start with a very hot skillet, so the crust can form cleanly. (3) Maintain the oil at a moderate heat once the cooking starts so that the crust develops slowly and becomes crunchy rather than hard and brittle.

One of the knacks to shallow-frying is to pour in more oil than needed at the beginning to "wash down" the skillet. After heating the oil, pour out the excess. In doing so, you cool the skillet momentarily and thus make sure the ingredients aren't browned instantly. And, when you add more oil, dribble it into the skillet from the side, so that it has time to heat as it seeps down toward the center of the pan.

荷 包 蛋 POCKET EGGS

These fried eggs, which make an unusual brunch dish, are folded over into half-moon pockets, encasing each soft center within a delightful crunchy exterior. The splashed-on vinegary sauce is refreshing. *Serves 2 to 4.*

Sauce:	2 tablespoons oil
1½ tablespoons light soy sauce	4 eggs
2 teaspoons sugar	Sprinkling salt
2 teaspoons cider vinegar	

Combine the sauce ingredients in a bowl and stir until the sugar is dissolved. Set it by the stove along with a lid to cover the skillet.

Heat a large, heavy skillet over high heat until very hot; add the oil, swirl, and heat until hot. Pour out about ½ tablespoon oil into a small dish and lower the heat slightly. Break the eggs into the pan and fry them about 45 seconds to 1 minute until the whites are jelled around the edges and the bottoms are light brown. Sprinkle a little salt over the yolks. Slip a spatula under each and fold it over into a crescent shape, pressing the edge gently with the tip of the spatula until it is sealed. Let them shallow-fry for about 20 seconds. Dribble in the reserved oil, flip the eggs, and shallow-fry them another 20 seconds or longer if you like the eggs firmer.

Turn heat to high, give the sauce a stir, and splash it over the eggs with one hand and clamp on the lid with the other. Turn off the heat immediately; swirl the pan a few times as it sizzles and sputters. Transfer the eggs with a spatula to a plate, with the sauce, and serve.

乾 煎 蝦 SHRIMP IN HOISIN AND GARLIC SAUCE

Shrimp shallow-fry extremely well, especially with the shells on. Here they are marinated, rolled in cornstarch, and shallow-fried until crusty outside but extremely tender inside. Covered with a rich sauce, they are absolutely delicious. *They serve 2 to 3 as a main course with rice and a light stir-fried vegetable or salad.*

1 pound large shrimp, about 24

Marinade:
1 teaspoon light soy sauce
¼ teaspoon salt
1 tablespoon dry sherry

½ cup cornstarch
2 tablespoons oil
4 large cloves garlic, lightly
    smashed and peeled

Sauce:
2 tablespoons hoisin sauce
2 tablespoons catsup
2 tablespoons light soy sauce
1 tablespoon dry sherry
¼ teaspoon salt
½ teaspoon sugar
¼ cup water

1 teaspoon cornstarch dissolved in
    1 tablespoon water and
    1 tablespoon sesame oil
4 tablespoons oil
Garnish: Fresh coriander leaves or
    shredded scallions

Preparations and sauce-making

For shell-on shrimp, you should always select shrimp that do not have obvious black veins, since you can't devein them. The vein is tasteless, however.

Remove the legs and rinse the shrimp in cold water; pat them dry thoroughly. Place them in a bowl and toss with the marinade and let them marinate for about 15 minutes. Pile the cornstarch on a plate and roll the shrimp in it until nicely coated.

Mix the sauce ingredients well, till the sugar dissolves. Heat a small skillet or saucepan over high heat until hot; add 2 tablespoons oil, swirl, and heat until hot. Reduce heat to medium low and sear the garlic cloves for about 45 seconds, pressing them with a spatula to extract the flavor. Pour the sauce into the pan; let this liquid simmer, stirring constantly, for another 45 seconds. Discard the garlic. Give the cornstarch mixture a good stir and blend it into the sauce with a circular motion until the sauce thickens smoothly. Turn off the heat, cover, and let sauce sit while you fry the shrimp.

Shallow-frying

Heat a large, heavy skillet over high heat until very hot; add 4 tablespoons oil, swirl, and heat until hot. Pour out half the oil into a small bowl. Return skillet to heat, reduce heat to medium low, and lay the shrimp one by one in the oil. Brown them slowly on one side for about 3 minutes, gently shaking the pan or pushing the shrimp all the while. Flip them over, dribble in the reserved oil from the side, and brown the shrimp for 2 minutes more. Toward the end, heat the sauce over very low heat, stirring.

Pour the hot sauce over the shrimp, increase the heat to medium high, and let the sauce sizzle for a few seconds, turning the shrimp over a few times. Then scoop out the shrimp to a platter, arrange them in swirling circles, and pour the sauce over them. Garnish with coriander leaves or shredded scallions.

To the Chinese, licking, biting, and spitting are all done in the name of good eating, so let yourself go and bite into the shrimp. Roll it on your tongue to taste the sauce; then separate the shell from the meat with your teeth and spit the shell out or remove it with your fingers.

VARIATIONS

The sauce-sizzling procedure may be omitted: after shallow-frying, place the shrimp on the serving platter and pour the sauce over them.

The shrimp may also be shelled and done exactly the same way, but decrease the shallow-frying time by about 1 minute for each side.

煎
魚 **BUTTERFISH IN GINGER AND SCALLION SAUCE**

Fish, with its natural thin, firm skin, is another ideal ingredient for the slow method of shallow-frying. Here the fish will turn out crusty with a strong flavor of scallions. The sauce, which is reduced, is one of those thin, tasty ones that go well with shallow-fried dishes. As with the preceding shrimp, the film of cornstarch prevents the fish from sticking and helps form a good crust. *Serves 2 to 3 as a main course.*

4 butterfish or 1 whole flounder, about 1½ pounds	*Sauce:*
2 tablespoons cornstarch	½ teaspoon salt
2 medium whole scallions, finely chopped	½ teaspoon sugar
	3 tablespoons light soy sauce
2 teaspoons minced peeled ginger	2 tablespoons dry sherry
7 tablespoons oil	¼ cup water

The fish should be cleaned, but leave heads and tails on. Rinse and dry them well and dust them lightly with the cornstarch. Prepare the scallions and ginger. Mix the sauce seasonings until the salt and sugar are dissolved. Place everything near the stove.

Heat a large, heavy skillet over high heat until very hot; add 5 tablespoons oil, swirl, and heat for 30 seconds. Remove about 2 tablespoons of the oil to a dish and return the pan to the heat. Adjust heat to medium low and slip in the fish; brown them slowly for about 5 minutes. Flip them when golden brown, dribble in the reserved oil on the side of the pan, and brown them for another 5 minutes.

In the meantime, make the sauce. Heat a small skillet or saucepan over high heat until hot, add 2 tablespoons oil, and heat until hot. Reduce the heat to medium and rapidly stir-fry the scallions and ginger for about 30 seconds. Add the sauce seasonings and bring to a boil, stirring. Turn off the heat.

When the fish are firm and nicely browned, turn up the heat and pour in the sauce; let it bubble vigorously for about 30 seconds. Quickly but gently turn the fish and baste while the sauce sizzles into the fish. Remove the fish to a hot serving platter, scrape the specks of scallion and ginger on top, and serve.

Deep-frying

In most cuisines, deep-frying is used only for one purpose: to cook food in deep oil until the center is done and the crust is crisp and golden brown.

It is not so in Chinese cooking. Out of their love for variety and deep interest in textures, the Chinese bring diversity to the simple process of deep-frying. Foods look different because of the different ways they are cut, taste different because of marinating and saucing, and vary in texture through coating, precooking, drying, salting, and through the manipulation of oil temperature. This play on different kinds of crispness, however subtle, is carried so far that one Fukien specialty actually calls for passing deep-fried pieces of fish through cool liquid lard before serving, so that the crust may acquire an unusual emollient smoothness. And, out of their love for multiple-phase cooking, the Chinese give deep-frying a lot of latitude and a certain amount of prestige: it serves not only as a preparational step but also as one of several steps in many of China's gastronomic specialties.

Cutting

Except in recipes calling for a whole fish or fowl, ingredients are cut into manageable sizes—small chunks, medium cubes, or large but thin slices, so that the heat may penetrate to the center easily. When ingredients are minced or ground, they are formed into balls or rolls, in which case they are mixed with dissolved cornstarch or beaten eggs or encased in egg sheets, dough wrappers, or caul fat.

Marinating and coating

After being cut, the ingredient is marinated in a mixture of salt and sherry or in a soy sauce mixture, which seasons as well as tenderizes. Then it is dredged in a dry coating or enclosed in a batter consisting of cornstarch, flour, nuts, and various egg mixtures.

Deep-frying

The oil temperature and length of time for frying vary according to whether the ingredient is meat, poultry, or seafood; how it is cut; and whether it contains bones. Unlike the Japanese, the Chinese deep-fry only a very few vegetables. A well-dredged or battered ingredient is often fried until brown, removed from the oil to drain and cool, and is then fried again. The resting period gives the food a chance to cook with its own heat while the moisture in the coating evaporates so that it is crisper than normal. This also makes cooking in advance possible, so that just before serving only the final fast immersion is needed.

Sauces

Any sauce is cooked separately, with thickening, so that it glazes but never soaks the crisp coating. It is then added either by the rapid tumbling of the stir-frying technique, as with Sweet and Sour Pineapple Pork, or by blanketing, as with Deep-fried Whole Fish with Meat and Vegetable Sauce. When a deep-fried ingredient is served without a sauce it is usually accompanied by roasted salt-pepper (*page 501*).

General rules

Before proceeding to the sample recipes, there are some general rules for good deep-frying:

1. The pan should be heavy enough so that the oil will not burn easily, deep enough so that it holds a substantial amount of oil, and wide enough so that small ingredients can float and large ingredients can bathe and turn with ease. The ideal utensil is a Chinese wok or a large, deep skillet, but any heavy, deep utensil can be used, such as an enameled casse-

role, a Dutch oven, a soup kettle, or a roasting pan. If your wok is of thin metal, regulate the heat to prevent the oil from smoking.

2. Even if you are well versed in using chopsticks, you should have one of the long wooden-handled skimmers for separating, turning, anchoring, and straining the ingredients. The Chinese implement is better than a slotted spoon because it is wide and flat and its handle is exceptionally long; thus you can cook standing away from the sputtering oil. It is sold in all Chinese stores.

3. Always use plenty of oil so that the ingredients may bathe and be basted generously. Four cups in a wok or deep pot is about right for most small ingredients, and 6 for large ones. Skimping on oil invites uneven cooking; furthermore, there is no waste, since the oil can be strained and used time and time again. If you must deep-fry in a smaller quantity of oil, use a smaller pan and fry the food in batches if cut small; baste and turn more often if in large chunks.

4. As a general rule, the oil must be very hot when the ingredient goes in, so that the coating will form instantly without separation. Then the heat can be lowered to medium, with high heat again at the end. I don't fry with a thermometer; I judge the oil temperature by old-fashioned ways: first heat the pan until hot, and then heat the oil until it ripples and feels hot to the palm of your hand held about 3 inches above the oil. Then test it by throwing in a small cube of fresh bread, a small piece of scallion green, or a drop of batter if that is involved. If it sizzles instantly, the oil is very hot, in the range of 375 degrees; if it foams snappily, it is medium hot, about 350 degrees; if it does not foam, the oil is too cold for deep-frying.

5. So that the oil temperature doesn't drop too drastically, always scatter in small cuts in batches; slip in any large ingredient, such as a whole fish, slowly; and bring any chilled ingredient to room temperature before deep-frying it. A drastically lowered oil temperature will make the oil soak the coating; the result will be greasy.

鳳尾蝦 FANTAIL SHRIMP

Plain and simple, this shrimp is closest to the Western conception of deep-frying. Since the shrimp isn't pretreated or covered with a sauce, the batter becomes important. I am offering you three versions: the egg batter is crisp and fluffy, thicker than the second; the flour and cornstarch batter is crunchy and puffy; and the sesame seed batter is nutty and brittle. *This recipe serves 2 to 3 as a main course with a vegetable and rice.* The shrimp are also excellent appetizers; in that case, buy medium shrimp.

1 pound large or jumbo shrimp

Egg batter:
1 cup flour
1 tablespoon baking powder
½ teaspoon salt
¼ cup oil
1 egg, lightly beaten
¾ cup water

Flour and cornstarch batter:
6 tablespoons flour
6 tablespoons cornstarch
2 teaspoons baking powder
½ teaspoon salt
9 tablespoons water
3 tablespoons oil

Sesame seed batter:
1 cup flour
2 teaspoons baking powder
½ teaspoon salt
1 cup water
3 tablespoons sesame seeds

4 cups oil
Roasted salt-pepper (*page 501*)

Rinse, dry, shell, and devein the shrimp if necessary, but leave the tails on. Split the shrimp along the inner curve, but do not cut all the way through. Spread each shrimp out flat and tap with the broad side of a cleaver or knife. (Cutting along the inner curve prevents the shrimp from curling out of shape during the cooking.)

Make any one of the batters by measuring out the dry ingredients into a mixing bowl and then adding the liquid ones, singly and little by little, stirring until the mixture is a smooth, thick batter. For the third batter, fold in the sesame seeds last. Place the batter by the shrimp near the stove.

Heat the wok or heavy, deep pot; then add and heat the oil until a drop of batter foams instantly, about 375 degrees. Lower the heat a little. Then hold 1 shrimp by its tail and dip it into the batter to coat evenly; slip it into the hot oil. Repeat rapidly with the rest of the shrimp and deep-fry them for 3 minutes. Turn the shrimp constantly, with a gentle motion, after they're all in the oil. When they are golden brown, remove them with chopsticks, a skimmer, or a slotted spoon to paper towels to drain.

Arrange the shrimp on a serving platter and sprinkle a little roasted salt-pepper on top.

The shrimp may be done 10 to 15 minutes in advance and kept hot and crisp in a 200-degree oven. Or decrease the frying time by 30 to 45 seconds; then drain on paper towels. When ready to serve, refry until brown and crisp, about 30 seconds.

炸 子 鷄 FIVE-FRAGRANCE DEEP-FRIED CHICKEN

This recipe is one of the best examples of regular deep-frying, showing the bone-in chunk cutting, the marinating, and the double-frying procedure. The chicken is dark in color and smells and tastes wonderfully of anise. It is delicious hot, at room temperature, or cold. *As a main course, it would serve 3 or 4 with a light stir-fried vegetable.*

1 frying chicken, about 2½
    pounds, chopped

4 cups oil
Roasted salt-pepper (*page 501*)

Marinade:
3 tablespoons light soy sauce
1 tablespoon dark soy sauce
1 tablespoon dry sherry
½ teaspoon sugar
1 teaspoon five-fragrance powder
1 egg white
1 heaping tablespoon cornstarch

Chopping the chicken through the bones
This is the classic bone-chopping method for a whole chicken. Rinse and dry the chicken thoroughly; discard the tail and the fat from the cavity. Disjoint the chicken at the shoulders and thighs. Cut off and discard the wing tips; then chop each wing into 3 pieces, leaving the joint intact. Chop each whole leg into 5 pieces—twice across the thigh and twice across the drumstick, also leaving the big joint intact. The joints are covered with gristle—they are tastier when kept intact, if you like their chewy brittleness.

Turn the chicken on its side and chop through it at the base of the ribs to separate the breast from the back. Chop both breast and back lengthwise in half and then chop these crosswise into 5 or 6 pieces. The chicken will be bony; if any bones protrude too much, trim them off by anchoring your knife over them and banging the top of the knife with a mallet; you could also simply remove them. Do not skin the meat, however; the protection is needed. Discard any bone splinters.

Put the chicken pieces in a bowl; add the 2 kinds of soy sauce, sherry, sugar, and five-fragrance powder; toss well. Add the egg white and mix evenly; then sprinkle in the cornstarch and mix until smooth. Marinate for about 30 minutes. This should not be done in advance and chilled—it would dull the aroma.

Deep-frying

Heat a wok or heavy pot over high heat until hot; add 4 cups oil and heat until it foams a cube of bread snappily, about 350 degrees. Scatter in the chicken in about 3 batches, then stir them gently with a skimmer or chopsticks. The oil will be bubbling vigorously. Fry, stirring and turning, for about 3 minutes; the chicken will darken slightly.

Turn off the heat and scoop out the chicken onto paper towels. Let it rest for a minute or so. Then reheat the oil over high heat until very hot. Return all the chicken pieces and let them brown very rapidly for 1 to 1½ minutes, stirring constantly.

Drain again on paper towels and then serve the chicken with roasted salt-pepper on the side or sprinkled lightly on top.

甜 SWEET AND SOUR PINEAPPLE PORK
酸
菠
蘿
肉

This Sweet and Sour Pineapple Pork is a good example of glazing deep-fried food with a thickened sauce by a brief stir-frying tumble. The pork and sauce are cooked separately, then tossed together just before serving. The egg yolk in the marinade gives the crust a marvelous fluffy crispness. The meat may be cooked in several different ways, which you will find under Variations.

This makes a main course for 2 or 3 people when served with rice and a refreshing vegetable, such as Stir-fried Green Beans, Cauliflower, Broccoli, or Asparagus. A green salad would also go well with it.

1 pound boneless loin of pork, cubed

4 cups oil
¼ cup cornstarch mixed with
¼ cup all-purpose flour

Marinade:
½ teaspoon salt
2 teaspoons light soy sauce
1 teaspoon sesame oil
1 tablespoon cornstarch dissolved
in 1 tablespoon water
1 egg yolk, beaten

BASIC SWEET AND SOUR SAUCE

Seasonings:
5 tablespoons sugar
½ teaspoon salt
4 tablespoons distilled white
   vinegar
3 tablespoons light soy sauce
2 tablespoons dry sherry
3 tablespoons catsup

1 large clove garlic, lightly crushed
   and peeled
1 tablespoon cornstarch dissolved
   in 3 tablespoons water
1 tablespoon sesame oil
½ cup water
1 cup canned pineapple cubes
   (or see Variations)

2 tablespoons oil

Trim the meat of excess fat; then lightly pound the meat all over with the blunt edge of a cleaver or heavy knife to loosen its fibers and make it tenderer. Cut it lengthwise into strips about ¾ to 1 inch wide, then cut the strips crosswise into ¾- to 1-inch cubes. Place them in a mixing bowl. To marinate: Sprinkle in the salt and soy sauce and toss to coat evenly. Add the teaspoon sesame oil to the dissolved cornstarch and pour over the meat with the beaten egg yolk; stir in circular motions to coat the meat well. Let the meat marinate for 30 minutes or longer. The marinating may be done hours in advance; cover and refrigerate, and bring to room temperature before the final cooking.

Making the sauce
Neither too sweet nor too sour, too thin nor too thick, this is an excellent base sauce for all sweet and sour dishes. It may be made in advance at your leisure and reheated just before using. It keeps, covered and refrigerated, for days and freezes for weeks without losing its flavor.

Mix the sauce seasonings in a bowl, stirring until the sugar is dissolved. Crush and peel the garlic. Dissolve 1 tablespoon of cornstarch in 3 tablespoons of water and add 1 tablespoon sesame oil. Measure out ½ cup of water and set it aside. Drain the pineapple cubes and set aside.

Heat a large, heavy skillet over high heat until hot; then turn heat to medium. Add 2 tablespoons oil, swirl, and toss in the garlic, flipping and pressing it in the oil a few times. Then pour in the sauce seasonings slowly as you stir with the back of a spoon in a circular motion until the liquid comes to a boil. Turn heat low, add the cornstarch mixture, stirring circularly, until the sauce begins to thicken. Then add the water slowly as you stir in circular motions until the sauce is smooth and bubbly. Turn off the heat.

Final cooking

Heat a wok or large, heavy saucepan over high heat until hot; add 4 cups oil and heat until it foams a cube of bread snappily, about 350 degrees. While the oil is heating, dredge the marinated meat cubes in the cornstarch and flour mixture. Shake off excess flour and drop them into the hot oil and fry for about 1 minute, stirring constantly. Lower the heat slightly and continue to fry, stirring, for 2 more minutes. Turn off the heat and scoop out the meat with a skimmer or slotted spoon to drain on paper towels for about 1 minute. (If you haven't made the sauce yet, use this lull to do so.)

Reheat the oil to 350 degrees; scatter in the meat again, and fry, stirring now and then, for 2 more minutes until the coating is crisp and brown and the meat is thoroughly cooked.

In the meantime, bring the sauce back to a simmer over low heat; discard the garlic. Turn heat to medium high, add the pineapple cubes, and stir for 30 seconds or so to heat them through. Scoop out the meat from the oil with a skimmer or slotted spoon, pause over the pan to drain, then scatter the cubes into the sauce; turn heat high and stir in fast flipping and turning motions with a spoon or spatula to glaze the meat. Pour immediately into a hot serving dish.

VARIATIONS

The meat may be marinated in 2 teaspoons light soy sauce, ¼ teaspoon salt, and ½ teaspoon sugar for 30 minutes, then coated with any one of the batters on *page 94*.

Or simmer the meat for 3 minutes in 1 cup boiling water with a slice of ginger and 2 teaspoons light soy sauce. Drain and let cool, then mix with 1 beaten egg, dredge in ½ cup cornstarch or the cornstarch and flour mixture, and then deep-fry for about 2 to 3 minutes until the crust is brown and crisp. Add to the sauce as before.

As for the sauce ingredient, instead of pineapple you could use 1 cup preserved lichee fruit, kumquats, or mixed sweet pickles.

Or stir-fry 1 cup sliced onions, 1 cup sliced green peppers, and ½ cup sliced carrots in 2 tablespoons oil with ½ teaspoon salt for about 2½ minutes over high heat. Add the precooked sweet and sour sauce, bring to bubbling, add the pork, and toss to glaze as with the pineapple.

廣東「紅燒」魚 DEEP-FRIED WHOLE FISH WITH MEAT AND VEGETABLE SAUCE

The blanketing sauce for a deep-fried fish may be sweet and sour, as in the preceding recipe, or this meat and vegetable sauce.

The long list of ingredients creates a false impression of complexity; actually it is not at all complicated or hard to make. In reality, this recipe involves cooking two dishes, then combining them into one. The fish and sauce can be cooked separately at the same time, but until you can do this easily, make the sauce first and then reheat it just before the fish is ready for the blanketing. *It serves 3 or 4 as a main course, and would be more than adequate for 6 when served with other dishes in a Chinese meal.*

SAUCE INGREDIENTS
¼ pound lean loin of pork,
    shredded

Marinade:
1 teaspoon light soy sauce
1 teaspoon dry sherry
1 teaspoon cornstarch
1 teaspoon oil

4 large black Chinese mushrooms
    (presoaked)
¼ cup Golden Needles (presoaked)
1 cup shredded Chinese or celery
    cabbage
½ cup shredded bamboo shoots

Seasonings:
1½ tablespoons light soy sauce
1½ tablespoons dry sherry
½ teaspoon salt
½ teaspoon sugar
Dash black pepper

1½ cups chicken or meat stock
2 tablespoons cornstarch dissolved
    in 3 tablespoons stock or water
1 tablespoon sesame oil
4 tablespoons oil
2 quarter-sized slices peeled ginger,
    shredded
½ to 1 teaspoon salt to taste

THE FISH
1 sea bass or striped bass,
    about 2 pounds
½ teaspoon salt
¼ cup cornstarch
1 egg, well beaten
¼ cup all-purpose flour
6 cups oil
Garnish: 2 or 3 sprigs fresh
    coriander, chopped

Preparations

Slice the pork thin against the grain, and then shred the slices. Toss them into a bowl, add the marinade ingredients, and mix well. Let the meat marinate as you prepare the other ingredients.

In separate bowls cover the mushrooms and Golden Needles with hot water and soak for 30 minutes. Then rinse and lightly squeeze them dry. Destem and cut the mushrooms into shreds. Gather up the Golden Needles; then hold them together, cut off the knobby ends, and cut them in half.

Wash and shake dry a few tender stalks of Chinese or celery cabbage; cut them diagonally into shreds about 1½ inches long. Rinse and drain the shredded bamboo shoots. Place all the vegetables and the chopped coriander on a working platter.

Combine the seasonings in a bowl and stir until the salt and sugar are dissolved. Measure out the stock; dissolve the cornstarch in a separate bowl, add the sesame oil, and mix; and assemble everything within reach of the stove.

The fish should be cleaned and scaled, with the head and tail on. Rinse and dry it thoroughly. Make 3 slanting cuts about an inch apart on both sides of the fish; these cuts facilitate even cooking. Sprinkle ½ teaspoon salt over the fish and rub it in. All these preparations may be done ahead of time. The fish must be coated just before the deep-frying.

Cooking the sauce

Heat a large, heavy skillet over high heat until hot; add 2 tablespoons of the oil, swirl, and heat about 30 seconds. Scatter in the ginger, mushrooms, Golden Needles, Chinese cabbage, and bamboo shoots. Stir briskly a few times; add salt to taste; then stir vigorously for about 2 minutes until they are bright and glistening. Remove and set aside.

Clean the pan and heat it until very hot. Add 2 more tablespoons oil, swirl, and heat for a second. Scatter in the meat and stir rapidly in swishing and shaking motions to separate the shreds. Then stir in fast turning motions for about 30 seconds until the meat is no longer pink. Return the vegetables to the pan and stir to mingle well. Add the seasonings and mix well. Pour in the stock, even out the contents, cover, and steam-cook vigorously over medium-low heat for about 2 minutes. Lower the heat and add the cornstarch mixture slowly, stirring in a circular motion until the sauce is smoothly thickened. Turn off the heat. If you are doing this an hour or so ahead of time cover the pan. Reheat over low heat just before the fish is ready.

Deep-frying the fish

Sprinkle ¼ cup cornstarch over the fish on both sides, smoothing it all over with your fingers. Place it on a large tray or platter. Pour on the beaten egg and pat it all over the fish. Sprinkle with the flour, coating the fish evenly. Let the coating set a few minutes.

Heat until very hot a wok or any large pan that will hold the fish comfortably—this heating is crucial, since it prevents the fish from sticking to the pan. Add 6 cups oil and heat until it foams a cube of bread instantly, about 375 degrees. Lower in the fish slowly, head first, with a skimmer or large spatula, so the oil temperature isn't suddenly reduced. Deep-fry it for about 6 minutes on each side: 1 minute of high heat to firm the fish, 4 minutes of medium heat to cook the fish, and 1 more minute of high heat to crisp the coating. Baste it constantly with a large spoon and shift it gently now and then. The fish should be firm, brown, and crisp. Remove it from the oil and place it on a serving platter.

In the meantime, reheat the sauce; give it a few circular stirs to smooth out the consistency, then pour over the fish, sprinkle on the coriander, and serve.

Turning and removing a fish

Turning a whole fish in a large quantity of oil and removing it to a platter may seem troublesome activities if you're not used to them. If you are using a wok, make absolutely certain that the base ring is securely anchored over the burner. The easiest way to turn a whole fish while deep-frying is to slip a large spatula under the middle of the fish, lift and pull it slightly toward you, then ease it over with the help of chopsticks, a wooden spoon, or another spatula over the top. And the simplest way to remove the fish after deep-frying is to turn off the heat, then slip 2 spatulas under, lift it up, pause to drain over the pan, and slide it gently over to the serving platter.

COOKING WITH WET HEAT

Steaming is the most delicate and least demanding of all Chinese cooking techniques. And, while being inherently simple, steaming accomplishes great deeds and renders a multitude of services to Chinese cuisine.

A self-basting method, steaming preserves the natural flavors when the ingredients are unseasoned and intensifies the tastes when the ingredients are seasoned. Since a traditional Chinese stove, which is a walled hearth with openings on top, offers no enclosed compartment to retain even, dry heat for baking, steaming, with its steady, penetrating wet heat, becomes the logical means by which to expand and develop dough into soft, fluffy breads, cakes, and dumplings. By the same token, leftovers and pre-cooked foods can be reheated by steaming, which preserves the flavor and texture of freshly cured meats, and rejuvenates dried meats and vegetables. In the old days, purists did not simmer clear-simmered dishes over direct heat; they steamed them.

Steaming also contributes to the artistic aspects of Chinese cooking. In general, the aesthetic appeal of Chinese cuisine is keyed to fine cutting and contrast of natural colors. But, when a formal arrangement is wanted, steaming provides the means to soften ingredients for shaping, to solidify minced and mixed ingredients for molding, and to cook set arrangements without disturbance, such as Floral Bean-Curd Soup.

In steaming the food is contained in a dish and suspended over boiling water in a covered pot, which is set over high heat to generate a steady flow of intense steam. There are three important requirements: (1) the water should be boiling before the food is placed in the pot, so that it is "seared" immediately with high heat; (2) the food should be well suspended above the boiling water so that the water doesn't bubble over it, washing away the flavor and spoiling the texture; (3) the steaming pot should be large enough to contain enough water and provide enough space for the intense steam to circulate around the food. There are Chinese and Western steamers made for this purpose. You certainly should know how to use them if you have them, but you should also know how to devise your own when the ready-made are too small or shallow for the ingredients, such as a whole fish or fowl or a large piece of meat.

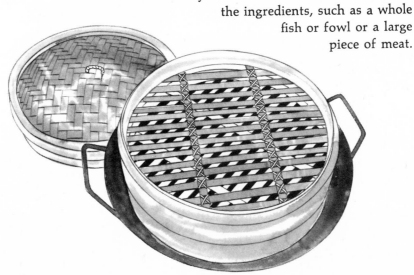

Chinese steamers

The Chinese bamboo steamers, available in Chinese stores across the United States, come in sizes ranging from miniature to gigantic—the first made explicitly for small dumplings and the latter for restaurant use. They are round trays with woven bamboo bottoms that fit tightly one over another in sets of 2 or 3 tiers; a solid wooden cover goes on top. The steamer should be set snugly inside a base pan, either a wok or a soup kettle, that is about 2 inches wider. If you wish to get a set, the practical size is a 12-inch steamer with 2 tiers and a cover—one tier for steaming a dish and the other for miscellaneous uses, such as warming dumplings or pancakes for Mo-shu Pork, rejuvenating Chinese sausages, or reheating leftovers.

Fresh or seasoned ingredients must be contained in a dish, which is placed on the woven bottom. Pancakes, dumplings, and cakes can be placed on a wet cloth or cabbage leaves laid on the tray; this protection prevents sticking as well as too much direct moisture.

Besides bamboo steamers, the Chinese also manufacture in Taiwan an aluminum steamer. It comes in 2 tiers with a base pot and a cover. The base pot may be used for cooking rice or simmering soup or meat while the upper compartments are used for steaming or warming something simultaneously.

Homemade steamers

To devise your own implements, take stock of all your large pots and pans and all the heatproof dishes you have. Place a cake rack, a trivet, a small bowl (with a little water in it), or an empty can with both ends removed in the center of the base pot as a rack and test out your steaming dishes to see which rack holds what dish properly. The base pot must be deep enough to hold at least 2 inches of water in the bottom and still have about 2 inches of space above the elevated food for the heat to circulate freely. It must be wide enough so that the steaming dish can be put in place and removed easily. If the food, such as a large chicken or a small turkey, rises above the pot, making it impossible to put the lid in place, create a dome of double-strength aluminum foil over it—allowing plenty of room for the heat to circulate—and tuck it securely under the rim of the base pan, permitting a little steam to escape so as not to create too much pressure and condensation within. A wok, roasting pan, or fish poacher, is ideal for steaming a large whole fish. And, in general, a wok is capable of handling most steamed dishes. There are steaming racks made for woks, but if you don't have one, use a small round roasting rack (about 10 inches in diameter) or even a can with both ends removed, about the size of a tunafish can.

Other points about steaming

The water line should come no higher than 1 inch from the top of the rack for a shallow plate and no higher than half the depth of a bowl if your ingredients are in one. Vigorously boiling water bubbles up about an inch, so always give yourself this inch as leeway.

A steady volume of steam should be maintained throughout the cooking time. Have a kettle of boiling water ready so you can add more water to the base pan when necessary. If the space between the dish and the pot is tight, insert a small funnel and add the water through it to prevent spilling water inadvertently into the dish.

Retrieving the hot dish is sometimes a problem. When you are steaming a heavy item and there's not much leeway for a firm grip, make a sling first: cross 2 kitchen towels or 2 strips of strong cloth and place them under the steaming dish. Drape them over the pot, cover, and tuck them on top of the lid. When the food is done, retrieve the dish by lifting it out with the sling.

清 STEAMED WHOLE FISH
蒸
魚

An excellent example of basic steaming for purity of flavor and texture is the steamed whole fish. While seasonings are purposely omitted, the spray of hot oil is crucial; it heightens the color and accentuates taste and aroma. You will get a wonderful whiff of freshly seared scallions when you pour it over the fish. It's that special touch that takes blandness to delicacy. If you by any chance don't eat it all, it is superb cold. The juices form a *gelée* and the meat is firm but succulent. *This recipe serves 3 to 4 as a main course.* It would go beautifully with Stir-fried Broccoli Flowerets or Spinach—something bright green.

1 sea bass, striped bass, whitefish,
   or trout, about 2 pounds
½ teaspoon salt
2 tablespoons dry sherry
4 quarter-sized slices peeled ginger,
   shredded
2 large whole scallions, cut into
   ½-inch-long shreds
2 tablespoons oil

Individual dip sauce:
1 tablespoon light soy sauce
1 teaspoon distilled white vinegar
¼ teaspoon minced peeled ginger

Have the fish cleaned and scaled but leave the head and tail on: a fish looks more important and its flavor is preserved better when it is whole. Rinse and dry it thoroughly. Make 3 diagonal slashes 1 inch apart on each side of the fish; they facilitate even cooking.

Place the fish on a heatproof platter. Dissolve the salt in the sherry and rub the liquid over and inside the fish; scatter the shredded ginger on top.

Place a suitable rack in the center of a wok or roasting pan and fill the pan with boiling water to within 1 inch of the top of the rack. Bring the water to a boil again, lower the heat, and place the platter on the rack. Then cover, turn heat to medium high, and steam the fish about 15 minutes, adding more boiling water if necessary. The fish is cooked when the eyes are white and the tip of a thin knife inserted into the thickest part of the fish comes out clean.

Remove the platter from the pot and slip it on top of a large serving platter. Scatter the shredded scallions on top of the fish. Then heat the oil in a small pan over very low heat until very hot but not smoking. Stand as far away as possible and pour the hot oil over the entire surface of the fish. Serve with the dip sauce on the side.

VARIATIONS

Here are a few tasty variations on the classic steamed fish.

WITH CLAMS—Scrub the shells of 12 small littlenecks or cherrystones well. Soak them in salted water with a clean iron nail for a couple of hours—the metal forces them to spit out the sand, a trick our cook Ar-chang told me that works well. Rinse the clams and place them around the fish, which has been prepared for steaming as in the master recipe, during the last 6 minutes of steaming time. When they are done (opened), scatter the scallions over the fish, sear with hot oil, and serve with the dip sauce on the side.

WITH BEAN CURD—Clean and score the fish but omit the salt-sherry rubbing. Lay the fish on the heatproof plate and scatter the shredded ginger on top. Cover 2 or 3 fresh bean-curd squares with hot water and soak for 15 minutes to soften them; then drain and cut them into large cubes. Place them around the fish. Mix 2 tablespoons light soy sauce, 2 tablespoons dry sherry, and ½ teaspoon salt, and pour over the fish. Steam, then scatter the scallions on top and sear with hot oil. Serve some Chenkong or red-wine vinegar on the side.

WITH BEAN CURD, GARLIC, AND FERMENTED BLACK BEANS—Clean, score the fish, omitting salt-sherry rubbing; lay on a heatproof platter with the presoaked bean-curd cubes around it (see above); omit the shredded ginger. Rinse 1 tablespoon fermented black beans briefly in cold water, drain, and chop coarsely with 1 or 2 cloves peeled garlic. Combine with 2 tablespoons light soy sauce, 1 tablespoon dry sherry, ½ teaspoon sugar, ¼ teaspoon salt, and 1 teaspoon minced ginger. Spread this over the fish, dribbling a little of it over the bean-curd cubes. Steam, scatter top of fish with 2 tablespoons finely chopped scallions, then sear with hot oil as before and serve without any dip sauce.

WITH BEAN CURD, BEAN PASTE, AND CHILI PEPPERS—Clean, score the fish, omitting salt-sherry rubbing; lay it on the heatproof platter with the presoaked bean-curd cubes (see above). Combine 1 tablespoon bean paste, 1 tablespoon light soy sauce, 1 tablespoon dry sherry, and ½ teaspoon sugar in a small bowl. Heat a small skillet over high heat until hot; then add 3 tablespoons oil, swirl, and heat a few seconds. Turn heat to medium low, toss in 4 small dried chili peppers, and flip and press them in the hot oil until they darken. Turn heat to medium, scatter in 1 tablespoon rinsed and coarsely chopped fermented black beans, 1 large clove minced garlic, 1 teaspoon minced peeled ginger, and 1 finely chopped large scallion. Stir briskly for about 45 seconds until they are bright and aromatic. Add this mixture to the seasonings in the bowl and stir to mingle well. Let the sauce cool a little, then pour it over the fish and dribble a little over the bean-curd cubes. Steam and serve without a dip sauce.

檸
檬
鷄 ## LEMON CHICKEN

Velveted and slippery-coated ingredients are ideal for steaming with rich seasonings for a very tasty, creamy result. This recipe gives you a lovely lemon-flavored sauce over a smooth succulent chicken. *It serves 2 to 4 as a main course with rice and something cool and green.*

1 pound sliced chicken breast,
    velvet coated (*page 75*)

8 thin lemon slices
Garnish: Sprig of fresh parsley or
    minced parsley

Sauce:
2 heaping tablespoons hoisin sauce
2 teaspoons bean paste
1 tablespoon light soy sauce
1 tablespoon dry sherry
1 teaspoon sugar
¼ teaspoon salt
1 tablespoon fresh lemon juice
1 teaspoon minced or grated
    lemon peel
1 tablespoon oil

Follow the preliminary steps for velveting the chicken according to the master recipe, but do not put it through the warm oil. Place it on a heat-proof platter, spreading out the meat evenly, without too much overlapping, so that the sauce can melt and flavor all the pieces.

Mix the sauce ingredients in a bowl until smooth; then spoon it all over the chicken and surround with the lemon slices. Steam over medium-high heat for 25 minutes, replenishing the boiling water if necessary. Put the hot platter on top of a larger serving platter and garnish the chicken with a sprig of parsley or dot the lemon slices with a little minced parsley.

蒸　MEAT PIE
肉
餅　While Westerners bake a meat loaf, the Chinese steam one, in the shape
of a shallow pie. March-chopped until smooth and mixed with moisture-
giving ribs of lettuce, the meat is light and succulent. This makes a delicious simple meal when served with a stir-fried vegetable and some fluffy
rice with which to soak up the marvelous juices. *It would serve 4 easily
as a main course.*

1 pound ground lean pork
2 tablespoons light soy sauce
1 tablespoon dry sherry
¼ teaspoon salt
¼ teaspoon sugar
Sprinkling black pepper

1 tablespoon cornstarch, dissolved
　in ¼ cup chicken or meat
　stock, with 1 tablespoon
　sesame oil
½ cup finely minced ribs of
　romaine or iceberg lettuce
⅛ teaspoon salt

Preparations

March-chop the ground meat on a chopping board—chopping in
close strokes across the mound, flipping it, and chopping across the other
side. Do this 4 or 5 times, until the meat is very smooth.

Place it in a large bowl, add the soy sauce, sherry, ¼ teaspoon salt,
sugar, and black pepper; mix well. Add the dissolved cornstarch and stir
vigorously in a circular motion until it is evenly blended. The meat, when
pinched between your fingers, should feel soft and wet. If dry and caky,
add a little more stock and stir some more.

Cut the thick bottom parts and ribs of the lettuce into fine shreds;
hold them in a bundle and mince, to make ½ cup. They offer no flavor but
release juices to moisturize the meat during cooking. Toss them lightly with
⅛ teaspoon salt, add to the meat, and mix in a circular motion. The meat
pie should not be made in advance; its flavor would dissipate and its texture would harden.

Place the meat mixture in a soup or pie plate and smooth it into a
mound with a wet knife. Steam over medium-high heat for 30 minutes. Remove the plate to a serving platter and serve.

VARIATIONS

There are many variations on this basic recipe. You may add ½ cup
chopped fresh mushrooms or dried Chinese ones that have been presoaked
30 minutes, rinsed, and destemmed. Or you could add 2 tablespoons finely
minced cooked Smithfield ham (*page 492*) or smoked knuckle. You could

also decrease the amount of meat and add a proportionate amount of flaked crabmeat or minced shrimp with 1 teaspoon minced ginger and 1 tablespoon finely chopped scallions.

In its uncooked state the meat is an excellent filling for dumplings and eggplant. Fill and then steam.

釀黃瓜 STUFFED CUCUMBERS IN PARSLEY SAUCE

Cooked stuffed cucumbers, rarely served here, are common in China. Steamed, they become translucent and moist; they are unusual and delicious. The parsley sauce is clear and delicate; it does not overshadow the refreshing flavor of the cucumbers. This delicate dish would go well with Vinegar-splashed Chicken, Flavor-potted Chicken, or Red-cooked Wine Duck. *Served alone, it would be enough for 2 people.*

¼ pound small shrimp, shelled
¼ pound ground pork

Seasonings:
1½ tablespoons light soy sauce
1 tablespoon dry sherry
⅛ teaspoon salt
Pinch sugar
Sprinkling black pepper

2 teaspoons cornstarch, dissolved
   in 3 tablespoons water with
   2 teaspoons oil
¼ cup finely chopped lettuce ribs
Sprinkling salt
2 large cucumbers
Sprinkling cornstarch

Sauce:
¾ cup liquid, from steamed
   cucumbers plus stock or water
2 tablespoons oil
2 heaping tablespoons minced
   fresh parsley
⅛ teaspoon salt
½ teaspoon light soy sauce
1½ teaspoons cornstarch, dissolved in 1 tablespoon water
   and 2 teaspoons sesame oil

Preparations

Rinse the shelled shrimp and spread them out still wet on a chopping board. Cut them fine. Then pile them together and march-chop, flipping them over each time, until they form a smooth paste. Wet your knife with cold water whenever necessary to prevent the glutinous consistency of the shrimp from caking the blade.

Add the ground meat and march-chop the two ingredients until the mixture is smooth. Put it into a bowl. Add the seasonings and stir; then add the dissolved cornstarch and stir vigorously in a circular motion until well blended. Cut the lettuce ribs as in the preceding recipe, toss with a sprinkling of salt, and fold into the meat gently. These steps can be done a little in advance; if refrigerated, bring the mixture to room temperature **before** stuffing the cucumbers.

Trim off the ends of the cucumbers, then peel and halve them lengthwise. Scrape out the seeds with a small spoon. Dust the hollowed-out centers with a little cornstarch so the filling will adhere.

Divide the shrimp and meat mixture into 4 parts and fill the cucumbers with it, mounding the filling and smoothing it with a wet knife. Then cut each crosswise into 4 or 6 pieces. Set them on a heatproof plate.

Steaming

Steam the stuffed cucumbers over medium-high heat for 20 minutes. Turn the heat off. Carefully pour off the juice from the plate into a measuring cup and return the plate of cucumbers to the steamer; cover to keep them hot while you make the sauce.

Sauce

Add stock or water to the cucumber liquid to make up ¾ cup. Heat a small skillet over high heat until hot; add 2 tablespoons oil, swirl, and heat for 10 seconds. Lower heat to medium and scatter in the minced parsley; sear it quickly by stirring it briskly for about 20 seconds. Add the salt, stir, then turn heat to medium high and pour in the cucumber liquid. When it boils, add the light soy sauce. Turn heat to low, give the dissolved cornstarch a big stir, and add while stirring in a circular motion until the sauce is smoothly thickened. Turn off the heat.

Transfer the steamed cucumbers to a hot serving dish, pour the sauce over them, and serve.

— FLORAL BEAN-CURD SOUP

品
豆
腐
湯

This simple soup illustrates the way steaming is used to facilitate decoration. The bean-curd squares are mashed, seasoned with shrimp, formed into a mound, and decorated before the steaming. The "floral" mound floats when boiling stock is added. *The soup serves 4 as a first course and more than 6 with other Chinese dishes.*

¼ pound small shrimp, shelled

4 squares fresh bean curd

1½ teaspoons salt

Dash white pepper

1 tablespoon cornstarch dissolved
  in 2 tablespoons water

1 tablespoon oil

3 egg whites, well beaten

For the flowers:

A thin slice cooked Smithfield ham
  (*page 492*), or any cooked ham

A few pieces parboiled wedge-cut
  carrots (*see end of recipe*)

A few tiny spinach leaves, stems
  intact

5 cups rich, well-seasoned chicken
  stock

The mound

March-chop the shrimp into a smooth paste as in the preceding recipe; place in a large bowl.

Put the bean-curd squares on the board and mash them well by pressing down on them with the flat of a cleaver or knife or rice them with a potato ricer until there are no lumps. Add to the shrimp. Sprinkle in the salt and pepper and mix well. Stir in the dissolved cornstarch, the oil, and the beaten egg whites in a circular motion until the mixture is very light, fluffy, and smooth. If there are any bean-curd lumps, mash them with the back of a spoon. Pile the mixture on a heatproof plate and smooth it into a pie with a wet knife.

The flowers

Shred the ham into 1-inch-long shreds and arrange them here and there on the mound in starlike clusters—these symbolize chrysanthemums. Create their leaves by pressing down 1 or 2 tiny spinach leaves below the "flower heads." Press down a few wedge-cut parboiled carrots (see below) here and there—these are peach blossoms. Make sure all the decorations are pressed lightly into the pie so they won't come off. Then steam the pie for 5 to 6 minutes over medium-low heat.

Finishing the soup

While the pie is steaming, bring the 5 cups chicken stock to a boil; taste for seasoning, then cover and keep it hot over very low heat. The broth must be rich, because the taste of the soup depends entirely upon it. When the pie is done, slide it carefully into a large serving bowl and pour in the simmering stock. The pie is so light that it floats a little.

Serve the soup by cutting the pie with a knife or spoon into wedges for the soup bowls; then add a little of the broth.

TO WEDGE-CUT CARROTS—Peel a small carrot. Using a small, sharp knife, cut 4 or 5 V-shaped grooves along the length of the carrot, and then slice the carrot into ⅛-inch slices to make carrot flowers. Parboil them for about 1 minute in rapidly boiling water and then drain them.

VARIATIONS

The shrimp may be replaced with puréed chicken breast (*page 19*). If you wish to make the soup more elaborate and substantial, velvet ½ pound sliced chicken breast or medium shrimp in water. Drain and place slices in the bottom of the tureen before you slip in the bean-curd mound and pour in the broth. It looks rather pretty and intriguing if you use a glass bowl for serving this soup so that people can see that the floral bean-curd mound floats over the other ingredients in the bottom.

COOKING WITH DRY HEAT

Roasting

Although the Chinese excel in roasting duck, roasting as a method of cooking is not a common practice. Requiring an oven, which does not exist in the standard Chinese stove, it has never been integrated into home cooking. The classic commercial oven, fired by charcoal, not only resembles a kiln but also requires the skill associated with master potters to control it. Historically, roasting began as a commercial specialty, and it remains one today. The tradition of dining out in roast-specialty restaurants or purchasing roasts from butchers and "roasting houses" for home consumption is as prevalent now as it was centuries ago. This tradition followed the Chinese abroad, often creating mob scenes in those Chinatown stores where roasted ducks, fillets of pork, and racks of spareribs, enticingly hooked above the chopping-board counters, are sold by weight. These are also popular items in Chinese restaurants all over the world.

The variety, however, is very limited; the ingredients are confined primarily to pork and duck. Overshadowed by the superb roast duck, chicken is done by this method only occasionally as a variation. Beef and lamb are never roasted: beef is scarce in China and lamb is disliked by most Chinese because of its strong odor.

The goal in roasting pork is to achieve a moist texture and a penetrating flavor. The first is accomplished by cutting the meat in strips for faster cooking so that it won't be dried out from prolonged dry heat, and the latter by marinating.

With roast duck, the main goal is to make the skin extraordinarily crisp. But flavor is not neglected. Besides conventional marinating, some recipes call for sewing up a marinade in the cavity of the bird, as in the magnificent Cantonese Fire Duck. Sealed in this way, the marinade flavors and moisturizes the meat while the natural juices collect in it and make it into a highly tasty sauce. After the duck is cooked, the marinade is poured out. It is sprinkled over the duck after it has been chopped.

To make the skin of a roast duck crisp, no time and effort are spared. A series of preparational procedures are applied to extract the fat and make the skin dry: First scalding with boiling liquid to remove the skin oil, then drying with air for many hours to make it hard and taut, and then coating and drying it with a sugared mixture to make it crunchy and deep brown. The most unusual preparation is stretching the skin by blowing air through the neck between skin and meat until the duck is as inflated as a balloon— this is done for the renowned Peking Duck. The ingenuity of stretching is pure logic. Stretching lifts the skin away from the meat and, most important, breaks the structure of the fat tissues of the skin so that they melt easily and drip away completely during the cooking, leaving the skin cracklingly dry.

The Chinese always roast meat and poultry vertically in the oven, hung up by hooks. The idea is that if the meats are free standing, they receive much better circulating heat on all sides and the excess fat is drained more thoroughly. While most home ovens are not tall enough to handle a duck vertically, with modifications you can still make excellent meats and spectacular ducks at home.

Besides roasting in the oven, the Chinese also roast poultry enclosed in hot salt on top of the stove. Chicken or duck, either filled with a marinating sauce or rubbed with it, is wrapped in cheesecloth and buried inside a mountain of scorchingly hot salt and "roasted" until it is tender and succulent. In China the preferred ingredient for this method is chicken, but I have experimented with Cornish hens and found them wonderful, especially the fresh one-pounders that are carried by many butchers and better supermarkets.

Smoking

Smoking is popular all over China, where it is a flavoring process rather than a cooking method. Ingredients are generally precooked in one way or another—most frequently salt-pepper-cured and steamed—before they are smoked briefly over tea leaves, rice, and brown sugar to acquire a deep color and a special flavor. The ingredients are not limited to meats, fowls, and fish as in the Western cuisine—smoked eggs, pressed bean curd, liver, tripe, shrimp, ducks' tongues and feet, and salt-pepper-boiled fresh soy beans are all well-known specialties of different regions. But the most prominent is fowl—and duck is especially delicious. See Salt-cured Duck in the poultry chapter for an excellent smoked variation.

啤 BEER-ROASTED DUCK
酒
烤
鴨

Every Chinese cook seems to have a pet version of simplified Peking Duck. Although inflating a duck can be done rather easily with a plastic or glass straw or with a bicycle pump if you have one, it does involve getting a specially eviscerated duck with the head intact, which can be bought only from Chinatown groceries or a poultry farm. But, salted overnight, dried for long hours, and rubbed with beer, the skin of a supermarket duck can be made just as incredibly crisp as the original. This duck may be served as is or with the traditional Peking Duck accompaniments of steamed pancakes, hoisin sauce, and scallion frills. *It would serve 4 as a main course with vegetables,* and would go beautifully, for instance, with any of the Chicken Fu Yung Vegetables or the plain stir-fried vegetables.

The Peking Duck, as well as another roast duck specialty, Cantonese Fire Duck, can be found in the poultry chapter.

1¾ tablespoons salt	Chinese Pancakes (*page 452*),
¼ teaspoon Szechuan peppercorns	optional
1 duck, about 4½ to 5 pounds	Hoisin Sauce Petals (*page 299*),
1 twelve-ounce bottle of beer,	optional
any brand	Scallion Frills (*page 299*), optional

Combine the salt and Szechuan peppercorns in a small skillet and toast over low heat for about 5 minutes, until the salt is slightly browned and the peppercorns faintly smoking, stirring them occasionally with a spatula. Let them cool.

Rinse and drain the duck; discard the fat from the cavity and trim off the wing tips and the tail. Rub the duck thoroughly, inside and out, with the salt-pepper mixture. Wrap it in aluminum foil and refrigerate overnight.

Unwrap the duck and drain off the liquid. Make a long hook from a coat hanger: stretch the larger support part of the hanger to make a narrow loop; then insert the sharp end into the base of the neck and hook the loop end over a nail by a window, on the back porch, in a ventilated basement, or even over the frame of the shower. Let the duck hang for 6 to 8 hours, until the skin is dry and firm.

Line a roasting pan with aluminum foil to give reflected heat, and place a roasting rack in it. Place the duck on the rack breast down and pour one third of the beer over it slowly as you rub it into the skin. Turn the duck over and pour and rub the rest of the beer over the breast, thighs, legs, and wings.

The oven should be preheated to 400 degrees and the oven rack placed at the middle level. Slide in the duck and roast for 1½ hours at 400 degrees, then 30 minutes at 425 degrees, and finally another 30 minutes at 450 degrees. By then the duck skin should be puffy and brown and crisp.

Remove the roasting pan from the oven and drain off the fat from inside the duck. Transfer the duck to a chopping board and let it cool slightly for easier handling. Then chop it the Chinese way (*page 14*) and reassemble it into a symbolic duck shape, piling the back pieces down the center of the platter, breast pieces on top, skin up. Place wings and legs where they should be. Or you could carve the duck at the table, Western style. Either way, you will love this duck.

叉 燒 肉 ROAST PORK

This simple recipe covers the fundamentals of roasting meat. It is a Cantonese specialty and a basic ingredient for some dishes. Sliced, it is an ever-popular appetizer. Cut into various forms, it is used as the main ingredient for dishes that call for roast pork, such as Roast Pork Almond Ding, Yangchow Fried Rice, and Roast Pork and Bean Sprouts Lo Mein, etc. A common error in making Roast Pork is using salt in the marinade, which toughens the meat. Leery about chemicals, I substitute catsup for the traditional red food dye. It gives the meat a deeper color and thickens the marinade for better coating.

2 pounds boneless pork loin

Marinade:
3 tablespoons light soy sauce
2 tablespoons bean paste
1 tablespoon dry sherry
2 tablespoons catsup
2 tablespoons pineapple or orange juice
1 tablespoon sugar
1 tablespoon malt sugar, honey, or Karo syrup
2 cloves garlic, crushed, peeled, and coarsely chopped
½ teaspoon five-fragrance powder

Trim the meat of excess fat. Slice it lengthwise, with the grain, into strips about 2 inches wide, 1 inch thick, and 5 to 6 inches long. Place them flat in a shallow pan. Stir the marinade ingredients in a bowl until well blended and pour over the meat, rubbing it well into both sides. Cover and marinate for about 3 hours at room temperature, turning the strips a few times. You could also refrigerate the meat and bring it to room temperature before roasting, but it shouldn't be marinated longer than 6 hours—prolonged soaking damages the firm texture.

Remove all the racks from your oven but the topmost one. Pour a few inches of water into a roasting or broiling pan and place it on the floor of the oven to catch the dripping and prevent smoking. Preheat the oven to 350 degrees.

Insert a meat hook, drapery hook, or even a bent strong paper clip into one end of each meat strip (1 hook per strip) and hook the strips onto the top rack over the drip pan in one line. Roast the strips for 1 hour. Then increase heat to 400 degrees and roast for 10 more minutes.

Remove meat and take out the hooks. Let the strips cool and firm slightly and then slice them crosswise, against the grain, to serve as an appetizer or main dish. The pork is good hot, at room temperature, or cold. It freezes well for months. If you like roast pork, double or triple the recipe and roast by hanging the meat in several rows so that you always have some on hand.

To reheat cold or frozen roast pork as an appetizer, cut the desired amount into slices and place them in an overlapping line in a snug shallow ovenproof dish. Pour a little meat or chicken stock over the meat (about ⅛ inch) and heat in a moderate oven or under a slow broiler until the liquid is steaming, the meat is hot inside, and the top surface is crisp. If you have no stock you could season some water with soy sauce and honey or syrup to taste.

叉
燒
排
骨

BARBECUED SPARERIBS

"Invented" here as a substitute for other cuts of pork during the meat shortage of World War II, barbecued spareribs have become one of the most popular Chinese appetizers. For a tasty result, one must buy lean ribs in whole racks from a butcher; the packaged ones sold in the supermarket are generally unacceptable—there is too much gristle and fat. *This recipe would serve 4 as a main course, more if used as an appetizer.*

2 racks of spareribs, each about
2 pounds

Marinade:
½ cup light soy sauce
2 teaspoons bean paste
½ cup hoisin sauce
2 tablespoons dry sherry
1 teaspoon sugar
1 tablespoon catsup
1 tablespoon orange, pineapple, or
grapefruit juice
1 teaspoon honey
3 cloves garlic, peeled and
coarsely chopped

Trim off the excess fat and gristle from the thick edge of the spareribs. Remove the overlapping piece of meat on the bony side, if any, and save it for making meat stock. Lay the ribs flat on a tray or platter. Mix the marinade ingredients and stir until well blended. Brush half over the ribs, coating them evenly; then turn them over and brush the other half of the marinade on. Cover and let the ribs marinate for 2 hours at room temperature or 4 hours in the refrigerator, turning and basting them a few times. Just as with the roast pork, the ribs should not be overmarinated.

Prepare the oven as for the roast pork: remove all racks but the topmost one, place a drip pan on the floor of the oven with an inch of water in it, and preheat the oven to 375 degrees.

Insert 4 hooks along the length of each rack of spareribs at regular intervals, then hook them onto the top oven rack above the drip pan in 2 rows. Roast the spareribs for 45 minutes, replenishing the water in the drip pan if necessary. You may interrupt the cooking now and freeze the ribs. Bring them to room temperature before you finish them in any one of the three ways described below.

When ready to finish the spareribs either: (1) increase the heat to about 420 degrees for 15 minutes to brown and crisp them; (2) transfer them to the broiler and broil 5 minutes on the bony side, 6 to 7 minutes on the meat side; or (3) put them aside and finish them outside if you have a charcoal grill, broiling them until crisp.

Separate the ribs and serve them with plum ("duck") sauce and Chinese hot mustard (*page 495*).

BARBECUED BEEF

Thinking that had beef been in abundance in China, as it is here in the United States, some form of luscious Chinese roast beef would have been created, I arduously went on an experimentation spree. The results were disastrous and unmentionable, except for this recipe, which is surprisingly delicious. Marinated and broiled, the meat has a robust garlic flavor, and it is very succulent. It reminds me a little of the tasty scorched beef I had in a Muslim restaurant in Peking as a child. *This would serve 6 to 8 as a main course* and would go well with such vegetables as Stir-fried Cauliflower, Green Beans, or Celery.

3 pounds London broil or flank
    steak

Marinade:
1 tablespoon sugar
1 teaspoon five-fragrance powder
4 large cloves garlic, coarsely
    chopped
⅓ cup light soy sauce
⅓ cup dry sherry
½ cup hoisin sauce
1 tablespoon bean paste (*page 486*)

Cut the London broil in half through the thickness; do not cut the flat flank steak. Place the beef in a shallow dish. Mix the marinade ingredients well and pour over the meat, rubbing well into all sides with your fingers. Cover and marinate at room temperature for 1 hour or refrigerate for 2 hours and bring to room temperature before roasting.

Turn the broiler up high till it is very hot. Remove the meat from the marinade and place it on the broiler tray. Broil for 7 minutes about 6 inches below the flame (or less—see below). Turn the meat and broil another 5 minutes. Then place the tray closer to the flame and broil another minute or so to slightly char the surface. Remove it to a chopping board and let it cool slightly before you cut it crosswise, against the grain, into desired slices for serving as a main dish, an appetizer, or for sandwiches. It is also an excellent cold meat if sliced very thin. It will be just rosy inside—the Chinese do not eat rare beef. If you like it rarer, decrease the broiling time, placing meat closer to the flame.

THE RECIPES

INTRODUCTION

Now that you are familiar with the basic techniques and have built up considerable confidence and dexterity by doing the recipes in the first part of this book, here are hundreds of recipes, both traditional and special, that I have developed and put down carefully so that you should be able to accomplish them with relative ease and superb results. But where to begin, how to select, how to choose and combine from so many dishes, you may well ask.

First of all, I have always tried to describe exactly what a dish is going to taste like so that you will know just what to expect in terms of taste and texture—how mild or spicy, how soft or crunchy—and these pointers should help you in your selections. I have also given the number of people a recipe will serve in terms of a Western-style meal, where you have one main dish accompanied by rice and/or a vegetable, perhaps preceded by a soup. In this country, to some people, a dish containing a pound of meat plus secondary ingredients would serve four nicely while others might deem it adequate for only two people; the final judgment must be yours. In a Chinese meal the same recipe would be ample for two or three times the number of people because you would serve at least three other dishes all at the same time, along with a soup. But until you are really proficient and have acquired an insatiable appetite for Chinese food, let it enter your diet little by little. Attempting Chinese cooking gradually, without pressure, perhaps even sharing the preparation with a friend or a spouse, gives you time to practice the techniques until they become second nature, as they are to those who grew up on it.

Chinese food blends beautifully with Western meals, so don't hesitate to incorporate a dish here and there into your luncheon, supper, or dinner. It is time that these tastes became a part of the great melting pot that is American cuisine, just as so many other strains have been blended in. There is nothing better than Chinese-cooked vegetables, as almost any Westerner will agree once he has been introduced to them. All the year-round standbys like carrots, broccoli, green beans, and cauliflower will seem suddenly fresh and exciting when you try some of the recipes here. Work a Chinese soup or an appetizer or a cold-stirred salad into an otherwise Western meal. There is no conflict: you will find that Egg Fu Yung or the Open-Face Omelet with Shrimp Sauce blends into your usual fare as well as a French soufflé; Yangchow Fried Rice as well as a Spanish paella; Lo Mein or Noodles with Bean-paste Meat Sauce as well as an Italian pasta; and the Szechuan Eggplants as well as a Greek moussaka. And in no time at all you will find that cooking an assortment of appetizers for a cocktail party or a simplified Chinese meal of one main dish and two vegetables really requires no more time and effort than cooking anything else—in fact less, once you get the feel of it. With this in mind, I have often mentioned what vegetable dishes would complement a meat, poultry, or seafood dish.

In a real Chinese meal, of course, the complementarity is based on the play between one dish and another—involving texture, flavor, color, size, and shape of the ingredients. There are generally four dishes, plus rice and soup. Those four dishes should represent the food spectrum of meat, poultry, seafood, and vegetable. The cooking techniques come into play in creating the different textures. Except in restaurants, where menus are predominantly the fast stir-fried dishes, one never would find four stir-fried dishes. Flavor should be varied—the delicate with the spicy, the saucy with the trim dishes. Cutting should balance out too, so that you have, for instance, one "whole" dish, like a steamed sea bass, one shredded dish, one chunky dish, one diced. Color is important to the aesthetic aspect of the meal, in the sense that you would not want four pale dishes or four of robust hue. This play of balance and contrast, then, works not only within a dish, but also in the arrangement of the meal itself.

Cooking a Chinese meal is not difficult if it is well planned, and a well-planned meal involves different techniques. Since the techniques are of different tempos, they enable you to synchronize the stages of cooking at a relatively leisurely pace. I have tried to indicate ahead-of-time points whenever possible and, once you get a feel for orchestrating the different techniques, you will be as adept as you are at cooking that simple but necessarily well-orchestrated meal, a standard American breakfast.

I will outline below three kinds of Chinese meals, giving general suggestions and specific examples. These merely scratch the surface of the recipes in the book, but you will at least get a sense of what is involved. Then vary them according to your own good common sense. As to what to drink with a Chinese meal, you will find that a dry white wine goes extremely well with this kind of food. Some people like beer but I find it a little too heavy. It may surprise you to learn that the Chinese never drink tea *with* their meals because tea cleanses away instead of enhancing the flavor of the food; they serve it only at the end.

Three Chinese meals

O N E—a standard family-style meal, which of course is also beautifully suited to entertaining. You are going to combine dishes of different techniques so that they can be synchronized for serving all at once. For instance, any clear-simmered or red-cooked meat can be done ahead of time and then reheated. A deep-fried dish, such as the Five-fragrance Deep-fried Chicken, can be prefried and then refried momentarily just before serving. A steamed dish such as a Steamed Whole Fish can be cooking while you stir-fry a vegetable. The rice can always be cooked at least 30 minutes ahead of time. The soup could be a simmered one, needing only last-minute reheating, or a quick soup, such as the Hot and Sour Soup, Egg Drop, or Purple Seaweed. The vegetable can be anything you like, as long as it provides contrast in taste, texture, and color.

T W O—a "meal without ceremony," an abbreviation of a banquet. This would usually be considered a dinner party here, with several separate courses. First come four assorted cold hors d'oeuvres, which you can do long ahead of time. Like the basic family meal, they should be composed of poultry, meat, seafood, and vegetables. For instance, a lovely combination would be Salt-cured Beef Brisket (cooked several days ahead), Scallion-Oil Shrimp (up to a day in advance), Chicken in Sesame Paste, and Spicy Minced Watercress.

While your guests are enjoying these, a simmered or steamed dish can be cooking. The selection is slightly fancier than that for a family-style meal, with one or two "anchoring" dishes that will have been done well ahead, such as Flavor-potted Chicken or Salt-roasted Chicken and Sea Bass in Pine-Nut Sauce—a deep-fried dish that can be mostly prepared ahead of time. Just before everyone has finished the hors d'oeuvres, you can slip away and make a spicy stir-fried meat you have chosen to balance the richness of the fish and poultry—an excellent one would be Chili-Pepper Beef or Twice-cooked Pork. A light vegetable (either cold, such as Cold-stirred Bean Sprouts, or Sliced Zucchini with Shredded Carrots, which can be stir-fried in advance and served at room temperature), would complement the richness and spiciness. The soup in this menu should also be light—such as Pork and Cucumber Soup or Chicken and Watercress Soup. Follow such a meal with fresh fruit or try one of the Chinese desserts.

T H R E E—The traditional banquet is always elaborate and often resplendent, taking days of preparation and involving in the old days up to 46 courses; now most banquets range from 12 to 16 courses. It is almost impossible, of course, to duplicate them, given our lifestyle today. Still, one might want to try a mini-banquet, so I've outlined a simple one below, using the traditional form. One point must be taken into consideration: a banquet is done dish by dish, each one constituting a course. Therefore, there is no getting around the fact that the hostess has to disappear into the kitchen often.

Start with an assortment of cold hors d'oeuvres, which should be on one large platter in a beautiful arrangement. Here again one takes into account the basic combination of meat, chicken, vegetable, and seafood— you could present only four or offer many more if you wish. An elegant arrangement might be Pepper-Salt-Water Beef Liver, Hoisin-sauced Pork, Shrimp in Mustard Sauce, Spicy Cold Celery Cabbage, Tea Eggs, and boned White-cut Chicken with a chosen sauce. This sumptuous platter is traditionally served in the middle of the table, but there is no reason why you shouldn't serve it with drinks before the guests come to the table.

A traditional banquet would then produce four hot stir-frys, highly flavored stir-fried dishes in small portions, usually meat by-products and small or finely cut ingredients. The portions in this book would serve 10 to 12 people. Since it is too difficult to prepare so many at once, make only one or two, such as Sweet and Sour "Boneless" Spareribs and Shrimp with Peas and Ham, and these should always be served at the table.

The soup, which follows, should be an elegant one, such as Chicken Fu Yung Swift's Nest Soup, The Whole Winter Melon Pond, the Yin-Yang Spinach and Chicken Soup, or the Wu-Soong Crab Gunn.

Then the main "anchoring" course appears, the star of the dinner. Although traditionally it is a rare delicacy, such as "Shark's Fin" or "Mountain Turtle," by which the banquet is then labeled, I recommend an elegant duck dish, partly because I love duck and partly because the rare delicacies are simply too expensive and too inaccessible. There are a number of good duck recipes to choose from for this course—such as Peking Duck (or its simpler version, Beer-roasted Duck), Boneless Whole Duck with Meat and Chestnut Stuffing, or Crisp Eight-Treasure Duck.

Follow this with a meat course, such as Casserole of Clear-Simmered Lion's Head, Clear-simmered Pork, or Red-cooked Fresh Ham. The meat for this course needs no last-minute attention.

In contrast to Western meals, a Chinese banquet has the fish after the poultry and the meat. An elegant and easy to make stir-fried fish is the Fillet of Flounder in Wine-Rice Sauce; a more elaborate one is the Seafood Kow. More traditional dishes are the Rainbow Fish or a fancy steamed fish.

At this point, a traditional banquet would go on, and on, with sweets as an interlude to be followed by an assortment of "rice-sending" dishes (made up of highly seasoned foods that entice you to eat more rice) accompanied by another soup. Rice is then served, signaling the end of the meal.

But for a mini-banquet, follow the fish course with a dessert— either Chinese, such as Almond Jelly with Lichees and Loquats, which is cold, or Steamed Pears with Cassia-Blossom Honey, which is hot; or a favorite Western concoction.

You might notice that there are no vegetable dishes in a formal banquet: this is tradition. Some vegetables may appear within a dish, but they don't appear alone. Also, since the rice course is eliminated here, serve rice instead with any dish it would be appropriate with, or pancakes or steamed buns. The introductory notes to each recipe will guide you in your choice.

Aside from these traditionally structured meals, you might try a dinner based on the Chrysanthemum or Lamb Pot, a wonderful communal dish, or branch out into experiments of your own. Many of the meat and poultry recipes would be superb in a buffet. And because oil, not butter, is used for stir-frying vegetables you will find they are excellent cold as well as hot. Another good idea would be a casual dinner based on the steamed pancakes so that each guest could stuff his own and sample a variety of flavorful shredded or diced stir-fried dishes.

There is really no limit to the way you can use this cuisine, one of the greatest in the world and one of the most flexible. With the interest lately in low-fat cooking, you will find it extraordinarily healthy in that respect, and since the price of meat and fish is so high today, you will also find many of these recipes economical—they use relatively small quantities of meats but in an inventive and expansive way .

A final word of caution, however, on the matter of quantity: when you want to increase a recipe, you *must not* simply double the amount of meat and sauce that is called for in a stir-fried dish. The heat will not then envelop the ingredients properly; it will just boil away the excessive amount of liquid, turning everything into a watery, stewed mess. Double stir-fried recipes by doing them twice and then combining. If you want to reduce the amounts, however, you may do so slightly; but a general rule of thumb would be: if you are halving the solid ingredients, reduce the seasonings and liquids by only a quarter. And if you have to hold any dish for a few minutes, put it over simmering water—never in the oven.

Such cautions, and the talk of orchestration, focus of course on the fundamental aspect of a Chinese meal: it is a meal of multiple dishes, to be served communally. This is a tradition rooted in Chinese society, one that honors the concept of a large, closely knit family, and it is one that persists, in the most common restaurant or the most lavish state banquet. For even in those multicourse banquets, the single dish is presented in the center of the table. I want you to enjoy these recipes in whatever way makes you feel comfortable with them, but I think it's important to know about this essential circularity and communality of Chinese eating, because it reflects our attitude toward food. In both cooking and eating, the emphasis is on variety; you don't indulge in one thing, and you draw from the center of the table. You pick and choose as appetite or whim may prompt you, selecting your own choice pieces, at moments even popping a special morsel onto someone else's plate. Many Westerners are shy at first about using their eating implement to also serve themselves, shy even about "reaching," but once this culture shock disappears, they find a marvelous gusto in this way of participating in good food. From such a simple discovery as that to the triumph of skinning a whole chicken and then stuffing it with exotic Chinese vegetables, you will come to love this food as I do and will continue to work adventures with it.

HOT
HORS D'OEUVRES
AND COLD
PLATTERS

There are no Chinese hot hors d'oeuvres if the phrase is used to mean neat finger food to serve at a standing reception, such as a cocktail party. The Chinese simply do not entertain at home standing up. The standard greeting to guests is *Chin tsuo*, which means, "Please sit down." It's not that the Chinese don't appreciate the good fellowship of milling around, sipping and nibbling in between floating pleasantries—in fact they love doing this—but they indulge only in public places, such as a temple mall or a city bazaar. There friends saunter from one food stall to another, nibbling such exotic foods as a piece of deep-fried bean curd coated with chili paste, a morsel of roasted squid, a succulent smoked duck tongue, or a slice of cured and meat-filled pig's stomach, as tasty as the best country ham in the world.

But if the French phrase is taken to mean tempting preliminaries before the main courses, the Chinese cuisine has an immense variety to offer. In Chinese meals appetizers are not confined to first courses necessarily. Most of them can be main dishes served in larger amounts but are ideal appetite rousers when they are cooked or served in small portions and dainty cuttings. Banquets are always initiated with "appetite teasers" and "wine chasers." These are either assorted cold meats, seafood, and fresh pickled or marinated vegetables, known as the "cold plates," or they are richly flavored small portions of rapidly stir-fried or flavor-potted meats, seafood, and innards such as livers, tripe, and gizzards, known as the "hot stir-frys." While the latter require some preparation and planning, the first are always abundant in every good Chinese kitchen. I never had to poke deeply into Ar-chang's covered bowls, jars, and bottles to gratify any sudden gastronomic urge. The kitchen at home, his domain, was always filled with all kinds of cold nibble treasures, from specially prepared strips of pork with bean paste to thin slivers of honeyed ham, marinated vegetables, and leftover red-cooked or steamed poultry or fish, which were often pressed into luscious aspics.

The recipes in this chapter are diversified—some are ideal as finger food, others are more conducive to being formal first courses. But all of them are excellent for serving as preliminaries or on buffet platters, and most can also be main dishes. And, besides these appetizers, there are numerous other dishes throughout the book that are ideal first courses.

Chinese hors d'oeuvres blend well with Western meals. Walnut Sesame-Seed Chicken, Fish or Shrimp Toast, Crabmeat Wontons, Shrimp Balls or Deep-fried Meatballs, and various kinds of rolls are excellent finger food. Chicken in Mustard Sauce, Red-cooked Chinese Black Mushrooms, Cucumbers in Hot Bean Sauce or Spicy Cold Celery Cabbage would make a wonderful assorted platter to precede a dinner. And a platter of Aromatic Beef, Crisp Pork Knuckles, Scallion-Oil Shrimp, Odd-Flavored Sauce Chicken, Chilled Lima Beans, Hot and Sour Cucumbers, and Spicy Minced Watercress will bring a new look and flavor to a buffet table.

芥末鷄絲　CHICKEN IN MUSTARD SAUCE

While hot mustard is a standard table condiment in all Cantonese restaurants here, it is the northern school of cooking that excels in blending it into a delicious sauce for cold appetizers. One of the best is this chicken combined with transparent mung-bean-paste sheets. It's a great dish—the flavor is sparklingly piquant, the meat velvety, and the bean-sheet shreds are silky, with bounce. Besides having it as an appetizer, you could also serve it as a cold dish, chilled in the sauce. *Serves 6 as a single appetizer, more with an assortment.*

1 pound shredded chicken breast,
   velveted (*page 75*)
3 transparent mung-bean-paste
   sheets

Sauce:
3 tablespoons light soy sauce
2 teaspoons hot mustard (*page 495*)
⅛ teaspoon salt
¼ teaspoon sugar
1 teaspoon Chenkong, cider, or
   red-wine vinegar
1½ tablespoons sesame oil
1½ tablespoons oil

1 tablespoon finely chopped fresh
coriander or parsley

Velvet the chicken in oil, but swish it about 30 seconds longer than called for, until the meat is completely cooked. Drain and spread the shreds on a plate to cool.

Meanwhile, place the bean-paste sheets in a large container and cover with boiling water. Soak them for 30 minutes or until they are soft and chalk white. They may be soaked a few hours at room temperature or pre-soaked and kept in the refrigerator overnight until ready to use. But, once they are chilled, the texture hardens to a gristlelike brittleness. In that case, drain and pour boiling water over them to cover for 20 to 30 minutes until they become, once again, silky with bounce.

Remove them to the cutting board and cut them into coarse shreds 2 inches long and ½ inch wide. Place them in a mixing bowl. Add the cooled velveted chicken.

Combine the sauce ingredients, stirring until the salt and sugar are dissolved and the mustard is well blended in. Pour the sauce into the mixing bowl, toss the chicken and mung-bean-sheet shreds well, then mound them in a serving dish. Sprinkle with the coriander or parsley and serve.

VARIATIONS

A cup of shredded cucumbers with the green skin on may be added for a touch of color and crispness. Wash and dry a small firm cucumber; trim off the ends, cut it in half lengthwise, and scrape out the seeds. Cut diagonally into 2-inch-long slices, then cut the slices into shreds. Macerate them with ¼ teaspoon salt for 15 minutes in the refrigerator; squeeze lightly to drain, then mix with the cooled chicken. In this case, so as not to interfere with the contrast of white chicken and green cucumbers, spread the shredded bean sheets in a serving dish as a base, top with the chicken mixture, and pour on the sauce at the table. Toss well before serving. A few parsley leaves may be used as garnish, but not coriander. It is too strong; it would overshadow the delicate, refreshing fragrance of the cucumber.

Instead of velveted chicken, white-cut (*page 51*) or boiled chicken breast may be used. To boil boned chicken breast, bring 1½ cups water to a boil with a slice of ginger. Add the chicken breasts and let them boil vigorously for about 5 to 6 minutes, turning frequently until the thickest part of the meat is no longer puffy and bouncy when pressed with a spoon or chopsticks. Cover the pan, turn off the heat, and let the chicken steep for about 15 minutes. Drain and let the breasts cool and firm before cutting them into fine shreds. This, of course, may be done in advance: cover and chill before cutting.

涼拌鷄絲 COLD-STIRRED CHICKEN, TOMATO, AND CELERY

Beautiful and refreshing, this chicken "salad" makes a colorful display as an appetizer or a cold dish. If you want it cold, chill and toss with the sauce at the table. *Serves 4 as a single appetizer; more with an assortment.*

½ pound shredded velveted,
    white-cut, or boiled chicken
    breast
2 large tomatoes
2 cups shredded celery

Sauce:
2 tablespoons light soy sauce
1 teaspoon sugar
2 tablespoons sesame oil
1 large clove garlic, lightly
    smashed and peeled

1 heaping tablespoon coarsely
chopped coriander

Velvet the chicken (*page 75*), turning it in the oil 30 seconds longer than called for; drain and spread it out to cool. If you use white-cut chicken (*page 51*) or boiled chicken breast (*see above*), cool, then cut it into thin shreds *with* the grain.

Peel the tomatoes by spearing each with a fork through the stem end and holding it over a gas flame; turn it quickly around for a minute to loosen the skin. Cut the tomatoes in half vertically and peel—the skin slips off easily. Or place the tomatoes in a bowl, cover with boiling water for 1 minute, then plunge them into cold water until cold. Cut them in half and slip the skin off. Then cut the tomatoes into ¼-inch-thick slices, then into ¼-inch-wide shreds. Set them aside on a dish.

Scrape the celery and cut on a slant into thin 2-inch-long shreds. Parboil them in 2 cups boiling water for 2 minutes. Drain into a colander and spray with cold water until completely cold. Drain well by pressing with your hand.

Place the celery shreds on a serving platter in a wide flat mound. Spread the tomato shreds on top, leaving a 1/2-inch border of celery. Scatter the chicken shreds over the tomatoes, leaving again a narrow border of tomatoes. Sprinkle the top with the coriander.

Mix the sauce ingredients in a small pretty bowl until the sugar is completely dissolved. Bring it to the table, then pour the sauce over the mound, without the garlic, and toss before serving.

VARIATIONS

For a spicier flavor, add some hot mustard, *page 495*, to taste, or use any of the sauces for white-cut chicken on *page 52*.

One-half pound of spinach may be substituted for the celery. Scald the spinach in a small pot of boiling water for 5 seconds; spray with cold water until cold. Drain well, pressing to extract the water, and cut coarsely.

桃
仁
芝
蔴
炸
鷄
片

WALNUT SESAME-SEED CHICKEN

While Westerners usually use bread crumbs for a crunchy effect, the Chinese make more use of nuts. The following recipe makes wonderful finger food when cut fine after frying. *Serves 6 as a single appetizer; more with an assortment.*

1/4 pound walnuts	1 egg white, lightly beaten
5 tablespoons unroasted sesame seeds	2 tablespoons cornstarch
1 pound chicken breast, boned and skinned	4 cups oil
1 teaspoon salt	Roasted salt-pepper (*page 501*), optional

Blanch the walnuts: pour boiling water over them and let them soak 5 minutes. Then peel off any brown skin. Rock-mince them until fine and mix them with the sesame seeds on a plate.

Freeze the chicken if you have the time; this makes cutting easier. Then slice the breasts crosswise into thin but wide pieces by tilting your knife to get a larger surface.

Put the chicken slices in a bowl. Combine the salt, egg white, and cornstarch, and stir till smooth. Pour this coating over the chicken and mix thoroughly. Then coat the pieces with the nut mixture and lay them flat on plates. Let them set for about 1 hour. This step may be done ahead of time; refrigerate the pieces.

Heat a wok or heavy pot over high heat until hot; add the oil and heat to 325 degrees, or until a cube of bread foams slowly. Slip in chicken slices without crowding them and fry them about 2 minutes, turning gently once, until they are crisp and brown. Watch them carefully, for if the oil becomes too hot the nut coating will darken too fast.

Scoop out the slices and let them drain on paper towels. Deep-fry the rest of the slices in manageable batches.

Cut each piece into thin strips about ¼ inch wide and sprinkle them very lightly with salt or roasted salt-pepper. Serve hot; the coating is scrumptious.

棒 子 鷄 翅 "DRUMSTICK" CHICKEN WINGS

Chicken wings deserve far more recognition than they are usually given. To me, they are the best part of the chicken, since the meat is juicy and tender, what the Chinese call "live" meat. They cook easily, acquire flavor readily, and have that nice contrasting texture of soft meat and firm skin. With just a little care and finesse, you can do wonders with them. Here they are coated with a glazy sauce. Use either—it is hard to say which is better. *Serves 4 as a single appetizer; more with an assortment.*

12 large chicken wings
1 tablespoon dark soy sauce

Sauce 1:
2 tablespoons dark soy sauce
2 tablespoons dry sherry
2 tablespoons cider vinegar
1 tablespoon oil
1 tablespoon sesame oil
⅛ teaspoon roasted and ground
    Szechuan peppercorns
    (*page 500*)
2 tablespoons sugar

Sauce 2:
2 tablespoons dark soy sauce
2 tablespoons Worcestershire sauce
1 teaspoon cider vinegar
2 tablespoons oil
1 large clove garlic, lightly
    smashed and peeled
2 tablespoons sugar

2 cups oil

Cut off and discard the wing tips. Disjoint the upper part of the wing at the first joint and save the lower section for the next recipe. 1) With

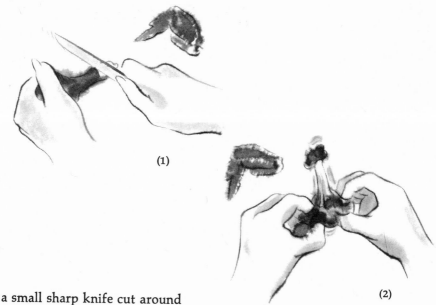

a small sharp knife cut around
the tip of the smaller end of the bone to
release the skin and meat. 2) Pull this meat down toward the large end with
your fingers, first cutting through any tendons or gristle to free the meat.
At the end you will have one big ball of meat with the skin holding the
meat from the inside; the ball will resemble a drumstick. This is very easy
to do, and it doesn't take more than 10 minutes to make all 12 drumsticks.

Simmering

Select a small, deep pot that will accommodate the drumsticks snugly
when stood upright with the exposed bones up. Add 1 tablespoon soy sauce
and coat each ball of meat evenly; then cover the balls with boiling water
and set the pot over high heat. When the liquid boils again, turn heat to
medium to maintain a strong simmering; cover and simmer for 15 minutes.
Turn off the heat, remove the cover, and let the chicken balls cool as you
make the glazing sauce, either the first or the second. The first has a subtle
taste of Szechuan pepper; the second has the stronger flavors of Worcestershire sauce and garlic. You could do the simmering in advance; let the
chicken wings steep in the liquid, covered, and if you refrigerate, bring
them to room temperature before continuing.

Sauce 1

Combine the soy sauce, sherry, and vinegar in a small bowl and set
it within reach near the stove. Heat a small skillet over high heat until hot,

add the oils and turn heat to medium. Add the ground Szechuan pepper-corns and stir a few times. Add the sugar and stir until it is dissolved. Then pour in the soy sauce mixture very slowly with one hand as you stir the sugared oil with the other very rapidly (this prevents the sugar from lumping). Let the sauce foam into caramel bubbles, stirring until it is smooth and thick. Turn heat to the lowest point possible, cover, and keep sauce hot while you deep-fry the chicken.

Sauce 2

Combine the soy sauce, Worcestershire sauce, and vinegar in a small bowl and set it within reach of the stove. Heat a small skillet over high heat until hot; add the oil and turn heat to medium. Sear the garlic on both sides, pressing it down with the back of a spatula all over the pan to extract its flavor. Remove and discard it. Add the sugar and stir until it is dissolved. Add the soy and Worcestershire mixture very slowly, stirring the sugar-oil rapidly with your other hand, so the sugar doesn't lump. Keep the sauce hot, covered, over extremely low heat while you deep-fry the chicken.

Deep-frying

Heat a wok or heavy pot over high heat until hot; add the 2 cups oil and heat until it foams a cube of bread instantly, about 375 degrees. Take a handful of the chicken by the bones, blot them dry lightly with a paper towel, and carefully plunge them into hot oil. Continue in the same way with the rest of them. Stand back and turn each piece with a spoon or chopsticks so that the meat ends are completely submerged in the foaming oil. Deep-fry for about 4 minutes, until the meat is firm and brown. Turn off the heat.

Glazing

Meanwhile, turn the heat up to medium under the sauce; stir until it foams. Then scoop the wings one by one from oil to sauce and turn until the knob of meat is well glazed. Put them on a serving platter, slip paper frills over the bones if you wish, and serve.

釀 鷄 翅 BONELESS STUFFED CHICKEN WINGS

These chicken wings are crisp outside and moist inside. The stuffing gives each bite a refreshing taste of scallion and ham. It is a very dainty dish, and a perfect example of how a little care transforms the insignificant into the unusual. *Serves 6 as a single appetizer; more with an assortment.*

12 large chicken wings, minus
    top part

Marinade:
2 tablespoons light soy sauce
1 teaspoon sugar
1 whole star anise

The batter:
2 tablespoons cornstarch
1 tablespoon flour
¼ teaspoon salt
1 well-beaten egg
1 tablespoon water

The stuffing:
6 large white parts of scallions,
    each about 2¾ inches long
12 shreds cooked Smithfield (*page
    492*) or baked ham, about
    ¼ inch thick and 2¾ inches
    long

2 cups oil

Preparations—simmering and boiling

Combine the soy sauce and sugar in a small pot that will accommodate the chicken wings snugly, and stir to dissolve the sugar. Add the chicken wings and the star anise, and set over high heat. Pour over boiling water to cover. When it boils again, stir to mingle the sauce, cover, and simmer over medium heat for 10 minutes, turning the wings occasionally. Then let the chicken wings steep in the sauce until cool enough to handle.

Bone each wing by slicing lengthwise on the side where the skin is of a finer texture. Lift and twist out the 2 bones, making certain that you don't break the skin on the other side. Repeat until all wings are boned. You could simmer and bone the chicken wings up to a day in advance if you like. Cover and refrigerate, but bring to room temperature before continuing.

Deep-frying

When you are ready to deep-fry the chicken wings, make the batter: Combine the cornstarch, flour, and salt, then stir in the beaten egg and mix until smooth. Add the water and stir until well blended. Let it sit a little.

Cut each scallion "white" lengthwise in half and shred the ham. Put half a scallion and 1 shred of ham inside each wing. Place them on a platter and put the batter within reach of the stove.

Heat the 2 cups oil in a wok or heavy pot until it foams a cube of bread instantly, about 375 degrees. Dip each wing in the batter to coat it thickly and evenly and then drop it into the hot oil; do all rapidly. Fry the wings for about 3 minutes, turning them occasionally, until they are nicely brown and crisp outside. Drain the chicken wings on paper towels and cut each wing into 2 pieces; serve with toothpicks for a cocktail party or arrange them in a pyramid for a main dish.

炸 DEEP-FRIED CHICKEN GIZZARDS
鷄
肫

Chicken gizzards and livers are excellent appetizers when they are deep-fried and glazed, respectively. *Serves 4 as a single appetizer; more with an assortment.*

1 pound chicken gizzards

Seasonings:
1 tablespoon light soy sauce
1 tablespoon dry sherry
1 teaspoon sugar
⅛ teaspoon five-fragrance powder
2 quarter-sized slices peeled ginger
1 small whole scallion, cut into
   3 pieces

Cornstarch for coating
2 cups oil
Roasted salt-pepper (*page 501*) or
   salt

Trim off the fat and thick skin of each gizzard; score the rounded top side in small diamond patterns halfway through the gizzard. Put the gizzards into a small saucepan, add the seasonings and boiling water to cover. When it boils again, turn the heat low, cover, and simmer for 5 minutes, stirring a few times. Let the gizzards cool in the sauce till at room temperature; then drain and roll in the cornstarch.

Heat a wok or heavy pot till hot, add the oil, and heat until a piece of scallion foams instantly, about 375 degrees. Shake off any excess cornstarch and deep-fry the gizzards for about 2 minutes, until they are crisp, stirring them constantly. Scoop them out with a slotted spoon to dry briefly on paper towels, and serve them hot or at room temperature with a very light sprinkling of roasted salt-pepper or regular salt.

醋
溜
鷄
肝

GLAZED CHICKEN LIVERS

These dark, gleaming chicken livers have a mellow flavor with a whiff of vinegar and a glaze that clings. *Serves 4 as a single appetizer; more with an assortment. It also makes a delicious main dish.*

1 pound chicken livers	*Sauce:*
2 quarter-sized slices peeled ginger	2 tablespoons oil
1 small whole scallion, cut into	2 tablespoons dark soy sauce
3 pieces	2 tablespoons sugar
1 tablespoon dark soy sauce	1 tablespoon dry sherry
	1 tablespoon sesame oil
	1 tablespoon cider vinegar

Cut each chicken liver in two, and place them in a small pot with the ginger, scallion, and soy sauce; pour boiling water over them to cover. When it boils again, turn heat to low, cover, and simmer for 5 minutes. Drain the livers and discard the ginger and scallion.

Heat a wok or large, heavy skillet over high heat until hot; add the oil, swirl, and heat for 30 seconds. Toss in the chicken livers and stir rapidly for 10 seconds. Add the soy sauce, sugar, and sherry, and stir until the sauce is all but absorbed by the livers. Sprinkle in the sesame oil and stir once. Splash the vinegar around the pan, and as it sizzles into steam, give the livers a few fast turns and pour them into a serving dish.

鷄
肝
捲

BACON-WRAPPED
CHICKEN-LIVER ROLLS

Marinated and simmered for a steeped flavor and moist texture, these chicken livers are further lightened by the crisp water chestnuts. Wrapped in bacon, coated with cornstarch, steamed, and then deep-fried just before serving, they make a delicious hot hors d'oeuvre. *Serves 6 as a single appetizer; more with an assortment.*

24 chicken livers	2 quarter-sized slices peeled ginger
	1 small whole scallion, cut in two
Marinade:	1 point star anise, crushed
2 tablespoons light soy sauce	24 slices water chestnuts, each
1 teaspoon sugar	about ⅛ inch thick (about
1 tablespoon dry sherry	8 whole water chestnuts)

| 12 strips bacon, cut in half crosswise | 1 egg, lightly beaten |
| | Cornstarch for coating |

4 cups oil

Preparations—simmering and steaming

Cut each chicken liver in half. Marinate the livers with the soy sauce, sugar, and sherry for 10 minutes. Then put them in a small pot with the ginger, scallion, and crushed star anise; pour boiling water over to cover. When it boils again, cover and simmer for 5 minutes. Cool the livers in the sauce to room temperature and then drain and blot them with paper towels. If you wish to do this step ahead of time, leave the livers in the sauce to steep, and cover. Refrigerate; bring to room temperature before continuing.

Sandwich a slice of water chestnut between 2 chicken-liver halves near one end of a bacon strip. Roll the bacon up around the filling; repeat until all bundles are made. Carefully dip each into the beaten egg and coat lightly with cornstarch. (The bundle won't come apart—no toothpicks are necessary.) Place them on a plate and steam them over high heat for about 10 minutes, until the coating is set and a little translucent. Transfer the bacon bundles to a dry plate to firm and cool. You may do this hours or even a day ahead of time. Cover and refrigerate; bring to room temperature before the final step. Then roll the bacon bundles in cornstarch just before frying them.

Deep-frying

Heat the oil in a wok or deep, heavy pot over high heat to 375 degrees, or until a cube of bread foams instantly. Fry the bacon bundles about 4 to 5 minutes, turning them constantly, until they are brown and crisp outside. Scoop them out onto paper towels to drain and serve them whole or cut in half.

HOISIN-SAUCED PORK

This is to eastern regional cooking in China what roast pork is to southern. It is a solid piece of marinated meat that is simmered instead of roasted and then sliced thin and small to go with sips of wine or thicker and larger to be a main-course dish. The meat is excellent for sandwiches. Its flavor is rich from the garlic, five-fragrance powder, and the piquant hoisin sauce. *Slice the amount you need, allowing 3 to 4 small pieces per person for an appetizer, 4 to 5 if used as a main course.* It keeps well. This is one of the cold treasures that are marvelous to have on hand.

2 pounds boneless pork loin roast
   in 1 piece

Marinade:
4 tablespoons hoisin sauce
1 teaspoon five-fragrance powder
2 large cloves garlic, crushed and
   peeled

Simmering ingredients:
4 tablespoons light soy sauce
4 quarter-sized slices ginger
2 small whole scallions, each cut
   in two
2 cups boiling water

Select a small pot that will accommodate the meat snugly and measure into it the hoisin sauce, then the five-fragrance powder and the crushed garlic; mingle well. Roll the meat in the marinade and rub it in well with your fingers. Cover and marinate the meat for at least 4 hours in the refrigerator.

Add the soy sauce, ginger, and scallions to the marinated meat and set the pot over high heat; add the boiling water and stir to mingle. When the liquid comes to a boil, adjust heat to maintain a strong simmering—small bubbles foaming around the meat—and cover and simmer for 1 hour, turning the meat a few times.

Turn off the heat and let the meat steep in the sauce for 15 minutes. Then put both in a bowl, cover, and chill in the refrigerator until cold. Scoop off any congealed fat. Slice the meat thin against the grain and serve as it is or with a little of the sauce spooned on top.

VARIATION

A 2-pound piece of beef, either rump, loin, or bottom round, may be substituted for the pork roast. Increase the simmering time to 2 hours.

白
雲
山
猪
蹄

CRISP PORK KNUCKLES

The Cantonese school of cooking has nothing to contribute to cold hors d'oeuvres except these fabulous pork knuckles. These are very crisp, with the interwoven textures of crunchy skin, brittle sinew, and firm meat. Cooked for a relatively short time but "cleansed" for long hours in "live" running cold water, which eliminates the grease, the knuckles acquire an amazing quality of cool crispness as refreshing as firm cucumbers. (This is not a recipe to make during a drought.) They are then boned and steeped in one of two traditional sauces—one clean and cool, the other sweet and sour. The first time, make both so you can decide which you prefer. *Serves 4 as a single appetizer; more with an assortment.*

4 pounds pork knuckles   Boiling water to cover

MARINADE SAUCES

Pepper-salt-water: *Sugar-vinegar:*
¼ teaspoon Szechuan peppercorns   1 tablespoon salt
3 tablespoons salt   4 tablespoons sugar
1½ cups boiling water   4 tablespoons distilled white
                                              vinegar
                                           1 cup cold water

Place the knuckles in a heavy pot and pour boiling water over them to cover. Bring the water to a boil again over high heat, then adjust heat to maintain a strong simmer, cover, and simmer for 1 hour.

While the knuckles are simmering, make your sauces:

Measure the peppercorns and salt into 1½ cups boiling water in a small pot set over medium heat. Stir until the salt is dissolved. Remove to cool.

Combine the salt, sugar, and vinegar with 1 cup cold water and cook, stirring, over medium heat until the water boils and the salt and sugar are dissolved. Remove to cool.

At the end of the simmering time, remove the knuckles from the broth and put them in a deep bowl or pot; place this under a faucet. Turn on the cold water and let it fill the pot, showering over the knuckles with sufficient force to cleanse them steadily with fresh water for about 30 minutes. Then turn the faucet to a trickle and let the meat soak for about 2½ hours.

Remove the knuckles from
the water and bone them. First
cut a slit across the skin, then
insert the point of a sharp knife
to the bone and cut with a careful
scraping motion to free all the
tendons and meat from the bone
in 1 piece. Divide the meat into
2 glass jars. Fill one with the pepper-
salt-water marinade, and the other
with the sugar-vinegar marinade. Screw on the lids and refrigerate for at least 6 hours or overnight.

To serve, cut the meat into very thin slices and dribble some of the marinade on top.

炸肉圓 DEEP-FRIED MEATBALLS WITH SPINACH FILLING

These spinach-filled balls are excellent steamed or deep-fried. Make them large for a main dish or small for appetizers. *Serves 4 as a single appetizer; more with an assortment.*

¾ cup fresh or frozen chopped
    spinach
1 tablespoon light soy sauce
1 teaspoon sugar
1 tablespoon sesame oil
1 pound ground lean pork

Seasonings for meat:
1 tablespoon minced scallion white
1 tablespoon dark soy sauce
2 teaspoons dry sherry
½ teaspoon sugar
½ teaspoon salt
⅛ teaspoon black pepper
1 tablespoon sesame oil
1 egg, well beaten
1 tablespoon cornstarch
1 tablespoon flour

4 cups oil

Making the meatballs

If using fresh spinach, wash about ½ pound of it and blanch it about 30 seconds in a lot of boiling water. Drain, press dry, and chop. If using frozen spinach, thaw it and march-chop it a few times to refine its consistency. Put it in a mixing bowl, add the soy sauce and sugar, stir, and set it aside to marinate as you proceed with the meat. The sesame oil should be added just before the meatballs are made to prevent dissipation of its fragrance.

March-chop the ground meat until smooth: scoop into a mixing bowl and add the minced scallion bulbs, soy sauce, sherry, sugar, salt, pepper, and sesame oil; blend well. Add the beaten egg and mix well; sprinkle in the cornstarch and flour and mix in circular motions until completely smooth. Turn the mixture onto a plate and roughly divide it into 16 portions.

Squeeze the spinach lightly to remove excess moisture; add 1 tablespoon sesame oil and mix well. Divide into 16 portions.

Grease your palms with oil; place one portion of the meat in your palm and flatten it into a small round with your fingers. Put a portion of spinach in the center, fold the meat over it, and roll it lightly into a ball. Repeat until all the balls are made. If you prefer the meatballs slightly hard and crusty outside, wet your palms with water instead of oil. This step may be done in advance; cover, refrigerate, and bring to room temperature before the final cooking.

Deep-frying the meatballs

Heat a wok or heavy pot over high heat until hot; add the oil and heat until a cube of bread foams instantly, about 375 degrees. Deep-fry the balls in 2 batches, spinning them constantly, for 2 minutes, then lower the heat to medium and fry them all together for about 4 minutes, until they are brown. Spin them constantly for even cooking. Drain them on paper towels and serve immediately.

VARIATIONS (*steamed versions*)

Steam the meatballs over high heat for 15 minutes; transfer them to a serving dish with the natural juice.

Make PEARL BALLS—Soak ½ cup glutinous rice in warm water to cover for 3 hours and drain. Roll each ball in the rice and steam for 40 minutes.

Make RAINBOW MEATBALLS—Omit the spinach filling and form the mixture into 12 balls. Roll four of them in 2 tablespoons mashed hard-boiled egg yolks, four in 2 tablespoons lightly salted minced parsley, and four in 2 tablespoons minced cooked Smithfield ham. Steam them for 15 minutes.

甜
酸
出
骨
排

SWEET AND SOUR ''BONELESS'' SPARERIBS

It may sound inconceivable to bone spareribs, but it is extremely easy to do if they are simmered first. Dark and glistening, these thickly glazed ribs are moist, tasty, and slightly crunchy. Their sweet and sour taste is faintly laced with the flavor of sesame oil and caramelized sugar. This is not only a good appetizer but also a scrumptious main dish. *Serves 4 as a single appetizer; more with an assortment.*

1½ pounds meaty small spareribs

Marinade:
1 tablespoon dark soy sauce
1 tablespoon dry sherry
1 teaspoon sugar
3 quarter-sized slices peeled ginger
1 small whole scallion, cut in two

Sauce:
3 tablespoons oil
2 tablespoons sugar
2 tablespoons dark soy sauce
1 tablespoon dry sherry
1 tablespoon cider vinegar
⅛ teaspoon salt
1 tablespoon sesame oil

Chop the ribs into 1-inch pieces (*see page 16*). Put them into a small pot, add the marinade, stir to coat every piece, cover, and marinate for 15 minutes. Add boiling water to cover, and when it boils again, turn the heat low to maintain a gentle simmering with small bubbles shooting up. Cover and simmer for 45 minutes. Drain the ribs in a colander and let them sit to cool slightly. Then extract the bones from the meat by pulling and twisting. They come out easily, since the meat has stiffened and shrunk from the bones. This may be done in advance. Cover and let the meat sit at room temperature or refrigerate, covered, and bring to room temperature before the final cooking.

Heat a wok or large, heavy skillet over high heat until hot; add the oil, swirl, and heat for 30 seconds. Add the sugar and stir with the back of a spoon. When it puffs into syrupy bubbles, turn the heat to medium low and add the soy sauce, sherry, vinegar, and salt, stirring all the time. When the sauce is smooth, add the meat, turn heat to medium high, and stir rapidly until the sauce has sizzled into the meat. Add the sesame oil, give the ribs a few big turns, and put them into a serving dish. Pass around with toothpicks or serve as an appetizer at the table.

酸
辣
排
骨
HOT AND SOUR RIBS

If you like spareribs and a hot sweet and sour taste, you will love this dish. Dainty and crunchy, these ribs are a superb preliminary to a good dinner. *Serves 4, or more with an assortment.*

1½ pounds meaty spareribs

Marinade:
1 tablespoon light soy sauce
⅛ teaspoon salt

1 tablespoon cornstarch dissolved
    in 3 tablespoons water
½ cup cornstarch for coating
3 cups oil

Sauce:
1 tablespoon shredded fresh hot
  peppers or 4 whole dried chili
  peppers
1 large clove garlic, minced
1 teaspoon minced peeled ginger
1 tablespoon finely chopped
  scallions
3 tablespoons sugar dissolved in
  3 tablespoons distilled vinegar

1 teaspoon chopped fresh coriander

Preparing and deep-frying the ribs

Chop the ribs into 1-inch pieces (*page 16*). Put them in a bowl, add the marinade, toss well, and let the ribs marinate for about 5 minutes. Add the dissolved cornstarch and mingle well, then toss the coated ribs in the dry cornstarch in a plastic bag. Put on a plate. You should do this just before the deep-frying.

Heat a wok, a large, deep skillet, or a wide, heavy saucepan until hot; add the oil and heat until it foams a cube of bread snappily, about 350 degrees. Shake off any excess cornstarch, and drop the ribs into the hot oil a few at a time. Deep-fry for about 6 minutes, lowering the heat slightly after the initial 2 minutes. The ribs should be tossed and turned with a skimmer or slotted spoon for even frying. Turn off the heat and scoop them out to drain and cool on a plate for about 2 minutes. Reheat the oil over high heat until hot, pour the ribs back into the oil, and deep-fry them again, stirring and turning, for about 1½ to 2 minutes, until they are crisp and brown. Remove from oil and drain.

Making the sauce

Pour out the oil except for about 2 tablespoons. Scatter in the shredded hot peppers and stir rapidly for 30 seconds; if dried chili peppers are used, press and turn them over low heat until blackened. Add the garlic, ginger, and scallions, and stir in fast turning and flipping motions for a few seconds until the scallions are aromatic. Shower in the ribs and stir vigorously to season them with the aromatic agents. Then give the sugar-vinegar mixture a few big stirs, dash it in, and stir briskly in sweeping and turning folds to coat the ribs evenly. Pour into a serving dish and garnish with chopped coriander.

五香排骨　GLAZED FIVE-FRAGRANCE SPARERIBS

These dark, glistening morsels are aromatic of that powerful ingredient, the five-fragrance powder. They are sugary and sticky, and you won't be able to stop eating them. *Serves 3 to 4 as a single appetizer; more with an assortment.*

1½ pounds meaty spareribs

Simmer sauce:
2 tablespoons dark soy sauce
1 tablespoon dry sherry
1 teaspoon sugar
½ teaspoon five-fragrance powder

1½ cups boiling water
2 tablespoons dark soy sauce
2 tablespoons dry sherry
3 tablespoons oil
1 medium clove garlic, crushed
    and peeled
2 tablespoons sugar

Garnish: Fresh parsley and Radish
Fans (*page 160*), optional

Chop the ribs into 1-inch pieces (*page 16*). Put them in a small pot and marinate in the simmer sauce for 15 minutes. Add the boiling water and bring the simmer sauce to a boil. Adjust heat to medium low to maintain a strong simmer; then cover and simmer for 30 minutes, turning the meat now and then. Drain the simmer sauce into a bowl and set the ribs aside. (If you want to do this step ahead of time, cover meat and sauce; if you refrigerate them, bring them to room temperature before continuing.)

Measure out ¼ cup of sauce and combine it with 2 tablespoons dark soy sauce and 2 tablespoons dry sherry. Set it within reach for making the glazing sauce.

Heat a wok or large, heavy skillet over high heat until hot; add the oil, swirl, and heat for 10 seconds. Press and turn the garlic in the oil with the back of a spatula. Stir in the sugar until it is dissolved. Then add the simmer sauce a little at a time (it will splatter—stand back) and stir until it puffs into thick caramel bubbles. Then pour in the ribs and tumble them vigorously until the sauce coats all of them, with no sauce left in the pan. Scoop the ribs onto a serving platter and garnish with parsley and Radish Fans if you wish.

五
香
牛
肉

AROMATIC BEEF

There are two ways to make this cold beef—either cut the meat into large chunks, simmer, chill, and then slice it paper thin with sauce spooned over, or cut the meat into small cubes, simmer until very well done, chill until firm, then cut the jellied meat into slices. The first is firm, the latter soft.

Shin beef is preferred by the Chinese because the meat is marbled with sinew, which gives it a soft, resilient texture. The sinew also thickens the sauce into a natural *gelée*. The meat keeps well, and its flavor actually improves by the second or third day. *Serves 6 to 8 as a single appetizer; more with an assortment. Cut the amount you need, allowing 3 to 4 small slices per person.* Leftover meat could be used for a mixed cold platter or as part of a cold-stirred vegetable dish. It also makes excellent sandwich meat.

2 pounds boneless shin beef in
    1 piece
2 tablespoons oil
2 quarter-sized slices peeled ginger,
    each ¼ inch thick
2 large whole scallions, cut into
    2-inch lengths
⅓ cup dark soy sauce

½ cup dry sherry
½ teaspoon salt
3 tablespoons crushed rock sugar
    or 2 tablespoons granulated
    sugar
1 whole star anise
4 to 5 cups boiling water

Trim off any membranes and cut the meat in half lengthwise.

Heat a large heavy pot over high heat until hot; add the oil, swirl, and heat for 30 seconds. Toss in the ginger and scallions and stir briskly for 30 seconds; add the meat and sear both sides until they stiffen and turn grayish brown. Lower the heat, pour in the soy sauce, and turn the meat rapidly for coloring. Raise the heat, add the sherry, salt, sugar, star anise, and boiling water to cover. Stir briefly, and then turn the heat low to maintain a gentle simmering. Cover and simmer for 1½ to 2 hours, turning the meat every 30 minutes. Adjust the flavor during the last 30 minutes by adding either a little more soy sauce or granulated sugar to taste—the flavor should be extremely mellow.

The exact amount of water and precise timing are difficult to determine because they depend on the age of the meat. As a rule, the water should cover the meat initially and when the meat is done it should be well saturated by the sauce. If it looks dry at any time, add a little boiling water. The meat should be well cooked, but not done to the point of falling apart; the texture should be firm, neither soft nor hard.

Transfer the meat to a deep bowl, pour the sauce over it, cover, and let the meat marinate until cool. Then refrigerate it, covered, until very firm. Take out the amount you need and cut it into thin slices, across the grain. Serve the slices as they are or with a little of the jellied sauce spread on top.

VARIATION

For a jellied version, cut the meat into ½-inch cubes before simmering it. Cook the meat until very well done, at the point of falling apart. Leave the cubes alone or mash with a fork until the meat and the simmering sauce are more or less smooth. Put the meat mixture into a square or rectangular shallow dish, cover, and chill until firm. Turn it onto a chopping board and slice it crosswise into small pieces and serve over lettuce leaves as an appetizer or cut it into larger and thicker slices for serving as a cold main dish.

鹽
水
蝦

SALT-WATER SHRIMP

When small shrimp are very briefly cooked with the protection of their shells, the meat is wonderfully tender and full of flavor. The taste is clean and refreshing. *Serves 4 as a single appetizer; more with an assortment.*

1 pound very small shrimp with shells on	1 whole star anise
3 cups water	1½ tablespoons salt
4 quarter-sized slices peeled ginger, each about ¼ inch thick	Garnish: Fresh coriander or parsley leaves

Remove the legs of the shrimp. Rinse the shrimp lightly in cold water. Bring 3 cups water to a boil with the ginger, star anise, and salt in a medium-sized pot over high heat. Add the shrimp and stir to scatter them evenly under the water. When the water comes to a boil again, turn off the heat and let them steep, covered, for 5 minutes. Pour everything into a deep bowl or jar, and cover it. Chill for 5 hours or overnight, drain, and serve. Garnish with either coriander or parsley leaves.

These shrimp are meant to be eaten slowly between sips of wine and good conversation. They shouldn't be shelled with your fingers; put one in your mouth whole, then bite and suck out the flavorful liquid within the shell. Roll the shrimp on your tongue and shell it with your teeth, spitting out the shell with as much decorum as possible.

VARIATION

When the shrimp are cold, drain and cover them with pale dry sherry. Marinate them for 6 hours or overnight, until they are winy; thus they become the well-known Intoxicated Shrimp.

芥末蝦   SHRIMP IN MUSTARD SAUCE

Velveted as a complete cooking process, these fluffy shrimp are then tossed with a spirited sauce and served lukewarm. If you wish to present a more substantial-looking platter, pile the shrimp in the center and surround with vegetables, such as Sweet and Sour Cucumber Skins, Spicy Minced Watercress, or Chilled Lima Beans. *Serves 4; more with the accompaniments.*

1 pound velveted small shrimp
  (*page 81*)

Sauce:
2 tablespoons light soy sauce
1 tablespoon dry sherry
1 to 2 teaspoons hot mustard
  (*page 495*)
1 tablespoon sesame oil
½ teaspoon sugar

Garnish: 1 tablespoon finely
  chopped fresh coriander

Marinate and set the shrimp as in the master recipe. Velvet them either in oil or water, but increase the cooking time by about 45 seconds until they are completely cooked. Drain and place them in a bowl. This may be done an hour or so in advance; cover but don't refrigerate, lest they harden.

Mix the sauce ingredients well. Pour over the shrimp, tossing gently to mix well. Sprinkle with the green coriander and serve. If you want them cold, refrigerate at this point.

VARIATION
Velveted chicken in shreds (*page 75*) may be done exactly the same way with excellent results. This also is good cold: toss with the sauce and refrigerate.

芫茜蝦   CORIANDERED SHRIMP IN EGG-WHITE BATTER

Refreshingly seasoned with minced coriander, these light and crusty shrimp make an excellent hot hors d'oeuvre, *serving 4 if alone, or a main course, serving 2 or 3 people.*

1 pound medium shrimp, shelled,
   with tails on
1 teaspoon salt
2 tablespoons finely minced
   fresh coriander
1 tablespoon cornstarch

Batter:
3 egg whites
½ teaspoon salt
3 tablespoons cornstarch

2 cups oil
Roasted salt-pepper (*page 501*)

Cut the shrimp along the inner curve to flatten them—but do not go all the way through (*see page 94*). Tap each lightly with the broad side of a heavy knife so that they won't curve into balls during the cooking.

Place the shrimp in a bowl, sprinkle with salt, coriander, and cornstarch, and mix thoroughly. Let them marinate for 10 to 15 minutes.

Whip the egg whites with the salt; add the cornstarch gradually when eggs are fluffy. Continue whipping until stiff. Place the shrimp and batter by the stove.

Heat a wok or large, heavy skillet over high heat until hot. Add the oil and heat until it foams a coriander leaf gently, about 325 degrees; lower the heat to maintain it at this moderate temperature throughout the cooking time. Pick up a shrimp by its tail, dip it into the batter, and slip it into the oil; repeat in quick succession with 8 or 9 more shrimp. Deep-fry them for about 2 minutes, until they look crusty and golden; turn them once. Remove from oil to drain, and deep-fry the other batches.

Arrange the shrimp in a swirling pattern with their pink tails clustered in the center. Sprinkle lightly with the roasted salt-pepper and serve immediately.

蝦
球
SHRIMP BALLS

Crisp outside and fluffy and succulent inside, these minced-shrimp balls make delicious appetizers or a main dish. Moisturized by minced water chestnuts and fluffed by the well-beaten egg white, this is an excellent base mixture with which to make Shrimp Toast or Shrimp Balls and Transparent-Noodle Soup. *Serves 4 to 6 as a single appetizer; more with an assortment.*

1 pound small or medium shrimp
3 water chestnuts
1 large scallion, white part only
1 teaspoon salt

1 tablespoon dry sherry
1 large egg white, beaten until
   very foamy
3 tablespoons cornstarch

2 quarter-sized slices peeled ginger

3 tablespoons water

2 teaspoons sesame oil

4 to 6 cups oil

Roasted salt-pepper (*page 501*)

Preparations

Shell the shrimp and devein if veins are large. Mince fine by chopping them into small pieces first, then mince with one or two cleavers or heavy knives until smooth. Or grind them, using the coarse blade, then follow by march-chopping until the consistency is smooth but not puréed. What you want is a smooth-textured consistency; not a pasty one. Place the minced shrimp in a large mixing bowl.

Smash the water chestnuts with the flat of a cleaver or heavy knife in a pulling motion; scrape up the pulp and mince it very fine. Cut the white section of a large scallion into fine shreds; hold the shreds together and chop very closely into fine pieces.

Add the water chestnuts, scallions, salt, and sherry to the shrimp, and mix in circular motions until well blended. Add the well-beaten egg white and stir in fast circular motions with a wooden spoon or chopsticks until smooth.

Measure the cornstarch into a bowl. Smash the ginger, scrape up the pulp, and mince it fine. Place this in a small bowl, add 3 tablespoons water, and squash the ginger with the back of a small spoon or squeeze with your fingers. Filter the juice into the cornstarch through a fine strainer, pressing down with a spoon to extract the last of the liquid. Stir to dissolve the cornstarch, then pour over the shrimp, and stir in circular motions until the shrimp mixture is smooth and fluffy. Turn it onto a plate and divide it into about 18 portions—the balls should approximate walnuts in size.

Grease your fingers and palms with oil. Take one shrimp portion and roll it lightly in the palms of your hands until it is round and smooth. Put it on a plate and repeat until all balls are made, dabbing oil on your hands when necessary. Balls made for deep-frying shouldn't be rolled with wet hands; the water makes the crust of the balls a little rubbery. The shrimp balls may be formed a few hours in advance. Cover and refrigerate; bring to room temperature before final cooking.

Deep-frying

Preheat the oven to 325 degrees and have a shallow tray ready. Heat a wok or a wide, heavy pot until hot; add the oil and heat until it foams a cube of bread gently, about 325 degrees. Drop in half of the balls and deep-fry them for about 3 minutes until they are brown and crisp, turning with a slotted spoon so that they spin constantly in the hot oil for even frying. Lower the heat if they brown too fast. Drain and place them on the tray and keep them hot in the oven while you fry the second batch. Place the shrimp balls in a serving dish, sprinkle lightly with the roasted salt-pepper, and serve immediately. They must be kept hot during the cooking and served immediately, since, once cooled, they tend to shrink and wrinkle.

VARIATIONS

If you don't have water chestnuts, substitute ½ cup finely minced iceberg or romaine lettuce ribs. Two tablespoons finely minced cooked Smithfield ham (*page 492*) may be added for a stronger flavor. In that case be very sparing with the roasted salt-pepper.

蝦
土
斯　SHRIMP TOAST

Neat and delicious, these are ideal finger food with drinks. *Serves 8 as a single appetizer; many more with an assortment.*

1 recipe shrimp mixture (*preceding recipe*)	8 thin slices stale white bread
	4 cups oil

The bread should be at least 2 days old; stale, the slices absorb less oil. Trim off the crusts and leave them whole or cut each into 2 triangles. Divide the shrimp mixture into appropriate portions.

Oil a table knife and spread the shrimp firmly over the bread, smoothing each portion into a nice mound. Cut each whole piece into 3 long strips or into 4 squares (leave the triangles as they are if you've made them).

Preheat the oven to 350 degrees and have a shallow tray ready. Heat a wok or wide, heavy pot over high heat until hot; add the oil and heat until it foams a cube of bread snappily, about 350 degrees. Slip in half of the shrimp toasts, shrimp side down, and deep-fry them for 2 minutes. Turn them over gently and fry for 45 seconds to 1 minute until the bread is brown and crisp. Drain on paper towels and place them on the tray to keep hot in the oven while you fry the second batch. Arrange them on a serving platter or tray and serve immediately.

VARIATION

For a large cocktail party, cut 20 slices of very thin white bread with a 1½-inch round cookie cutter into 80 small disks. Divide the shrimp mixture into 40 portions and spread each portion over a disk, then press another disk lightly over the top to form them into 40 Shrimp Rounds.

Preheat the oven and heat oil as for Shrimp Toast, and deep-fry them 2 minutes on each side in 2 or 3 batches until the bread is brown and crisp.

You may deep-fry them for 1½ minutes on each side just before the arrival of your guests, then reheat them for about 5 minutes in a 400-degree oven in batches for replenishment as your party continues.

紙 包 魚 PAPER-WRAPPED FISH

Deep-fried, sealed inside paper packages, these delicate fish fillets are succulent and tasty from the seasoning ham. They are excellent sit-down appetizers as well as a main dish when served with other dishes in a Chinese meal. *Serves 6 as a sit-down appetizer; more with an assortment.*

1 pound fillet of flounder or sole	24 six-inch squares of waxed paper
1 teaspoon salt	2 tablespoons sesame oil
2 tablespoons dry sherry	6 thin slices peeled ginger, finely
¼ pound finely minced cooked	shredded
Smithfield ham (*page 492*) or	3 large whole scallions, in 1½-
substitute	inch-long shreds

4 cups oil for deep-frying

Preparations

Cut each fillet lengthwise in two; then cut them crosswise, to make 24 pieces in all. Put them in a bowl, sprinkle with salt and sherry, and toss.

Slice, shred, and mince the ham; then polish by rock-mincing until almost powdery. Add to the fish and stir to mingle well.

Place a square of waxed paper with 1 point facing you. Brush center of the paper with sesame oil. Place a piece of fish in the center, scatter a few slivers of ginger and scallions over the fish, fold the corner closest to you over the fish, fold over the 2 side corners, fold over once, then tuck in the flap securely, making a neat, tight envelope so that it won't come apart during the deep-frying. Repeat until all 24 packages are made. This may be done a few hours in advance. Refrigerate until ready to deep-fry.

Deep-frying

Heat the 4 cups oil in a wok or wide, deep pot over high heat until it foams a cube of bread instantly, about 375 degrees. Gradually scatter in half the packages and deep-fry them for about 3 minutes, turning occasionally. Remove them from the oil and drain on paper towels. Do the other half. Place neatly in rows on a serving platter or arrange them in a swirling pile. Serve immediately.

To eat, untuck the flap with your fork or chopsticks, and spread out the paper. You'll be greeted with the tantalizing fragrance of the scallions and sesame oil.

魚 FISH TOAST
土
斯

The fish is moist and fluffy. It is delicate but not bland, each bite nicely seasoned by the ham and parsley. The ham is the main seasoning agent—only a very tasty cured ham, meat from a smoked knuckle, or a very good baked ham should be used. *Serves 6 to 8 as a single appetizer; more with an assortment.*

½ pound fillet of flounder, sole, or pike (any fine-textured fish)	2 tablespoons finely minced parsley
¼ cup water	1 egg white, well beaten but not stiff
2 teaspoons dry sherry	1 tablespoon cornstarch
½ teaspoon salt	1 tablespoon oil
2 tablespoons finely minced cooked Smithfield ham (*page 492*) or substitute	8 thin slices stale white bread (at least 2 days old)
	4 cups oil

Preparations

Lay the fillet, membrane side down, on a chopping board, and with the tip of a wet cleaver scrape the fish lightly in short outward strokes. Discard any stringy membrane or tiny bones if any. When finished, pile the fish scrapings together, sprinkle with 1 tablespoon of the water, and mince-chop until the meat is fine and fluffy, adding the rest of the water a tablespoon at a time. Scoop the fish into a mixing bowl and add the sherry, salt, ham, and parsley. Mix well. Add the egg white and mix in circular motions, then add the cornstarch and the oil and blend in circular motions until the mixture is smooth. Let it sit and fluff for a few minutes, then turn it onto a plate and divide it roughly into 8 or 16 portions according to how you want to cut the bread.

Remove the crust from the bread (it must be at least 2 days old, or else it will be too absorbent). Leave the slices as they are or cut each into 2 triangles. Spoon the fish onto the bread and spread it firmly into a smooth mound with a table knife dipped in oil. You may do this in advance. Cover and refrigerate, but bring to room temperature before cooking.

Deep-frying

Heat a wok or heavy pot over high heat until hot; add the oil and heat until a cube of bread foams slowly, about 325 degrees. Slide the toast in, fish side down, and fry in batches without crowding for about 1½ minutes. Turn them over and fry for about 30 to 40 seconds until the bread is brown and crisp. Drain on paper towels. Serve the whole ones cut into long strips or squares and the triangles as they are or cut in two.

VARIATION

A nice variation is to press a sprinkling of raw sesame seeds or blanched walnut halves on top of the fish before frying.

蟹
肉
雲
吞

CRABMEAT WONTONS

Fried wontons make a good hot hors d'oeuvre—they are neat and crisp outside and succulent inside. The filling may be varied by using pork, pork combined with shrimp or crabmeat, seafood alone, or curried beef. They may be made in advance and reheated in a hot oven or refried just before serving. *Serves 6 as a single appetizer; more with an assortment.*

6 ounces fresh, frozen, or canned
    crabmeat
¼ pound ground lean pork
1 tablespoon minced parsley or
    scallion bulbs
2 tablespoons oil
1 tablespoon light soy sauce
1 tablespoon dry sherry
½ teaspoon sugar

¼ teaspoon salt
A dash black pepper
1 teaspoon cornstarch dissolved in
    2 teaspoons water and 1 tea-
    spoon sesame oil
24 thin wonton wrappers, either
    commercially made or home-
    made
2 cups oil

Thaw the crabmeat if frozen and flake it into small pieces. March-chop the ground pork a few times. Mince the parsley or scallion bulbs. Put these in separate piles on a working platter.

Heat a wok or large, heavy skillet over high heat for 30 seconds; add the oil, swirl, and heat for 30 seconds. Scatter in the minced parsley or scallions and stir quickly a few times. Add the pork and stir until it turns gray. Add the crabmeat, soy sauce, sherry, sugar, salt, and pepper; stir for about 1 minute to mingle well. Give the dissolved cornstarch a big stir and pour into the pan; adjust the heat to low and stir until the mixture is smooth. Pour onto a plate to cool, roughly dividing the mixture into 24 portions.

Either make the wonton wrappers according to the recipe on *page 463* or buy them from a Chinese grocer. The recipe for homemade wrappers is for 40—use 24 for this recipe and freeze the rest for future use or wrap them in aluminum foil, refrigerate, and make Wonton Soup (*page 464*) the next day.

1) Place a wrapper in front of you with a point toward you; spoon one portion of the filling into the center. Dip your fingers in water and moisten the edges of the wrapper. 2) Then fold the point nearest you over to the far point, making a triangle. Press the edges down. 3) Pull the 2 bottom corners forward and down to meet at the center of the bottom edge; wet one corner and press it over the other to make the wonton. Repeat with the other wontons.

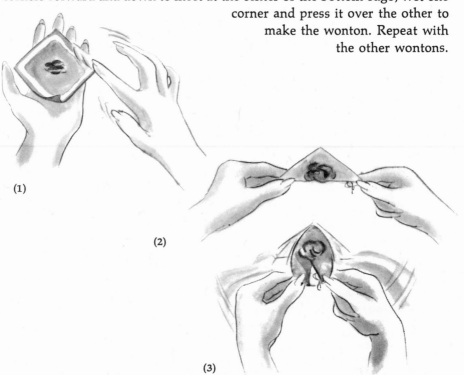

(1)

(2)

(3)

Heat a wok or heavy pot over high heat until hot; add the oil and heat until a cube of bread foams immediately, about 375 degrees. Drop in the wontons and fry them for about 2 minutes, turning, until nicely browned. Scoop them out and drain on paper towels.

If you do them a little in advance, deep-fry them until light brown, remove from oil, and drain on paper towels. When ready to serve, reheat the oil and fry until brown and crisp. You may also reheat them by placing them in a hot oven (450 degrees) for about 5 minutes, until the wrappers are crisp.

辣 白 菜   SPICY COLD CELERY CABBAGE

This is a very popular Chinese condiment. The spectacular smooth, crisp texture is attained by soaking in salted water. Don't make it, however, unless the celery cabbage is in season and is tender. It is a cool, biting dish, absolutely delicious. *Serves 6 to 8 as a single appetizer or accompaniment to meat; more with an assortment.*

4 tablespoons salt
1 cup boiling water
5 cups cold water
2 pounds celery cabbage

Sauce:
3 tablespoons sugar
3 tablespoons cider vinegar
2 tablespoons oil
1 tablespoon sesame oil
1 teaspoon Szechuan peppercorns
4 dried red chili peppers

Dissolve the salt in 1 cup boiling water; pour it into a large salad bowl or kettle and add 5 cups cold water. Set it aside to cool completely.

Cut off the root end of the cabbage and separate the stalks; wash them well in cold water. Cut them lengthwise into 1-inch-wide strips—stacking several together shortens the task considerably. Gather the strips into even bundles and cut them into 2-inch-long pieces. Put them in the salt water; anchor with a plate, and soak them for 6 hours at room temperature or in the refrigerator overnight—longer will make the cabbage too soft.

Squeeze the cabbage very dry with your hands and scatter the sections into a bowl. Dissolve the sugar in the vinegar and pour this over the cabbage; toss to cover evenly. Set a small skillet over medium-low heat, add the oil and sesame oil, and heat for 30 seconds. Add the peppercorns and chili peppers and fry, stirring and pressing, for 1 minute. Turn the heat very low and continue to fry, pressing with a spatula now and then, until the peppers have blackened. Strain the oil over the cabbage; add the peppers but discard the peppercorns. Toss well, cover, and refrigerate until very cold. The taste improves if it is marinated overnight.

涼
拌
紅
蘿
蔔

RADISH FANS OR FLOWERS

Radishes don't absorb flavors unless they are crushed or sliced. Here, cut thin two-thirds of the way through, they are either flattened into fan shapes or pulled into spreading petals as symbolic flowers. *Serves 3 to 4 as a single appetizer, but best served with an accompaniment of cold meats.*

1 pound large red radishes
½ teaspoon salt

Sauce:
2 tablespoons light soy sauce
2 tablespoons distilled white
   vinegar
1 tablespoon sugar
1 tablespoon sesame oil

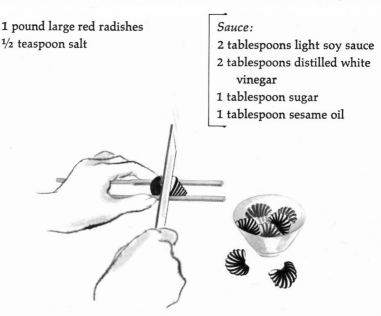

Wash the radishes and trim off the two ends. Place a radish on its side between the square ends of a pair of chopsticks. Anchor the chopsticks with one hand while you slice very thin with a sharp knife down through the radish as far as the anchoring chopsticks permit. You will find that tilting the radish forward for the initial slicings will prevent the knife from cutting it all the way through and that turning the radish midway through slicing will give you a better grip. Repeat until all radishes are cut.

Place them in a large bowl; sprinkle in the salt and toss to mingle well. Combine the sauce ingredients and stir until the sugar is dissolved. Pour over the radishes, mix well, cover, and chill for 1 hour or longer.

Flatten the radishes into oblong fans or pull the slices apart slightly to make spreading petals.

VARIATIONS

One or two crushed cloves of garlic may be added to the sauce. If you like a milder taste, use cider or red-wine vinegar instead of the sharper distilled white vinegar.

涼
拌
東
洋
菜

COLD-STIRRED AGAR-AGAR

Agar-agar, a processed seaweed, has no taste of its own but plenty of resilient texture and bulk. Being spongy, it absorbs seasonings; when mingled and eaten with minced dried shrimp, tasty ham, and crisp spinach, it makes a refreshing exotic salad of brilliant colors and contrasting textures. The dried shrimp add a spark of extra taste, but you may omit them. *Serves 4 as a single appetizer; more if part of a buffet.*

¼ cup dried shrimp	*Sauce:*
1 ounce agar-agar	2 tablespoons light soy sauce
1 pound fresh spinach	2 tablespoons red-wine or cider
1 teaspoon salt	vinegar
1 teaspoon sugar	2 tablespoons oil or sesame oil
¼ pound baked ham in 1 piece	2 tablespoons sugar

Place the dried shrimp in a small dish and cover with boiling water; let them soak for about 1 hour, until soft.

Meanwhile, soak the agar-agar in cold water for 30 minutes. Rinse it in cold water, squeeze dry, and cut into 1½-inch-long pieces.

When the shrimp are soft, drain and rock-mince them until fine.

Wash the spinach well and remove stems. Bring a small pot of water to a boil with the salt and sugar and wilt the spinach for 30 seconds. Drain in a colander and spray with cold water to arrest the cooking. When the spinach is completely cold, press down to extract excess water and chop medium fine.

Cut the ham into shreds about 1½ inches long, ¼ inch wide.

Arrange the green spinach, white agar-agar, and red ham attractively on a serving platter in separate mounds or in swirling circles. Scatter the minced shrimp over the spinach and agar-agar.

Make the sauce by blending the soy sauce, vinegar, and oil in a small bowl and adding the sugar bit by bit last—to personal taste—and stir until the sugar is dissolved. Serve the sauce along with the salad; pour it over and toss lightly just before serving.

涼
拌
素
菜

EGG SHREDS AND COLD-STIRRED VEGETABLES

Impressive and appetizing, this cold-stirred, or tossed, vegetable dish is the closest to a grand Western salad. Egg shreds, made of shredded egg sheets, add a lovely color as well as a delightful fluffiness. *Serves 6 to 8 as a single appetizer; more as part of a cold assortment or buffet.*

2 tablespoons dried mo-er
   mushrooms
1½ cups shredded carrots
2 cups shredded white
   radishes
½ teaspoon salt

2 cups egg shreds:
3 eggs
¼ teaspoon salt
1 tablespoon oil

2 cups shredded cucumbers
   (preferably unwaxed)
Mustard sauce (*page 131*)

Preparations

Place the mo-er mushrooms in a large bowl; add 1 cup boiling water, anchor down with a small plate, and soak them for 30 minutes. Rinse them well in cold water, pinching off and discarding hard "eyes" if any. Shake them dry; pile them loosely, and cut into narrow shreds. Set them aside on a dish. Mo-er mushrooms may be soaked and cleaned hours or a day or two in advance. Cover with cold water and refrigerate. When ready to use, drain, rinse, and shred.

Peel a large carrot; cut it diagonally into slices about 2 inches long and ⅛ inch thick. Make a slanting stack of the slices and cut them into shreds.

Rinse the radishes and trim off the ends. Cut them into shreds the size of the carrot shreds. Place the carrots and the radishes in 2 separate bowls; sprinkle each with ¼ teaspoon salt and toss well. Let them chill in the refrigerator for at least 10 minutes—this softens them so the sauce will penetrate.

Egg sheets

Beat the eggs well with ¼ teaspoon salt. Heat a 9-inch skillet until very hot. Add the oil, swirl, and then pour the oil into a small dish. Turn heat low under the skillet. Pour in a third of the beaten eggs and swirl the pan to spread the eggs over the entire bottom. If there are holes, dip a chopstick or spoon in the eggs and fill them in. When the egg sheet is light brown on the bottom and solidified on the surface, about 45 seconds, peel it loose at the edge, tilt the pan, and slip it onto a plate to cool. Return half of the poured-out oil back to the pan, swirl, and pour in half the remaining eggs; make this egg sheet and then a final one. Spread all three out separately to cool.

When they are completely cold, fold each into a half moon, then fold over once more in the same direction. Then cut each crosswise into ⅛-inch-wide pieces. Toss them lightly with your fingers until they loosen into a pile of long fluffy shreds. Set them aside on a plate.

Wash and dry a large firm, slender cucumber. It is better to have an unwaxed cucumber for this recipe, but if unavailable, use the waxed. Trim off the ends; cut it lengthwise in half and scrape out the seeds with a small spoon. Turn the hollowed side down and cut diagonally into slices ⅛ inch thick and 2½ inches long. Flatten the slices into slanting stacks and cut them into fine shreds.

Assembling

Select a large, round serving patter. Place the yellow egg shreds in the center in a fluffy pile, then circle it with separate piles of black mo-er mushrooms, white radishes, orange carrots, and green cucumber.

Make the mustard sauce. Taste and adjust it to your personal taste by adding a little more mustard or vinegar. Bring the sauce to the table with the vegetable platter. Just before serving, pour the sauce over the platter and toss lightly.

VARIATIONS

The white radishes may be replaced with 2 cups fresh bean sprouts and the cucumbers with 2 cups shredded celery stalks. Parboil each separately in boiling water for 10 seconds. Spray with cold water to stop cooking, and drain well.

Chili-pepper oil (*page 489*) may be added or substituted for the mustard.

This may be also made into a Chinese chicken salad. Add 2 cups shredded boiled (*page 133*) or white-cut (*page 51*) chicken breast and decrease the vegetables and eggs by ½ cup.

涼拌白蘿蔔 COLD-STIRRED WHITE RADISHES

Serves 4 to 6 as a side dish.

2 cups peeled and shredded white radishes or Chinese white turnips 1 teaspoon salt	Sauce: 2 teaspoons light soy sauce ½ teaspoon sugar 1 tablespoon sesame oil

Peel and slice the white radishes and then shred them. Place them in a bowl and sprinkle them with the salt; stir. Cover and macerate the radishes for about 30 minutes to extract some of their water.

Drain off the liquid and add the sauce seasonings; stir to blend well.

Cover and chill until cold and crisp. Serve the radishes as a side dish or as a garnish for a platter of assorted cold meats.

VARIATIONS

Add a few drops of chili-pepper oil (*page 489*) or a little roasted, crushed Szechuan peppercorns (*page 500*) if you like the flavor hot. The radishes are also very good with dried shrimp. Soak a tablespoon of dried small shrimp in hot water for 30 minutes; then rock-mince them and sprinkle them on top of the radishes. Toss at the table before eating.

糖
醋
蒜
頭

SWEET AND SOUR ''CURED'' GARLIC

There is no limit to garlic's virtues. Even though it is used primarily as a seasoning, garlic is also a delectable vegetable as well as one of the oldest and most effective anti-pest agents.

Late in the spring, just as the bugs were beginning to be active in the garden, Ar-chang, our family cook, would frame the kitchen doors with small bouquets of long-stemmed garlic. While he regularly fed us his delicious garlic soup, made with balls of turnip and dried scallops, my nurse, Liu-ma, bottled her cured garlic each week throughout the spring and summer.

Cured garlic, plump with a rich marinade, is one of the best relishes in the world. Mellowed by the sauce over a long period of time, the cloves are mild, sweet, and tasty.

6 large heads garlic

Marinade:
½ cup dark soy sauce
½ cup sweet sherry
½ cup cider vinegar
¼ cup sugar

Separate the cloves but do not remove the peel.

Measure the marinade ingredients into a small pot and stir to dissolve the sugar. Add the garlic cloves, set the pot over medium-low heat, and slowly bring to a boil as you stir every once in a while. Let it simmer vigorously for 1 minute, then pour cloves and marinade into a large jar. When cool, cover and let the cloves marinate for 2 days at room temperature, then chill in the refrigerator about 20 days before eating them. The garlic keeps indefinitely and the flavor improves as time goes on.

For the robust, there's nothing better than eating them whole. For the delicate, peel and mince the cloves and serve them doused with their own sauce—as a seasoning dip for plain boiled meat. Just as with flavor-pot brine, the sauce may be kept "alive" indefinitely for curing additional garlic; just add more of the sauce ingredients.

酸
辣
黃
瓜

HOT AND SOUR CUCUMBERS

Tumbled in hot oil only long enough to brighten the skin and turned with seasonings briefly, these cucumbers are chilled before the vinegar is added so that the acidity will not discolor the vivid green skin. Cold, crisp, and tangy, they are refreshing in look and taste. *Serves 4 as a single appetizer or an accompaniment to meat; more with an assortment.*

2 firm slender cucumbers, prefer-
    ably unwaxed, a little over
      1 pound

Sauce:
1 tablespoon light soy sauce
2 tablespoons sugar
½ teaspoon salt

3 tablespoons oil
1 large clove garlic, lightly crushed
    and peeled
2 to 4 dried chili peppers
2 tablespoons distilled white
    vinegar

Wash and dry the cucumbers; trim off the ends and cut them in half lengthwise. Scrape out the seeds with a small spoon and cut each half lengthwise into 4 strips. Gather up the strips and cut each into 4 sections. Since the cooking time is extremely short, measure out the soy sauce into a cup and combine the sugar and salt in another.

Heat a skillet over high heat until hot; add the oil, swirl, and turn heat low. Add the garlic and chili peppers (2 for a mild dish, 4 for hot), press them against the pan, flipping, until the garlic is light brown and the peppers have darkened.

Turn heat high, shower in the cucumbers, and stir immediately in fast sweeping turns to tumble and roll them in the hot oil, about 25 seconds, until the skin is bright green. Sprinkle in the soy sauce and scatter the sugar mixture over the top. Stir briskly in abrupt flipping and turning motions to spin them in the hot pan for 5 seconds to melt but not darken the sugar. Pour immediately into a dish. Let the cucumbers cool, cover, and then refrigerate until thoroughly chilled, stirring a few times for even marinating.

Transfer the cucumbers to a serving dish without the seasoned liquid, garlic, or peppers. Add the vinegar, toss to mix well, and serve.

辣
醬
黃
瓜 CUCUMBERS IN HOT BEAN SAUCE

Macerated briefly with salt so that the seasoning sauce may penetrate a little deeper into the vegetables, these cucumbers are reddish tinted and speckled with tiny dots of preserved chili peppers and ground Szechuan peppercorns. Hot and tasty, they are indeed one of the best "pickles" in the world. *Serve as part of an assortment, not alone.*

2 firm, slender cucumbers, preferably unwaxed, a little over
   1 pound
2½ teaspoons salt

Sauce:
1 tablespoon sugar
1 teaspoon salt
1 tablespoon distilled white vinegar
2 heaping teaspoons hot bean
   sauce
1 tablespoon oil
2 teaspoons sesame oil
2 medium cloves garlic, smashed
   and peeled
¼ to ½ teaspoon roasted and
   crushed Szechuan peppercorns
   (*page 500*)

Wash and dry the cucumbers; then prepare and cut them into rectangular pieces as in preceding recipe. Place them in a bowl and sprinkle them with 2½ teaspoons salt, tossing to mix well. Macerate in the refrigerator for 1 hour. Pour them into a colander and drain thoroughly. Put them in a bowl.

Mix the sauce ingredients together until the sugar and salt are dissolved. Pour the sauce over the cucumbers and toss gently. Cover and chill until thoroughly cold and very crisp.

炒
利
馬
豆 CHILLED LIMA BEANS

Fast and easy, this is a marvelous nibbler with drinks, particularly wine. Serve with toothpicks. You could also use this dish as a cold accompaniment to a main course.

1 ten-ounce package large frozen
   lima beans
2 tablespoons oil
1 teaspoon salt

1 tablespoon sugar
½ cup chicken stock or water
1 teaspoon sesame oil

Remove the beans from the package, let them defrost a little, and separate them with your fingers.

Heat a skillet over high heat until hot; add the oil, swirl, and heat for 30 seconds. Scatter in the beans and stir-fry briskly for 30 seconds until the frost is dissolved and the color of the beans brightens into icy green. Sprinkle in the salt and sugar and stir rapidly for another 30 seconds to season them evenly. Add the stock or water, even out the beans, turn heat to medium low to maintain a strong simmer, cover, and simmer for 5 minutes.

Uncover, turn heat high and stir rapidly for about 30 seconds until the small amount of foaming liquid has evaporated. Add the sesame oil, give the beans a few fast turns, and pour into a serving dish. Cover, refrigerate, and serve chilled. The beans are also very delicious hot, but chilling settles the flavor and firms the texture, making them richer and nuttier.

VARIATIONS

Increase the oil to 3 tablespoons and add 1 cup diced bamboo shoots from the beginning for a contrast of texture.

Two points of a star anise may also be added, after the stock or water, for a whiff of subtle licorice flavor.

乾
煸
· 茄
子 EGGPLANTS WITH GARLIC SAUCE

Through deep-frying first, a substitute for the old Chinese practice of drying them in the sun for a whole day, eggplants acquire a hardened exterior that prevents the purple skin from discoloring and the pulp from collapsing. They become firm, slightly brittle, and extremely tasty—and they are a great appetizer when chilled. Also delicious hot, this recipe can be used as a vegetable dish.

Highly aromatic of garlic and ginger, the eggplants are tasty but not sour. Each piece is neat, dark, and glazed, giving you a crunchy texture well coated by a rich sauce. If you like eggplants hot and spicy, substitute chili-pepper oil for the sesame oil in the sauce. *Serves 8 as a rich single appetizer; more with an assortment.*

2 eggplants, each about ½ pound
2 cloves garlic, smashed, peeled,
    and coarsely chopped
1 teaspoon minced ginger

Sauce seasonings:
2 tablespoons dark soy sauce
2 tablespoons sugar
1 teaspoon sesame oil

1 tablespoon cider vinegar
2 cups oil for deep frying

Trim off the stems of the eggplants; rinse and dry them. Cut them lengthwise to make 1-inch-wide wedges, and then cut the wedges into 1½- to 2-inch-long pieces.

Set the chopped garlic aside with the minced ginger. Combine the soy sauce with the sugar and sesame oil; stir until the sugar is dissolved. Place the vinegar nearby, place a large strainer over a pot or bowl, and spread out a few paper towels for draining.

Heat a wok or heavy pot over high heat until hot; add the oil and heat until a cube of bread foams instantly, about 375 degrees. Scatter in all the eggplant pieces and stirring, basting, and turning occasionally, fry them about 8 minutes more, until the white pulp is quite brown. Turn off the heat, scoop out the eggplant into the strainer, and let drain, pressing the pieces lightly with the back of a spoon. Put the eggplant on the paper towels, cover with another towel, and press lightly with your hands to extract any more excess oil, being careful not to squash it. Let cool and harden as you make the sauce.

Drain off all but 1½ tablespoons oil from the wok or pot, heat over medium heat, add the ginger and garlic, and sear them rapidly for 20 seconds. Add the eggplant and stir rapidly with a spatula, scooping and turning, for about 1 minute. Turn the heat high; give the soy sauce mixture a big stir, and pour it over the eggplant, stirring rapidly. Toss and turn the eggplant until the sauce is all but absorbed by the vegetable. Splash the vinegar quickly around the edge of the pan. As it sizzles into steam, give the eggplant a few fast turns and pour into a dish. Cover and chill until cold before serving. The dish may be done a day in advance.

MUSHROOM SHRIMP BLOSSOMS

These shrimp-filled mushrooms are steamed and served with a delicate sauce. *They would make an excellent light appetizer for 3 or 4 people; for more as part of a buffet.*

12 large dried black Chinese
    mushrooms (presoaked)

Mushroom seasonings:
2 teaspoons light soy sauce
1 teaspoon dry sherry
½ teaspoon sugar
¼ teaspoon salt
¾ cup water
1 tablespoon sesame oil

Cornstarch for dusting
½ pound small shrimp

Shrimp seasonings:
1 quarter-sized slice peeled ginger,
    minced
1 small white of scallion, minced
1 teaspoon dry sherry
½ teaspoon salt
A pinch black pepper
1 teaspoon cornstarch
1 small egg white, beaten slightly
1 teaspoon oil

1 tablespoon minced cooked
    Smithfield ham (*page 492*)
12 coriander or parsley leaves

Sauce:
½ cup simmering stock
2 tablespoons dry sherry
¼ teaspoon sugar
¼ to ½ teaspoon salt

2 teaspoons cornstarch dissolved
    in 2 teaspoons water and
    1 teaspoon sesame oil

Preparations

Select mushrooms with thick caps and deep curved rims. Pour over them 1 cup hot water and soak for 30 minutes. Squeeze them over the bowl and rinse them briefly to remove any sand; squeeze them lightly to dry, then cut off the stems. Put the caps into a small saucepan, add the soaking water without the sandy residue at the bottom, and bring to a boil over medium-low heat. Add the mushroom seasonings, turn heat low to maintain a gentle simmering, cover, and simmer 20 minutes. Then put the caps in a bowl and press them with a smaller plate over the saucepan to extract excess liquid. Save the liquid for the sauce.

Dust the inside of the mushroom caps with cornstarch.

While the mushrooms are simmering, or later, prepare the filling: Shell and briefly rinse the shrimp; chop them coarse. Then with 1 or 2 wet cleavers mince-chop them until their consistency hovers between a mince and a paste. Put them in a bowl and add the ginger, scallion, sherry, salt, and pepper, and stir to mingle well. Add 1 teaspoon cornstarch and mix it in well. Add the egg white, stir, then add the oil; stir until the mixture is smooth. Turn it onto a plate and divide it into 12 portions.

Fill each cap with the shrimp in a very offhand fashion, so the surface is uneven—then the stuffing will puff out during the steaming to approximate the petals of flowers. Sprinkle each with a little minced ham, and press a coriander or parsley leaf in the center of each. You may prepare and fill the mushrooms hours ahead of time; cover and refrigerate. Bring them to room temperature before steaming.

Steaming the mushrooms and making the sauce

Place the mushrooms on a heatproof plate and steam them over high heat for 10 minutes.

In the meantime, make the sauce: Bring the mushroom-simmering stock to a gentle boil over medium-low heat; add the sherry, sugar, and salt to taste. Stir in the cornstarch mixture till stock is slightly thickened. Turn off the heat and cover to keep sauce warm. When the mushrooms are done, remove them from the steamer and tilt the plate to drain off any juice into the saucepan. Slide the mushrooms onto a serving platter, stir the sauce and warm it a little if necessary, and pour it over the mushrooms.

紅
燒
冬
菇

RED-COOKED CHINESE
BLACK MUSHROOMS

Each mushroom is plump and juicy, full of its own natural good flavor, fortified by simmering in its own soaking water. The flavor is subtly sweet from the rock sugar. Like most mushrooms, these require a substantial amount of oil to bring out their full flavor. *Serves 4 as a single appetizer, but better as part of an assortment.* Combine these glistening black mushrooms with the pale-yellow Stir-fried Celery, side by side on a large platter for a lovely dish, either appetizer or vegetable.

¼ pound medium-sized dried Chinese black mushrooms, about 20 of them	1 tablespoon crushed rock sugar (or ¾ tablespoon granulated sugar)
5 tablespoons oil	½ cup mushroom water
2 tablespoons dark soy sauce	1 tablespoon sesame oil

Place the mushrooms in a deep bowl, cover with 1 cup boiling water, and soak for 30 minutes, anchoring them down with a small plate. Squeeze them dry, letting the liquid drip back into the bowl. Then rinse the mushrooms and cut off and discard the stems. Set aside ½ cup of the soaking water without the residue at the bottom of the bowl.

Heat a saucepan over high heat until hot; add the oil, swirl, and heat for 15 seconds. Add the mushrooms and stir rapidly for about 2 minutes. Add the soy sauce and sugar; stir to blend. Add the mushroom-soaking water and when it boils turn heat low to maintain a very gentle simmering. Cover and simmer for 25 to 30 minutes, stirring occasionally, until most of the liquid has been absorbed by the mushrooms. Turn heat to medium, add the sesame oil, and give the mushrooms a few fast turns. Pour them into a serving dish and serve hot, at room temperature, or cold.

SOUPS

In China, no meal is served without a soup. Not only are the soups full of good things, but a soup acts as the beverage during the meal. Contrary to the custom of Chinese restaurants in this country, water or tea is never served with a meal in China. Presiding over the surrounding dishes, a large bowl or tureen is invariably placed in the center of the table and diners spoon a little soup into their soup or rice bowls from time to time throughout the meal.

The ingredients for soups range widely, from commonplace ones such as bean curd and cabbage to exotic and intricate ones such as mountain creek turtle, shark's fin, and bird's nest. I have included swift's nest soup in this book, since the ingredients are easy to obtain and the soup is quite simple to make, but other delicacies, such as the turtle soup and shark's fin soup, I have excluded, since the proper ingredients are impossible to obtain in the United States and their preparation is extremely tedious.

Actually, though shark's fin soup is a familiar item on restaurant menus here and recipes are freely offered in many Chinese cookbooks, none of them is the real thing. Since the genuine soup is very costly and time-consuming to make, restaurants resort to buying the ordinary presoaked fins sold by Chinese grocers and the cookbooks recommend canned fins. These inferior fins, thin and hard, generally taste no better than the gristle in chicken wings. To make this superb soup properly, you must start with the very expensive yellow fin from the Philippines and be prepared to devote 4 days to soaking it and 1 day to simmering and cleaning it before you can finally cook it over extremely low heat for many hours in a freshly made rich stock. Only then will you have bright, translucent, plump, and softly resilient shark's fin. My advice is to avoid this much-touted soup in the restaurants and forgo making it at home; wait till you can go to China.

The soups I have selected here and in the first part of the book are diversified, basically easy to make, and in all instances quite delicious to eat. Don't limit their use to an all-Chinese meal; they blend beautifully with American food. You'll be delighted when you substitute Fish "Gunn" for chowder; Yin-Yang Spinach and Chicken Soup or Crabmeat Cream of Corn Soup for a Western cream soup; and Hot and Sour Shad Soup or Fish and Clam Soup for a bouillabaisse.

酸
辣
湯　　HOT AND SOUR SOUP

Of northern origin, this soup became popular in all regions of China. Over there, it is not authentic unless the silky congealed chicken or duck blood is used. While it does contribute to creating a very smooth texture, the soup is not lesser without it. This is what I call a "mixed" soup, and true to form, it is flexible. Besides pork, it may be made with chicken, beef, veal, small shrimp, or fillets of fish. The vegetables may be varied too, out of convenience, such as substituting fresh mushrooms for the dried Chinese mushrooms and shredded peeled broccoli stem for the bamboo shoots. Sharp and peppery, it's an ideal cold-weather soup; it warms you from within, giving you a glowing sense of comfort. *Serves 4 as a first course.*

¼ pound lean pork, loin or butt

Slippery-coating:
1 teaspoon light soy sauce
1 teaspoon dry sherry
2 teaspoons cornstarch
2 teaspoons sesame oil

4 dried black Chinese mushrooms
　　(presoaked)
1 tablespoon dried mo-er mush-
　　rooms (presoaked)
16 to 20 Golden Needles
　　(presoaked)
¼ cup shredded bamboo shoots
1 square fresh bean curd
2 tablespoons cornstarch dissolved
　　in 3 tablespoons water and
　　1 tablespoon sesame oil

1 egg, beaten with 1 teaspoon
　　sesame oil

Seasonings:
1½ tablespoons light soy sauce
2 tablespoons Chenkong, cider, or
　　red-wine vinegar
½ to 1 teaspoon black pepper,
　　to taste
1 teaspoon chili-pepper oil
　　(*page 489*), optional

4 cups chicken or meat stock
2 teaspoons minced fresh coriander
　　or 1 small whole scallion,
　　finely chopped

Preparations

Cut the meat against the grain into ¼-inch-thick slices; stack them, then shred them. Place them in a bowl; add the slippery-coating ingredients in the order listed. Let it set in the refrigerator until ready to use.

Place the black mushrooms, the mo-er mushrooms, and Golden Needles in separate bowls. Pour about ½ cup hot water over each and let them soak for 30 minutes. When soft, rinse the black mushrooms briefly, squeeze dry very lightly, destem, and shred to about the same size as the meat. Rinse and shred the mo-er mushrooms the same way, discarding any hard "eyes." Rinse and squeeze the Golden Needles lightly dry, sort them out into a bundle, cut off the knobby ends, then cut them crosswise in two. Rinse and drain the shredded bamboo shoots; cut the bean curd into ¼-inch shreds about 2 inches long. Place the ingredients on your working platter in separate piles and set aside. All these preparations may be done hours in advance; cover and refrigerate.

When ready to cook, dissolve the cornstarch and beat the egg in separate bowls. Measure the seasonings into the final serving bowl and set aside.

Cooking the soup

Bring the stock to a boil in a soup pot over high heat: Add the black Chinese mushrooms, the Golden Needles, and the bamboo shoots. Adjust heat to low and simmer, covered, for 5 minutes. Stir in the meat, raise heat, and when it boils again, add the bean curd and mo-er mushrooms. Lower heat, cover, and simmer for about 3 minutes. Give the cornstarch mixture a big stir and add to the soup slowly with one hand as you stir with the other until it is satiny smooth. Turn off the heat. Pour the beaten egg over the surface in a wide circle; as it congeals into floating ribbons, stir gently a few times to break them into chiffony flakes.

Pour the soup into the serving bowl that has the seasonings in it. Scatter the coriander or scallions on top, and stir the soup up from the bottom a few times at table before serving individual portions.

Placing the seasonings for mixed soups directly into the serving bowl is an established cooking habit of professional cooks in China. Ar-chang would never deviate from this practice, insisting the soup is more flavorful because the "fragrance" is intact in the serving bowl. I fully agree but you may season to taste after the soup is poured into the serving bowl.

STIR-FRIED VERSION

This is often done with "mixed" soups, especially when stock is not available. To give the soup a more vivid flavor, the meat and vegetables are stir-fried in oil with seasonings, then water is added instead of stock for a brief simmering.

Prepare everything exactly as before. When ready to cook, heat the soup pot over high heat until hot. Add 3 tablespoons oil, swirl, and heat for about 30 seconds. Scatter in the meat and stir quickly in swishing and shaking motions to break the lumps; toss the shreds rapidly for about 45 seconds in turning and folding motions all over the pan until they are no longer pink. Add the vegetables and stir them together for 30 seconds. Sprinkle in 1 tablespoon light soy sauce, 1 tablespoon dark soy sauce, and 1/2 teaspoon salt; stir well, then pour in 4 cups water and add the bean curd. When the water comes to a boil, turn heat to medium low to maintain a gentle simmering, cover, and simmer for 3 minutes. Adjust the flavor by adding more soy sauce to taste; then the black pepper and vinegar. Add the cornstarch, then the beaten egg as before. Pour into the serving bowl and scatter the coriander or scallion on top. While this version may be a little less rich, the flavor is nonetheless vivid.

粉絲肉圓湯 MEATBALL AND TRANSPARENT-NOODLE SOUP

One of the best "meaty" soups is that made with meatballs and transparent noodles. The meatballs are fun to make, and the minced water chestnuts add a bit of crunchiness plus making them light, resulting in a substantial soup that is not at all heavy. *Serves 4 as a first course.*

Meatballs:
3 water chestnuts, finely minced
1/2 pound ground pork
1 tablespoon light soy sauce
1 teaspoon dry sherry
1/2 teaspoon sugar
1/4 teaspoon salt
Sprinkling black pepper
1 egg, lightly beaten
1 tablespoon cornstarch dissolved
   in 3 tablespoons water and
   1 tablespoon sesame oil

4 cups water or stock seasoned
   with 2 tablespoons light soy
   sauce and 1/4 teaspoon salt to
   taste
2 ounces transparent noodles
   (presoaked)
1 heaping tablespoon coriander
   or parsley leaves
1 tablespoon sesame oil
Dash of black pepper

Cover the transparent noodles with 2 cups hot water and soak for at least 10 minutes. Set aside.

Meatballs

Mince the water chestnuts and put them in a large mixing bowl.

March-chop the ground pork a few times to loosen its formation; combine it with the water chestnuts; add the soy sauce, sherry, sugar, salt, and pepper and stir until well mixed. Add the beaten egg; stir in a circular motion until well blended; then pour in the dissolved cornstarch and stir the same way until the meat is very smooth. This may be done hours in advance; cover and refrigerate.

When ready to make the meatballs, bring the mixture to room temperature for a few minutes, then stir vigorously in circular motions until the mixture is soft and fluffy. Scrape it onto a platter and roughly divide it into 16 portions.

Measure 4 cups cold water or stock into a large pot with the seasonings and set it within reach. Wet your hands and keep the faucet running with cold water. Scoop up one portion of meat and place it in the palm of your slightly cupped left hand; then throw it lightly to the palm of your slightly cupped right hand. Bounce the meat back and forth like this a number of times, wetting your hands when they feel caky and dry. When the meatball is smooth and round, drop it into the soup pot. Repeat the process for the rest of the meat. The standard way is to grab a fistful of meat in one hand and squeeze it up through a curled index finger and then scrape off the top with a wet spoon—it's messy and not nearly as gay and lighthearted as bouncing the balls from palm to palm.

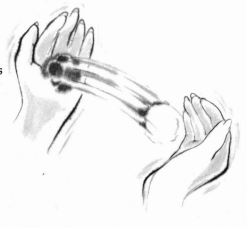

Soup

When ready to cook the soup, drain the soaked noodles. Rinse a few stalks of coriander and shake them dry; pinch off the leaves with a little of the brittle stems and set them aside on a plate. To people who aren't used to coriander's "odd" aroma and taste, it seems medicinal. To me, it's a heady gastronomic perfume. But you may substitute parsley.

Set the pot with the meatballs over medium heat and bring to a boil; skim the surface of any foam. Add the drained noodles, lower the heat, cover, and simmer gently for 5 minutes. Season to taste with additional salt or soy sauce if necessary; add the sesame oil. Pour the soup into a serving bowl or tureen, letting the meatballs nestle here and there over the fluffy noodles, or scoop up the silky threads and drape them gracefully on one side of the bowl, next to the mound of smooth balls of meat. Sprinkle on top a little black pepper and a scattering of fresh coriander leaves.

陰
陽
菠
菜
鷄
蓉
湯

YIN-YANG SPINACH AND CHICKEN SOUP

A Fukien concoction, this is actually two soups in one, and it stands on the border between soup and soupy main dish. The two soups are made separately, then poured together into one bowl to form the curved symbol of Yin and Yang. It is elegant and delicious. *Serves 4 to 6 as a first course.*

Chicken mixture:

½ pound boneless and skinless
    chicken breast
1 tablespoon water
½ teaspoon salt
2 teaspoons dry sherry
4 egg whites, well beaten but not
    stiff
2 cups hot chicken stock
2 tablespoons cornstarch dissolved
    in 4 tablespoons cold stock and
    1 tablespoon oil

Spinach mixture:

1 ten-ounce package chopped
    frozen spinach, defrosted, or
    fresh spinach
1 tablespoon oil
1 teaspoon salt
½ teaspoon sugar
2 cups hot chicken stock
1½ tablespoons cornstarch
    dissolved in 3 tablespoons cold
    stock and 1 tablespoon sesame
    oil

Preparations

Trim off any fat or gristle from the chicken breast. Rinse and lay it on a chopping board, membrane side down. Hold one end firmly as you "scrape-mince" the meat with the tip end of a cleaver or sharp kitchen spoon (see illustration, *page 18*). Discard the tendon in the center of the fillet. Sprinkle 1 tablespoon of water on the scraped meat and march-chop it very fine, flipping the meat over several times until it is fluffy, a soft purée. Put it in a bowl, stir in the salt and sherry, then fold in the beaten egg whites. Mix vigorously in circular motions until the mixture is smooth and fluffy. You may do this hours in advance—cover and refrigerate until ready to use.

March-chop the defrosted spinach until it has the consistency of a purée. If you use fresh spinach, buy a little less than a pound. Wash it well and then parboil it in a large pot of boiling water for about 45 seconds; pour into a colander and spray with cold water until cold, then drain. Chop it fine, then march-chop until it is puréed. As with the scraped chicken, this preparation can be done hours ahead of time.

When ready to start the soup, bring 4 cups stock to a boil in a medium-sized saucepan and keep it hot on the stove. This will be for both the chicken and the spinach.

Spinach mixture

Heat a medium-sized saucepan over high heat until hot, add 1 tablespoon oil, swirl, and heat until hot. Add the spinach and stir rapidly for 30 seconds. Add the salt and sugar, stir, and then measure out and pour in 2 cups of the hot stock. When it comes to a boil, taste and adjust seasonings. Turn the heat very low and stir in the dissolved cornstarch, and mix until smooth and creamy. Cover and keep hot over very low heat while you complete the chicken.

Chicken mixture

Bring the remaining 2 cups stock to a boil over high heat, then turn heat to low and stir in the puréed chicken. When it is well blended and the meat turns white, about 1 minute, stir in the dissolved cornstarch and blend in circular motions until very smooth.

Assembly

Immediately, holding a pot in each hand, pour the two soups simultaneously into a large serving bowl from opposite directions, moving your hands clockwise slowly as you pour so that they form a natural curved pattern. Then dot the wide end of the white chicken part with 1 teaspoon of the green spinach mixture and the green spinach part with 1 teaspoon of the white chicken mixture to complete the symbol of Yin and Yang. Stir to mingle at the table just before serving in individual soup bowls. For a heightened flavor, 2 teaspoons finely minced cooked Smithfield ham (*page 492*) may be used as the dots.

FISH ''GUNN''

"Gunn" is thick and hearty, something like a Western chowder. It comes in various combinations of ingredients, and the flavor may be delicate, piquant, or smashingly sharp and peppery, according to one's preference.

In China, Fish "Gunn" is traditionally made with "yellow fish"—a type of croaker that contains pebbles in its head and luscious meat on its body. Whiting, flavorful and thick-meated, is an excellent substitute. Substantial and well seasoned, this is a great dish, brimming with delicious ingredients and flavor. *It would serve 4 to 6 as a soup course, 4 as a light supper accompanied by hot crusty bread and wine.*

6 whitings, about 2½ to 3 pounds

Stock:
2 large slices peeled ginger
1 large whole scallion, cut in
   3 pieces
4 cups water
1 teaspoon salt

¼ pound fresh mushrooms
1 ten-ounce package frozen large
   lima beans, thawed
2 squares bean curd
1 teaspoon minced peeled ginger
2 heaping tablespoons finely
   chopped scallions or parsley

2 tablespoons cornstarch dissolved
   in 2 tablespoons water and
   2 teaspoons sesame oil
2 eggs, well beaten with ½ teaspoon salt and 1 teaspoon oil
3 tablespoons oil
¼ teaspoon salt
2 tablespoons light soy sauce
1 tablespoon dry sherry
Black pepper to taste
1 tablespoon minced coriander
   (optional)
Chenkong, red-wine, or cider
   vinegar to taste (optional)
Chili-pepper oil to taste (*page 489*),
   (optional)

Preparing the fish and stock

Small whitings, weighing about ½ pound each, are dressed, packed 2 to 3 to a package, and sold in supermarkets almost all year round. Get 6 whitings. Rinse and cut each crosswise into 1½-inch-wide pieces. Place them in a wide saucepan in a single layer, add the ginger, scallions, water, and salt, and bring to a boil. Turn heat to medium low, cover, and simmer for about 4 minutes. Turn off the heat and steep for 5 minutes. Transfer the fish with a slotted spoon to a dish, reserving the broth.

When the fish is cool enough for handling, peel off the skin and lift out the firm lumps of meat from the triangular center bone. Whitings have no small bones within the meat except tiny rolls on the side under the fins, which you remove and discard. Place the meat in a dish, cover, and set aside.

Return the skin, tails, and center bones to the broth; bring it to a boil, cover, and simmer over very low heat for 30 minutes. Filter the broth through a fine strainer into a bowl, discarding the residue. Cover and set aside. Boning the meat and making the stock may be done hours in advance. If chilled, bring them to room temperature before the final cooking.

Other preparations

In the meantime, clean the mushrooms and cut each into 3 or 4 slices. Remove and discard the skins of the lima beans so that by squeezing the inner pod slips out—this is a fast and simple operation. Cover the bean-curd squares with hot water and soak for 10 minutes to soften them. Cube them by cutting them 4 times one way, 4 times the other. Mince the ginger and chop the scallion or parsley fine. Place everything in separate piles on your working platter. The preparation of the vegetables may be done hours in advance (but not the bean curd); cover and refrigerate. When ready to cook, soak and cut the bean curd, dissolve the cornstarch, and beat the eggs.

Making the soup

Heat a wok or large saucepan over high heat until hot. Add the 3 tablespoons oil, swirl, and heat for a second. Scatter in the ginger and scallions and stir rapidly a few times; add the mushrooms and beans and stir in fast turning motions to sear them evenly. Sprinkle in ¼ teaspoon salt, then toss them rapidly for about 45 seconds until they are radiant and glistening with oil. Lower the heat to medium, scatter the bean-curd cubes over the surface; sprinkle in the soy sauce, and turn gently with a spatula a few times. Add the fish stock; when it boils, turn heat low, cover, and simmer for 5 minutes.

Add the fish and sherry, even out the contents, and let everything simmer for another minute. Add the dissolved cornstarch and stir in circular motions until the broth is thickened. Turn off the heat, pour the beaten eggs in a wide circle; stir gently a few times when the eggs form into chiffony ribbons.

Pour the soup into a serving bowl or tureen, dashing in the black pepper to taste, and dot the center with the minced coriander. If you have a spicy palate, add vinegar and chili-pepper oil or serve them on the side for individuals to add to their own taste.

蟹肉粟米羹 CRABMEAT CREAM OF CORN SOUP

This soup falls into the general category of being a "gunn." Here the fluffy consistency is created by the cream of corn. This is a delicate, creamy soup, speckled with red-white crabmeat, golden corn, and green scallions and parsley. The flavor is even better if you have the time and patience to shell 4 freshly steamed or boiled female crabs, to obtain their tasty meat and rich roe. *Serves 6 as a first course, 4 as a supper dish.*

½ pound fresh, frozen, or canned crabmeat

2 heaping tablespoons finely chopped scallions

1 teaspoon minced peeled ginger

2 cups chicken stock or water

1 seventeen-ounce can cream-style corn (about 2 cups)

1 tablespoon cornstarch dissolved in 2 tablespoons water with 2 teaspoons sesame oil

1 large egg, beaten with ¼ tablespoon salt and 1 teaspoon oil

2 tablespoons oil

½ teaspoon salt

1 tablespoon dry sherry

1 to 2 tablespoons light soy sauce, to taste

Sprinkling of white pepper

2 tablespoons finely chopped fresh parsley

Cider vinegar to taste (optional)

If using frozen king crabmeat, thaw it. Break it into coarse flakes. Place it with the scallions and ginger on your working platter. Have ready the stock, corn, dissolved cornstarch, and beaten egg. Gather all ingredients within reach of the stove.

Heat a medium-sized soup pot over high heat until hot; add the 2 tablespoons oil, swirl, and heat for a second. Scatter in the scallions and ginger and stir rapidly a few times. Add the crabmeat and stir; sprinkle in the salt and sherry, and stir vigorously for about 45 seconds. Pour in the stock or water, the corn, and the soy sauce to taste, stirring until the soup comes to a boil. Turn heat low and let it simmer for about 1 minute.

Give the cornstarch mixture a big stir and pour it in, stirring in a circular motion as the soup thickens. Turn off the heat and pour the egg in a wide circle over the surface; stir gently a few times when it forms into floating ribbons. Adjust seasonings by adding a little more salt or soy sauce if necessary.

Pour into a serving bowl, sprinkle with pepper, and dot the center with the parsley. Stir to blend well at table before serving. If you like a sharper flavor, add vinegar to taste.

VARIATIONS
Substitute minced velveted chicken or shrimp for the crabmeat.

蛋 EGG-ROLL CARTWHEEL SOUP
卷
湯

The egg rolls in this soup are made with egg sheets that are stuffed, steamed, cut into cartwheels, and then poached in the soup. They could also be served alone with a sauce or coated with dissolved cornstarch and deep-fried as an appetizer.

This is an intriguing-looking soup, with its swirls of yellow and patches of green. The meat filling is fluffy; the simmered egg sheets are soft but delightfully resilient; and the spinach is crisp. Rapid parboiling in sugared water eliminates its tart taste and prevents it from diluting the flavor of the good stock. *Serves 6 as a first course.*

2 egg sheets (*page 162*)

Filling:
½ pound ground pork, beef, or veal
1 tablespoon light soy sauce
1 teaspoon dry sherry
½ teaspoon sugar
¼ teaspoon salt
Sprinkling black pepper
1 egg, lightly beaten
1 tablespoon cornstarch dissolved
   in 3 tablespoons water and
   2 tablespoons sesame oil

Paste: 2 teaspoons cornstarch dissolved in 2 teaspoons water
2 cups packed fresh spinach
1 teaspoon sugar
5 cups meat or chicken stock
Salt or light soy sauce, to taste

Make the egg sheets and set aside.

Make the filling: First march-chop the ground meat a few times to loosen its formation; then put it in a bowl and add the soy sauce, sherry, sugar, salt, and pepper; mix well. Add the beaten egg in a circular motion until well blended. Then pour in the dissolved cornstarch and stir circularly until the meat is very smooth. Let it sit for about 10 minutes to "fluff out."

Egg rolls

Place an egg sheet on a flat surface; give the meat a few big stirs and then cover the sheet with half of the filling, to within about ¾ inch from the edge. Brush the edge with half of the cornstarch paste. Then lift the edge closest to you and roll the sheet lightly but firmly across to the other end, pushing back any filling that escapes. Press down the far edge to seal the roll. Do the other. Place them both, seam down, on a heatproof plate and steam over high heat for 15 minutes. Remove, drain, and slip them onto a clean plate to firm up. These may be done hours in advance; when cool, cover and refrigerate.

Spinach

When ready to cook, bring a small pot of water to a boil with 1 teaspoon sugar. Wash the spinach well, pinching off any long, tough stems. Plunge them into the boiling water, stir to submerge them, then immediately pour the spinach and water into a colander.

Press it with your hands, lightly, to extract excess water, and set aside to drain further.

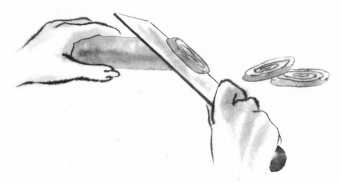

Final cooking

Slice the egg rolls diagonally into ½-inch-thick cartwheels.

Bring the stock to a boil over high heat, then turn heat low to maintain a gentle simmering—small bubbles shooting up. Scatter in the cartwheels, cover and simmer for about 2 minutes. Add the spinach to the soup. Cover and simmer about 1 minute, season to taste with salt or light soy sauce, and pour the soup into a serving bowl or tureen.

VARIATIONS

Instead of using ground meat in the cartwheel filling, try minced chicken, shrimp, or crabmeat, alone or combined.

五
綵
湯
THE RAINBOW SOUP

This is a soup that puts leftover poultry and pork to good use. It is beautiful-looking, ideal for entertaining. You create a colorful mound of ingredients with a delicate stock poured around it. *It serves 4 to 6 people.*

1 large dried Chinese
    black mushroom (presoaked)
2 ounces transparent noodles
    (presoaked)
1 cup chicken stock
1 tablespoon light soy sauce
3 cups packed fresh spinach
¾ cup shredded cooked chicken or
    turkey breast
¾ cup shredded Roast Pork
    (*page 116*)

¾ cup shredded cooked Smithfield
    ham (*page 492*) or boiled ham
¾ cup shredded egg sheets
    (*page 162*)
2 tablespoons oil
2 quarter-sized slices peeled ginger
¼ teaspoon salt
A pinch of sugar
4 to 5 cups chicken stock

Soak the mushroom in hot water for 30 minutes. Rinse, destem, and set aside.

Soak the transparent noodles in cold water for 15 minutes. Drain and simmer them with 1 cup stock and the soy sauce over extremely low heat for 5 minutes. Drain and set them aside.

Wash spinach well, pinching off any long, tough stems. Drain.

Cut the chicken, pork, ham, and egg sheets into 3-inch-long shreds and place them in separate neat groups on your working platter.

Lightly oil a heatproof bowl about 8 inches wide and 3 inches deep. Place the mushroom cap in the center, black top down. Fan the chicken shreds around a quarter of the circumference of the bowl, the shreds going straight up the side of the bowl, with the other ends resting on the inside of the mushroom cap. Spread the ham next to the chicken in the same way, then the shredded egg sheets, and finally the pork—so forming a complete circle. Fill the center with the simmered transparent noodles.

Steam over moderately high heat for 20 minutes. Turn off the heat and keep the bowl in the steamer, covered, while you prepare the spinach and the stock.

Heat a wok or large skillet over high heat until hot, add the oil, swirl to cover the entire surface. Throw in the ginger and press against the pan. Scatter in the spinach, and stir rapidly for 10 seconds. Add the salt and sugar and stir for another 10 seconds. Pour into a dish and set aside.

Bring the stock to a boil, and keep it hot over extremely low heat. Taste for seasoning.

Remove the bowl bearing the shreds; invert a large serving bowl over it; flip the two bowls over. Scatter the spinach, without the juice, around the base of the mound, and fill the bowl with the hot stock, pouring gently from the side.

酸
辣
鰣
魚
湯

HOT AND SOUR SHAD SOUP

When shad is in season, be sure you try this marvelous specialty from eastern China. It is an "eating" soup—the shad is the star and the broth is the supporting feature.

Shad is a very rich fish, and its meat is extremely fine. The vinegar cuts the heaviness, making this a delicious spicy soup. Steaming the fillet first, instead of simmering it, gives it a concentrated richness. *Serves 6 as a first course.*

2 pounds boned shad
1 tablespoon light soy sauce
1 tablespoon dry sherry
3 quarter-sized slices peeled
    fresh ginger
1 large whole scallion, cut into
    3 pieces
4 cups seasoned chicken stock

Seasonings:
1 tablespoon light soy sauce
2 tablespoons Chenkong or
    red-wine vinegar
¼ teaspoon black pepper
2 teaspoons sesame oil

1 tablespoon minced fresh
    coriander, parsley, or
    scallion greens

Cut the boned shad into about 6 pieces and place in a shallow heat-proof dish. Sprinkle both sides with soy sauce and sherry. Scatter the ginger and scallions on top and steam over high heat for 20 minutes. While it is steaming, bring the seasoned chicken stock to a simmer, add the seasonings; let it barely simmer, covered, until the fish is done. Then pour the soup into a deep serving bowl, add the shad and its juice. Scatter the minced coriander on top, and serve.

蛤
蜊
魚
湯

FISH AND CLAM SOUP

Impressive and delicious, this soup is a masterpiece of finesse and understanding about the nature of food. It requires a rich meat stock, a fish, shucked small cherrystone clams, and a head of celery cabbage. It involves three simple procedures: steaming the vegetable separately so that it retains its crisp texture and doesn't dilute the stock; poaching the delicate fish in a rich stock; and merely scalding the clams, so that they are plump with juice and extremely tender. It is a perfect example of the basic principle of Chinese cooking—exploit the simple subtleties to create a grand finale of complex distinctions. *The soup serves 6 generously as a first course.*

1 sea bass or striped bass, about 2 pounds	2 quarter-sized slices peeled fresh ginger
24 small cherrystone clams, shucked	1 whole scallion
1 tablespoon minced cooked Smithfield ham (*page 492*),	1 medium-sized slender celery cabbage
1 small whole scallion or a few sprigs parsley, finely minced	½ teaspoon salt
6 cups rich meat stock	1 tablespoon oil
	2 tablespoons dry sherry
	Salt to taste

Have the fish cleaned but leave the head and tail on. Rinse the fish well and then score it on both sides with 3 slanting cuts across the thick midsection. Set it aside.

Place the clams in a bowl; strain the juice through cheesecloth into another bowl. Place the minced ham and scallion in separate piles on a plate.

Bring the stock to a boil over medium heat in a large wok, a fish poacher, or a roasting pan—anything that will hold the fish comfortably. Add the strained clam juice, ginger, and the whole scallion; then slither in the fish. When the stock boils again, turn the heat low and skim off any foam. Cover and let the fish poach gently over low heat for 15 minutes.

In the meantime, cut off and discard the tough end and outer leaves of the celery cabbage. Holding the remaining cabbage firmly, cut it crosswise into 1½-inch sections, trying not to let them fall apart. If necessary, insert toothpicks crosswise to hold the sections. Rinse each one in cold water and shake dry. Place them on a heatproof plate, sprinkle with ½ teaspoon salt and 1 tablespoon oil, and steam over high heat for 10 minutes. Turn off the heat but keep the cabbage hot inside.

When the fish is done, transfer it to a large serving bowl with two spatulas. Surround the fish with the celery-cabbage sections on both sides, removing the toothpicks if used, and place the clams between the fish and the cabbage. Bring the stock to a boil, add the dry sherry and salt to taste. Then pour the stock over the clams and the fish, discarding the ginger and scallion. Sprinkle the minced ham on the cabbage, the parsley in the center, on the fish.

VARIATION

If you wish, you could serve it with a dip sauce on the side for each person—made of 1 tablespoon light soy sauce mixed with 1 teaspoon sesame oil, 1 teaspoon cider or wine vinegar, and ½ teaspoon minced ginger.

鍋
巴
湯

SIZZLING GO BA SOUP

When hot liquid is poured over freshly fried go ba, or rice patties, it makes a wonderful sizzling sound. This richly embellished soup is one of the best created in Chinese cuisine. Thickened with dissolved cornstarch, the soup softens but doesn't soak through the crisp rice patties. A great eating treat. *Serves 6 as a first course.*

¼ pound loin of pork

Marinade for meat:
2 teaspoons light soy sauce
1 teaspoon dry sherry
2 teaspoons cornstarch

¼ pound medium shrimp

Marinade for shrimp:
½ teaspoon salt
1 teaspoon dry sherry
1 teaspoon cornstarch

3 tablespoons oil

1 large whole scallion, cut into
    4 pieces
½ cup sliced bamboo shoots
6 to 8 dried black Chinese
    mushrooms (presoaked)
½ cup frozen green peas,
    defrosted, or fresh peas
1 tablespoon dry sherry
4 cups chicken stock
¼ teaspoon salt
1½ tablespoons light soy sauce
1½ tablespoons cornstarch
    dissolved in 3 tablespoons
    water
10 to 12 rice patties, or go ba
    (*page 430*)
Sprinkling black pepper

Preparations

Cut the meat crosswise into paper-thin slices about as long as the shrimp, add the marinade, and refrigerate for at least 30 minutes.

Shell the shrimp; cut each in two through the back, rinse vein off, add the marinade, and refrigerate for at least 30 minutes.

Rinse and drain the sliced bamboo shoots. Cover the mushrooms with hot water and soak for 30 minutes; rinse, squeeze dry, destem, and cut into ¼-inch-wide pieces. Defrost the peas. Place all the vegetables with the scallions on a plate. (If you use fresh peas, parboil them in a cup of boiling water in a small saucepan for 5 to 7 minutes depending on how young they are. Eat one—if it is crisp but tender, it is done.)

You may do all of this in advance, but once you start the soup you must cook uninterrupted and serve immediately.

Making the soup

Heat a wok or large pot over high heat until hot; add the oil, swirl, and heat for 30 seconds. Toss in the scallions and stir briskly a few seconds until they are bright green. Add the bamboo shoots, mushrooms, and peas, and stir rapidly about 30 seconds to mingle well. Splash in the sherry and then add the stock.

When the stock comes to a boil, turn heat to medium low to maintain a gentle simmering. Scatter in the meat and stir to separate and whiten the pieces, about 1 minute. Then add the shrimp and stir 30 seconds, until they are pink. Add the salt and soy sauce. Turn heat low, give the dissolved cornstarch a big stir, pour into the pan, and stir in circular motions until the broth is smoothly thickened. Turn off the heat, cover, and keep hot.

Deep-frying the rice patties and serving the soup

Heat a pot of oil and deep-fry the rice patties as on *page 431*. Just before the last of the patties are fried and ready, bring the soup to a simmer, add the pepper, and pour into a hot bowl. Place the patties in another soup bowl or tureen and bring the two bowls to the table. Pour the hot soup over the patties and listen for the delightful sizzling sound. Toss them lightly, then serve in individual bowls.

VARIATION

The most elegant version of this soup is made in China with a special kind of dried mushroom known as K'o-mo. They are very small but exceptionally flavorful and fragrant. These mushrooms are native specialties of Inner Mongolia and Kiling province and not yet available in the United States. But I have found go-ba soup made with fresh mushrooms to be extremely delicious: Stir-fry 1 pound sliced mushrooms exactly as on *page 383*, adding ½ cup peas during the last 30 seconds of cooking. Then add the stock, soy sauce to taste, and the dissolved cornstarch, and continue to conclusion as before.

沙 CASEROLE OF CHICKEN SOUP
鍋
鷄　A frying chicken can be made into a substantial soup, or a main course,
湯　when its delicate flavor is enhanced with oil and seasonings and combined
　　with interesting secondary ingredients. Make it in a casserole and serve it
　　directly from stove to table.

This chicken is tender and flavorful; the broth is tasty of the mushrooms. The transparent noodles are silky, the steamed eggs smooth, and the bamboo shoots firm and crisp. *Serves 4 as a light supper or lunch dish with crusty bread.*

8 medium dried black Chinese
    mushrooms (presoaked)
2 ounces transparent noodles
    (presoaked)
1 cup roll-cut bamboo shoots
4 eggs, well beaten

Seasonings for eggs:
1 teaspoon salt
1 tablespoon oil
1 tablespoon minced cooked
    Smithfield ham (*page 492*)
    optional

1 frying chicken, about 3 pounds
3½ to 4 cups water
3 tablespoons oil

Seasonings for fryer:
3 quarter-sized slices peeled ginger
1 medium whole scallion, cut in
    two
1 tablespoon light soy sauce
¼ teaspoon salt

Preparations

Pour ¾ cup hot water over the mushrooms and soak for 30 minutes. Squeeze them dry lightly over the soaking bowl and save the liquid. Rinse the mushrooms briefly, destem, and set the mushroom caps aside. Cover the transparent noodles with cold water, soak for 30 minutes, and set them aside. Rinse the canned bamboo shoots in cold water and roll-cut them into small chunks. Group them with the mushrooms on a plate.

Beat the eggs well with the salt and oil, and add the minced ham if you have some on hand. Grease a small, deep bowl with oil; pour the beaten eggs in and steam over medium heat for 15 minutes, until the eggs are firm. Loosen the edges with a small paring knife and turn the egg mound onto your chopping board to cool. Quarter it and then cut each quarter into chunky pieces. Set them aside.

Remove the fat from the cavity; rinse and dry the chicken. Disjoint it (*see page 14*) by cutting through the shoulder and thigh joints; discard the wing tips and chop the wings and the legs each into 3 pieces, keeping the joint intact. Turn the body and split it in half lengthwise at the ribs. Chop the breast and the back lengthwise into 2 strips, and then each strip crosswise into 4 or 5 pieces.

All these steps may be done in advance.

Cooking the soup

When ready to start the soup, drain the mushroom liquid into a measuring cup, without the residue, and add boiling water to make 4 cups.

Heat a wok or large, heavy skillet over high heat until hot; add the oil, swirl, and heat for 30 seconds. Scatter in the ginger and scallions and stir a few times, then add the chicken. Sear for about 2 minutes, until all pieces are richly yellow but not browned. Add the soy sauce and salt, turning the chicken rapidly to coat it evenly. Transfer the chicken and juice to an earthenware or heavy enameled casserole. Add the hot mushroom liquid and water, the mushroom caps, and the bamboo shoots.

Set the pot on medium heat, and when the liquid boils, cover and simmer over medium-low heat for 20 minutes. Drain the transparent noodles, add to the pot, cover, and simmer another 5 minutes. Add the steamed eggs and simmer, covered, another 5 minutes. Adjust seasonings to taste at this point by adding either a little salt or light soy sauce. Cover and bring the soup to a bubbling boil, and then serve immediately.

猪蹄腐竹湯 PORK KNUCKLES AND SOYBEAN-STICK SOUP

The combination of pork and soybean sticks makes this soup very rich and milky, and the smoked knuckle lends a good, deep flavor without making the soup too smoky. If you like, serve on the side a dip sauce of light soy sauce with a sprinkling of freshly ground Szechuan peppercorns or minced fresh coriander to offer a contrasting taste to the meat. *Serves 6 to 8 as a first course.*

4 soybean sticks (*page 487*)	4 quarter-sized slices peeled ginger,
1 teaspoon baking soda	each ½ inch thick
3 fresh pork knuckles	2 large scallions
1 smoked pork knuckle or ham	2½ quarts cold water
hock	Salt to taste

Soybean sticks

Break each dry soybean stick into 4 or 5 pieces; place them in a large bowl and sprinkle the baking soda on top. Cover with warm water, stir, and let them soak for 2 hours, placing a small plate on top to keep them submerged so that they soften and expand evenly. After the first hour, change the water and turn any that look dry. After 2 hours, drain and rinse them well in warm water; put them in a bowl and cover with lukewarm water until ready to use.

Soup

Put the fresh and smoked knuckles, ginger, and scallions into a large, heavy pot. Add 2½ quarts cold water and bring to a boil over high heat.

Turn the heat low and skim off any foam. Adjust heat to maintain a low but firm simmering, with tiny bubbles shooting steadily to the surface. Cover and simmer for 1½ hours, stirring once in a while. Skim off foam, and season with salt to taste. Drain the soybean sticks and add them to the pot, tucking them next to the meat here and there. Cover and simmer for another hour, or until the soybean sticks are completely loosened and soft. Skim off the foam, taste for seasoning again, then discard the ginger, scallions, and the knuckle bones if you wish. The meat may be served in its natural chunks or cut into small pieces.

Substitutes for soybean sticks

If you wish, 1½ cups raw blanched peanuts may be added from the beginning, or 2 to 3 cups peeled and roll-cut turnips may be added during the last 40 minutes of simmering.

鷄
蓉
燕
窩
湯

CHICKEN FU YUNG SWIFT'S NEST SOUP

This is a gastronomic exercise in matching a delicate but savory taste to a brittle texture; one complements the other with perfect balance. With no taste of its own, the bird's nest depends on other ingredients for flavor. Nevertheless, the seasonings shouldn't be strong or they will overwhelm the lightness of the nests. Using a rich stock for flavor, fu yung chicken for a creamy consistency, and minced Smithfield ham for accent, this fluffy white soup is really a marvel of sophistication. *It serves 6 as a first course.*

1 cup loosely packed ground
    bird's nest
1 small knob peeled ginger (about
    1 inch square), crushed
1 pound boneless and skinless
    chicken breast
3 tablespoons water

4 cups rich chicken stock
⅛ teaspoon white pepper
Salt to taste
2 tablespoons cornstarch
    dissolved in 3 tablespoons
    stock
1 tablespoon minced cooked
    Smithfield ham (*page 492*)

Marinade:
1 teaspoon salt
2 teaspoons cornstarch dissolved
    in 1 tablespoon water
2 egg whites, beaten until frothy

Preparing the bird's nest

Soak the bird's nest in warm water for 2 to 3 hours. Pour into a colander and rinse well with cold water, tossing. Pick off any impurities.

Place the nest in a saucepan, cover with warm water, and bring to a boil with the ginger (crushed with the flat of a knife). Turn heat to medium high and let the water bubble gently for 5 minutes; the parboiling will remove the faint fishy taste of the nest. (This step was always done in China in the old days with a rich stock and ginger, since the rare and precious bird's nest was considered too important to be "degraded" by water.) You may do this hours or even a day in advance; after draining, cover the bird's nest with cold water and refrigerate. Drain just before making the soup.

Preparing the fu yung chicken

Scrape and mince the chicken breast as on *page 17*, adding the 3 tablespoons water as you march-chop it until pasty. Put it in a bowl and stir in the salt. Add the cornstarch mixture and stir well, then add the beaten egg whites and stir in a circular motion until mixture is fluffy. This can be done a few hours in advance. Cover and refrigerate; bring out a few minutes before making the soup.

Soup

Bring the rich chicken stock to a boil in a large soup pot; add the drained bird's nest. When the stock comes to a boil again, turn heat to medium low, cover, and simmer for 5 minutes. Add the white pepper and salt to taste. Turn heat low, give the dissolved cornstarch a big stir; and pour into the pot, stirring until the broth thickens. Add the chicken fu yung slowly with one hand as you stir in a circular motion with the other. Turn off the heat and stir continuously until the chicken is white and the entire mixture is smooth and fluffy. Pour into a tureen or serving bowl and sprinkle the minced ham on top.

冬瓜盅　THE WHOLE WINTER MELON POND

This is a truly "big affair" for a banquet—a very delicate soup with a very impressive bearing. It is not at all complicated, but it does take a good deal of time. You can do all the preparations except cutting the melon a day in advance, however. *This soup can easily serve 10 people as a sumptuous soup course.*

1 whole winter melon, about
    7 or 8 pounds
10 dried black Chinese mushrooms
1/2 cup diced cooked Smithfield
    ham (*page 492*)

1 cup diced bamboo shoots
1/2 cup diced water chestnuts
    (optional)
1 cup canned gingko nuts
6 to 7 cups rich chicken stock

2 cups diced chicken breast,
    velveted in water (*page 77*)
Light soy sauce and salt to taste
1 cup frozen peas, parboiled
    2 minutes, or cooked fresh peas
    (*page 372*)

1 tablespoon minced cooked
    Smithfield ham

Melon

Select a well-formed oblong-shaped winter melon with a small stem on top. Scrub it clean under cold running water to remove any dirt and the white film. Using a sharp knife, cut off a lid about 2½ inches deep from the top. With a paring knife make tiny V-cuts along the edge of the melon to give it a serrated finish. Scrape the melon and the lid to remove seeds and stringy pulp. If you feel an artistic urge, carve some designs along the borders or over the shell of the melon by scraping off the green skin with the tip of a small, sharp knife.

Place the melon upright in a large, deep heatproof bowl to hold its bottom securely. The steaming pot must be large enough so that you can place the melon in it and remove it safely after cooking. If your largest pot is tight, make a basketlike sling with lengths of strong cloth and slip it underneath the melon-supporting bowl, so that you can lower it in, drape the sling loosely over one side of the pot during cooking, and gather it up and lift out the melon, in its bowl, safely after steaming.

Broth

Prepare the broth and its assorted ingredients for the inside of the melon. The mushrooms should be covered with hot water and soaked for 30 minutes. Rinse, destem. Then cut the ham, mushroom caps, bamboo shoots, and water chestnuts into small dice. Rinse the gingko nuts. Put all these ingredients into a soup pot. Add the rich stock and bring to a boil over high heat. Lower the heat to maintain a gentle simmer, cover, and simmer for 30 minutes. While this is simmering, velvet the diced chicken and set it aside.

This may be done hours or a day in advance. Cover and refrigerate until ready to use.

Making the soup

Place the slinged bowl with melon into a tall soup kettle. Pour boiling water around the outside of the base bowl to within an inch of its rim and bring it to a boil over high heat. Then fill the melon with the stock and vegetables, about three-quarters full.

Cover the melon with its own lid; adjust the heat to medium, cover the soup kettle, and steam for 3 hours, replenishing the water whenever necessary to maintain a strong steam.

Remove kettle and melon covers and add the velveted chicken to the soup. Season to taste with a little soy sauce and salt. Re-cover everything and steam for another 2 hours. This soup is done when the melon pulp is soft and translucent.

Serving the soup

Very carefully remove the melon (in bowl) by the sling; this takes strength. Put into a larger bowl. Tuck the sling down at the side of the melon and camouflage with watercress or parsley—*don't* try to remove it; that melon is extremely hot and should be handled as little as possible.

Remove the melon top and stir in the parboiled peas. Adjust seasoning if necessary, but remember that it is to be a delicate soup. Sprinkle 1 tablespoon minced ham on top with a little on the serrated edge for a decorative touch, and serve, scooping some of the melon pulp into the soup bowls along with the delicious broth plus its ingredients.

VARIATIONS

You could add to, or use instead of, the chicken some velveted pork and shrimp. Fresh or canned mushrooms may be substituted for the black mushrooms. If you use fresh ones, slice and stir-fry them briefly in a little oil with a sprinkling of salt to preserve their flavor and texture before simmering them in the broth.

The Fire Pot

Originating with the Mongols as a way to keep food hot throughout the meal in the bitterly cold winter months, the fire pot, called *ho-go* in Chinese, has been much refined over the centuries in China. The object itself underwent a transformation from a pot over a crude brazier to a beautiful and ingenious utensil, made of brass, copper, pewter, or stainless steel, with a built-in compartment for charcoal or Sterno. And from the robust fare of mutton or beef, coarse vegetables, and hearty noodles, the contents have been refined and widened to include assorted meats, poultry, seafood, leafy vegetables, and vegetarian products. Nevertheless, the fire pot offers a basically simple way of eating; there is no cooking art involved. The flavor is rather plain, but one can make an impressive display of finely cut ingredients, especially for the Chrysanthemum Pot.

You really must have the pot itself, which is available in two varieties. There is the traditional funneled pot, which is fueled by charcoal, and the chafing-dish pot, which you can heat with Sterno. The latter is more practical, since you need to give the first a good deal of attention. Fire pots are sold in many better department stores or Chinese utensil stores, or they can be bought by mail order. Some cookbooks recommend using an electric pot or skillet instead. I disagree emphatically, since part of the charm of a fire-pot dinner is the elegance of the table, and an electric appliance with a dangling electric cord does nothing for that effect.

The meal begins when the pot, containing boiling stock and some basic vegetables and vegetarian products, is placed in the center of the table. The pot is surrounded by platters of thin-cut raw meats, poultry, seafood, and leafy vegetables. Each guest is provided with a plate, a fork or chopsticks to cook his own ingredients in the broth, a small dish for the basic dip sauce, plus a soup bowl and spoon. At the very end of the meal, when all the broth-cooked ingredients have been eaten, everyone fills his bowl with the tasty broth.

There are many fire-pot versions, but the most popular are the sumptuous Chrysanthemum Pot and the simpler but very tasty Lamb Pot.

菊 CHRYSANTHEMUM POT
花
鍋

This is so named because it's traditionally served in the autumn, when the weather is cool and the chrysanthemums are in full bloom. The flowers are used not only in great sprays around the room but also, stems removed, as decorations on the platters themselves.

The ingredients, and the quantity, depend on your preference and the number of people. As a general guide, calculate about ½ pound of meat and fish per person. If you don't like one of the ingredients listed below, drop it or replace it with another, such as veal for beef or oysters for clams. There should be enough variety, however, to make the meal interesting and exuberant.

A standard-sized fire pot can take care of 8 to 10 people, most easily used if the guests are sitting at a round table.

Precede the fire pot with some tasty or crisp hot hors d'oeuvres, such as Sweet and Sour "Boneless" Spareribs, Paper-wrapped Fish, Crab-meat Wontons, and Deep-fried Eggplants with Curry Beef Filling. With an hors d'oeuvre, the fire pot then makes an impressive one-dish meal for entertaining. *This recipe will be fine for 8 to 10 people.*

1 pound boneless and skinless
    chicken breast
1 pound fillet of beef or flank steak
1 pound large shrimp
1 pound fillet of sole, flounder,
    or pike
2 to 3 dozen small clams
1 pound squid or canned abalone
2 pounds fresh spinach
8 to 10 cups chicken stock

Vegetables for the pot:
2 ounces presoaked transparent
    noodles
1 pound celery cabbage
4 to 5 squares bean curd

Dip sauce (1 serving):
1 tablespoon light soy sauce
1 teaspoon sesame oil
¼ teaspoon finely minced peeled
    ginger

Seasonings for dip sauce
(put in separate dishes):
4 to 6 tablespoons chopped fresh
    coriander
1 to 2 tablespoons roasted and
    crushed Szechuan peppercorns
    (page 500)
3 to 4 tablespoons chili-pepper oil
    (page 489)
3 to 4 tablespoons chili-pepper
    sauce
3 to 4 tablespoons Chinese hot
    mustard *(page 495)*
3 to 4 tablespoons Chenkong or
    red-wine vinegar

Garnishes for the platters:
A bunch of watercress
Some Carrot Flowers *(page 111)*
Some Radish Flowers *(page 160)*
Chrysanthemums, stems removed

Cutting and arranging the ingredients

Everything must be sliced into large but thin pieces, so that while they are a reasonable size they will also cook very quickly. Since the emphasis here is on neat, precise cutting, do wrap the chicken breast and beef and freeze them for about 3 hours until they are very firm but not solid. Tilt the knife and cut on a slant in a shaving motion so that you will get larger slices out of thin meat, such as the flank steak.

The platters should be attractive and large enough to show off the meats without crowding them. The most effective way to arrange the sliced meats is to place each type on a separate platter in overlapping circles. The circle pattern is simple and neat, and it tends to make a small quantity of an ingredient look like much more. Besides, then the center of the platter is left free for chrysanthemums.

C H I C K E N—Freeze the boned breast until firm and slice from the top crosswise into paper-thin slices. Make an overlapping circle on a platter.

B E E F—Freeze until firm; turn the tubular fillet of beef on its side, slice crosswise into thin slices. If you use flank steak, cut the meat lengthwise in half before slicing it on a slant in shaving motions from the top into paper-thin slices. Arrange in a circle on a platter.

S H R I M P—Rinse, shell, and devein if necessary, but leave the tails on—they are attractive. Cut through the back of each, but not all the way through. Spread them out flat and arrange in a circle on a platter with the tails outward.

F I S H—Cut each fillet lengthwise along the center indentation into two strips; then cut all strips crosswise into 2-inch-wide pieces. Arrange in a circle on a platter.

C L A M S—Open the clams, but leave them on the half shell. Loosen the meat from the attaching muscles. Place the clam shells on a bed of watercress on a platter.

S Q U I D—Peel off the membranes and cut off the tentacles. Cut the body open, discard the transparent cartilage, and peel away the membranes on the inside. Rinse well and drain. Score each squid on one side in a crosswise pattern and then cut it lengthwise into 2 pieces. Place them in a circle and pile the separated tentacles in the center. If you use abalone, slice into thin pieces.

S P I N A C H—Wash the spinach well and drain it. Place it in a bowl or on a platter.

All the cutting and arranging, of course, may be done hours in advance; cover all the platters and refrigerate. When you are ready to bring them to the table, put the chrysanthemum flowers in the center of the platters bearing the chicken, beef, shrimp, and fish, and on the sides of the platters bearing the clams and those with the squid. Scatter a few Carrot Flowers and Radish Flowers here and there to accentuate the colors.

Preparing the sauce and the pot
Make the dip sauce individually in small saucers. Put the additional seasonings into 6 small cups on an attractive tray for easy passing around at the table.

Soak the transparent noodles in cold water for 30 minutes; drain them. Trim off the root end of the celery cabbage and cut it crosswise into 1½-inch pieces. Separate the pieces. Rinse them well and shake dry. Cut each bean curd square in two and then make ¼-inch-thick slices. Add all of this to the stock and bring to a boil over high heat. Then cover and turn off the heat. You may do this a little in advance and reheat just before putting it into the fire pot. However, the cabbage will become too limp if you leave it a long time.

When ready to serve bring all the platters of meats and vegetables and sauces to the table. Place the fire pot on the trivet and light the Sterno. Scoop the vegetables from the stock into the pot and fill it about three-quarters full of stock, reserving the rest, keeping it hot on the stove, for replenishment later. Cover the pot and place it in the center of the table. When the stock bubbles again, begin the meal.

Cooking time for the ingredients

Everyone starts by taking whatever ingredient he wants from the platter with chopsticks or a fork and swishing it in the bubbling broth. Nothing requires more than 2 minutes: the chicken takes about 1 to 1½ minutes to be white and succulent; the beef mere seconds, especially for those who like rare meat; the shrimp 1 to 1½ minutes to be pink and succulent; the fish 1 to 1½ minutes to be white and firm; the clams a few seconds to curl into juicy balls; the squid body a few seconds to curl into crisp pieces; the tentacles 1 to 1½ minutes to stiffen and crisp; and the spinach a second or two.

When all the meats have been eaten, add the rest of the stock, scoop out the cabbage, bean curd, and noodles into the soup bowls and ladle in some of the tasty broth. Steamed Chinese buns or hot Western rolls may be served at this point.

涮
羊
肉

LAMB POT

This is a characteristically northern fire-pot dish—very robust. It is hearty enough to make a substantial meal, but you may precede it with some hors d'oeuvres, such as Fish or Shrimp Toast, or a platter of assorted cold appetizers, such as Scallion-Oil Shrimp, Chicken in Sesame-Paste Sauce, Spicy Minced Watercress, and Peppercorn-Oil "Choked" Celery. Just as with the Chrysanthemum Pot, allow ½ pound solid meat per person. *Serves 8, as a main course.*

1 leg of lamb, about 5½ pounds
10 cups lamb stock made from
    the bone
1 small peeled knob ginger (about
    1 inch square), smashed
1 small turnip, peeled
Salt

Marinade:
4 tablespoons light soy sauce
6 whole scallions, finely chopped

Vegetables for the pot:
1½ pounds celery cabbage
    (*see preceding recipe*)
4 squares fresh bean curd (*see
    preceding recipe*)
2 ounces transparent noodles
    (*see preceding recipe*)
2 pounds fresh spinach
1 pound cooked egg noodles (*page
    432*) or linguini

Dip sauce (1 serving):
1 tablespoon light soy sauce
1 teaspoon sesame oil

Seasonings for dip sauce:
3 to 4 tablespoons chopped fresh
    coriander
3 to 6 cloves garlic, mashed
3 to 6 tablespoons chili-pepper oil
    (*page 489*)
1 to 2 tablespoons roasted and
    crushed Szechuan peppercorns
    (*page 500*)

Preparing the meat and the stock

Have the butcher trim off the fat and bone the meat or do it yourself as you would fresh ham (*page 49*). Cut the meat in two lengthwise; wrap in foil and freeze until firm—this takes about 4 hours.

Place the bone in a large kettle; add 12 cups water, the ginger, and the turnip to eliminate the strong taste. Bring to a boil over high heat, skim off any foam, season lightly with salt, cover, turn heat very low, and simmer for about 2 hours.

Remove the meat from the freezer. Then cut each piece crosswise into paper-thin slices and arrange them neatly in a single layer on as many platters as necessary for marinating. Sprinkle or brush the soy sauce over the meat and scatter the scallions on top. Cover and refrigerate the platters until ready to serve.

When the stock is tasty, skim off most of the fat and strain the stock into a large pot. It is now ready for the addition of cabbage, bean curd, and transparent noodles (the egg noodles will not be added until the very end when everything has been eaten), but do not add these vegetables much in advance of serving, since the cabbage will become too soft. After putting them in, bring the stock to a boil and turn off the heat and cover.

Assembling and serving the pot

Arrange the table: Make the individual dip sauces in small saucers; put the seasonings in 4 small bowls on a tray; pile the cooked egg noodles and raw spinach in separate bowls; put out the platters of sliced lamb.

Bring the stock back to a boil. Place the fire pot on a trivet and light the Sterno. Scoop the celery cabbage, bean curd, and transparent noodles into the pot and then fill the pot with three-quarters of the hot stock, keeping the rest hot on the stove for later in the meal. Cover and bring the fire pot to the table; place it in the center. When the stock bubbles again, begin the meal.

Each diner, using chopsticks or a fork, will alternately take pieces of lamb and leaves of spinach and swish them in the pot; both take mere seconds—the lamb is ready when it turns slightly gray. As the last of the meat, vegetables, bean curd, and transparent noodles are being eaten, add to the pot the cooked egg noodles and the rest of the hot stock. Cover the pot and simmer a few minutes. Then fill each person's bowl with some noodles, broth, and whatever vegetables and slivers of meat are left in the pot.

Instead of using noodles at the end, you could serve Chinese Plain Buns or some hot crusty French or Italian bread with the wonderful broth.

SEAFOOD
AND FISH

Seafood is always abundant in China. Bordered on the east and south by an extensive coastline, veined with four gigantic rivers, dotted with lakes, and covered with a network of canals from the eastern province of Kiangsu all the way to the northern city of Tientsin, China is generously supplied with an enormous variety of fish and shellfish all year round. And this bounty is treated with great gastronomic reverence—for instance, the Chinese will bathe a fish in hot liquid so that its natural juices slowly gather beneath the skin or salt-whip shrimp into a clear, crisp delicacy. In this chapter you will also discover the marvelous gusto with which the Chinese eat shrimp with shells on and lobster cut up and richly sauced.

Although of course it's preferable to have fresh fish and shellfish for all these dishes, that is not always possible, and you can certainly use canned or frozen crabmeat, frozen shrimp, or even frozen fillets of sole or flounder for many of the recipes. Lobster and whole fish, however, must be fresh. For those lucky enough to be able to catch or buy fresh fish, there is a good variety here to choose from—I have recipes for trout, butterfish, smelt, soft-shell crabs, clams, and even squid. I think you will find Fillet of Flounder in Wine-Rice Sauce as elegant as a French Sole Veronique and Shrimp with Mo-er Mushrooms and Cucumbers as light and easy to make as a Shrimp Salad.

Shrimp

木
耳
炒
蝦

SHRIMP WITH MO-ER MUSHROOMS AND CUCUMBERS

This is light, bright, and refreshing. The emphasis is on natural flavor, texture, and color. Not "treated" in any way, the shrimp are briefly seared and steam-cooked before they are combined with vegetables in a delicate and aromatic sauce. *Serves 2 or 3 with rice as a main course.*

1 pound medium shrimp, shelled
2 tablespoons dried mo-er
    mushrooms (presoaked)
1 large firm, slender cucumber
1 large clove garlic, crushed and
    peeled
2 quarter-sized slices peeled ginger,
    minced
1 tablespoon finely chopped fresh
    coriander or parsley

Sauce:
2 tablespoons light soy sauce
1 tablespoon dry sherry
¼ teaspoon salt
¼ teaspoon sugar
Sprinkling black pepper

¼ cup water
1 teaspoon cornstarch dissolved in
    1 tablespoon water
2 teaspoons sesame oil

5 tablespoons oil
½ teaspoon salt
1 tablespoon dry sherry

Preparations

Shell the shrimp and devein if necessary; rinse and blot dry. Pour 1 cup hot water over the mo-er mushrooms and soak for 15 minutes. Rinse in cold water, pinching off any hard "eyes," and drain. Cut off the ends of the cucumber; rinse and dry. To make a green-white pattern, peel the cucumber lengthwise at 1-inch intervals with a vegetable peeler or paring knife. Then cut it in half lengthwise and scrape out the seeds with a small spoon. Cut the halves diagonally into thin slices about ¼ inch thick and 1½ inches long. Place everything with the garlic, ginger, and coriander in separate piles on your working platter. Combine and mix the sauce ingredients in a bowl. Measure out the water; dissolve the cornstarch and add to it the sesame oil.

Stir-frying

Heat a wok or large, heavy skillet over high heat until hot; add 2 tablespoons of the oil, swirl, and heat for 30 seconds. Scatter in the mo-er mushrooms and cucumbers and stir rapidly a few times; sprinkle in ½ teaspoon salt and the sherry and stir vigorously for about 30 seconds until they are gleaming with oil. Pour them into a dish.

Clean the pan and reset it over high heat. Heat until hot, add the remaining 3 tablespoons oil, swirl, and heat for a few seconds. Throw in the garlic and press it in the oil; scrape in the ginger and coriander and stir rapidly a few times. Add the shrimp and stir in fast flipping and turning motions for 1 minute, until they are well seared and pink. Give the sauce ingredients a big stir, pour over the shrimp, toss to season them evenly, add the water, turn heat to medium low, and steam-cook for 1 to 1½ minutes.

Turn heat high, add the mo-er mushrooms and cucumber and toss to mix them well. Add the cornstarch mixture and stir in fast sweeping turns until the shrimp and vegetables are gleaming and lightly glazy. Pour into a hot serving dish.

辣醬炒蝦仁　FLUFFY SPICY SHRIMP

Coated with a whole egg so the texture is fluffy, this shrimp is then stir-fried with a chili sauce.

You need very small shrimp for this dish, called *hsia-jein* in Chinese, meaning they are as tiny as the young pit of a small fruit. Sold under the name TT shrimp commercially here, they are available frozen. If you cannot get any, buy the smallest shrimp you can; then cut each crosswise once. As with all highly seasoned dishes, the ingredients should be small or finely cut so that the flavors may penetrate more deeply. Moist and flavorful, this dish should be served with a vegetable that provides a refreshing taste and texture, and a contrasting color. Natural, crisp, and icy green, Stir-fried Celery is an ideal candidate. *This serves 2 to 4 with rice.*

1 pound very small shrimp

Fluffy coating:
½ teaspoon salt
2 tablespoons dry sherry
Sprinkling black pepper
1 egg, well beaten
2 tablespoons cornstarch
1 tablespoon oil

2 large whole scallions, finely
   chopped
2 teaspoons finely minced
   peeled ginger
1 medium clove garlic, minced

Sauce:
2 teaspoons hot bean sauce
2 tablespoons light soy sauce
2 tablespoons catsup
2 teaspoons sugar
2 teaspoons cider vinegar
2 tablespoons dry sherry
1 tablespoon sesame oil
2 teaspoons cornstarch dissolved
   in ¼ cup water

2 cups oil for the velveting

Preparations and velveting

Rinse, drain, and shell the shrimp. If using the frozen TT shrimp, defrost them thoroughly. Place the shrimp in a bowl, and add the salt, sherry, and black pepper. Mix well. Beat the egg and add it to the shrimp, sprinkle in the cornstarch, and mix well. Add the oil and stir till smooth. Let the shrimp set in the coating, refrigerated, for at least 30 minutes.

Place the chopped scallions, minced ginger, and minced garlic in a dish. Measure the sauce ingredients into a bowl and stir until the sugar is dissolved. Set a strainer over a pot.

Heat a wok or large skillet until very hot; add the oil and heat until it barely foams a cube of bread, about 280 degrees. Scatter in the shrimp and swish and turn them rapidly but gently with a spatula until their color whitens: it takes about 40 seconds. Pour shrimp and oil into the strainer to drain; then set shrimp on a plate. Reserve the oil for general cooking. This procedure may *not* be done in advance—the whole-egg coating would thicken and lose its fluffiness if cooled.

Stir-frying

Clean the pan if necessary and reset it over high heat; add 2 table-spoons of the drained oil. Toss in the scallions, ginger, and garlic, and stir rapidly for 30 seconds. Then give the sauce a big stir and pour it into the pan. Turn the heat down low and stir for 5 seconds. Then raise the heat, add the velveted shrimp, and toss and turn them until they are well coated by the sauce. Scoop into a hot serving dish.

VARIATION

Cubed or very small bay scallops may be done the same way; they are excellent.

玻
璃
蝦

CRYSTAL SHRIMP

The deliberate alteration of the texture of food, a prominent feature of Chinese cuisine, cannot be better demonstrated than by this recipe. Salt-whipped and rinsed repeatedly until they are thoroughly cleansed of their sticky substance, the shrimp become brittle, clean, and as clear as crystal in texture as well as color. Once treated and velveted, they are capable of endless variations—a unique crisp substitute for many of the shrimp dishes in this book, either whole, stir-fried with vegetables, or cut up and tossed with rich or spicy sauces.

Here the shrimp are unseasoned and served with a fluffy bed of crunchy black mo-er mushrooms and dainty streaks of green scallions. Thus the pearly sheen of white meat and pink border is completely preserved. Though delicate, this is a very tasty dish, with no fuss. You might precede it with a flavorful soup, such as the Hot and Sour Soup, and accompany it with a vegetable such as the stir-fried Broccoli Flowerets in Black Bean Sauce. *Serves 2 to 4.*

1 pound medium shrimp
3 teaspoons salt

Velvet coating:
½ teaspoon salt
1 egg white, well beaten
1 tablespoon cornstarch

4 tablespoons dried mo-er mushrooms (presoaked)
1 large clove garlic, crushed and peeled

2 quarter-sized slices peeled ginger
4 whole scallions, diagonally cut into 1½-inch-long pieces
½ teaspoon salt

Sauce:
½ teaspoon salt
1 tablespoon dry sherry
2 teaspoons cornstarch dissolved in ½ cup stock
2 teaspoons sesame oil

4 cups oil for velveting

Preparations and velveting
Slice the shrimp three-quarters of the way through along the outside curve; remove the vein. Put them in a large, deep mixing bowl and sprinkle in 1 teaspoon salt. Holding a pair of chopsticks as a whisk or using a wooden spoon, stir the shrimp rapidly in a circular, whipping fashion for 1 minute so that all the shrimp skid, bounce, and turn against the side of the bowl. Put them in a colander and spray with cold water for 1 minute, tossing them with your hands. Drain and repeat the salt-whipping for 1

minute with the next teaspoon of salt; rinse again for 1 minute, and repeat the process a third time. Shake them in a colander and roll them dry in a kitchen towel. Put them in a mixing bowl; add the ½ teaspoon salt, egg white, and cornstarch, and mix well. Cover and let them set in the refrigerator for at least 1 hour. You may do this in the morning and then complete the cooking in the evening.

Cover the mo-er mushrooms with hot water and soak for 15 minutes. Rinse and remove any hard "eyes." Have the garlic, ginger, and scallions ready. Combine the sauce ingredients in a bowl and mix well.

Heat a wok or large, heavy pot over high heat until hot; add the 4 cups oil and heat until it foams a cube of bread instantly, about 375 degrees. Scatter in the shrimp and stir quickly to separate them. Then baste and turn them rapidly for about 40 seconds until each is curled into a large petal of pearly white meat with a vivid pink border. Drain them immediately by either pouring both oil and shrimp into a strainer set over a pot or by spooning the shrimp rapidly into a strainer held over the pan. Put the shrimp on a plate.

Stir-frying

Pour out the oil and reserve it for general cooking. Clean the pan. Reset it over high heat; return 3 tablespoons oil to it, swirl, heat for 30 seconds, and then toss in the garlic and ginger, pressing them in the hot oil. Shower in the mo-er mushrooms and scallions and stir in sweeping motions until the mushrooms are gleaming and the scallions aromatic; add ½ teaspoon salt and stir rapidly to season evenly. Give the sauce ingredients a big stir, pour into the pan, and stir vigorously until smooth and glazy. Add the shrimp and give them a few fast folds and pour into a serving dish, discarding the garlic and ginger and placing most of the shrimp on top.

VARIATION

IN PARSLEY SAUCE—Press a clove of crushed garlic in 3 tablespoons hot oil. Add 2 heaping tablespoons finely chopped parsley and 1 teaspoon minced ginger and stir-fry them for a few seconds with ½ teaspoon salt. Add 1 cup chicken or meat stock and bring it to a simmer. Lower the heat and slowly add 1 tablespoon cornstarch that has been dissolved in 2 tablespoons stock, stirring until the sauce is smoothly thickened. Add salt to taste. Turn heat to medium high, add the shrimp, give them a few fast tumbles, then pour into a serving dish, discarding the garlic. Not embellished by vegetables, this dish should be served with some on the side, along with fluffy rice.

蝦龍糊 SHRIMP IN LOBSTER SAUCE

This is a very popular dish in the United States, and it is so named because the sauce is the same as that in Lobster Cantonese, not because the sauce contains any lobster meat. The shrimp are not velveted—they are blistered in hot oil to acquire a protective shield, then steam-cooked vigorously with the meat sauce, resulting in a succulent crispness. Since the dish is saucy, it goes very well with rice. Serve with a firm vegetable, such as Stir-fried Broccoli Flowerets or Green Beans. *Serves 2 to 4.*

1 pound medium shrimp
¼ pound ground lean pork

Dry seasonings:
1 tablespoon fermented black beans
2 medium cloves garlic, coarsely
    chopped
1 quarter-sized slice peeled ginger,
    finely minced
2 small scallions, including green
    part, finely chopped

Liquid seasonings:
1 tablespoon dry sherry
1½ tablespoons light soy sauce
½ teaspoon salt
¼ teaspoon sugar

½ cup water
1 tablespoon cornstarch dissolved
    in 2 tablespoons water and
    2 teaspoons sesame oil
1 egg, well beaten

2 cups oil

Preparations

Shell the shrimp and devein by cutting along the outer curve ⅛ inch deep; rinse briefly; then blot dry. Place them at one end of your working platter.

March-chop the ground pork until its formation is loosened. Put it next to the shrimp. Place the fermented black beans in a strainer and rinse briefly in cold water; then chop them coarsely. Put them with the garlic, ginger, and half the scallions at one end of the working platter; put the rest of the scallions on a separate dish for later use.

Combine the liquid seasonings in a small bowl and stir until the sugar is dissolved. Dissolve the cornstarch and add the sesame oil; beat the egg in a separate bowl.

Stir-frying

Heat a wok or large skillet over high heat till hot; add 2 cups oil and heat until it foams a cube of bread instantly, about 375 degrees. Scatter in the shrimp and toss and baste them rapidly for about 30 seconds until they whiten, stiffen, and are covered with minute blisters when examined closely. Drain the shrimp and oil immediately into a strainer set over a pot. Turn the shrimp onto a plate.

Reset the pan over high heat; add 2 tablespoons of the drained oil, swirl, and shower in the fermented black beans, garlic, ginger, and scallions. Stir rapidly for about 30 seconds. Add the pork and stir rapidly in poking and swishing motions to separate the meat until it loses all pinkness. Add the shrimp, then the liquid-seasonings mixture, and stir for 15 seconds to coat evenly. Pour in the ½ cup water, cover, and steam-cook vigorously over high heat for 3 minutes. Uncover, turn heat to medium low, adjust seasoning by adding a little soy sauce to taste, and then give the dissolved cornstarch a big stir and add to the sauce, stirring until it thickens. Turn the heat extremely low and pour the beaten egg all over the surface. Pause for 30 seconds to let it firm but not harden. Turn heat high, give the contents a few gentle, sweeping folds, and pour into a serving dish. Scatter the remaining chopped scallions over the top.

一 ONE SHRIMP TWO FLAVORS

蝦
二
味

Velveted first, these shrimp are served half white and half seasoned with the reddish hoisin sauce. It's especially pretty if you serve them on a silver platter with a vegetable in the middle, either Stir-fried Spinach or Broccoli Flowerets, Red-cooked Chinese Mushrooms, or Mushrooms in Oyster Sauce. *That way it would serve 4 as a main course.*

1½ pounds very small shrimp (or TT shrimp)	2 tablespoons oil
	6 small whole scallions, finely chopped
Velvet coating:	6 quarter-sized slices peeled ginger, minced
½ teaspoon salt	½ teaspoon salt
1 egg white, well beaten	1 tablespoon dry sherry
1½ tablespoons cornstarch	1 teaspoon sesame oil
	2 tablespoons hoisin sauce (or 1 tablespoon hoisin sauce and 1 tablespoon catsup)
2 cups oil for velveting	

Put the shelled shrimp in a bowl, add the velvet coating, and stir to mingle until smooth. Marinate in the refrigerator for at least 1 hour.

Velvet the shrimp in the oil according to the master recipe (*page*

81), for only about 15 seconds, until the coating whitens. Drain immediately. You may do the velveting up to 1 hour in advance; do not refrigerate.

Heat a wok or large, heavy skillet over high heat until hot; add 2
tablespoons oil, swirl, and heat for 30 seconds. Scatter in the scallions and
ginger and stir quickly a few times. Add the shrimp and stir, tossing and
turning, for a few seconds to heat them through. Sprinkle in the salt,
sherry, and sesame oil. Give the shrimp a few fast turns and pour half of
them into one side of a hot serving dish.

Add the hoisin sauce to the pan and stir in light, tossing motions
with a spatula, until the shrimp are coated evenly. Pour them into the
serving dish next to the other shrimp, and serve.

VARIATIONS

If you wish, add a few drops of chili-pepper oil (*page 489*) to the red
shrimp to give them spice.

If you serve them with any of the vegetables mentioned above, cook
the vegetable first, drain off liquid, place it in the center of a serving
platter, and keep hot by setting the platter over a pot of simmering water
until the shrimp are completed.

蘆筍蝦 SHRIMP WITH ASPARAGUS

This is a simple stir-fried dish of lovely pink velveted shrimp and bright-
green asparagus. *It serves 2 to 4.*

1 pound small shrimp, velveted (*page 81*)	½ teaspoon salt
8 to 10 young stalks asparagus, roll-cut	¼ teaspoon sugar
2 tablespoons oil	¼ cup water
2 quarter-sized slices peeled ginger, each about ⅛ inch thick	1½ tablespoons light soy sauce
	1 tablespoon sesame oil

Velvet the shrimp according to the master recipe. This may be done
up to 1 hour in advance—do not refrigerate.

Break off the tough ends of the asparagus. Rinse the stalks thoroughly and roll-cut them into 1-inch pieces, leaving the buds intact.

Heat a wok or large, heavy skillet over high heat until hot; add 2
tablespoons oil, swirl, and heat for a few seconds. Add the ginger and press
it around in the oil quickly, then add the asparagus and toss vigorously for

about 1 minute. Sprinkle in the salt and stir; then add the sugar and stir a few seconds more. Add the water, cover, and let the asparagus steam-cook over high heat for 1 minute.

Add the shrimp and stir and toss a few times. Add the soy sauce and stir vigorously to season evenly. Sprinkle in the sesame oil, give the contents a few big turns, and then pour the shrimp and asparagus into a serving dish, discarding the ginger slices.

If the shrimp have been velveted in advance, spread them on top of the asparagus after adding the water so that they may steam-cook until hot with the vegetable. Then add the soy sauce and sesame oil, stir well, discard the ginger, and serve.

VARIATION

If you prefer a stronger flavor, add 1 clove minced garlic and 1 tablespoon rinsed and chopped fermented black beans to the ginger in the initial stir-frying step.

青豆蝦仁 SHRIMP WITH PEAS AND HAM

A delicate stir-fried dish of dainty ingredients—the pinkish-white shrimp fluffy, the green peas firm, and the red ham very tasty. With nothing to turn watery or limp, this is a good dish for a buffet. *It serves 2 to 4 as a main course.*

1 pound very small shrimp	2 cups oil
or TT shrimp	1 cup frozen or fresh peas
	½ cup finely cubed cooked
Velvet coating:	Smithfield ham (*page 492*)
1 tablespoon dry sherry	2 tablespoons oil
1 egg white, beaten well but not	1 quarter-sized slice peeled
frothy	ginger, minced
1 tablespoon cornstarch	1½ teaspoons salt
1 tablespoon oil	1 tablespoon dry sherry
	2 teaspoons sesame oil

Velveting the shrimp

Rinse, dry, and shell the shrimp (if using frozen TT shrimp, thaw, rinse, and dry thoroughly). Put them in a bowl, season with 1 tablespoon sherry, then add the egg white and cornstarch, and mix well. Add 1 tablespoon oil and stir until smooth. Let the shrimp set, refrigerated, for at least 1 hour.

Velvet the shrimp in 2 cups warm oil (about 280 degrees) for about 20 seconds, according to the master recipe on *page 81*. Drain immediately. You may velvet the shrimp up to 1 hour in advance; do not refrigerate.

Parboil frozen peas in boiling water about 40 seconds; fresh peas for about 3 minutes. Drain and spray with cold water to stop the cooking. Cut the ham into tiny cubes and place them with the peas on your cooking platter. Gather together all the other ingredients.

Stir-frying

Heat a wok or large, heavy skillet until hot; add 2 tablespoons oil, swirl, and heat for 30 seconds. Toss in the ginger and press it in the oil. Add the peas and stir them spiritedly a few times; then sprinkle in ½ teaspoon of the salt and the sherry and stir rapidly. Add the shrimp and toss lightly; add the other teaspoon of salt and stir. Scatter in the ham, dribble in the sesame oil, and stir in sweeping motions for about 30 seconds. Pour into a hot serving dish.

菠蘿蝦 SWEET AND SOUR PINEAPPLE SHRIMP

Here is deep-fried shrimp glazed with a pungent sauce. *It serves 2 or 3 and should be accompanied by a refreshing, simple stir-fried vegetable.*

1 pound medium shrimp
Batter (*page 94*)

Sauce:
1 cup basic sweet and sour sauce
   (*page 97*)
1 teaspoon cornstarch dissolved in
   2 teaspoons water
1 cup canned small pineapple
   chunks

Shell the shrimp and make a slit about ⅛-inch deep along the outer curve. Rinse them briefly to remove the vein and dry thoroughly. Put them in the batter. Deep-fry in hot oil as on *page 94* until nicely browned, in 2 or 3 batches, and drain on paper towels. Don't do this in advance.

Make the sauce according to the master recipe. You may do this ahead of time. Thicken it slightly with the dissolved cornstarch, then add the pineapple cubes. Heat up the sauce over low heat until the pineapple cubes are thoroughly warmed. Scatter in the fried shrimp, turn heat high, and give the shrimp a few big gentle tumbles to saturate each one with the sauce. Serve immediately, so that while the shrimp are glazed they remain crisp.

VARIATIONS

Instead of pineapple cubes, use 1 cup canned kumquats, mandarin oranges, or canned lichee fruit, well drained.

Fish

豆
豉
魚
片

FILLET OF FLOUNDER IN BLACK-BEAN SAUCE

This white, fluffy, delicate-looking fish, colorfully studded with speckles of fermented black beans, red pimientos, and green scallions, is deceptive— it looks too fragile and refined to be so robustly flavorful and aromatic. A spoonful of heated oil is added just before it is put into the serving dish to give it a high gloss and to bring out the aroma of raw scallions.

This goes very well with the dark Mushrooms in Oyster Sauce and crisp Stir-fried Green Beans or Celery. *It serves 2 to 4.*

1 pound fillets of flounder, velveted
    in water (*see next recipe*)
2 tablespoons fermented black
    beans
2 large cloves garlic, minced
1 tablespoon minced peeled ginger
2 tablespoons finely diced
    pimientos

Sauce:
1 teaspoon cornstarch
½ cup chicken stock
1 teaspoon dry sherry
½ teaspoon salt
½ teaspoon sesame oil
Sprinkling black pepper

2 tablespoons finely chopped
    scallion bulbs
3 tablespoons oil

Preparations and velveting

Marinate and velvet the fish in water. Do not velvet in advance.

Place the fermented black beans in a strainer; rinse briefly, drain, and chop fine. Put them with the garlic and ginger in a small dish. Combine the sauce ingredients and mix until smooth. Chop the scallion bulbs fine and set aside in a dish. Dice the pimientos and add to the scallions.

When ready to cook, heat 1 tablespoon oil in a small pan. Turn off the heat, but keep it handy, so that just before the conclusion of the dish you can reach over and reheat it instantly.

Stir-frying

Heat a large, heavy skillet over high heat; add remaining 2 tablespoons oil and swirl for 30 seconds. Shower in the black beans, garlic, and ginger, and stir rapidly for about 15 seconds to explode their aroma and flavor. Turn heat low, give the sauce a big stir and pour it into the pan. Stir in fast circular motions with the back of a spoon until the sauce is glazy and smooth. Add the fish, raise the heat a little, and turn each piece gently but quickly with a spatula a few times. Scatter in the pimientos and scallions, then the hot oil over the top. Pour the fish into a hot serving dish.

糟
溜
魚
片   FILLET OF FLOUNDER IN
WINE-RICE SAUCE

Cooking with wine is a time-honored Chinese practice. Wine is used to enrich a sauce, to diminish the fishiness of seafood, to lighten the heaviness of meat, and to anchor the delicate flavors of vegetables. In China the wine used for cooking comes from Shaohsing and is named for that city. It resembles dry sherry in color and taste, and that is a standard substitute in the United States. Besides wine, Chinese cooking also uses wine rice and wine lees (wine rice is a white liquid mixture of fermented glutinous rice, and wine lees are a concentrated red paste) to create a richer wine flavor and a thicker consistency. Here the velveted fish fillets are served in this white glazy wine-rice sauce sprinkled with crisp black mo-er mushrooms.

This is a delicious and elegant dish. Preceded by some appetizers and accompanied by vegetables and rice, it would make a lovely dinner. While the appetizers could and should be highly seasoned, the vegetables should be delicate and firm, such as Stir-fried Asparagus or Sliced Zucchini and Shredded Carrots, so that the wine flavor is not intruded upon and the liquid consistency is not repeated. The sauce is so good you will want rice to absorb the last of it. *Serves 2 to 4.*

1 pound fillets of flounder

Velvet coating:
½ teaspoon salt
1 tablespoon dry sherry
⅛ teaspoon white pepper
1 egg white, well beaten
1½ tablespoons cornstarch
1 tablespoon oil

2 tablespoons dried mo-er mushrooms (presoaked)
1 small clove garlic
2 quarter-sized slices peeled ginger

Wine-rice sauce:
1 cup wine rice (*page 503*)
¼ cup dry sherry
1 teaspoon salt
1 teaspoon sugar
1½ tablespoons cornstarch
dissolved in 1 cup cold water

3 tablespoons oil
½ teaspoon salt

Preparations and velveting

Halve each fillet lengthwise. Cut each half crosswise into 2-inch pieces. Put these in a bowl; add salt, sherry, and pepper, and mix well. Add the egg white, then the cornstarch and oil; toss gently until the pieces are smoothly coated. Let the fish set, covered and refrigerated, for at least 2 hours. The longer it sets, the smoother it will be.

Cover the mo-er mushrooms with 1 cup hot water and let soak for 15 minutes. Rinse well and discard any hard "eyes." Then squeeze dry. Mince the garlic and ginger. Place everything on your working platter.

Mix the wine-rice sauce: Pour the wine rice onto a piece of double-fold cheesecloth over a measuring cup. Gather the cloth up and wring out the juice into the cup; then add water to make a full cup. Pour this into a bowl, add the sherry, salt, sugar, dissolved cornstarch; stir until the salt and sugar are dissolved. The sauce should not be mixed in advance, lest the wine fragrance be weakened.

Bring 4 cups water to a boil in a large pot; turn heat down to maintain a gentle simmer; then give the fish a few gentle stirs and pour them into the water, stirring gently to separate the pieces. Turn heat to medium high; when the water comes to a boil in about 2 minutes, drain the fish by pouring into a colander. The fish is white and glistening; it is ready for the wine sauce. Don't do the velveting in advance.

Stir-frying

Heat a large, heavy skillet over high heat until hot; add 2 tablespoons of the oil, swirl, and heat 30 seconds. Scrape in the garlic and ginger and stir rapidly a few times. Turn heat to medium and then add the mo-er mushrooms, tossing them vigorously for 30 seconds. Sprinkle in ½ teaspoon salt and stir a few more times. Turn heat to low, give the wine-rice sauce a big stir, and pour it slowly into the pan. Stir in circular motions until the sauce is smooth and thickened. Push the mushrooms to the side and add the fish in a single layer. Tilt the pan, add 1 tablespoon oil, and baste the fish. Turn the pieces quickly but gently, then remove to a hot serving platter with a spatula; pour the sauce and mo-er mushrooms on top.

VARIATION

If you don't have wine rice on hand, make the mock one—it's almost as delicious as the genuine. Mix 2 tablespoons cornstarch with ⅔ cup dry sherry. Add 4 teaspoons sugar, 1¼ teaspoons salt, and 1½ cups cold water. Mix until the sugar and salt are dissolved and use as the wine-rice mixture.

炒 FILLET OF FLOUNDER WITH VEGETABLES
魚
片

Once velveted, the fillets remain neat and tender when gently stir-fried with vegetables in a glazy sauce. This is an excellent main dish, in which the succulent fish contrasts with the crisp vegetables. *It would serve 3 to 4, and should be accompanied by rice.*

1 pound fillets of flounder	*Sauce:*
Velvet coating (*page 214*)	1 tablespoon oyster sauce
6 large dried black Chinese	1 tablespoon light soy sauce
mushrooms (presoaked)	1 tablespoon dry sherry
½ cup sliced bamboo shoots	¼ teaspoon salt
1 cup stringed fresh snow peas	½ teaspoon sugar
2 quarter-sized slices peeled ginger	1 tablespoon cornstarch dissolved
1 medium clove garlic, crushed	in 1 cup chicken stock and
and peeled	1 tablespoon sesame oil

4 cups oil for velveting
4 tablespoons oil
½ teaspoon salt
1 tablespoon dry sherry
2 tablespoons chicken stock or
    water

Cut and marinate the fish as on *page 215.*

Pour hot water over the mushrooms and soak for 30 minutes. Rinse and squeeze dry. Cut them in half. Rinse and drain the sliced bamboo shoots thoroughly. Rinse and dry the snow peas; string by snipping off the tips and pulling along the edge. Place these, plus ginger and garlic, in separate piles on a working platter. Combine the sauce ingredients and mix until the salt and sugar are dissolved.

When ready to cook, velvet the fish as on *page 215,* but using the 4 cups oil. When the oil has drained off, turn the fish onto a plate. The velveting cannot be done in advance.

Heat a large, heavy skillet over high heat till hot; add 4 tablespoons oil, swirl, and heat 30 seconds. Toss in the ginger and garlic and press them in the oil. Scatter in the mushrooms and bamboo shoots and stir in fast tossing and turning motions for about 1 minute. Add ½ teaspoon salt and 1 tablespoon sherry and stir a few times. Then add the stock, even out the contents, cover, and steam-cook vigorously for about 1 minute. Uncover and add the snow peas; stir in rapid flipping motions for 30 seconds until they are bright green; discard the garlic.

Turn the heat to medium low and add the fish slices. Give the sauce ingredients a big stir and pour into the pan. Then immediately slide a spatula under the vegetables and fish and turn them gently; baste until saturated with the glazy sauce. Pour into a hot serving dish.

咖哩魚片　FILLET OF FLOUNDER IN CURRY SAUCE

Here the velveted fish is covered by a smooth curry sauce studded with minced onions, celery, and carrots. *This dish serves 2 to 4* with plenty of fluffy rice and one or two refreshing vegetables.

1 pound fillets of flounder, velveted in water (*page 214*)	1 tablespoon curry powder
1 small clove garlic, minced	½ teaspoon salt
¼ cup minced onions	1 tablespoon light soy sauce
¼ cup minced celery	1 teaspoon sugar
¼ cup minced carrots	2 teaspoons cornstarch dissolved in
3 tablespoons oil	1 cup water and 2 teaspoons sesame oil

Marinate and velvet the fillets in water. Put the minced ingredients together on a plate. The velveting shouldn't be done in advance.

Heat a wok or large, heavy skillet over high heat until hot; add 3 tablespoons oil, swirl, and heat for a few seconds. Scatter in the garlic, onions, celery, and carrots and stir rapidly for about 1 minute. Add the curry powder, salt, soy sauce, and sugar, and stir for about 30 seconds. Turn heat low and give the dissolved cornstarch a big stir; then pour it into the pan and stir with the back of a spoon in a circular motion until smooth. Add the fish and let it simmer, basting frequently, for about 30 seconds. Pour into a hot serving dish.

五
綵
魚
RAINBOW FISH

This banquet specialty from the eastern region of China is very beautiful and delicious. It calls for velveting and glazing the shredded fillet in a tasty and aromatic parsley sauce. Sprinkled with minced red ham, it is then assembled with separately stir-fried black mo-er mushrooms and green spinach into a "rainbow" of bright colors. *It serves 4 as a main course.*

1 pound fillets of flounder

Velvet coating:
¼ teaspoon salt
⅛ teaspoon white pepper
1 teaspoon dry sherry
1 egg white, well beaten
1 tablespoon cornstarch
2 teaspoons oil

2 tablespoons dried mo-er
    mushrooms (presoaked)
1 recipe Stir-fried Spinach
    (*page 370*)

Sauce for the fish:
2 tablespoons oil
1 large clove garlic, minced
1 teaspoon minced peeled ginger
2 tablespoons finely chopped
    parsley
½ teaspoon salt
1 cup chicken or meat stock
1 tablespoon cornstarch dissolved
    in 2 tablespoons stock

1 tablespoon minced cooked
    Smithfield ham (*page 492*) or a
    substitute

2 cups oil for velveting
1 tablespoon dry sherry
½ teaspoon salt

Preparations

Cut each fillet lengthwise in two; then cut each strip crosswise in two. Then cut them lengthwise, with the grain, into ¼-inch-wide shreds. The fillet must not be shredded crosswise against the grain—the shreds would flake into messy small pieces during cooking.

Place the shreds in a mixing bowl. Add the salt, pepper, and sherry, mixing gently; add the beaten egg white, mix, then sprinkle in the cornstarch and mix until smooth. Add the oil and blend well. The easiest way to mix is with your fingers. Cover and marinate in the refrigerator for at least 2 hours—the longer the marinating time the smoother the fish will be.

Cover the mo-er mushrooms with 1 cup hot water and soak for 30 minutes; when ready to cook, rinse and discard any hard "eyes." Pile them on the board and cut them into coarse shreds.

Wash the spinach and set it aside. Mince the garlic, ginger, and parsley for the sauce. Measure out the stock, dissolve the cornstarch, have the minced ham on a separate dish.

Velveting and stir-frying

Heat a wok or large, heavy skillet over high heat until very hot. Add 2 cups oil and heat until it foams a snip of parsley slowly, about 280 degrees. Scatter in the coated fish shreds and scoop and turn them rapidly and gently in the hot oil with a spatula for about 30 seconds, until they are white, fluffy, and gleaming. Drain them immediately into a strainer set over a pot. Once the oil has drained off, turn the fish onto a dish.

Return 2 tablespoons oil to the wok; scatter in the mo-er mushrooms and stir vigorously to sear them in oil. Splash in 1 tablespoon sherry, add ½ teaspoon salt, then give the mushrooms a few more vigorous stirs. Remove to one end of a large dish and keep them hot by setting the dish over a pot of steaming rice or a pot of boiling water.

Rinse and dry the wok and stir-fry the spinach as in the recipe. Keep it hot by dishing it out next to the mo-er mushrooms.

For the sauce: Rinse and dry the wok and heat till hot over high heat. Add 2 tablespoons oil, swirl, and heat very briefly. Scatter in the minced garlic, ginger, and parsley, and stir vigorously for a few seconds until the parsley is deep green and fragrant, lowering the heat a little to prevent scorching. Sprinkle in ½ teaspoon salt and stir a few times; then add the stock and when it comes to a boil, turn heat low. Give the dissolved cornstarch a big stir and pour it in slowly with one hand while you stir with the other until the sauce is glazy and smooth.

Turn the heat a little higher; add the fish and stir gently in scooping and folding motions to heat it and saturate it with the sauce. Pour it into a mound in the center of a large serving dish. Circle the base with the black mo-er mushrooms, then surround the mushrooms with the green spinach without the juice. Scatter the red ham over the parsley-speckled white fish, and serve.

VARIATION

If you want the dish to be really fancy: Get a fish head and tail from your fishman—either sea bass or striped bass. Rinse the head and tail and rub them with a little sherry to eliminate any fishy odor and a little oil for a shiny effect. Steam them for 15 minutes. Turn off the heat and keep it hot while you cook the fillet, mushrooms, and spinach to conclusion. Then place the fish head at one end of a large oval platter and the tail on the other end. Mound and spread the fish in the center between head and tail, then

decorate both sides, one
with the mo-er mushrooms
and the other with the
spinach, making a slight
curve to resemble the
natural outline of a whole
fish.

Or, instead of mo-er mushrooms, use shredded egg sheets
(*page 162*), which will make
the dish daintier and more fragile looking.

白
水
魚

STEEP-POACHED WHOLE FISH

Steep-poaching is a simple but marvelous method for capturing the natural flavor of a fish. The fish is put into boiling water and then steeped instead of simmered until done. It is served with a variety of seasonings in separate cups—they lend that special touch which makes eating a plain fish colorful. *It would serve 4 people as a main course with vegetables.* Szechuan Eggplants would go beautifully with this.

1 sea bass, striped bass, or white-
    fish, about 3 pounds
4 large slices peeled ginger, each
    about ⅛ inch thick
1 large whole scallion, cut in two
3 tablespoons oil
	Dipping sauce:
	Light soy sauce
	Sesame oil
	Chenkong or red-wine vinegar
	Minced ginger soaked in 2 to
	    3 tablespoons white wine
	Finely chopped coriander
	Horseradish, hot mustard, hot
	    bean sauce, or chili-pepper oil

Have the fish cleaned and scaled but leave the head and tail on; rinse well. With the ginger and scallion bring to a boil enough water to cover the fish—in a wok, fish poacher, or roasting pan. Slither the fish in and immediately turn the heat to the lowest possible point; cover and steep in the hot water for 25 minutes. The water should not be permitted to simmer.

Test for doneness by sticking the tip of a knife into the thickest part of the fish. If it goes in easily and no pinkish liquid seeps out, the fish is done. If it isn't ready, steep 5 minutes longer.

While the fish is taking its hot bath, put 6 glass custard cups on a small attractive tray. Put into them, separately, a little light soy sauce, a little sesame oil, some Chenkong or red-wine vinegar, minced ginger soaked in 2 to 3 tablespoons white wine, finely chopped fresh coriander, and either horseradish, hot mustard (*page 495*), hot bean sauce, or chili-pepper oil (*page 489*).

Just before the fish is done, heat the oil in a small saucepan over low heat until hot but not smoking. Remove the fish from the water with 2 spatulas, tilt to drain momentarily, and place it on a hot serving platter. Stand back and pour the hot oil over the fish to give it a shiny glaze and heightened flavor. Pass the seasonings tray for each person to make his or her own dip sauce, in small individual saucers.

紅燒釀魚 RED-COOKED SEA BASS WITH MEAT STUFFING

First fried to crisp and firm the skin, the fish is then simmered in the dark soy-sauce seasonings for a penetrating flavor. It's saucy and good with rice. Make either Stir-fried Cabbage and Carrots or Sliced Zucchini with Shredded Carrots to provide a light change of taste for this rich dish. *It serves 4 as a main course.*

1 sea bass or striped bass, about 2½ pounds
4 to 5 tablespoons flour for dusting

4 tablespoons oil
1 large clove garlic, lightly smashed and peeled

Stuffing:
¼ pound ground lean pork
2 teaspoons light soy sauce
2 teaspoons dry sherry
¼ teaspoon sugar
3 minced water chestnuts or 2 tablespoons minced lettuce ribs
2 quarter-sized slices peeled ginger, minced
Sprinkling black pepper
½ teaspoon cornstarch dissolved in 1 teaspoon water

Sauce:
4 tablespoons dark soy sauce
2 tablespoons dry sherry
1½ cups water
4 quarter-sized slices peeled ginger
1 large whole scallion, cut into 3 pieces
1 teaspoon sugar

1 tablespoon sesame oil
Garnish: Chopped coriander or sprigs of parsley

Preparing and stuffing the fish
Have the fish cleaned and scaled, but leave the head and tail on. Rinse and dry it inside and outside. Score the fish (see illustration *page 226*)

on the slant 3 times on each side, about 1 inch apart. Dust the entire fish, outside and inside, with the flour.

March-chop the ground pork until its formation is loosened and the consistency is fluffy. Put it in a bowl, add the soy sauce, sherry, and sugar, and mix well. Add the minced water chestnuts to the meat; if you use lettuce ribs, chop them fine and toss with a pinch of salt before you add them to the meat. Add the minced ginger, a sprinkling of black pepper, and the dissolved cornstarch; stir in circular motions until the mixture is smooth. Spoon the stuffing into the cavity of the fish and press the fish lightly to enclose the stuffing. It cannot be skewered.

Browning the fish

Heat a wok or large, heavy skillet over high heat until very hot; add the 4 tablespoons oil, swirl, and heat for 30 seconds. Throw in the garlic and press it around in the oil; then lower in the fish and brown it for 3 minutes, turning down the heat if the flour coating is browning too fast. Turn the fish over with 2 spatulas and brown it 2 minutes on the other side.

Red-cooking the fish

When the fish is crisp and brown, pour the soy sauce and sherry over it and add the water, ginger, and scallions. When the sauce boils, stir in the sugar to dissolve it. Turn heat down to medium, tilt the pan, and baste the fish with the sauce a few times. Lower the heat to maintain a gentle simmering; cover and let the fish simmer for about 10 minutes. Baste the fish a few times again, cover, and simmer another 8 minutes.

Remove the fish carefully to a serving platter. Add the sesame oil to the sauce and bring it to a boil over high heat. Pour it immediately over the fish and serve garnished with a little chopped coriander or sprigs of parsley.

VARIATIONS

For the pork stuffing you may substitute any minced seafood, such as shrimp, crabmeat, clams, or oysters. In that case, reduce the simmering time from a total of 18 minutes to 15.

If you like the sauce richer, add 2 additional tablespoons dry sherry and 2 teaspoons sugar to taste when you add the sesame oil.

Two squares of bean curd may be added to give more substance. Presoak them in hot water for 5 minutes; cut each into 6 or 8 cubes and scatter them around the fish during the last 5 minutes of simmering.

豆
豉
全
魚

WHOLE SEA BASS IN BLACK-BEAN SAUCE

This is an earthy dish, full of the rich flavors of fermented black beans, garlic, ginger, and scallions. The whole fish is shallow-fried, then simmered with the seasoning sauce. It is dark red and saucy, like Red-cooked Sea Bass with Meat Stuffing, but it has a more pronounced taste. *Serves 4 as a main course.* Choose a bright-green stir-fried vegetable.

1 sea bass, about 2½ pounds
½ teaspoon salt
Cornstarch for dusting

Dry seasonings:
2 large cloves garlic, coarsely
  chopped
2 tablespoons fermented black
  beans, rinsed and coarsely
  chopped
4 quarter-sized slices peeled ginger,
  coarsely chopped
1 large whole scallion, finely
  chopped

Liquid seasonings:
2 tablespoons dark soy sauce
2 tablespoons dry sherry
1 teaspoon sugar
¾ cup water

2 teaspoons cornstarch dissolved in
  2 tablespoons water with
  2 teaspoons sesame oil

4 tablespoons oil

Preparations

Have the fish cleaned and scaled, but leave the head and tail on. Rinse and dry it. Score the fish 3 times on a slant on each side, about 1 inch apart. Sprinkle and rub the salt over the inside and outside. Dust the fish lightly and evenly with the cornstarch.

Prepare the dry seasonings and put them on your working platter. Mix the liquid seasonings and stir until the sugar is dissolved. Dissolve the cornstarch in a separate bowl.

Shallow-frying and simmering

Heat a large skillet that will accommodate the fish over high heat until very hot; add the 4 tablespoons oil, swirl, and heat for 30 seconds. Slither the fish into the skillet and brown it for 2 minutes. Gently turn the fish over, with 2 spatulas if necessary, and brown it on the other side for 2 minutes. Remove it to a plate.

Add to the skillet all the dry seasonings and stir and toss to explode their flavors. Add the liquid-seasoning mixture and bring to a boil. Return fish to the pan, lower the heat to maintain a very gentle simmering, cover, and simmer for 6 minutes. Turn the fish over gently, cover, and simmer another 6 minutes. Remove it to a hot serving platter.

Give the cornstarch mixture a big stir, add it to the sauce, and stir in a circular motion until it thickens smoothly. Pour it over the fish, scraping all the speckles of dry seasonings on top.

VARIATION

For a hot and spicy sea bass, substitute for the black beans 1 tablespoon hot bean sauce, and add 2 teaspoons Chenkong vinegar or red-wine vinegar and a pinch of sugar to the liquid seasonings.

糖醋魚 SWEET AND SOUR SEA BASS

This is the classic version of a sweet and sour fish; it is deep-fried and then glazed with the vegetable-rich sauce. *It serves 4 people as a main course.*

1 sea bass, about 2½ pounds
¼ teaspoon salt dissolved in
    2 tablespoons dry sherry
4 tablespoons cornstarch
4 tablespoons all-purpose flour

Sauce vegetables:
4 quarter-sized slices peeled ginger,
    shredded
1 medium clove garlic, lightly
    smashed and peeled
4 large dried black Chinese
    mushrooms (presoaked)
¼ cup shredded carrots
½ cup shredded bamboo shoots
½ cup frozen or fresh green peas

Sauce seasonings:
5 tablespoons sugar
3 tablespoons cider vinegar
2 tablespoons dark soy sauce
1 tablespoon catsup
1 teaspoon salt

1 tablespoon cornstarch dissolved
    in 1 cup water
1 tablespoon sesame oil

4 to 6 cups oil
Garnish: Sprigs of fresh coriander
    or parsley

Preparations

Have the fish scaled and cleaned, but leave it whole. Rinse and dry it; score it on a slant 3 times on each side, about 1 inch apart. Rub the salt-sherry all over it. Combine the cornstarch and flour and coat the fish all over. Let it set as you prepare the sauce vegetables and seasonings. It may be done an hour or two in advance; cover and refrigerate.

Prepare all the vegetables: Cover the mushrooms first with hot water and soak for 30 minutes. Rinse, destem, then shred. Prepare the ginger and garlic. Put frozen peas in a strainer and dip-cook them 1 minute in boiling water; parboil fresh ones about 3 minutes. Run them under cold water to halt the cooking. Shred the carrots and bamboo shoots. Place in piles on a working platter.

Combine all sauce seasonings in a bowl, stirring until the sugar is dissolved. Dissolve the cornstarch in a separate bowl with the water and then stir in the sesame oil. Place both bowls next to the vegetables.

Deep-frying the fish

Heat a wok or roasting pan over high heat until hot; add the oil, and heat until a cube of bread foams instantly, about 375 degrees. Gently slither in the fish and deep-fry it about 7 minutes on each side, basting and shifting occasionally. Remove with 2 spatulas, tilting it briefly over the pot to drain, and put it on a hot serving platter.

Making the sauce

In the meantime, after turning the fish, heat a skillet or large saucepan over high heat until hot. Take 4 tablespoons oil from the fish-frying pan, swirl, then toss in the ginger and garlic and sear quickly. Lower the heat a little, add the mushrooms, carrots, and bamboo shoots, and stir rapidly for 2½ minutes. Add the peas and toss for 30 seconds. Pour in the sauce seasonings and stir a few times. Discard the garlic and turn heat low, give the dissolved cornstarch a big stir and pour it into the sauce with one hand as you stir the sauce and vegetables with the other in a circular motion, until they are smooth and glazy. Turn off the heat and cover.

Bring sauce back to a bubble after the fish is drained and placed on the serving platter. Pour the sauce over the fish, draping the shredded vegetables over the top. Garnish with coriander or parsley and serve.

If you don't feel at ease cooking the fish and sauce simultaneously, do the sauce first and reheat over low heat after the fish is ready.

松子魚 SEA BASS IN PINE-NUT SAUCE

This is also a deep-fried sweet and sour fish, but not in the usual sense of the term; here the reddish sauce is embellished with speckles of pearly pine nuts instead of vegetables or fruits. Scored with numerous slashes on both sides and deep-fried until the slashes are stiffened and branched out, the fish is served gracefully curved, straight up, looking as though it were ready to glide away. It's a beautiful presentation, particularly if you serve the fish on a large oval silver platter. This dish indeed justifies the Chinese practice of cooking a fish whole. *It serves 4 as a main dish with one or two green vegetables.*

1 sea bass or striped bass,
    about 2½ pounds

Coating:
4 tablespoons cornstarch
4 tablespoons all-purpose flour
½ teaspoon salt
Sprinkling black pepper
2 tablespoons dry sherry
1 egg white, well beaten

Sauce:
4 tablespoons sugar
4 tablespoons cider vinegar
2 tablespoons light soy sauce
2 tablespoons dry sherry
4 tablespoons catsup

1 tablespoon cornstarch dissolved
    in 1½ cups water and
    1 tablespoon oil

6 cups oil
½ cup pine nuts
Garnish: Sprigs of coriander or
    parsley

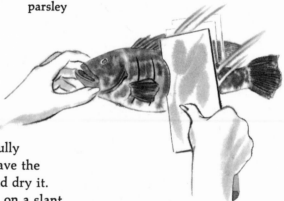

Preparations
    Have the fish carefully cleaned and scaled, but leave the head and tail on. Rinse and dry it. Score the fish 7 to 8 times on a slant across each side. Place on a large plate.

    Combine the coating ingredients and mix until smooth. Pour over the fish and coat evenly on both sides from head to tail, including the inside of the slashes. Let it set as you prepare the sauce and pine nuts. This may be done a few hours in advance; cover and refrigerate until ready for the final cooking.

    Measure the sauce ingredients into a small saucepan; heat them over very low heat, stirring with the back of a spoon until the sugar is dissolved. Give the dissolved cornstarch a big stir, pour into the pan, and stir in a circular motion until the sauce is smooth and glazy. Turn off the heat and reheat just before the fish is ready for glazing.

Deep-frying

Select a pan that will accommodate the fish comfortably—a wok or a roasting pan. Heat it over high heat until very hot; then add the oil and heat until it foams a cube of bread very slowly, about 280 to 300 degrees. Put the pine nuts in a strainer and dip the strainer into the oil; stir the submerged nuts for about 30 to 40 seconds, until their color deepens slightly. Remove immediately and drain on paper towels.

Continue to heat the oil until it foams a cube of bread instantly, about 375 degrees. Dab the fish with any loose coating. Grasp the fish by the tail and, supporting the head with a large spoon, ease the fish into the hot oil. Pause for a few seconds in a suspended position for the hot oil to fry and expand the slashes on the upper part of the fish before you release the tail and let it submerge in the hot oil. Fry it for about 6 minutes on each side over high heat until it is brown and crisp; baste it now and then.

Turn off the heat and remove the fish by slipping a skimmer and a spatula underneath it, pausing over the pan to drain. Place it on its stomach in the center of a serving platter, pressing down lightly on the head. The fish will curve naturally on the platter, with its head turned one way and its tail the other.

Finishing the sauce

In the meantime, during the last minute of deep-frying, reheat the sauce over very low heat. Give it a few circular stirs and pour over the fish. Shower the platter with the pine nuts and garnish with sprigs of coriander or parsley. Carry the fish to the table and be ready for a torrent of compliments.

煎 SHALLOW-FRIED BROOK TROUT
魚

Shallow-fried over low heat, then sizzled over high heat with seasonings, these delicate trout are crusty, aromatic, and very tasty. *They serve 2 as a main course.* Stir-fried Spinach would be a good accompaniment.

2 brook trout, each about ¾ pound
1 teaspoon salt
2 tablespoons cornstarch

Sauce:
2 tablespoons light soy sauce
2 tablespoons dry sherry
2 tablespoons Chenkong or
    red-wine vinegar
2 teaspoons sugar
2 tablespoons sesame oil

5 tablespoons oil
1 tablespoon coarsely minced
    peeled ginger
4 small whole scallions, coarsely
    chopped

Have the fish cleaned but leave them whole. Score them on a slant 3 times on each side. Rub them with the salt and dust well with the cornstarch, inside the slashes as well.

Combine the sauce seasonings in a small bowl.

Heat a large, heavy skillet over high heat until very hot; add the 5 tablespoons oil, swirl, and heat for 30 seconds. Scatter in the ginger and scallions and stir briskly until the scallions are bright green and aromatic. Push them to the side of the pan and slither in the fish; brown them 1 minute on each side. Turn the heat to low and shallow-fry each side about 4 minutes, until crisp and brown.

Give the sauce a big stir, turn heat high, and splash the sauce directly onto the fish, basting and turning them once as the sauce sizzles.

Remove them with a spatula to a hot serving dish, scraping on top the darkened ginger and scallions without too much of the pan oil.

五 FIVE-FRAGRANCE SMELTS
香
小
魚

When small fish such as smelts are marinated and then deep-fried without any coating, they acquire a firm, crisp texture and a resounding taste. They make an excellent appetizer or main dish, either hot, at room temperature, or cold. The fragile bones, steeped in the marinade for many hours and then deep-fried, are thoroughly edible and add a good crunchiness.

The marinade, incidentally, is an excellent splash-on sauce for any shallow-fried fish or a deep-fried vegetable such as eggplant or zucchini.

This serves 3 or 4 as a main course with a stir-fried vegetable such as Chinese or celery cabbage and perhaps a green salad.

1½ pounds small smelts, without the heads

Marinade:
2 tablespoons dark soy sauce
1 tablespoon light soy sauce
3 tablespoons dry sherry
1½ tablespoons sugar
2 teaspoons distilled white vinegar
¼ teaspoon salt
½ teaspoon five-fragrance powder
2 teaspoons minced peeled ginger
1 large whole scallion, finely
   chopped

2 cups oil
Garnish: Sprigs of fresh coriander
   or parsley

Rinse and dry the fish thoroughly. Combine the marinade ingredients in a large bowl and stir until the sugar is completely dissolved. Add the fish and toss to coat well. Cover and marinate them in the refrigerator for 4 to 6 hours, turning them a few times.

Blot the fish dry. Heat a wok or large, heavy skillet over high heat until very hot; add the oil and heat until it foams a cube of bread instantly, about 375 degrees. Add one-third of the fish and deep-fry, basting and turning, for about 4 minutes, until the fish are crisp and brown. Remove them to drain on a plate with paper towels in a low oven, about 200 degrees, and repeat with the other batches.

Place them on a hot serving platter and garnish with the coriander or parsley. If they are to be served as finger food, cut each into 2 pieces and serve with toothpicks.

青葱燻魚　SCALLION-SMOKED FLOUNDER OR FLUKE

In this dish the fish is salted, steamed, and then smoked so that it acquires a wonderfully exotic flavor. You must have good ventilation in your kitchen, or the odor of smoke will linger a long time.

This fish is delicious hot, at room temperature, or cold, and it may be served as an appetizer. *It serves 3 or 4 people as a main course with a vegetable.* Try it with Chicken Fu Yung broccoli, for instance.

1 whole flounder or fluke,
about 2½ pounds
1-inch knob ginger, peeled and
smashed
1 tablespoon roasted salt-pepper
(*page 501*)

8 large whole scallions, bulbs
lightly crushed
Sesame oil for brushing
Garnish: Fresh parsley sprigs

Smoking ingredients:
½ cup brown sugar
½ cup rice
¼ cup black tea leaves

Have the fish cleaned but leave the head and tail on. Rinse and dry thoroughly. Rub the ginger and then the salt-pepper on both sides and inside as well. Wrap the fish in aluminum foil and refrigerate for 2 hours.

Place 3 chopsticks lengthwise on a heatproof platter; place the fish on top of the chopsticks so that during the steaming it will not lie in any moisture.

Steam the fish over high heat for 10 minutes. Remove it to a dry plate.

Line a wok or large pot and its cover with heavy-duty aluminum foil. Mix the smoking ingredients and spread them in the center of the pan. Place an oiled rack in it and lay the whole scallions perpendicular to the bars. Put the fish on top of the scallions. Cover the pot and coil wet towels around the seam of the cover.

Set the pan over medium-high heat for 2 minutes; turn heat low and smoke for about 8 minutes. Uncover (open a window if possible), turn the fish over, cover, and smoke about 6 minutes more.

Put the smoked fish on a chopping board and brush it on both sides lightly with the sesame oil. Serve it whole, garnished with sprigs of parsley, or cut it crosswise into 4 large pieces and serve reassembled into a whole fish.

VARIATIONS

A large red snapper may be used instead of flounder. And add 1 teaspoon roasted and crushed Szechuan peppercorns (*page 500*) to the smoking ingredients if you like an herbier flavor.

Lobster

炒 LOBSTER CANTONESE
龍
蝦

Here lobster is chopped into small pieces and steam-cooked with ground pork and seasonings. It acquires additional flavor but is not masked.

By normal standards a 1½-pound lobster barely satisfies one lobster lover. But made more substantial by the meat sauce, Lobster Cantonese *will serve* 2 accompanied by a green salad, a stir-fried vegetable such as cauliflower, broccoli, or green beans, and plenty of rice.

1 live lobster, about 1½ pounds   1 tablespoon sesame oil
3 tablespoons oil   1 egg, lightly beaten

Sauce:
2 teaspoons minced peeled
     ginger
2 small whole scallions, finely
     chopped
1 medium clove garlic, minced
1 tablespoon fermented black
     beans, rinsed and coarsely
     chopped
¼ pound ground lean pork
2 tablespoons dry sherry
1 tablespoon light soy sauce
¾ cup stock or water
A dash black pepper
2 teaspoons cornstarch dissolved
     in 1 tablespoon water

Preparations

As with crabs, lobster must be bought alive—once dead, the meat loses strength and becomes pasty and mushy. Since chopping anything alive calls for steely nerves that most of us don't care to develop, I suggest that you kill the lobster first: plunge it into a large pot of boiling water for about 1 minute until it is still but not cooked. Drain it. Then snap off the claws and reserve. 1) Remove and discard the legs (or save for another purpose); 2) chop off and discard the tip of the head where eyes and antennae are located; 3) then split the lobster in half lengthwise. Remove and discard the stomach sac—a pouch about 1 inch long that is in the head—but keep intact the greenish tomalley and any roe. 4) Then chop the body crosswise into 1½-inch pieces and chop each claw into 3 pieces by chopping first between the pincers, then once across the base of the claw.

March-chop the ground pork until its formation is loosened and fluffy; place it on your working platter with the ginger, scallions, garlic, and fermented black beans. Measure out the stock or water. Dissolve the cornstarch in a separate bowl. Beat the egg and gather all the seasonings within reach of the stove.

Stir-frying

Heat a wok or large, heavy skillet over high heat until hot; add the oil, swirl, and heat for a few seconds. Scatter in the ginger, scallions, garlic, and fermented black beans and stir quickly for 30 seconds. Add the meat and stir vigorously in poking and pressing motions to break up the lumps; keep stirring until the meat has lost all pinkness.

Add the lobster chunks, splash in the sherry and stir a few times as it steams up; then add the soy sauce, stock or water, and pepper; even out everything in the pan. Turn the tail pieces meat side down, cover, and steam-cook over medium heat for 3 minutes. Uncover and give the contents a few sweeping turns. Lower the heat, stir the dissolved cornstarch once again, and pour it into the sauce. Add the sesame oil and stir until the sauce thickens. Pour the beaten egg over the lobster in a circular motion, then immediately turn off the heat and let the egg slide into the sauce and firm into a flowing consistency. Then scoop the lobster and sauce into a serving dish, placing the tail pieces and pincers over the top.

CRAB VARIATION

Substitute for the lobster 4 large or 6 small blue crabs, and in the fall try to get females, since they will then contain the scrumptious roes. It's easy to tell—the females are modestly covered with a wide "apron" over their abdomens; the male's apron is long and narrow.

The crabs should be cleansed in a sinkful of cold water for 30 minutes. 1) Pick them up with tongs or gloved hand and plunge them into a large pot of boiling water for about 30 seconds to kill them (but not to cook them). Remove, drain, and scrub them.

2) Lift up and twist off the apron; 3) snap off the claws and crack them. 4) Then separate the shell from the body by inserting a finger in the small depression at the back of the crab, and pull the body back as you hold

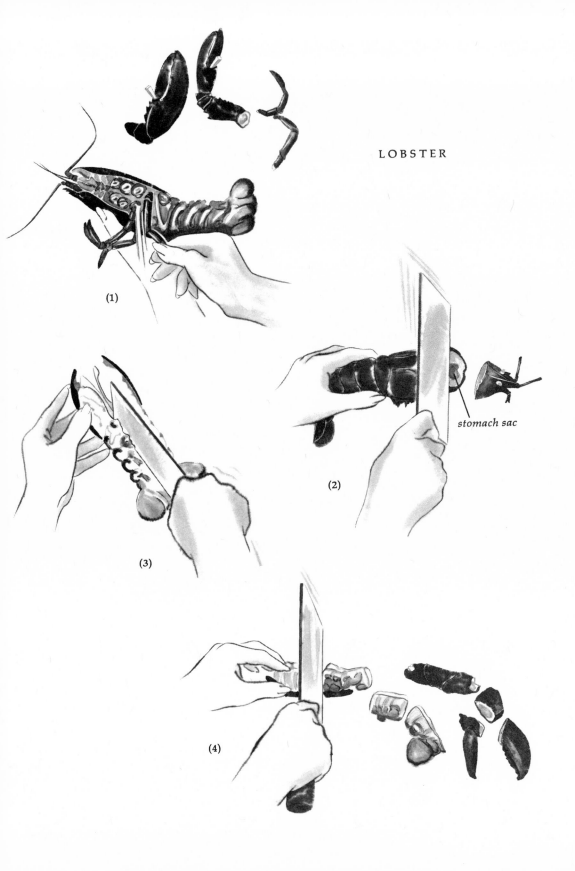

LOBSTER

(1)

(2)

stomach sac

(3)

(4)

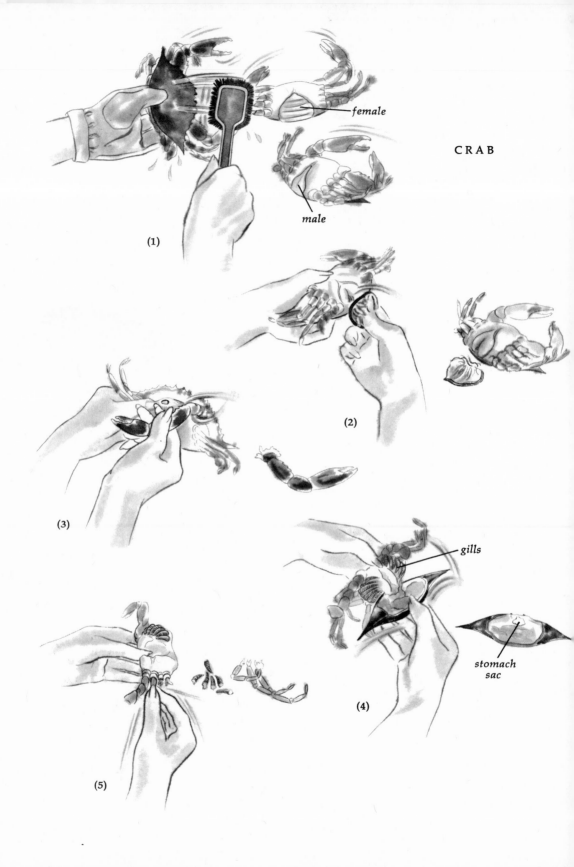

CRAB

(1)

female

male

(2)

(3)

(4)

gills

stomach
sac

(5)

the shell firmly in your other hand. 5) Remove and discard both sets of feathery gills, rinse off sand and mud if any, and snap off the small legs. Leave the shell with its tomalley and any roe intact but remove and discard the stomach sac, which is located between and attached to the eyes. Quarter the bodies and cook the crabs the same way as the lobster.

Eating both lobster and crab: The only way to do it is to dig right in, pulling out the lobster tail meat and the claws with a fork or chopsticks and using fingers, tongue, and teeth on the complicated pieces and the smaller crabs, turning to a small lobster pick for help when necessary. They are seductive—their flavor and texture are so superb that they induce you to pick and search for the next morsels with great anticipation.

乾燒龍蝦 DRY-COOKED LOBSTER

In contrast to the saucy and more delicate-looking Lobster Cantonese, this lobster is robust, its sauce all but absorbed, leaving it gleamingly red and speckled with bright green scallions. Just as with the preceding recipe, *this serves 2* with rice and vegetable.

1 live lobster, about 1½ pounds

Sauce:
2 tablespoons dark soy sauce
2 tablespoons dry sherry
2 teaspoons bean paste (*page 486*)
2 tablespoons catsup
¼ teaspoon salt
½ teaspoon sugar

3 tablespoons oil
2 quarter-sized slices peeled
   ginger, minced
2 large cloves garlic, finely
   chopped
2 large whole scallions, finely
   chopped
¾ cup stock or water
1 tablespoon sesame oil

Prepare and chop the lobster as in the preceding recipe.

Mix the sauce ingredients in a small bowl.

Heat a wok or large, heavy skillet over high heat until hot; add 3 tablespoons oil, swirl, and heat for a few seconds. Turn heat to medium and stir-fry the ginger, garlic, and scallions for about 30 seconds until they are fully aromatic. Turn heat high and add the chopped lobster; flip and stir for 1 minute. Splash in the sauce and turn the lobster pieces in it a few times. Add the stock or water, even out the contents, cover, and steam-cook over medium-high heat for 3 minutes. Uncover; stir the lobster rapidly until the sauce is all but gone. Dribble in the sesame oil, give the lobster a few big turns, and pour into a hot serving dish. In this recipe, too, crabs may be substituted.

清蒸龍蝦 STEAMED LOBSTER

This lobster is chopped, reassembled, and steamed with seasonings—a delicate dish of succulent meat. The final touch of oil-seared raw scallion shreds gives this lovely-looking dish a beautiful fragrance and shine. *It serves 2 as a main course with a vegetable.*

1 live lobster, about 1½ pounds

Seasonings:
1 clove garlic, minced
2 quarter-sized slices peeled ginger, minced
1 tablespoon light soy sauce
2 tablespoons dry sherry
¼ teaspoon salt
1 tablespoon sesame or vegetable oil

1 large whole scallion, cut into 1½-inch-long shreds
1 tablespoon oil

Prepare and chop the lobster as described on *page 231.* Reassemble it in the form of a whole lobster, shell side down, on a heatproof platter.

Combine the seasonings and stir until the salt is dissolved. Spoon this mixture over the lobster and steam over high heat for 15 minutes. Remove the platter from the steamer, put it on another platter or a trivet, and scatter the shredded scallions over the meat.

Heat 1 tablespoon oil in a small pan until very hot but not smoking. Stand back and pour it over the scallions and lobster and serve the dish immediately, steaming hot and aromatic of scallions.

VARIATIONS

You may omit the seasonings and accompany the lobster with a dip sauce: For each person mix 2 teaspoons light soy sauce, 2 teaspoons Chenkong or red-wine vinegar, and ¼ teaspoon minced ginger.

For a stronger flavoring in the steaming sauce, add 2 tablespoons briefly rinsed and finely chopped fermented black beans.

Naturally, crabs may be steamed this way with excellent results; they are especially good steamed plain, then eaten with the vinegar dip sauce.

海鮮球 SEAFOOD KOW

"Kow" is the Cantonese pronunciation for the Chinese word for "ball," which is found in the titles of many Cantonese dishes, meaning that the main ingredients are cut into chunky pieces and stir-fried with large cuts of crisp vegetables. The Cantonese school of cooking excels in this line of cooking—extravagant materials are masterfully bound by a light sauce so that each ingredient glows in its own glory in taste, texture, and color.

This is an exuberant dish of vivid colors—red lobster meat, pink shrimp, and white scallops nestled over green-white Chinese cabbage, yellow bamboo shoots, deep-green snow peas, and bands of gleaming black mushrooms. Well balanced with vegetables, *this makes a delicious dinner for 4*, preceded by soup or appetizers and accompanied with rice or bread.

1 live lobster, about 1½ pounds
6 large dried black Chinese
    mushrooms (presoaked)
8 medium shrimp
¼ pound scallops
½ cup sliced bamboo shoots
½ pound tender stalks of Chinese
    cabbage or Swiss chard, sliced
    diagonally into pieces about
    ¼ inch thick and 2 inches long
½ cup snow peas, stringed
1 slice peeled ginger, about
    ¼ inch thick, smashed
1 large clove garlic, lightly
    smashed and peeled

Sauce:
½ teaspoon salt
½ teaspoon sugar
1½ tablespoons oyster sauce
1½ tablespoons light soy sauce
1 tablespoon dry sherry
1 tablespoon cornstarch dissolved
    in ¾ cup stock

½ cup oil
½ teaspoon salt
1 tablespoon dry sherry
1 tablespoon sesame oil

Preparations

Bring a large pot of water to a boil and immerse the live lobster head first; cover and boil over medium-high heat for about 15 minutes. Remove and let it cool enough to handle. Snap off and crack the claws; remove the meat in as large chunks as possible. Snap off the head and legs, and save them for a delicious snack. Snap and twist off the last section of the tail, then detach the meat from the shell by pushing the meat through the larger end with fingers or a chopstick—this is very easy to do. Cut the meat into ¾- to 1-inch cubes and set them on your working platter.

Cover the mushrooms with hot water and soak for 30 minutes; then rinse, destem, and cut in half.

Shell the shrimp and devein if necessary by cutting ⅛ inch deep along the back; rinse briefly, then blot dry. Rinse and drain the scallops. If large sea scallops are used, cut each crosswise in two. Place seafood, and vegetables, ginger, and garlic in separate piles on the working platter. Combine the sauce ingredients in a bowl and have the salt, sherry, and sesame oil within reach.

All these preparations may be done hours ahead; cover and refrigerate the seafood and vegetables until ready to cook. Let the lobster meat come to room temperature before the final stir-frying.

Oil-blistering and stir-frying

Heat a wok or large, heavy skillet over high heat until very hot; add the oil, and heat until it foams a cube of bread instantly, about 375 degrees. Scatter in the shrimp and toss and baste them rapidly for 30 seconds to firm and blister their surface. Drain the shrimp and oil immediately into a strainer that is set over a pot. Return the shrimp to your working platter.

Reset the pan over high heat; return 3 tablespoons of the drained oil to it. Toss in the ginger and garlic and press them around the pan. Shower in the mushrooms, bamboo shoots, cabbage, and snow peas, and stir vigorously to sear them in the hot oil. Sprinkle in ½ teaspoon salt and 1 tablespoon sherry and give them a few fast turns. Scatter the shrimp, lobster meat, and scallops on top, lower the heat to medium high, cover, and let them steam-cook for 1 minute.

Uncover and stir the contents in fast flipping and turning motions a few times. Give the premixed sauce a big stir and pour it into the pan. Stir in fast tossing motions by sliding your spatula around and under the ingredients, lifting and turning them swiftly until the sauce is glazy. Add the sesame oil and give the seafood and vegetables a few sweeping folds, then pour into a hot serving dish, discarding the ginger and garlic.

VARIATIONS

A double amount of lobster meat may be used instead of shrimp and scallops—then the dish becomes Lobster Kow. Or, instead of lobster meat, you may substitute lumps of Alaska king crabmeat. You could also make the dish with only shrimp or scallops. Vegetables, of course, may be interchanged: sliced fresh mushrooms or canned whole button mushrooms instead of the black mushrooms; sliced celery stalks or peeled broccoli stems instead of the bamboo shoots and snow peas. Canned miniature ears of corn may also be added to or substituted for any of the vegetables.

When the dish is poured over freshly fried rice patties (*page 431*) it becomes Sizzling Seafood Go Ba, which I introduced to the U.S. dining public in 1955, when I first went into the restaurant business.

Crabs

吴
淞
蟹
羹

WU-SOONG CRAB ''GUNN''

Crabs are delicious no matter how they're cooked, but when those of a special kind are treated to an unusual preparational procedure, the result is extraordinary. "Gunn," the Chinese equivalent of a bisque or chowder, is found in all the regional Chinese styles of cooking, but only the people living in and around Wu-Soong, a suburb of Shanghai, are lucky enough to make a gunn with the remarkable flavor of the miniature crabs found in the bay at the mouth of the Yangtze River.

Known locally as "insect crabs," they measure about an inch in diameter. They appear only in the early spring, when they swarm around the boulders in the shallow waters of the Yangtze Bay. Their translucent, tiny bodies contain almost no meat, but a concentration of savory juice. The crabs used to be pounded and the juice filtered to make the most delectable of all gunns. I never made the gunn here until I discovered the tiny soft-shell crabs that are available in the early spring. They are beyond mere substitution—they are excellent.

This dish deserves the best of everything—the best stock, the finest tureen, and an appreciative audience. *It serves 4 as a rich soup course.*

1 pound very small soft-shell crabs	2 tablespoons cornstarch dissolved in 2 tablespoons cold stock and 2 teaspoons oil
2 quarter-sized slices peeled ginger, finely minced	2 large egg whites, well beaten
1 large whole scallion, coarsely chopped	2 teaspoons oil
3½ cups chicken stock	1 tablespoon finely minced cooked Smithfield ham (*page 492*)
3 tablespoons dry sherry	2 teaspoons chopped fresh coriander or parsley
1 tablespoon light soy sauce	
Salt to taste	

Preparations

Select the smallest soft-shell crabs you can get. Have them cleaned, quartered, and packed carefully so they're protected from the air; use them as soon as possible.

Before starting the soup, have 3 cups of stock ready in a heavy pot, preferably earthenware, and have ½ cup stock for blending with the crabs.

Dissolve the cornstarch. Beat the egg whites till frothy in a small bowl; add 2 teaspoons oil and blend well. Drape a large linen napkin or cotton cloth over a large bowl.

Put the quartered crabs, the ginger, scallion, and ½ cup stock into an electric blender and blend until the mixture is pasty and smooth. If you have no blender, do this with a mortar and pestle or pound them in a pot with the handle of a cleaver or a rolling pin without handles.

Pour half the puréed crabs into the center of the napkin, gather up the ends, twirl the cloth, and wring the juice into the bowl—get every last drop. Discard the residue and repeat with the other half. You should do this just before cooking, since the delicate flavor will dissipate if you do it in advance.

Cooking the "gunn"

Combine the crab juice with the stock and bring the liquid to a gentle boil over medium-low heat. Skim off any foam and add the sherry and soy sauce, then salt to taste. (Depending on how well you've seasoned your stock, no more than ½ teaspoon should be needed, since you will add Smithfield ham later.) Give the dissolved cornstarch a big stir. Pour it into the pot and stir in a circular motion until the soup is smoothly thickened.

Turn off the heat and pour in the beaten egg whites in a wide circle pattern. As they float into chiffony ribbons, stir gently to break them into silky petals. Pour the soup immediately into a tureen, sprinkle the surface with the minced ham, and make a dainty bouquet of the minced coriander or parsley in the center.

炸軟壳蟹　DEEP-FRIED SOFT-SHELL CRABS

Each bite of these deep-fried crabs gives the texture of fluffy coating, thin, crunchy shells, and luscious meat. Mushroom-smothered Bean Curd and Spicy Minced Watercress would go very well with this. *It would serve 2 or 3 people as a main course.*

4 large or 6 medium-sized
    soft-shell crabs
Batter (*page 94*)
4 cups oil

Either:
Roasted salt-pepper (*page 501*)

Or individual dip sauce:
1 tablespoon light soy sauce
1 teaspoon Chenkong, red-wine,
    or cider vinegar
½ teaspoon minced peeled ginger

Garnish: Fresh parsley sprigs

Preparations

Have the fishman clean and quarter the crabs, removing the spongy gills. Rinse and pat dry.

Mix the batter. Prepare the roasted salt-pepper or the dip sauce for each person.

Deep-frying

Heat a wok or heavy pot over high heat until hot; add the oil and heat until it foams a cube of bread instantly, about 375 degrees. Dip the crabs piece by piece into the batter and then slip into the hot oil. Deep-fry them, turning constantly, for about 3 minutes. Drain on paper towels, pile on a hot serving dish, and garnish with parsley.

煎軟壳蟹 SHALLOW-FRIED SOFT-SHELL CRABS

These crusty crabs, flavored with a subtly sweet and sour sauce, *would serve 3 or 4 people as a main course* with some Stir-fried Green Beans or Lima Beans and a green salad.

4 large or 6 medium-sized
   soft-shell crabs
½ cup cornstarch

Sauce:
3 tablespoons light soy sauce
3 tablespoons dry sherry
1 tablespoon cider vinegar
1 tablespoon sugar
1 small scallion, including green
   part, finely chopped
2 quarter-sized slices peeled ginger,
   minced
1 teaspoon cornstarch dissolved in
   ¼ cup water

6 tablespoons oil
1 tablespoon sesame oil
1 tablespoon chopped coriander or
   parsley

Preparations

Have the fishman clean and quarter the crabs, removing the spongy gills under the shells. Coat each quarter with cornstarch. Combine the sauce seasonings and mix until the sugar is dissolved. Add the scallions and ginger and the cornstarch mixture and stir well.

Shallow-frying

Heat a large, heavy skillet over high heat until very hot; add 6 tablespoons oil, swirl, and heat for 30 seconds. Pour half of the oil into a small dish and reserve. Turn heat to medium, shake the excess cornstarch off the crabs, add them to the skillet, and shallow-fry them for about 3 minutes until brown and crisp on the bottom. Then dribble the reserved oil back into the pan from the side. Flip the crabs over and brown them on the other side for about 3 minutes, lowering the heat if they brown too fast.

Turn heat high, pour in the sauce, and let it sizzle for about 1 minute, flipping the crabs over once and cooking until they all but absorb the sauce. Sprinkle in the sesame oil and transfer the crabs to a serving dish. Serve immediately with the chopped coriander or parsley sprinkled on top.

Oysters and Clams

酥
炸
蠔
CANTONESE DEEP-FRIED OYSTERS

Cleansed in salt and dipped in boiling water to seal in the juice before being coated and deep-fried, these oysters are succulent inside and crisp outside. The batter is excellent—light and crunchy. It would be very good for shrimp and such vegetables as sliced mushrooms, eggplant, or zucchini. *The oysters make a delicious hors d'oeuvre or a lovely meal for 4 when served with stir-fried Broccoli Flowerets in Black-Bean Sauce or Spicy Cold Celery Cabbage.*

24 shucked oysters

1 teaspoon salt

½ teaspoon black pepper

4 cups oil

Roasted salt-pepper (*page 501*)

Batter:

1 cup all-purpose flour

1 teaspoon salt

2 teaspoons baking powder

⅔ cup water

1 egg, well beaten

1 tablespoon oil

Preparations

Drain the oysters and place them in a bowl. Sprinkle in 1 teaspoon salt and rub gently and thoroughly for about a minute. Pour oysters into a strainer under a gentle stream of cold water; rinse them until they are no longer slippery. Set aside on a plate.

Bring 6 cups water to a rolling boil in a large pot. Dip the strainer in and out of the boiling water for about 10 seconds, snapping the handle in fast up and down motions to toss and turn the oysters; the oysters should be grayish white and firm. Drain thoroughly and turn them onto a dish. Sprinkle and toss lightly with the black pepper.

Make the batter: Measure the flour into a large bowl; add the salt and baking powder and stir to mingle. Add the water slowly as you stir in a circular motion until smooth. Add the beaten egg and stir again in a circular motion; then add the oil and stir until the batter is smooth. The consistency should be that of a smooth pancake batter, neither too thin nor too thick. Place the oysters next to the batter by the stove. Have a soup spoon ready.

Deep-frying

Heat a wok or large, heavy pot over high heat until hot; add the oil and heat until it foams a cube of bread instantly, about 375 degrees. Scatter 12 oysters into the batter, toss to coat them, scoop out one in the spoon, scraping the spoon against the rim of the bowl to remove excess batter. Then slip the oyster into the oil, and rapidly add the rest one by one. Let them puff and brown for about 2 minutes, turning them gently, until they are golden brown and crisp. Remove to drain on paper towels and skim off any floating balls of batter. Continue with the second batch.

Arrange the oysters on a serving platter and either sprinkle lightly with the roasted salt-pepper or serve it on the side.

豆
豉
蛤
蜊
CLAMS IN BLACK-BEAN SAUCE

These clams are stir-fried in their shells with high seasonings and then steam-cooked briefly until the shells open. *They serve 2 as a main course with rice, and 4 to 6 as an appetizer.*

24 very small littleneck or
   cherrystone clams

Sauce:
3 tablespoons oil
2 large cloves garlic, coarsely
   chopped
1-inch knob peeled ginger,
   coarsely chopped
1 large whole scallion, coarsely
   chopped
1 heaping tablespoon fermented
   black beans, coarsely chopped
1 tablespoon light soy sauce
2 tablespoons dry sherry
½ teaspoon sugar
½ cup water
2 teaspoons cornstarch dissolved
   in 4 teaspoons water with
   2 teaspoons sesame oil

Garnish: Fresh coriander or
   parsley

Soak the clams in lightly salted water with a clean nail for 2 hours to extract any sand. Scrub the shells and rinse well.

Heat a wok or large, heavy skillet over high heat until hot; add the oil, swirl, and heat for 30 seconds. Splash in the chopped garlic, ginger, scallions, and black beans, and stir rapidly until they exude their heavenly aromas. Add the clams and stir for 1 minute. Sprinkle in the soy sauce, sherry, and sugar; stir; then pour in the water. Cover immediately and steam-cook vigorously over medium-high heat for about 4 minutes, until all the clams have opened.

Uncover, give the dissolved cornstarch a big stir, and pour into the sauce, stirring until it is smoothly thickened. Scoop the clams and sauce into a serving dish and garnish with some chopped coriander or parsley.

Squid

炒
鱿
魚

STIR-FRIED SQUID WITH PEPPERS AND MUSHROOMS

The tender pieces of white squid are beautifully embellished with the crisp green peppers and fluffy black mushrooms. Frilling makes the vegetables resemble flower petals. A beautiful dish with a delicate taste, *this would serve 2 or 3 people as a main course.*

1½ pounds fresh squid

Marinade:
1 tablespoon dry sherry
1 tablespoon scallion-ginger juice
 (*page 332*)
1 tablespoon cornstarch

2 small green peppers
8 small dried black Chinese
 mushrooms (presoaked)

2 cups oil
2 quarter-sized slices peeled ginger
1 tablespoon dry sherry
1 teaspoon salt

Preparations
1) Remove the head and tentacles; save for another use. 2) Peel off the purple membrane and slit each squid; 3) remove the cartilage. Rinse well and

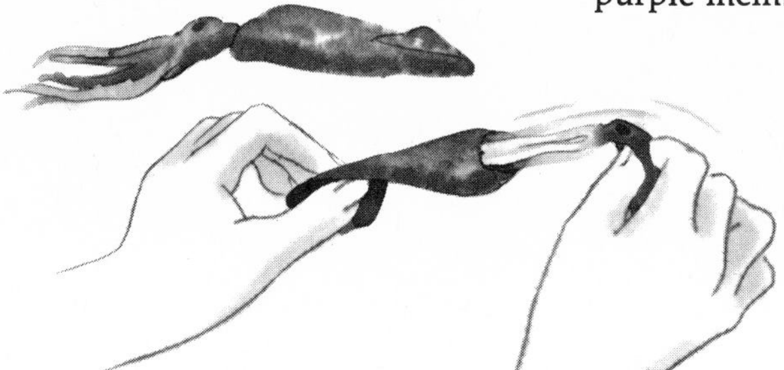

(1)

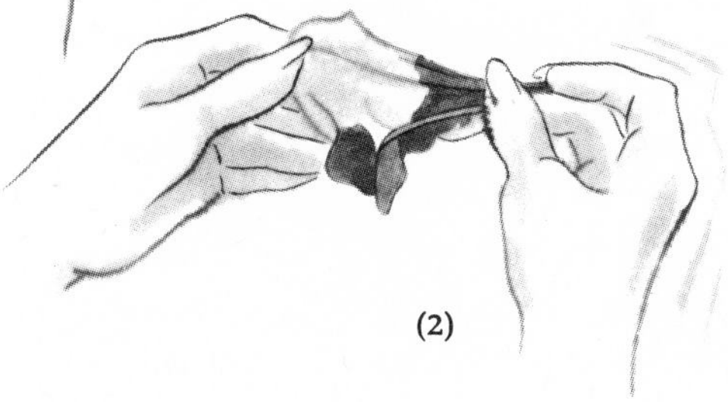

(2)

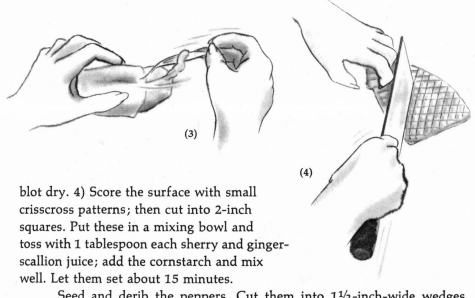

blot dry. 4) Score the surface with small crisscross patterns; then cut into 2-inch squares. Put these in a mixing bowl and toss with 1 tablespoon each sherry and ginger-scallion juice; add the cornstarch and mix well. Let them set about 15 minutes.

Seed and derib the peppers. Cut them into 1½-inch-wide wedges and "frill" one long edge—make very closely spaced slits about ¾ inch down into the pepper. Then cut each wedge in two. Cover the mushrooms and soak with hot water for 30 minutes; rinse and destem. Then cut them in half and frill the outer edge as done with the pepper wedges.

Velveting the squid

Heat a wok or large, heavy skillet over high heat until hot; add the oil and heat until a cube of bread foams slowly, about 280 degrees. Scatter in the squid and stir quickly in scooping and turning motions for about 45 seconds, until the pieces curl and become white. Drain immediately, either by pouring both oil and squid into a strainer over a bowl or by scooping the squid into a strainer held over the oil. Then set them on a plate.

These preparations may all be done up to an hour in advance; do not refrigerate the velveted squid.

Stir-frying

Heat the wok or skillet over high heat; add 3 tablespoons oil, heat 30 seconds, then toss in the ginger and press in the oil. Add the peppers and mushrooms and toss rapidly to coat them with oil. Splash in 1 tablespoon sherry and stir, tossing and turning, for 2 minutes. Add the squid and stir quickly a few times, then add the salt and give the squid and vegetables sweeping turns for about 30 seconds, or longer if squid was velveted in advance. Pour into a hot serving dish.

VARIATIONS

The vegetables may be varied with fresh mushrooms, canned straw mushrooms, stringed and sliced celery stalks, sliced cucumbers, or stringed snow peas. A small amount of cooked Smithfield ham (*page 492*), either slivered or minced, may be added for a stronger flavor and a brighter color.

POULTRY
AND EGGS

O f the different species of poultry, chicken is the most valued
in China. It is more expensive there than pork and has a prestige seldom
conferred on it in other cuisines. In China a chicken is never a nameless
bird. It is known by its place of origin, such as a province or city; by its
outstanding weight, such as the 9-kilogram chicken; or by a special feature,
such as the black-boned chicken. One always buys it alive, by age and
type needed for a particular method of cooking. Loved by all Chinese and
deemed a nourishing tonic for one's vigor, chicken is done more ways in
Chinese cooking than in any other cuisine. Since chickens here are plenti-
ful and amazingly reasonable, all the more reason to present an extensive
sampling of the way Chinese cooking methods and seasonings enhance
the qualities of this bird.

While China is famous for its roast duck, in general cooking ducks
are mostly simmered, since an oven is not a standard piece of equipment in
home kitchens. Multiple methods are frequently applied in cooking ducks
—for instance, a duck is often simmered or steamed before being boned
and then deep-fried so that it acquires a crackling crispness comparable to
that of roast duck.

In this chapter, the longest in the book, I have tried to give a great
range of recipes, from the simple stir-fried chicken-breast recipes to the
exotic boneless stuffed duck. And since I am very fond of squab and Rock
Cornish hen, there are a number of delicious recipes for them too.

Chicken

芝
蔴
醬
拌
鷄
絲

CHICKEN IN SESAME-PASTE SAUCE

Seasoned by one of the most scrumptious sauces of Chinese cuisine, this "chicken salad" is rich and full of nutty flavor and aroma. It is simple to make; the meat can be leftover white-cut chicken (*page 51*) or fast-boiled chicken breasts (*page 133*). *It serves 2 for lunch or supper and 4 to 6 as a cold appetizer.*

2 cups boneless white-cut chicken
    with the skin on, hand-torn or
    shredded
1 large firm cucumber

Sauce:
1 heaping tablespoon sesame paste
1 tablespoon oil
2 tablespoons dark soy sauce
2 teaspoons sugar
1/8 teaspoon roasted and crushed
    Szechuan peppercorns
    (*page 500*)
1 tablespoon sesame oil

Garnish: Sprigs of fresh coriander
or parsley

The general appearance of this dish is fluffy and offhand, so the chicken should be torn in rather coarse shreds, about 1½ inches long. If you shred with a knife, cut the shreds rather thick. Once the meat is cooked, it should be shredded *with* the grain to prevent the shreds from breaking into small pieces. Peel and halve the cucumber; remove seeds. Then cut the halves into diagonal slices before shredding the same length as the chicken shreds. Combine the chicken and cucumber shreds in a bowl.

Since sesame paste is quite hard, you must soften it a little first. Scrape 1 tablespoon of the paste from the bottle with a spoon and put it in a small bowl. Heat 1 tablespoon oil in a small pan until hot but not smoking. Add it to the paste and stir by pressing with the back of a spoon against the side of the bowl until there are no more lumps. Add the soy sauce and sugar and blend them into the sauce well. Sprinkle in the crushed Szechuan peppercorns and the sesame oil. Stir until the sauce has the consistency of a very smooth, thin paste. Pour it over the chicken and cucumber shreds and stir to coat them evenly. Transfer the salad to a serving plate and garnish with sprigs of coriander or parsley. You may cover and chill this hours in advance.

VARIATION
Substitute celery for cucumbers if you like. String and shred 3 large stalks; then parboil them in lightly salted water for 1½ to 2 minutes until they are softened but not soggy. Rinse immediately in cold water and drain thoroughly. Add them to the chicken.

麻辣鷄 PEPPERY-NUMB CHICKEN

This cold dish is light and refreshing, with an exotic numbness from the ground Szechuan peppercorns. The smooth texture of meat and vegetable is deliberately offset by the sprinkling of textured seasonings, so that you chew and savor the lingering flavors of the refreshing scallions, the hint of ginger, and the numbing aftertaste of the peppercorns. For lovers of hot food, add ½ to 1 teaspoon chili powder or cayenne pepper. Just as with the preceding recipe, *it serves 2 as a main dish and 4 to 6 as an appetizer.*

2 cups boneless white-cut or boiled
    chicken breast, skinned and
    cut into 1½-inch shreds
2 packed cups shredded iceberg
    or romaine lettuce

Sauce:
1 medium whole scallion, finely
    chopped
4 quarter-sized slices peeled ginger,
    minced
1 teaspoon roasted and crushed
    Szechuan peppercorns
    (*page 500*)
¼ teaspoon salt
2 tablespoons light soy sauce
2 teaspoons Chenkong, red-wine,
    or cider vinegar
½ teaspoon sugar
2 tablespoons sesame oil
1 tablespoon oil

Combine the shredded chicken and lettuce in a bowl.

The sauce
Combine the scallion, ginger, crushed peppercorns, and salt in a mortar and mash them well with a pestle, or put them in a bowl and crush

them with the handle of a cleaver. Add the soy sauce, vinegar, and sugar. Add the sesame and vegetable oils and blend well. Add the sauce to the chicken and lettuce, toss and mingle until evenly coated. Pour into a serving dish and serve.

松子黃燜鷄 RED-COOKED PINE-NUT CHICKEN

Pine nuts are particularly favored by the refined cuisine of eastern China. Here, mingled with ground pork as a covering for the chicken, they loosen the consistency of the ground meat and give each bite a remarkable fluffiness.

Involving boning, shallow-frying, and red-cooking, this is a "big affair" dish, ideal for entertaining, since even though the chicken is cut into small pieces, it is extremely rich, meant *to be shared by up to 10 people in small quantities, with other dishes;* Stir-fried Chinese Cabbage, Asparagus, or Bean Sprouts would go well with this.

1 fryer, about 3 pounds, or
    2 pounds boneless chicken
    breasts

Coating:
2 tablespoons cornstarch
4 tablespoons water
1 egg yolk

Meat mixture:
½ pound ground pork
½ cup pine nuts
½ teaspoon salt
2 tablespoons minced scallion
    bulbs
2 quarter-sized slices peeled ginger,
    minced
2 egg yolks, lightly beaten

2 tablespoons oil

Sauce:
4 tablespoons dark soy sauce
4 tablespoons dry sherry
½ teaspoon roasted and crushed
    Szechuan peppercorns
    (*page 500*)
1¼ cups chicken stock
1¼ tablespoons sugar

Garnishes:
Sprigs of fresh coriander or parsley
Carved Tomato Roses (see end of
    recipe)

Preparations

Remove the fat from the cavity and discard the tail. Rinse and dry the chicken, then 1) disjoint the wings and 2) legs at the thighs. 3) Cut through the meat at the ridge of the breast and scrape against the breast-bone on both sides to remove the meat in one piece with the skin attached.

Repeat on the other side. Cut through the joint to separate thigh and leg;
4) make an incision through the meat along the center bone of each, and
around the ends; cut and pull to free the bones. Keep skin on. You should
have thigh meat in 1 piece and leg meat in 1 piece. Do the same with the
other leg. Save the wings, bones, and carcass for making stock.

Turn the chicken skin side down and pound it lightly with the back
of a cleaver or heavy knife to loosen the fibers, especially the leg meat. Cut
each thigh and leg piece into 3 lengthwise pieces. Cut each breast half into
4 crosswise pieces. Now you have a total of 20 rectangular pieces. Put them
on a plate, skin side down. (If you can't be bothered with boning a chicken,
use 2 pounds boneless chicken breast with the skin on. Cut the meat into
20 rectangular pieces.)

TO MAKE THE COATING—Dissolve the cornstarch in the
water and beat in the egg yolk; mix well. Pour half of it over the chicken,
smoothing with your fingers; then turn the pieces and coat the other side
with the coating already ·on the plate. Save the other half for the final
coating.

TO MAKE THE MEAT MIXTURE—First march-chop the ground
meat, turning it a few times, until fluffy. Add the rest of the ingredients
and stir thoroughly.

Divide the pork mixture into 20 portions. Pat and smooth the mixture
onto the meat side of the chicken pieces and then dip the mounded pieces in
the remaining coating. Repeat till all pieces are covered and coated.

The boning and cutting may be done in advance, but not the coating
and covering—air will dry and coagulate the egg yolks and destroy the
smooth fluffiness of the dish.

Shallow-frying and red-cooking

Heat a large, heavy skillet over high heat until very hot; add the oil,
swirl, and heat for 30 seconds. Lower the heat to medium, add half the
chicken pieces, pork-covered side down, and shallow-fry them for 1½ to 2
minutes. Turn them over and shallow-fry another 1½ minutes. Remove
them to a plate and fry the remaining batch. Then push the pieces to one
side and put the first batch back in the skillet, pork side up—all the pieces
should be in 1 layer.

Pour the soy sauce and sherry over the surface of the pieces, sprinkle
in the crushed peppercorns, and add the stock. When the sauce bubbles,
sprinkle in the sugar, tilt the pan, and baste the top with the sauce a few
seconds. Turn heat low, cover, and let the chicken simmer very gently for
45 minutes. Turn the pieces over halfway through the cooking and baste
every once in a while.

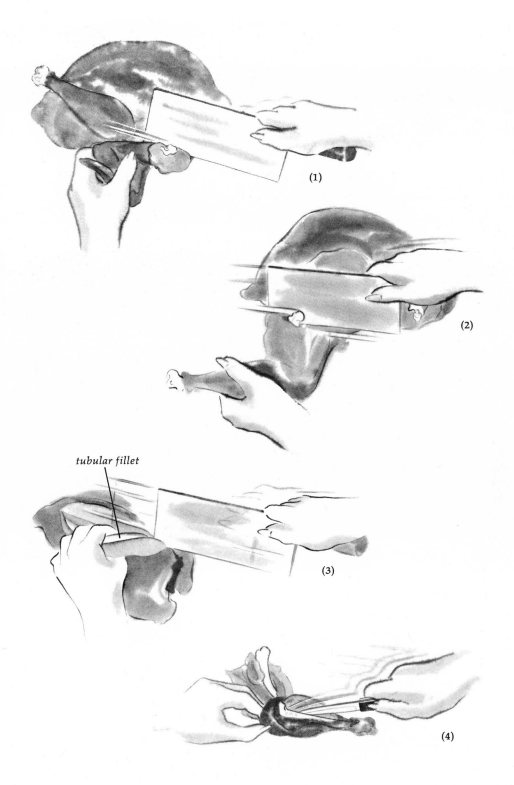

tubular fillet

(1)

(2)

(3)

(4)

Turn off the heat and remove the chicken to a hot serving platter, pork side up; pour the sauce over and garnish the two ends of the platter with sprigs of coriander or parsley and Carved Tomato Roses.

CARVED TOMATO ROSES—By cutting in a continuous circular strip, remove the peel from 2 large or 4 small ripe but firm tomatoes. Coil each strip of peel tightly, then let them loosen and spread into symbolic roses. Tuck some coriander or parsley on the side as leaves.

IMPROMPTU STOCK—If you don't have chicken stock on hand for the sauce, bring 4 cups water to a boil with the carcass, wings, a slice of ginger, and a small whole scallion. Cover and simmer for 1 hour or longer over low heat. Season lightly with salt to taste, strain the amount you need, and bottle the rest for other uses.

紅燒粟子鷄 RED-COOKED CHICKEN WITH CHESTNUTS

Chestnuts combine well with red-cooked meats and poultry. Absorbing the rich sauce and seasonings, they become plump and flavorful while they enrich the meat and sauce with a subtle sweetness. This dish is a rich brown color, the flavor sweet and winy with a hint of star anise. *It will serve 4 people as a main course;* it should be served with rice, steamed buns, or hot rolls and a light vegetable, such as Stir-fried Bean Sprouts or Chinese Cabbage.

1 cup dried blanched chestnuts or
    fresh chestnuts

½ teaspoon baking soda
3 tablespoons oil

4 quarter-sized slices peeled ginger
2 medium whole scallions, each
    cut into 4 pieces
1 roasting chicken, 3½ to 4
    pounds, chopped through
    bones (*page 14*)

5 tablespoons dark soy sauce
½ cup dry sherry
2 tablespoons sugar
¼ teaspoon salt
1 whole star anise
1 cup water

Chestnuts

I love chestnuts but hate the tedious work of shelling and peeling them. Therefore, I usually buy the dried blanched chestnuts, available in Chinese grocery stores and in some American markets. Put them in a deep bowl, sprinkle the baking soda over them, cover with 2 cups boiling water, stir well, and soak for 1 hour. Rinse them in warm water to remove the soda, then pick off any red inner skins from the creases with a toothpick. Bring them to a boil with 2 cups water in a small saucepan; turn heat low to maintain a gentle simmering, cover, and simmer for 1 hour. By that time the chestnuts should be firm but tender and sweet. Turn off heat and set aside; if doing this hours or a day ahead of time, drain the chestnuts, cover, and refrigerate.

For fresh chestnuts, cut a shallow cross in the flat side and then boil them in water to cover for 5 minutes. Peel them as soon as possible, and if any inner skin remains, soak them further in boiling water. The trick is to peel them hot.

Simmering the chicken and chestnuts

Heat a large, heavy pot over high heat until hot; add the oil, swirl, and heat for 30 seconds. Toss in the ginger and scallions. Then add the chopped chicken and sear the pieces until the skin is yellow, tossing and turning them continuously. Add the soy sauce, half of the dry sherry, the sugar, and the salt. Stir for about 1 minute to color the chicken. Add the star anise and 1 cup water and stir to mingle well. Turn heat low to maintain a strong simmering, cover, and simmer for 20 minutes, turning the chicken a few times.

Add the remaining sherry and stir a little. Add the chestnuts, and stir to scatter them into the sauce. Cover and simmer 15 minutes, stirring them gently once for even cooking. Pour into a hot serving dish.

VARIATION

When you add the chestnuts, add also 8 to 10 medium-sized dried black Chinese mushrooms, which have been covered with hot water and soaked for 30 minutes, then rinsed, destemmed, and cut in half.

紅 RED-COOKED DRUMSTICKS
燜
鷄
腿

The drumsticks are briefly marinated and deep-fried, and then fast simmered so that they acquire flavor and color but still retain their firm, neat
form. Embellished with silky straw mushrooms and crunchy spring bamboo shoots, they make a lovely presentation, everything glistening under
the tasty glaze sauce. *It is a marvelous main course for 4* when served with
rice to soak up the delicious sauce and one of the simple stir-fried vegetables, such as lima beans, celery, or celery cabbage.

8 drumsticks, about 2 pounds

Marinade:
4 tablespoons dark soy sauce
2 tablespoons light soy sauce

1 eleven-ounce can spring bamboo
    shoots (about 2 cups roll-cut)
1 eight-ounce can straw mush-
    rooms (about 1 cup)
4 cups oil

Sauce:
Soy sauce left over from the
    marinade
1 tablespoon dry sherry
1 tablespoon sugar
⅛ teaspoon salt

3 tablespoons oil
2 quarter-sized slices peeled ginger,
    coarsely chopped
1 large whole scallion, including
    green part, cut into 6 pieces
2 cups chicken stock or water
2 teaspoons cornstarch dissolved
    in 1 tablespoon water
1 tablespoon sesame oil

Preparations and deep-frying
    Place the drumsticks in a bowl; add the soy sauces and toss to color
and season them all over. Let them marinate for 10 to 15 minutes. Meanwhile rinse the bamboo shoots, roll-cut them into 1½-inch pieces, and place
them in a colander to drain well. Rinse and drain the mushrooms. Place
them in separate piles on the working platter with the scallions and ginger.
    Heat a wok or large, deep pot over high heat until hot; add the 4
cups oil and heat until it foams a snip of scallion instantly, about 375 degrees. While the oil is heating, toss and turn the meat a few times in the
soy sauce. When oil is ready, pick up the bone end of a drumstick with a
pair of chopsticks or tongs, shake off the excess liquid, then stand back and
slip it quickly into the hot oil. Repeat, quickly, with the rest. Let them
deep-fry, foaming vigorously, for 2½ minutes, evening out the contents

with chopsticks or a wooden spoon so that every drumstick is submerged in oil. Turn off the heat, remove the drumsticks, and place them on a plate.

Reheat the oil. Scatter in the bamboo shoots and let them deep-fry for 45 seconds to extract the water and firm the texture. Turn off the heat, hold a strainer over the pot, and spoon the bamboo shoots rapidly into it to drain. Put them back on the working platter.

Both the drumsticks and bamboo shoots may be deep-fried 1 to 2 hours in advance; cover the meat until ready for the final cooking. Do not refrigerate, for the meat will harden.

Add the sherry, sugar, and salt to the marinade bowl and stir until the sugar and salt are dissolved. Dissolve the cornstarch, measure out the stock or water, and have the sesame oil within reach.

Simmering

Heat a large, deep skillet or Dutch oven, one that will accommodate the meat in a single layer, until hot. Add 3 tablespoons oil, swirl, and heat for 30 seconds. Scatter in the ginger and scallions and stir a few times. Add the straw mushrooms and stir a few times, then scrape them to the edge of the pan. Place the drumsticks in the pan, snugly in one layer. Scatter the bamboo shoots on top of the chicken, pour over the seasoning sauce, then add the stock or water. When the sauce boils, turn heat to medium low to maintain a strong simmer, cover, and simmer for 30 minutes. Turn off the heat. As with all red-cooked dishes, this may be done hours or even a day in advance. Cover and refrigerate; reheat over low heat just before serving.

The prettiest way to serve this dish is on an oval silver platter. Arrange the drumsticks down the center in 2 rows, bony end to meat end, tucking the bony end underneath. Scoop up the vegetables with a slotted spoon without the sauce and place them in 2 mounds at either end of the drumstick row.

Bring the sauce in the pan to a simmer over medium heat; add the dissolved cornstarch and stir in a circular motion until the sauce is smoothly thickened. Add the sesame oil, give a big stir, and pour the sauce over the chicken and vegetables.

VARIATIONS

Two pounds disjointed drumsticks and thighs or disjointed wings, without the wing tips, may be used instead of drumsticks alone. Or use a broiler or small fryer; disjoint and then chop the body (see *page 14*). Prepare and cook it exactly as the drumsticks, but add 1 tablespoon light soy sauce to the marinade and 1 tablespoon dry sherry, 1 teaspoon sugar, and a pinch of salt to the seasoning sauce. And increase the simmering liquid by ½ to ¾ cup.

雲南汽鍋蒸鷄　STEAMED CHICKEN IN YUNNAN POT

A Yunnan pot is ingenious, and unique. It resembles a porcelain casserole from the outside, but it contains a central chimney inside that tapers to a point below the well-fitted lid. The ingredients are scattered around the chimney and the pot is then covered and placed inside a steaming pot so that the steam rises through the chimney, hits the lid, and forms into a fine mist that sprays the ingredients until done. Poultry cooked in this pot is a marvel of superb flavor and succulence. Unusually beautiful, the pot is a worthy investment for any good kitchen. It is sold in some Chinatown stores and it may also be purchased by mail order.

This is an "eating" soup. Individual soy-sauce dippers should be provided along with a few aromatic seasonings for each person to create an individual sauce. *It serves 6 as a first course, in Chinese soup bowls. And it may be served as a main dish for 4* with rice or bread and a green vegetable.

1 roasting chicken, about 4 pounds
4 quarter-sized slices peeled ginger
1 large scallion, cut into 2-inch
   pieces
3 cups chicken stock
1 tablespoon dry sherry
1 teaspoon salt

Dip sauce:
Light soy sauce
Sesame oil
Chopped fresh coriander or parsley
Minced peeled ginger
Roasted and crushed Szechuan
   peppercorns (*page 500*)

Chopping the chicken

Remove the fat from the cavity and the tail; rinse and dry the chicken. Following illustrations on *page 15*, disjoint the wings and thighs. Discard the wing tips, chop each wing into 3 pieces, leaving the joint intact. Chop each leg and thigh into 5 pieces, keeping the joint intact. Turn the chicken on its side and chop along the base of the ribs to separate the breast from the back. Chop the breast in two lengthwise and then crosswise into pieces about the size of the leg and wing pieces. Reserve the back and giblets for other uses.

Parboiling and cooking

Remove any chipped bones from the chicken and rinse the pieces if it seems necessary. Bring 6 cups of water to a boil in a large saucepan over high heat; add the chicken, and when the water boils again, let it boil rapidly for 1 minute. Turn off the heat and pick up the chicken pieces with chopsticks or a pair of tongs and swish them in the water to rinse off the foam; then scatter them around the chimney of the Yunnan pot. This parboiling procedure cleanses the chicken, making the subsequent broth very clear. Scatter the ginger and scallions over the chicken pieces and add the chicken stock. Put the lid on, place the pot in a large soup pot over a rack and pour in boiling water to about one-half the height of the Yunnan pot. Cover the steaming pot and steam over medium-high heat for about 2 hours, replenishing with boiling water whenever necessary. (This may be done hours in advance, the chicken resteamed until piping hot before serving. In that case, cool and then refrigerate the chicken in its Yunnan pot. Remove some of the fat before resteaming.)

Remove the pot from the steamer after 2 hours. Skim off some of the fat and discard the ginger and scallion. Season the broth with the sherry and salt. Replace the lid and bring the Yunnan pot to the table. The chicken and broth may be ladled into individual soup bowls or you serve the chicken first and then the soup in small bowls. You will find the meat tender and moist and the clear golden broth superbly flavorful.

The dip sauce

Put tablespoons of light soy sauce in individual small saucers and place these at each setting. Put a few tablespoons sesame oil, chopped coriander or parsley, minced peeled ginger, and ground Szechuan peppercorns in 4 saucers or dainty cups on a small tray and pass around for each person to season his or her own sauce.

VARIATIONS

You could add 8 to 10 large dried black Chinese mushrooms that have been covered with hot water and soaked for 30 minutes, then rinsed and destemmed.

Instead of chicken, you could use 3 one-pound fresh Cornish hens or 4 squabs, each quartered. In that case, reduce the steaming time to 1 hour.

If you prefer a stronger flavor, add ¼ pound sliced cooked Smithfield ham for the last hour of cooking (*page 492*).

魚
香
子
鷄

PEPPER-GINGER CHICKEN

The young chicken is boiled, chopped into small pieces, marinated, then stir-fried with hot peppers, ginger, and liquid seasonings over high heat until the spicy flavor is cooked into the meat. It's a fast dish that takes only minutes to cook at mealtime, since the preparations may be done in advance. It is very saucy and goes well with rice. *Serves 4 easily with a light stir-fried vegetable.*

1 small broiler, about 2½ pounds

Marinade:
2 tablespoons light soy sauce
1 tablespoon dry sherry
½ teaspoon salt
1 tablespoon cornstarch

2 tablespoons shredded fresh hot
    peppers
4 tablespoons shredded peeled
    ginger
2 small whole scallions, shredded
4 tablespoons oil

Sauce:
¼ teaspoon salt
1 tablespoon sugar
1½ teaspoons cornstarch
1 tablespoon light soy sauce
3 tablespoons Chenkong or
    red-wine vinegar
¼ teaspoon black pepper
½ teaspoon roasted and crushed
    Szechuan peppercorns
    (*page 500*)
1 cup stock
1 teaspoon sesame oil

Preparations

Remove and discard the fat and tail of the chicken; rinse and drain. Place the chicken in a snug pot, add boiling water to cover, and set over high heat. When the water boils again, turn heat medium high to maintain a strong boil and let it boil for 10 minutes, turning the chicken from side to side. Remove the chicken to a colander, reserving 1 cup of the broth for the sauce. Spray the chicken with cold water to stop the cooking. When the chicken is cool, chop it through the bones (*page 15*) into small pieces, about 1 inch wide and 1½ inches long. Put them in a large bowl. This may be done hours or 1 day in advance; if so, cover and refrigerate.

Add the marinade ingredients, the cornstarch last; toss to season evenly. Marinate for 10 minutes at room temperature or cover and refrigerate for 1 hour.

Shred the hot peppers, ginger, and scallions into fine shreds about 1 inch long. Combine sauce ingredients; stir until sugar is dissolved.

Stir-frying

Heat a wok or large, heavy skillet over high heat until hot; add the oil, swirl, and heat for 30 seconds. Scatter in the peppers, ginger, and scallions, and stir vigorously for about 5 seconds. Add the chicken pieces and stir rapidly and vigorously in fast turning motions for 1 minute, then pour the sauce over. When it boils, lower the heat slightly and stir in fast and rapid turns for 2 minutes until the meat is thoroughly cooked and deeply flavored. Pour into a serving dish.

VARIATION

If fresh hot peppers are not available, use 2 to 4 dried chili peppers. Press and flip them in oil over moderate heat until blackened, then turn up the heat, add the ginger and scallions, and continue with the recipe.

核桃鷄丁 CHICKEN WITH WALNUTS

This is a lovely dish of succulent chicken, crisp celery, and crunchy walnuts. It is lightly seasoned, so nothing detracts from the sweet nuttiness of the deep-fried walnuts, but its flavor does depend on a good chicken stock—the dish will be on the bland side if the stock is thin, but delicately flavorful if it is rich and well seasoned.

It serves 2 to 3 for a main course and, since it does not turn "watery" sitting around, it is ideal for a buffet table.

1 pound velveted chicken breast,
   in ½-inch cubes (*page 75*)
⅔ cup walnut halves
1 cup oil
2 cups cubed celery
2 quarter-sized slices peeled ginger
½ teaspoon salt

½ cup rich chicken stock
2 tablespoons dry sherry
2 tablespoons light soy sauce
2 teaspoons cornstarch dissolved
   in 1 tablespoon water and
   1 teaspoon sesame oil

Preparations

Velvet the chicken. It can be done an hour or so in advance; do not refrigerate.

The dark skin of the walnuts is rather tart. Remove it by soaking the walnuts in boiling water for 5 minutes and then peeling them with tweezers.

Heat 1 cup oil in a small saucepan over high heat until it foams a cube of bread gently, about 325 degrees. Pour in the walnuts, and stir them constantly for about 1½ minutes, lowering the heat slightly after the first 30 seconds, until their color turns a light brown. Be careful; walnuts burn easily. Immediately strain the walnuts, reserving the oil, without the residue, for future use. Then spread the walnuts on paper towels to drain and crisp. Their color will deepen a little more, since walnuts absorb oil and continue to cook until they're cool. This step can be done in advance.

Snap off the ends of 4 to 5 celery stalks; then pull off the stringy fibers. Cube the celery by cutting the stalks lengthwise into ½-inch-wide strips, then crosswise into ½-inch cubes. Put celery, ginger, and chicken on your working platter. Dissolve the cornstarch in a small bowl and add the sesame oil.

Stir-frying

Heat a wok or large, heavy skillet over high heat until hot; add 3 tablespoons of drained oil, swirl, and heat until hot. Throw in the ginger slices, press them in the oil, then shower in the celery cubes and stir them vigorously for about 30 seconds until they deepen to a bright green. Sprinkle in the salt and stir rapidly a few times. Add the stock, turn heat to medium-high, cover, and let it steam-cook for 1½ minutes. Scatter the velveted chicken over the top, cover, and steam-cook for another 30 seconds. If the chicken has been done in advance and is completely cold, add it to the pan 30 seconds earlier.

Remove the cover, give the contents a few vigorous stirs. There should be some stock left in the pan. Sprinkle in the sherry and soy sauce and toss lightly. Give the dissolved cornstarch a big stir and pour it over the chicken and celery, stirring in fast sweeping turns until the liquid thickens into a smooth glaze. Pour into a hot serving dish, scatter the walnuts over the top, and mingle at table before eating.

VARIATIONS

Velveted shrimp (*page 81*) or slippery-coated beef or veal (*page 85*) may be substituted for the chicken with excellent results. And green peppers may be used in place of or combined with the celery. If you happen to have small amounts of bamboo shoots, Chinese black mushrooms, fresh mushrooms, or button mushrooms on hand, cube and combine them and proportionately decrease either the celery or green peppers to make a total of 2 cups of vegetables.

豆 SHREDDED CHICKEN WITH
芽 BEAN SPROUTS
一
鷄
絲

Bean sprouts are easy to grow but they need care in the cooking; they contain a raw beany odor and taste when undercooked, and they become soggy when overcooked. A little ginger and sherry do wonders—they eliminate these undesirable qualities, enabling one to stir-fry the sprouts very briefly so that they retain their marvelous plumpness and crispness.

This is a colorful dish, in which the white velveted chicken and bean sprouts are intermingled with tasty red ham and bright-green snow peas. Refreshing in color and taste, it goes especially well with spicy shrimp or fish and a red-cooked or highly seasoned meat in a multi-course dinner. *As a main course, it can easily serve 4, with rice.*

1 pound boneless and skinless
    chicken breast, shredded and
    velveted (*page 75*)
3 cups fresh bean sprouts
4 quarter-sized slices peeled ginger,
    shredded
½ cup finely shredded fresh
    snow peas
¼ cup finely shredded cooked
    Smithfield ham (*page 492*) or
    substitute

Sauce:
1 teaspoon salt
¼ teaspoon sugar
1 tablespoon dry sherry
⅓ cup chicken stock
1 tablespoon cornstarch dissolved
    in 2 tablespoons water
2 teaspoons oil

3 tablespoons oil

Velvet the chicken and set aside on a working platter.

Rinse the bean sprouts in a pot of cold water, stirring to loosen the husks and broken tails, then tilting the pot to float them out; drain well. Put the bean sprouts, ginger, shredded snow peas and ham with the chicken on the working platter. Combine the sauce ingredients and blend well. All this may be done in advance; do not refrigerate the velveted chicken.

Heat a wok or large, heavy skillet over high heat until hot; add the oil, swirl, and heat for a few seconds. Scatter in the ginger and toss rapidly. Add the bean sprouts and snow peas and stir in fast sweeping and tossing motions for about 30 seconds. Add the chicken and ham and stir another 30 seconds. Give the sauce ingredients a big stir, pour into the pan, and stir rapidly until the contents are lightly glazed. Pour into a hot serving dish.

VARIATIONS

Substitute for the snow peas either thinly shredded green peppers, French-cut string beans, or peeled and shredded broccoli stems. If you don't like ham, substitute ½ cup finely shredded carrots. Salt to taste before serving.

陳
皮
鷄
TANGERINE-PEEL CHICKEN

To my Szechuan grandmother, this dish embodies her criterion for good seasoning—a manifold flavor separating into distinctive tastes.

    The chicken is chunky and dry-textured. The initial flavor is a stimulating hotness. Then that breaks down into the subtly bitter tangerine peel, the numbing Szechuan peppercorns, the sharp ginger, the aromatic scallions, and the sweet mellowness of the wine rice and liquid seasonings. This dish is also delicious cold. *It serves 2 to 4 with rice and a vegetable; Stir-fried Celery would be excellent with it.*

1 pound boneless and skinless
    chicken, white or dark meat,
    or both, cubed
2 tablespoons oil
2 tablespoons sesame oil
1 teaspoon salt

Dry seasonings:
2 pieces dried tangerine peel
    (total 3 inches wide)
4 dried chili peppers
1 medium whole scallion, finely
    chopped
4 quarter-sized slices peeled ginger,
    minced
½ teaspoon roasted and crushed
    Szechuan peppercorns
    (page 500)

Liquid seasonings:
2 tablespoons wine rice
2 tablespoons dry sherry
2 tablespoons dark soy sauce
2 teaspoons sugar

Preparations

If you are using dark meat, pound it lightly with the back of a cleaver or heavy knife to loosen the fibers. Cut both white and dark meat into ½- to ¾-inch cubes.

Soak the tangerine peel in hot water for 15 minutes. Cut lengthwise into shreds about ⅛ inch wide. Place them, and the dried peppers, scallion, ginger, and Szechuan peppercorns, on a small plate.

Place a piece of double-fold cheesecloth over a small bowl; measure into it 2 tablespoons of wine rice and then wring the cheesecloth to extract all its liquid. Discard the residue. Add the rest of the liquid seasonings to the bowl and stir until the sugar is dissolved.

All these preparations may be done hours in advance, although the wine rice will lose its flavor if left in the sauce too long.

Stir-frying

Heat a wok or large, heavy skillet over high heat until hot, add the oil and the sesame oil, swirl, and heat for 30 seconds. Scatter in the chicken and stir and flip rapidly to separate the cubes. Lower the heat to medium, sprinkle in the salt, and stir in fast scooping and turning motions for about 2 minutes, until the meat loses all pinkness and the pan is pretty dry. Scrape in all the dry seasonings and stir briskly to mingle. Then pour in the liquid seasonings and stir briefly. Turn heat extremely low, cover, and let the meat smother in this low heat for 15 minutes.

Turn heat high and stir rapidly in sweeping motions until the meat is evenly colored and most of the sauce has cooked into it. Pour into a hot serving dish, letting the red chili peppers show on top.

VARIATION

Use a 2½-pound broiler instead of boneless chicken. Chop it through the bones into 1-inch pieces (*see page 14*) and proceed with the steps outlined above, with these changes:

Add ¼ cup water to the liquid seasonings and increase the wine rice, sherry, and soy sauce each by 1 tablespoon. Add a little more sugar to taste. And, instead of smothering it over very low heat, let it simmer, covered, very gently for 20 to 25 minutes until done and the bones have enriched the sauce.

魚 香 鷄 絲　FISH-FRAGRANCE SAUCED CHICKEN

The delicious sauce that coats this chicken is not actually flavored with fish; it was originally created to go with fish—hence its name. It has become a famous sauce of Szechuan cooking.

This recipe produces light-brown shredded chicken, the mildly hot, faintly sweet and sour sauce just glazing the shreds. *Preceded by appetizers and accompanied by vegetables, perhaps one hot and one cold, this dish will serve 3 to 4 with rice or hot bread on the side.*

1 pound shredded chicken breast, velveted (*page 75*)	*Seasonings:*
2 tablespoons oil	1 teaspoon sugar
2 quarter-sized slices peeled ginger, minced	¼ teaspoon roasted and crushed Szechuan peppercorns (*page 500*)
2 small whole scallions, finely chopped	Sprinkling black pepper
2 medium cloves garlic, peeled and well mashed with a garlic press or cleaver	1 tablespoon dark soy sauce
	2 teaspoons Chenkong or red-wine vinegar
	1 teaspoon chili oil
	1 teaspoon cornstarch dissolved in 1 tablespoon water

Preparations

Velvet the chicken. It may be done up to an hour beforehand; cover but do not refrigerate.

Place the ginger, scallions, and garlic on a small plate. Combine the seasonings in a bowl and stir until the sugar is dissolved.

Stir-frying

Heat a wok or large, heavy skillet over high heat until hot; add the 2 tablespoons oil, swirl, and heat for 30 seconds. Scrape in the ginger, scallions, and garlic, and stir rapidly for a few seconds to explode their aromas. Scatter in the chicken and stir in fast tossing motions to blend. Give the seasonings a big stir, pour over the chicken, and stir in sweeping motions until the sauce coats the chicken evenly. Pour into a hot serving dish.

VARIATIONS

Shredded velveted fillet of flounder (*page 214*), velveted small shrimp (*page 81*), shredded slippery-coated flank steak (*page 85*), or blanched liver (*page 365*) may be done exactly as the chicken is.

If you use shredded slippery-coated pork loin (*page 85*), let it steam-cook 3 minutes with ¼ cup water before you add the seasonings.

芙蓉鷄 FU YUNG CHICKEN

Fu Yung, a species of Chinese hibiscus, is a fragile pale-white flower with fluffy petals. Its name is invoked by the Chinese when puréed breast of chicken is combined with whipped egg whites. Fu Yung occupies an important position in Chinese cuisine, representing a line of elegant dishes from soups and main dishes to sauces. It is not to be confused with the popular Egg Fu Yung of Chinese restaurants in the United States. Stretching the term beyond reason, the early Chinese immigrants named their deep-fried omelets "fu yung" simply because eggs were involved.

In this dish, the puréed chicken–egg-white mixture becomes thick and creamy, white and very fluffy; the mo-er mushrooms and snow peas add lovely color and contrasting texture. The key is a very hot pan and warm oil, so the chicken puffs, away from the metal. *It serves 2 with rice.*

½ pound boneless and skinless
    chicken breast
1 tablespoon water

Marinade:
1 teaspoon salt
1 tablespoon dry sherry
1 tablespoon cornstarch dissolved
    in 2 tablespoons water
6 egg whites, well beaten

1 heaping tablespoon dried mo-er
    mushrooms (presoaked)
10 to 12 fresh snow peas
¾ teaspoon salt
1 tablespoon dry sherry

1 cup chicken stock
1 tablespoon cornstarch dissolved
    in 2 tablespoons water
¾ cup oil

Preparations

Place the chicken breast on a chopping board, smooth (membrane) side down. Using a sharp knife or spoon, scrape across the surface to shave off the meat, discarding the tendon and membrane. Pile the meat and mince it. Then wet a cleaver or heavy knife and march-chop the meat repeatedly, turning the mass every few times, until the consistency is a purée. Add the tablespoon of water a little at a time and wet your knife every now and then. Place the puréed chicken in a large bowl.

Add to it 1 teaspoon salt, 1 tablespoon sherry, and 1 tablespoon dissolved cornstarch; stir in a circular motion to mix well. Then stir in the well-beaten egg whites little by little, and stir vigorously in a circular motion until the chicken mixture is smooth and fluffy. Let it marinate in the refrigerator for 30 minutes or longer. (This can be done hours ahead. Cover well, then bring to room temperature and restir until fluffy just before the cooking.)

In the meantime, cover the mo-er mushrooms with hot water and soak for 30 minutes, rinse them, and pinch off any hard "eyes." Squeeze them dry.

Rinse and string the snow peas. Blanch them in boiling water for 30 seconds, then pour them immediately into a colander and spray with cold water. Drain and place them with the mo-er mushrooms on a plate. Have the seasonings, chicken stock, and dissolved cornstarch ready.

Cooking

Heat a wok or large, heavy skillet over high heat till very hot; add the oil, minus 2 tablespoons for later use. Turn heat low and heat until the oil is warm but not hot, about 280 degrees. Give the chicken mixture a few vigorous stirs and pour it into the oil. Stir immediately with the tip of a spatula in fast scraping motions to lift the mass from the bottom of the pan. Then flip it over and repeat the scraping to prevent it from sticking and browning. Scoop and turn the mixture rapidly until it is completely white. Pour it into a dish, oil and all.

Clean the pan and heat it over high heat. Add the remaining 2 tablespoons oil, swirl, and heat until hot. Add the mo-er mushrooms and stir a few times; then add the snow peas, ¾ teaspoon salt, and 1 tablespoon sherry. Stir rapidly to mingle. Pour in the chicken stock. When it boils, lower the heat and add the dissolved cornstarch, stirring until the liquid begins to thicken. Using a slotted spoon, scoop up the fu yung chicken *without* the oil, put it into the pan, and stir rapidly in scooping and turning motions until the consistency is creamy and the contents glazed. Pour into a hot serving dish, letting the black mo-er mushrooms and the green snow peas peep out here and there.

VARIATION

If you'd like a stronger flavor, sprinkle 2 tablespoons finely minced cooked Smithfield ham (*page 492*) on top.

CHIANG-BO CHICKEN

Chiang-bo means to explode ingredients in sweet bean paste. This is a simple last-minute dish. Brown in color and thickly coated by the mellow sweet bean paste, the chicken and bamboo shoots make a lovely contrast of soft and crunchy. Accompany it with a sharp, cool vegetable. *This would serve 2 to 3 as a main course.*

1 pound diced chicken breast, velveted in oil or water (*page 75*)	5 tablespoons oil 1 cup diced bamboo shoots 2 quarter-sized slices peeled ginger, minced
Sauce: 1 tablespoon dark soy sauce 1 tablespoon dry sherry 2 tablespoons sweet bean paste ½ teaspoon sugar	1 small whole scallion, finely chopped

Velvet the chicken; it may be done in advance.

Combine the sauce ingredients in a small bowl, mixing them well.

Heat a wok or large, heavy skillet over high heat until hot; add 2 tablespoons of the oil, swirl, and heat for 30 seconds. Turn heat to medium and add the bamboo shoots; stir briskly for about 1 minute to firm and dry them—but don't let them scorch. Drain in a strainer, then set them aside.

Clean the pan, then add the remaining 3 tablespoons oil. Heat until hot and scatter in the ginger and scallions, then the velveted chicken and the reserved bamboo shoots. Stir and toss them together rapidly for a few seconds if the chicken has just been velveted or until heated through if it has been done before. Scrape in the sauce and stir in sweeping, folding motions until the chicken and vegetables are coated evenly. Pour into a hot serving dish.

VARIATIONS

For a hot flavor, add 1 to 2 teaspoons chili-pepper oil (*page 489*) when you stir-fry the chicken and bamboo shoots together.

If you don't have any sweet bean paste, use 1 tablespoon regular bean paste with 1 tablespoon hoisin sauce.

松
子
黃
瓜
鷄
丁
CHICKEN WITH PINE NUTS AND PICKLED CUCUMBERS

Used as flavoring agents as well as secondary ingredients, the sweet pine nuts and the crisp pickled cucumbers give this dainty dish a remarkable dual personality—it is both light and rich, delicate and flavorful. This is delicious hot, at room temperature, or cold. It's versatile, too: it may be served as a main course or a cold appetizer. *It would serve 3 or 4 with rice and accompaniments* such as eggplants and a stir-fried green vegetable.

1 pound diced chicken breast, velveted in water (*page 77*)	*Seasonings:*
	¼ teaspoon salt
1 six-ounce can pickled cucumbers, diced	2 tablespoons dry sherry
	1 teaspoon sugar
1 teaspoon sesame oil	
3 tablespoons oil	¾ cup pine nuts

Velvet the chicken in water and set it aside. This may be done hours in advance; cover and refrigerate until ready to use.

Drain the pickled cucumbers and cut them into ¼-inch dice. Put them in a bowl, add the sesame oil, and stir.

Heat a wok or large, heavy skillet over high heat until hot; add 3 tablespoons oil, swirl, and heat for about 30 seconds. Turn heat to medium high, scatter in the chicken, and stir rapidly a few times—if the chicken has been chilled, stir for about 1 minute to heat it through. Add the seasonings and stir to flavor the meat evenly. Add the diced cucumbers and stir in sweeping and tossing motions for 30 to 45 seconds to mingle them well. Pour into a serving dish and shower the top with the pine nuts. Toss well at the table before eating.

鷄
鬆   CHICKEN SOONG

Inspired by the famous Squab Soong of Canton, this diced chicken is creamily blended with vegetables and served either with a crown of crisp rice sticks or with whole lettuce leaves to use as wrappers for the chicken. *It serves 3 to 4 as a main course.*

1 pound diced chicken breast,
    velveted in oil (*page 75*)
6 medium dried black Chinese
    mushrooms (presoaked)
10 water chestnuts, diced
¾ cup fresh or frozen peas,
    parboiled
1 quarter-sized slice peeled ginger
3 tablespoons oil
½ teaspoon salt

Seasonings:
1 tablespoon light soy sauce
2 tablespoons dry sherry
¼ teaspoon sugar

2 teaspoons cornstarch dissolved
    in 2 tablespoons water
1 tablespoon sesame oil
2 ounces rice sticks (see below) or
    8 lettuce leaves

Preparations

Velvet the chicken and set it aside. Reserve the oil for deep-frying the rice sticks.

Cover the mushrooms with hot water and soak for 30 minutes; rinse, destem, and dice.

Prepare the water chestnuts and peas (parboil fresh 3 minutes; frozen 1 minute) and put with the mushrooms and ginger. Combine the seasonings, dissolve the cornstarch in a separate bowl, and place the sesame oil within reach.

Rice sticks generally come in 1-pound packages, divided into 4 wads. Break 1 wad in half lengthwise for 2 ounces. Reheat the velveting oil until it foams a cube of bread instantly, about 375 degrees. Pull the wad of rice sticks gently to flatten it into a thin lacy net, then drop it into the hot oil. Fry on one side for 3 seconds—they puff out immediately—and then gently turn them with a spatula and slotted spoon and fry them another 3 seconds. Scoop the net out immediately to drain on paper towels.

You may do all these preparations ahead of time.

Stir-frying

Heat a wok or large, heavy skillet over high heat until hot; add 3 tablespoons oil, swirl, and heat for 30 seconds. Toss in the ginger and press it against the pan. Add the mushrooms and stir for 1 minute; add the water chestnuts, peas, and salt, and stir rapidly for 30 seconds. Add the velveted chicken and stir vigorously in fast sweeping motions to mix well.

Discard the ginger, add the premixed seasonings, and stir to coat all the ingredients. Taste and add a little more soy sauce if you need it. Lower the heat and give the cornstarch mixture a big stir; pour it into the pan, stirring in a circular motion until it thickens the sauce smoothly. Add the sesame oil, give the contents a few sweeping folds, and pour onto a hot serving platter in a mound. Break up the rice sticks and make a circle around the chicken or scatter them over the top. Mingle lightly at the table before serving each person. Or arrange small lettuce leaves around the chicken and let everyone fill a leaf, fold it over, and eat as a sandwich.

VARIATIONS

Velveted diced shrimp (*page 81*), steamed lobster meat (*page 236*), or fresh or frozen crabmeat, cut into small cubes, may be substituted for the chicken.

If you want to use meat, marinate 1 pound ground pork or beef that has been march-chopped a few times with 1 tablespoon light soy sauce, 1 tablespoon dry sherry, 1 tablespoon cornstarch dissolved in 2 tablespoons water, and 1 tablespoon oil. Add to the pan after searing the vegetables and stir and poke vigorously until meat has no lumps. Add ⅓ cup water, turn heat to medium high, cover, and steam-cook the pork for 3 minutes, the beef for 2 minutes. Add the seasonings and 1 teaspoon sesame oil, but omit the dissolved cornstarch. A sprinkling of freshly ground black pepper will perk up the meat.

If you like a spicy flavor, add a minced clove of garlic with the ginger and 2 teaspoons chili paste or sauce to the seasonings.

鮮菇鷄片 CHICKEN WITH FRESH MUSHROOMS

Light and simple, this is a delicious dish with a distinctive mushroom flavor. *It serves 2 to 3 as a main course.*

1 pound sliced chicken breast, velveted (*page 75*)	½ teaspoon salt
½ cup sliced bamboo shoots	1 tablespoon light soy sauce
½ pound sliced fresh mushrooms	2 teaspoons cornstarch dissolved in 2 tablespoons chicken stock or water
4 tablespoons oil	
2 quarter-sized slices peeled ginger	2 teaspoons sesame oil

Velvet the sliced chicken breast (may be done up to 1 hour in advance; do not refrigerate). Rinse and drain the sliced bamboo shoots. Wipe the mushrooms with a damp paper towel; dry and slice them.

Heat a wok or large, heavy skillet over high heat until hot; add 2 tablespoons of the oil, swirl, and heat for 30 seconds. Scatter in the bamboo shoots and stir rapidly for about 1 minute to evaporate their moisture and eliminate the canned odor—lower the heat if necessary to prevent scorching. Remove to a plate.

Dry the pan, add the 2 remaining tablespoons oil, swirl, and heat over high heat until hot. Toss in the ginger slices and press them against the pan. Add the mushrooms and stir and flip them rapidly for about 30 seconds, until their color brightens. Add the bamboo shoots and the salt and stir briskly with the mushrooms for 1 minute. Then add the chicken and stir to mingle well; add the soy sauce and stir briskly to season evenly. Pour in the cornstarch mixture and stir until the contents are smoothly coated. Add the sesame oil, flip the contents a few times, and pour into a hot serving dish.

VARIATIONS

Instead of fresh mushrooms, well-drained canned button or straw mushrooms may be substituted. And instead of bamboo shoots you could use fresh snow peas or peeled broccoli stems to give some green color to the dish.

If you use snow peas, string and rinse them briefly. Dip them in boiling water for 10 seconds and drain. Use 3 tablespoons oil to stir-fry the mushrooms; then add the snow peas.

If you use broccoli stems, peel and cut them on the slant into thin slices. Stir-fry them with the mushrooms and continue.

醋溜鶏 VINEGAR-SPLASHED CHICKEN

Dark, gleaming, and coarse-looking, this is a flavorful dish full of lingering good tastes. Splashed in as a final touch, the vinegar sizzles to a fine mist that perfumes the chicken without making it sour. Once the chicken is boned and marinated, it takes only 7 minutes to cook. All meat and highly seasoned, it should be served with rice and a delicate and cool-looking vegetable, two of the best ones for it being Stir-fried Celery Cabbage and Stir-fried Shredded Cabbage with Carrots. *It serves 3 to 4 as a main course.*

1 broiler or fryer, about 3 pounds

Marinade:
2 tablespoons dark soy sauce
1 tablespoon light soy sauce
1 tablespoon dry sherry
1 tablespoon sugar
¼ teaspoon salt
½ teaspoon roasted and crushed
    Szechuan peppercorns
    (*page 500*)

1 tablespoon minced peeled ginger
2 large cloves garlic, minced
2 medium whole scallions,
    finely chopped
1 teaspoon sesame oil
1 tablespoon Chenkong or
    red-wine vinegar
3 tablespoons oil

Boning and marinating the chicken

Rinse and dry the chicken; remove and discard the fat and tail. Disjoint the wings, legs, and thighs. Remove the breast meat by cutting against the breast ridge, scraping against the frame with your knife while you pull the meat off in 2 large pieces. (Keep skin on.) Cut against the bones of the thighs and legs; then cut around the bones to free the meat in whole pieces. Again, skin should remain. Do the same with the upper and lower wings, discarding the wing tips. Turn the meat skin side down; pound lightly all over to loosen the fibers, then cut it, with skin attached, into 1-inch pieces. Save the bones for making stock. Boning may be done hours in advance, following the illustrations on *page 253.*

Place the meat in a mixing bowl; add the marinade, mix well, cover, and marinate for 15 minutes at room temperature or 30 minutes in the refrigerator.

When ready to cook, mince the ginger and garlic; chop the scallions; and have the sesame oil and vinegar ready.

Stir-frying

Heat a large, heavy skillet over high heat until hot; add the oil, swirl, and heat for a second. Scatter in the ginger, garlic, and scallions, and stir briskly for a second or two to bring out their fragrance. Pour in the chicken and marinade and stir vigorously for about 2 minutes; turn heat to low, cover, and simmer for 3 minutes. Uncover, turn heat high, and stir in fast turning motions for 1½ minutes to coat the chicken evenly as the sauce reduces to a thick glaze. Sprinkle in the sesame oil and give the chicken a few fast folds; then gather it to the center of the pan. Splash the vinegar around it and stir briskly in fast folding motions 2 or 3 times, then pour into a hot serving dish without the excess oil. It looks especially inviting if you place the chicken in the center of an oval platter and pile up at each end a mound of the dainty shreds of pale cabbage and bright-orange carrots. Both the chicken and vegetables are delicious hot or cold.

VARIATION

If you like spiciness, add 4 dried red chili peppers with the ginger, garlic, and scallions. Turn heat low and press and turn them in the hot oil until the peppers are scarlet, then continue as described above.

豆豉鷄 CHICKEN IN BLACK-BEAN SAUCE

This is a darkly glazed dish of succulent chicken and crisp vegetables, with a hearty taste of garlic and black beans. *It would serve 4 as a main course* with rice and a vegetable such as Stir-fried Green Peas or Lima Beans.

1 fryer or broiler, about 2½ pounds, cut through the bones into 1-inch pieces (*page 14*)	*Seasonings:* 2 tablespoons dark soy sauce 2 tablespoons dry sherry 1 teaspoon sugar
1 large onion, cut into 1-inch squares	1 cup water
2 medium green peppers, cut into 1-inch squares	
2 quarter-sized slices peeled ginger, minced	1½ tablespoons cornstarch dissolved in 3 tablespoons water
2 tablespoons fermented black beans, rinsed and chopped coarsely	4 tablespoons oil ½ teaspoon salt 1 tablespoon sesame oil
2 large cloves garlic, coarsely chopped	

Preparations

Put the cut-up chicken on your working platter with the onions, peppers, ginger, black beans, and garlic, all in separate piles. Mix the seasonings; dissolve the cornstarch in a separate bowl; have the sesame oil nearby. All this may be done hours ahead of time. Cover and refrigerate the chicken and vegetables. Bring to room temperature before stir-frying.

Stir-frying

Heat a wok or large, heavy skillet over high heat until hot; add 2 tablespoons oil, swirl, and heat for 30 seconds. Scatter in the onions and peppers and stir-fry vigorously with the salt for about 1 minute. Remove to a dish.

Add the remaining 2 tablespoons oil to the hot pan, heat a few seconds, then sear the ginger, black beans, and garlic for a few seconds, stirring all the time. Add the chicken and toss and stir until all the pieces are yellow-whitish—about 2 to 3 minutes. Add the seasonings mixture, stir, and when it bubbles, turn heat to medium, cover, and let the chicken steam-cook vigorously for 10 minutes, stirring the pieces every now and then.

Uncover, turn heat high, add the onions and peppers, and stir in sweeping and tossing motions for 1 minute. Give the cornstarch mixture a big stir and pour it into the pan, stirring in a circular motion until the chicken and vegetables are smoothly glazed. Add the sesame oil, give the contents a few sweeping folds, and pour into a hot serving dish.

炒 CHICKEN KOW
鷄
球
Bright and pretty, this dish takes no time at all to whip up if you velvet the chicken in water hours or even a day in advance. *It serves 4 as a main course with rice.*

1 pound cubed chicken, velveted
    in water (*page 77*)
2 tablespoons dried mo-er
    mushrooms (presoaked)
½ cup sliced bamboo shoots
1½ cups sliced celery stalks
2 quarter-sized slices peeled ginger
1 medium clove garlic, lightly
    crushed and peeled
4 tablespoons oil
¾ teaspoon salt
1 tablespoon dry sherry
½ cup chicken stock or water

Sauce:
1 tablespoon oyster sauce
1 tablespoon light soy sauce
¼ teaspoon salt
⅛ teaspoon sugar

2 teaspoons cornstarch dissolved
    in 2 tablespoons water and
    2 teaspoons sesame oil

Preparations
Velvet the chicken and set it on your working platter. Cover the mo-er mushrooms with hot water and soak for 30 minutes; rinse well, shake dry, and discard any hard "eyes." Rinse the bamboo shoots and blot dry on paper towels. Rinse the celery stalks, string, and then cut them

diagonally into slices about 2 inches long and ½ inch wide. Place them, with the ginger, garlic, and chicken, on your working platter, in separate piles. Combine the sauce ingredients and stir until the salt and sugar are dissolved. Dissolve the cornstarch; add the sesame oil.

Stir-frying

Heat a wok or large, heavy skillet over high heat until hot; add 2 tablespoons of the oil, swirl, and heat for 30 seconds. Add the ginger and garlic, and press them around in the pan. Scatter in the bamboo shoots and stir rapidly a few times to extract the water. Then add the mo-er mushrooms, ¼ teaspoon salt, and the sherry. Stir vigorously for about 1 minute, then pour the vegetables into a dish.

Add the remaining 2 tablespoons oil to the pan, swirl, and scatter in the celery. Stir rapidly for 30 seconds to sear it well. Sprinkle in the remaining ½ teaspoon salt and toss. Add the chicken stock or water, even out the contents, turn heat to medium low to maintain a strong simmer, cover, and simmer for about 1½ to 2 minutes until the celery is a little translucent, tender but still crisp.

Uncover and turn heat high. Add the stir-fried bamboo shoots and mo-er mushrooms and the chicken and toss rapidly a few times to mingle all the ingredients. Pour in the sauce and stir vigorously. Give the dissolved cornstarch mixture a big stir, add to the pan, and stir in fast circular motions until the sauce is smooth and glazy. Pour into a hot serving dish.

VARIATIONS

Peeled broccoli stems (1½ cups) may be substituted for the celery. Cut the stems diagonally into pieces the same size but steam-cook only 1½ minutes.

If you wish to use fresh snow peas, snip off the ends and string if necessary. Before cooking the other vegetables, tumble them in 2 tablespoons oil for 5 seconds with ¼ teaspoon salt. Pour them into a dish. Add the remaining oil, then the ginger and garlic, and stir-fry the bamboo shoots and mo-er mushrooms as before, then add ½ cup stock or water and bring to a boil. Add the chicken, snow peas, sauce, and cornstarch mixture and bring the dish to conclusion as before.

 ## PHOENIX-DRAGON CHICKEN

In Chinese mythology, the phoenix is a bird symbolic of feminine beauty, the dragon a symbol of male virility. When the delicate white meat of chicken breast, considered feminine, is coupled with hearty red ham, regarded as masculine, the dish is usually given, mostly by the Cantonese chefs, a fanciful name such as "Phoenix meeting Dragon in a lanterned court" to indicate that they have joined in harmony and bliss. I have simplified the name but not the bliss.

Ham indeed complements and enhances chicken meat in color and flavor. Here it is put between 2 layers of chicken-breast meat, which are then enclosed inside a crunchy batter, deep-fried, and served over a crispy vegetable sauce. *This party dish would serve 6 to 8 easily as a main course.* Without the sauce it makes a marvelous hot hors d'oeuvre, with a sprinkling of roasted salt-pepper.

4 large whole chicken breasts,
   skinned and boned
8 thin slices cooked Smithfield ham
   (*page 492*) or boiled ham

Batter:
1 cup all-purpose flour
¼ teaspoon salt
2 teaspoons baking powder
1 egg
¾ cup water

Vegetable sauce:
2 quarter-sized slices peeled ginger,
   minced
1 medium clove garlic, lightly
   smashed and peeled
½ cup shredded bamboo shoots
1 tablespoon dried mo-er
   mushrooms (presoaked)
2 cups fresh bean sprouts

Sauce seasonings:
½ teaspoon salt
1 tablespoon dry sherry
1 tablespoon light soy sauce
¾ cup chicken stock
Sprinkling black pepper

1 tablespoon cornstarch dissolved
   in 3 tablespoons stock or water
4 cups oil
1 tablespoon sesame oil

Preparations

After boning the breasts, freeze till firm, about 2 to 3 hours—they will be infinitely easier to prepare.

Remove the fillets and cut off the thin tapered ends of the breasts— use some other time. Lay 1 of the 8 oblong pieces of meat across a cutting board. Pressing one hand on top, start at the thicker side and slice horizontally through the middle of the meat to within ½ inch of the far end, yielding 2 flaps of meat with the end attached. Repeat with the other breast halves.

Cut the cooked Smithfield ham against the grain into ⅛-inch-thick pieces. Open the flaps of each piece of chicken, line neatly with a slice of ham, and then close. If you use baked ham, slice it a little thicker than ⅛ inch since it is milder in taste than the Smithfield.

MAKE THE BATTER—Measure the flour into a bowl; add the salt and baking powder. Break the egg into another bowl, add the water and beat lightly until mingled. Add the egg mixture to the flour, little by little, as you stir in circular motions until it is as smooth as a thin pancake batter. Set the batter aside to fluff out while you finish the preparations.

PREPARE THE SAUCE INGREDIENTS—Mince the ginger and peel the garlic; rinse and drain the bamboo shoots and cut into fine shreds. Pour over the mo-er mushrooms ½ cup hot water and soak for 15 minutes. Rinse them well in cold water, discarding hard "eyes," and shred them. Place everything on a working platter in separate piles. Toss the bean sprouts in a pot of cold water and pick out the husks and broken tails. Pour into a colander and let them drain well.

Gather the sauce seasonings within reach of the stove and dissolve the cornstarch. All of these preparations may be done in advance. Cover and refrigerate the chicken.

Deep-frying

Heat a wok or large, wide pot over high heat until hot; add the 4 cups oil and heat until it foams a drop of batter snappily, about 350 degrees. Give the batter a big stir; then dip 1 chicken-breast "sandwich" into the batter, holding together the open end. Let the excess batter drip off a little, then quickly slip into the hot oil. Do three others. Fry them for 1 minute, then gently turn, lower the heat to medium, and fry them for 3 minutes, turning constantly, until they are firm, crisp, and brown. Remove from oil with a skimmer or a slotted spoon and place them on paper towels. Coat and fry the other 4 "sandwiches." When all are done, turn off heat and leave the oil in the pot for the final deep-frying.

Making the sauce

Heat a skillet over high heat until hot; add 3 tablespoons oil, swirl, and heat for 30 seconds. Scrape in the ginger and garlic, stir a few times, then add the bamboo shoots and stir rapidly for about 30 seconds. Add the mo-er mushrooms and stir to mingle well. Sprinkle in ½ teaspoon salt and the sherry and stir rapidly a few times. Shower in the bean sprouts and stir vigorously in fast flipping and turning motions for about 30 seconds; then add the soy sauce, stirring, and then the stock, a little more salt to taste, and a sprinkling of black pepper. Clap a cover over the pan and let it steam-cook vigorously for about 30 seconds. Turn heat low and discard the garlic; give the dissolved cornstarch a big stir, pour it into the pan, and stir until the sauce is smooth and glazy. Add the sesame oil, give the contents a few fast folds, and pour onto a hot serving platter.

Finishing the dish

In the meantime, while the vegetables are being steam-cooked, reheat the deep-frying oil over medium heat. When the sauce is completed, turn heat high and bring the oil back to 350 degrees. Refry all the chicken together for about 1 minute, turning constantly, until very crisp and brown. Remove them to paper towels to drain. Then cut each crosswise into 4 slices and place them on top of the vegetables on the serving platter. Serve everyone at table some chicken and spoonfuls of the vegetable sauce on the side.

辣 子 鷄 CHILI-PEPPER CHICKEN

A chunky, spicy Szechuan dish, using a whole chicken, boned, so that you have both white and dark meat. The chicken cubes are first deep-fried, then tumbled in chili oil and seasonings. Dark and glistening, the chicken is tender but firm. It is aromatic of vinegar, but the taste isn't at all sour. It is delicious hot or cold. *It serves 4 with a vegetable and rice.* Mushroom-smothered Bean Curd and Stir-fried Spinach would go well with it.

1 broiler, about 2½ pounds

Coating:
½ teaspoon salt
¼ teaspoon roasted and crushed
    Szechuan peppercorns
    (*page 500*)
1 egg white, well beaten
1 tablespoon cornstarch

6 dried chili peppers
1 tablespoon minced peeled ginger
1 large whole scallion, finely
    chopped

Liquid seasonings:
1 tablespoon sugar
½ teaspoon salt
2 tablespoons Chenkong or
    cider vinegar
2 tablespoons dark soy sauce
1 tablespoon dry sherry

2 cups oil
2 teaspoons sesame oil

Preparations

Bone the meat as described on *page 252*, skin the meat, and save the wings, bones, carcass, and skin for soup stock.

Pound the leg and thigh meat from the inside with the back of a cleaver or heavy knife to loosen the fibers. Score the other side of the meat (which was next to the skin) lightly with crisscross hatchings. Give the breast meat a few firm but light slaps with the broad side of the cleaver or knife and score the smooth side. Then cut all the meat into about ¾-inch cubes. Put the meat in a bowl, sprinkle in the salt and Szechuan pepper-corns, stir lightly, then mix in the beaten egg white and the cornstarch, stirring until smooth. Let the chicken rest for 15 minutes. You could do this in advance; refrigerate, covered, and bring to room temperature before the deep-frying.

Put the chili peppers, ginger, and scallions on a small plate and mix the liquid seasonings until the sugar is dissolved.

Deep-frying

Heat a wok or large, heavy skillet over high heat until hot; add the 2 cups oil and heat until a cube of bread foams instantly, about 375 degrees. Scatter in the chicken and deep-fry the cubes about 2½ minutes, until light brown, turning them constantly. Drain the chicken and oil in a strainer over a bowl. You cannot do this step in advance.

Stir-frying

Return 2 tablespoons oil to the pan and heat over medium-low heat; toss in the chili peppers, press them with a spatula, and flip and press them in the oil until they are blackened.

Turn the heat high, scatter in the ginger, scallions, and chicken, and stir briskly a few seconds. Pour in the liquid seasonings; stir rapidly in turning and folding motions until the chicken is well coated by the foaming sauce. Add the sesame oil, give a few fast turns, and pour into a hot serving dish, arranging the blackened peppers on top here and there.

香
酥
鷄

SZECHUAN CRUNCHY CHICKEN

This chicken is called *hsiang-su* in Chinese, meaning fragrant and crunchy. It is a specialty of the Szechuan school of cooking. Salted, steamed, dusted with flour, and then deep-fried, this chicken indeed lives up to its name. Very much overshadowed by the famous duck of the same name, it is usually made only as a second choice. But it is delicious and certainly deserves recognition on its own.

This chicken is traditionally accompanied by Chinese Pancakes or buns, but it is also good with rice. It should be served with a delicate vegetable. *It serves 4 to 6.*

1 roasting chicken, about 4 pounds
1 tablespoon dry sherry
1 teaspoon Szechuan peppercorns
2 tablespoons salt
½ teaspoon five-fragrance powder
4 medium whole scallions, each cut
    into 4 sections
2 quarter-sized slices peeled ginger,
    coarsely chopped

1 tablespoon dark soy sauce
¼ cup flour
6 cups oil
Garnish: Sprigs of fresh coriander
    or parsley
Roasted salt-pepper (*page 501*)
Chinese Pancakes or Flower Rolls,
    optional

Preparations

Rinse and dry the chicken. Remove the fat from the cavity and cut off the tail. Press down on the breast bone hard with the palms of your hands to snap it and flatten the frame. Brush the sherry over the chicken, smearing a little inside the cavity too.

Put the peppercorns and salt into a skillet and roast over low heat for about 5 minutes, stirring and shaking occasionally, until the salt is slightly browned and the peppercorns faintly smoking. Pour the mixture onto a chopping board and when cool, crush the peppercorns with the broad side of a cleaver or heavy knife. Add the five-fragrance powder and mix well. Rub this mixture all over the chicken, inside and outside, particularly over the breast, thighs, and legs. Place the chicken in a bowl, cover, and let it macerate in the refrigerator for at least 6 hours or overnight; drain off whatever juice has accumulated.

Steaming and deep-frying

Transfer the chicken to a heatproof bowl and put the scallions and ginger inside the cavity. Steam the chicken over medium heat for about 2 hours, until very tender; replenish boiling water when necessary. Drain the chicken well, brush off the peppercorns from the surface, remove scallions and ginger from the cavity, and blot dry. Brush the soy sauce all over; dust the chicken lightly with flour.

Heat a wok or large, heavy pot over high heat until hot; add the oil and heat until it foams a cube of bread instantly, about 375 degrees. Slip in the chicken breast side down and deep-fry, basting constantly, for 2½ minutes. Turn it over carefully and fry for another minute, basting. Turn off the heat, lift the chicken up to drain with a skimmer or 2 spatulas, then slip it onto a serving platter.

Garnish with sprigs of fresh coriander or parsley. Serve the roasted salt-pepper on the side. The chicken should not be cut—it would break into messy pieces under pressure of the knife. It is so crunchily tender that the meat and bones fall apart easily with the tug of a fork or chopsticks.

Sprinkle or dip the meat lightly in the salt-pepper mixture and eat it with rice. Or wrap it in steamed pancakes and eat them as sandwiches, allowing 3 pancakes for each person. If you don't have pancakes on hand and don't feel like making them, a fast and easy substitute is to trim the crusts off slices of thin white bread and steam them over high heat for 5 minutes.

VARIATION

If you prefer boneless chicken, decrease the steaming time to about 1½ hours. Let the chicken drain and cool thoroughly; then quarter it and bone it from the inside, leaving the skin as intact as possible. Dip the quarters in a well-beaten large egg, then coat evenly with cornstarch, and let the coated chicken set in the refrigerator for 1 hour or longer. Then heat 4 cups oil and deep-fry for 2 minutes on each side, until the chicken is crisp and brown. Cut each piece into 4 or 5 slices and serve with a sprinkling of roasted salt-pepper.

鹽焗鷄 SALT-ROASTED CHICKEN

Within the small realm of roasting, the Chinese do not limit the technique to the indirect dry heat generated by an oven. For instance, at home, where there is no oven, a cook will "roast" by burying the ingredient in salt within a wok on top of the stove or encase it in clay and bury it in hot ashes. In this recipe, the chicken meat is succulent and the skin has a very unusual texture: it is firm but not really crisp; soft but not moist. The chicken is not at all salty. As with Fire Duck, the marinade "stuffing" creates an exchange of flavors. The cheesecloth serves two crucial functions: it retains heat and it separates the bird from the salt to eliminate the danger of its becoming too salty.

This chicken is also wonderful cold—one is very aware of the marinade flavoring in the meat. *Serves 4 to 6.* It would go well with Winter Melon Stuffed with Ham and Stir-fried Spinach.

1 roasting chicken, about 4
    pounds
Marinade: The one for Cantonese
    Fire Duck (*page 302*)

3 tablespoons dry sherry, vodka,
    or gin
Cheesecloth
5 pounds kosher salt

Remove and discard the fat from the cavity. Rinse and dry the chicken thoroughly inside and out. Sew up the neck cavity.

Make the marinade as described for Cantonese Fire Duck, and cool it before you pour it into the cavity and truss the opening very lightly with a skewer or sew with a needle and thread.

Brush the surface of the chicken with the dry sherry, vodka, or gin and place the chicken on a rack in an airy place to dry for 2 to 3 hours. Then wrap it firmly with a single layer of cheesecloth (the overlap on top, so it's easy to remove later), and it is ready for "roasting."

Heat the salt in a wok or large, heavy pot until the salt is very hot. Turn off the heat, pour half the salt into a bowl, and place the chicken on the salt in the pan. Cover the top with the reserved salt. Cover the pot and set it over medium heat for 3 minutes. Then adjust the heat to low and roast the chicken for 2 hours, or transfer the pot to a preheated 350-degree oven and roast for 1½ hours.

When done, remove the chicken from the salt and put it on a chopping board. Carefully unwrap the cheesecloth. Untruss the cavity and drain off the marinade into a bowl. Either cut the chicken in the Chinese manner, as done for the Fire Duck, or carve it Western style. Serve it with the marinade.

VARIATION
Two fresh Cornish hens, each a little over 1 pound, may be done the same way. Sew up the neck skin, fill with the marinade, sew up the cavities, wrap in cheesecloth, bury inside the hot salt, and roast for about 1 hour. They are absolutely magnificent. The drying step is optional.

Skinning a whole fowl
This is not as difficult as it sounds. You are going to remove the skin of a chicken or duck whole, so that the bones may be removed and the meat marinated and combined with other ingredients to make a stuffing for the skin. It's fun and exciting to do and it adds such prestige that a mere fryer becomes a banquet specialty, worthy of any elegant occasion.

Soaking the bird in tap water for 30 minutes before the skinning will loosen the skin and make it more resilient. Do *not* remove the tail until after the cooking.

For equipment, you will need a small, sharp paring knife and a cleaver to crack the leg bones.

Remove the bird from the water and pat it dry. Give it an overall massage to loosen the skin, taking great care not to puncture the skin.

Now, starting with the neck: 1) With your fingers and the tip of the paring knife slid between membrane and skin, cut and pull the skin free of connecting tissue and meat. Roll the skin downward as you go (almost inside out), until you reach the wings. 2) Using the paring knife, cut through the joint to detach the wing, and keep rolling and cutting away the skin from meat until you reach the second joint of the wing. 3) Cut through this and remove the meat plus bone of the upper part of the wing; you now have the wing tip still within skin but only a pocket of skin for the upper part. Do the same for the other wing.

Continue with the main body of the bird, always cutting just in front of the rolled-back skin, which you hold firmly with the other hand. The cutting is particularly delicate over the back, where the skin is tight over the bones. The action should be almost a vertical cutting—keep lifting the skin up and back and carefully scrape the edge of the paring knife against the bones (not the skin!).

4) When you reach the thighs, cut through the joint to detach the whole leg; then roll the skin down to the tip of the leg bones. Put the skinned fowl across your board with the attached skin off to your right, lift the cleaver carefully and chop through the lower leg bone decisively, keeping knobby end plus about 1½ inches of bone with the skin. If you find it easier, place the blade on the bone and bang the top of your cleaver with a mallet. Turn the bird around with the skin off to the left and do the same with the other leg.

Roll the skin down to the cavity and reveal the tiny tail bone, which is attached to the spine. Cut through this bone (leaving the tail still on) and then around the edge of the cavity to free the skin completely. Turn the skin right side up and you have a whole chicken or duck skin with wing tips and partial leg bones, ready for luscious stuffing. There may be little holes until you have practiced a few times, especially if you've used a tender young chicken, but don't despair—patch them with dabs of beaten egg.

BONELESS WHOLE CHICKEN WITH RICE STUFFING

This chicken is skinned, and the skin is filled with chicken meat, glutinous rice, and vegetables. The re-formed chicken is then steamed, coated with a batter, and deep-fried until crisp and brown. It is a rich dish and *will serve*

(1)

(2)

(3)

(4)

4 to 6 as a main course with several refreshing vegetables, such as Vinegar-slithered Green Cabbage, Stir-fried Green Beans, or Stir-fried Pickled Vegetables.

1 large fryer or a small roasting
    chicken, 3 to 3½ pounds

Velvet coating:
1½ tablespoons light soy sauce
1 egg white, well beaten
1 tablespoon cornstarch
1 tablespoon oil

2 cups oil

Stuffing:
6 large dried black Chinese
    mushrooms (presoaked)
1 large whole scallion, finely
    chopped
2 quarter-sized slices peeled ginger,
    minced
3 tablespoons diced cooked
    Smithfield ham (*page 492*) or
    substitute
¼ cup diced bamboo shoots
1 cup glutinous rice
2 tablespoons oil
2 tablespoons light soy sauce
A dash freshly ground black
    pepper
2 cups chicken broth made from
    the chicken bones (*see below*)
1 tablespoon sesame oil

Batter:
¼ cup flour combined with
    ¼ cup cornstarch
1 egg, well beaten
1 tablespoon dark soy sauce

6 cups oil for deep-frying
Garnishes: Sprigs of parsley and
    Carved Tomato Roses
    (*page 254*)
Roasted salt-pepper (*page 501*)

Preparations

Skin the chicken according to instructions above.

    THE STOCK—Bone the meat and trim off any fat and gristle. Chop the carcass into small pieces and put them with all the other bones and trimmings from the meat in a small pot. Add 2½ cups water, 2 slices ginger, 1 scallion, and 1 teaspoon salt and bring to a boil. Cover and simmer over very low heat for at least 30 minutes. Strain the liquid and set aside.

Both skinning and stock making may be done hours or even a day in advance. Cover meat, skin, and stock, and refrigerate. Heat the stock before adding it to the stuffing.

VELVETING THE CHICKEN MEAT—Cut the chicken meat into ¼-inch dice. Mix the diced chicken with the velvet coating, adding each ingredient and stirring before adding the next. Set aside or refrigerate awhile. Velvet it in 2 cups oil according to the master recipe, *page 75.*

PREPARING THE OTHER STUFFING INGREDIENTS— Pour over the mushrooms ½ cup hot water and soak for 30 minutes. Rinse, destem, and slice the mushrooms. Save the soaking water. Chop the scallion and mince the ginger. Dice the ham and bamboo shoots. Put everything in separate piles on your working platter. Rinse the glutinous rice in a strainer and let it drain.

Heat a wok or large, heavy skillet over high heat until hot; add 2 tablespoons oil, swirl, and heat 30 seconds. Toss in the scallions and ginger and press them to explode their aroma. Add the mushrooms, ham, and bamboo shoots, and stir and turn them rapidly a few times. Add ¼ cup of the mushroom liquid, without the residue at the bottom. Stir vigorously a few times, then add the glutinous rice and stir to mingle well. Add the soy sauce and a sprinkling of black pepper. Add the velveted chicken and stir and toss briefly. Pour in the hot chicken stock; when it boils, stir in the sesame oil. Adjust heat to very low to maintain a very gentle simmering. Cover and simmer 15 minutes, stirring now and then to loosen the rice from the bottom of the pan. Then turn heat to the lowest point possible, cover, and let the stuffing mixture steam for another 15 minutes. Pour it into a mixing bowl and let it cool enough to handle before you stuff the chicken.

First fill the wings with stuffing and sew up the neck opening with strong thread. Then fill the body and legs; pat, shape, and mold it with your hands to make the stuffed skin assume its original form.

Sew up the cavity.
The filled chicken should be
pretty firm, but not to the point of
bursting. This may be done in advance; cover and leave it at room temperature for a couple of hours or refrigerate if kept longer.

Cooking the chicken

Place the stuffed chicken on a heatproof plate and steam over high heat for 30 minutes to cook the skin and to give the skin and stuffing a unity. Remove it and drain off any liquid. Combine the batter ingredients and mix to a smooth paste. Spread over the chicken and coat it evenly.

Heat a wok or large, heavy pot over high heat until hot; then add the 6 cups oil and heat until a cube of bread foams instantly, about 375 degrees. To help retrieve chicken later and to prevent scorching, carefully lower the chicken into the hot oil, breast up, with a Chinese skimmer or large spatula and leave it underneath. Deep-fry, basting exposed breast often, until chicken is brown and crisp—about 15 to 20 minutes.

Carefully lift the chicken out with the skimmer (or use another as well), pausing briefly over the pot to drain off the excess oil, and put it on a hot serving platter. Remove the strings and cut or snip off the tail. Garnish the platter with sprigs of parsley and Carved Tomato Roses (*page 254*) and serve a dish of roasted salt-pepper on the side. At the table, sprinkle a little of the salt-pepper over the chicken and then cut the chicken lengthwise down the center. Cut each half crosswise into desired portions.

VARIATIONS

This chicken may also be steamed and covered with a glazy sauce—crispness replaced by richness.

Fill and sew up the chicken as before, then brush 1 tablespoon dark soy sauce all over the bird. Place it, breast side down, inside a wide heatproof bowl, and steam over medium-high heat for 45 minutes. Drain the liquid off into a bowl and return the chicken to the steamer, covered, to keep it warm while preparing the sauce.

Add stock to the drained-off liquid to make 1 cup and bring it to a simmer in a saucepan. Add 1 tablespoon dry sherry, ½ to 1 tablespoon dark soy sauce, and ½ to 1 teaspoon sugar to taste, then thicken with 2 teaspoons cornstarch dissolved in 2 tablespoons stock and 2 teaspoons sesame oil. Stir over low heat until smooth. Invert the chicken on a serving platter, pour the sauce on top, and serve—Stir-fried Spinach is especially good with it.

FOR DUCK—Duck is frequently prepared this way, but since duck meat is tougher than chicken, it must be simmered until tender before being combined with the rice stuffing.

After skinning the duck, bone the meat and trim away all tough fibers. Add the meat to the chopped carcass, cover with 3½ cups water, and simmer them together for 30 minutes. Strain the stock; cut the meat into ½-inch cubes.

Heat a wok or large, heavy skillet over high heat for 30 seconds; add 2 tablespoons oil, swirl, and heat for 30 seconds. Toss in the meat and stir and flip the pieces a few seconds. Add 1½ tablespoons dark soy sauce, 1 tablespoon dry sherry, and ⅛ teaspoon sugar. Stir to coat the meat evenly, then add 1 cup of the strained broth. Turn heat very low to maintain a very gentle simmering, cover, and simmer for 30 minutes, until the meat is very tender. Add it to the rice mixture and proceed as with the chicken recipe, but increase the steaming time by 15 minutes to extract the fat from the skin. The duck skin will be even crunchier than the chicken skin, since it is thicker and fatter.

Of course, duck may also be steamed and glazed with sauce as in the chicken variation. But be sure you skim off all the grease from the liquid before adding stock to make up the desired cup.

EXOTIC SUBSTITUTES /
ADDITIONS FOR
STUFFING

2 tablespoons chopped fresh
coriander instead of the
scallions will give a stronger
aroma.

½ cup gingko nuts or lotus seeds
will lend a mealy texture.

½ cup pitted Chinese red dates
will lend a fruity sweetness.

Turkey

椒
鹽
火
鷄

SALT-PEPPER CURED TURKEY

This is a magnificent recipe that is astoundingly simple to make. Inspired by the traditional wind-cured chickens that were salted and hung up to cure by Liu-ma every winter for the Chinese New Year feasting, I tried to duplicate the effect with turkey. A small but meaty turkey is cured for a week, then steamed and chilled; it yields a large quantity of the most scrumptious meat imaginable. Macerated by salt, the meat is firm and silky with a rich flavor all its own. It does not dry out, remaining luscious for more than a week—that is, if it doesn't disappear in no time at all. It is delicious from neck to tail and can be used not only as a "big affair" dish, but also as something special for buffets, picnics, or just general snacking.

1 teaspoon Szechuan peppercorns   1 small turkey, about 6 pounds
4½ tablespoons salt

Measure the peppercorns into a small frying pan and cover them with the salt. Set the pan over very low heat and roast for about 6 minutes until the peppercorns are smoking a little and the salt is slightly browned, shaking the pan and tossing the salt and pepper with a spatula occasionally. Pour the mixture into a dish to cool.

Rinse and drain the turkey and its neck and giblets. Place the turkey in a suitable shallow pan or container, and put the miscellaneous parts around it. When the salt mixture is cool enough to handle, rub it all over the bird thoroughly, inside and outside, particularly over the meaty breasts, thighs, and legs. Roll the neck and giblets in the salt that has scattered off the turkey into the pan. Cover the pan securely with aluminum foil and refrigerate for 7 days, turning the turkey a few times for even salting.

Drain and discard the liquid and brush off the surface peppercorns from the turkey. Rinse and dry the pan and replace the bird inside, scattering the miscellaneous parts around it. Set up a steaming pot—a large, deep roasting pan or soup kettle. Place the turkey pan on a rack, cover, and steam for 45 minutes over high heat, replenishing the water every 10 to 15 minutes to maintain vigorous steam (see key below). Turn off the heat and let the turkey sit tightly covered, for 15 minutes. This is plenty of time; the meat will be silky. Stick a wooden spoon or pair of chopsticks through its cavity, lift the turkey up to drain a little, then place it, plus neck and giblets, on a platter. Strain and save the delicious juice for cooking noodles or seasoning vegetables. When the turkey is cool, cover with aluminum foil and refrigerate until thoroughly chilled before serving.

• *The key:* While the cooking procedure is simplicity itself, care must be given to the steaming process. The steaming pot must be large so that it contains a substantial quantity of water to generate a strong steam and deep enough for the steam to circulate freely over the turkey. The pan containing the turkey must be well raised so that no water bubbles inside to dilute the flavor. A kettle of boiling water should be kept in readiness over low heat for replenishment. If the space between the pan containing the turkey and the steaming pot is tight, insert a funnel into the crack and add the boiling water through it to prevent the water from spilling into the turkey pan.

Duck

醬鴨 SHANGHAI DUCK

Every region and big city in China has its own duck specialty, and Shanghai is no exception. This delicious firm duck is usually served at room temperature or cold as a preliminary, but it certainly makes a magnificent main course too. The eastern cuisine indulges in some chemicals such as saltpeter or rice soaked in red food coloring to cure and color its meat and poultry, but since I never use them, I have substituted the reddish hoisin sauce for the red rice here—with excellent results.

As a main course, this duck would serve 4, with rice. It goes beautifully with Stir-fried Chinese Cabbage or Marinated Celery Cabbage and White Radishes.

1 duck, about 5 pounds
2 tablespoons salt

Sauce:

2 large whole scallions, each
    cut in two
4 quarter-sized slices peeled ginger,
    each ¼ inch thick
½ stick cinnamon
2 whole star anise
3 cups water
2 tablespoons dark soy sauce
1 tablespoon dry sherry
2 tablespoons hoisin sauce
3 tablespoons crushed rock sugar

1 tablespoon sesame oil

Preparations

Remove the fat from the cavity of the duck. Bring a large pot of water to a boil and slither in the duck. When the water boils again, swish the duck to rid it of any foam and drain it. Remove the tail. Rinse the duck in cold water and pat it dry. This procedure cleans the duck and tightens the skin for better coloring later.

Rub the salt over the outside and inside of the duck. Let it macerate on a plate while you prepare the sauce for simmering.

Put the scallions, ginger, cinnamon stick, and star anise in a double-fold piece of cheesecloth and tie the bundle securely. Place it in a heavy pot just large enough to take the duck; add the 3 cups water and bring to a boil over moderate heat. Cover and simmer over very low heat for 1 hour, pressing and turning the herby bundle occasionally to extract the flavors. Then remove the bundle, press it between 2 small plates over the pot, and discard the residue. This may be done ahead of time.

Simmering

Bring the liquid to a boil again; then add the soy sauce, sherry, hoisin sauce, and rock sugar, and stir until the sugar dissolves. Lower in the duck, breast down. Turn heat to medium to maintain a strong simmer, cover, and simmer the duck for 45 minutes, basting and shifting occasionally to color it and prevent it from scorching. Then turn the duck breast up and simmer covered another 40 minutes, basting and shifting occasionally. Turn off the heat.

Now comes the special basting; it may seem strange at first, but the process is designed to give the duck a beautiful glaze, so do it despite any misgivings. Place a colander over an empty pot and set it next to the one containing the duck. Lift the duck into the colander. Skim off most of the fat from the sauce, add the sesame oil, and bring the sauce to a boil over high heat. Turn off the heat and pour the hot sauce over the duck. Then transfer the colander with duck to the empty pot and bring the sauce again to a boil, and pour it over the duck again. Repeat this showering from pot to pot 4 or 5 times, until the duck is shiny and glazed.

Place the duck on a serving platter and serve whole for table carving, or let it cool and firm a few moments before chopping it the Chinese way (*page 15*). Before serving, brush the small remaining amount of sauce over the duck if you wish.

If you want the duck cold, pour the sauce over it, cover with aluminum foil, and chill thoroughly before chopping or carving.

鹵 鴨 FLAVOR-POTTED DUCK

This duck is first chilled to dry the skin, then deep-fried, and finally plunged into the flavor-pot sauce to simmer quietly. It is deeply colored from the soy-sauce coating and the deep-frying. The skin is firm and slightly chewy and the meat is subtly herby and full of its natural flavor. The duck is good hot, at room temperature, and especially delicious cold. *Serves 4 as a main course.* Spicy Minced Watercress and Stir-fried Shredded Turnip Salad would be lovely with it when served cold.

1 duck, 4½ to 5 pounds	2 large whole scallions
2 tablespoons dark soy sauce	6 cups oil
Flavor-pot Sauce (*page 61*)	Sesame oil
4 quarter-sized slices peeled ginger	

Drying the duck

Remove fat from the cavity, cut off the tail and excess neck skin. Rinse and dry the duck thoroughly. Place in a colander and chill in the refrigerator for about 2 hours. Brush the soy sauce all over the duck, especially over the breast and legs. Pop it back in the colander and let it dry in the refrigerator for 2 to 3 hours or longer. Dry the cavity well before frying.

You can do this a day ahead of time. This drying process is very important: unless the duck skin is dry, the soy-sauce coloring will not be even, and unless the soy sauce is dried onto the skin, it will not only come off during deep-frying but will also make the oil spatter dangerously.

Deep-frying and simmering

When ready to cook, bring the flavor-pot sauce, with the ginger and scallions, to a boil in a large, heavy pot that will accommodate the duck snugly. Lower heat, cover, and keep it hot until ready to use.

Heat a wok or large, heavy pot over high heat until hot; add the 6 cups oil, and heat until a cube of bread foams instantly, about 375 degrees. Slide in the duck breast side up and deep-fry for 2 minutes, basting the breast continuously—lower the heat slightly if the oil spatters. Turn the duck over and deep-fry for another 2 minutes, basting the back as before. Drain and remove the duck and slip it breast down into the Flavor-pot Sauce. Turn heat high to let the sauce boil; then turn heat low to maintain a gentle simmering, cover, and simmer for 1½ hours, turning the duck every 30 minutes.

Drain the duck and remove to a chopping board to firm and cool. Then brush it all over with sesame oil and chop it the Chinese way (*page 15*) or carve it the Western way.

Turning and draining notes

It's not the easiest thing to deep-fry and turn a large whole duck in a large amount of hot oil. If you do it in a wok, make absolutely certain that the base ring of the wok is placed securely over the burner so there is no possibility of unbalancing the wok or splashing the hot oil while you are turning the duck.

The safest way to turn the duck is to slip a skimmer or large slotted spoon underneath, tilt, then gently ease it over with the help of chopsticks, a spatula, or wooden spoon. To drain, lift it above the oil with a skimmer or slotted spoon and anchor the top with a spatula; tilt it and let the oil pour out from the cavity.

VARIATION

If you want a stronger flavor and a glazed look, make this sauce: Heat ½ cup of the sauce, skimmed of fat, with ½ cup chicken stock. When it comes to a boil, add 1 tablespoon dry sherry and 2 teaspoons sugar; stir until the sugar is dissolved. Then thicken it with 2 teaspoons cornstarch dissolved in 1 tablespoon water. Stir until the sauce is smooth, then pour over the duck.

SZECHUAN CRUNCHY DUCK

Aromatic, flavorful, and extremely crunchy, this is a famous Szechuan specialty that deserves all its fame and glory. Just as with Peking Duck, it is traditionally served with Chinese Pancakes or Flower Rolls to offset the richness of the skin. *It serves 4 as a main course*, and might be accompanied by Sweet and Sour Red Cabbage and Stir-fried Cauliflower.

1 duck, 4½ to 5 pounds

Salting mixture:
2½ tablespoons salt
1 teaspoon Szechuan peppercorns
1 teaspoon five-fragrance powder

4 quarter-sized slices peeled ginger
4 whole scallions, each cut into
    4 pieces

1 tablespoon dark soy sauce
⅓ cup flour
6 cups oil
Garnish: Coriander or parsley
    sprigs
Chinese Pancakes or Flower Rolls
    (*pages 452 and 447*), allowing
    3 pancakes or 2 buns for
    each person
Roasted salt-pepper (*page 501*)

Macerating

Rinse and dry the duck thoroughly, discarding the fat and tail. Press down on the breast bone hard with the palms of your hands to snap the bone and flatten the duck, as for Szechuan Crunchy Chicken.

Roast the salt and peppercorns in a dry skillet over low heat for about 5 minutes, stirring occasionally, crush, combine with five-fragrance powder, and rub all over the duck. Let duck sit in the refrigerator for 6 hours or overnight as on *page 281*.

Steaming and deep-frying

Drain off the liquid and transfer duck to a large, wide heatproof bowl. Place the ginger and scallions inside the cavity and steam the duck over rapidly boiling water in a huge pot or roasting pan for 3 hours, replenishing with boiling water when necessary. The long hours of steaming are crucial. Unless the duck is extremely well cooked, it will not be juicy and flavorful inside and the skin will not be as crunchy as it should be.

When done, drain and remove the duck to a plate. Discard the ginger and scallions in the cavity; blot the duck dry. Remove all the surface peppercorns; brush with the soy sauce and dust with the flour, tapping off the excess.

Heat a wok, large pot, or roasting pan until hot; add the oil and heat until it foams a cube of bread instantly, about 375 degrees. Lower the duck in gradually and deep-fry, basting continuously, for about 3 minutes, turning once. Turn off the heat; drain and remove the duck to a plate for a minute. Reheat the oil and deep-fry the duck for 2 more minutes, basting constantly, until it is brown and crackly. Remove from the oil, drain well, place it on a serving platter, and garnish with coriander or parsley. Arrange the Pancakes or Flower Buns around or at the sides of the duck, and serve with a dish of roasted salt-pepper on the side.

Just as with the chicken, it should be served whole at the table. Pull the meat off the bones and eat wrapped in the Pancakes or Flower Rolls.

臨 水 鴨 SALT-CURED DUCK

This salted and steamed duck, magnificent in its rich, pure flavor, is a variation of the famous salted duck of Nanking, which is delicious but salty and hard. I think this version is really better. The duck should be served cold; it makes a wonderful dish for a summer meal, buffet, or as an appetizer or delicious snack. It takes 3 days to salt, but there's no labor—this is a very simple dish to make.

2½ tablespoons salt
1 teaspoon Szechuan peppercorns
1 duck, about 5 pounds
4 quarter-sized slices peeled ginger,
   each lightly smashed

2 large whole scallions, each
   cut in four

Salting

Roast the salt and peppercorns in a small, dry skillet over low heat for about 5 minutes, stirring and shifting, until the salt is slightly browned and the peppercorns are faintly smoking. Spread the mixture on a chopping board and let it cool. Then crush the peppercorns with the broad side of a cleaver or a rolling pin.

Remove the fat from the cavity of the duck and cut off the tail and excess neck skin. Rinse and dry the duck. Press down on the breastbone with your palms to snap the bone and flatten the duck. Rub the salt-pepper mixture all over the duck, inside the cavity as well. Put the duck in a large bowl and refrigerate for 3 days, turning it once a day so that it marinates in the salt water that accumulates in the bottom of the bowl.

Steaming

Drain the duck and place it in a clean heatproof bowl. Put half the ginger and scallions in the cavity and place the rest on top. Steam the duck over medium heat for 1½ hours, replenishing the water when necessary.

Remove and discard the ginger and scallions. Tilt the duck over the steaming bowl (save the juice), then put it on a plate, cover, and chill it until firm and cold before chopping it the Chinese way (*page 15*) or carving it Western style.

Refrigerate the juice, then degrease it. It makes an excellent seasoning agent for vegetables such as bean curd, celery cabbage, or turnips. Dilute it with water to make a soup base for poaching sliced cucumbers or winter melon, or for simmering transparent noodles.

VARIATION

Smoking the duck: After steaming and discarding the ginger and scallions, blot the duck lightly with paper towels. Line a wok and its cover with heavy-duty aluminum foil. Spread a mixture of ½ cup brown sugar (or ½ cup hickory flakes), ½ cup raw rice, and ½ cup black tea leaves over the bottom of the foil-lined pan. Make a rack by crisscrossing four chopsticks to form a lattice—place them far apart. If your wok isn't large enough to handle a whole duck, use a large pot or roasting pan. Line the pan and its cover with heavy-duty aluminum foil and place an oiled roasting rack over the smoking agents. Put the duck on this rack, cover, and coil 2 wet towels around the seam. Turn heat to medium and smoke the duck for 5 minutes. Reduce heat to low and smoke another 10 minutes. Turn off the heat and let the smoke subside a little, then uncover (near a window if possible) and remove the duck to a chopping board. Brush it lightly with sesame oil all over and chop or carve it into desired pieces. It is excellent hot, at room temperature, or cold.

掛
爐
鴨

PEKING DUCK

Peking Duck, a triumph of natural flavor, emphasizes in particular the crackling skin. The duck is first inflated with air between the skin and meat. This stretches the skin, lifting it from the moisture of the meat, breaking the fat formation, and providing space for the fat to melt and drip out during the roasting. Then the skin is scalded with boiling water; this astringent procedure makes the skin drier and tauter than normal. The duck is then dried with a coating of sugar water so that it acquires a deep, rich coloring and a subtle caramel aroma.

To prevent air from escaping, one needs a duck with the head on, available from Chinatown butchers or a poultry farm. In China, specially grown ducks are used exclusively for this dish. They are kept in individual cages and force-fed so that they grow plump with no development of muscle. But Long Island ducks are excellent substitutes, since they are direct descendants of the Peking species.

At a glance, it seems too complicated and troublesome to make Peking Duck at home. True, it is time consuming, but it is not at all difficult. The air-blowing technique is ingenious, and great fun to do. After all, it is quite an experience to blow air into a duck. Once someone came upon me doing it and cried out in horror: "Good lord! She's doing a mouth-to-neck resuscitation with a dead duck!"

It should always be served with Chinese pancakes, hoisin sauce over lettuce petals, and scallion frills. Allow 3 pancakes and hoisin petals and about 1 scallion frill for each person when it is the main course, and one pancake for each when the duck is served with many other dishes. You should always have on hand a few extra pancakes, however. *As a main course for a sumptuous dinner, Peking Duck serves 4 to 6. As part of a small Chinese banquet, it serves 8 to 12.* It goes beautifully with Stir-fried Bean Sprouts and Stir-fried Asparagus.

1 duck, about 5½ to 6 pounds, with head on
2 tablespoons malt sugar (*page 499*) or honey
1 cup boiling water

Chinese Pancakes (*page 452*)
Romaine or iceberg lettuce leaves for petals
Hoisin sauce
12 scallions

Preparations

Have your poultry man or Chinese butcher make the cavity hole as small as possible when he eviscerates the duck. Tell him that you want the neck skin intact with only a tiny slit made about 2 inches above the base of the neck. And have him remove and discard the cavity fat and oil sacs from the tail.

Rinse the duck and drain. Massage the entire body by rubbing the skin back and forth; this loosens the skin from the meat. Make sure you do not puncture the skin, or you won't be able to inflate the duck with air.

Insert a large plastic or glass straw or bamboo tube through the neck hole to the tip of the breast area. Loop string over this area, below the hole, and tie loosely (you need this in place for tightening it fast later). Hold your hand over the neck and tube and blow air in until the duck is as taut as a drum, stopping now and then to rub and roll the skin to even out the distribution of air. Ease out the tube and quickly draw the string tight below the hole. Secure with more loops of string if necessary. Then insert a meat hook, or a hook fashioned out of a wire hanger (*page 115*), securely through the neck bone above the string. While the head is always served along with the meat in China so that one may relish the delicious brain and tongue, you may, at this stage, cut it off and discard it.

If you can't bring yourself to inflate the duck this way, use a clean bicycle, balloon, or football pump with a rubber hose attachment. Insert the hose and inflate the duck as described above.

Bring 3 to 4 quarts of water to a boil in a large, deep pot. Hold the duck by the hook and dip it in and out of the boiling water, turning it from side to side, while you ladle water over the exposed skin. Do this for about 5 minutes until the skin is white and acquires a dull look. Then hang the duck up to dry 6 hours or longer in a draft near a window, over a shower rod, on a back porch, or in a ventilated basement, spreading paper on the floor to catch the drippings.

Combine the malt sugar or honey with 1 cup boiling water in a small saucepan; bring it to a boil over low heat, stirring until the sugar is completely dissolved. Use a brush and paint the sugar water all over the duck, except on the lower wing tips, until well coated. Let the duck dry for 4 to 6 more hours, until it is creamy brown and looks parchment-dry. It is now ready for roasting. This should be done 1 day in advance; wrap and refrigerate the duck overnight and hang it up to dry again for a few hours before the final cooking.

In the meantime, make the Chinese Pancakes according to the recipe and set aside. Reheat them by steaming for about 10 minutes just before serving. Make the Hoisin Sauce Petals and Scallion Frills as follows:

HOISIN SAUCE PETALS—
Cut firm lettuce leaves into petals 2
inches wide, with a cookie cutter, sharp
knife, or scissors. Arrange them on
a plate and spoon a heaping teaspoon
of premixed hoisin sauce (*page 493*)
into the center and refrigerate until needed.

SCALLION FRILLS—Cut 3 inches
of the white portion of each scallion,
reserving the green ends for another use.
Cut ¾-inch deep slits all around both
ends of each piece of scallion, leaving
about an inch of solid

scallion in the center. Place them in ice water and refrigerate for an hour or longer; the shredded ends will curl and stiffen, making balls of lovely green-white frills. These can also be used to garnish elegant seafood dishes, such as the Steamed Whole Fish.

Roasting

If your oven is large and tall, remove all the racks except the topmost one. Cover a large pan with aluminum foil for reflected heat and to catch the drippings, and place it in the bottom of the oven. Preheat the oven to 425 degrees. Wrap the lower wing tips with aluminum foil and hook the duck vertically over the top rack in the center of the oven over the drip pan and roast it for 15 minutes. Reduce the heat to 350 degrees and roast for 1 hour and 15 minutes. Remove the foil from the wings and roast at 375 degrees for another 15 to 20 minutes until the duck is evenly browned. To prevent the grease from smoking in the drip pan, draw it out with a bulb baster when necessary.

If your oven is not tall enough for hanging a duck, place it on a roasting rack, breast side up, in the foil-lined pan. Place the pan on the middle rack of the oven and roast at 425 degrees for 15 minutes. Turn it breast side down and roast for another 15 minutes. Then turn the duck again, reduce heat to 350 degrees, and roast for 1 hour. Remove the wrappings from the wing tips, turn the heat to 375 degrees, and brown the duck for 15 to 20 minutes, drawing off the grease with a bulb baster when necessary.

Every oven has its own idiosyncrasies, so gauge the timing and temperature by watching the duck rather closely—the idea is to lightly brown the duck at the beginning, then with lower heat to cook it through, and finally, with high heat, to give it a deep brown color.

Serving

Remove the duck to a chopping board and have a stack of paper towels ready to wipe away the grease as you cut it. And have a working platter within reach.

Disjoint the wings and drumsticks and place them apart at either end of the serving platter, outlining the form of a whole duck. Then carve away all the skin on the duck with a very thin layer of meat, trying to make the slices as large as possible. Place them on your working platter. Then remove all the meat from the carcass and cut it into pieces about 1 by 1½ inches. Arrange the meat strips neatly in the center of the serving platter between the wings and legs, tucking the odd slivers beneath the large pieces of meat. Then cut the strips of skin crosswise into comparable pieces and lay these over the meat, so that you are creating a symbolic whole duck. Place the hoisin petals around the duck and the scallion frills inserted between them. Serve the pancakes on a separate platter or in a small bamboo steamer.

Let everyone take a pancake, a piece of skin, and a piece of meat, cover with a hoisin petal, fold it up, and eat it as a sandwich, the raw scallion frill inside too. The scallions may also be used as brushes with which to smear the hoisin sauce over the meat if you don't like to eat lettuce with the duck. Of course, you could also munch on the scallion separately.

VARIATION

Not as crackly as the recipe above, this simplified version, using a 5-pound regular supermarket duck and omitting the air-pumping procedure, is nonetheless a very crisp and delicious duck. Served with all the traditional trimmings, it can be magnanimously accepted as Peking Duck with, as the Chinese say, one eye open and the other closed.

Rinse and drain the duck; remove the fat from the cavity and trim off the excess neck skin. Insert a meat hook, or a fashioned wire hook, through the base of the neck bone. Make sure it's secure. Then follow through with the scalding, drying, sugar coating, drying, roasting, and carving as outlined in the recipe.

廣東火鴨 CANTONESE FIRE DUCK

A fantastically delicious duck that is crisp outside and marinade-tasting inside, this Cantonese specialty is roasted with a marinade sewn inside the cavity. "Stuffing" the marinade within the duck not only seasons the meat deeply but also enables the duck juices to collect and enrich the liquid seasonings into one of the most flavorful sauces in the world. After roasting, the sauce is poured out and served over the duck after carving.

This recipe also requires a duck with the head on to prevent the marinade from seeping out. While in China it is also inflated as is the Peking Duck, we can omit that procedure without really altering the spectacular result very much. Unlike Peking Duck, which must be eaten while hot, Cantonese Fire Duck is delicious hot, at room temperature, or cold. It makes a marvelous cold delicacy for a picnic. *It may be served as a main course for 4* with, for example, such vegetables as Stir-fried Shredded Cabbage with Carrots and Szechuan Eggplants.

1 duck, about 5 to 6 pounds

Marinade:
2 tablespoons oil
2 tablespoons minced fresh
    coriander or parsley
2 medium whole scallions, finely
    chopped
1 or 2 large cloves garlic,
    peeled and minced
1 point of a star anise
¼ teaspoon roasted and crushed
    Szechuan peppercorns
    (*page 500*)
2 tablespoons light soy sauce
1 tablespoon dry sherry
1 tablespoon bean paste
¼ teaspoon salt
2½ teaspoons sugar
¼ cup water or stock

2 tablespoons malt sugar (*page*
    499) or honey
2 quarts boiling water

Preparations

Remove the fat and the oil sacs—two smooth flat ovals about the size of kidney beans attached to the tail bone; then rinse the duck and pat the inside dry. Tie a heavy piece of string at the base of the neck and insert a hook securely into the neck bone above it.

MAKE THE MARINADE—Heat a small skillet over high heat until hot; add the oil, swirl, and heat for 5 seconds. Splash in the coriander, scallions, and garlic, and stir rapidly for 10 seconds, then add the remaining marinade ingredients. Adjust the heat to medium low and stir until well blended. Cover and let it simmer over very low heat for 3 minutes. Turn off the heat and let the marinade cool. Then tilt the duck and fill the cavity with the marinade. Fold the fatty skin inward and truss the opening very tightly with skewers, or sew with needle and thread.

Dissolve the malt sugar or honey in 2 quarts boiling water in a large wok or roasting pan over high heat. Holding the duck by the hook, lower it about halfway into the sugar water and scald it, turning it and basting it, for 5 to 7 minutes, just as done for the Peking Duck. Then place it on a rack in an airy spot for 4 hours.

Roasting

Leave one oven rack at the middle level and one at the bottom level. Cover a large pan with aluminum foil and pour in about ½ inch water. Put it on the bottom rack as a drip pan. Preheat the oven to 425 degrees. Remove the hook from the duck, wrap the wing tips with foil, and place the duck directly on the middle-level rack, breast side up, and roast for 30 minutes. Lower the heat to 350 degrees and roast for 1½ hours until the skin is waxy and a deep-brown color. Remove the foil from the wing tips during the last 20 minutes of roasting.

When done, transfer the duck to a chopping board. Remove the hook and skewers and drain off the marinade into a bowl.

Serving

Chop and reassemble the duck the Chinese way (*page 16*), spooning the marinade on top, or carve it Western style. In that case, pass the marinade separately.

Boning a whole fowl

This is essentially the same process as skinning a whole fowl, except that only the bones are removed, leaving the meat attached to the skin.

Again you start with the neck; but instead of cutting between the skin and meat, 1) cut against the bones with your paring knife at the neck cavity and spine to free the meat from the carcass, pulling the skin with

(1)

the meat as you go. Cut the breast and back bones with poultry shears whenever they get in your way. 2) Now you want to remove the bones from the upper part of the wings. To do this cut through the wing joint to detach the upper part of the wing and then cut against the bones to free the meat and skin until the second joint is exposed. Cut through this upper joint and remove the upper wing bone, leaving the lower wing and wing tip intact. Repeat with the other wing.

3) Cut against the breast bone, spine, and back. 4) Free the meat all the way to the thighs. For each leg, disjoint the thigh bone and then cut against the bones almost to the end of the drumstick. Fold back the skin and meat and chop through the leg bone, leaving about 1½ inches at the end, as described on *page 284*.

Cut and scrape against the carcass all the way to the cavity. Cut

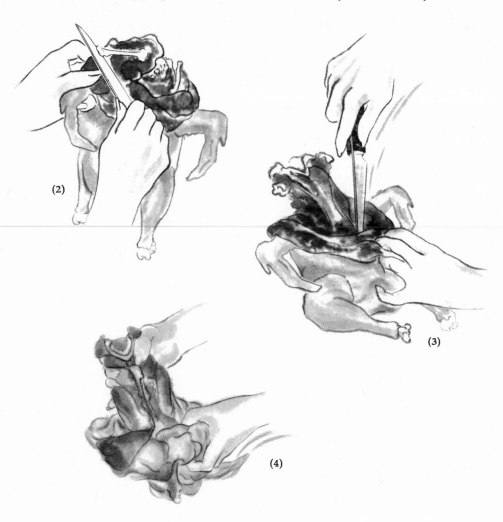

(2)

(3)

(4)

through the tail bone to detach it from the spine, leaving the tail intact. Then cut around the edge of the cavity to release the skin and meat from the carcass. Turn it skin side out and you have a whole boneless bird, ready for stuffing as in the following two recipes.

香
酥
八
寶
鴨

CRISP EIGHT-TREASURE DUCK

Steamed and then deep-fried until golden brown, this boneless whole duck results in a spectacular creation of crisp skin, succulent meat, and a delicious eight-ingredient stuffing that is moist and delicately herbal from the marvelous duck-liver sausage. It is not a simple dish to make, but it is tension free, since all the preparations and cooking procedures may be done leisurely in advance at different stages. *It makes a memorable, rich main course for 4.* Accompany it with refreshingly crisp vegetables.

1 duck, about 5 pounds, boned
    as above

Stuffing:
1 cup glutinous rice
4 links Chinese duck-liver sausages
    (*page 497*)
6 large dried black Chinese
    mushrooms (presoaked)
¼ cup diced cooked Smithfield
    ham (*page 492*) or substitute
¼ cup diced bamboo shoots
¼ cup diced water chestnuts
¼ cup fresh or frozen peas
½ cup gingko nuts

Stuffing seasonings:
1 medium whole scallion, finely
    chopped, or 1 heaping table-
    spoon finely chopped fresh
    coriander
1 tablespoon dry sherry
½ teaspoon salt
1 tablespoon light soy sauce
⅛ to ¼ teaspoon black pepper

3 tablespoons oil
2 tablespoons dark soy sauce
¼ cup flour
6 cups oil
Garnishes: Sprigs of fresh cori-
    ander or parsley, Tomato Roses
    (*page 254*), or Radish Fans or
    Flowers (*page 160*)

Boning the duck

Bone the duck and set it aside. You may bone it hours or a few days in advance. Wrap and refrigerate or freeze it until needed.

Stuffing

Rinse the glutinous rice and drain. Bring it to a boil in a small sauce-pan with 1¼ cups water. Turn heat low, cover, and simmer for 10 minutes.

Lay the duck-liver sausages on top, cover, and simmer for another 10 minutes. Turn off the heat and let the rice and sausages steep for 10 minutes. Then remove the sausages and cut them into ¼-inch dice. Stir them into the rice. This may be done either a few hours in advance (cover and leave at room temperature) or 1 day in advance (cover and refrigerate; then bring back to a creamy consistency by setting the saucepan inside a larger pot of boiling water until the rice and sausages are softened).

Pour hot water over the mushrooms and soak for 30 minutes. Rinse, destem, then cut into ¼-inch dice. Dice the ham; rinse and drain the diced bamboo shoots; dice the water chestnuts; parboil fresh peas 2 minutes or thaw the frozen peas; rinse and drain the gingko nuts. Place all these ingredients in separate piles on your working platter.

Chop the scallion or coriander fine and put in a small dish; gather all the seasoning ingredients within reach.

Heat a wok or large, heavy skillet over high heat until hot; add 3 tablespoons oil, swirl, and heat for 30 seconds. Scrape in the scallion or coriander and stir rapidly for a second to explode its aroma. Add the mushrooms and stir a few times, then shower in all the remaining ingredients on your working platter. Stir them vigorously in fast flipping and turning motions for about 30 seconds; add the seasonings and stir vigorously for 1 minute to blend them. Turn off the heat, add the sausage-rice mixture, and stir to mingle them well. Let the stuffing cool.

When it is cool enough for handling, stuff the wings from the neck opening. Fold over the neck skin and sew the neck opening securely, then stuff the body and legs through the cavity until duck is filled but not to the point of bursting. Sew up the cavity.

This may be done a few hours in advance.

Steaming

Place the duck in a large heatproof bowl and steam over high heat for 1 hour, replenishing the water when necessary. Remove to a plate and blot dry. Brush it all over with the dark soy sauce, sprinkle with the flour, and coat evenly. It is now ready for the final cooking. If you do this in advance, brush on only half of the soy sauce and don't coat it with flour. The duck can sit at room temperature for 1 to 2 hours. When ready to deep-fry, brush on the rest of the soy sauce and coat with flour.

Deep-frying

Heat a wok or large pot until hot; pour in 6 cups oil, and heat until it foams a cube of bread instantly, about 375 degrees. Carefully lower in the duck with the help of a skimmer or spatula, and deep-fry it over high heat for about 5 to 6 minutes, basting continuously and turning once (*see page 294*, until it is crisp and golden brown. Turn off the heat, lift the duck with 2 slotted spoons or spatulas, pause to drain, and place it on a serving platter.

Serve the duck whole with garnishes on the side. Cut it into quarters for 4 servings, or cut lengthwise in half, then crosswise into as many pieces as desired.

VARIATIONS

A 4½- to 5-pound roasting chicken may be done exactly the same way. If duck-liver sausages are not available, substitute regular Chinese sausages.

紅 燒 釀 鴨 BONELESS WHOLE DUCK WITH MEAT AND CHESTNUT STUFFING

This is a superb dish—a stuffed duck that is red-cooked, making it saucy and succulent. *It is rich enough to serve 6 as a main course.* Spicy Cold Celery Cabbage or Spicy Minced Watercress would go well with it.

1 duck, about 5 pounds, boned
    as on *page 303*
1 pound boneless pork loin,
    cut into ¼-inch dice

Slippery-coating:
1 tablespoon light soy sauce
1 tablespoon dry sherry
1 tablespoon cornstarch

3 tablespoons oil
1 large whole scallion, coarsely
    chopped
8 large dried black Chinese
    mushrooms, presoaked, then
    diced
½ cup diced water chestnuts or
    bamboo shoots

½ cup diced cooked Smithfield
    ham (*page 492*) or substitute
1 cup simmered blanched dried
    chestnuts (*page 255*), coarsely
    chopped
2 tablespoons oil

Seasonings:
2 quarter-sized slices peeled ginger
4 tablespoons dark soy sauce
1 tablespoon light soy sauce
5 tablespoons dry sherry
2 tablespoons sugar
2 whole star anise

1⅓ cups duck stock (*see below*)

Stuffing

Put the diced pork in a bowl, add the soy sauce, sherry, and cornstarch, and mix well. Heat a wok or large, heavy skillet over high heat until hot; add 3 tablespoons oil, swirl, and heat for 30 seconds. Scatter in the chopped scallion and stir a few times; then add the pork and stir and toss until all pinkness is gone, about 45 seconds. Add the diced mushrooms and water chestnuts or bamboo shoots and stir rapidly for 30 seconds to mingle well. Pour the mixture into a bowl, add the ham and chestnuts, and toss to mingle. Let the stuffing cool; then stuff and truss the duck as in the preceding recipe. Just as with the Crisp Eight-Treasure Duck, this may be boned and stuffed a few hours in advance, but no more than that.

Searing and simmering the duck

Heat a wok, large heavy pot, or roasting pan over high heat until hot; add 2 tablespoons oil, swirl, and heat for 30 seconds. Lower in the duck and sear it all over, turning it from side to side, until the skin is lightly browned and the duck is as taut as a drum. Remove it to a plate and drain off the oil.

In simmering the duck, you need to suspend it very slightly, so it doesn't scorch. Do this with wooden chopsticks: if using a wok, break the chopsticks at the point where the flat turns round and lay the flat ends in the bottom of the wok. If using a roasting pan, lay the whole chopsticks on the bottom.

Place the duck breast side up on the chopsticks and set the pan over high heat. Add the sauce seasonings. As they begin to boil, baste the duck rapidly for a few seconds. Add the stock; when it boils, turn heat low to maintain a steady, very gentle simmering; then cover and simmer for 40 minutes. Turn the duck breast down, cover, and simmer for about 1½ hours, until tender.

Turn the duck breast up, increase heat to medium high, and baste it continuously for 2 to 3 minutes, until it is glistening and the sauce has reduced and thickened. Turn off the heat and transfer the duck to a shallow platter or wide bowl and remove the trussing threads.

Skim the fat from the sauce and bring it back to a boil. Pour it over the duck. Serve the duck whole, cutting it into desired portions at the table. Actually, it is so tender that it can be torn apart easily with chopsticks.

DUCK STOCK—Chop the neck and bones into small pieces and place in a small saucepan. Add a slice of ginger, a small whole scallion, and 2 cups cold water. Bring to a boil, turn heat low to maintain a gentle simmering, cover, and simmer about 30 minutes. Season with a little salt to taste. Strain the broth through a sieve and skim off the fat. If you are making this in advance, leave a little fat on as a sealer and then freeze. Remove the hard fat later.

窩
燒
鴨

PRESSED DUCK

One of the most popular dishes in Chinese restaurants here, this Cantonese specialty originated in the north and was brought south at the end of the Ming dynasty in the seventeenth century, when the Manchus took control and many people fled the north.

Simmered and boned, flattened, coated and steamed, then deep-fried, this crunchy duck may be served with a brown sauce and chopped almonds or a sweet and sour sauce with fruits. It does involve several different procedures, but each may be done in advance at leisure. *It serves 4 as a main course.* Stir-fried Green Beans and Cucumbers Simmered with Dried Shrimp would go well with it.

1 duck, about 4½ pounds
1 tablespoon salt
1 whole star anise, broken into
    points
2 slices peeled ginger
1 small scallion, cut in two
8 cups boiling water
2 egg whites, lightly beaten
½ cup water-chestnut flour (*page
    502*), combined with ½ cup
    cornstarch

Brown sauce:
1 cup strained duck stock (*below*)
1 tablespoon dry sherry
2 to 3 teaspoons light soy sauce
1 tablespoon cornstarch dissolved
    in 2 tablespoons water and
    2 teaspoons sesame oil

¼ to ½ cup finely chopped
    almonds
6 to 8 whole lettuce leaves
6 cups oil

Preparations

Discard the fat from the cavity, trim off the excess neck skin and tail, and rinse the duck. Then split it in half lengthwise, through the breast, and rub the halves well with the salt on both sides. Place the duck halves in a pot that fits them snugly with the star-anise points, ginger, and scallion; pour in about 8 cups boiling water to cover. Bring the water to a boil again over high heat; then turn heat very low, cover, and simmer gently for about 1¼ hours. Remove duck halves to a plate to cool, and reserve the broth for the brown sauce. (This step may be done hours or 1 day in advance. Cover and refrigerate both the duck and broth in separate containers.)

When the duck is completely cool, remove all the bones from the inside, keeping meat and skin intact. Place the meat between 2 pieces of waxed paper or aluminum foil and press down lightly with the palms of your hands to loosen the meat and squash the fat so that the texture is lighter and crisper when deep-fried. Cut each half crosswise just beyond the thighs, so you have 4 slabs of duck meat.

Dip the pieces of meat in the beaten egg whites, then coat evenly with the water-chestnut flour and cornstarch mixture. Place them on a heat-proof plate and steam over medium heat for 20 minutes. Transfer to a dry plate. This may be done several hours in advance. Cover and refrigerate.

Strain 1 cup duck broth into a measuring cup, skimming off any fat; it must be totally fat free. Of course, if you have done the simmering in advance and refrigerated the broth, merely scoop off the congealed fat.

Just before the duck is ready for deep-frying, make the brown sauce: Bring the broth to a simmer in a small saucepan, season with sherry and soy sauce; add more to taste if you wish. Give the dissolved cornstarch mixture a big stir and pour it into the seasoned broth, stirring in circular motions until smooth. Turn off the heat, cover, and keep it hot.

Chop the almonds in a nut chopper or smash them with the broad side of a cleaver, then rock-chop until fine. Or blend for a minute or so in a blender till fine. Place them on a dish and set aside. Arrange the lettuce leaves in a swirling and overlapping circle in the center of a serving platter so that they resemble a lotus-blossom cup. Set it aside.

Deep-frying

Heat a wok or large pot over high heat until hot; add the 6 cups oil and heat until it foams a cube of bread instantly, about 375 degrees. Slip in the steamed duck and fry for about 5 mintues until all the pieces are crisp and brown, basting and turning them constantly. Drain and place them on a cutting board; let them cool and firm slightly before cutting each into 5 or 6 slices. Arrange them in a mound in the center of the lettuce cup. Stir and bring the sauce back to a simmer, pour over the duck, and shower the top with the chopped almonds. Serve immediately.

VARIATIONS

Instead of the brown sauce, cover the pressed duck with sweet and sour pineapple, lichee, or mandarin orange sauce (*page 97*).

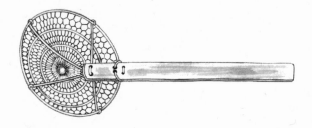

醬
爆
鴨

CHIANG-BO DUCK

This is a stir-fried dish using half a simmered and boned duck, with a tasty bean-paste sauce. Use the other half of the duck, if you like, in the Duck Salad recipe that follows. It is delicious with rice, and *will serve 2 or 3 as a main course.*

Half a simmered and boned duck, (*page 309*), shredded
2 cups shredded green peppers (2 or 3 peppers)
1 cup shredded bamboo shoots
2 dried chili peppers
1 clove garlic, lightly smashed and peeled
4 quarter-sized slices peeled ginger, shredded
1 large whole scallion, shredded into 1½-inch-long pieces

Sauce:
1 tablespoon bean paste
1 tablespoon sweet bean paste or hoisin sauce
1 tablespoon dry sherry
¼ teaspoon sugar to taste

⅓ cup stock or water
1 tablespoon cornstarch dissolved in 3 tablespoons stock or water and 2 teaspoons sesame oil

4 tablespoons oil

Preparations

Cut the duck, skin on, into shreds about ¼ inch wide and 1½ inches long. Cut the green peppers in half lengthwise; seed, derib, trim off the curved ends, and cut them into thin shreds about 1½ inches long. Rinse and blot dry the shredded bamboo shoots. Place them with the chili peppers, garlic, ginger, and shredded scallion in different piles on your working platter. Combine the sauce ingredients and stir until they are smoothly blended. Measure the stock or water, and make the cornstarch mixture in a separate bowl.

Stir-frying

Heat a wok or large, heavy skillet over high heat until hot; add 2 tablespoons oil, swirl, and heat for 30 seconds. Add the green peppers and bamboo shoots and stir them vigorously in flipping and turning motions for about 1½ minutes. Pour them into a dish.

Add the 2 remaining tablespoons oil to the pan; turn heat low, toss in the chili peppers, and press and flip until they are darkened. Turn heat high, add the garlic, ginger, and scallions. Stir rapidly for a few times until the scallions are a gleaming bright green. Add the sauce and stir rapidly in circular motions to mingle with the aromatic seasonings. Then toss in the duck meat and vegetables, add the stock or water, and stir briskly in fast and light tossing and turning motions for 1 minute to heat up the meat and season the contents evenly. Add the dissolved cornstarch mixture and stir rapidly until the meat and vegetables are smoothly and evenly glazed. Pour into a hot serving dish.

VARIATIONS

For the vegetables, you could use, instead, shredded celery and shredded peeled broccoli stems. The chili peppers may be omitted or increased.

涼
拌
鴨
絲
DUCK SALAD

This sharp salad is full of flavor and crunch. *It may be served as a light dinner for 2, as an appetizer for a dinner party, or as a cold dish for a buffet or multi-course dinner.*

Half of a simmered and boned duck (*page 309*), shredded	2 cups fresh bean sprouts
2 cups shredded celery	¼ cup shredded peeled carrots
	Mustard Sauce (*page 131*)

Cut the duck into coarse shreds about ¼ inch wide and 1½ inches long with the skin on. Set aside.

Scrape the celery stalks and then cut all into shreds 1½ inches long and ¼ inch thick. Parboil them in a small pot of lightly salted water for 15 seconds; pour into a colander and spray with cold water until completely cold. Drain well and set aside.

Toss the bean sprouts in a pot of cold water, removing the husks and broken tails. Plunge them into a small pot of boiling water and blanch for 5 seconds. Pour into a colander, spray with cold water until completely cold, shaking the colander and pressing down lightly with your hand to drain well.

Cut a peeled carrot diagonally into slices 1½ inches long and ⅛ inch thick. Then cut the slices into fine shreds. Add them to the bean sprouts, and toss to mingle well.

Pile the bean sprouts and carrots in the center of a serving platter in a mound. Divide the duck shreds into 4 portions and place them around the center mound in 4 neat bundles far apart. Divide the celery shreds into 4 portions and place them, in neat bundles, between the duck shreds.

Make the Mustard Sauce, stirring until the salt and sugar are dissolved. Pour it into a small bowl. Toss the salad at the table.

VARIATIONS

Besides the Mustard Sauce, you may use any of the sauces for White-cut Chicken.

Squab and Cornish Hen

蠔
油
白
鴿

SQUAB IN OYSTER SAUCE

Squab are uniquely delicious: there is a silkiness to the meat that no other kind of poultry offers. The Cantonese excel in preparations of them, either as in this recipe, a stir-fry, or as in the following one, where they are deep-fried whole.

In this recipe, the oyster sauce gives the squab a rich, glowing color as well as a deep, mellow flavor. *It serves 2 with rice and a vegetable.*

2 squab
1 medium clove garlic, lightly
    smashed and peeled
2 quarter-sized slices peeled ginger

Seasonings:
2 tablespoons oyster sauce
1 tablespoon light soy sauce
1 tablespoon dry sherry
1 teaspoon sugar

2 tablespoons oil
1 cup chicken stock
1 tablespoon cornstarch dissolved
    in 4 tablespoons water with
    1 teaspoon dark soy sauce and
    1 tablespoon oil

Split each squab in half lengthwise, over the breast; then chop each half crosswise into 3 pieces, once at the thigh and once under the wing.

Place the chopped squab with the garlic and ginger on your working platter. Mix the seasonings until the sugar is dissolved.

Heat a wok or large, heavy skillet over high heat until hot; add the oil, swirl, and heat for 30 seconds. Toss in the garlic and ginger, stir and press in the oil, then add the cut-up squab. Sear rapidly until the pieces are nicely browned, about 3 minutes. Add the seasonings and stir for 1 minute. Add the stock, turn heat to medium low to maintain a strong simmering, cover, and simmer for 10 minutes, stirring once.

Uncover and toss and turn the squab a few times; then give the cornstarch mixture a big stir and add it to the pan, stirring until the sauce is smoothly thickened. Pour into a hot serving dish.

VARIATION

Fresh 1-pound Cornish hens may be substituted for the squab. Don't use the large frozen ones.

油淋白鴿 OIL-SHOWERED SQUAB

These squab are first soaked in the Flavor-pot Sauce, dried with a honey coating, then deep-fried. The skin is extremely crisp and the meat satiny. The herbal flavor-pot steeping subtly enhances the delicate gamy taste of the squab. *They may be served as a first course for 4 or a main course for 2.* Any of the Chicken Fu Yung vegetables or the Spinach and Bean Curd Gunn would be excellent with this.

2 squab
Flavor-pot Sauce (*page 61*)

4 cups oil
Lemon wedges
Roasted salt-pepper (*page 501*)

Crisp-skin coating:
1½ teaspoons cornstarch
½ teaspoon dry sherry
½ teaspoon Chenkong or cider
 vinegar
1 tablespoon honey

Flavor-potting and drying

Rinse and dry the squab. Tie the necks securely with string (or, if there's no neck skin left, make a sling for them under the wings). Bring the master Flavor-pot Sauce to a boil; add the squab, letting the strings hang over the side of the pot. Cover and when the sauce boils again, turn off the heat and let the squab soak for 1 hour, turning them once during that time. Remove from the sauce and pat dry.

Combine the coating ingredients, mixing until smooth. Brush this mixture all over the squab and hang them up in a draft to dry for 4 hours or longer until ready to deep-fry.

Deep-frying

Heat a wok or heavy pot over high heat until hot; add the 4 cups oil and heat until it foams a cube of bread snappily, about 350 degrees. Hold the squab by the strings and dip them in and out of the hot oil, turning and twirling them, while you baste them; make sure that plenty of hot oil seeps through the neck cavity into the squab. Do this for about 5 minutes, until the skin is crisp and brown. You may set them in a frying basket but they must not be submerged for any length of time—the coating chars easily.

Halve, quarter, or cut each into 6 pieces as in preceding recipe. Serve with lemon wedges and roasted salt-pepper either lightly sprinkled on top or in a small bowl.

VARIATIONS

If you don't have Flavor-pot Sauce on hand or wish a change of taste, do the squab this way: Dissolve ½ teaspoon salt in 1 tablespoon dry sherry, add 1 teaspoon finely minced ginger, and rub this mixture all over the squab, inside and outside. Let them marinate for 10 to 15 minutes in a heatproof bowl, then steam them over high heat for 5 minutes. Drain, blot dry, and brush off the surface ginger. Mix 1 tablespoon dark soy sauce with 1 tablespoon honey and brush this all over the squab. Dust and coat them lightly with a film of cornstarch. Hang them up to dry for 4 hours or more, then deep-fry until crisp and brown.

Fresh 1-pound Cornish hens may be substituted for the squab.

CORNISH HEN IN LEMON SAUCE

Weighing a little over 1 pound each, fresh (not frozen) Cornish hens are excellent poultry. Ever since they came onto the market, I have substituted them for the costly squab with great success. Here they are seared and then simmered with seasonings and fresh lemon juice until succulent and aromatic. *They serve 4 to 6 as a main course.*

4 fresh Cornish hens, each a little   4 tablespoons oil
    over a pound   ¾ cup chicken stock

Marinade:
3 tablespoons fresh lemon juice
2 tablespoons dark soy sauce
2 tablespoons light soy sauce
2 tablespoons dry sherry
1 teaspoon sugar
2 teaspoons sesame oil

Rinse and dry the Cornish hens; chop off the tails. Rinse and dry the livers and gizzards; cut each in half.

Combine the marinade ingredients in a large bowl, stirring until the sugar is dissolved. Add the hens, gizzards, and livers, and rub well all over; cover and let them marinate for 30 minutes at room temperature, turning the hens a few times. If you marinate them any longer, the lemon-juice flavor will dissipate a bit.

Heat a large, heavy skillet until hot; add the oil, swirl, and heat for 30 seconds. Lower the heat to medium, drain the hens, add them to the skillet with livers and gizzards, and sear, turning, until they are lightly brown on all sides. Pour the leftover marinade over the birds, then the stock. When it comes to a boil, turn heat low to maintain a strong but gentle simmer, cover, and simmer for 15 minutes, turning once. You won't need more time for this succulent bird.

Turn off the heat; drain and remove the hens to a chopping board. Quarter or chop each into 6 pieces as on *page 313*. Pile them neatly into a mound on a serving platter. Bring the sauce back to a simmer, pour over the hens, and serve. Needless to say, squab may be done exactly the same way.

Eggs

茶
葉
蛋

TEA EGGS

Tea eggs are so good that they shouldn't be made in small quantities. Not only does their flavor improve with time but they also disappear swiftly. They are excellent as snacks, appetizers, or for a buffet or picnic. They were a vendor's specialty in China, sold on the streets, in market places, theaters, and even in the Chinese opera houses.

Even though they are hard-boiled eggs, because of the tea leaves and the long simmering time within the shells their texture is extremely soft and smooth. The cracks in the shells enable the sauce to seep in, not only giving the eggs a beautiful design but also flavoring them deeply.

2 dozen small eggs	2 whole star anise
4 tablespoons salt	4 black-tea bags or 4 teaspoons
3 tablespoons light soy sauce	loose black tea

Rinse the eggs in cold water carefully to remove any blemishes. To prevent cracking, puncture the wider end of the eggs with a straight pin. Bring 6 cups water to a boil, turn down the heat to maintain a slow simmering, and lower the eggs into the water with a spoon. Simmer them about 5 minutes. Place the pot under a running cold faucet until the pot is full of cold water. Soak the eggs in the cold water for a minute, then tap each of them lightly with the back of a spoon until they are covered with a network of fine cracks.

Put the eggs back in the pot and pour enough cold water over them to cover. Add the seasonings and bring to a slow boil over medium heat; adjust the heat to maintain a very gentle simmering, then cover and simmer for 1½ to 2 hours. Remove eggs to a bowl.

Remove the tea bags and adjust the brine with soy sauce if necessary; it should be a little salty with a subtle aroma of star anise. If using loose tea, strain sauce through cheesecloth.

If you wish to eat the eggs immediately, shell the amount you want and soak them in the sauce for at least 30 minutes. Then serve, cut in halves or quarters, wetting the yolk with the sauce.

If you are going to eat the eggs later, soak and then chill them in the sauce, shells still on. If you want them hot later, rewarm over slow heat until piping hot.

蟹 肉 炒 蛋　STIR-FRIED EGGS WITH CRABMEAT

A delicate but tasty dish using just those basics of Chinese flavoring— ginger, sherry, and scallions. *It serves 4 as a luncheon dish.*

5 tablespoons oil	½ teaspoon salt
2 quarter-sized slices peeled ginger, minced	1 tablespoon dry sherry
1 small scallion, including green part, finely chopped	6 eggs, well beaten, with ½ teaspoon salt
½ pound fresh or frozen crabmeat, flaked	Sprinkling black pepper

Heat a wok or large, heavy skillet over high heat until hot; add 2 tablespoons of the oil, swirl, and heat for 30 seconds. Toss in the ginger, scallions, and crabmeat. Stir rapidly to mingle well. Sprinkle in the salt and the sherry and stir a few times. Pour into a dish and reserve.

Clean the pan and heat again over high heat until very hot. Add the remaining 3 tablespoons oil, swirl, and heat for 30 seconds or a little longer —but don't let the oil smoke.

Pour in the beaten eggs and as they puff up around the edges push the mass away from you as you tilt the pan toward you, so the liquid eggs on top slide down into the hot pan. Repeat this pushing of eggs and tilting of pan in opposite directions rapidly, until the eggs have become soft and fluffy—this takes no more than 15 seconds or so. Add the crabmeat and stir in fast, light motions to break up the eggs a little and mingle in the crabmeat. Add the black pepper, give the eggs and crabmeat a few final stirs, and pour into a hot serving dish.

VARIATIONS

Add ½ cup fresh green peas parboiled 4 minutes or thoroughly defrosted ones with the crabmeat for a touch of color and texture.

Velveted small shrimp (*page 81*) or velveted fish (*page 214*), flaked, may be used instead of the crabmeat. Since you will be using only ½ pound of seafood, cut the velveting ingredients in proportion.

蝦 仁 漲 蛋   OPEN-FACE OMELET WITH SHRIMP SAUCE

Delicious and pretty, this omelet, water-oil fried, offers a fluffy chewiness. *It's ideal for brunch or a luncheon and would serve 4.*

1 whole scallion, finely chopped
½ cup sliced small fresh
   mushrooms
½ pound velveted shrimp
   (*page 81*)
½ cup fresh or frozen peas,
   parboiled 4 minutes or
   30 seconds

Liquid seasonings:
1 tablespoon light soy sauce
2 teaspoons dry sherry
⅓ cup chicken stock

1 teaspoon cornstarch dissolved
   in 1 tablespoon water with
   2 teaspoons sesame oil
4 tablespoons oil
6 eggs, beaten well with
   1 teaspoon salt
¼ cup water with 1 tablespoon oil
Garnish: Minced fresh coriander
   or parsley (optional)

Shrimp mixture

Assemble the scallion, mushrooms, velveted shrimp, and peas on your working platter. Combine the soy sauce, sherry, and stock in a small bowl. Beat the eggs with the salt until light and fluffy. Dissolve the cornstarch. Mix the water with the oil. Group all these bowls near the stove.

Heat a wok or large, heavy skillet over high heat until hot; add 2 tablespoons of the oil, swirl, and heat for 30 seconds. Throw in the scallions and stir and toss for 10 seconds. Add the mushrooms and flip them rapidly for about 1 minute. Add the shrimp; then stir and toss a few seconds. Add the peas and the liquid seasonings and stir for 1 minute. Add the dissolved cornstarch and stir until the sauce thickens slightly. Set the mixture aside on a dish.

Omelet

Heat a large, heavy skillet over high heat until hot; add the remaining 2 tablespoons oil and swirl, making sure you oil up to the rim of the pan. Pour in the beaten eggs swiftly. Let them sit as the bottom firms and a puffed ring forms around the edge. Then turn heat to medium low. Cover and cook the eggs for about 2½ minutes, until the surface has jelled but is still soft.

Spread the shrimp sauce over the center of the omelet. Loosen the edge with a spatula, then dribble the oiled water in from the side of the pan, shifting the pan gently to distribute the water evenly underneath the omelet. Turn heat a little higher, cover, and cook about 3 minutes, until the water has evaporated and the eggs have browned on the bottom.

Loosen the omelet with 1 or 2 spatulas and carefully slide it to a serving platter. Garnish the top with a little minced coriander or parsley if you wish. Slice the omelet as you would a pie or cut out portions with a large spoon.

VARIATIONS

As a substitute for the shrimp, you could use ½ pound crabmeat or velveted cubed fillet of flounder (*page 214*).

廣
東
蓉
蛋

OLD-FASHIONED EGG FU YUNG

The Old-fashioned Egg Fu Yung, as old as the history of Chinese cuisine in the United States, may not be totally authentic, since in China it is never served with a sauce, but it is delicious and extremely easy to make. *Serves 2 to 4.*

Brown sauce:
1¼ cups chicken or meat stock
1 tablespoon dry sherry
2 to 3 teaspoons light soy sauce
Sprinkling black pepper
1 tablespoon cornstarch dissolved
    in 3 tablespoons water and
    2 teaspoons sesame oil
1 cup finely diced cooked chicken

½ cup finely diced onions
½ cup fresh bean sprouts
¼ cup defrosted frozen peas or
    fresh, parboiled 3 minutes
¼ cup sliced fresh or canned
    mushrooms
1 teaspoon salt
⅛ teaspoon black pepper
4 eggs, well beaten

3 cups oil

Preparations

Make the brown sauce: Bring the stock to a simmer in a small sauce-pan; add the sherry, soy sauce, and pepper. Turn heat low, give the corn-starch mixture a big stir, pour it into the broth, stirring in circular motions until it is thickened and smooth. Turn off the heat, cover, and keep it hot.

Combine the chicken with all the vegetables and seasonings in a large bowl, adding the beaten eggs last. Mix well.

Deep-frying

Heat a wok or deep, heavy pot over high heat for 30 seconds; add the oil and heat until a cube of bread foams snappily, about 350 degrees. Ladle in a fourth of the egg mixture; when it forms an omelet, ladle in another one. Deep-fry until the bottoms are light brown, then turn and brown the other side. Sandwich each between 2 spatulas, pressing lightly to extract excess oil, and lift out to a hot serving platter. Do the other 2 omelets. Reheat the sauce until piping hot, stirring, and pour it over the omelets.

VARIATIONS

The filling may be varied with cooked turkey meat, roast pork, crab-meat, or lobster, cooked or raw small shrimp, or cubed fish fillet. Shredded celery and bamboo shoots may be added to or substituted for the vege-tables, but don't omit the bean sprouts—they give the eggs the right amount of moisture and lend a light crunchiness that is essential.

EGG DUMPLINGS WITH DICED MUSHROOMS AND PEAS

Egg dumplings may be filled with a variety of fillings, from minced shrimp, fillet of fish, or chicken breast to ground beef or pork. They may be simmered in clear soup, with transparent noodles, or steam-cooked with stir-fried vegetables, as below.

When fried beaten eggs are later simmered in liquid, they acquire a fluffy, chewy texture. The filling is firm but juicy. The peas add color and the black mushrooms lend a light fragrance. *Makes 12 to 14 dumplings.*

Filling:
¼ pound ground lean pork
1 tablespoon minced lettuce ribs
1 tablespoon light soy sauce
1 tablespoon dry sherry
¼ teaspoon salt
A pinch sugar
A dash black pepper
½ teaspoon cornstarch
2 teaspoons sesame oil

1 ten-ounce package frozen peas, defrosted or 1½ cups fresh (parboiled 5 minutes)
8 large dried black Chinese mushrooms, presoaked, then diced
4 eggs, well beaten
Oil for making dumplings
3 tablespoons oil
½ teaspoon salt
½ cup water combined with 2 teaspoons light soy sauce

Preparations

March-chop the ground meat until the texture is fluffy. Combine with the minced lettuce ribs in a mixing bowl, then add the other filling ingredients and mix until smooth. Prepare the peas and pour hot water over the mushrooms and soak for 30 minutes. Rinse, destem, and dice them. Beat the eggs in a separate bowl just before the dumplings are to be made.

Making the dumplings

Heat a small skillet (about 6 inches wide) over low heat until hot. Pour a teaspoon of oil in the center and tilt the pan slightly to make an oil circle about 3 inches in diameter. When the oil is hot, add a tablespoon of beaten egg and let it spread into a small pancake about 3 inches wide, then let it jell softly. Place a teaspoon of filling a little off center, fold over the egg, and press down with the tip of a spatula to seal the edge. Remove immediately. If any egg should run, fold over the edge or cut with a spatula and discard. The dumpling resembles a half moon. Repeat until 12 to 14 dumplings are made, each time greasing the pan with about ½ teaspoon oil.

The dumplings can be made hours in advance—cover and refrigerate; bring out just before the final cooking.

Stir-frying

Heat a wok or large, heavy skillet over high heat until hot; add 3 tablespoons oil, swirl, and heat for 30 seconds. Turn heat to medium, throw in the diced mushrooms, and stir rapidly for 30 seconds. Add the peas and salt and stir to mingle well. Spread the dumplings over the vegetables; pour the soy sauce and water on top of them. Turn heat to medium low to maintain a strong simmering, then cover and steam-cook for 5 minutes. Transfer to a serving dish, placing some of the green peas and black mushrooms on top.

燴 魚 捲　FILLET OF FISH CARTWHEELS

Cut diagonally to reveal swirls of white fish and yellow eggs, these "cartwheels" make a lovely appetizer or first course. The fish is delicate and moist, the egg wrappers slightly brown and crunchy outside, soft inside. *These cartwheels make a lovely appetizer for 8 or a light meal for 2 with vegetables.*

2 egg-sheet wrappers (*page 162*)
½ pound fillet of flounder or sole

Marinade:
1 medium whole scallion, finely
　　chopped
2 quarter-sized slices peeled ginger,
　　minced
½ teaspoon salt
1 teaspoon dry sherry
¼ teaspoon black pepper

1 tablespoon cornstarch dissolved
　　in 1 tablespoon water
3 tablespoons oil
Roasted salt-pepper (*page 501*)

Make the egg-sheet wrappers and set them aside.

Rinse the fillet and drain it; do not pat it dry. Lay it smooth side down and scrape it with a sharp knife or spoon to shave off the meat, discarding any stringy membranes or bones. Pile up the fish and march-chop it repeatedly until the texture is smooth. Add the marinade and mix well.

Divide the fish into 2 portions and spread evenly over each wrapper; then roll these into 2 rolls. Brush the entire surface with the dissolved cornstarch.

Heat a large, heavy skillet over high heat until hot; add the oil, swirl, and heat for 30 seconds. Pour out half the oil, add the rolls, and cook them for 1 minute on each side. Turn heat low, cover, and shallow-fry each side for 3 minutes. They need this much time so that the center will cook.

Dribble in the reserved oil from the side of the pan, turn heat up to medium, and shallow-fry each side about 30 seconds longer, to brown the surface and draw out some of the oil that was absorbed by the eggs.

Remove the rolls to a chopping board and let them cool and firm a little. Then cut each roll diagonally into 8 slanting pieces, tilting your knife or cleaver slightly so the initial pressure of the cut is on the side—this way you won't squash the soft filling.

Arrange the cartwheels, flat, in a circular pattern on a hot serving platter with a light sprinkling of roasted salt-pepper on top.

MEAT

Meat in the Chinese cuisine is predominantly pork. Scarcity of grazing land and therefore cattle left the Chinese with but a few established beef dishes. Lamb, in great supply in the northern regions, is a staple for the Chinese Muslims, but most other Chinese shun it because they feel its flavor is too strong. The northern cuisine has produced such excellent dishes as Scallion Exploded Lamb and Lamb Pot.

The repertoire for beef has widened considerably today among the Chinese living abroad. After all, what applies to pork is also ideally suited to beef, with only minor adjustments in timing. Slippery-coating is a remarkable preparational technique for beef, making tougher cuts of meat as tender as fillet.

In this chapter I have included not only a large number of spicy stir-fried dishes, many of them Szechuan, but also a selection of unusual and delicious simmered meats that have not been properly introduced before.

Pork

紅
燒
蹄
膀
RED-COOKED FRESH HAM

With its meaty fragrance, this red-cooked fresh ham is a masterpiece of savory flavors, subtly herby with a deep wine taste. Here, through long simmering, the incomparable natural flavor of pork is brought to a peak. It has a size and impressive presence that, as my mother used to say, will anchor the table and focus the meal.

Rock sugar is indispensable to the well-being of this scrumptious meat—it is mellower than regular granulated sugar and it gives the sauce a lovely glossiness. It comes in rocky lumps; wrap a few in a towel and shatter with a hammer into tiny crystal pebbles, then measure with a spoon. The sherry is used at two stages—a smaller amount at first to neutralize the odor of raw meat, followed by a large quantity to enrich the sauce.

The ham is a glowing reddish brown. The skin, passionately loved by many Chinese, is soft but resilient; and the fat, no longer greasy, is as light as custard. A good accompaniment would be a pyramid of steamed Chinese buns (*page 447*) or hot Western bread, with which to soak up all the ambrosial sauce. A platter of Spicy Cold Celery Cabbage and Stir-fried Broccoli Flowerets or Asparagus would be excellent to lighten the meal. *It is ideal for a party of 8.*

Fresh ham, the shank end, about
   7½ pounds
2 tablespoons oil
6 quarter-sized slices peeled ginger
4 large whole scallions, cut in half

Sauce:
1 cup dark soy sauce
¾ cup dry sherry
5 cups boiling water
1 teaspoon salt
4 to 5 tablespoons crushed
   rock sugar
2 whole star anise
1 stick cinnamon, broken in two

Heat until hot a large, heavy pot that will hold the meat comfortably; add the oil, swirl to cover the bottom and sides of the pan, and heat for 30 seconds. Toss in the ginger and scallions, press them in the oil, then add the ham and sear it, turning, until the surface has whitened.

Add 1 cup dark soy sauce and ¼ cup of the dry sherry. Turn the ham from side to side to color it all over. Add the boiling water, then scatter in the salt, 4 tablespoons rock sugar, star anise, and cinnamon sticks; stir until the liquid boils again. Adjust the heat to maintain a very gentle simmering, cover, and simmer for 5 hours, turning the meat every hour, each time basting it with a spoon a few times. Then add another ½ cup dry sherry. Taste the sauce and adjust the flavor, adding the remaining tablespoon rock sugar or to taste. Cover and simmer 30 minutes more. Once the meat is tender, it should be turned with care so as not to tear the skin and fat. Slip a large spatula under the ham, anchor chopsticks or a wooden spoon on the side or top, then lift and pull the spatula toward yourself, easing the meat over to the other side.

The ham is now almost ready to fall apart, moist and glistening. Raise the heat to bring the sauce to a gentle bubble and baste the meat continuously for about 5 minutes to deepen the color of the meat and thicken the sauce. Turn off the heat. Slipping a spatula underneath and holding the side with chopsticks, a wooden spoon, or another spatula, remove the ham to a serving dish. Use either a wide, shallow bowl or a large, deep platter so that the ham may preside over the dish with its imposing presence. Skim the surface fat from the sauce, bring it to a boil, then pour it over the meat, discarding the ginger, scallions, star anise, and cinnamon sticks.

The ham can be pulled apart easily with chopsticks or a fork. It should be served with plenty of the rich sauce.

VARIATIONS

Leftovers: Remove the bone and add a little water to the sauce; then the leftover meat may be simmered with vegetables for another meal. Broad beans, deep-fried green beans, turnips, carrots, and a combination of Chinese black mushrooms, Golden Needles, and roll-cut bamboo shoots are all suitable "extenders" to use.

The meat is also delicious when jelled. Chill the sauce to congeal the fat, scrape it off, then heat the sauce till melted. Flatten the meat in a dish, pour the sauce over it, and chill until firm. Slice thin and serve it on a bed of lettuce or surround it with Hot and Sour Cucumbers or radishes. It resembles head cheese if you leave some skin and fat in it.

紅燒猪肉 RED-COOKED CUBES OF PORK

As casual and versatile as the fresh ham is classic and imposing, these red-cooked cubes of pork make the most basic of all Chinese stews. The light-brown-sauced meat and vegetables are mellow. The meat is very smooth, the bamboo shoots crisp. It can be cooked plain or combined with a variety of secondary ingredients (see Variations for a number of suggestions). As with all red-cooked dishes, it not only reheats well but the flavor improves also.

Since this is on the rich side, a good menu would be to precede it with Cold-stirred Egg Shreds and Vegetables and accompany it with Stir-fried Spinach, Green Beans, or Chinese Cabbage. A side dish of Spicy Minced Watercress would add a sparkle of refreshing hotness. *As a main course it serves 4 to 6 with rice, buns, or bread.*

3 pounds boneless pork-loin roast or butt	4 quarter-sized slices peeled ginger
2 tablespoons oil	2 whole scallions, each cut into 4 pieces

5 tablespoons dark soy sauce

4 tablespoons dry sherry

1½ to 2 tablespoons crushed rock sugar or granulated sugar to taste

½ teaspoon salt

1 whole star anise

1 cup boiling water

1-pound-3-ounce can spring bamboo shoots

Cut the meat lengthwise into 1½-inch-wide strips; then cut the strips crosswise into 1½-inch cubes.

Heat a heavy stewing pot or casserole over high heat until hot; add the oil, swirl, and heat for 30 seconds. Add the ginger and scallions; give them a fast stir and then add the meat; toss and turn the cubes until all the pinkness is gone. Add the seasonings and stir to color the meat evenly. Then add the boiling water and stir. When it boils again, adjust heat to maintain a gentle, steady simmering, cover, and simmer for 1 hour, turning the meat a few times.

In the meantime, roll-cut the spring bamboo shoots into 1½-inch-long pieces. Rinse and drain.

After the meat has cooked for 1 hour, mingle in the bamboo shoots and let the stew simmer covered for another 30 minutes, turning once or twice.

Uncover, turn heat high, and let the meat and vegetables bubble for a minute or so to darken their color and to thicken the sauce—stirring gently with a spoon. Pour into a hot serving dish.

VARIATIONS

The flavor may be subtly heightened by adding 4 tablespoons Tientsin preserved vegetables, *page 501,* and if you add 1 cup water and 1 tablespoon soy sauce then any of the following may be substituted for the bamboo shoots:

12 to 16 medium Chinese black mushrooms: Soak them in hot water for 30 minutes, rinse, and destem. Add them to the stew during the last 30 minutes of cooking time.

1 cup dried Golden Needles: Cover them with hot water and soak for 30 minutes. Rinse briefly in cold water, squeeze dry lightly, and snip off the knobby ends. Add them during the last 30 minutes of cooking time.

4 pieces of pressed bean curd: Cut each into 1½-inch cubes and add during the last 45 minutes of cooking time.

3 bean sticks: Break each stick into 4 pieces and place them in a large container. Sprinkle in ½ teaspoon baking soda and cover with 6 to 8 cups hot water. Anchor with a plate and soak them for about 1 hour until they are soft. Rinse well in warm water to eliminate the soda taste and soak again in warm water for another 30 minutes before cutting each piece into 1½-inch sections. Add them during the last 45 minutes of cooking time.

4 to 6 shelled hard-boiled eggs: Add them during the last 45 minutes of cooking time. The eggs may be cut with tiny slits in 4 places around the middle for deeper absorption of flavor. Leftover eggs may be served as a cold appetizer or a snack.

1 pound string beans: Rinse and dry the beans and snip off the ends. Deep-fry them until wrinkled, as on *page 73*. Add them during the last 20 minutes of cooking time.

1 pound broad beans: Rinse and dry the beans; snip off the ends and snap each in two. Add them during the last 45 minutes.

Cut 5 to 6 canned small abalone into chunky pieces and add them during the last 5 minutes, just to heat them through. They add a subtle sea flavor and a wonderful silky texture. Do not use the large ones—they are tough and their texture is woody.

For variety, you could add several of these ingredients in smaller quantities. Bamboo shoots, mushrooms, and Golden Needles combine well, and so do bamboo shoots, mushrooms, and pressed bean curd or bean sticks. Turnips and carrots are good together. Do not put in more than 3 items, however, since overdoing it would degenerate this lovely dish into a "chop suey stew."

Like all red-cooked dishes, this one may be cooked ahead of time and reheated thoroughly over low heat just before serving.

FRESH SALTED PRESSED PORK

Chenkong, a city 150 miles west of Shanghai, gives China in addition to its outstanding rice vinegar an extraordinary pork, salted with salt and saltpeter, which is known as *hsiao* meat.

There were rules for the making and cutting of this pork in the old days. The first stated that the cut should be a 10-pound pork shoulder or fresh ham.

The meat was speared all over with a thin wooden pick; then a mixture of salt and saltpeter was massaged well into these holes with one's fingers. The treated pork was then placed in a pan to steep: for 1 day in the summer, 2 days in the spring or autumn, and 3 days in the winter.

After the maceration, the meat was soaked in cold water for hours until it was caked with foam, at which time it was scraped with a cleaver in feathery strokes until it was clean and fresh. Then it was placed in a snug pot, anchored down with a thick piece of wood and a heavy rock, and boiled all but submerged in the traditional flavor-pot brine: for 2½ hours in the summer, 3 hours in the spring or autumn, and 4 hours in the winter. During the cooking, the meat was turned every 30 minutes.

After that, the meat was removed to a rectangular molding pan smaller than the meat, so the meat was squeezed into a neat rectangular shape; it was also weighted by a board and rock. Thus confined, it sat for hours until it was firm and thoroughly cold.

After being pressed, the meat was finally dissected into 3 different cuts: the innermost meat, totally lean, was known as the "lantern stick meat"; the surrounding meat—muscle, sinew, and a little fat—was known as the "luscious eyeball"; and the outer portion, a thin strip of meat topped with fat and then skin, was known as the "white jade belt." This last section was the most treasured, since it contained the shockingly luscious combination of resilient skin, satiny and slightly brittle fat, and firm but dewy meat.

My mother's abhorrence of chemicals, shared by me, led Ar-chang to this modified and simplified freshly salted pork, which makes, beyond doubt, one of the tastiest cold cuts in the world.

The texture is fantastic—strong heat, rapid simmering, and weighting all contribute to giving the meat, fat, and skin an amazing crunchy firmness. The dip sauce adds a sparkling piquancy, but the meat is also delicious without it. It is a perfect buffet, picnic, or luncheon meat. Star-anised Fava Beans, Stir-fried Spinach, or Stir-fried Celery would all go well with this. *As a main course, this would serve 10 to 12.*

1 boned whole pork shoulder, about 4 pounds, with the skin on 4 tablespoons salt	*Dip sauce:* Chenkong vinegar Minced ginger

Cut the meat lengthwise into 4 strips. Rub the salt well into the meat all over. Place the strips in a container, cover, and refrigerate for 2 days, turning once.

Rinse the meat briefly in cold water to remove some of the salt. Select a heavy pot that will accommodate the meat snugly in one layer.

Bring 4 cups water to a boil in the pot and add the meat skin side up. When it boils again, adjust heat to medium low to maintain a strong simmering. Then cover and simmer vigorously for 1 hour, turning the meat once during the first 30 minutes and several more times during the last 30 minutes. By the end of the hour all the water should have boiled away, leaving a thin layer of thick, salty foam on the bottom. If there is some liquid left, the heat has been too low—cook until the water has evaporated.

Remove the meat strips and force them into a shallow baking pan—

one that is too snug for the meat. Cover with a flat lid or another baking pan and put on top of that about 15 pounds of weights—books, bricks, whatever. Weight the meat for 2 to 3 hours until it is shaped and firm. Transfer to a plate, cover, and chill until completely cold.

Take the amount you need and cut the strips crosswise into ⅛-inch slices. Serve with the vinegar and ginger sauce on the side, allowing about 1 tablespoon vinegar and ½ teaspoon finely minced ginger for each person.

The meat keeps well in the refrigerator for a week to 10 days.

VARIATION

If a whole shoulder seems to be too much meat for you as an initial experiment, select a large shoulder that will yield about 5 pounds of meat when boned. Use 3 pounds for red-cooking (*page 326*) and 2 pounds for salting. In that case, decrease the salt to 2 tablespoons and the water to 2 cups.

白切肉 SLICED PORK WITH TIGER SAUCE

The stalwart northerners of China offer us not only a robust cuisine but strong titles as well, such as "exploded" and "scorched" meats, and this charmingly ferocious sauce, aptly named the tiger sauce. It is puréed garlic further spiced with chili-pepper oil, though fluffed and tamed a little by the thick sesame oil. Definitely not for refined tastes or occasions, but a vivid treat for those with lion-hearted appetites. It is really too strong for a main course, but is good for a multi-course Chinese dinner, where it may be relished in small portions with a variety of other tastes and textures. Any of the light stir-fried cabbage dishes would go well with it. *Serves 10 on a buffet.*

1 pound boneless loin of pork
   in 1 piece
2 quarter-sized slices peeled ginger
1 small whole scallion

Sauce:
6 to 10 large cloves garlic, peeled
   and crushed
¼ teaspoon salt dissolved in
   1 tablespoon water
2 tablespoons dark soy sauce
1 tablespoon chili-pepper oil
   (*page 489*)
1 tablespoon sesame oil

Garnish: Sprigs of fresh coriander
   or parsley

Put the pork with the ginger and scallion in a saucepan that fits the meat snugly. Pour in boiling water to cover to 1 inch above the meat. When it boils again, turn heat to medium low to maintain a strong simmering, cover, and simmer for about 40 to 45 minutes, until no pink juice runs out when meat is poked with a chopstick. Remove to a plate to let it drain, firm, and cool.

While the meat is sitting, make the sauce: Smash the peeled garlic well with the broad side of a cleaver or knife. Put the cloves in a mortar (or any small metal bowl—something that won't break) and grind them fine, with a pestle, the handle of the cleaver, or a handleless rolling pin. They should have the consistency of a purée.

Put the garlic paste in a bowl, add the other seasonings, and stir until smooth. Cover until ready to use. The sauce may be made a few hours in advance.

When ready to serve, slice the meat crosswise into paper-thin slices, arrange them in overlapping lines or circles on a platter, and pour the sauce on top. Garnish with a few sprigs of coriander or parsley. This overlapping arrangement is important—most pieces are then lightly covered rather than soaked by the strong sauce. The garlic, of course, may be decreased to 3 or 4 cloves.

沙鍋獅子頭 CASSEROLE OF CLEAR-SIMMERED LION'S HEAD

These meatballs are so named because of their huge size. Their wonderful light texture will never be apparent when such unmentionable foreign substances as breadcrumbs or cornflakes are added, as is done in some poor recipes. It is the result of blending minute grains of pork fat with the lean meat, where they act not only as little cushions but also as moisturizers for the meat throughout the cooking.

The authentic version from Yangchow, where the dish originated and gained national fame, calls for equal parts of lean meat and fat, each to be hand-minced separately. With our consciousness of time and cholesterol, this requirement is hard to comply with. By using moderately fatty pork and resorting to machine grinding with the final polish of hand march-chopping, you can still make the most luscious meatballs on earth.

This is basically a carefree dish to make, since once the meatballs are simmering in the pot they require no attention and, in fact, they should be left undisturbed. There are some requirements, however: you must use a rich meat or chicken stock, so that even though the meatballs are lightly seasoned they will be very savory; you must use a wide casserole, so that the meatballs may be placed in one layer without crowding; and you should use an attractive casserole, preferably earthenware, so that it may be served directly from the stove to the table to retain the heat.

Lion's Head is ideal for a buffet table. Set over Sterno or a candle, in its original casserole or a chafing dish, it remains hot and delicious for hours. In spite of their melting consistency, the meatballs do not fall apart during prolonged or repeated heating. However, if this is to be cooked in advance and reheated for a prolonged buffet affair over table heating, use only the Chinese cabbage. Too much cooking would turn the delicate celery cabbage sour. The broth, by now a rich sauce thick with juicy cabbage, should be served along with the meat. Plenty of rice or crusty bread should accompany the dish. *It would serve 4 to 6 as a main course and 8 to 12 as part of a buffet, where each guest spoons off only part of a meatball.*

2 pounds ground pork, loin or butt

Seasonings:
2½ tablespoons light soy sauce
2 tablespoons dry sherry
¼ teaspoon salt
½ teaspoon sugar
3 tablespoons scallion-ginger juice
   (see below)

2 egg whites, well beaten
2 tablespoons cornstarch dissolved
   in ½ cup cold meat or
   chicken stock
2 quarter-sized slices peeled ginger
1½ pounds Chinese or celery
   cabbage, cut into 2-inch pieces
3 tablespoons cornstarch dissolved
   in 5 tablespoons water
2½ cups meat or chicken stock
2 tablespoons oil
1 teaspoon salt

Scallion-ginger juice

Cut a medium whole scallion into 4 sections; hold in a bundle and chop closely into fine pieces. Smash 3 quarter-sized slices of peeled ginger with the broad side of a cleaver, then chop the pulp a few times to break it into fine minces. Soak the scallions and ginger in 3 tablespoons water for 10 to 15 minutes, covered, then strain the juice through a strainer, pressing the aromatics to extract all the liquid.

Preparations

March-chop the meat until the formation is loosened and the texture is smooth and fine, but not pasty. Place it in a large mixing bowl, add the soy sauce, sherry, salt, sugar, and scallion-ginger juice, and mix well. The best way—to me the only way—to mix a large quantity of meat is to use your fingers. Dig your hand into the meat and scoop up a handful and scatter it back rapidly while you lightly squeeze and rub with your finger tips. Repeat the action quickly a few times to season the meat evenly. Add the beaten egg whites and the 2 tablespoons dissolved cornstarch and mix vigorously in a circular motion until the meat is smooth and fluffy, using either your hand, chopsticks, or a wooden spoon. Cover and let it set in the refrigerator for 30 minutes or longer.

Peel and slice the ginger. If using Chinese cabbage, cut off the root end, wash the stalks, and shake off excess water. Pile them together and cut them crosswise into 2-inch pieces. For celery cabbage remove tough outer leaves, cut off root stem, slice into 2-inch sections, toss in a colander under running water, and shake dry lightly. Up to this point, you could do all this hours before cooking.

Stir-frying and simmering

Dissolve the 3 tablespoons cornstarch in a large bowl. Heat the stock in a casserole, preferably earthenware, over low heat as you stir-fry the cabbage.

Heat a large, heavy skillet over high heat until hot; add 2 tablespoons oil, swirl, and heat for 30 seconds. Toss in the ginger, press it in the oil briefly, scatter in the cabbage, and stir briskly a few times. Sprinkle in the salt and stir in fast tossing motions for about 1 minute. Turn off the heat and scrape about three-quarters of the cabbage, without the pan liquid, into the casserole, leaving the remaining portion in the pan or a dish for later use. Keep the stock faintly simmering over low heat as you form the meatballs.

Divide the meat roughly into 4 portions. Give the dissolved cornstarch a big stir and then wet the palms of your hands with the mixture. Scoop up one portion of the meat and bounce it rapidly between your hands lightly (see illustration *page 176*) a few times to form it into a smooth ball, dipping your hands in the cornstarch mixture in between bouncing, to coat it well with the starch. Drop it gently into the casserole of simmering cabbage. Repeat until all four balls are made and placed inside the casserole, side by side, not overlapping. Cover the top with the remaining cabbage, and bring it to a gentle boil over medium heat. Adjust heat to maintain a very gentle simmering, cover, and simmer for 3 hours. Make sure the meatballs are well enclosed by the cabbage so that they will not scorch on the bottom or harden or discolor on the top.

Turn off the heat and skim off as much fat as possible. Bring the mixture back to a gentle boil, cover, and take the casserole to the table to serve. Lion's Head may be done a few hours or 1 day in advance. Reheat over extremely low heat until the meatballs are hot all the way through.

Omit the skimming if you chill it overnight; the congealed fat can be scraped off before reheating.

Doubling the recipe

If you wish to double the meat to 4 pounds for a large crowd, change the seasonings to: 5 tablespoons light soy sauce, 4 tablespoons dry sherry, 1 teaspoon salt, 1½ teaspoons sugar, 4 tablespoons scallion-ginger juice. Use 3 egg whites and 3 tablespoons cornstarch dissolved in 1 cup stock. Increase the simmering stock to 4 cups and the cabbage to 2½ pounds. Stir-fry the cabbage in 3 tablespoons oil with 4 slices ginger and 1½ teaspoons salt. The scallion and ginger for the juice need not be increased; add an extra tablespoon water and soak a few minutes longer, rubbing them with your fingers before straining. For forming the balls use 5 tablespoons cornstarch to 8 tablespoons water.

回 TWICE-COOKED PORK
鍋
肉

This Szechuan specialty involves simmering the meat first, then stir-frying it in a hot sauce with green peppers. Reddish in color and spicy in flavor, the meat is firm and the peppers crisp. It is not saucy, but glisteningly moist. *It would serve 4 as a main course* with appetizers, rice, and any of the light stir-fried vegetables, particularly the cabbage ones.

1 pound boneless pork loin in 1 piece	*Sauce:* 1 tablespoon hot bean paste
2 quarter-sized slices peeled ginger	(*page 486*)
2 medium-sized green peppers	2 tablespoons sweet bean paste
2 large cloves garlic, crushed and peeled	(*page 486*) 1 tablespoon dark soy sauce
2 medium-sized whole scallions, cut into 2-inch pieces	1 tablespoon dry sherry 1½ to 2 teaspoons sugar to taste 2 tablespoons water

4 tablespoons oil
¼ teaspoon salt
1 teaspoon sesame oil

Simmering

Do not trim the fat from the meat—the meat would be dry if completely lean. Cover with boiling water to 1 inch above the meat in a small pot, add the ginger, and bring to a boil. Skim off any foam, turn heat to medium low to maintain a strong simmering, cover, and simmer for 40 minutes. Drain the meat, then cover and chill it in the refrigerator for a few hours until it is very firm. You may cook and chill the meat a day or two in advance, but do not slice it until you are ready to stir-fry it.

Stir-frying

Cut the meat lengthwise into 2 strips; then cut the strips crosswise into ⅛-inch-thick slices. Seed, derib, and cut the green peppers into pieces approximating the size and shape of the meat, trimming off the curved tips so the pieces lie almost flat. Do the garlic and scallions. Then put the peppers, garlic, scallions, and meat in separate piles on your working platter. Mix the sauce ingredients in a bowl and set out the sesame oil.

Heat a wok or large, heavy skillet over high heat until hot; add 2 tablespoons oil, swirl, and heat for 30 seconds. Lower the heat to medium, toss in the peppers, sprinkle in the salt, and stir rapidly for about 2 minutes; pour them into a dish. They should be softly crisp, not limp.

Add the remaining 2 tablespoons oil to the pan; toss in the garlic cloves and press them in the oil. Reduce heat to medium, add the pork and scallions, and toss and turn them briskly for about 3 minutes, until the meat is stiff and brown.

Add the peppers without any oil residue, and stir and toss in sweeping motions to mingle them well. Turn heat high, pour in the sauce, and stir in fast folding motions until the contents are well coated by the sauce. Add the sesame oil, give a few rapid turns, and pour into a hot serving dish.

VARIATIONS

Two pieces of pressed bean curd (*page 486*) may be added for a satiny touch. Cut them on a slant from the top to yield wider pieces approximating the size and shape of the meat and peppers. One-half cup sliced bamboo shoots may also be added, but don't use any vegetables that will yield moisture to dilute the sauce or soften the general firm characteristics of this spunky dish.

If you want to put some leftover rare roast beef to good use, slice it against the grain, then cut the slices into pieces like the pork and proceed as before, only decreasing the stir-frying with garlic and scallions to 1 minute.

PORK WITH PEPPERS AND BAMBOO SHOOTS

This is a dainty, light, and refreshing dish. The meat and vegetables are stir-fried separately, then blended without any thickening. *It makes a good dinner for 2 if you precede it with a thick soup, such as Shrimp "Gunn," and accompany it with rice.*

½ pound boneless pork, loin or
  butt

Marinade:
1 tablespoon dark soy sauce
1 tablespoon dry sherry
½ teaspoon sugar

1 large green pepper
½ cup shredded bamboo shoots
3 tablespoons oil
1 tablespoon light soy sauce
1 tablespoon dry sherry
Pinch of salt
¼ teaspoon sugar
¼ cup boiling water
2 teaspoons sesame oil

Preparations

Freeze the meat until firm to make the cutting easier. Cut meat cross-wise into slices a little thinner than ¼ inch thick. Line them up into a slanting stack and cut them crosswise into thin shreds about 1½ inches long. Toss them in bowl to separate them. Add the marinade, mix well, and let them marinate while you prepare the vegetables.

Cut the green pepper in half, remove seeds and ribs; trim off the curved ends. Then shred the pepper lengthwise into strips the same size as the meat. Rinse and shred the bamboo shoots. If you use the canned shredded ones, rinse and drain well.

Stir-frying

Heat a wok or large, heavy skillet over high heat until hot; add 1 tablespoon oil, swirl, and heat for 30 seconds. Toss in the vegetables and stir in fast flipping and turning motions for about 30 seconds. Add the soy sauce, sherry, salt, and sugar and stir rapidly in the same motions for 1 minute. Scrape the vegetables into a dish.

Clean the pan and heat it until very hot. Add the remaining 2 table-spoons oil, swirl, and heat 30 seconds. Scatter in the meat and stir in fast shaking, poking, and tossing motions to separate the shreds, about 1 minute. Add the boiling water, even out the meat, cover, and steam-cook vigorously over medium-high heat for about 1½ to 2 minutes, until the pan begins to crackle.

Uncover, stir the meat a few times, then pour in the vegetables. Stir them in fast turning motions for about 30 seconds. Add the sesame oil, give mixture a few sweeping folds, and pour into a hot serving dish.

VARIATIONS

A half cup of shredded carrots, celery, or tender unwaxed cucumber skins may be added to the dish or equal amounts substituted for the pepper or bamboo shoots.

Beef may be used instead of pork: Shred ½ pound flank steak against the grain and let it stand in the marinade, adding 2 teaspoons cornstarch and 2 teaspoons oil. Slippery-coat it through 1 cup hot oil as described on *page 85,* and drain. Stir-fry the vegetables as before, then add the beef and blend. This results in a softer version of the dish, since there is a little cornstarch to keep the beef from toughening.

木
樨
肉
MO-SHU PORK

In Chinese *Mo-shu* means yellow cassia blossoms. They are symbolized here by the tiny pieces of scrambled eggs that are mingled into this shredded meat and vegetable dish. It is northern in origin, traditionally served with steamed pancakes into which one rolls the meat, but it's just as good with rice. It's both fluffy and full of crunch. *There is enough filling for 12 pancakes, and they make a nice meal for 4 with appetizers and dessert.*

½ pound boneless pork, loin or
    butt

Marinade:
2 teaspoons light soy sauce
1 teaspoon dry sherry
2 teaspoons cornstarch dissolved
    in 1 tablespoon water

Scrambled eggs:
1½ tablespoons oil
2 eggs, well beaten with
    ¼ teaspoon salt

¼ cup Golden Needles (about 30)
2 tablespoons mo-er mushrooms
½ cup shredded bamboo shoots
4 tablespoons oil
½ teaspoon salt
⅓ cup chicken stock or water
2 to 3 teaspoons light soy sauce
2 teaspoons dry sherry
½ teaspoon sugar
1 teaspoon sesame oil
Optional: Chinese Pancakes
    (*page 452*)

Preparations

Cut the meat against the grain into slices a little thinner than ¼ inch thick, then into julienne shreds about 1½ inches long. Toss them in a mixing bowl with your fingers, separating the shreds. Add the marinade, mix well, and let the meat marinate for 30 minutes. These steps may be done in advance and the meat refrigerated.

Cover the Golden Needles and mo-er mushrooms separately with hot water and soak for 30 minutes. Rinse them well and drain. Cut off and discard the knobby ends of the Golden Needles; then cut them in half. Tear the mo-er mushrooms into small pieces, discarding the hard "eyes" if any. Rinse and drain the shredded bamboo shoots. Place all the vegetables on your working platter. Beat the eggs with the salt.

Stir-frying

Heat a wok or large, heavy skillet over high heat until very hot; add 1½ tablespoons oil, swirl, and heat for 30 seconds. Pour in the eggs and swirl the pan quickly. The instant the eggs puff up around the edges push them away from you with a spatula as you tilt the pan toward you, so that the liquid eggs on top slide down into the hot pan. Repeat this pushing and tilting a few times with lightning speed until the eggs are no longer running but have become soft and fluffy, then poke and shake them rapidly with the tip of the spatula to break them into tiny pieces. Scrape them immediately into a dish. The actions should be extremely fast, so the eggs won't have any time to toughen.

Wipe the pan and add 2 tablespoons oil, swirl, and heat for a few seconds over high heat until hot. Scatter in the vegetables and stir rapidly in scooping, turning, and tossing motions a few times to sear them in oil. Sprinkle in ½ teaspoon salt and stir vigorously, in motions as before, for about 1½ minutes. Remove them to a dish.

Wipe the pan and add the last 2 tablespoons oil, swirl, and heat until hot. Scatter in the meat and stir, shake, and toss rapidly for about 1 minute, until all the pinkness is gone. Add the stock or water, even out the contents, cover, and let the meat steam-cook vigorously for about 1½ minutes. Add the vegetables, then the soy sauce, sherry, and sugar, and stir rapidly for 30 seconds to mingle them. Scatter in the scrambled eggs and stir them in fast tossing and turning motions for another 30 seconds. Sprinkle the top with the sesame oil, give the contents a few sweeping folds, and pour into a hot serving dish. Serve with Chinese Pancakes or rice.

VARIATIONS

Omit the scrambled eggs and you have a delicious meat and vegetable dish. And instead of bamboo shoots you could use shredded peeled broccoli stems, Chinese, celery, or green cabbage. In that case, increase the stir-frying by 1 minute or longer until the vegetables are soft but not completely limp.

A half-pound shredded breast of chicken, flank steak, or the small shrimp known as TT shrimp may be substituted for the pork. In these cases, omit the steam-cooking procedure. Scramble the eggs, stir-fry the vegetables, then stir-fry the chicken, beef, or shrimp for about 1 minute until done. Proceed directly to adding the vegetables and eggs.

公 SPICY PORK WITH PEANUTS
保
鷄
丁

A hot dish of charred chili peppers, satiny meat, and crunchy peanuts, this is full of spirit and chewy goodness. The dash of vinegar in the sauce gives it a teasing aroma. It is definitely a dish to be eaten with plenty of rice and vegetables. The refreshing Sliced Zucchini and Shredded Carrots is an excellent accompaniment, since, even though also stir-fried, it may be done ahead of time for room-temperature serving. *Dainty but meaty, this recipe serves 3 or 4 as a main dish.*

1 pound boneless pork, loin or
    butt, diced

Marinade:
1 tablespoon dark soy sauce
1 tablespoon cornstarch
1 tablespoon oil

4 cups water
2 tablespoons oil
4 dried chili peppers
3 quarter-sized slices peeled ginger,
    minced

Sauce:
1 teaspoon cornstarch
1 tablespoon dry sherry
1½ tablespoons dark soy sauce
2 teaspoons Chenkong or
    red-wine vinegar
2 teaspoons sugar
¼ teaspoon salt
1 teaspoon sesame oil

½ cup salted peanuts

Preparations

Slice, shred, and finally dice the meat into ¼-inch cubes. Place the meat in a bowl, add the soy sauce, and mix well; add the cornstarch and stir until smoothly coated, then add the oil and stir in circular motions to blend well. Marinate for 30 minutes or longer in the refrigerator.

Bring 4 cups water to a rolling boil in a saucepan; give the marinated meat a few big circular stirs, then drop it into the boiling water. Stir gently to separate the pieces for about 1 minute, until it comes to a boil again. Stir and let it cook for another minute. Pour into a colander to drain. Transfer the meat, now cooked and satiny, to a dish. This may be done hours in advance. Cover and refrigerate; bring to room temperature before final cooking.

Place the chili peppers and minced ginger on a small dish. Just before cooking, mix the sauce ingredients until the cornstarch and sugar are dissolved. Any sauce involving vinegar should be done at the last moment—otherwise the piquant aroma would dissipate. Set the peanuts nearby.

Stir-frying

Heat a wok or large, heavy skillet over high heat until hot; add the oil, swirl, and turn heat to low. Toss in the chili peppers and press them in the oil, flipping back and forth, until they are darkened.

Scatter in the ginger and stir briskly a few times. Then turn heat high, add the meat, and stir briskly in turning and tossing motions for about 45 seconds to skid and roll the pieces in the spicy oil. Give the sauce mixture a big stir, pour over the meat, and stir in sweeping and turning motions until the sauce coats the meat evenly. Pour it into a serving dish and shower the top with the peanuts. Mingle them at the table before serving.

VARIATIONS

Velveted chicken (*page 75*) or shrimp (*page 81*) or slippery-coated beef (*page 85*) may be substituted for the pork. And, instead of peanuts, you could use cashew nuts, walnuts, or pine nuts. The hotness may be adjusted to personal preference. A good guide: 4 chili peppers are medium hot, 6 are hot, and 7 to 8 are devastating.

The texture of the meat can be varied. If you like your meat natural, marinate with the soy sauce only, and then stir-fry it in 3 tablespoons oil until the diced meat is no longer pink. Add ⅓ cup meat or chicken stock and steam-cook for about 3 minutes over medium heat. Remove to a dish. Darken the chili peppers in 1 tablespoon oil, return the meat, and cook to conclusion as before. Instead of being satiny, the meat is tender but firm.

PORK IN HOT BEAN SAUCE

Coated with sauce and rich in color, the dainty pieces of meat and vegetables are tasty and subtly hot. This dish is moist and thick, and goes extremely well with rice and a stir-fried cabbage. *Serves 2.*

½ pound lean pork, loin or
    butt, diced

Marinade:
2 teaspoons dark soy sauce
2 teaspoons dry sherry
2 teaspoons cornstarch
2 teaspoons oil

1 large clove garlic, lightly
    smashed and peeled
1 large green pepper, diced
    (about 1 cup)
½ cup diced bamboo shoots
1 large whole scallion, finely
    chopped
2 quarter-sized slices peeled ginger

Sauce:
2 teaspoons bean paste
2 teaspoons hoisin sauce
2 teaspoons sugar
1 tablespoon dry sherry
2 teaspoons dark soy sauce
2 teaspoons hot bean sauce
2 teaspoons sesame oil

3 cups water
4 tablespoons oil

Preparations

Put the diced pork in a bowl and add the soy sauce and sherry; mix well. Sprinkle in the cornstarch and stir; then add the oil and toss and mix until the meat is evenly coated. Refrigerate for 30 minutes. Prepare the garlic, green pepper, bamboo shoots, scallion, and ginger and place them on your working platter. Mix the sauce ingredients in a bowl. All these preparations may be done hours ahead of time.

Bring 3 cups of water to a boil; scatter in the meat and stir for about 2 minutes. Drain and set aside in a dish. If you do this hours in advance, cover and refrigerate but bring the meat to room temperature before the final cooking.

Stir-frying

Heat a wok or large, heavy skillet over high heat until hot; add 3 tablespoons of the oil, swirl, and heat until hot. Toss in the garlic, press in the oil, then add the peppers and bamboo shoots. Stir briskly for about 1½ to 2 minutes until the peppers are softened and the bamboo shoots are well seared. Lower the heat slightly, if necessary, after the initial 30 seconds so that the vegetables won't burn. Scrape them on top of the reserved meat, discarding the garlic.

Add the remaining 1 tablespoon oil, swirl, and heat over medium-low heat. Toss in the scallions and ginger and stir a few times. Add the sauce mixture and stir with the back of a spoon or spatula in fast circular motions for about 30 seconds to mingle everything well. Turn heat high, pour in the meat and vegetables, and stir briskly in fast turning and flipping motions to coat them evenly. Pour into a hot serving dish.

VARIATIONS

The hot bean sauce may be replaced by 1 to 2 teaspoons chili-pepper oil or chili sauce or paste; in that case add 1 extra teaspoon soy sauce to the sauce mixture.

雪 SHREDDED PORK WITH RED-IN-SNOW
裏
紅 This is a dish from Shanghai, characteristic of the eastern school of cook-
炒 ing, being light and dainty. The meat is tender, the bamboo shoots crisp,
and the tiny shreds of red-in-snow are extremely crunchy. This incompara-
肉 ble preserved vegetable makes the dish marvelously refreshing. The dish
絲 is excellent with rice or as a topping for noodles (*page 434*). *It serves*
3 or 4 as a main course.

1 pound lean pork, loin or butt, shredded	1½ cups shredded spring or regular bamboo shoots
	¾ cup canned red-in-snow
Slippery-coating	1 tablespoon light soy sauce
1 tablespoon light soy sauce	¾ teaspoon sugar
1 teaspoon sugar	⅓ cup boiling water
2 teaspoons cornstarch	1 teaspoon sesame oil

3 tablespoons oil

Shred the meat, toss it lightly in a bowl, then add the marinade ingredients, stirring in the cornstarch last until meat is smoothly coated. Let
the meat marinate for 15 minutes or longer.

Heat a wok or large, heavy skillet over high heat until hot; add the
oil, swirl, and heat for 30 seconds. Scatter in the meat and stir briskly for
2 minutes, first in fast circular motions to separate the shreds, then in
sweeping and turning motions to cook them thoroughly.

Add the bamboo shoots and red-in-snow and stir rapidly for 30
seconds. Sprinkle in the soy sauce, sugar, and water; mingle well. Turn
heat to medium low, cover, and steam-cook for 2 minutes. By then there
should be only a little liquid in the pan. Adjust the flavor by adding a pinch
or two of sugar if needed. Turn heat high and add the sesame oil; give the
contents a few sweeping turns and pour into a hot serving dish.

兩 ONE PORK TWO TASTES
味
肉 This simple deep-fried meat is served with two seasonings. It would be
very good accompanied with a salad, Stir-fried Fresh Mushrooms, and
Simmered Radish Balls. *As a main course it serves 4.*

Cut into strips, the pork makes excellent finger food for a cocktail
party; sprinkle a little roasted salt-pepper on top.

1 pound boneless loin of pork

Marinade:
1 tablespoon light soy sauce
1 tablespoon dry sherry
¼ teaspoon sugar

1 egg white
Cornstarch for dusting

Sweet and sour sauce:
1 tablespoon sesame oil
1 heaping tablespoon finely
   chopped fresh coriander
1 tablespoon dry sherry
2 tablespoons dark soy sauce
3 tablespoons cider vinegar
5 tablespoons chicken or meat
   stock
4 tablespoons sugar

4 cups oil
2 tablespoons roasted salt-pepper
(*page 501*)

Cut the meat crosswise into ¼-inch-thick slices. Smash the meat lightly with the broad side of a cleaver to flatten the slices. Put them in a mixing bowl, add the marinade, toss well, and marinate for 15 minutes. Add the egg white, stir well, then coat each piece with the cornstarch. Shake off excess and set the pieces aside, flat on a plate, while you make the sauce.

Heat a small saucepan over medium heat until hot; add the sesame oil and heat for 5 seconds. Throw in the minced coriander and stir rapidly for 15 seconds. Add the liquid ingredients and sugar and bring to a boil, stirring. Cover and turn off the heat.

Place 2 tablespoons roasted salt-pepper in a small dish and set aside.

Heat a wok or large, heavy skillet until hot; add the oil and heat until a cube of bread foams instantly, about 375 degrees. Slip in the pork, piece by piece, and deep-fry all of them about 2 minutes, until they are brown and crisp, turning constantly. Drain and place them on a serving platter. Meanwhile, reheat the sauce and pour it into a bowl. Serve the meat with the sauce and the salt-pepper on the side so each person may select and flavor the meat individually on his or her own plate.

椒鹽肉 SALT-PEPPER PORK

This recipe involves three techniques: the meat is first steamed with seasonings to acquire flavor, then coated with dissolved cornstarch and shallow-fried to acquire a protective crust, and finally recoated with dissolved cornstarch and deep-fried to achieve crunchiness. Sliced and served with a sprinkling of roasted salt-pepper, each piece is juicy in the center and brittle around the edges. The dish is meaty without being heavy. *It may be served as an appetizer for 4 or 5 people to share, or a main course for 2 or 3 persons.* For a larger group you can double all the ingredients. Try it with hoisin sauce and Chinese Pancakes (*page 452*). Each person then takes a piece or two of the meat, smears on some sauce, wraps it up, and eats it like Peking Duck or Mo-shu Pork.

1 pound boneless pork, loin or
    butt, in one piece

Marinade:
1 tablespoon light soy sauce
1 tablespoon dry sherry
¼ teaspoon salt
1 medium whole scallion, coarsely
    chopped
2 quarter-sized slices peeled ginger,
    coarsely minced

4 tablespoons cornstarch dissolved
    in 4 tablespoons water
1 tablespoon oil
2 cups oil
Roasted salt-pepper (*page 501*)

Steaming

Mix the marinade in a heatproof bowl; add the meat, turn to coat it evenly, and marinate for 30 minutes, turning once. Set the bowl in a steamer and steam over high heat for 1 hour, replenishing water when necessary to maintain a strong circulating heat. Remove the meat from the juice to drain. This may be done a few hours in advance; cover but don't chill. Refrigerate the juice until the fat is congealed, discard, and save the tasty liquid as a soup base.

Cut the meat in half lengthwise. Coat the 2 strips well with the dissolved cornstarch. Save the remaining mixture.

Shallow-frying

Heat a large, heavy skillet over high heat until very hot; add 1 tablespoon oil, swirl, and heat until hot. Add the meat and shallow-fry for about 1 minute on each side over medium-high heat. The pieces should be firm and slightly brown. Remove them to a plate.

Deep-frying

Heat a small pot over high heat until hot; add 2 cups oil and heat until it foams a cube of bread instantly. Coat the pork again, with the remaining dissolved cornstarch, drop it into the hot oil, and deep-fry for about 2 minutes. Drain and let the pieces cool a little before cutting them crosswise into slices. Place them on a serving plate, sprinkle lightly with roasted salt-pepper, and serve.

杏仁叉燒丁 ROAST PORK ALMOND DING

There comes a time when you have no more than about ½ pound of roast pork odds and ends. Rather than snacking on them, dice the meat and combine it with vegetables and nuts. *This becomes a substantial and delicious meal for 2 to share.*

½ pound roast pork, diced
2 tablespoons oil
1 small clove garlic, lightly
    smashed and peeled
2 quarter-sized slices peeled ginger
1 cup diced celery
½ cup diced bamboo shoots or
    peeled broccoli stems
¼ teaspoon salt
1 tablespoon dry sherry
⅓ cup water

Sauce:
⅛ teaspoon salt
½ teaspoon sugar
1 tablespoon light soy sauce
2 teaspoons oyster sauce
2 teaspoons cornstarch dissolved
    in 2 tablespoons water
1 teaspoon sesame oil

¼ to ½ cup blanched almonds,
    walnuts, or cashews

Dice the pork into ¼-inch cubes; remove strings from celery, if necessary, and dice; dice the bamboo shoots; have the garlic and ginger ready. Combine the sauce ingredients and stir until the sugar is dissolved.

Heat a wok or large, heavy skillet over high heat until hot; add the oil, swirl, and heat for 30 seconds. Throw in the garlic and ginger and press them on the pan. Add the vegetables, sprinkle in ¼ teaspoon salt, and stir rapidly a few seconds. Add the meat, then the sherry, and stir briskly in fast turning motions a few times. Add the water, even out the contents, cover, and let it steam-cook vigorously over medium-high heat for about 3 minutes, until the meat is softened, the celery is tender but still firm, and the liquid is all but evaporated. Discard the garlic and ginger. Pour in the sauce ingredients and stir in fast sweeping and turning motions a few times until the sauce is completely glazed over the meat and vegetables. Pour into a hot serving dish, shower the top with the nuts, and toss at the table before serving.

VARIATION
Leftover rare London broil or roast beef may be done the same way.

金橘肉圓 DEEP-FRIED MEATBALLS WITH KUMQUATS

Deep-fried meatballs are tossed in a reddish sweet and sour sauce with green peppers and golden kumquats. *This would serve 4* and goes especially well with Stir-fried Celery Cabbage or Cauliflower.

1 recipe meatballs (*page 144*),
    without the spinach filling
4 cups oil
1 medium-sized green pepper,
    in ½-inch squares
¼ teaspoon salt

16 preserved kumquats
1 recipe sweet and sour sauce
    (*page 97*)
1 teaspoon cornstarch dissolved
    in 2 teaspoons water

Divide the meatball mixture into 16 portions and form into balls. This may be done hours in advance. Then deep-fry them as indicated in the recipe and drain on paper towels. Do not do the deep-frying in advance.

Heat a wok or large, heavy skillet over high heat until hot; add 1½ tablespoons of the oil, swirl, and heat for 15 seconds. Scatter in the green peppers and salt and stir rapidly for about 2 minutes, lowering the heat a little after the initial few seconds, stirring until the peppers are softened but not too limp. Add the kumquats and let them roll in the hot pan a few times. Pour in the sweet and sour sauce, and when it is hot, turn heat low, stir in the dissolved cornstarch, and keep stirring until it begins to thicken. Add the meatballs, turn heat high, and stir rapidly in sweeping motions until the sauce glazes the contents smoothly. Pour into a hot serving dish.

豆豉排骨 SPARERIBS IN GARLIC AND BLACK-BEAN SAUCE

This is a simple and delicious simmered dish. The dark, glazed ribs have that robust bite of black beans—a dish with a hearty personality. *It serves 2 or 3 as a main course* with any one of the stir-fried crisp or leafy vegetables.

1½ pounds meaty spareribs,
    chopped
3 tablespoons oil
2 large cloves garlic, lightly
    smashed and peeled

2 tablespoons fermented black
    beans, lightly rinsed and
    coarsely chopped
2 quarter-sized slices peeled ginger,
    minced

2 large whole scallions, finely
    chopped

Sauce seasonings:
2 tablespoons dark soy sauce
2 tablespoons dry sherry
1 teaspoon sugar

1¼ cups boiling water

Separate the ribs first, then chop each, meat side down, into 3 pieces.

Heat a wok or large, heavy skillet over high heat until hot; add the oil, swirl, and heat for 30 seconds. Scatter in the garlic, fermented black beans, ginger, and scallions, and stir rapidly for 30 seconds. Add the ribs and stir vigorously in sweeping and turning motions until every piece has whitened and is well seasoned by the aromatics. Add the sauce seasonings and boiling water. When the liquid boils, turn the heat low to maintain a gentle simmering, cover, and simmer for 45 minutes. Turn heat to medium high and stir vigorously until the liquid is all but evaporated. Scoop the ribs out into a hot serving dish, without any remaining oil. Scrape up the aromatic bits and scatter them over the ribs.

一
二
三
四
五
排
骨

"ONE, TWO, THREE, FOUR, FIVE" SPARERIBS

This is a light-hearted title for an extremely easy and delectable dish—the 1 to 5 referring to the simmering ingredients. The sauce-coated meat is succulent, with a deep sweet and sour flavor. *The dish serves 2 or 3 amply when accompanied by rice and a stir-fried leafy vegetable or a crisp salad.* The ribs are also good as an appetizer.

1½ pounds meaty spareribs

Simmering ingredients:
1 tablespoon dry sherry
2 tablespoons dark soy sauce
3 tablespoons cider vinegar
4 tablespoons sugar
5 tablespoons water

Separate the ribs first; then chop each, meat side down, into 3 pieces. Put them in a skillet or saucepan and set it over high heat; add the simmering ingredients and stir to mingle. When the liquid comes to a boil, adjust heat to maintain a very gentle simmering, and cover and simmer for 40 minutes. Stir and turn the spareribs from time to time.

Uncover and turn heat high to bring the sauce to a sizzling boil; stir rapidly until the sauce is all but evaporated.

酥 CRUNCHY RIBS
炸
排
骨

Simmered, coated with a thick batter, and then deep-fried, these ribs are wonderfully crunchy and subtly aromatic of the light sprinkling of roasted salt-pepper. *They could serve 2 and should be well balanced by vegetables.* Good ones would be Chilled Sweet and Sour Red Onions and Stir-fried Spinach. Since the ribs are neat, they also make good finger food.

1 pound meaty spareribs
2 quarter-sized slices peeled ginger
1 large whole scallion

Batter:
¼ teaspoon salt
2 heaping tablespoons
   breadcrumbs
¾ teaspoon baking powder
2 tablespoons flour
2 tablespoons cornstarch
5 tablespoons water

2 cups oil
Roasted salt-pepper (*page 501*)

Separate the ribs, then chop each, meat side down, into 3 pieces. Place them in a small saucepan with the ginger and scallion, pour boiling water to come 1 inch above the ribs. Bring it to a boil over high heat, adjust heat to maintain a gentle, steady simmer, cover, and simmer for about 30 minutes, until the meat is tender but a little on the firm side. Drain the ribs, reserving the liquid for stock.

Make the batter by combining all the dry ingredients in a large bowl and then adding the water slowly. Mix until smooth. Add the ribs, stir to coat them well, then give the batter a few moments to thicken and adhere to the meat.

Heat a wok or large, heavy skillet over high heat until hot; add the oil and heat until it foams a drop of batter instantly, about 375 degrees.

Dip a small spoon in the oil to grease it, then spoon up the coated ribs, without too much excess batter, and slip them in quick succession into the hot oil. Flip them over quickly and fry until both sides are dark brown and crunchy—it takes only about a minute since this batter browns easily. Scoop them out with a skimmer or slotted spoon to drain on paper towels. Pile on a serving dish and sprinkle lightly with the salt-pepper.

四川糖醋排骨 SZECHUAN SWEET AND SOUR SPARERIBS

Not saucy but glazy, this is a delightful deviation from the standard sweet and sour fare. The long simmering in the small quantity of water makes the meat tender and full of its own meaty flavor. *The dish serves 2 or 3 with rice and platters of leafy and crisp stir-fried vegetables,* such as the Chinese cabbage and the celery.

1½ pounds meaty spareribs	*Sauce:*
2 tablespoons oil	2 tablespoons bean paste
4 quarter-sized slices peeled ginger	2 tablespoons dark soy sauce
1 cup boiling water	2 tablespoons dry sherry
	2 tablespoons cider vinegar
	2 tablespoons sugar
	2 teaspoons sesame oil

1 medium whole scallion, coarsely
chopped

Separate the ribs first, then chop each, meat side down, into 3 pieces.

Heat a wok or large, heavy skillet over high heat until hot; add the oil, swirl, and heat for 30 seconds. Toss in the ginger slices and press them in the oil. Then add the ribs and stir-fry in turning and flipping motions until all are white. Add the boiling water, adjust the heat to maintain a very gentle but steady simmering, cover, and simmer for 45 minutes.

In the meantime, mix the sauce ingredients together in a bowl, stirring until the sugar is dissolved. Chop the scallion.

At the end of 45 minutes, the ribs should be tender and there should be very little liquid left in the pan. Turn the heat high and tumble the ribs a few times. Then give the sauce mixture a big stir and pour it over the meat; stir vigorously until it thickens and glazes the meat. Scatter in the chopped scallions, give the contents a few fast turns, and scrape the ribs and scallions into a hot serving dish—without the oil.

Beef

燒
牛
肉

CHINESE POT ROAST

A long-simmered piece of beef that is magnificently firm and smooth. It should be balanced with at least two vegetables, perhaps Stir-fried Cauliflower and Steamed Eggplant or Sweet and Sour Red Cabbage. Serve with rice for the sauce. *This is one of those versatile meat dishes that will serve 4 to 6 for one meal or can be refrigerated for use as cold cuts or appetizers.*

2 tablespoons oil
2 pounds rump, loin, or bottom
    round roast

Seasonings:
1 large clove garlic, crushed
    and peeled
2 quarter-sized slices peeled ginger
3 tablespoons dark soy sauce
3 tablespoons dry sherry
1 cup boiling water
1 tablespoon sugar
½ teaspoon salt
1 whole star anise

Heat a large, heavy pot over high heat until hot; add oil, swirl, and heat for 30 seconds. Turn heat to medium; toss in the garlic and ginger; then add the meat and brown on all sides. Add the soy sauce and sherry, turning the meat a few times to color it; then add boiling water, sugar, salt, star anise. When the liquid boils again, adjust heat to medium low to maintain a slow but steady simmering, cover, and simmer for 2 hours, turning the meat now and then.

Remove the roast to a chopping board to cool and firm; then slice it crosswise into the desired thickness. Skim most of the oil from the sauce and serve the sauce on the side or over the meat.

If you want to serve the roast cold, let it cool in the sauce first and then refrigerate it covered. Scrape off the congealed fat. Remove the meat, cut it lengthwise into two pieces and then slice these crosswise very thin. Spread a little of the succulent jellied sauce over the cold slices of meat. The meat is excellent for sandwiches.

京
葱
牛
肉
絲

BEEF WITH LEEKS

Leeks, larger and meatier and sweeter than scallions, are used a great deal in the northern parts of China. Traditionally they are combined raw with this highly seasoned meat, serving as a cushion to be tossed at table before being eaten. Finding them too coarse, I modify by stir-frying them with a little salt and sugar, which makes them brighter in color and silkier in texture. Served around the reddish-colored meat, they make a lovely presentation. *This recipe serves 3 or 4 as a main course with rice.*

1 pound flank steak, shredded

Marinade:
1 tablespoon light soy sauce
1 tablespoon cornstarch dissolved
    in 1½ tablespoons water
1 tablespoon oil

2 cups oil
1 pound leeks, shredded, rinsed

¼ teaspoon salt
¼ teaspoon sugar

Seasonings:
2 tablespoons sweet bean paste
1 tablespoon dry sherry
2 teaspoons light soy sauce
2 teaspoons sugar
1 teaspoon sesame oil

Preparations and oil-showering

Cut meat with the grain into 2-inch strips. Then cut crosswise against the grain into ⅛-inch slices, then stack and shred. Toss the shreds of meat in a mixing bowl, separating any that stick. Season them with the soy sauce, add the dissolved cornstarch and oil, and stir until smoothly coated. Let the meat marinate in the refrigerator for 30 minutes or longer.

Leeks are gritty and should be washed thoroughly, but to make shredding easier, cut before washing. Trim off the roots and all but 1 inch of the green, rinse off any sand, and cut them into thin diagonal slices. Flatten the slices into overlapping stacks, and cut them into narrow shreds. Rinse them thoroughly in a colander, then drain.

Mix the seasoning ingredients in a small bowl until smooth. Have a strainer and empty pot within reach.

Heat a wok or large, heavy skillet over high heat until very hot; add 2 cups oil and heat until a piece of leek foams snappily, about 350 degrees. Add the meat and stir in fast circular motions for about 10 seconds to separate the shreds. Hold the strainer over the pan and rapidly spoon the meat into it to drain. The meat will appear red at first, but it continues to cook with the showerings of hot oil as you spoon all the meat in. Drain well and put aside on a dish. Pour out all the oil into the empty pot. When cool, strain, and rebottle for general cooking.

Stir-frying

Wipe the pan, return 2 tablespoons oil, and set it over high heat until hot. Scatter in the leeks, sprinkle in the salt, and stir in fast tossing and flipping motions to sear them for 1 minute. Add ¼ teaspoon sugar and stir briskly for another minute to season them evenly. Pour them into a dish.

Add 1 tablespoon oil to the pan; lower the heat to medium. Scrape in the seasoning ingredients with a spoon and stir them in fast circular motions for a second or so. Return the meat, turn heat high, and stir-fry in fast sweeping motions for 20 to 30 seconds to coat the meat with the sauce evenly. Pour into a serving dish, piling it into a nice mound. Scatter the green leeks around it and serve. Toss at table to mingle the meat and leeks before eating.

VARIATIONS

One-half pound scallions, shredded, may be substituted for leeks. Toss them in the hot oil 30 seconds with the salt, then another 30 with the sugar. Or shred 2 cups of lettuce, romaine or iceberg, and place it flat on the serving dish; pour the meat on top. You could also use as a substitute 3 cups bean sprouts. Place the bean sprouts in a strainer and dip them in a pot of boiling water for 30 seconds, then put the strainer under cold running water to stop the cooking. Drain well and spread them on the serving dish; top with the meat.

You could use pork instead of beef. Marinate the meat and then stir-fry it in 3 tablespoons oil over high heat for about 1½ minutes to separate the shreds; add ¼ cup stock or water, even out the meat, cover, and steam-cook over medium-low heat for about 2 minutes, until most of the liquid has evaporated. Then add the sauce seasonings and serve with the leeks as before.

Instead of rice, serve steamed Chinese Pancakes (*page 452*), which you fill, roll up, and eat as you eat Mo-shu Pork.

士 FILET MIGNON KOW
的
球　It amuses me no end when a Chinese dish is endowed with a French title —it's a dead giveaway that the dish was invented abroad. But this has become a "classic" Cantonese specialty in all the Chinese restaurants in

the United States. It's pretty and delicious, especially if you like plenty of crisp Chinese vegetables. *It makes an excellent dinner for 4 preceded by soup or appetizers, accompanied by rice, and concluded with a nice dessert.*

1 pound filet mignon
6 large dried black Chinese
    mushrooms (presoaked)
1 cup sliced Chinese cabbage
½ cup sliced bamboo shoots
¼ cup thinly sliced water
    chestnuts
1 cup fresh snow peas
5 tablespoons oil
1 tablespoon dry sherry
2 quarter-sized slices peeled ginger
½ teaspoon salt

Sauce:
2 tablespoons light soy sauce
1 tablespoon oyster sauce
2 tablespoons dry sherry
¼ teaspoon sugar
2 teaspoons cornstarch dissolved
    in ¼ cup strained mushroom
    water
2 teaspoons sesame oil

Preparations

Cut the filet mignon lengthwise in half; then roll-cut each strip into about 1¼-inch-long chunks.

Cover the mushrooms with 1 cup hot water and soak for 30 minutes. Squeeze water from the presoaked mushrooms back into the soaking bowl and reserve the liquid. Rinse the mushrooms briefly, squeeze dry, destem them, and cut each in two.

Rinse and dry the tender heart and a few inner stalks of a Chinese cabbage, reserving leaves and outer stalks for another use. Quarter the heart and cut the young stalks diagonally into narrow pieces about 1½ inches long. Slice the bamboo shoots and water chestnuts. The water chestnut slices should be about ⅛ inch thick.

String the snow peas and dip them, in a strainer, into boiling water for 30 seconds; then drain them.

Place the meat, all the vegetables, and the ginger slices in separate piles on your working platter. Dissolve the cornstarch in ¼ cup of the mushroom liquid (without the sandy residue) and then mix with the other sauce ingredients.

All these preparations may be done hours ahead of time. Cover and refrigerate the meat and vegetables.

Stir-frying

Heat a wok or large, heavy skillet over high heat until hot; add 2 tablespoons of the oil, swirl, and heat for 30 seconds. Add the meat and stir and toss quickly to sear all surfaces—no more than 45 seconds or so; then splash in the sherry and give the meat a few fast turns. Transfer to a dish.

Add the remaining 3 tablespoons oil to the pan and heat until hot. Toss in the ginger slices and press them in the oil. Add all the vegetables except the snow peas and stir vigorously in sweeping and tossing motions for 1 minute. Add the salt and stir; scatter the meat and juice over, cover the pan, and let it steam-cook over medium heat for another minute.

Toss in the snow peas and stir vigorously a few times to mix the meat and vegetables well. Add the sauce seasonings and stir in sweeping folds until the sauce is smooth. Pour into a serving dish.

VARIATION

If you don't like oyster sauce, omit and increase the soy sauce to 3 tablespoons. The flavor, then, is a little more delicate.

芹
菜
牛
肉
絲

CHILI-PEPPER BEEF

Shredded beef is stir-fried with hot spices and crisp vegetables. It is a spirited dish, tingling hot but not numbing. *It makes a nice main course for 2 with rice.*

½ pound flank steak, shredded
   (*page 351*)

½ cup shredded bamboo shoots,
   in 1½-inch-long shreds

Slippery-coating:
1 teaspoon dark soy sauce
1½ teaspoons cornstarch dissolved
   in 2 teaspoons water
1½ teaspoons oil

4 dried red chili peppers
2 quarter-sized slices peeled ginger,
   shredded
1 large clove garlic, finely chopped
1½ cups shredded celery, in
   1½-inch-long shreds

Sauce:
2 tablespoons dark soy sauce
1 tablespoon dry sherry
2 teaspoons Chenkong vinegar
   or red-wine vinegar
2 teaspoons sugar
½ teaspoon roasted and ground
   Szechuan peppercorns
   (*page 500*)
1 teaspoon cornstarch dissolved
   in 2 teaspoons water
2 teaspoons sesame oil

1 cup oil

Preparations and slippery-coating

Toss the shredded beef into a mixing bowl, separating the pieces if any are attached. Add the coating and mix until smooth; refrigerate 30 minutes or longer.

Assemble the chili peppers, ginger, garlic, celery, and bamboo shoots in separate piles on your working platter. Combine the sauce ingredients and mix well. Place a strainer over a pot.

Heat a wok or large, heavy skillet over high heat until very hot; add 1 cup oil and heat until it foams a piece of scallion snappily, about 350 degrees. Add the meat, and stir briskly with chopsticks or a spoon in fast circular motions 5 or 6 times to separate the shreds, then pour the meat and oil immediately into the strainer. Drain briefly and set meat on a dish. These vegetable preparations and the slippery-coating may be done in advance; do not refrigerate the meat.

Stir-frying

Return 2 tablespoons oil to the pan and set it over low heat. Toss in the chili peppers and press and turn them until blackened. Turn heat to medium, scatter in the ginger and garlic and stir quickly a few times. Turn heat high and shower in the celery and bamboo shoots and toss and stir rapidly about 1½ minutes. Add the beef and stir briskly another minute. Give the sauce ingredients a big stir and pour them into the pan, stirring in fast sweeping and turning motions to coat the ingredients evenly. Pour into a hot serving dish.

VARIATIONS

You may substitute peeled and shredded broccoli stalks for the bamboo shoots.

And instead of beef you may use shredded loin of pork. In that case, marinate the pork as you did the beef. Heat a wok or large, heavy skillet till hot, add 2 tablespoons oil, heat, then stir-fry the pork for 1 minute, until all pinkness is gone. Add ¼ cup water, cover, and steam-cook vigorously over medium heat for about 2 minutes, until most of the liquid is gone. Set meat aside. Then proceed with stir-frying the vegetables, combining the two, and adding the sauce as described above.

咖哩牛肉片 STIR-FRIED CURRY BEEF

Curry is as Indian as soy sauce is Chinese. But since the Chinese began using the combination of spices that is called curry powder at the turn of the century, the small line of Chinese curry dishes has become so Chinese that it is doubtful Indians would recognize its origin.

Here meat is coated with a cornstarch marinade and stir-fried only seconds with the curry-sauced vegetables to become a fast and easy dish of sparkling taste, succulent meat, and flavorful vegetables. Since it's saucy, it's scrumptious with rice. *It serves 2 as a main course with rice and a delicate vegetable,* such as Stir-fried Bean Sprouts.

½ pound flank steak, sliced

Marinade:
1 tablespoon light soy sauce
½ teaspoon sugar
1 tablespoon cornstarch dissolved
   in 1 tablespoon water
1 tablespoon oil

3 tablespoons oil

2 large cloves garlic, finely
   chopped
½ cup minced onions
1 tablespoon curry powder
1½ cups sliced celery
1 cup sliced carrots
½ teaspoon salt
1 tablespoon light soy sauce
1 teaspoon sugar
1 cup water

Preparations

Cut the meat lengthwise into 3 strips, then crosswise into ⅛-inch-thick slices. Place them in a bowl, add the soy sauce and sugar, and toss to season well. Add the dissolved cornstarch and oil, and mix until smooth. Let it set for 15 minutes while you prepare the vegetables. If you wish to do this in advance, cover, refrigerate, and bring out a few minutes before the final cooking.

Chop the garlic and mince the onions. Scrape any outer celery stalks; cut them diagonally into ¼-inch-thick slices about 1½ inches long. Peel the carrots and cut them diagonally into slices about ⅛ inch thick and 1½ inches long. Place all the ingredients on your working platter in separate piles. If doing in advance, cover and refrigerate.

Stir-frying

Heat a wok or large, heavy skillet over high heat until hot; add the oil, swirl, and heat until hot. Scrape in the garlic, toss rapidly once in the hot oil, shower in the minced onions, and stir briskly for about 30 seconds until they are aromatic. Sprinkle in the curry powder and toss vigorously a few times. Add the celery and carrots and stir in fast flipping and turning motions to sear and coat them with the curried oil. Add the salt, soy sauce, and sugar and stir. Pour in the water, even out the contents, cover, and cook for 5 minutes over medium-low heat.

Uncover, scatter the marinated meat over the vegetables, cover, and let them steam-cook for about 1½ minutes. Uncover, turn heat high, and stir-fry vigorously in fast flipping and turning motions for about 30 seconds until the sauce glazes everything evenly. Pour into a hot serving dish.

洋葱炒牛肉 BEEF AND ONIONS

This is a fast and easy beefy dish with a pleasing sweetness to the sauce. The crisp onions add a delightful crunchiness. *Serves 2 or 3 with a salad and a vegetable,* such as the Stir-fried Spinach or Shredded Cabbage with Carrots.

½ pound flank steak, shredded
   (*page 351*)

Marinade:
2 teaspoons dark soy sauce
¼ teaspoon sugar
2 teaspoons cornstarch
2 teaspoons oil

5 tablespoons oil
2 to 3 large onions, shredded
   lengthwise (2 cups)

¼ teaspoon salt
1 large clove garlic, lightly
   smashed and peeled

Sauce:
1½ tablespoons dark soy sauce
1 tablespoon dry sherry
2 teaspoons sugar
1 tablespoon cornstarch dissolved
   in ⅓ cup water
2 teaspoons sesame oil

Toss the shredded meat in a bowl, separating the shreds if any are attached. Mix in the soy sauce and sugar; add the cornstarch and mingle until smooth; then pour in the oil and mix thoroughly. Refrigerate the marinated meat for 15 to 30 minutes or longer.

Shred the onions, always cutting them lengthwise. Peel the garlic. Combine the sauce ingredients in a bowl and stir until the sugar is dissolved.

Heat a wok or large, heavy skillet over high heat until hot; add 2 tablespoons oil, swirl, and heat for 30 seconds. Scatter in the onions and stir briskly to skid and turn them in the hot oil for about 1½ minutes until they are translucent but not limp. Sprinkle in the salt, stir quickly a few times, then pour into a dish.

Wipe the pan and heat it over high heat until hot. Add the remaining

3 tablespoons oil, swirl, and heat about 30 seconds. Toss in the garlic and press it in the oil. Then scatter in the meat and stir in fast shaking and flipping motions for about 30 seconds or until most of the meat is no longer pink. Discard the garlic. Add the onions and toss them rapidly in sweeping and turning motions for 30 seconds to blend them well. Give the sauce a big stir and pour into the pan, stirring in fast scooping and turning motions until the sauce is smoothly thickened. Pour into a hot serving dish.

SPICY BEEF

Hot and tasty, this is strictly for spice lovers. Marinated, then stir-fried until the moisture is "baked" away from the heat of the pan, the meat acquires a unique chewy crispness. You eat slowly and savor the full flavor of the seasonings. *This would serve 4 as a main course* and should be accompanied by some delicate vegetables—for instance, Cucumbers Simmered with Dried Shrimp and Stir-fried Green Peas.

1 pound flank steak, shredded
    (page 351)

Marinade:
4 tablespoons dark soy sauce
1 tablespoon dry sherry
1 teaspoon sugar

½ cup oil

4 dried chili peppers
2 cups shredded celery stalks
½ cup peeled and shredded carrots
1 teaspoon salt
2 teaspoons sesame oil
½ teaspoon crushed roasted
    Szechuan peppercorns
    (page 500)

Toss the shredded meat in a bowl, separating the shreds. Combine the marinade and stir until the sugar is dissolved. Pour over the meat. Marinate 30 minutes at room temperature or cover and refrigerate for 1 hour or longer.

Heat a wok or large, heavy skillet over high heat until hot; add 5 tablespoons of the oil, swirl, and heat for 30 seconds. Scatter in the meat and stir-fry briskly for 5 minutes until the meat is dark. Turn heat to medium low and continue to stir in swooping and turning motions for another 5 to 6 minutes, until the meat is dry and slightly brittle. Pour it into a dish.

Add the remaining 3 tablespoons oil to the pan and heat over medium-low heat. Add the chili peppers and press and flip them in the oil until they darken. Turn the heat high, scatter in the vegetables, and stir vigorously a few times. Add the salt and stir rapidly for 1½ minutes. Return the beef shreds to the pan without the oil and stir them with the vegetables for another 30 seconds. Sprinkle in the sesame oil, then the peppercorns, give a few sweeping turns, and pour into a hot serving dish, permitting the chili peppers to show here and there.

辣 SPICY BEEF WITH VEGETABLES
醬
牛 This dish is vividly colorful and dainty, and the dash of vinegar in the
肉 sauce gives it a seductive aroma that is known in Chinese as an "appetite
絲 arouser." Here the slivers of tender beef are well embellished by the crisp
green celery, crunchy black mo-er mushrooms, and brittle orange carrots. There is a good tangy sauce. *With rice, it would make a good main course for 2 people.*

½ pound flank steak, shredded
   (page 351)

Marinade:
1 teaspoon light soy sauce
2 teaspoons cornstarch dissolved
   in 1 tablespoon water
1 teaspoon oil

1 heaping tablespoon dried mo-er
   mushrooms (presoaked)
1½ cups shredded celery
1 cup shredded carrots
1 large clove garlic, minced
2 quarter-sized slices peeled ginger,
   minced
½ teaspoon salt

Sauce:
1 tablespoon bean paste
1 teaspoon Szechuan chili sauce
   or paste
1 teaspoon light soy sauce
1 tablespoon dry sherry
1½ teaspoons Chenkong vinegar
   or red-wine vinegar
¼ teaspoon salt
1 teaspoon sugar
1 teaspoon cornstarch dissolved
   in 2 teaspoons water
2 teaspoons sesame oil

1 cup oil

Toss the shredded meat in a bowl, separating the shreds. Add the marinade and stir until well blended. Let the meat sit, refrigerated, for 30 minutes or longer.

Soak the mo-er mushrooms for 30 minutes in hot water. Then rinse and discard any hard "eyes." Shred them and then put them with the celery, carrots, garlic, and ginger on the working platter. Combine the sauce ingredients and mix well. Put a strainer over a pot.

Heat a wok or large, heavy skillet over high heat until very hot; add 1 cup oil and heat until very hot, about 375 degrees. Scatter in the beef and swish and toss rapidly for about 10 seconds until most of the meat has lost its pinkness. Pour the meat and oil into the strainer. When the oil has drained off, turn the meat onto a plate. This slippery-coating may be done in advance, but do not refrigerate the meat.

Wipe the pan, return 3 tablespoons of oil, and heat over high heat until hot. Scatter in the minced garlic and ginger and stir a few times. Add the vegetables and toss rapidly in flipping and turning motions a few times. Sprinkle in the salt and continue to toss for about 1 minute until they are well seared by the oil. Return the meat to the pan and stir vigorously to mingle them well. Give the sauce a big stir and pour into the pan; stir rapidly in flipping and turning motions for about 5 to 10 seconds, until the meat and vegetables are evenly coated. Turn into a hot serving dish.

菜
花
炒
牛
肉

BEEF WITH CAULIFLOWER AND CARTWHEELED CUCUMBERS

This recipe demonstrates the steam-cooking method for slippery-coated beef, used only when the secondary ingredients call for steam-cooking with liquid. It eliminates the preliminary slippery-coating in oil or water, and it makes the beef very tender.

It is fast and easy, and it makes an excellent one-dish main course since the meat is well balanced with vegetables. *It serves 2 amply.*

½ pound cauliflower (about
    2 cups)
2 tablespoons oil
1 small clove garlic, lightly
    smashed and peeled
2 quarter-sized slices peeled ginger
1 long, slender cucumber
½ pound flank steak, sliced

Marinade:
1 tablespoon light soy sauce
¼ teaspoon sugar
1 tablespoon cornstarch dissolved
    in 1 tablespoon water
1 tablespoon oil

¼ teaspoon salt
⅓ cup water

Seasonings:
1 tablespoon oyster sauce
2 teaspoons light soy sauce
1 teaspoon sesame oil

Preparations

Break the cauliflower into individual flowerets; trim off excessive stems. If flowerets are large, cut them in half so that the cluster is flat on one side. Bring 2 cups water to a rolling boil, add the flowerets, and boil for 2 minutes. Drain, spray with cold water, and place them on your working platter. This may be done up to an hour in advance, but cover well to prevent the flowerets from drying and discoloring.

Prepare the garlic and ginger. Rinse and dry the cucumber; trim off the ends. Using a small, sharp knife, peel lengthwise strips off around the cucumber, spacing the peelings about an inch apart. Cut the cucumber in half lengthwise and scrape out the seeds. With hollowed side down, cut each half crosswise into slices a little thicker than 1/8 inch.

Cut the meat lengthwise into 3 strips, then cut each strip crosswise into 1/8-inch-thick slices. Toss the meat in a bowl. Sprinkle in 1 tablespoon soy sauce and the sugar, toss lightly, then add the dissolved cornstarch and oil and stir till the meat is smoothly coated. Let it marinate for 15 minutes or longer. It's more succulent when not chilled.

Prepare or measure out everything else and combine the seasonings in a small bowl. Group everything near the stove when ready to cook.

Stir-frying

Heat a wok or large, heavy skillet over high heat until hot; add 2 tablespoons oil, swirl, and heat for a second or two. Then lower the heat to medium low so that the oil will not be hot enough to scorch the cauliflower. Toss in the garlic and ginger, pressing them rapidly in the oil. Add the cauliflower flowerets and stir in fast turning and flipping motions to roll them in the oil. Sprinkle in the salt and stir a few times; then add the 1/3 cup water, even out the contents, cover, and steam-cook gently for 2 minutes. Uncover, spread the marinated meat over the cauliflower, cover, and steam-cook another 2 minutes undisturbed.

Uncover, turn heat high, add the cucumbers, and stir briskly in fast turning motions for about 15 seconds. Give the seasonings a big stir and pour into the pan; stir vigorously for another 15 seconds. Pour into a hot serving dish.

粉
蒸
牛
肉

RICE-POWDER STEAMED BEEF

This is a marvelous Szechuan specialty. The tender meat is fluffily coated by a marinade-seasoned toasted rice powder. It is a subtly spicy dish. Unfortunately, rice powder is hard to get and is often rancid, but cream-of-rice cereal makes an excellent substitute. *Serves 2 with a crisp salad and light vegetable,* such as Stir-fried Celery, Spinach, or Chinese Cabbage. It also makes an excellent appetizer in a chafing dish, from which people may help themselves with toothpicks.

½ pound flank steak

⅓ cup cream-of-rice cereal
1½ tablespoons water combined
    with 2 tablespoons oil

Marinade:
1 tablespoon dark soy sauce
1 tablespoon light soy sauce
1 tablespoon dry sherry
2 teaspoons hot bean sauce
1 teaspoon sugar
⅛ teaspoon salt
½ teaspoon five-fragrance powder
1 tablespoon minced scallion white
1 teaspoon minced peeled ginger
1 tablespoon cornstarch dissolved
    in 1 tablespoon water
1 tablespoon sesame oil

Preparations

Cut meat lengthwise into 3 strips and then cut strips crosswise into ⅛-inch-thick slices. Place them in a bowl, add all the marinade but the dissolved cornstarch and sesame oil. Mix well to coat all pieces evenly; then add the last 2 items, mixing until smooth.

Roast the cream of rice in a small pan over low heat for 5 minutes, stirring occasionally, until it is lightly browned. Pour it into a dish to cool. When it is cold, pour it over the meat and stir to coat the slices well. Add the water-oil mixture and stir until smooth. This may be done a few hours in advance; cover, refrigerate, and bring to room temperature before steaming.

Steaming

Scatter the coated meat on a heatproof plate, spreading it as thin as possible so that all pieces may receive the wet heat. Steam over high heat for 15 to 17 minutes, until the coating is dark, moist, and creamy. If some pieces are covered with a little hard and dry coating, turn them over, cover, and steam a minute or two longer. Well coated and durable, this meat may be presteamed and reheated just before serving. When ready, slip the plate on top of a serving platter or transfer the beef to a hot serving plate or chafing dish.

VARIATIONS

Thin slices of loin of pork or spareribs, chopped into 1-inch pieces, may be substituted for the beef. For pork loin, increase the steaming time to 45 minutes over medium-high heat, turning the pieces after the initial 25 minutes. Steam the spareribs for 1½ hours, omitting the cornstarch mixture from the marinade.

The spiciness may be increased by adding 1 teaspoon chili-pepper oil (*page 489*) or chili powder.

蘆筍炒牛肉   BEEF AND ASPARAGUS

Stir-fried, then steam-cooked briefly, asparagus is marvelous combined with beef. The oyster sauce does not make the dish fishy; it merely strengthens the flavor. *This would serve 3 or 4 people as a main course.*

1 pound flank steak

Marinade:
1 tablespoon light soy sauce
1 tablespoon dry sherry
½ teaspoon sugar
1½ tablespoons cornstarch
    dissolved in 2 tablespoons
    water
1 tablespoon oil

1 pound asparagus
1 quarter-sized slice peeled ginger
1 medium clove garlic, lightly
    smashed and peeled

2 cups oil
½ teaspoon salt
½ teaspoon sugar
1 tablespoon dry sherry
⅓ cup stock or water

Sauce:
1 tablespoon light soy sauce
1 tablespoon oyster sauce
2 teaspoons cornstarch dissolved
    in 3 tablespoons water and
    2 teaspoons sesame oil

Preparations and slippery-coating

Cut the meat lengthwise into 3 strips. Cut the strips crosswise into ¼-inch-thick slices. Place them in a bowl. Add the marinade and mix until well blended. Let the meat marinate in the refrigerator for 30 minutes or longer.

Wash the asparagus well; snap off the tough ends, then roll-cut the stalks into 1½-inch pieces, leaving the tips intact. Place them on your working platter with the ginger and garlic. Combine the sauce seasonings, and have the other ingredients and a strainer within reach.

Heat a wok or large, heavy skillet over high heat until very hot; add the 2 cups oil and heat until hot, about 375 degrees. Scatter in the beef, swish, and toss for about 10 seconds, until the meat is superficially whitened. Hold the strainer over the pan and spoon the meat rapidly into it, drain for a moment, then turn it onto a plate. These preparations may be done up to an hour in advance, but don't refrigerate the meat. When oil is cool, rebottle it for general cooking.

Stir-frying
Set wok or skillet over high heat, add 2 tablespoons oil, and heat about 30 seconds. Toss in the ginger and garlic and press them rapidly in the oil. Scatter in the asparagus and toss it briskly for about 1 minute, until the color brightens. Sprinkle in the salt and sugar and stir well; dash in the sherry and stir a few more times. Pour in the stock or water, even out the contents, cover, and steam-cook vigorously for 1 minute. Uncover, add the beef, and toss the two in fast turning and flipping motions a few times. Add the sauce and stir contents in rapid sweeping motions until the sauce is thickened and smoothly glazed onto the meat and vegetables. Pour into a hot serving dish.

Liver and Kidneys

黄
瓜
木
耳
炒
猪
肝

LIVER WITH CUCUMBERS AND MO-ER MUSHROOMS

The parboiling eliminates the liver's mealiness, making its texture firm and clean. The marinade gives it a wonderful flavor without overshadowing the more delicate flavor of the crisp cucumbers and the crunchy mo-er mushrooms. You will be absolutely astonished by the wonderful textures, good flavor, and garden-fresh aroma. *It serves 3 to 4 people amply as a main course.*

1 pound pork or beef liver

Marinade:
2 tablespoons light soy sauce
1 tablespoon dry sherry
½ teaspoon sugar
½ teaspoon salt
A dash black pepper
2 teaspoons cornstarch
2 teaspoons sesame oil

2 tablespoons mo-er mushrooms
    (presoaked)
1 firm, slender cucumber
5 tablespoons oil
1 tablespoon dry sherry
1 tablespoon stock or water
½ teaspoon salt
2 whole scallions, cut into
    1½-inch pieces
3 quarter-sized slices peeled ginger,
    shredded

Preparations

Cut the liver lengthwise into 1½-inch-wide strips. Cut the strips crosswise into ⅛-inch-thick slices.

Bring 1 quart water to a boil, scatter in the liver slices, and stir until the water begins to puff into a boil again. Drain the liver into a colander and spray with cold water to stop the cooking. Shake off excess water and put the liver into a bowl; add the marinade. Stir the slices, then let them marinate while you prepare the vegetables.

Cover the mo-er mushrooms with hot water and soak for 30 minutes. Then rinse and tear into petals if large, discarding any hard "eyes."

Rinse, dry, and trim off the ends of the cucumber; do not peel. Cut it in half lengthwise and scoop out the seeds. Slice the halves (hollowed side down) on a slant into thin pieces.

The liver and mushrooms may be prepared hours ahead of time— cover and refrigerate. The cucumber, however, should be sliced just before the stir-frying to preserve its refreshing aroma.

Stir-frying

Heat a wok or large, heavy skillet over high heat until hot; add 3 tablespoons oil, swirl, and heat for 30 seconds. Scatter in the mo-er mushrooms and toss quickly to coat them with oil. Add the sherry and stock or water and stir vigorously until the liquid evaporates. Add the cucumber slices and stir vigorously a few times; then sprinkle in the salt and stir in rapid sweeping and turning motions for about 30 seconds. Put the vegetables at both ends of a hot serving platter.

Rinse and dry the pan and set it over high heat; add the remaining 2 tablespoons oil, and heat until very hot but not smoking. Toss in the scallions and ginger and skid them in the oil. Then add the liver and stir rapidly in folding and turning motions about 45 seconds, until the meat is heated through and the marinade is all but absorbed. Put the liver slices in the center of the serving platter, and toss with the vegetables at the table to mingle before serving.

VARIATIONS

One-half cup snow peas, sliced bamboo shoots, hearts of palm, peeled and macerated broccoli stems (*see page 378*), celery, or water chestnuts may be added to the mo-er mushrooms and the cucumbers with an additional ½ teaspoon salt to taste.

豆豉猪肝　LIVER IN BLACK-BEAN SAUCE

This is a robust version of the preceding recipe. It's a dish that calls for plenty of fluffy rice. *It will serve 3 to 4 people comfortably as a main course.*

1 pound pork or beef liver
1 large onion
2 medium green peppers
5 tablespoons oil
½ teaspoon salt

Sauce:
2 large cloves garlic, coarsely
    chopped
1 tablespoon fermented black
    beans, rinsed and coarsely
    chopped
2 quarter-sized slices peeled ginger,
    minced
1 small whole scallion, coarsely
    chopped
2 tablespoons dark soy sauce
2 tablespoons dry sherry
1 teaspoon sugar

1 tablespoon cornstarch dissolved
    in 3 tablespoons water
1 tablespoon sesame oil

Preparations

Slice and parboil the liver as in the preceding recipe. Peel and wedge-cut the onion so that the pieces are about 1½ inches wide. Halve peppers lengthwise, seed and derib them, then cut them into pieces about 1½ inches wide, trimming off the curved ends (but using them in the recipe).

Prepare the sauce seasonings: Group all the solid ingredients in separate piles on your working platter. Combine the soy sauce with the sherry and sugar and stir until the sugar dissolves. Put the dissolved cornstarch and the sesame oil near the stove.

Stir-frying

Heat a wok or heavy skillet over high heat until hot; add 2 tablespoons oil, swirl, and heat for 30 seconds. Scatter in the onions and peppers and stir and toss vigorously until they are gleaming with oil. Sprinkle in the salt and stir for about 1½ minutes until the onions are slightly translucent and very fragrant. Pour the vegetables into a dish.

Wipe the pan, add the remaining 3 tablespoons oil, and heat until hot but not smoking. Scrape in the garlic, black beans, ginger, and scallions, and stir about 30 seconds to sear them. Add the liver and stir and flip another 30 seconds. Splash in the liquid seasonings mixture and toss and turn to coat the meat; then add the vegetables without the oil and give a few sweeping turns to mingle them in. Give the cornstarch mixture a big stir and pour it into the pan in a circular motion, stirring the contents until they are lightly glazed. Sprinkle in the sesame oil, toss once or twice, and pour into a hot serving dish.

涼拌腰片 PORK KIDNEYS IN SESAME-PASTE SAUCE

Pork kidneys are really delicious when they are put first under running water and then soaked in cold water with shallots. This treatment eliminates their mealiness and strong odor. This excellent recipe uses pork kidneys for a cold saladlike dish, perfect for a buffet. It has wonderful textures—firm kidneys, crunchy mo-er mushrooms, and crisp cucumbers—and a heavenly taste. It is rich and should be enjoyed only in small portions. *Serves 8 to 10 on a buffet.*

4 large pork kidneys, about
    1 pound
4 shallots, each peeled and
    quartered
2 heaping tablespoons mo-er
    mushrooms (presoaked)
1 firm, slender cucumber, sliced
½ teaspoon salt

Sauce:
2 tablespoons sesame paste
    dissolved in 2 tablespoons
    boiling water
2 tablespoons dark soy sauce
1 teaspoon sugar
1 tablespoon sesame oil
1 tablespoon oil
2 quarter-sized slices peeled ginger,
    minced
½ teaspoon roasted and crushed
    Szechuan peppercorns
    (*page 500*)

Preparations

Remove membrane and any balls of fat from the kidneys. To make the slicing easier, freeze about 2 hours, until they are firm but not frozen hard. Split each kidney in half horizontally by pressing it down on the cutting board while cutting it through the middle, knife parallel to the board. Cut out the white cores.

Turn the kidneys cut side down and cut them vertically (crosswise) into paper-thin slices. Place them in a colander and spray with cold water for 2 minutes. Then put them in a large, deep bowl, add the shallots, and fill the bowl with cold water. Soak the kidneys for 30 minutes or longer, while you prepare the vegetables, both of which need 30 minutes to set.

Cover the mo-er mushrooms with hot water and soak for 30 minutes. Meanwhile, peel and halve the cucumber lengthwise; scrape out the seeds. Turn the cut side down and cut into very thin slices crosswise. Put the slices into a bowl, stir in ½ teaspoon salt, and macerate 30 minutes in the refrigerator. When the mo-er mushrooms are soft, tear the clusters into smaller petals and discard any hard "eyes." Bring 2 cups water to a boil with ½ teaspoon salt; blanch the mo-er mushrooms for 30 seconds. Drain and squeeze dry.

Soften the sesame paste by stirring it vigorously with 2 tablespoons boiling water until smooth. (If you like peanuts, use 3 tablespoons chunky peanut butter creamed with 3 tablespoons boiling water instead.) Add to the paste the soy sauce, sugar, and sesame oil, and stir until the mixture is creamy.

Heat a small skillet over medium heat for 10 seconds; add 1 tablespoon oil, swirl, and heat for 5 seconds. Sprinkle in the minced ginger and Szechuan peppercorns and stir for 15 seconds. Turn heat very low and add the sesame paste mixture; stir until the sugar has dissolved and the sauce is smooth. Turn off heat, cover the pan, and set aside.

Put the kidneys back in the colander and run them under cold water for 5 minutes, stirring occasionally. They are ready to be cooked when the water from them runs clear. Drain, and discard the shallots.

Bring 2 quarts water to a rolling boil in a large pot. Add the kidneys, let water come to a boil again, and stir for 1 minute, letting them tumble about in the water. Pour water and kidneys into the colander set in the sink and then spray the kidneys with cold water until completely cold. Their texture should be firm and slightly bouncy, their color gray, and there should be no trace of "pink" juice when they are squeezed. Press them to extract any excess water.

Squeeze the cucumber slices lightly to extract liquid, drain, and put them in a large bowl. Add the mo-er mushrooms and kidneys; pour in the sauce and toss well. Then transfer to a serving platter. This "salad" is good at room temperature served immediately or it may be made hours ahead of time and served chilled.

VEGETABLES

There is a far greater variety of vegetables in China than here. Aside from having a wider range of types and numerous forms of dried and processed vegetarian products, bean curd being particularly notable, the Chinese also relish parts of vegetables generally discarded in Western cooking, such as radish greens, cucumber skins, or the red roots of spinach. For lack of proper refrigeration and transportation, however, many regional specialties never travel beyond their own provincial boundaries. Consequently, the unique flavor and texture of the blue turnips of Tientsin in the north might be totally unknown to a southerner, and by the same token, a northerner might never taste the bitter melons of the south.

The Chinese cook vegetables primarily by the stir-frying method, and the results are spectacular. The brief searing in hot oil followed by vigorous steam-cooking with a small amount of liquid gives fresh vegetables a plump crispness and vivid coloring that are really extraordinary. After trying green beans and broccoli this way, you may never want to boil them again. Seldom ever turning soggy or becoming discolored, stir-fried vegetables are delicious hot and cold.

I have kept most of the vegetable dishes here simple, and unless you wish to make special trips to the Chinese grocer, you will be able to enjoy vegetables the Chinese way from produce found right in the supermarket— Chilled Sweet and Sour Onions and Spicy Minced Watercress being good examples of the transformations wrought by Chinese cooking methods and seasonings.

炒菠菜 STIR-FRIED SPINACH

Spinach, containing a good deal of salt and iron, sometimes leaves one with a puckery aftertaste unless a little sugar is added. It needs a good amount of oil to give it luster and a smooth texture, garlic and sesame oil to enrich the flavor, and a very brief parboiling to prevent it from turning watery. This soft, shiny spinach is delicious hot or cold. *Serves 2 to 4.*

2 pounds spinach	¾ teaspoon salt
4 tablespoons oil	1 teaspoon sugar
2 large cloves garlic, lightly crushed and peeled	2 teaspoons sesame oil

Wash the spinach well. If it has roots, separate them and cut into 2 or 4 pieces—they are extremely sweet and succulent. Chop stems if long.

Bring a large pot of water to a rolling boil, add the spinach, and stir to submerge it. When the water begins to boil again, in about a minute, pour the spinach into a colander and spray with cold water to stop the cooking. Press down lightly to extract excess water.

Heat a wok or large, heavy skillet over high heat until hot; add the oil, swirl, and heat about 30 seconds till hot. Toss in the garlic cloves and press them against the pan a few times. Add the spinach and poke and shake to separate the mass; then stir in fast turning motions to coat it with oil. Sprinkle in the salt and sugar and stir briskly for about 1 minute. Add the sesame oil, give a few fast turns, and pour into a hot serving dish, discarding the garlic.

炒 青 豆   STIR-FRIED GREEN PEAS

While there is nothing to compare with eating fresh peas at their peak season, for year-round enjoyment there is nothing quite as convenient as frozen peas. Rapidly stir-fried and briefly steam-cooked, these peas are firm and tender, each one a burst of sweetness. Unlike fresh, you must not use the tiny frozen peas—they are too fragile; they tend to be creamy rather than slightly crisp. *Serves 2 to 4.*

1 ten-ounce package frozen green peas, thoroughly defrosted	½ teaspoon salt
3 tablespoons oil	¼ teaspoon sugar
	¼ cup chicken stock

Heat a wok or large, heavy skillet over high heat until hot; add the oil, swirl, and heat for 30 seconds. Pour in the peas and stir rapidly for 5 seconds. Add the salt, sugar, and stock; lower the heat, cover, and steam-cook for about 2 minutes. Uncover and stir lightly and rapidly until there is no more liquid, then pour into a hot serving dish.

VARIATIONS

Peas with black mushrooms and bamboo shoots—Stir the peas in 2 tablespoons oil for 5 seconds and pour into a dish. Add 2 more tablespoons oil to the pan and stir-fry 8 small dried black Chinese mushrooms (pre-soaked 30 minutes in ½ cup hot water, destemmed, and diced; save liquid) plus 1 cup diced bamboo shoots for 1 minute.

Return the peas to the pan, add 2 teaspoons light soy sauce or oyster sauce, ¼ teaspoon sugar, and the mushroom liquid, minus residue. Even out the contents, turn heat low, cover, and let vegetables steam-cook briskly for 2 minutes. Uncover and stir until there's only a bit of foaming liquid; then add 1 teaspoon sesame oil, give a few fast turns, and pour into a hot serving dish. This variation has a stronger flavor than the simple stir-fry dish, and the mushrooms and bamboo shoots offer contrasting texture. If you want the texture without the strong flavor, use ¾ teaspoon salt to taste instead of the soy sauce or oyster sauce.

Fresh peas—If you use fresh peas, shell 2 pounds of very fresh and young peas just before cooking—they lose flavor when shelled and chilled for any length of time. Stir them in hot oil as before, add a little more salt and sugar to taste, and increase the stock to ¾ cup. Cover and increase the steam-cooking time by 4 to 6 minutes depending on the tenderness and size of the peas.

青
豆
蟹
粉

GREEN PEAS IN CRABMEAT SAUCE

This is a beautiful, glazed-sauce dish of pinkish or white crabmeat laced with bright-green peas. It has a delicate taste. *Serves 2 to 4.*

1 ten-ounce package frozen large peas, thoroughly defrosted, or fresh peas	1 cup fresh or frozen crabmeat
3 tablespoons oil	1 tablespoon dry sherry
1 small whole scallion, finely chopped	1 teaspoon salt
2 quarter-sized slices peeled ginger, minced	1 cup chicken stock
	1 tablespoon cornstarch dissolved in 2 tablespoons water with 1 tablespoon oil

Defrost the frozen peas and set them aside. If you use fresh ones, shell 2 pounds and parboil them in about 1½ cups of water in a small saucepan for 5 to 7 minutes until they are tender but still firm and slightly crisp. Drain and set them aside.

Heat a wok or large, heavy skillet over high heat until hot; add the

oil, swirl, and heat for 30 seconds. Lower heat to medium high, add the scallion and ginger, and stir about 10 seconds. Add the crabmeat and stir; then splash in the sherry and stir once. Add the peas, sprinkle in the salt, and stir rapidly in turning and scooping motions to mingle well. Pour in the stock, cover, and steam-cook vigorously for 1 minute.

Uncover, give the cornstarch mixture a big stir, and pour it into the pan, stirring briskly until the saucy crabmeat and peas are smoothly glazed. Pour into a hot serving dish.

青豆肉粉 GREEN PEAS WITH MINCED PORK

Tender, tasty specks of meat act here as a coating and flavoring agent for the delicious peas. *Serves 2 to 4.*

½ pound ground pork	4 tablespoons oil
	1 ten-ounce package frozen peas,
Marinade:	thoroughly defrosted, or
1 tablespoon light soy sauce	parboiled fresh peas (*page 372*)
1 tablespoon dry sherry	¼ teaspoon salt
A dash black pepper	A pinch sugar
2 teaspoons cornstarch dissolved	⅓ cup water
in 1 tablespoon water	

March-chop the ground meat a few times to loosen its formation. Put it into a bowl and add the marinade; mix until smooth.

Heat a wok or large, heavy skillet over high heat until hot. Add 2 tablespoons of the oil, swirl, and heat for 30 seconds. Toss in the peas and glide them in the oil about 1 minute with the salt and sugar. Pour into a dish.

Add the other 2 tablespoons oil to the pan, swirl, and heat. Then add the pork, stirring and poking until pinkness is gone, about 30 seconds. Return peas to pan, add water, and stir-fry rapidly over medium heat for 2 minutes, until the consistency of the meat is creamy.

炒利馬豆 STIR-FRIED LIMA BEANS

Just as peas, frozen lima beans are a convenient year-round delicacy. I prefer the larger ones, known as Fordhook: they are more full bodied and flavorful than the tiny ones. Although the lima beans prepared this way have no surrounding liquid, they are moist, sweet, and creamy, and aromatic of the sesame oil. *Serves 2 to 4.*

3 tablespoons oil
1 ten-ounce package frozen lima
    beans, thoroughly defrosted
½ teaspoon salt

¼ teaspoon sugar
½ cup chicken stock or water
1 tablespoon sesame oil

Heat a wok or large, heavy skillet over high heat until hot; add the oil, swirl, and heat for 30 seconds. Add the lima beans and stir and flip about 30 seconds, until their color deepens into a bright green. Then add the salt, sugar, and stock, and stir to mingle. Cover and steam-cook vigorously for 2 minutes, until the pan crackles. Uncover, and stir the lima beans rapidly until the liquid has completely evaporated. Add the sesame oil, give a few sweeping turns, and pour into a hot serving dish.

VARIATIONS
Soak 4 medium dried black Chinese mushrooms for 30 minutes in 1 cup hot water. Rinse, squeeze dry, and destem; then dice them. Instead of using ½ cup stock for the steam-cooking, use ¾ cup of the mushroom soaking water (pouring off carefully to leave behind the residue in the bottom). Add the diced mushrooms to the oil with the lima beans. You may also add ½ cup diced bamboo shoots and ¼ cup finely chopped red-in-snow to give the dish a crunchiness, but do add a little more sugar to taste, since the preserved vegetable is on the salty side.

雪裏紅炒利馬豆　LIMA BEANS IN MEAT AND RED-IN-SNOW SAUCE

A light and refreshing mingling of flavors and textures. It is excellent with rice or as a topping for soup noodles (*page 434*). *As a vegetable dish it serves 2 to 4.*

1 ten-ounce package frozen lima
    beans, thoroughly defrosted
¼ pound ground lean pork
½ cup red-in-snow, finely chopped
½ cup finely diced bamboo shoots
5 tablespoons oil

Seasonings:
1 tablespoon dry sherry
1 tablespoon light soy sauce
¼ teaspoon salt
1½ teaspoons sugar
½ cup water

2 teaspoons sesame oil

Peel off the outer skins of the lima beans (*page 180*). March-chop the ground meat to loosen its formation. Finely chop the red-in-snow. Dice the bamboo shoots. Place everything in separate piles on your working platter. Mix the seasonings together in a small bowl.

Heat a wok or large, heavy skillet over high heat until hot; add 2 tablespoons of the oil, swirl, and heat for 30 seconds. Scatter in the lima beans and stir briskly for about 30 seconds, until they are brightly green. Pour immediately into a dish.

Add the remaining 3 tablespoons oil to the pan and heat a few seconds till hot. Add the meat and stir and poke rapidly to break up the lumps; stir until all pinkness is gone, about 40 seconds. Add the red-in-snow and bamboo shoots and stir briefly to mingle. Then stir in the seasonings and return the lima beans without the oil, smoothing contents into an even layer. Turn heat low to maintain a very gentle simmer, cover, and simmer for 2½ minutes. Uncover, turn heat to medium high, add the sesame oil, and give the contents a few turns, then pour into a hot serving dish.

炒　STIR-FRIED CAULIFLOWER

菜

花　Each lovely, white floweret is tender but still firm and slightly crunchy. *Serves 2 to 4.*

1 medium head cauliflower, about 2 pounds	1 teaspoon salt
3 tablespoons oil	¾ cup chicken stock or water

Break the head into flowerets, and trim off any long or thick stems—they have a strong cabbage smell. Leave the smaller flowerets intact and cut the larger ones in half so they're all about the same size. Rinse and drain.

Heat a wok or large, heavy skillet over high heat until hot; turn heat to medium, add the oil, swirl, and heat for about 15 seconds—like cabbage, cauliflower scorches easily if the oil is too hot. Add the flowerets and stir quickly to coat them with oil; then sprinkle in the salt and stir briefly. Add the stock and make sure all stems are in the liquid. When it boils, cover, and simmer vigorously for 5 minutes.

Uncover, turn heat high, and stir gently but rapidly until there is just a little foaming liquid in the skillet. Pour into a hot serving dish.

VARIATION

For a touch of color and that wonderful aroma of sesame, add 1 medium scallion, finely chopped, and 1 teaspoon sesame oil during the last few seconds of stir-frying just before you serve.

炒
芹
菜　STIR-FRIED CELERY

Plain, seasoned only with salt, this celery retains much of its own refreshing flavor. Briefly stir-fried and steam-cooked in hot oil, it also acquires a
delightful "nutty" aftertaste. Icy green with a bright overcast of yellow,
it's an inviting vegetable that goes especially well with red-cooked or spicy
meats, poultry, or seafood. It is also excellent when cold or chilled. *Serves
4 amply.*

1 bunch celery, about 2 pounds	1 teaspoon salt
3 tablespoons oil	¼ cup water

Cut off the root end and separate the stalks; wash thoroughly to
remove all clinging soil. Scrape any tough outer stalks so they won't be
stringy. Hold stalks in bundles and cut them crosswise into ¼-inch-wide
pieces.

Heat a wok or large, heavy skillet over high heat until hot; add the
oil; swirl, and heat for a few seconds. Scatter in the celery and stir rapidly
for about 2 minutes in fast turning and tossing motions until it acquires a
general glistening and translucent look. Sprinkle in the salt and stir for 30
seconds to season the pieces evenly. Pour in the water in a circle; turn heat
to medium low, cover, and steam-cook for 2½ minutes. Uncover, turn heat
high, and stir vigorously for about 30 seconds until there is no liquid in the
pan. Pour into a hot serving dish.

炒
芥
蘭　STIR-FRIED BROCCOLI FLOWERETS

Broccoli is the only vegetable that offers two distinct varieties—one has
not only the tender, nuttily rich flowerets, but also the stems, which,
peeled, sliced, and macerated, make a wonderful substitute for bamboo
shoots or a delicious vegetable by themselves. *Serves 2 to 4.*

1 bunch broccoli, about 2 pounds	¼ teaspoon sugar
3 tablespoons oil	½ cup chicken stock or water
2 quarter-sized slices peeled ginger	1 tablespoon sesame oil
1 teaspoon salt	

Break off the flowerets and peel the skin from their small stems as
much as possible. Rinse and drain well. Set aside the large stems for the
recipe on *page 378*.

Heat a wok or large, heavy skillet over high heat until hot; add the

oil, swirl, and heat for 30 seconds. Toss in the ginger slices and press them in the oil; then add the broccoli and stir and toss for 5 seconds. Turn heat to medium high and toss and turn the flowerets very quickly until they turn a brilliant green.

Add the salt and sugar and stir briefly. Then add the stock or water, cover, and steam-cook vigorously over medium-high heat for 2½ minutes. Uncover—you'll be amazed by the clean fragrance—and stir the flowerets rapidly until all liquid is gone. Dribble in the sesame oil, give a few rapid folds, and pour into a hot serving dish. The broccoli is delectable hot, at room temperature, or cold.

豆
豉
芥
蘭

BROCCOLI FLOWERETS IN BLACK-BEAN SAUCE

Serves 2 to 4.

1 bunch broccoli, about 2 pounds	3 tablespoons oil
1 heaping tablespoon fermented black beans	1 teaspoon salt
	1 teaspoon sugar
1 to 2 large cloves garlic, coarsely chopped	½ cup chicken stock or water
	1 teaspoon cornstarch dissolved in 3 tablespoons water and
2 quarter-sized slices peeled ginger, coarsely chopped	1 teaspoon sesame oil

Prepare the flowerets as in the preceding recipe; save the stems for salting (*see page 378*).

Rinse the fermented black beans briefly in water and shake dry; chop them coarse. Prepare and measure out the other ingredients.

Heat a wok or large, heavy skillet over high heat until hot; add the oil, swirl, and heat for 30 seconds. Splash in the black beans, garlic, and ginger and stir briskly for 15 seconds. Add the flowerets and stir and flip for 5 seconds. Lower the heat to medium and continue to stir in fast turning motions until their color deepens. Add the salt, sugar, then the stock or water; cover and steam-cook sizzlingly for 2½ minutes.

Uncover, stir a few times, then pour the dissolved cornstarch over the flowerets and toss until the sauce thickens. Pour into a hot serving dish and serve immediately—it is good only when piping hot.

炒
芥
蘭
枝

STIR-FRIED BROCCOLI STEMS

Serves 2 to 4.

2 cups sliced broccoli stems

1 teaspoon salt
2 tablespoons sesame oil

Macerating broccoli stems

Peel off the tough outer skin of the stems with a sharp paring knife. Cut the stems into diagonal slices about ⅛ inch thick and 2 inches long. Put the slices in a bowl, sprinkle in the salt, and toss well with your fingers. Chill in the refrigerator for 1 hour.

The stems are now ready to be eaten as is, with a little oil, or with sesame oil. If you want to use them in a recipe, rinse them very briefly and pat them dry.

If you are not going to use them within a few days, put them in the pickling brine (*page 397*), where they can stay for weeks. They would be delicious in Stir-fried Pickled Vegetables.

Stir-frying the stems

Heat a wok or large, heavy skillet over high heat until hot; add the sesame oil and swirl. Immediately splash in the macerated stems and stir with lightning speed in sweeping and turning motions for 15 seconds— they're only to be tumbled in the oil, not cooked. Pour immediately into a serving dish. They are excellent hot and even better when chilled.

VARIATIONS

To make them spicier, use 1 tablespoon chili-pepper oil (*page 489*) and 1 tablespoon sesame oil; tumble the same way.

Done either plain or spicy, the cooked broccoli stems are wonderful sparklers for other dishes. You could shred and add them to a green salad or mince and mix them with cottage cheese.

炒
蘆
筍

STIR-FRIED ASPARAGUS

The stir-frying method seems to have been invented for asparagus. Seared rapidly to heighten the color, then vigorously steam-cooked to give the stalks a firm tenderness, the asparagus is quite simply magnificent in color, texture, and taste. *Serves 2 to 4.*

1 pound asparagus	¾ cup chicken stock or water
2 tablespoons oil	2 teaspoons sesame oil
½ teaspoon salt	

Wash the asparagus under cold water, especially the tips, where sand often lodges within the buds. Snap off the tough ends. Roll-cut the spears into ¾-inch-long pieces.

Heat a wok or large, heavy skillet over high heat until hot; add the oil, swirl, and heat for 30 seconds. Turn heat to medium high, scatter in the asparagus, and stir rapidly to roll them in the hot oil; their color will brighten vividly. Sprinkle in the salt and stir once or twice; then pour in the stock, cover, and steam-cook vigorously for 5 minutes. Uncover, dribble in the sesame oil, and stir in sweeping motions until the tiny amount of liquid has completely evaporated. Pour into a hot serving dish.

芙蓉菜鹵 CHICKEN FU YUNG SAUCE FOR VEGETABLES

This is a sauce version of that northern specialty Fu Yung Chicken. The scraped chicken, in lesser quantity, is blended into stock instead of being stir-fried. The sauce is only briefly stir-fried with the chosen vegetable at the end of its cooking time. With a little minced Smithfield ham sprinkled on top, this creamy sauce lends elegance to many vegetables, such as peas, lima beans, cauliflower, broccoli, and asparagus.

¼ pound boneless and skinless chicken breast	2 teaspoons cornstarch dissolved in 2 teaspoons water
¼ teaspoon salt	4 egg whites, beaten until light and frothy
1 teaspoon dry sherry	

Place the chicken breast, smooth side down, on a chopping board and scrape it with a sharp knife or spoon in light strokes; discard tendon and any membrane. Pile the shaved meat and cut it closely; then sprinkle a teaspoon of water over it and march-chop with a wet knife or cleaver until the consistency is pasty.

Put the meat in a large, deep bowl; add the salt, sherry, and dissolved cornstarch and mix until smooth. Then add the beaten egg whites little by little, stirring vigorously until the mixture is completely smooth. Let the mixture marinate in the refrigerator for 30 minutes or longer—this can be done hours ahead of time. Before you add it to any vegetable bring it to room temperature and stir vigorously to fluff it up.

芙
蓉
素
菜

CHICKEN FU YUNG VEGETABLES

The sauce is white, fluffy, and creamy. With the garnishing of red ham, it makes a very pretty dish with any of these green or white vegetables. *Serves 2 to 4.*

1 recipe stir-fried vegetable (peas,
   lima beans, cauliflower,
   broccoli, asparagus)
1 cup chicken stock
1½ teaspoons cornstarch dissolved
   in 1 tablespoon water

Chicken Fu Yung Sauce (*preceding
   recipe*)
2 teaspoons oil
2 tablespoons minced cooked
   Smithfield ham (*page 492*) or
   substitute

Just before concluding any of the stir-fried recipes (say, before adding sesame oil), pour 1 cup stock into the pan and bring to a boil. Lower heat, add the dissolved cornstarch, and stir until sauce begins to thicken. Then add the Chicken Fu Yung Sauce and stir and fold until the chicken is white and the sauce creamy. Stir in the oil to give sheen to the sauce and pour into a hot serving dish. Sprinkle the top with the Smithfield ham or a substitute.

乾
煸
四
季
豆

DRY-SEARED GREEN BEANS

In this dish all the ingredients are dry and chewy, with a lingering flavor. It is unusual and delicious. The beans are wrinkled but crisp, and each is speckled with a little adhering meat, shrimp, and preserved vegetables. *Serves 4.*

1½ pounds green beans
1 cup oil
¼ pound ground pork
1 tablespoon dried shrimp
1 tablespoon minced Szechuan
   preserved mustard stems

Seasonings:
2 tablespoons light soy sauce
2 tablespoons dry sherry
½ teaspoon salt
½ teaspoon sugar
2 tablespoons water
1 tablespoon sesame oil

1 tablespoon finely chopped
scallion greens

Rinse and dry the green beans; break off the ends. March-chop the ground meat a few times to loosen its formation. Cover the dried shrimp with boiling water and soak for 30 minutes; drain and mince fine. Slice off a small piece of the preserved mustard stems; rinse briefly to remove some of its pepperiness and then mince it fine, to make 1 tablespoon. Chop the scallion greens. Put everything in separate piles on your working platter. Measure out the seasonings into a small bowl and mix well.

Heat the cup of oil in a wok or large, heavy skillet until it foams a cube of bread instantly, about 375 degrees. Scatter in the green beans and deep-fry until they are wrinkled and a little blistered, stirring constantly, and lowering the heat slightly if necessary. Pour beans and oil into a strainer over a small pot.

Return 3 tablespoons oil to the pan, scatter in the meat, and stir quickly in poking and pressing motions to break the lumps. Stir until it begins to brown; then add the minced shrimp and preserved mustard stem and stir well. Shower in the green beans; stir in scooping and turning motions a few times. Add the seasonings, then the scallion greens, and stir vigorously in sweeping motions until the liquid is absorbed by the ingredients. Pour into a hot serving dish.

VARIATION

If you omit the shrimp, substitute Tientsin preserved vegetable for the Szechuan preserved mustard stems, and add 1 teaspoon chili-pepper oil to the seasonings, you will have a magnificent hot and garlicky dish.

SLICED ZUCCHINI WITH SHREDDED CARROTS

This is a very pretty and delicate dish. The zucchini are silky with a slight crispness along the edges and the carrot shreds are firm. It is an excellent dish hot, at room temperature, or chilled. *Serves 3 to 4.*

1 pound zucchini	1 teaspoon salt
1 cup shredded carrots	2 quarter-sized slices peeled ginger
4 tablespoons oil	

Wash and dry the zucchini, and trim off the ends. Do not peel. Cut each crosswise into 1½-inch-long sections; then cut each section lengthwise into ¼-inch-thick slices.

Peel the thick end of a large carrot. Cut it diagonally into thin slices about 1½ inches long; then stack the slices and shred them. You should shred enough carrots to make up 1 cup.

Heat a wok or large, heavy skillet over high heat until hot; add 1 tablespoon of the oil, swirl, and heat for 30 seconds. Scatter in the carrots and stir briskly a few times; add ⅛ teaspoon salt and stir rapidly for 30 seconds. Pour the carrots into a dish.

Add the other 3 tablespoons oil to the skillet and heat for a few seconds until hot. Then toss in the ginger and press the slices in the oil. Add the zucchini and stir and flip briskly for 30 seconds, to coat the slices with oil. Sprinkle in the remaining salt and stir rapidly in scooping and turning motions for 1½ minutes. Add the carrots and stir both vegetables a few times to mix them. Then pour into a hot serving dish.

涼拌芽菜 COLD-STIRRED BEAN SPROUTS

The tails of the bean sprouts (the final tip) were always removed in China. Carrying vivid memories of Liu-ma and her squad of helpers plucking the bean sprouts while sharing hot tea and gossip in the lull of the afternoon, I embarked on such an endeavor that began and ended there and then—it took no less than 1 hour and 3 minutes to pluck 1 pound of bean sprouts, which then took less than 1 minute to cook and less than 5 to eat.

This is a delightfully refreshing salad, even if the bean sprouts aren't as neat and dainty as they should be. *Serves 3 to 4.*

4 cups fresh bean sprouts
   (about ⅔ pound)
½ cup finely shredded carrots
1½ teaspoons salt

Sauce:
2 tablespoons sugar
2 tablespoons distilled white
   vinegar
2 tablespoons oil or sesame oil

Preparing the bean sprouts

Rinse the bean sprouts in a large pot of cold water, stirring them to loosen any husks, broken roots, or wilted sprouts; to remove these unwanted pieces, tilt the pot to float them off, then drain the bean sprouts into a colander.

Bring 4 cups water to a boil; add the bean sprouts and stir to submerge them in the boiling water for 30 seconds. Drain them immediately into a colander and spray with cold water until they are cold. Shake dry and place them in a bowl with the shredded carrots.

Making the salad

Mix the sauce ingredients in a small bowl until the sugar is dissolved. Toss the bean sprouts and carrots with the salt, add the sauce, and mix well. Cover and chill the salad until thoroughly cold. Serve the salad with the liquid unless part of a cold platter; in that case, drain off the liquid.

炒
芽
菜

STIR-FRIED BEAN SPROUTS

In this traditional recipe, the bean sprouts are seasoned with a whiff of garlic and scallions and lightly glazed with dissolved cornstarch. *Serves 3 to 4.*

4 cups fresh bean sprouts
   (about ⅔ pound)
3 tablespoons oil
1 large clove garlic, lightly
   smashed and peeled
2 quarter-sized slices peeled ginger
1 large whole scallion, finely
   chopped

1 teaspoon salt
¼ teaspoon sugar
Dash black pepper
1 teaspoon cornstarch dissolved
   in 2 tablespoons water
1 teaspoon sesame oil

Toss bean sprouts in a pot of cold water, tilting the pot to float out the husks and broken tails. Pour into a colander, spray with water, and drain. Then parboil them in boiling water for 30 seconds and drain. This eliminates the raw beany taste as well as preventing them from turning watery.

Heat a wok or deep, heavy skillet over high heat until hot; add the oil, swirl, and heat for 30 seconds. Add the garlic and ginger and press them in the oil; then toss in the scallions and stir once or twice. Add the bean sprouts, then the salt, sugar, and a dash of black pepper. Stir rapidly in tossing and turning motions for 30 seconds. Give the dissolved cornstarch a big stir and pour it over the sprouts. Then add the sesame oil and stir briskly until the sprouts are smoothly glazed. Pour immediately into a hot serving dish.

炒
鮮
菇

STIR-FRIED FRESH MUSHROOMS

A simple, all-mushroom dish, excellent both hot and cold. The mushrooms are creamy in color and delightfully firm and slightly crunchy, especially when they are chilled. *Serves 3 to 4.*

1 pound large fresh mushrooms
4 tablespoons oil

1 to 1½ teaspoons salt (to taste)

Rub the mushrooms with a wet paper towel if they are dirty and trim off the very ends of the stems. Slice them into ¼-inch-wide sections, stems attached.

Heat a wok or large, heavy skillet over high heat until hot; add the oil, swirl, and turn heat to medium. Scatter in the mushrooms and toss lightly and rapidly for about 2 minutes; then add the salt and stir another 30 seconds. Pour into a hot serving dish.

炒 雙 菇　MUSHROOMS IN OYSTER SAUCE

Dark and glistening, the two kinds of mushrooms offer two distinct textures—the straw mushrooms are silky and soft, the button mushrooms firm and slightly crunchy. Of course, you could also use just one kind of mushroom with an equally tasty result. *Serves 2 to 4.*

1 cup straw mushrooms	1 teaspoon light soy sauce
1 cup small canned button	1 tablespoon oyster sauce
mushrooms	1 teaspoon cornstarch dissolved
2 tablespoons oil	in 2 tablespoons water
1 whole scallion, finely chopped	2 teaspoons sesame oil

Rinse both canned mushrooms and drain.

Heat a wok or large, heavy skillet over high heat until hot; add the oil, swirl, and heat for 30 seconds. Scatter in the scallions and stir a few times; then add the mushrooms and stir and toss for about 1 minute. Add the soy sauce and oyster sauce and stir for another minute. Add the cornstarch mixture and sesame oil; stir until the mushrooms are glazed. Pour into a hot serving dish.

椒 油 熗 芹 菜　PEPPERCORN-OIL ''CHOKED'' CELERY

A northern specialty, this gorgeous dish combines light-green celery with sherry-soaked pink dried shrimp. The celery is parboiled, then marinated, or "choked," with the shrimp and peppercorn oil. *Serves 2 to 4.*

2 tablespoons dried shrimp	1½ teaspoons salt
2 tablespoons dry sherry	3 tablespoons Szechuan pepper-
1 bunch celery	corn oil

Put the shrimp in a small bowl, add the sherry, cover, and soak overnight or for 8 hours. The sherry not only softens the shrimp but also neutralizes their strong smell. Thirty minutes before using them, add 2 tablespoons boiling water to the sherry, cover, and continue to soak.

Reserving the outer stalks for another use, wash and string the inner stalks of the celery; you can do this by snapping either end and pulling the fibers off. Cut the stalks on the slant into pieces about ½ inch wide and 2 inches long. You should have about 3 cups.

Bring 4 cups water to a boil. Scatter in the celery and boil vigorously for about 3 minutes. Drain into a colander and spray with cold water to stop the cooking. Put the celery in a large bowl, sprinkle with salt, and toss.

Pour shrimp and soaking liquid into the celery; add the peppercorn oil and mingle well. Cover and chill until thoroughly cold. Pour into a serving dish and serve as an appetizer or cold vegetable dish.

VARIATION

Here the celery and shrimp are stir-fried for a hot dish. Soak the shrimp in the sherry and add the boiling water as in preceding recipe. Increase the celery to 4 cups. Heat a wok or heavy skillet over high heat until hot; add 3 tablespoons peppercorn oil, swirl, and heat for 30 seconds. Scatter in the celery and stir-fry briskly with 1½ teaspoons salt for a few seconds until the color deepens. Add the shrimp and liquid, plus another ½ cup water.

Turn heat to medium to maintain a vigorous simmer, cover, and simmer for 5 minutes. Season with a little more salt if necessary and pour into a hot serving dish.

The celery and shrimp are softer than in the cold dish, and the flavor is more pronounced because of the "smothering" under cover.

肉末炒芹菜　SHREDDED CELERY IN HOT MEAT SAUCE

In this dish, the translucent celery is soft with a faint crunchiness left, and it is speckled with the tasty meat. The hot bean paste gives the clinging glaze a mellow, hot flavor. *Serves 3 to 4.*

4 cups shredded celery	*Seasonings:*
¼ pound ground pork	2 tablespoons hot bean paste
4 tablespoons oil	1 tablespoon light soy sauce
¼ teaspoon salt	1 tablespoon dry sherry
1 large clove garlic, lightly smashed and peeled	¼ teaspoon sugar
2 quarter-sized slices peeled ginger, minced	½ cup chicken or meat stock
	1 teaspoon sesame oil

Scrape off any strings from the tough outer stalks of a bunch of celery. The easiest way to shred celery is to cut it while still in a whole bunch. If it is very long, cut off the narrow tips for another use. Then trim

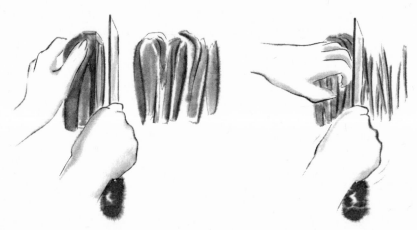

off the leaves and root end but don't let the stalks separate. Cut the whole mass thin on the straight, in strips about 1½ inches long, from the root end. Then cut these slices lengthwise into 1½-inch-long shreds. Place them in a colander, rinse thoroughly, and drain.

March-chop the meat a few times to loosen its formation. Prepare the other ingredients, mixing the seasonings in a small bowl.

Heat a wok or large, heavy skillet over high heat until hot; add 2 tablespoons of the oil, swirl, and heat for 30 seconds. Scatter in the celery shreds and stir briskly a few times; then add the salt and keep stirring for about 1 minute. Put the celery in a dish.

Clean the pan and heat it again till hot. Pour in the other 2 tablespoons oil, swirl, and heat for 30 seconds. Toss in the garlic and press it in the oil, flipping a few times; then add the ginger and the meat and stir and poke to break up the lumps. Pour in the seasonings and stir to mingle well; then add the celery and stir briskly a few times to incorporate. Pour in the stock and even out the contents. Turn heat to medium low, cover, and steam-cook vigorously for about 1½ to 2 minutes, until there is very little liquid left.

Uncover, turn heat high, and stir until the liquid is completely gone. Add the sesame oil, give a few fast turns, and pour into a hot serving dish, discarding the garlic.

乾燒冬筍 DRY-COOKED BAMBOO SHOOTS WITH MINCED DRIED SHRIMP

The bamboo shoots are dry and crunchy, and they have that concentrated savory taste of the dried shrimp. They go well with rich meat dishes such as the Red-Cooked Ham or Duck. *Serves 2 to 4.*

2 tablespoons dried shrimp
   (presoaked)
4 cups sliced bamboo shoots
1 cup oil
¾ teaspoon salt

1 tablespoon dry sherry
2 tablespoons soaking water from
   the shrimp
½ teaspoon sugar
1 tablespoon sesame oil

Soak the shrimp in 5 tablespoons boiling water for 1 hour. Mince, reserve liquid. The bamboo shoots should be in slices about ⅛ inch thick and 2 inches long. Rinse, and roll them dry in a kitchen towel.

Heat a wok or large, heavy skillet over high heat until hot; add the oil and heat until it foams a cube of bread instantly, about 375 degrees. Scatter in the bamboo shoots and deep-fry, stirring for about 3 minutes to extract their water. Drain off all but 1 tablespoon of the oil.

Add to the bamboo shoots in the pan the salt, sherry, minced shrimp, shrimp water, and sugar; stir to mingle well. Cover and steam-cook vigorously over high heat, for about 1½ minutes. Uncover, stir rapidly until there is no more liquid in the pan, and then add the sesame oil; give a few big turns and pour the bamboo shoots into a hot serving dish.

海鮮醬冬筍   BAMBOO SHOOTS IN HOISIN SAUCE

Reddish brown in color, the bamboo shoots are resiliently crisp. Rich, this is an excellent accompaniment to delicate main dishes such as steamed or steep-poached fish. *Serves 4.*

4 cups sliced bamboo shoots
1 cup oil
1 teaspoon salt
½ teaspoon sugar
3 tablespoons hoisin sauce

1 tablespoon dry sherry
2 tablespoons stock or water
1 teaspoon cornstarch dissolved in
   3 tablespoons stock or water
2 teaspoons sesame oil

Cut the bamboo shoots into slices 2 inches long and ⅛ inch thick. Rinse, and roll them dry in a kitchen towel.

Heat a wok or large, heavy skillet over high heat until hot; add the oil, heat until it foams a cube of bread instantly, about 375 degrees. Scatter in the bamboo shoots and deep-fry them, stirring, for about 3 minutes, to soften and extract their water. Drain through a strainer placed over a pot and return 1 tablespoon of the oil to the wok or skillet. Set over medium heat.

Add to the oil the hoisin sauce, sherry, and stock or water, and mingle well with the back of a spoon or a spatula. Return the bamboo shoots to the sauce and stir rapidly to cover them evenly. Let them sizzle in the sauce about 15 seconds, then give the dissolved cornstarch a big stir and add it to the sauce, stirring and tossing while the sauce glazes. Add the sesame oil and stir a few times; then pour into a hot serving dish.

VARIATION

If you like a hotter taste, use 2 tablespoons regular oil plus 1 table-spoon of chili-pepper oil (*page 489*) for the searing.

 ## STIR-FRIED CHINESE CABBAGE (BOK-CHOY)

Simple and plain—just the right kind of natural dish to go well with a rich or spicy main course. *Serves 2 to 4.*

1½ pounds Chinese cabbage	3 tablespoons oil
1 tablespoon oil	1 teaspoon salt or to taste
Pinch baking soda	¼ teaspoon sugar
2 or 3 quarter-sized slices peeled ginger	2 teaspoons sesame oil (optional)

Separate the white stalks of the cabbage and wash well. Trim the uneven ends and then cut them diagonally into pieces 1 inch thick and about 2 inches long.

Bring 4 cups water to a boil in a large saucepan with 1 tablespoon oil; toss a generous pinch of baking soda in the water and swish to dissolve it. Shower in the cabbage. When the green brightens, in about 30 seconds, pour water and vegetable immediately into a colander to drain. Spray with cold water to stop the cooking if parboiling in advance.

Heat a wok or large, heavy skillet over high heat until hot; add the oil, swirl, and heat for a second. Throw in the pieces of ginger and press them around the pan. Add the cabbage and toss vigorously for 30 seconds. Add the salt and sugar and stir rapidly for 2 minutes, until the cabbage has an overall translucent look and is tender, plump, and slightly crunchy. Add the sesame oil if you like a nutty aroma, give the contents a few fast folds, and pour into a hot serving dish.

炒 黃 芽 白 菜 STIR-FRIED CELERY CABBAGE

Just as natural and refreshing as the Chinese cabbage, this fragile-looking celery cabbage goes exceptionally well with tasty Vinegar-splashed Chicken. It provides a wonderful contrast in color, flavor, and texture. *Serves 2 to 4.*

1½ pounds celery cabbage	1 teaspoon salt, to taste
3 tablespoons oil	¼ teaspoon sugar
2 quarter-sized slices peeled ginger	2 teaspoons sesame oil

Cut off the root end and cut the cabbage crosswise into 1-inch sections. Toss them into a colander, loosening the folds. Spray with cold water, rinsing well, and drain.

Heat a wok or large, heavy skillet over high heat until hot; add the oil, swirl, and heat for a second. Throw in the ginger, and press slices around the pan. Shower in the cabbage and toss rapidly to turn and tumble it in the hot oil for 30 seconds. Sprinkle in the salt and sugar, then stir vigorously for about 2 minutes until the stalks are translucent and shiny, and leaves are green and yellow—as springlike as daffodils. Add the sesame oil, toss a few times, then pour into a hot serving dish.

椒 鹽 白 菜 蘿 蔔 絲 MARINATED CELERY CABBAGE WITH WHITE RADISHES

This cold dish is wonderfully refreshing: its crisp texture is well matched by a cool, aromatic flavor. *Serves 3 to 4.*

4 cups (loosely packed) shredded celery cabbage	½ teaspoon roasted and crushed Szechuan peppercorns (*page 500*)
1 cup shredded white radishes or icicle turnips (white Chinese turnips)	2 tablespoons chopped fresh coriander leaves
1½ teaspoons salt	2 tablespoons sesame oil

Remove the cabbage's tough outer leaves and shred the inner leaves by stacking them and cutting closely crosswise. Cut off the ends of the radishes and slice lengthwise; then shred the slices. If you are using icicle turnips, peel them first.

Put the vegetables in a large bowl, add the salt and ground peppercorns, and toss well with your hands. Cover and refrigerate for 4 to 6 hours, stirring now and then.

Just before serving, drain off the macerating liquid, add the coriander and the sesame oil, and toss well. Serve as a salad or as part of an assorted cold platter.

VARIATION

Add 1 teaspoon chili sauce or paste or chili-pepper oil, if you'd like it hot.

STIR-FRIED GREEN CABBAGE

Serves 4 or more.

1 small head green cabbage, about 1 pound
3 tablespoons oil
1 teaspoon salt

3 tablespoons chicken or meat stock
1 teaspoon sesame oil

Remove the cabbage's tough outer leaves and discard the stem. Quarter the cabbage, cut out the core, and shred as for cole slaw. Toss the shreds in a colander to separate them; then rinse and drain. If you shred the cabbage ahead of time, rinse and drain just before stir-frying—when completely dry, the cabbage scorches in the hot oil and becomes spotted.

Heat a wok or large, heavy skillet over high heat until hot; add the oil, swirl, and heat for 30 seconds. Add the cabbage shreds and stir and toss them till glazed with oil. Add the salt and mingle. Pour in the stock and smooth out the cabbage in an even layer. Turn heat low, cover, and steam-cook for 2 minutes. Uncover, turn up heat, and stir briskly for about 30 seconds; taste to see if you need more salt and check the texture—the cabbage should be soft with some crunchiness left in it. Add the sesame oil, give a few fast turns, and pour into a hot serving dish.

STIR-FRIED SHREDDED CABBAGE WITH CARROTS

Cabbage is hearty by nature, but here, cut into thin, long shreds and salted before stir-frying, it acquires a refined look as well as a refreshing lightness. Brightened by slivers of orange carrots, it is dainty and delicate, an excellent balancer for hot and spicy meats. It is delicious hot or cold and it may be served as a vegetable dish or a salad. *Serves 4 or more.*

1 pound green cabbage

2 teaspoons salt

1 carrot

3 tablespoons oil

1¼ teaspoons salt to taste

¾ teaspoon sugar

2 teaspoons sesame oil

Preparations

Discard the tough outer leaves and the stem of the cabbage. Quarter it and cut out the solid rooty core. Cut the quarters crosswise into very fine shreds, as for cole slaw. Toss them into a colander, rinse well in cold water, then place them in a large mixing bowl. Sprinkle in 2 teaspoons salt, mix, then cover with cold water. Let the cabbage macerate for about 1 hour.

When ready to cook, wash and peel a carrot; cut it diagonally into thin, long slices, about ⅛ inch thick and 1½ inches long; set it aside on a dish. Pour the cabbage into a colander, spray briefly with cold water, then drain.

Stir-frying

Heat a wok or skillet over high heat until hot; add the oil, swirl, and heat for a second or two. Scatter in the carrots and stir rapidly a few times until the color deepens. Add the cabbage and stir vigorously a few times to sear it in the hot oil evenly. Sprinkle in the salt and sugar; stir in fast tossing motions to blend well. Add the sesame oil, give a few fast folds and pour immediately into a serving dish. The whole process shouldn't take more than 2 minutes.

醋溜包心菜　VINEGAR-SLITHERED GREEN CABBAGE

This stir-fried cabbage tossed in a hot and sour sauce at the end is delicious either hot or cold. *Serves 4 or more.*

1 small head green cabbage, about

    1 pound

3 tablespoons oil

4 dried red chili peppers

Sauce:

½ teaspoon salt

2 tablespoons sugar

1 teaspoon cornstarch

2 tablespoons cider vinegar

2 tablespoons light soy sauce

1 tablespoon dry sherry

Remove the cabbage's tough outer leaves and cut off the stem. Quarter the cabbage and cut out the core. Cut the leaves into pieces about 1 inch square, toss in a colander to separate, and then rinse and drain (do not rinse and drain until shortly before the stir-frying).

Mix the sauce ingredients in a bowl until the sugar and cornstarch are dissolved.

Heat a wok or large, heavy skillet over high heat until hot. Add the oil, turn heat low, and toss in the peppers. Press and turn them in the oil until they are deep red—do not let them blacken, since they won't look as pretty with the cabbage. Then turn heat high, scatter in the cabbage, and stir and flip for about 2 minutes in the hot oil.

Add the sauce and stir in folding motions for 30 seconds; then pour into a hot serving dish.

糖醋紅包心菜　SWEET AND SOUR RED CABBAGE

A simple stir-fried cabbage that is good hot and even better cold. Soft but not watery, the cabbage is mildly sweet and sour. Because of the vinegar, it retains a lovely bright-red color. When the cabbage is chilled, the texture hardens to a light crispness. *Serves 4 or more.*

1 small head red cabbage, about 1½ pounds	2 tablespoons cider vinegar
3 tablespoons oil	2 tablespoons sugar
1 medium clove garlic, lightly smashed and peeled	½ cup water
1 teaspoon salt	2 tablespoons light soy sauce
	2 teaspoons sesame oil

Discard the cabbage's tough outer leaves and cut off the stem. Quarter the cabbage and cut out the core. Shred the leaves as for cole slaw. Toss the shreds in a colander to separate; then rinse and shake dry (do not do this until shortly before the stir-frying).

Heat a wok or large, heavy skillet over high heat until hot; add the oil, swirl, and heat for 30 seconds. Press the garlic in the oil, then scatter in the cabbage and stir and toss rapidly until the shreds are glistening with oil. Add the salt and stir; then add the vinegar. As the cabbage brightens from deep purple to vivid red, add the sugar and toss to mingle. Pour in the water, even out the cabbage, cover, and steam-cook vigorously for about 3 minutes, until the pan begins to crackle.

Uncover, add the soy sauce, and stir in folding motions until there is hardly any liquid in the pan. Sprinkle in the sesame oil, give a few big turns, and pour into a serving dish.

糖
醋
紅
洋
葱

CHILLED SWEET AND SOUR RED ONIONS

These onions are crisp and crunchy, and they are delectable. They are wonderful as part of a cold platter. *Serves 3 to 4.*

1 pound red onions
2 tablespoons oil
1 large clove garlic, lightly smashed
    and peeled
¼ teaspoon salt

Sauce:
1 tablespoon dark soy sauce
2 tablespoons cider vinegar
2 tablespoons sugar

Trim off the root ends of the onions and peel them. Cut each onion into 1-inch-wide wedges and separate the layers. Combine the sauce ingredients in a bowl and stir until the sugar is dissolved.

Heat a wok or large, heavy skillet over high heat until hot; add the oil, swirl, and heat for 30 seconds. Toss in the garlic and press it in the oil. Then scatter in the onions and stir rapidly in turning motions for about 30 to 40 seconds, until they are glistening with oil and have a slight translucent look. Sprinkle in the salt and stir briskly a few times. Splash in the sauce and, as it sizzles, stir the onions briskly a few times; then pour immediately into a dish. Let them cool a few minutes, then cover and refrigerate until well chilled.

蝦
米
燒
黃
瓜

CUCUMBERS SIMMERED WITH DRIED SHRIMP

While the texture of huge cucumbers is too coarse for cold-stirring or fast stir-frying, it adapts beautifully when simmered. These cucumbers, seasoned with the tasty sea flavor of dried shrimp, are plump and translucent. *Serves 4 or more.*

1 heaping tablespoon dried shrimp
3 huge cucumbers

2 tablespoons oil
1 teaspoon salt

Cover the shrimp with 5 tablespoons boiling water and soak for 1 hour. Remove them to a dish, leaving the liquid in the bowl.

Cut off the ends of the cucumbers and peel them. Cut them lengthwise, scoop out seeds, and then cut each half into 4 lengthwise strips. Gather up the strips and cut them into 4 pieces crosswise.

Heat a wok or large, heavy skillet over high heat until hot; add the

oil, swirl, and heat for 15 seconds. Add the cucumbers and stir rapidly a few times; then add the salt and continue to stir another 5 seconds. Add the shrimp, then the soaking liquid without any residue; stir briefly.

Turn heat to medium low to maintain a strong simmering, cover, and simmer for 15 minutes. By that time the shrimp are soft, the cucumbers tender, and there is very little liquid left in the pan. Pour immediately into a hot serving dish.

甜
酸
黃
瓜
皮

SWEET AND SOUR CUCUMBER SKINS

An unusual tangy cold vegetable—a Peking specialty. Barely cooked, the cucumber skins are wonderfully crisp. The sauce is sweet and sour with a touch of hotness. The vinegar is added after the cucumber and sauce are cool to prevent the acid from dulling the bright green skin. You really should have unwaxed cucumbers for this. In a pinch, however, you can use the waxed kind.

Serve these as a vegetable dish, part of an assorted cold platter, or, shredded, as a spicy touch to a green salad. *Enough for 4 or more.*

6 slender, medium-sized cucumbers	*Sauce:*
2 tablespoons sesame oil	1 tablespoon light soy sauce
1 clove garlic, lightly smashed and peeled	4 tablespoons sugar
	½ teaspoon salt
2 small fresh hot peppers, seeded and shredded	4 tablespoons cider vinegar

Wash (or scrub under running water with a vegetable brush if waxy) and dry the cucumbers and cut off both ends. Peel the skin lengthwise into 1-inch-wide strips with a thin layer of the white pulp. Cut the cucumber skins crosswise into 1½-inch-long pieces. Save the insides for salads.

Combine the soy sauce, sugar, and salt in a bowl; stir to mingle until the sugar is dissolved. Prepare and measure out the other ingredients.

Heat a wok or large, heavy skillet over high heat until hot; add the sesame oil, swirl, and heat for 10 seconds. Toss in the garlic and press it in the oil on both sides; then add the shredded peppers and stir rapidly for about 15 seconds. Toss in the cucumber skins and stir and flip vigorously to tumble them in the oil. Pour in the sauce seasonings, stir rapidly for 30 seconds, and then pour immediately into a serving dish. When it is cool, add the vinegar and toss well. Cover and refrigerate until thoroughly chilled.

火腿釀冬瓜 WINTER MELON STUFFED WITH HAM

Even though winter melon is used primarily for soups, it makes a lovely "vegetable" by itself. Here, with Smithfield ham slices inserted into it and the melon then steamed, it becomes a delicate and elegant dish. Well saturated with the thick sauce, it literally melts in your mouth. The scallions and black pepper are crucial, giving the delicate dish a nice lift. *Serves 4 or more.*

2-pound slice winter melon	½ teaspoon salt, to taste
1 piece (about 4 ounces) cooked Smithfield ham (*page 492*)	1 tablespoon cornstarch dissolved in 3 tablespoons stock
½ cup chicken stock	Freshly ground black pepper
1½ tablespoons oil	
1 tablespoon finely chopped scallion greens	

Winter melon is usually sold by the pound in a curved wedge, the center much wider than the ends. Remove the pulp and seeds, peel off the rind, and trim off the tips. Rinse and blot dry.

Cut the melon crosswise into 1-inch-wide pieces; then make a slit in the center of each about halfway to three-quarters down. In the widest section, cut the pieces in two and then create the pockets. You should have about 20 pieces of melon.

Cut the ham in thin slices against the grain, about the size of the melon pieces. Insert 1 piece of ham into each slit, with an edge showing at the top. This step may be done up to a day in advance. Cover and refrigerate. Bring out the melon just before the steaming.

Put the melon pieces, ham edge up, in a shallow heatproof bowl, pour over the stock, and steam over high heat for 20 minutes.

Remove the bowl and transfer the melon pieces with a slotted spoon to a hot serving dish, arranging them attractively in a circular nestling pattern. Pour out juice into a measuring cup. Put the dish inside the hot steamer, covered, as you prepare the sauce.

You should have about 1 cup of the hot, steaming juice; if not, add a little more chicken stock to make that cup.

Heat a small skillet or enameled saucepan over high heat until hot; add the oil, swirl, and heat for 10 seconds. Scatter in the scallion greens and stir briskly to bring out their aroma. Then add the steaming juice and the salt and stir until the sauce comes to a simmer. Lower heat to maintain a faint simmer, add the dissolved cornstarch, and stir until the sauce is thick and smooth. Pour over the melon pieces and grind a good amount of black pepper on top.

爆
淹
西
洋
菜
SPICY MINCED WATERCRESS

If watercress is seared in hot oil, no matter how briefly, without a preliminary macerating, the fluffy leaves wilt and the stringy stems are tasteless and chewy. However, if the watercress is minced and macerated, then stir-fried very quickly, and finally chilled, its texture becomes remarkably crisp, even if it is then simmered with liquid. This is a magnificent cold relish as is or a delightful seasoning agent for other vegetables, such as bamboo shoots, broccoli stems, lima beans, or bean curd. *Serves 3 to 4.*

2 bunches watercress, minced
1 teaspoon salt
3 tablespoons oil

1 large dried chili pepper
2 teaspoons sesame oil

Rinse the watercress in cold water and shake dry. Holding the bunch firmly, mince both leaves and stems. Put the minced watercress in a bowl, sprinkle in the salt, and toss well; macerate it for 30 minutes in the refrigerator. Squeeze dry and place on a dish.

Heat a skillet over high heat until hot; add the oil, swirl, and turn heat to medium low. Brown the chili pepper in the oil for about 40 seconds, flipping and pressing it. Turn heat high, scatter in the watercress, and stir-fry rapidly in scooping motions for 30 seconds. Add the sesame oil, give a few sweeping turns, and pour into a dish. Refrigerate until the watercress is thoroughly cold.

炒
蘿
蔔
絲
STIR-FRIED SHREDDED RADISH SALAD

Macerating and then briefly searing white radishes lighten their texture, making them crunchy when chilled. *Serves 3 to 4.*

1 pound white radishes, shredded
1 tablespoon salt
2 tablespoons oil
1 medium whole scallion, finely
   chopped

¼ teaspoon roasted and crushed
   Szechuan peppercorns
   (*page 500*)
1 teaspoon sesame oil

Wash and dry the radishes and trim off the ends. Slice them thin; then shred the slices. Toss them in a bowl with 1 tablespoon salt until they become moist. Let them macerate in the refrigerator for 2 to 3 hours. Squeeze dry and discard the liquid just before the stir-frying.

Heat a wok or large, heavy skillet over high heat until hot; add the oil, swirl, and heat for 30 seconds. Scatter in the radishes and stir rapidly for 10 seconds. Add the chopped scallions and the peppercorns and stir another 10 seconds. Dribble in the sesame oil, give a few big turns, and pour into a dish. Cover and chill until thoroughly cold before serving.

冬菜燒蘿蔔球　SIMMERED RADISH BALLS

Here radishes are simmered and then tumbled in a sauce. They are translucent, sauce-glazed, and speckled with tiny dots of the faintly garlicky preserved vegetable. They make a very unusual side dish and would go beautifully with pork dishes. *Serves 4 or more.*

20 large red radishes	1 tablespoon dry sherry
1 cup chicken stock	2 teaspoons cornstarch dissolved
½ teaspoon salt	in 2 teaspoons water
3 tablespoons oil	2 teaspoons sesame oil
2 tablespoons Tientsin preserved	
vegetable	

Peel the radishes; rinse and drain. Put them in a small saucepan, add the stock and salt, and bring to a boil. Adjust the heat to maintain a gentle simmering, cover, and simmer for 30 minutes, until the radishes are soft and translucent. Turn off the heat and set aside.

Heat a wok or large, heavy skillet over high heat until hot; add the oil, swirl, and heat for 30 seconds. Scatter in the preserved vegetable and stir briskly in the hot oil; splash in the sherry and mingle well. Pour the radishes and stock into the skillet and let the stock sizzle for about 1 minute as you stir and turn constantly. Add the dissolved cornstarch and stir until the sauce thickens. Add the sesame oil, give a few rapid turns, and pour into a hot serving dish.

泡菜　PICKLED VEGETABLES

Home pickling was so important in Chinese households that special porcelain urns were made from the kilns of Kwangsi province. Measuring about 3 feet in height and 1 foot in diameter, the beautiful blue-white jar, resembling a vase, was ingeniously designed for perfect functioning.

Around the neck was a deep cup into which water was poured. When the cover, shaped like a deep rice bowl, was placed over this cup its rim was submerged in about 2 inches of water, thereby preventing air from seeping in but allowing the gas of fermentation to escape through the water as the brine aged.

Just as Liu-ma always preserved the garlic (*see page 164*) so did she also supply the household with a good variety of excellent pickles all year round.

THE BRINE
4 tablespoons salt
2 tablespoons Szechuan pepper-
    corns
4 dried chili peppers
1 cup boiling water
7 cups cold water
6 quarter-sized slices peeled ginger
2 tablespoons gin or vodka

Combine the salt, Szechuan peppercorns, and chili peppers in a gallon jar; pour in the boiling water and stir until the salt is dissolved. Let the water cool a little, then add the cold water and stir. Add the ginger and gin. The brine is now ready for pickling. If you don't have a gallon jar, make the brine in a large pot and divide it among smaller bottles.

Any firm or root vegetable may be pickled. The variety and quantity of vegetables used is up to you. The only point to remember is that they must all be submerged in the brine.

Once pickled, the vegetables are refreshingly crisp. They are wonderful eaten as is with a little sesame oil or they can be stir-fried to make delectable hot vegetable dishes or a spicy contrast to meat or chicken.

Here is a good combination to start with, using this amount of brine.

THE VEGETABLES

1 to 1½ pounds green cabbage	½ to 1 pound green beans
3 to 4 carrots	4 to 8 gherkins (small fresh
1 to 1½ pounds white turnips	cucumbers, 3 inches long)
	2 to 4 broccoli stems

Wash and dry all the vegetables well. Cut off the stem and any wilted leaves from the cabbage; quarter it, core it, and separate the leaves. Halve or quarter the carrots lengthwise according to their thickness. Trim off the root ends of the turnips and quarter the small ones or cut the larger ones into 5 or 6 wedges. Snap off the ends of the green beans. Trim off the stem ends of the gherkins. Peel the broccoli stems and either leave them whole or slice them in half lengthwise.

Scatter the larger cabbage leaves in the brine and weight them with the turnips and carrots. Then put in the green beans, broccoli stems, gherkins, and the tender inner leaves of the cabbage. Stir with chopsticks or a wooden spoon and press down the vegetables so that all are covered by the brine. Screw the jar lid on lightly and chill in the refrigerator for 4 days. By then the tender inner cabbage leaves and the gherkins, broccoli stems, and green beans will have lost their raw taste and will be ready for eating. The others will be just right on the sixth or seventh day.

To keep the jar filled, replenish with small amounts of the same vegetables or a chosen few; they should be added to the bottom of the jar, poking them down with chopsticks, so the pickled ones at the top will be easy to remove. Add a little salt and gin with each replenishment to strengthen the brine.

The brine keeps well for months. If it turns slightly cloudy and sour, strain it through cheesecloth and add some salt, Szechuan peppercorns, chili peppers, and gin. Or make a small amount of fresh brine and add it to the strained old brine. There are no set measurements—this is old-fashioned brine that doesn't like to be scientifically measured. It's up to your personal taste.

The vegetables should not stay in the brine more than 3 weeks—they will lose their crispness and turn too sour.

炒 泡 菜   STIR-FRIED PICKLED VEGETABLES

If the vegetables have been in the brine about 2 weeks, and are slightly sour, rinse them briefly and shake dry; add 1 or 1½ teaspoons of sugar when you stir-fry them. Crisp and crunchy, these pickled vegetables are remarkably refreshing. They are subtly hot and spicy. *Serves 4 or more.*

3 tablespoons oil	½ cup finely diced broccoli stems
1 cup finely diced cabbage	¼ cup finely diced carrots
1 cup finely diced turnips	¼ cup finely diced gherkins
½ cup finely diced green beans	1 tablespoon sesame oil

Heat a wok or large, heavy skillet over high heat until hot; add the oil, swirl, and heat for 30 seconds. Splash in the diced pickled vegetables and sugar if necessary and stir rapidly in scooping and turning motions to coat them with oil. The moment their colors brighten and deepen, add the sesame oil. Give a few fast turns and pour into a serving dish. They are delicious hot, at room temperature, or chilled.

肉丁炒泡菜 STIR-FRIED PICKLED VEGETABLES WITH PORK

In this recipe, the mildly seasoned pork combines beautifully with the lightly salty, spicy vegetables. It is a crunchy dish, and good hot, at room temperature, and cold. *Serves 4 or more.*

1 cup finely chopped cabbage
½ cup finely diced carrots
½ cup finely diced string beans or
  broccoli stems
3 tablespoons oil
½ pound boneless lean pork loin,
  finely diced

1 tablespoon light soy sauce
1 teaspoon dry sherry
¼ teaspoon sugar
4 tablespoons water
2 teaspoons sesame oil

If the vegetables have been in brine about 2 weeks, and are slightly sour, rinse them briefly and shake dry; then add a little sugar when you stir-fry them.

Heat a wok or large, heavy skillet over high heat until hot; add 2 tablespoons of the oil and heat for 30 seconds. Splash in the cabbage, carrots, and beans or broccoli stems, and stir rapidly to coat them with oil. When their colors brighten and deepen, pour them immediately into a dish.

Wipe the pan clean, add the remaining tablespoon of oil, and heat for a few seconds until hot. Scatter in the diced pork and stir rapidly to separate the dice; stir and toss until all pinkness is gone, about 30 seconds. Add the soy sauce, sherry, and sugar; stir to mingle. Add the water and gather all the meat into the center of the pan. Turn heat low, cover, and cook for 2 minutes, until there is very little liquid left.

Uncover, turn heat high, and add the vegetables. Stir in sweeping motions to mingle the vegetables and pork. Add the sesame oil, give a few sweeping turns, and pour into a hot serving dish.

VARIATIONS
Use diced chicken breast or flank steak instead of pork.

釀茄子 DEEP-FRIED EGGPLANTS WITH CURRY BEEF FILLING

These deep-fried "sandwiches" are very hard to stop eating. The coating is crisp, the eggplants soft and creamy, and the filling scrumptious. *Serves 3 to 4.*

Beef filling:
½ pound ground lean beef
1 large whole scallion, finely
    chopped
1 tablespoon light soy sauce
1 teaspoon curry powder
¼ teaspoon salt
½ teaspoon sugar
⅛ teaspoon black pepper
1 tablespoon cornstarch

2 slender eggplants, about 1 pound

Coating:
1 egg, well beaten
1 cup breadcrumbs seasoned lightly
    with salt and pepper

4 cups oil

March-chop the ground beef a few times to loosen its formation. Place it in a bowl, add the seasonings and the cornstarch in the order listed, and stir circularly in one direction until well mingled. The consistency will be on the dry side.

Cut off the stems and peel the eggplants. Cut each crosswise into ⅓-inch-thick slices. Spread 1 slice thickly with a glob of meat filling, then cover with another slice, to make a sandwich. Leave the smaller end pieces as they are and cut the large sandwiches in two. Dip each sandwich in the beaten egg and then coat lightly but well with the breadcrumbs on all sides, using more than a cup if necessary. You can do this a few hours in advance; cover and refrigerate.

Heat a wok or heavy pot over high heat for 30 seconds; add the 4 cups oil and heat until it foams a cube of bread instantly, about 375 degrees. Lower in the eggplants piece by piece (do only half if pot is too crowded) and deep-fry them about 4 minutes, until they are golden brown and crisp, gently turning them all the while. When done, drain them on paper towels.

Serve them as hot appetizers or as a main dish.

VARIATION
Zucchini may be substituted for eggplant with equally delicious results. Since zucchini contains more moisture than eggplant, the sandwiches should be eaten immediately.

魚香茄子 SZECHUAN EGGPLANTS

This is a stimulating stir-fried dish, full of seductive aromas. Dark and gleaming, each piece of eggplant is plump and soft, and a wonderful complex of flavors comes through—hot, sour, salty, sweet. *Serves 3 to 4.*

1½ pounds small eggplants
4 tablespoons oil
1 tablespoon chili-pepper oil
  (*page 489*)
1 large clove garlic, coarsely minced
4 quarter-sized slices peeled ginger,
  coarsely minced
1 small whole scallion, finely
  chopped

Seasonings:
2 tablespoons bean paste
1 tablespoon dark soy sauce
2 tablespoons dry sherry
2 tablespoons cider vinegar
2 tablespoons sugar
½ teaspoon roasted and crushed
  Szechuan peppercorns
  (*page 500*)

1 teaspoon cornstarch dissolved
in 1 tablespoon water and
1 teaspoon sesame oil

Rinse and dry the eggplants and cut off the stems. Do not peel. Quarter them lengthwise and cut each quarter into 2-inch wedges. Place them with the garlic, ginger, and scallions on your working platter. Mix the seasonings in a bowl until the sugar is dissolved. In another bowl, dissolve the cornstarch with the water and sesame oil.

Heat a wok or large, heavy skillet over high heat for 30 seconds; add the 2 oils, swirl, and heat for 30 seconds. Scatter in the garlic, ginger, and scallions and stir rapidly for 15 seconds. Then add the eggplant wedges and stir with a spatula in flipping and light pressing motions for 2 minutes, to expose them to the oil. Turn heat to medium high and continue to flip and press lightly for 4 more minutes, until the wedges are slightly browned and flattened. Do not press them hard, lest they break and become messy.

Turn heat high; give the seasonings a stir and pour over the eggplants. Stir in scooping motions for 30 seconds; give the cornstarch mixture a stir and add to the sauce. Toss briefly, then pour into a hot serving dish.

蒸茄子 STEAMED EGGPLANT

Unpeeled eggplant, diamond-scored, steamed, and then seasoned with a garlicky sauce, is an impressive and very tasty dish. This is good hot, and even better cold. The eggplant is soft but not mushy. The scoring makes it dainty looking and allows the vegetable to absorb the delicious sauce. *Serves 2 to 4.*

1 eggplant, about 1¾ pounds

Sauce:
1 tablespoon oil
1 tablespoon sesame oil
2 large cloves garlic, minced
1 tablespoon minced peeled ginger
2 tablespoons cider vinegar
2 tablespoons light soy sauce
1 tablespoon sugar

Rinse and dry the eggplant; discard the stem. Cut eggplant in half lengthwise and then score the skin surface of both halves with ½-inch-wide crosshatching, going halfway through the thickness. Place the scored halves side by side on a shallow, heatproof platter and steam over high heat for about 30 to 40 minutes, until they have a slightly sunken look.

Drain off and discard the liquid in the platter. Transfer the eggplant halves carefully to a serving platter with spatulas or by sliding them off. Cover platter to keep eggplant warm.

Make the sauce. Heat a small skillet over high heat until hot; add the oils, swirl, and heat for 10 seconds. Scatter in the minced garlic and ginger, turn heat to medium, and stir for a few seconds until garlic is aromatic. Add the vinegar, soy sauce, and sugar, and turn off the heat; stir until the sugar is dissolved. Pour the sauce over the eggplant and serve.

蠔
油
豆
腐
BEAN CURD IN OYSTER SAUCE

A dark, chunky, glazed dish of smooth bean curd. The scallions lend a refreshing aroma and color. *Serves 2 to 4.*

4 squares fresh bean curd
3 tablespoons oil
2 quarter-sized slices peeled ginger, minced
1 tablespoon light soy sauce
½ cup chicken or meat stock

1 teaspoon cornstarch dissolved in 1 tablespoon water and 2 teaspoons sesame oil
2 tablespoons oyster sauce
2 whole scallions, in 1½-inch-long shreds

Cut each square of bean curd in two; then cut each half crosswise into 4 pieces. Cover the pieces with hot water and soak for 10 minutes, draining them just before adding them to the pan.

Heat a large, heavy skillet over high heat until hot; add the oil, swirl, and heat for 30 seconds. Scatter in the ginger and stir a few times. Drain the bean curd and quickly add them to the skillet, evening them out with a spatula and then sprinkling them with the soy sauce and stock. When the liquid comes to a boil, gently turn the bean curd over. Adjust heat to low, cover, and simmer about 4 minutes.

Add the dissolved cornstarch and stir gently until the sauce thickens. Add the oyster sauce and turn the bean curd a few times; then pour them into a hot serving dish. Scatter the top with the shredded scallions.

蝦仁豆腐 BEAN CURD WITH SHRIMP

In this dish the bean-curd cubes are extremely soft and smooth while the shrimp, not having been coated, are tender but slightly crisp. There is a creamy sauce. The dash of pepper gives the essentially light dish just a touch of zest. *Serves 2 to 4.*

4 squares fresh bean curd
½ pound medium shrimp
2 quarter-sized slices peeled
   ginger, minced
1 whole scallion, finely chopped

Seasonings:
2 tablespoons dry sherry
2 tablespoons light soy sauce
¼ teaspoon salt
¼ teaspoon sugar

½ cup chicken or meat stock
2 teaspoons cornstarch dissolved
   in 1 tablespoon water, then
   2 teaspoons sesame oil added
3 tablespoons oil
Sprinkling black pepper

Cut the bean curd into ½-inch cubes; cover cubes with hot water and soak for 10 to 15 minutes, and drain just before using.

Shell and devein the shrimp, rinse, and drain them. Cut them crosswise into ½-inch pieces. Place them with the ginger and scallion on your working platter. Mix the seasonings in a small bowl and have the stock and the dissolved cornstarch ready.

Heat a heavy skillet over high heat until hot; add the oil, swirl, and heat for 30 seconds. Scatter in the ginger and scallions and stir a few times. Then add the shrimp and give them a few fast stirs. Add the seasonings, and stir briskly until the shrimp begin to turn pink. Then add the stock. Turn the heat very low. Drain the bean curd cubes into a colander, shake off the water, and pour them over the shrimp. Stir gently to even out the contents, turn heat to medium low to maintain a vigorous simmering, cover, and simmer for 3 minutes.

Give the cornstarch mixture a big stir and pour it into the pan; stir gently until the sauce thickens. Pour into a hot serving dish and sprinkle the top with a few grindings of black pepper.

VARIATION

Instead of shrimp, substitute ½ pound crabmeat, either fresh or frozen, in flakes or chunks.

麻
婆
豆
腐

BEAN CURD WITH HOT MEAT SAUCE

This is a magnificent dish, gently spicy, with a final teasing touch of Szechuan peppercorns. It is smooth in texture and light in color, lightly glazed with sauce and speckled with the ground meat. *Serves 3 to 4.*

4 squares fresh bean curd
½ pound ground pork
4 quarter-sized slices peeled ginger,
    finely minced

Seasonings:
1 tablespoon dry sherry
1 tablespoon hot bean paste
1 tablespoon dark soy sauce

1 cup chicken or meat stock

Binding sauce:
2 teaspoons cornstarch dissolved
    in 1 tablespoon water
1 tablespoon dark soy sauce
2 teaspoons sesame oil

2 whole scallions, finely chopped
½ teaspoon roasted and crushed
    Szechuan peppercorns
    (*page 500*)
2 tablespoons oil

Cut the bean-curd squares into ½-inch cubes. Cover with hot water and soak for 10 to 15 minutes, draining them just before adding to the pan.

March-chop the ground pork a few times to loosen its formation. Mince the ginger, set out the seasonings and the stock, combine the binding-sauce ingredients, and place the scallions with the peppercorns in separate piles on a small plate.

Heat a skillet over high heat until hot; add the oil, swirl, and heat for 30 seconds. Stir the minced ginger in the oil a few times. Add the meat and poke and shake with the tip of a spatula until it is loosened; then stir it in pressing and scooping motions until all the pinkness is gone. Splash in the sherry, add the hot bean paste and soy sauce, and stir briskly to season the meat well. Lower the heat and stir in the stock.

Drain the bean-curd cubes in a colander, shake off excess water, and scatter them over the meat. Stir gently to even out the pan. When the contents bubble, adjust heat to medium low to maintain a strong simmering, cover, and simmer for 5 minutes, turning once by slipping a spatula under the bean curd and meat and flipping the mass over, being careful not to mash the bean curd.

Give the binding sauce a big stir and pour it in a circle over the bean-curd cubes; turn them very gently a few times until the sauce thickens. Scatter in the scallions, fold the bean curd and meat a few times, and then pour into a hot serving dish. Sprinkle the ground peppercorns on top.

VARIATIONS

The hotness can be heightened by adding 1 teaspoon chili-pepper oil (*page 489*) with the hot bean paste or completely eliminated by using regular bean paste instead of the hot. Don't omit the Szechuan peppercorns, however; they give the dish its distinctive personality.

釀 STUFFED BEAN CURD
豆
腐

The bean-curd texture is soft and the filling very juicy. A light sauce glazes the dish. It is both a delicate and substantial treat. *Serves 2 to 4.*

4 squares fresh bean curd
¼ pound ground pork

Marinade:
2 teaspoons finely chopped
   scallions
2 teaspoons light soy sauce
2 teaspoons dry sherry
⅛ teaspoon salt
Dash black pepper
1 teaspoon cornstarch dissolved
   in 1 tablespoon water

Sauce:
1 tablespoon light soy sauce
2 teaspoons cornstarch dissolved
   in 1 tablespoon water and
   1 teaspoon sesame oil

3 tablespoons oil
1 cup chicken or meat stock
2 small whole scallions, in
   1½-inch-long shreds

Cut each bean-curd square into 2 triangles; then cut a deep slit down the long side and one short side to within ¼ inch of third side. Repeat with all the triangles.

March-chop the ground pork a few times to loosen its formation. Put it in a bowl and add the marinade, mixing in the dissolved cornstarch last. Divide it into 8 portions and stuff a portion inside each bean-curd triangle, smoothing the edges with your fingers. Combine sauce ingredients.

Heat a large, heavy skillet over high heat until hot; add the oil, swirl, and heat for 30 seconds. Turn heat to medium low. First shallow-fry the triangles briefly on their meat-filled edges (standing up), a minute for each—this works, and the filling will not fall out. Then turn them flat and brown each side for about 1 minute. Add the stock and when it boils adjust heat to low to maintain a gentle simmering, cover, and simmer for 8 minutes, turning once. Remove the triangles carefully with a spatula to a hot serving platter without the liquid.

Add the sauce to the liquid in the pan. Stir over low heat until the mixture is smooth and thickened. Pour the sauce over the bean curd and scatter the shredded scallions on top.

冬菇燗豆腐 MUSHROOM-SMOTHERED BEAN CURD

This was a popular hot stir-fry appetizer in Peking restaurants. The mushroom flavor penetrates the daintily cut bean curd over low heat. Instead of having its customary custardlike texture, this bean curd is soft but firm. This is also a marvelous dish served cold. *Serves 2 to 4.*

3 squares fresh bean curd
8 medium-sized thick-capped dried
    black Chinese mushrooms
3 tablespoons oil
1 whole scallion, in 1½-inch-long
    shreds
2 quarter-sized slices peeled ginger,
    shredded

1 tablespoon dry sherry
2 tablespoons dark soy sauce
½ teaspoon sugar
½ cup mushroom-soaking
    liquid
1 tablespoon sesame oil

Quarter each bean-curd square; then cut each of these smaller squares into 2 triangles. Turn each triangle on its longest side and cut through the thickness to make 3 thin triangles from each. Set aside.

Cover the mushrooms with ¾ cup boiling water and soak for 1 hour. Lightly squeeze them to let their liquid drain back into the bowl; then rinse them briefly and squeeze dry. Destem and cut each cap into ½-inch-wide slices. Assemble the scallions, ginger, mushrooms, and bean-curd triangles on your working platter. Measure the mushroom liquid; if there isn't ½ cup, add a little stock or water.

Heat a large, heavy skillet over high heat until hot; add the oil, swirl, and heat for 15 seconds. Lower heat to medium, scatter in the scallions and ginger, and stir rapidly a few times. Add the sherry, soy sauce, sugar, and mushroom liquid; as it sizzles to a boil, add the mushrooms and bean-curd triangles. Turn them gently a few times. Adjust the heat to maintain a very gentle simmering, cover, and simmer for 10 to 12 minutes, turning the contents once midway.

By this time there should be little or no liquid in the skillet. Add the sesame oil and turn the bean-curd triangles once more; then pour into a hot serving dish.

菠菜豆腐羹　SPINACH AND BEAN-CURD ''GUNN''

Fluffy and smooth, this dish is a cross between a soup and a soupy main dish. It is delicate, and tastily embellished by the pork and ham. *Serves 2 to 4.*

5 ounces fresh parboiled or frozen chopped spinach, thoroughly defrosted	3 squares fresh bean curd
	2 tablespoons oil
	4 cups chicken or meat stock
¼ pound lean loin of pork	Salt to taste
	2 tablespoons cornstarch dissolved in 4 tablespoons water
Marinade:	2 tablespoons finely diced cooked Smithfield ham (*page 492*)
2 teaspoons light soy sauce	Sprinkling black pepper
1 teaspoon dry sherry	
1 teaspoon cornstarch	

Cut a 10-ounce package of frozen spinach in half. Thaw one half; reserve the other for another use. March-chop the thawed spinach until very finely minced. If using fresh spinach, wash it well, parboil 1 minute in boiling water, rinse, squeeze dry, and chop. Cut the pork against the grain into ⅛-inch-thick slices. They should be about 1½ inches long. Place them in a bowl with the marinade and marinate for 15 minutes.

Cut the bean-curd squares into ½-inch cubes, cover them with hot water, and soak for about 10 minutes; drain just before cooking.

Heat a wok or heavy pot over high heat until hot; add the oil, swirl, and heat for 30 seconds. Add the marinated pork slices and stir-fry briskly until all pinkness is gone. Add the stock. When it boils, add the drained bean-curd cubes and stir gently. Turn heat low to maintain a gentle simmering, cover, and simmer for 5 minutes. Season with salt to taste, then add the dissolved cornstarch and stir gently until dish is thickened.

Stir in the spinach and the diced ham and continue to stir gently for about 1 minute. Pour into a deep bowl or a tureen and serve with a sprinkling of black pepper.

家常豆腐 HOME-STYLE BEAN CURD

There are many versions of this dish; it's a matter of whose home and what regional style of cooking is involved. One fact is constant, however: the bean-curd cubes are first deep-fried, so that instead of being soft and smooth, they are firm and spongy. The common version is generally rather neutral—the bean curd is combined with slivers of meat, some vegetables, and a mellow soy-sauce mixture. My home-style, without any moist vegetables, is spicy, with a rich brown sauce. *Serves 2 to 4.*

4 squares fresh bean curd
¼ pound loin of pork

Marinade:
1 teaspoon light soy sauce
1 teaspoon dry sherry
1 teaspoon cornstarch

1 medium whole scallion, finely
    chopped
2 quarter-sized slices peeled ginger,
    minced
2 cloves garlic, minced
1 teaspoon fermented black beans,
    rinsed briefly and chopped

Seasonings:
2 tablespoons light soy sauce
1 tablespoon dry sherry
1 teaspoon salt
½ teaspoon sugar
1 cup chicken or meat stock

1 tablespoon cornstarch dissolved
    in 2 tablespoons water
1 cup oil
1 tablespoon hot bean paste
2 teaspoons sesame oil

Preparations and deep-frying

Cut each square of bean curd in half, and then each half into 4 crosswise pieces. Blot dry with paper towels.

Slice the pork loin against the grain into thin slices about the same dimensions as the bean-curd pieces. Mix the pork with the marinade. Prepare the scallion, ginger, garlic, and fermented black beans and place them on a plate. Combine the seasonings and stir until the sugar has dissolved. Make the cornstarch mixture and place the oil, hot bean paste, and sesame oil within reach.

Heat a wok or large, heavy skillet over high heat until hot. Add the oil and heat until it foams a cube of bread instantly, about 375 degrees. Turn heat to medium, scatter in the bean-curd pieces, and deep-fry them about 2 minutes, until they are light brown; turn them constantly. Drain on paper towels. This step may be done in advance, but do not refrigerate the deep-fried bean curd. The marinated meat may be refrigerated.

Stir-frying

Pour out all the oil but 3 tablespoons and heat over high heat. Add the marinated pork and stir briskly in swishing and turning motions for 1 minute until the slices are firm. Toss in the scallion, ginger, garlic, and black beans; stir rapidly to explode their aromas, then add the hot bean paste and stir to mingle well.

Add the deep-fried bean-curd pieces and the seasonings; stir to even out the pan. Turn heat to medium low to maintain a strong simmering, cover, and simmer for about 4 minutes. Gently stir in the cornstarch mixture until the sauce is thick and smooth. Add the sesame oil, give a big stir, and pour into a hot serving dish.

蝦米蘿蔔煮粉絲 TRANSPARENT NOODLES WITH DRIED SHRIMP AND TURNIPS

This is a delicate-looking dish of glistening noodles, translucent turnips, pink shrimp, and green scallions. The stock-sauce is flavored by the deep-sea taste of the dried shrimp. *Serves 2 to 4.*

2 tablespoons dried shrimp (presoaked)	2 cups shredded icicle turnips or white radishes
¼ cup boiling water	3 tablespoons oil
1 tablespoon dry sherry	1 medium whole scallion, finely chopped
¾ cup chicken stock (approximately)	1 to 1½ teaspoons salt
2 ounces transparent noodles (presoaked)	

Preparations

Pour ¼ cup boiling water over the dried shrimp and soak for 1 hour; they should have expanded and softened. Remove them 15 minutes before cooking and put them in a bowl with the sherry. Cover and let them marinate. Pour the shrimp-soaking liquid into a measuring cup and add about ¾ cup chicken stock to make 1 cup.

Soak the noodles in cold water for 30 minutes. Drain and cut them into 4 sections crosswise.

Peel and rinse the turnips or radishes. Slice them lengthwise into ¼-inch-thick pieces and then cut those into julienne strips—about 2 inches long. Set aside in a dish.

These preparations may be done ahead of time. Cover and refrigerate the drained noodles and the shredded turnips. Let the shrimp sit in the sherry.

Simmering

Heat a wok or large, heavy skillet over high heat until hot; add the oil, swirl, and heat for 30 seconds. Turn heat to medium, add the scallion and turnips, and stir rapidly to toss them with the oil. Scatter in the shrimp and sherry; stir briefly. Add 1 teaspoon salt, the stock, and the noodles and toss to even out the contents.

Turn heat low to maintain a gentle simmering, cover, and simmer for 10 minutes. Adjust seasoning with another ½ teaspoon salt if needed and pour into a hot serving dish.

Sprouting dry fava beans

While fresh fava beans are incomparable in their sweet tenderness, dried fava beans, available in pound packages in Chinese grocery stores and by mail order, are also very tasty and unusual. After being sprouted, they are nutty, sweet, and as mealy as roasted chestnuts. The drying process was first initiated for preservation, but it has long since established its gastronomical merit. The delicious sprouted beans are a popular nibbler in the eastern part of China. They are very inexpensive, and a pound will yield 6 cups of sprouted beans.

FIRST DAY—Rinse the pound of fava beans in cold water. Then spread them out on a tray or rimmed plate large enough so the beans are in a single layer. Cover them with an inch of cold water. Let them soak.

SECOND DAY—Drain the water and rinse the beans briefly in cold water. Cover them again with an inch of water.

THIRD DAY—Tiny sprouts begin to appear. Rinse the beans briefly in cold water. Leave just a little water on the bottom of the tray or plate. Wet a clean towel (preferably terry cloth) and cover the beans with it, wringing out the towel in fresh water twice during the day.

FOURTH DAY—Each bean has a ½-inch sprout, resembling a tiny elephant tusk. Rinse the beans gently and drain. Set aside the amount you wish to cook and store the rest, wet, in a covered jar or bowl—they keep well for about a week in the refrigerator if you sprinkle them with a little water every now and then.

Following are two excellent recipes. In each case, the beans are neat and firmly encased within the skin-shell, which splits open around the sprouts during the cooking. When eating them, bite into this shell and let the succulent center collapse in your mouth; do not eat the shells. These beans are wonderful wine chasers, absolutely delectable hot or cold.

炒 STIR-FRIED FAVA BEANS

笠
豆

This simple, delicious dish is good either hot or cold. *Serves 2 to 4.*

2 cups sprouted fava beans	1 teaspoon sugar
3 tablespoons oil	1½ cups water
1 teaspoon salt	1 teaspoon sesame oil

Heat a wok or a large, heavy skillet over high heat until hot; add the oil, swirl, and heat for 30 seconds. Add the beans and stir rapidly for 10 seconds to sear the skin-shells. Add the salt, sugar, and water, stir to mingle, and when the liquid boils, turn the heat to medium low to maintain a strong simmering. Cover and simmer for 25 minutes, until there is barely any water left in the pan.

Uncover and stir the beans lightly until there is no water left; then add the sesame oil and give a few sweeping turns. Pour the beans into a serving dish and either serve them hot or refrigerate and serve cold.

To eat them, pop them into your mouth, bite down on the hulls, and suck out the tasty centers. Spit out the hulls if you find them too chewy.

VARIATION

For a more exotic flavor, add ⅛ teaspoon roasted and crushed Szechuan peppercorns (*page 500*) after the simmering.

八
角
煮
蠶
豆

STAR-ANISED FAVA BEANS

Reddish brown and glistening, the beans have that rich, sweet mellowness of red-cooking ingredients. Their texture is softer and mealier than that produced in the stir-fried recipe. *Serves 2 to 4.*

2 cups sprouted fava beans	1 whole star anise
3 tablespoons oil	2 cups water
2 tablespoons dark soy sauce	1 teaspoon sesame oil
2 tablespoons sugar	

Heat a wok or large, heavy skillet over high heat until hot; add the oil, swirl, and heat for 30 seconds. Toss in the beans and stir them briskly for 10 seconds. Then add the soy sauce, 1 tablespoon of the sugar, the star anise, and the water, and stir to mingle. When the liquid boils, adjust heat to medium low to maintain a strong simmering, then cover and simmer for 40 minutes, until there is very little liquid left in the pan. Uncover, turn heat high, and add the remaining tablespoon sugar. Stir rapidly in turning and folding motions until the dissolving sugar darkens and coats the beans. Add the sesame oil, give the beans a few turns, and pour into a hot serving dish. The hulls will be softer than in the stir-fried version, so eat them if you wish.

麵
筋

WHEAT GLUTEN

Known as "muscles" or "sinews" of dough in Chinese, gluten is made by washing out the starch from dough until only the adhesive substance remains. Once made, it is either boiled or deep-fried before being finally cooked with seasonings and other ingredients. It is a main staple for Chinese vegetarians: to them, gluten is a symbolic meat.

A devout Buddhist and virtually a total vegetarian, Liu-ma regularly slipped into the kitchen and washed a batch of "sinews" for the enjoyment of the entire household. Since gluten is easy and fascinating to make, I was an eager helper. When I was little, it was a plaything to me, as much fun as making a dough animal or doll, but as I grew older, I marveled at the ingenuity of the first discoverer of this wonderful substance. Smooth-textured, it gives weight to a light vegetable dish; very absorbent, it acquires flavors beautifully from other ingredients. Much to Liu-ma's chagrin, Ar-chang often borrowed her vegetarian meat for stuffing with pork, simmering with red-cooked meats, or stir-frying with meat and vegetables.

| 2 pounds unbleached flour | 2¼ cups lukewarm water |
| (such as Hecker's) | |

Pour the flour into a large pot and add the water; stir and knead (punching, folding, and turning) until the mixture forms a smooth dough. Cover the pot and let the dough "sober" for 1 hour.

Place the pot under a fast-running faucet of tepid water and "wash" it by kneading and squeezing it with your hands continuously for 15 minutes, pouring out the water frequently so the dough is constantly being washed by fresh water. At first the dough will separate into slippery stringy pieces; then, as time passes, it becomes sticky and puffy. Finally, at the end of 15 minutes of washing and massaging, it forms into a ball of elastic gum. The washing is complete when the water is no longer milky but just slightly cloudy; when pulled and stretched, the gluten should show no white specks of starch.

Gluten is a "created" ingredient and its creation involves three stages: 1) making dough and washing it to retain only the gluten; 2) cooking the raw gluten by boiling or deep-frying it to let it acquire a definite texture; 3) cooking it with other ingredients to make a finished dish.

You may do the initial step days in advance. Submerge it in cold water, refrigerate, and change the water every day. Then either boil or deep-fry it before giving it its final cooking with seasonings. Since boiling and deep-frying produce completely different kinds of textures, I suggest the first time dividing the gluten and doing half one way, half the other, so that you may decide which you prefer.

Boiling

Bring a large pot of water to a boil. Divide the gluten in half by twisting it. Pull and twist half the gluten into 24 small pieces—they will be odd shaped, roughly 1½ inches in diameter. Put them on a plate without letting them touch one another, since once out of water they are sticky.

Pull each piece a little to spread it before you drop it into the water. Working quickly, pull and drop in all the gluten lumps. Boil for about 5 minutes, until they are floating on top of the water. Drain in a colander.

They are now ready for the final cooking. If you do the preceding step in advance, put them in a container, submerge in water, then cover and refrigerate. They keep well for a week if you change the water every day. You could also put them in a plastic bag and freeze them until needed.

Deep-frying

Break the other half of the gluten into 24 pieces as in preceding instructions.

Heat a small, heavy pot over high heat until hot; add 2 cups oil and heat until it foams a cube of bread instantly, about 375 degrees. Stretch the pieces of gluten as described above and drop them into the hot oil about 5 at a time. When they puff into large glistening balls, flip them over, and then turn them over repeatedly until lightly brown all over. Lower the heat if oil gets too hot. Remove to a plate and repeat the deep-frying until all are done.

Refrigerated, deep-fried gluten balls keep well for 1 week, covered. Sealed in a plastic bag and frozen, they will keep for months without losing their elastic texture.

• *What to expect:* Brown and crisp, these deep-fried gluten puffs are crunchy outside and soft and white inside. When cooled, they flatten and wrinkle a bit. Once cooked further with liquid and seasonings, they become silkily soft and chewy.

紅
燒
素
麵
筋 RED-COOKED VEGETARIAN WHEAT GLUTEN

The mellow flavor of the red-cooking ingredients permeates the soft gluten. This red-cooked dish is also excellent cold. *Serves as a vegetable dish 2 to 4; more as an hors d'oeuvre on an assorted platter.*

24 pieces boiled gluten (*see preceding recipe*)	4 tablespoons oil
½ cup sliced bamboo shoots	2 tablespoons dark soy sauce
12 small dried black Chinese mushrooms (presoaked)	1 tablespoon dry sherry
	½ teaspoon sugar
1 cup hot water	¾ cup mushroom-soaking liquid
	1 tablespoon sesame oil

Drain the boiled gluten. Rinse and drain the sliced bamboo shoots. Pour 1 cup hot water over the mushrooms and soak for 1 hour. Squeeze them over the soaking bowl and reserve the liquid. Rinse the mushrooms briefly, squeeze dry, and destem. Cut the caps into ½-inch-wide slices. Put the bamboo shoots, mushrooms, and gluten pieces in separate piles on your working platter. Measure out ¾ cup of the mushroom liquid, without the residue.

Heat a wok or large, heavy skillet over high heat until hot; add 1 tablespoon oil, swirl, and heat for 30 seconds. Scrape in the bamboo shoots and stir vigorously for 1 minute to extract their water. Pour into a dish.

Wipe the pan, heat it until hot, add the remaining 3 tablespoons oil, swirl, and heat until hot. Scatter in the mushrooms and gluten pieces and stir rapidly for about 30 seconds to coat them with oil. Lower the heat, add the soy sauce, sherry, and sugar. Return the bamboo shoots and stir briskly to season them. Add the mushroom liquid, even out the contents of the pan, turn heat low, cover, and simmer gently for 30 minutes.

Uncover, raise heat to make the liquid sizzle, and stir rapidly for about 10 seconds. Add the sesame oil, give the contents a few fast folds, and pour into a hot serving dish.

VARIATIONS

Use deep-fried gluten pieces. They are lighter in texture than the boiled ones, and a little slippery.

Add 1 star anise, broken into its points, if you like that deep, smoldering flavor of anise.

If you'd like meat in the dish, shred ¼ pound lean loin of pork against the grain; marinate the pork shreds in 1 teaspoon dark soy sauce and 1 teaspoon cornstarch dissolved in 2 teaspoons water. After you've fried the bamboo shoots, stir-fry the pork shreds in the 3 tablespoons oil until all the pinkness is gone, about 30 seconds; then add the mushrooms and gluten pieces. Continue recipe as above.

釀麵筋 WHEAT GLUTEN STUFFED WITH MEAT

If you wish to stuff gluten pieces with meat, you should tear the gluten into larger pieces—for the recipe on *page 413*, tear into 12 or 14 pieces rather than 24. The bounciness of the gluten makes it form into balls. When you deep-fry them they swell into large balls, and while they are still puffed, punch a hole in the side with your finger and move it around to hollow out the center—do not remove any dough, however.

This dish is substantial enough to use as a main dish; *it would serve 3 or 4 people with rice.* As a casing, the gluten is silkily firm; the filling is moist and tasty.

½ pound ground lean pork

Marinade:
2 teaspoons light soy sauce
2 teaspoons dry sherry
Sprinkling black pepper
1 teaspoon cornstarch dissolved
   in 2 teaspoons water
2 teaspoons sesame oil

12 to 14 hollowed-out deep-fried
   gluten balls
8 medium-sized dried black
   Chinese mushrooms (presoaked)
½ cup sliced bamboo shoots
1½ tablespoons dark soy sauce
¼ teaspoon sugar
1 cup chicken or meat stock
½ cup mushroom liquid

March-chop the ground meat a few times to loosen its formation. Put it in a bowl, stir in the marinade seasonings in the order listed. Divide the meat roughly into 12 to 14 portions; then stuff one portion inside a hollowed-out gluten ball. It will close by itself. Repeat with the others. You may stuff them hours in advance; cover and refrigerate.

After the mushrooms have soaked 1 hour in about ¾ cup hot water, squeeze them lightly over the bowl to let their liquid drain back. Reserve the liquid. Rinse the mushrooms, squeeze dry, and destem. Rinse and drain the sliced bamboo shoots. Measure out the mushroom liquid without the residue, to give you ½ cup.

Put the stuffed gluten balls, mushrooms, and bamboo shoots in a medium-sized saucepan and set it over high heat. Add the soy sauce, sugar, stock, and mushroom liquid, and bring to a boil. Stir a few times, then turn heat low to maintain a very gentle simmering, cover, and simmer for 30 minutes, turning the gluten balls every now and then.

It is ready when the sauce has thickened and reduced by about half and the gluten and mushrooms look invitingly plump and succulent. Pour into a hot serving dish.

VEGETARIAN ''CHICKEN''

This cold bean-stick dish is one of the most delicious Chinese vegetarian "meats." Softened bean sticks are stir-fried, then pressed into a tight roll, steamed, and then chilled so they become as firm and smooth as the breast meat of chicken. *Serves 2 as a main dish, more as an appetizer.* Stir-fried Asparagus would be lovely with it.

½ pound soybean sticks	2 tablespoons dark soy sauce
1 tablespoon baking soda	½ teaspoon salt
4 tablespoons oil	1 teaspoon sugar
3 tablespoons light soy sauce	2 tablespoons sesame oil

Preparations

Bean sticks are sold in 1-pound packages. Take half and break them into several sections. Place them in a large bowl, sprinkle the soda over them, and cover with 8 cups hot water. When they begin to whiten and float to the top, anchor them down with a small plate and let them soak for about 4 hours.

Drain the bean sticks in a colander and rinse with warm water. Put them back in the bowl, cover with warm water, anchor, and let them soak another 4 hours, or even overnight. Just before the cooking, drain them again, spray with warm water, and press them lightly to extract excess water.

Stir-frying

Heat a wok or large, heavy skillet over high heat until hot; add the oil, swirl, and heat for 30 seconds. Scatter in the bean sticks and stir rapidly to coat them with oil. Add the soy sauces, salt, and sugar and stir briskly for about 30 seconds. Turn heat to medium low, cover, and let them steam-cook vigorously for about 10 minutes—the bean sticks will release enough liquid to prevent scorching. Uncover, stir in the sesame oil, and pour the bean sticks into a bowl. Let them cool.

Wrapping and steaming

You are going to wrap the bean sticks into a sausage shape. Have two 40-inch-long pieces of string ready, plus a clean kitchen towel about 20 inches long or a 20-inch-square cloth napkin. If using the towel, place it with the long side in front of you; if using the napkin, place it with a point in front of you.

Grab handfuls of the cooked bean sticks and squeeze dry lightly. Place them in a thin line: either 2 inches from long edge of towel or in the center of the napkin. Leave 2 inches of towel or napkin at each end. When all the bean sticks have been squeezed and arranged in this line, start rolling up the towel snugly, or fold napkin to far corner and then roll tightly. In either case you want to make a very firm, compact sausage shape. Tie one end of the cloth with both strings; then either wind the strings, together, around and around the roll, or crisscross them separately as you keep firm-

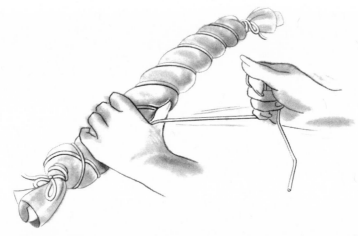

ing and squeezing the roll. It should be about 2 inches wide, 16 inches long. Tie the other end securely with the ends of the strings.

Coil the bean-stick sausage on a heatproof plate. Steam over high heat for 30 minutes.

Remove from the steamer and chill in the refrigerator until the bean-stick roll is thoroughly cold. Remove string, unroll the cloth, and slice the amount you need into ¼-inch-thick diagonal slices to serve as an appetizer or a cold main dish.

甜 SWEET AND SOUR WALNUTS
酸
核
桃

甜
酸
核
桃

This unusual and delicious dish is also known as sweet and sour "vege-tarian" pork. The brown coating is slightly resilient and very crisp, the walnuts crunchy, and the reddish sweet and sour sauce flavors both vege-tables and walnuts. It is delectable. *Serves 2 to 4.*

24 walnut halves

Batter:
4 tablespoons glutinous rice
    powder
4 tablespoons all-purpose flour
1 teaspoon baking powder
⅓ cup cold water

1 recipe sweet and sour sauce with
    vegetables (*page 97*)
2 cups oil

Preparations

Soak the walnuts for 5 minutes in boiling water and remove any clinging skin. Dry well and then deep-fry them as on *page 261*. Let them cool on paper towels.

Make the batter by mixing the glutinous rice powder, flour, and baking powder with the water until smooth.

Make the sweet and sour sauce and stir-fry the vegetables. Put the vegetables into the sweet and sour sauce, turn off the heat, cover, and set aside on the back burner.

The walnuts and the basic sweet and sour sauce may be done hours ahead of time but the vegetables shouldn't be done too much in advance lest they turn limp.

Deep-frying and assembly

Heat a wok or heavy pot over high heat until hot; add the oil and heat until it foams a cube of bread snappily, about 350 degrees. Turn heat to medium. Stir up batter if it's been sitting a while. Then, working quickly, coat each walnut in the batter and drop it into the oil. Deep-fry the walnuts, turning constantly, until the coating is puffy, brown, and crisp. Scoop out the nuts with a slotted spoon to drain on paper towels.

Bring the sauce to a sizzling boil over high heat; then scatter the fried walnuts into it and stir in quick folding motions just long enough to coat them. Pour into a hot serving dish and serve immediately, lest the coating become soggy in the sauce.

VARIATION

If you serve the deep-fried walnuts without the sauce, sprinkled with sugar, they make an unusual snack or dessert. See Cream of Yam with Sugared Walnuts.

RICE, NOODLES, AND DOUGH STUFFS

Rice

Rice is the staple of China, and for the majority of its people, except the northerners, it is the foundation of the Chinese diet. Unlike bread, a staple that plays a secondary role in Western cooking, rice is an integral part of every meal. Not only are many dishes created especially to "send down the rice," but also many tasty dishes cannot be fully appreciated without the contrast of the natural taste and fluffy texture of rice. And, beyond taste, rice is the bulk of a family meal. The main dishes are there to please the palate, but most Chinese feel that they haven't really eaten if they haven't had their bowls of pearly-white grains.

Naturally, such an important item plays a large part in the idioms of the Chinese language. When a family meal is served, it is announced that "rice is ready." A greeting between friends is the inquiry whether "rice has been eaten." The slang expression for a fool is a "colossal rice barrel."

Rice is eaten three times a day, and sometimes leftover rice is stir-fried or simmered for an afternoon snack. Rice is never wasted. Liu-ma, a devout Buddhist, used to intone to me that I would starve in the next life whenever a grain accidentally dropped from my rice bowl. Reincarnation notwithstanding, the lesson not to waste food, by design or accident, is one that is impressed on Chinese children very early. And there are methods for utilizing every grain. Broken ones are ground into powder for making noodles and dough, and even the browned crusts from the pots in which the rice has been cooked are saved for simmering into a porridge or deep-frying into the delicious puffed rice patties for the sizzling go-ba dishes.

Although there are numerous kinds of rice in the world, for everyday use we know really only three types: the long-grain, the short-grain, and the glutinous. The long-grains, used in virtually all Chinese restaurants in the United States, are firm after cooking and hold up well when stir-fried into fried rice. The oval short-grains are starchier, but well liked by the Chinese, particularly those in the eastern provinces. Short-grain rice is soft and creamy when cooked, and is excellent for making breakfast rice porridge and puffed rice patties. Glutinous rice is used mostly for stuffings and desserts.

白 PLAIN RICE
飯

There is a little more to boiling rice than meets the eye: the ratio of rice to water cannot really be set scientifically. While the base of 2 cups long-grain rice calls for 3 cups water for a perfect result, this does not mean that 1 cup rice requires only 1½ cups water or that 3 cups rice require 4½ cups of water. In fact, the first needs 1¾ cups of water and the second 4 cups. Perhaps for this reason the Chinese judge the ratio by the hand, not the cup. You place your hand flat on the rice in the pot. When the water comes three-quarters of the way up your hand, the ratio is correct. Try it—it works. Here, meanwhile, is the basic recipe done in cups. This recipe makes a lovely, light, fluffy rice, *yielding 3½ cups, enough for 4 people.*

1 cup long-grain rice   1¾ cups cold water

Measure the rice into a 3-quart heavy saucepan and rinse it repeatedly under cold water, raking it with your fingers until the water runs clear; drain thoroughly. Washing rice is a cooking ritual that is taken seriously by a Chinese cook—it signifies the beginning of a meal; it removes any husks or other impurities, eliminates superficial starch, and allows the grains to separate during cooking.

Pour in 1¾ cups cold water and bring to a boil over medium heat; let it bubble for 1 minute. Then immediately turn heat low to maintain a gentle simmering, cover tightly, and simmer for 20 minutes. You must watch to make sure the rice doesn't bubble longer than 1 minute, and you *must not peek* at the rice while it is simmering.

At the end of 20 minutes, turn the heat off and let the rice "smother" in its own heat for about 5 minutes (again, do not lift off the lid). If left undisturbed, the rice will still be fine up to 30 minutes. At the time you are ready to serve, uncover the rice and fluff it with a fork. This gives you 3½ cups cooked rice.

SHORT-GRAIN RICE

Because of its starchier content, short-grain rice needs a little less water than long-grain, but it is cooked exactly as in the above recipe. The ratio of water and rice is:

> 1 cup rice to 1½ cups water
> 2 cups rice to 2½ cups water
> 3 cups rice to 3⅞ cups water

REHEATING RICE

Once cooked, rice will stay hot in the saucepan for about 30 minutes, or it may be put into a serving dish, covered, and placed in a moderately hot oven for 30 minutes without drying out. If the rice is cold, it may be reheated in a double boiler or steamed in a bowl over high heat.

無 WU-HSI VEGETABLE RICE
錫
菜 Wu-hsi, my mother's home town, is a beautiful city midway between
飯 Shanghai and Nanking in the central eastern part of China. It is noted
for its lovely cobblestone streets, winding lanes, and cassia trees, whose fragrant yellow blossoms peek over the scalloped walls surrounding the residential compounds. In the mid-eighteenth century, when the Emperor Chi Lung made his famous tour of China, he stayed two weeks in the home of my mother's ancestors. The record of how Chin Tzuan-yuan, the leading scholar of his time, wined and dined his imperial visitor is long lost, but according to Liu-ma's folksy version, his highness was enchanted by this simple but delectable vegetable rice.

Her family having served my mother's family for generations, Liu-ma was a self-proclaimed spokesman for our ancestral history. Entirely at the disposal of her mood and selective memory, this rice was served to the emperor with Red-cooked Fresh Ham, Salt-Pepper Pork, Pork in Spicy Bean-paste Sauce, among other dishes. In truth, this rice goes well with anything, but it is a particularly good contrast to richly flavored dishes.

Laced with pieces of dark-green cabbage leaves and plump white stalks, the rice is very soft and creamy and faintly aromatic of the delicate sweet vegetable. *Serves 3 to 4.*

1 cup short-grain rice	1 teaspoon salt
½ pound Chinese cabbage	2 cups water
2 tablespoons oil	

Rinse and drain the rice as described on *page 422;* set it aside. Trim off the cabbage's root end; wash the stalks thoroughly. Cut them crosswise into 1-inch pieces.

Heat a heavy saucepan over high heat until hot; add the oil, swirl, and heat for 30 seconds. Add the cabbage and stir rapidly to coat the pieces with oil. Sprinkle in the salt and stir until the green leaves brighten. Then add the washed rice and the water; when the water boils, let it bubble vigorously for 3 minutes and stir with a fork or chopsticks occasionally. Turn heat to medium and let it bubble another 2 minutes, stirring a few times. Turn heat to lowest possible level, cover tightly, and let the rice "smother" for 25 minutes.

VARIATIONS

Add 2 cups cubed yams or sweet potatoes (about 1 inch to a side) with another ½ cup water if you'd like a touch of sweetness.

For a rich flavor, substitute 2 cups chicken stock for the water and add to the cabbage ½ cup diced cooked Smithfield ham or one of its substitutes (*page 492*).

Fried rice

Fried rice, created primarily as a way to reheat leftover cold rice, is an incidental in the Chinese diet. It is a snack, served in the afternoon or eaten on a train or in a restaurant; it is never served at a regular meal. Since it is seasoned and mingled with other ingredients, it would detract from rather than enhance the main dish.

But, although it is not a Chinese custom, fried rice has merit as a light luncheon dish or a side dish for a buffet. When well done, it is delicious, especially the delicate versions produced by the eastern school of cooking. These Yangchow-Shanghai rice dishes are not darkened by soy sauce as are the Cantonese; generally they are brilliant in color and have a light consistency, since shrimp or crabmeat is used rather than roast pork.

The only fixed requirement for a good fried rice is that the rice be cold and firm, so that it may be separated with wet hands to prevent lumping or mashing during the fast stir-frying process. Long-grain rice is better for these dishes than short-grain.

蛋 炒 飯 EGG FRIED RICE

Traveling by train in China was always an adventure in regional gastronomic delights. The "small-eats" one could buy from the vendors plying the station platforms included such items as glazed spareribs, soy-sauced chicken (called "barrel" chicken because of the containers), and, in the north, roasted lamb-head meat. Even though the trains had kitchens with a fairly good selection of dishes, most people bought food from the vendors and purchased from the train kitchen only the incomparable Egg Fried Rice, which was truly outstanding. Extremely fluffy and seductively aromatic of cooking eggs and raw scallions, it was, to me, worth a train trip just to have it.

The secret is a simple one—a matter of tilting a very hot pan over high heat with a nimble wrist so that the eggs become light and fluffy. *Serves 4 as a light, single dish.*

4 large eggs
2 to 2½ teaspoons salt
6 tablespoons oil
3½ cups cold cooked long-grain
    rice (1 cup uncooked)

2 large whole scallions, coarsely
    chopped

Beat the eggs well with ½ teaspoon salt. Have the rice and scallions ready.

Heat a wok or large, heavy skillet over high heat until hot; add 3 tablespoons of the oil, swirl, and heat for 30 seconds or a little longer—don't let the oil smoke, however. Pour in the eggs and, as they puff around the edges, push the mass with a spatula across to the back of the pan as you tilt it toward you; this allows the liquid eggs to slide down into the hot pan. Repeat this pushing and tilting quickly until the eggs are no longer runny but soft and fluffy. Slide them onto a dish and set aside.

Stir the rice a little with wet hands. Add the remaining 3 tablespoons oil to the hot pan and scatter in the rice; stir, poke, and flip with a spatula to coat each grain with oil. Add the other 1½ to 2 teaspoons salt to taste and stir briskly for 1 minute, just to warm the rice through. Then add the eggs and stir to mingle the two; the eggs should remain in decent-sized pieces. Add the chopped scallions, give the dish a few fast turns, and pour into a hot serving dish.

蝦 炒 飯 SHRIMP FRIED RICE

This is a gorgeous-looking dish—pink shrimp, yellow eggs, green scallions, white rice. It is a delicate but tasty fried rice. *Serves 3 or 4 as a single dish*

¼ pound shrimp

Coating:
¼ teaspoon salt
1 teaspoon cornstarch dissolved
   in 2 teaspoons water

5 tablespoons oil
3 large eggs, beaten with
   ¼ teaspoon salt
3½ cups cold cooked long-grain
   rice (1 cup uncooked)
½ to 1 teaspoon salt
2 large whole scallions, finely
   chopped

Shell the shrimp and devein if large. Cut them crosswise into ½-inch-wide pieces. Mix them with the coating and set aside if you wish or continue with recipe.

Heat a wok or large, heavy skillet over high heat until hot; add 2 tablespoons of the oil, swirl, and heat for 10 seconds. Turn heat to medium, scatter in the shrimp, and stir them briskly for about 1½ minutes until they are pink and firm. Pour into a dish and set aside.

Clean the pan and set it again over high heat; heat until very hot, then add the remaining 3 tablespoons oil, swirl, and heat until hot. Pour in the eggs, and as they puff around the edges, push the mass with a spatula to the far edge of the pan as you tilt the pan toward you, letting the runny eggs slide onto the hot surface. Push and tilt the eggs until they are no longer runny but soft and fluffy. Give them one big whirl and scrape into a dish.

Set the pan over medium heat—you don't need any more oil. Add the rice, and toss and poke with a spatula for 1 minute to heat it through. Sprinkle in ½ to 1 teaspoon salt to taste; add the scallions and stir rapidly to mingle. Add the shrimp and the eggs and stir rapidly in turning and folding motions for about 1 minute, until the eggs are in small pieces and well mingled with the rice and shrimp. Pour into a hot serving dish.

楊州炒飯 YANGCHOW FRIED RICE

This delicate fried-rice dish has an assortment of ingredients and is lightened by a cupful of bean sprouts or a scattering of shredded lettuce. If you use bean sprouts, pluck off the tails (the very end), since they would blemish an otherwise delicate and elegant dish. *Served as a single course, this would be enough for 4 to 6 people.*

¼ pound small shrimp

Coating:
¼ teaspoon salt
1 teaspoon cornstarch dissolved
   in 2 teaspoons water

6 tablespoons oil
½ cup diced cooked breast of
   chicken
½ cup diced cooked ham, roast
   pork (*page 116*), or Hoisin-
   Sauced Pork (*page 141*)
¼ cup defrosted frozen peas
1 cup plucked fresh bean sprouts
   or finely shredded romaine or
   iceberg lettuce
3½ cups cold cooked long-grain
   rice (1 cup uncooked)
1 medium whole scallion, finely
   chopped
½ to 1 teaspoon salt, to taste

Shell the shrimp and devein if necessary; slice them lengthwise in half and cut each half into ¼-inch pieces. Mix the shrimp with the coating and set aside while you prepare and set out all the other ingredients.

Heat a wok or large, heavy skillet over high heat until hot; add 3 tablespoons of the oil, swirl, and heat for 10 seconds. Turn heat to medium, add the shrimp, and stir briskly for about 1 minute, until they are pink and firm. Pour into a dish.

Clean the pan and reheat until hot. Add the remaining 3 tablespoons oil, swirl, and heat until hot. Toss in the chicken, ham, peas, bean sprouts, and shrimp (without any remaining oil); stir rapidly for about 1 minute. Then add the rice, scallions, and salt to taste. Stir briskly in tossing and turning motions for another minute, until the rice is heated through. Pour into a hot serving dish. If using shredded lettuce instead of bean sprouts, shower them over the rice when heated through; give a few sweeping turns, and then pour into the hot serving dish.

Rice porridge

Known as *hsi-fan*, "thin rice," rice porridge is the basis of breakfast for most Chinese. In the northern provinces wheat products and millet, barley, and cornmeal take its place. Made by simmering a small quantity of rice with a large amount of water, the resulting rice is a creamy gruel.

The porridge is served in individual bowls with an accompanying assortment of tasty and highly seasoned cold dishes, such as salted and preserved eggs, vegetables, or fish and leftover red-cooked or stir-fried meats and poultry.

This Chinese breakfast has gone out of style among most Chinese abroad. We have, by and large, readily and willingly adapted to the faster and easier Western meal of toast, bacon, and eggs. But, by using the porridge as a base to which you will add minced meat or flaked fish fillet, you can make this an exotic dish for brunch or a late supper. It is filling and delicious.

粥　PLAIN RICE PORRIDGE

Serves 4 people.

⅓ cup long-grain or short-grain rice	4 cups water

Rinse and drain the rice in a saucepan. Add 4 cups water and bring to a boil over high heat. Turn heat to medium low, cover the pan partially, and let the rice bounce gently in the bubbling liquid for 5 minutes. This procedure loosens the starch in the rice and blends water and rice without letting the mixture boil over, which would dissipate the creamy film of starch so necessary to making the porridge creamy.

After 5 minutes, give the rice a big stir, turn heat low to maintain a faint simmer, cover, and simmer for about 1 hour. The porridge is ready when there is no separation of liquid and rice. You will have about 3 cups porridge ready to be combined with meat or fish and vegetable garnishes. It may be prepared a few hours or 1 day in advance; reheat over extremely low heat until piping hot. A little water may be added to prevent scorching.

魚
片   FILLET OF FISH PORRIDGE
粥

Serves 4 or more.

½ pound fillet of sole, flounder,
   sea bass, or yellow pike
1 teaspoon salt
1 tablespoon sesame oil
1 recipe Plain Rice Porridge
   (*page 428*)

Salt and freshly ground pepper
   to taste
2 cups finely shredded romaine
   or iceberg lettuce
½ cup finely chopped fresh
   coriander or scallions

Cut the fillet into thin crosswise slices; add the salt and sesame oil; toss gently.

When the rice is ready, add the fish slices and stir gently for 30 seconds until they are white. Turn off the heat and season to taste with the salt and pepper. Cover and let the porridge steep a minute or two; then pour into a hot serving dish and serve the lettuce and coriander or scallions on the side for individual garnishing.

牛
肉   BEEF PORRIDGE
粥

Serves 4 or more.

1 recipe Plain Rice Porridge
   (*preceding recipe*)
½ pound ground beef

Marinade:
2 tablespoons light soy sauce
1 teaspoon cornstarch dissolved
   in 2 tablespoons water

1 large whole scallion, finely
   chopped
Salt and freshly ground black
   pepper to taste
½ to 2 cups finely shredded
   romaine or iceberg lettuce

Make the plain rice porridge. See end of preceding recipe for cooking-in-advance instructions.

March-chop the ground beef a few times to loosen its formation; add the marinade and mix well. You may do this long in advance; cover and refrigerate the meat and bring it out just before the final cooking.

When the porridge is ready, add the beef and stir gently to separate the lumps. Continue stirring until all pinkness is gone. Turn off the heat, cover, and let the rice and beef steep a minute or two. Pour into a serving dish, stir in the scallions, and add freshly ground pepper and salt to taste. Serve the shredded lettuce separately, so each person can garnish his or her own bowl.

VARIATIONS

Half a pound of boned chicken breast, scraped or slivered and marinated with 1 teaspoon salt, 2 teaspoons dry sherry, and 1 teaspoon cornstarch dissolved in 2 tablespoons water can be substituted for the beef, as can ½ pound chopped shrimp, marinated as above. Chopped fresh coriander would be an ideal garnish for the chicken or the shrimp.

鍋巴 GO BA (RICE PATTIES)

Go Ba, meaning "pot stickings," originated as a way of using the crust formed by soft rice in the cooking pot. After the rice is scraped out, the crust is left in the pot and dry-baked over low heat until brown and firm. It is then dried overnight, broken into pieces, and deep-fried until puffed and crisp. It is used as a base for all the sizzling dishes, either in a soup (*page 187*) or in a main dish (*page 238*).

Since Americans hardly ever cook rice soft enough to form a worthwhile crust on the pot, it is simpler to make Go Ba as a separate procedure. Besides its use in the sizzling dishes, it also makes a scrumptious snack. The little patties are white, fluffy, and crunchy—delicious eaten plain or sprinkled with a little salt. *Serves 4 as a snack.*

⅔ cup short-grain rice   ⅓ cup water

Making the patties

Put the rice into a small saucepan; rinse and drain. Add the water and bring to a boil over high heat. Turn the heat low, cover, and let it simmer for 20 minutes.

Heat a 10½- or 11-inch skillet over high heat until hot. Turn heat very low. Spread the rice in the skillet with the back of a large spoon, evening it out into a round cake that fills the bottom of the skillet. Let it dry-bake, without turning, for 1 hour, until the edge of the cake separates from the skillet and the cake can be lifted out in 1 piece. Place it on a tray and air-dry it for 6 hours or overnight. When it is hard and dry, break it into rough squares about 3 inches to a side; save all the broken pieces. Store the patties in a tin box, or in a plastic bag. They keep well for months; in fact, the drier they are, the puffier they will be when deep-fried.

Deep-frying the patties

Heat 2 cups oil in a saucepan until very hot, about 400 degrees. Test with a tiny piece of Go Ba—if it darts, whitens, and puffs instantly, the oil is hot enough. Drop in no more than 2 Go Ba at a time. When they whiten, expand, and puff up, in just a few seconds, turn them rapidly a few times, until just *slightly* browned—do not fry them more than 8 to 10 seconds. Remove with chopsticks or a slotted spoon immediately and drain on paper towels.

Go Ba are light and crisp when white, aromatic and crunchy when slightly browned. When you fry the little broken pieces, remove them almost immediately.

Go Ba really cannot be fried long in advance; they lose that magnificent crispness and that good sizzling sound when liquid is pouring over them. If you must, deep-fry them as close to serving time as possible and keep them hot in a 475- to 500-degree oven for as little time as possible.

Noodles

Since the climate of northern China is more suitable to growing wheat than rice, northerners depend on it for their daily staple of starch—in the form of noodles, buns, dumplings, pancakes, etc. To the rest of the country wheat products are primarily snacks, known as "dot hearts," a between-meals refreshment to only touch one's appetite. But there are exceptions. Noodles, symbolic of longevity, are frequently eaten as the main dish at birthday meals all over China. And in the eastern and southern regions, the noodles and pastries often are made of powdered rice, not wheat.

Like all noodles, the Chinese kinds are of various shapes and sizes, ranging from fresh to dry and pure wheat to wheat with eggs; the shapes range from fine threads to ribbons. The distinctive feature of all Chinese noodles is that, no matter what kind they are, they are never made short. After all, longevity implies length. Short noodles not only wouldn't stand up to Chinese methods of cooking, but they would also diminish the enjoyment the Chinese get from them—they love swishing and tossing the noodles in their steaming broth or tasty sauce before sucking them up, relishing the texture and flavor. Unlike most Westerners, the Chinese don't put much stock on eating noodles quietly, especially noodles in broth.

Even though all Chinese cooks prefer freshly made noodles, very few bother to make them at home. Basically simple, noodle making is nonetheless a demanding art. It requires a deep knowledge born of experience, since the precise ratio of flour to eggs to water varies according to the quality of the flour, the size of the eggs, even the temperature of the season. It also takes strength and patience to knead the stiff dough, a large working area to roll the dough into large paper-thin sheets, an area to dry them undisturbed, and an experienced hand to cut them into uniform thin noodles no more than $\frac{1}{16}$ inch wide.

Fortunately, fresh noodles are available today in all major Chinatowns of cities throughout the United States, supplied daily by the flourishing noodle factories that have become a mainstay of every large Chinese community. If you can, by all means buy a quantity, use what you need, and freeze the rest for future use. If you can't get fresh ones, you can use American or Italian packaged noodles and spaghettis; particularly good substitutes are the spaghettinis and the flat linguine.

The amount per serving depends on whether the noodles are to be served as a snack or as a meal and whether you love noodles as much as the northern Chinese. A half pound of fresh or dry noodles, after boiling, will yield about 4 cups, which is a nice quantity to handle and will be enough to feed between 2 and 4 people.

All Chinese noodle dishes begin with boiled noodles, which are rinsed in cold water to remove the loose starch and then drained well, before they are given a final cooking. If you need to boil them long ahead of time, rinse with cold water again just before using them.

Boiling fresh egg noodles

Bring a large pot of salted water to a rolling boil over high heat. Scatter in ½ pound of noodles. As the water foams to a boil again, lower the heat to medium high, stir to separate the strands, and let the water boil vigorously for 4 minutes. Pour noodles and water into a colander; then spray the noodles with cold water and drain well.

Boiling dry noodles and spaghetti

Bring a large pot of salted water to a rolling boil over high heat. Add the noodles and let them boil vigorously for about 9 to 10 minutes. They should be *al dente*—having just a little stiffness when you bite into them.

Rinse and drain as done with the fresh noodles.

The four categories of noodles

SOUP NOODLES—The boiled noodles are simmered in broth with garnishings of meat and vegetables or served in the broth and topped with a separately stir-fried meat and vegetable dish.

SAUCE NOODLES—The boiled noodles are served with a highly seasoned sauce on the side, with a variety of raw vegetable garnishes for each person to mingle according to personal taste. In the summer, this version is sometimes served chilled with various sauces and vegetables.

STIR-FRIED NOODLES—The boiled noodles are stir-fried with a variety of meats and vegetables.

SHALLOW-FRIED NOODLES—Known as "two-sides-brown" in Chinese, the boiled noodles are shallow-fried until brown and crisp on both sides, then crowned with a glazy topping of stir-fried meats and vegetables, so that while they acquire flavors from the thickened sauce they aren't soaked through. Only fresh egg noodles may be used for a good shallow-fried result.

鷄絲湯麵　SOUP NOODLES WITH CHICKEN

This is a classic recipe—in fact, the most widely known soup noodle dish in China. It is light and tasty, with a good contrast of flavors and textures. Serves 4 as a single dish.

4 large or 6 medium dried black Chinese mushrooms (pre-soaked)
1/2 cup shredded bamboo shoots or fresh snow peas
1 tablespoon oil
1 tablespoon light soy sauce
1 tablespoon dry sherry

4 cups chicken stock
1 to 1 1/2 cups shredded cooked breast of chicken or turkey
1/4 cup shredded cooked Smithfield ham (*page 492*) or substitute
1/2 pound noodles, boiled (*page 432*)
Salt to taste

Cover the mushrooms with hot water and soak for 30 minutes. Rinse, destem, and then shred the caps.

Parboil the bamboo shoots for 1 minute. Rinse in cold water to stop the cooking and drain well. If you use snow peas, snip off the ends, string, and parboil for 30 seconds. Rinse in cold water and shred them.

Heat a large, heavy pot or saucepan over high heat until hot; add the oil, swirl, and heat for 30 seconds. Add the shredded mushrooms and bamboo shoots and stir rapidly for 1 minute. Add the soy sauce and sherry and stir; then add the stock, chicken, and ham. When the stock comes to a boil, add the noodles and mingle well. Turn heat to medium and let them simmer for about 2 minutes. If you use snow peas, add them during the last minute of cooking. Season to taste with salt. When serving either from the pot itself or a tureen, scoop out first the noodles, then the meat and vegetables to put on top. Ladle in the stock.

VARIATIONS

There is no limit to what you can put in the topping. Since this is really a snack dish or a one-dish meal, use whatever you have on hand. The chicken may be replaced by cooked pork or beef, raw shrimp or crabmeat. And for the vegetables you could use spinach, Chinese cabbage, celery cabbage, Swiss chard, string beans, or tender young broccoli stems or flowerets. The vegetables should be raw to start with and shredded or cut into dainty pieces. In your choice, however, bear in mind that the topping should not overwhelm the noodles and the broth. The vegetables should always be stir-fried first in a small amount of oil with a little salt or light soy sauce to fortify their flavor and prevent them from turning limp.

Instead of wheat noodles rice noodles may be used. Soak them in warm water for 5 minutes; drain and proceed as above.

雪
菜
肉
絲
麵

SHREDDED PORK WITH RED-IN-SNOW NOODLES

Here the well-seasoned Shredded Pork with Red-in-Snow is stir-fried separately and then simmered briefly with the noodles in broth. *Serves 4.*

1 recipe Shredded Pork with
    Red-in-Snow (*page 342*)
½ pound noodles, boiled
    (*page 432*)

4 cups chicken or light meat stock
Light soy sauce or salt to taste

Prepare the pork dish and boil the noodles. Set aside. You may do both ahead of time; rinse the noodles just before using.

When you are ready to assemble the dish, bring the stock to a boil, add the noodles, and scatter the pork and vegetables on top. When the stock comes to a boil again, swish to even out the noodles, turn heat to medium low, and simmer for 3 to 5 minutes. Season to taste with a little soy sauce or salt if you find it necessary. Serve from the pot or from a tureen at the table into individual bowls.

VARIATION

Any highly seasoned stir-fried combination may be substituted; there are a number in the meat chapter. However, always omit the dissolved cornstarch if a recipe calls for a glazy sauce; it would cloud the broth and make the noodles heavy.

楊州窩麵 YANGCHOW NESTLED NOODLES

This dish is a glorification of soup noodles. It contains less liquid and more topping, so that instead of swimming in broth the noodles are nestled luxuriously in a tureen between a little rich soup in the bottom and assorted meats and vegetables on top. It is a wonderful one-dish meal, and all the preparations can be done hours in advance, leaving only 3 minutes of cooking at the end. *Serves 4 to 6.*

¼ pound thinly sliced breast of
    chicken

Marinade:
½ egg white (reserve other half
    for shrimp)
¼ teaspoon salt
1 teaspoon dry sherry
1 teaspoon cornstarch

¼ pound thinly sliced loin of pork

Marinade:
1 teaspoon light soy sauce
1 teaspoon dry sherry
1 teaspoon cornstarch

¼ pound small shrimp, shelled

Marinade:
½ egg white
¼ teaspoon salt
1 teaspoon dry sherry
1 teaspoon cornstarch

4 to 6 cups water
3 tablespoons oil
1 small clove garlic, crushed
    and peeled
2 quarter-sized slices peeled ginger
4 large or 6 medium dried black
    Chinese mushrooms (pre-
    soaked)
¼ cup shredded bamboo shoots
¼ cup shredded snow peas
¼ cup frozen peas, defrosted
2 tablespoons light soy sauce
1 tablespoon dry sherry
3 cups rich chicken or meat stock
½ pound noodles, boiled
    (*page 432*)
¼ cup shredded cooked Smithfield
    ham (*page 492*) or substitute
Light soy sauce or salt to taste

Preparations

Beat the egg white and divide it in two, and make the marinades. Marinate the chicken, pork, and shrimp in their respective marinades for 30 minutes.

Bring 4 cups water to a boil with 1 tablespoon oil. Turn heat to medium high, scatter in the chicken, and stir gently until white. Scoop into a strainer held over the pot, and then set aside on a large plate. Scatter the pork into the water, stir, and let it simmer for about 1½ minutes; scoop into a strainer and put it next to the chicken. Scatter in the shrimp and stir until firm and pinkish white, about 1 minute; scoop up, drain, and place with the meats. These steps may be done hours in advance; cover and refrigerate. Bring to room temperature before final cooking.

The noodles may be boiled in advance and refrigerated. Rinse to separate them before final cooking.

The mushrooms should be covered with hot water and soaked for 30 minutes, then rinsed, destemmed, and shredded.

The vegetables may also be prepared in advance. Cover and refrigerate.

Heat a wok or large, heavy skillet over high heat until hot; add remaining 2 tablespoons oil, swirl, and heat for 30 seconds. Toss in the garlic and ginger and press them in the oil. Then add the mushrooms, bamboo shoots, snow peas, and green peas, and stir briskly about 30 seconds. Add the 2 tablespoons soy sauce and sherry, give the contents a vigorous stir, and pour into a dish, discarding the garlic and ginger.

Final cooking and serving

Bring the stock to a boil in a large pot. Add the noodles, chicken, pork, shrimp, ham, and the stir-fried vegetables. When the stock comes to a boil again, turn heat low, cover, and simmer for about 3 minutes. Adjust taste with a little soy sauce or salt if necessary.

Pour into a tureen and arrange the meats and vegetables on top as much as possible. It is very impressive looking, so don't dish up in the kitchen first.

VARIATIONS

Use beef for the pork, sliced fresh mushrooms or canned straw mushrooms for the black ones, and defrosted frozen or parboiled fresh French-cut string beans for the snow peas.

四川牛肉麵 SZECHUAN RED-COOKED SPICY BEEF NOODLES

Rich and tasty, this is a well-known "small-eats" specialty from Szechuan province. The beef, of course, is a legitimate main dish, so you could serve it alone one night and use the leftovers for a noodle snack. In fact, all leftover red-cooked and braised meats and poultry are excellent with noodles, whether there is still some meat or just the lovely sauce. *Serves 4 to 6 as a snack.*

Seasonings:
5 tablespoons dark soy sauce
3 tablespoons dry sherry
½ teaspoon salt
1 tablespoon sugar
1 tablespoon hot bean paste

4 tablespoons oil
1 teaspoon Szechuan peppercorns
   (*page 500*)
2 large whole scallions, cut into
    2-inch pieces
4 quarter-sized slices peeled ginger
1 pound shin beef, in 1-inch cubes
6 cups boiling water
2 whole star anise
½ to 1 pound noodles, boiled
   (*page 432*)
Chili-pepper oil or chili sauce
   or paste (*pages 489 and 490*)

Mix the seasonings in a small bowl and set aside.

Heat a large, heavy saucepan over high heat until hot; add the oil, swirl, and turn heat to medium low. Scatter in the peppercorns and let them brown for about 1 minute, stirring and pressing them in the oil. Scrape them out and discard. Turn heat high, add the scallions, ginger, and meat; stir and flip for about 45 seconds until the meat is seared on all sides. Add the seasonings mixture and stir until the meat is well covered. Add the boiling water and the star anise and stir until it comes to a boil again.

Turn heat low to maintain a very gentle simmering, cover, and simmer for 1½ to 2 hours, until the meat is tender and the sinews are soft and translucent. Adjust the taste with a little soy sauce or sugar if necessary. This step may be done in advance. Cover and refrigerate if to be kept a long time. Reheat just before serving.

Boil the noodles and add them to the hot red-cooked beef, which should come to a boil over high heat. Lower heat, cover and simmer for about 3 minutes. Serve from a large bowl or a tureen into individual bowls. Have a little chili-pepper oil or chili sauce or paste on the side for those who like a really spicy taste.

炸
醬
麵
NOODLES WITH BEAN-PASTE MEAT SAUCE

Served with an array of crisp raw vegetables, this is a typical one-dish northern noodle meal. Although it involves the preparation of three separate components—the noodles, garnishes, and meat sauce—each can be done in advance. *Serves 6 to 8 generously.*

1 pound noodles, boiled (*page 432*)

Garnish:
1 large firm, slender cucumber
2 cups fresh bean sprouts
2 cups shredded romaine lettuce
1½ cups shredded celery
4 large cloves garlic, minced or
    mashed
1 teaspoon sesame oil

1 pound ground pork
4 tablespoons oil
1 large whole scallion, finely
    chopped
1 tablespoon dry sherry

Sauce:
5 tablespoons bean paste
2 teaspoons sugar
½ cup water

1 tablespoon sesame oil

Noodles

Cook fresh noodles or spaghetti or linguine according to the instructions. Rinse, drain, and set aside. When ready to serve, plunge them into a pot of boiling water to boil briefly till hot. Drain them well.

Garnishes

Cut off the ends and peel the cucumber; halve and deseed it. Cut the halves diagonally into 1½-inch-long slices; then shred them thin.

Rinse and drain the bean sprouts. Parboil them in boiling water for 30 seconds. Drain into a colander and spray with cold water. Drain well.

Separate the lettuce leaves; rinse and shake dry. Cut the larger leaves in half lengthwise; then shred them crosswise thin. Cut the tender core diagonally into thin slices and then shred these.

Wash, scrape, then cut the celery stalks diagonally into thin slices; shred the slices thin. Rinse in cold water and drain well.

Crush and peel the garlic; then either mince it or mash it in a garlic press. Mix with the sesame oil in a small dish.

Put each vegetable in a separate serving dish. If doing this step in advance, cover the dishes and refrigerate. Bring out just before serving.

Meat sauce

March-chop the pork a few times to loosen its formation. Place it with the finely chopped scallions on your working platter. Combine the bean paste with the sugar and water and stir well.

Heat a wok or large, heavy skillet over high heat until hot; add the 4 tablespoons oil, swirl, and heat for 30 seconds. Turn heat to medium and add the meat, stirring briskly in poking and pressing motions until the meat separates. Scatter in the scallions and stir a few times; then add the sherry and stir rapidly to mingle. Give the sauce ingredients a big stir, pour over the meat, and stir to even out the contents.

Turn heat low to maintain a gentle simmering, and simmer for 10 minutes or until the sauce has thickened, stirring now and then. At this point add a little sugar if sauce needs it—it should be on the salty side with a subtle sweet aftertaste.

Turn the heat high, add the sesame oil, and give a few fast folds before pouring into a serving dish. The sauce may be made ahead of time, covered, and chilled. Reheat over very low heat just before serving.

Serving

Place the vegetable garnishes in a circle in the center of the table with the hot meat sauce in the middle. Pile the hot noodles on a platter or in a deep bowl. Serve the noodles to each person and let him or her spoon on a little sauce and a sprinkling of vegetable garnishes. The mixture should be tossed well before being eaten.

涼
拌
麵
COLD-STIRRED NOODLES

In this dish of cold noodles the garnishes of cooked meats and vegetables and different sauces are served in separate dishes so that each person can mix according to individual taste. *Serves 3 to 4;* increase noodles as needed.

Noodles

Boil ½ pound noodles as on *page 432.* After draining, toss them with 1 tablespoon vegetable or sesame oil. Chill them, covered, until completely cold. Pile on a serving platter.

Meat

Shred 1 cup each of whatever cooked meats you have on hand or wish to make, such as white-cut chicken (*page 51*), leftover roast turkey, plain boiled loin of pork, Chinese pot roast (*page 350*), or boiled tongue. Arrange them attractively on one platter or on individual plates.

Vegetables

See the assortment suggested for the recipe on *page 437,* or make up your own shredded selection. Arrange them on one platter or on individual dishes.

Sauces

The most common sauce is a soy sauce and vinegar sauce. Combine about ¼ cup light soy sauce with ¼ cup vinegar, 2 tablespoons sesame oil, and 2 to 3 teaspoons sugar. Mix until the sugar dissolves. Use white distilled vinegar for a strong sour flavor, Chenkong vinegar for a mellow one, and red-wine vinegar for a mild one.

Other good sauces are peppery-numb sauce (*page 250*) or sesame-paste sauce (*page 249*).

Serving

Arrange everything in the center of the table, serve the noodles to each person, and let him or her choose meat, vegetables, and sauces according to individual taste.

叉燒撈麵 ROAST PORK AND BEAN SPROUTS LO MEIN

Lo mein, meaning stir-fried noodles in the Cantonese dialect, is very tasty when done with spirit. Speed and motions of cooking are always intimately related to the outcome of a dish, but they are nowhere as evident as in the stir-frying technique, and with no dish more particularly than the tossed noodles. Scooped, lifted, and showered back into the pan with lightning speed and energetic motions, these noodles are light and bouncy. Well seasoned and entwined with slivers of juicy meat and crunchy bean sprouts, they make a scrumptious snack, main course, or side dish. *Serves 3 to 4.*

½ pound roast pork (*page 116*)
    shredded
3 tablespoons oil
2 quarter-sized slices peeled ginger
1 small clove garlic, lightly
    crushed and peeled
1 large whole scallion, shredded
1 tablespoon dry sherry
4 cups fresh bean sprouts
    (about ⅔ pound)

Seasonings:
1½ tablespoons light soy sauce
1½ tablespoons oyster sauce
½ teaspoon salt
½ teaspoon sugar

½ pound noodles, boiled
    (*page 432*)

Preparations

Cut the pork into thin slices, then into thin shreds. Cut the scallion into 2-inch sections, then into shreds. Place the ginger, garlic, scallions, and meat at one end of a working platter.

Toss the bean sprouts in a pot of cold water; filter out the husks and broken tails; drain thoroughly. Place them at the other end of the working platter.

Combine the seasonings and stir until the salt and sugar are dissolved.

Boil, rinse, and drain the noodles. If you have done them in advance and chilled them, rinse in water and drain well just before the final cooking. Set everything within reach of the stove.

Stir-frying

Heat a wok or large, heavy skillet until hot; add the 3 tablespoons oil, and toss in the ginger and garlic, pressing them in the oil. Scatter in the scallions and meat and toss briskly for 1 minute to sear them with oil. Splash in the sherry and stir rapidly for another 30 seconds. Shower in the bean sprouts and stir in fast tossing motions to flip and spin them in the hot oil for 45 seconds. Pour in the seasonings and stir briskly a few times. Pick out and discard the ginger and garlic.

Add the noodles and immediately slide a spatula from the side of the pan beneath the noodles, meat, and vegetables. Scoop them up in the air, shake, and shower them back into the pan; repeat these fast sweeping motions in rapid-fire succession from all directions for 3 minutes, until the noodles are heated through, evenly tinted by the sauce, and well mingled with the meat and vegetables. Pour into a hot serving dish and serve immediately.

VARIATIONS

White-cut chicken or pork, velveted chicken and small shrimp, or slippery-coated beef may be substituted for the roast pork. You may also decrease the bean sprouts and add another shredded vegetable, such as bamboo shoots, mushrooms, or Chinese or celery cabbage.

煎 麵 SHALLOW-FRIED NOODLES

These are the "two-sides-brown"—fresh (not dried) egg noodles that are boiled, then coiled and shallow-fried until they are crunchy and brown. They are served topped with a glazed stir-fried dish, such as the two following this recipe. *Either would serve 3 to 4 people.*

½ pound fresh noodles, boiled   1 teaspoon salt
(*page 432*)   5 tablespoons oil

Boil the fresh noodles; rinse and drain them. Toss them with 1 teaspoon salt and then spread them out to dry on a platter for 1 hour or longer —until their surface moisture has evaporated. This may be done in advance and the noodles refrigerated.

Heat a large, heavy skillet over high heat until very hot; add the oil, swirl, and heat for 30 seconds. Pour half the oil into a small bowl and reserve. Add the noodles, coiling them into a large pancake, and let them shallow-fry for a few seconds over high heat. Then turn heat to medium low and continue to shallow-fry, undisturbed, for about 4 minutes, until the bottom is brown and crisp.

Flip the noodle nest over with a spatula and dribble the remaining oil in from the side. Shallow-fry another 4 minutes, until this side is as crisp as the other. Remove to a hot serving platter. It is now ready to be crowned with a topping.

CHICKEN AND SHRIMP TOPPING

This is a delicious, brightly colored glazy topping, which coats and clings to the crisp noodles, making them just crunchily soft. To prepare this topping or the next, cut and assemble all the ingredients in advance and then stir-fry while the noodles are being shallow-fried, so they are ready together.

½ pound small shrimp or   ½ pound shredded chicken breast
TT shrimp (*page 204*)

Marinade: *Marinade:*
½ teaspoon salt   ½ teaspoon salt
1 teaspoon dry sherry   1 teaspoon dry sherry
½ egg white, well beaten   ½ egg white, well beaten
1 teaspoon cornstarch   2 teaspoons cornstarch

Vegetables:
6 medium dried black Chinese
   mushrooms (presoaked)
¼ cup sliced bamboo shoots
2½ inches of carrot, grooved and
   cut crosswise into ⅛-inch
   rounds (*page 21*)
3 cups fresh spinach

4 tablespoons oil
2 whole scallions, cut into
   1½-inch sections
4 quarter-sized slices peeled ginger,
   shredded

Seasonings:
2 cups chicken stock
2 tablespoons light soy sauce
¼ to ½ teaspoon salt, to taste
¼ teaspoon sugar
⅛ to ¼ teaspoon black pepper

1½ tablespoons cornstarch
   dissolved in 2 tablespoons
   water
2 teaspoons sesame oil

Preparations

Rinse and shell the shrimp; cut each crosswise into 2 pieces. If you are using the small TT shrimp, leave them whole. Add the marinade, stir well, and refrigerate for at least 30 minutes.

Cut the boned and skinned chicken breast into crosswise slices, stack, and cut them into thin shreds. Add the marinade, mix well, and refrigerate for at least 30 minutes.

Cover the mushrooms with hot water, and soak for 30 minutes. Then rinse, squeeze dry, destem, and quarter them. Rinse and drain the bamboo shoots. Groove and slice the carrot as described. Wash the spinach and blanch it 30 seconds in boiling water; drain into a colander, spray with cold water, and press lightly to dry it a little. Prepare the ginger and scallions. Combine the seasonings in a bowl and stir until the sugar is dissolved. Have the dissolved cornstarch and sesame oil ready. All these preparations may be done hours in advance.

Stir-frying

Heat a wok or large, heavy skillet over high heat until hot; add the 4 tablespoons oil, swirl, and heat for 30 seconds. Scatter in the scallions and ginger and stir briskly for 30 seconds. Add all the vegetables and stir vigorously for 1 minute. Add the seasonings and stir to even out the contents. When the liquid boils, turn heat to medium, add the shrimp and chicken, and stir them in the hot broth until the shrimp are firm and pink and the chicken white—no more than a minute or two. Turn heat low, add the dissolved cornstarch and stir until the sauce is smooth and thick. Sprinkle in the sesame oil, give the contents a few big stirs, and pour over the browned noodles. Serve at once.

PORK AND BEAN SPROUTS TOPPING

Another, simpler topping, with tender meat and crisp bean sprouts.

½ pound loin of pork, finely
    shredded

Marinade:
1 teaspoon light soy sauce
2 teaspoons dry sherry
2 teaspoons cornstarch

4 tablespoons oil
2 whole scallions, in 1½-inch
    sections
2 quarter-sized slices ginger,
    shredded
3 cups bean sprouts, tightly packed

Seasonings:
2 cups chicken stock
2 tablespoons light soy sauce
¼ to ½ teaspoon salt, to taste
¼ teaspoon sugar
⅛ to ¼ teaspoon black pepper

2 tablespoons cornstarch dissolved
    in 2 tablespoons water
2 teaspoons sesame oil

Preparations
Add the marinade to the shredded meat, mix well, and refrigerate for at least 30 minutes. Prepare the scallions and ginger. Wash the bean sprouts and drain. Combine the seasonings in a bowl and stir until the sugar is dissolved. Mix the cornstarch and have the sesame oil ready.

Stir-frying
Heat a wok or large, heavy skillet over high heat until hot; add 4 tablespoons oil, swirl, and heat for 30 seconds. Scatter in the scallions and ginger and stir briskly for 30 seconds. Add the meat and stir vigorously in shaking and swishing motions for 1½ minutes, to separate, firm, and whiten the shreds. Add the bean sprouts and stir and toss for 1 minute. Pour in the seasonings and stir to even out the contents. When the liquid boils, let it bubble for 30 seconds, then turn heat low, add the dissolved cornstarch, and stir in circular motions until the sauce is smooth and glazy. Sprinkle in the sesame oil, give the contents a few big stirs, and pour over the browned noodles. Serve immediately.

VARIATIONS
Any glazy-sauced meat or seafood, such as Filet Mignon Kow or Seafood Kow, makes an excellent topping for the browned noodles.

These two toppings as well as those mentioned above are excellent with the crisply fried Go Ba (*page 431*).

炒 STIR-FRIED RICE STICKS WITH SHRIMP
米
粉

Rice sticks, also called rice noodles, aren't noodles in the pure sense of the word, but they do have a wonderful light, absorbent quality that is conducive to stir-frying.

These fragile, white "noodles" are broken into dainty pieces by the stir-frying motions and they acquire a light-brown hue from the seasonings. Their light texture blends wonderfully with the crisp cabbage and firm shrimp. *Serves 3 or 4.*

½ pound rice sticks
½ pound medium shrimp
5 tablespoons oil
1 small whole scallion, finely
 chopped
1 teaspoon salt
1 tablespoon dry sherry
2 quarter-sized slices peeled ginger

2 cups shredded Chinese or celery
 cabbage, or Swiss chard
1½ to 2 tablespoons light soy
 sauce to taste
½ cup chicken stock
¼ cup diced cooked Smithfield
 (*page 492*) or baked ham

Soak the rice sticks in cold water for about 15 minutes, until they are soft and separate naturally from their tight wad. Drain well. Shell the shrimp and devein if necessary; cut them crosswise into ½-inch-pieces. Prepare all the other ingredients. All this may be done in advance.

Heat a wok or large, heavy skillet over high heat until hot; add 2 tablespoons of the oil, swirl, and heat for 30 seconds. Add the shrimp and stir a few times; add the scallions, ¼ teaspoon of the salt, and the sherry. Stir briskly until the shrimp are pink and firm. Pour them into a dish.

Clean the pan and add the remaining 3 tablespoons oil. Toss in the ginger and press it briefly in the oil. Add the cabbage and stir rapidly for about 1 minute, until the color brightens. Add the remaining salt, the soy sauce, and the rice sticks; stir to mingle well. Add the stock, shrimp, and ham and stir briskly in tossing and turning motions until all the liquid is absorbed. Pour into a hot serving dish.

Dough Stuffs

Buns

發 YEAST DOUGH
麵

A yeast dough is the base for Chinese bread, for either Plain Buns or
Flower Rolls. Sometimes the buns are stuffed with meat, meat and vegetables, or a sweet red bean paste. The Plain Buns and Flower Rolls are
traditional accompaniments to red-cooked or deep-fried meats and poultry,
such as Red-cooked Fresh Ham or Szechuan Crunchy Duck, and the
stuffed buns are popular snacks.

1 teaspoon dry yeast	1 tablespoon sugar
2 tablespoons lukewarm water	1 cup lukewarm water
1 pound all-purpose flour (3½ cups unsifted flour)	1 teaspoon baking powder

Dissolve the yeast in 2 tablespoons lukewarm water, letting it sit for
5 minutes.

Pour the flour into a large stewing pot or a large bowl and stir in the
sugar. Make a well in the center and pour in the dissolved yeast and 1 cup
lukewarm water; stir with chopsticks or a wooden spoon until a lumpy
mass forms. Press and knead the mass to form a large ball.

Turn the dough onto a floured work surface and knead it, pushing
and turning with the heel of your hand, for 5 minutes. Dust it with flour
from time to time if too sticky. At the end of the kneading, it should be
smooth and springy.

Put the dough inside the pot or bowl, cover, and set it in a warm
area, such as the back of the stove or an unlit oven, for about 2 hours, until
the dough has risen to double its original size.

Remove it to a lightly floured work surface. Flatten it with the palm
of your hand to make a long oblong shape. Sprinkle the baking powder over
the surface. Fold the dough over; then knead vigorously for 5 minutes,
until it is smooth, satiny, and firm, with plenty of bounce. Dust the work
surface with flour when necessary. Now the dough is ready to be shaped.

饅
頭 PLAIN BUNS

These smooth oblong buns are fluffy and firm with a tinge of sweetness. They are "live" dough, full of a resilient buoyancy that you can sink your teeth into. Since they are steamed, not baked, they have no crust.

Divide the dough into 2 parts. Shape each into a log then, using the palms of your hands, roll each into a smooth sausage shape about 6 inches long. Cut each roll crosswise with a sharp knife into 6 pieces, yielding 12 in all.

Dust a tray or cookie sheet with flour and place the buns on it, giving each room to expand. Cover the tray with a dry cloth and place it in a warm area for the buns to rise to about double in size—this should take about 45 minutes. The buns should be puffed and taut and feel light. If the air is damp and cool, this rising may take longer than 45 minutes.

Set up your steamer and bring the water to a vigorous boil. Line a heatproof plate with a damp cloth and place 6 buns, not touching, on the cloth. Steam the buns over high heat for 15 minutes. Turn off the heat and wait a few seconds for the steam to subside before uncovering and removing the buns to a platter. If the pot is uncovered immediately, the drastic change of temperature will cause the buns to wrinkle on the surface.

Replenish the boiling water in the steamer and then steam the other 6 buns for 15 minutes. If you have a set of Chinese bamboo steamers, line 2 of the trays with damp cloths and do both batches at once.

Once steamed the buns will keep well wrapped in plastic for about 10 days in the refrigerator and weeks in the freezer. To reheat, steam them as above for 10 to 15 minutes until they are thoroughly hot.

花
捲 FLOWER ROLLS

Divide the dough into 2 parts. Roll each into a rectangular sheet about 12 inches long and 8 inches wide. Brush the tops of both with 1 tablespoon sesame oil. Then, tightly roll the sheets of dough lengthwise like jelly rolls, each about 1½ inches in diameter. Cut each roll crosswise with a sharp knife into 12 one-inch pieces.

Press 1 piece on top of another firmly. Then press a chopstick crosswise hard down the middle of the top piece; the rolled ends of the top piece will lift up. (In steaming, these folds, and those on the bottom too, will separate to look like flower petals.) Repeat with the other pieces until all 12 flower rolls are formed. Set them on a lightly floured tray or cookie sheet under a dry towel to rise for about 45 minutes, till double in size.

Steam them in 2 batches as with the Plain Buns above.

VARIATION

To dress these up a little, add ½ teaspoon salt to the sesame oil and brush the tops of the dough sheets as before. Then scatter 1 tablespoon minced cooked Smithfield or baked ham and 1 tablespoon finely chopped scallions over each sheet and roll up into a tight jelly-roll shape. Form the flower rolls and let them rise; then steam them.

 MEAT BUNS

Filling and satisfying, meat-filled buns are popular snacks all over China. Children look forward to them at home after school and wayfarers seek them out from food vendors and alley eating places. Wholesome, untouched by fancy, they are rib-sticking and scrumptious. They keep well and reheat easily. They are wonderful to take along on a picnic since they may be "steamed" wrapped in foil on a grill or lightly toasted over a low charcoal flame. *This recipe makes 20 buns.*

1 recipe yeast dough (*page 446*)	*Seasonings:*
1 pound ground pork	2½ tablespoons light soy sauce
1 large whole scallion, finely	1 tablespoon dry sherry
chopped	¼ teaspoon salt
	¼ teaspoon black pepper
	3 tablespoons sesame oil
	1 tablespoon cornstarch dissolved
	in 5 tablespoons water

March-chop the ground pork until its texture is smooth. Combine it with the scallion, add all the seasonings, and mix until well blended. Chill in the refrigerator for at least 30 minutes to firm it for neat handling. Divide into 20 portions.

Divide the dough in half and, using the palms of your hands, roll each into a 10-inch-long sausage. Cut each into 1-inch pieces. Dip the cut sides in flour and press the pieces with your palm to flatten them slightly. Roll each one out into a 4½-inch circle, making the center thicker than the rim.

Put a disk in your hand and place 1 portion of the filling in the

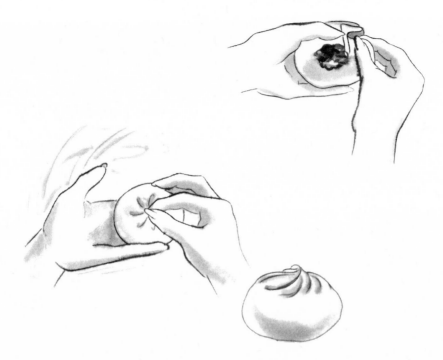

center. Flute the edge firmly all around the filling and bring the top folds together. Pinch and twirl them into a tiny "knot." Repeat until all 20 buns are made.

Put the buns, fluted side down, on a lightly floured cookie sheet, with a good amount of space between them. Cover them with a dry cloth and let them puff for about 30 to 40 minutes in a warm place. Turning them upside down prevents them from splitting at the fold while rising.

Turn 10 of the buns over and place them on a heatproof plate that is covered with a damp cloth. Steam the buns over high heat for 20 minutes. Let the steam subside a few seconds before uncovering the steaming pot so the buns won't wrinkle on top. Steam the other 10 buns.

The cooked buns keep well in the refrigerator for 3 to 4 days and if frozen they will keep from 2 to 3 weeks. Reheat by steaming for about 15 minutes, until piping hot.

VARIATIONS
One-third cup finely cubed jellied meat stock may be folded into the filling. During steaming this melts into luscious gravy, whereupon the buns are called "soup buns."

Ground beef may be used instead of pork. In that case, reduce the steaming time from 20 to 15 minutes.

菜肉包 MEAT AND VEGETABLE BUNS

This recipe makes 20 filled buns.

1 recipe yeast dough (*page 446*)
¾ pound ground pork or beef

Marinade:
2 tablespoons light soy sauce
2 tablespoons dry sherry
½ teaspoon salt
1 tablespoon cornstarch dissolved
    in 2 tablespoons water

3 tablespoons oil
2 quarter-sized slices peeled ginger,
    minced
1 medium whole scallion, finely
    chopped
2 tablespoons mo-er mushrooms or
    6 medium dried black Chinese
    mushrooms (presoaked)

1 ten-ounce package frozen
    chopped spinach, kale, or Swiss
    chard, defrosted and squeezed
    dry lightly, or 2 cups packed
    fresh vegetable, parboiled
    2 minutes

Seasonings:
2 tablespoons light soy sauce
½ teaspoon salt
1 teaspoon sugar
Sprinkling black pepper
3 tablespoons sesame oil

March-chop the ground meat a few times to loosen its formation; add the marinade and stir to mingle. Prepare the scallion and ginger. Cover the mo-er mushrooms or black mushrooms with hot water and soak for 30 minutes. Rinse and squeeze, destem if you use the black mushrooms, and chop fine. Squeeze the defrosted greens but not until absolutely dry—there should be some moisture left. If using fresh, chop after parboiling. Mix the seasonings in a small bowl.

Heat a wok or large, heavy skillet over high heat until hot; add the oil, swirl, and heat for 30 seconds. Scatter in the ginger and scallions and stir a few times. Add the meat and stir in poking, shaking, and pressing motions to break up the lumps. Add the mo-er or black mushrooms and the greens and stir briskly to mingle. Add the premixed seasonings and stir to flavor all the ingredients. Pour into a dish and divide the mixture into 20 portions. Let it cool completely before filling the dough.

Shape and cut the dough as described in the previous recipe. Fill and make fluted buns. Cover, and let them rise for 30 minutes, pinched side down, till about double in size. Turn them over and steam them as in the previous recipe.

VARIATIONS

The filling may be varied by adding or substituting ingredients.

For instance, you could use half pork and half coarsely minced shrimp or flaked crabmeat.

You could substitute ½ pound celery cabbage for the greens. Chop it fine, let it macerate with ½ teaspoon salt for 5 to 10 minutes; then squeeze it dry. Omit the salt in the seasonings.

About ½ cup finely minced bamboo shoots and finely chopped fresh button mushrooms or straw mushrooms may be substituted for the mo-er or black mushrooms.

桂花豆沙包 RED BEAN PASTE AND CASSIA BLOSSOM BUNS

Often served as a sweet course midway into a formal banquet in dainty fancy forms in the old days, these sweet buns are delicious snacks. *Makes 20 buns.*

1 recipe yeast dough (*page 446*)
3 tablespoons oil
2 cups canned red bean paste

2 teaspoons preserved cassia blossoms

Heat a large, heavy skillet over high heat for 30 seconds; add the oil, swirl, and heat for 30 seconds. Turn heat to medium low, add the red bean paste, and stir with the back of a spoon in circular motions for about 5 minutes, until it is hot and creamy. Pour into a dish and fold in the blossoms. Let the paste cool completely before dividing it into 20 portions and filling the buns.

Prepare and cut the dough into 20 pieces as on *page 448*. Flatten them and then roll each into a 3-inch circle. Place a portion of the filling in the center and either flute the edge and pinch to form a pleated bun like the ones in the two preceding recipes, or gather up the sides, pinch together firmly to close, and then roll in the palm of your hand to form it into an oblong or oval-shaped bun. Repeat for all the rest.

Let the buns rest and rise on a floured cookie sheet under a dry cloth for 30 minutes or longer, until about double in size. Then steam them 10 at a time on a heatproof plate for 15 minutes.

VARIATION

Decrease the amount of bean paste to 1½ cups and add ½ cup finely chopped walnuts after the bean paste is cold.

Pancakes

薄
餅　CHINESE PANCAKES

These are an important accessory in Chinese cooking. They are a must for quite a few excellent dishes, such as Peking Duck, Mo-shu Pork, and Beef with Leeks. *Makes 30 pancakes.*

2 cups flour	3 tablespoons oil for brushing
1 cup boiling water	

Measure the flour into a large bowl and add the boiling water gradually as you stir with chopsticks or a wooden spoon until the mixture resembles lumpy meal. Press the mass into a large ball.

Dust your work surface with flour and turn the dough out onto it. Knead it, pushing with the heels of your hands and turning it, for 5 minutes, until it is no longer sticky. Dust lightly with flour whenever necessary. Cover with a damp cloth and let it rest for 30 minutes.

Flour the work surface again and knead the dough another 5 minutes, until it is soft and smooth, dusting with flour when necessary. Shape the dough into a log, cut it in half lengthwise, and then roll each half back and forth with your palms to form a sausage shape about 15 inches long. Cut each sausage into 1-inch pieces and stand them up on their edges on a floured surface.

Brush 1 side of a piece of dough with oil and press this side onto another piece; then roll into a double pancake measuring about 6 inches in diameter. Repeat until you have made 15 double pancakes. Doubling is to cut the pan-baking time and effort in half.

Heat a heavy skillet over low heat until hot. Place a pancake in the center and "bake" it for about 1½ minutes, until the surface puffs into a bubble and the bottom is speckled with small light-brown spots. Flip and "bake" the other side about 45 seconds. These pancakes should be soft and slightly chewy. The crucial point in making them is the heat level: if the pan is too hot the pancakes will be covered with large burned spots and if it is not hot enough the pancake will dry out in cooking. Be careful to bake for only 1½ minutes and test for light-brown spots, and you'll have a perfect pancake.

Remove the double pancake to a plate while you put another one into the skillet; then peel off the finished top one to give you 2 individual pancakes. Fold each one to make a half moon and place on a plate. Repeat the "baking," peeling, and folding until all 30 pancakes are made, lowering heat if pancakes are browning too fast.

Steam the folded pancakes on a heatproof plate for 5 minutes before serving them. You may make them hours or days in advance, and you can freeze them. Wrap tightly in plastic for refrigerating or freezing. Reheat by steaming 10 to 15 minutes until soft and resilient.

葱油蛋餅 SCALLION EGG PANCAKES

These pancakes were often served with the morning rice porridge at home in China, and to me breakfast is still not quite complete without them. Thin, crisp, and aromatic of scallions, they also make a wonderful snack. *This batter will make about 8 small pancakes about 6 to 7 inches wide.*

1 cup all-purpose flour
½ teaspoon salt
1 large egg
¾ cup water

2 large whole scallions, finely chopped
2 tablespoons oil

Put the flour in a bowl and sprinkle in the salt. Beat the egg lightly and combine it with the water. Add the liquid to the flour gradually, stirring until it is no longer lumpy. Mix in the finely chopped scallions.

Heat a 6- to 7-inch heavy skillet over high heat until hot; add the oil, swirl, and heat for 30 seconds. Pour it into a small dish, leaving only a film on the bottom. Set heat at medium low and pour in about ⅛ cup of the batter with one hand as you tilt the pan with the other, forming a thin pancake that covers the whole surface of the pan. Cook for about 1½ minutes, until lightly brown on the bottom. Flip the pancake over and cook about another minute. Remove to a plate.

Cook the rest of the pancakes the same way, filming the pan each time with a little of the oil (about ½ teaspoon). Serve the pancakes with no condiments.

Dumplings

燒
賣
SHAO MAI (OPEN-FACED DUMPLINGS)

Also known as *dim siem* in the Cantonese dialect, these open-faced dumplings are made with a hot-water dough. The flat wrappers are available in Chinese grocery stores, but they are easy to make at home and are far superior to the commercial ones. The Shao Mai are delectable appetizers. You may make them in advance; well covered, they will keep in the refrigerator for 2 to 3 days. *This recipe makes 16 dumplings.*

Hot-water dough:
2 cups all-purpose flour
1 cup boiling water

Filling:
1 pound ground pork
¼ pound shrimp
1½ cups finely chopped celery
  cabbage or Chinese cabbage
½ teaspoon salt
2 quarter-sized slices peeled ginger,
  minced
1 small whole scallion, finely
  chopped
2 tablespoons light soy sauce
2 tablespoons dry sherry
¼ teaspoon salt
¼ teaspoon sugar
Sprinkling black pepper
1 tablespoon sesame oil
1 tablespoon cornstarch dissolved
  in 3 tablespoons water

Preparations
Make the dough: Measure the flour into a large bowl and pour in the boiling water as you stir with a wooden spoon or pair of chopsticks until it resembles lumpy meal. Let it rest while you make the filling.

March-chop the meat a few times to loosen its formation and put it in a bowl. Shell and devein the shrimp if necessary; slice them lengthwise through the back and then cut them crosswise into ¼-inch pieces. Add them to the meat.

Rinse and drain the cabbage. Cut the Chinese cabbage stalks lengthwise into narrow strips; then gather them up and dice them fine. If you are using celery cabbage, put the leafy strips on top of the firm ones so the latter don't scatter when you shred; then mince. Macerate the diced cabbage with ½ teaspoon salt for 5 minutes; squeeze dry lightly and add to the meat mixture with the rest of the ingredients. Stir until smooth and pasty. Divide the mixture into 16 portions.

Making and steaming the dumplings

After the dough has rested, knead it a few minutes until soft and smooth, dusting it with flour whenever necessary. Roll it out into a 16-inch-long sausage. Cut it with a sharp knife into 1-inch pieces. Dip the cut sides in flour and press them into small round cakes with the palm of your hand. Then roll them out into round wrappers 4 inches across.

Lay a wrapper on the outstretched fingers of your hand. Put a portion of the filling in the center and spread with a table knife to within ½ inch of the edge. Then gather the wrapper up with your fingers to make a little "basket." Using the back of the table knife, press it deep into the sides of the basket about 10 times, all around, as you lightly bounce the filled dough to firm it into the fluted dumpling shape. Keep smoothing any filling that threatens to gush over the side. Set the dumpling on the table and bounce it a few times so that the bottom is firm and even. Repeat until all the dumplings are formed.

Put the dumplings on a heatproof platter and steam them over medium-high heat for 20 minutes. They may be steamed in advance and then reheated by steaming for 5 to 10 minutes until thoroughly hot.

VARIATIONS

Scraped and minced chicken breast may be substituted for the pork. Ground beef, omitting the shrimp, is another excellent substitute. If you use beef, you could vary the seasonings by adding a little curry powder or by adding 1 tablespoon oyster sauce and decreasing the soy sauce by 1 tablespoon.

鍋 SHALLOW-FRIED DUMPLINGS
貼

Through the combined processes of shallow-frying and vigorous steam-cooking, these scrumptious filled dumplings acquire a dual texture: they are fluffily soft on top and crunchy-crisp on the bottom. Hearty and satisfying, they make an excellent meal in themselves, needing no more than a light broth with a float of leafy vegetables as accompaniment. *Makes 28 very small dumplings.*

1 recipe hot-water dough
(*page 454*)

Filling:
½ pound ground pork
1½ tablespoons light soy sauce
¾ teaspoon salt
⅛ teaspoon sugar
Sprinklings black pepper
2 quarter-sized slices peeled ginger, minced
1 small whole scallion, finely chopped
1 cup finely chopped celery cabbage
1 tablespoon cornstarch dissolved in ¼ cup water
1 tablespoon sesame oil

2 tablespoons oil
1 cup boiling water mixed with 2 tablespoons oil
Individual dip sauce: 1 tablespoon Chenkong or cider vinegar and ½ teaspoon minced ginger

Preparations

Make the dough and let it rest in the bowl while you prepare the filling.

March-chop the ground pork a few times to loosen its formation. Add the soy sauce, ½ teaspoon salt, sugar, a few sprinklings of black pepper, the ginger, and scallions; stir to mingle well.

Rinse and drain the celery cabbage stalks; cut them lengthwise into narrow strips and then chop them crosswise fine. Sprinkle with the remaining ¼ teaspoon salt, toss, and macerate for 5 minutes. Squeeze lightly to get rid of excess moisture and add to the meat. Add the dissolved cornstarch and sesame oil and stir in circular motions until the mixture is smooth and pasty.

Dust your work surface with flour and turn the dough out onto it.

Knead it, pushing it with the heels of your hands and turning it, for 5 minutes, until the dough is smooth. Cover it with a damp cloth and let it relax for 30 minutes. Then flour the work surface again and knead the dough for another 3 minutes, dusting with flour whenever necessary. Shape the dough into a log and roll it back and forth with the palms of your hands until it becomes a thin sausage measuring about 1 inch in diameter and 28 inches long. Cut it into 28 pieces. Keep them under the damp cloth as you work each piece of dough into a dumpling wrapper.

Dip the cut ends of one of the dough pieces in flour and press down with the palm of your hand. On a flour-dusted work surface roll it out into a 3¼-inch round; repeat until all the pieces are done. Keep them under the damp cloth as you shape and fill each wrapper.

With your fingers, pinch-pleat about one half of the circle into 5 small overlapping pleats, creating a shell with gathers on the top, a flat edge of dough on the bottom. Hold it in the palm of your hand and fill the shell with 1 teaspoon of filling, pushing it in with the back of the spoon until it completely fills the hollow, adding more if necessary. Fold the bottom edge to the pleated one and pinch the two together firmly to close the shell into a half-moon shape. Keep the filled dumplings under the damp cloth as you fill the rest. They should be spaced apart so that they won't stick to one another.

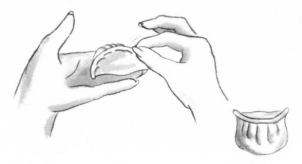

If you must, this may be done a few hours in advance. Dust the dumplings lightly with flour and set them on a lightly floured plate, not touching one another. Cover with a dry cloth and refrigerate. Bring to room temperature before cooking.

Cooking the dumplings

Heat a large, heavy skillet over high heat until hot; add 2 tablespoons oil, swirl, and heat for 30 seconds. Turn heat to medium, add the dumplings, pleated sides up, crowded together, and tilt the pan around a little to grease the sides of the outer dumplings with oil.

Combine the boiling water and oil. Turn heat under skillet to medium high, pour the oiled water over the dumplings and loosen any that are sticking to the side of the pan, cover, and steam-cook for 2 minutes. Turn heat to medium low and continue to cook for 8 minutes. Uncover, turn heat slightly higher to evaporate any remaining water, and let the dumplings fry for about 2 minutes, until the bottoms are golden brown. Tilt the pan a few times to prevent outer dumplings from sticking.

Turn off the heat. Remove dumplings with a spatula to a hot platter. Serve with the vinegar sauce on the side.

VARIATION

STEAMED DUMPLINGS—Make and fill the dumplings as above. Place them on a heatproof platter, not touching one another, and steam for 20 minutes—do them in batches if your equipment isn't large enough. Serve them with a dip sauce. A traditional one, for 1 person, is: 1 tablespoon light soy sauce, 1 teaspoon distilled white vinegar, ½ teaspoon sesame oil, and ½ teaspoon minced ginger.

Egg rolls

What are known as "egg rolls" in this country are called "spring rolls" in China. Since the first day of the Chinese new year is also the first day of spring according to the Chinese lunar calendar, these and other traditional pastries such as the New Year Dumplings were always served to the callers who came by on that day. They are also, however, popular year-round snacks for the Chinese and a standard appetizer for American patrons of Chinese restaurants here.

There are two kinds of commercially made egg-roll wrappers available in Chinese grocery stores—the Cantonese kind, which are smooth, resembling thin noodle dough, and the Shanghai kind, which are transparent, resembling rice paper. After deep-frying, the first are crisp and dry, the latter brittle and hard, since they absorb more oil. The Cantonese wrappers are 7-inch squares and are sold by the pound, each pound containing 14 wrappers. The Shanghai wrappers are circles and are sold in packages of 12. Both types keep well for about a week in the refrigerator and months in the freezer.

If you can't get the commercial wrappers, which are really quite good, make the Cantonese ones as described in this recipe. The Shanghai kind are extremely tricky and messy to make; they are hardly worth the time and effort.

廣東春捲皮 CANTONESE EGG-ROLL WRAPPERS

Makes 14 wrappers.

2 cups all-purpose flour	1 egg, lightly beaten
½ teaspoon salt	½ cup water
	Cornstarch for dusting

Sift the flour and salt into a large bowl. Make a well in the center. Beat the egg lightly and combine it with the water, mixing well. Pour the liquid into the well gradually as you stir with a pair of chopsticks or a wooden spoon until the mixture becomes a coarse meal. Push and knead it into a ball.

Turn the dough onto a floured work surface and knead and turn it for 6 to 7 minutes, until it is smooth. Sprinkle with flour when necessary. Cover with a damp cloth and let it rest for 15 to 30 minutes.

Roll the dough into a 14-inch-long sausage, using your hands, and cut it with a sharp knife into 1-inch pieces. Dip the cut sides in flour, press the circle with your hand, and then roll it out into a thin sheet no more than ⅟₁₆-inch thick. Trim the sheet with a sharp knife to make a 7-inch square. Smooth the top with a little cornstarch and put it on a plate. Roll, trim, dust with cornstarch, and stack all the pieces of dough. They may be done 2 to 3 days in advance; refrigerate them, well wrapped. They keep for weeks wrapped and frozen.

EGG-ROLL WONTON WRAPPERS
This dough also makes excellent wonton wrappers if you like them soft and fluffy. Divide the dough into 4 parts. Roll each into a sheet ⅟₁₆-inch thick; trim the edges and cut into 3-inch squares. Smooth the surface with cornstarch, stack what you need, then wrap the rest in small stacks and freeze.

鶏
絲
春
捲

CHICKEN EGG ROLLS

These egg rolls are filled with a smooth, moist filling, a departure from the usual filling of pork, shrimp, and cabbage. *Makes 14 rolls.*

1 pound shredded velveted chicken
   (*page 75*)
3 tablespoons oil
6 large or 8 medium dried black
   Chinese mushrooms (presoaked)
½ cup finely shredded bamboo
   shoots
2 cups fresh bean sprouts
½ teaspoon salt
3 tablespoons light soy sauce
2 teaspoons cornstarch dissolved
   in 2 tablespoons water

1 tablespoon sesame oil
1 pound commercial egg-roll
   wrappers or 1 recipe homemade
   (*page 459*)

Sealing mixture:
1 tablespoon cornstarch
2 tablespoons water
1 egg yolk

4 cups oil

Filling

After velveting the chicken, set it aside on a platter. Cover the mushrooms with hot water and let them soak 30 minutes. Rinse, squeeze dry, destem, and shred them. Have bamboo shoots and bean sprouts ready.

Heat a wok or large, heavy skillet over high heat until hot; add 3 tablespoons oil, swirl, and heat for 30 seconds. Add the shredded mushrooms and stir rapidly to sear them in the oil. Then add the bamboo shoots and bean sprouts and stir in tossing motions for about 2 minutes. Add the salt and soy sauce and stir to mingle. Give the dissolved cornstarch a big stir, pour over the vegetables, and stir until glazed. Add the sesame oil, give the contents a few fast turns, and pour over the chicken on the platter. Stir to mix, divide the mixture into 14 portions, and let them cool until completely cold before filling the egg rolls.

Sealing mixture

Dissolve 1 tablespoon cornstarch in 2 tablespoons water. Add the egg yolk left over from the velveting to the cornstarch mixture, stirring until smooth. Set aside.

Wrapping the egg rolls

1) Place a wrapper with 1 point of the diamond facing you. Take 1 portion of the filling and place it a little below the center (nearer you); form

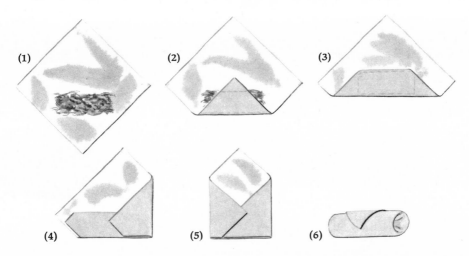

it with your fingers into a compact cyclinder about 4½ inches long, horizontal to you. 2) First fold the bottom flap over the filling, brush the edge with some of the egg-yolk sealer, and 3) fold again. 4) Then fold the right-hand flap over and brush with sealer. 5) Fold the left-hand flap over that (now the wrapper looks like an open envelope) and 6) then roll it firmly to the far point, pressing lightly to seal it into a firm roll. Repeat until all 14 egg rolls are made. You must deep-fry them now at least partially or the wrappers will be too soggy.

Deep-frying

Heat a wok or heavy pot over high heat; add the 4 cups oil and heat until a cube of bread foams instantly, about 375 degrees. Slide in half of the egg rolls and deep-fry them about 4 minutes, turning them constantly, until they are golden brown and crisp, lowering the heat slightly after the first 2 minutes. Remove with a slotted spoon to drain on paper towels, and deep-fry the second batch.

If you want to do this in advance, even up to a day ahead, deep-fry the egg rolls about 2 to 3 minutes, until very lightly brown. Drain, cool, cover, and refrigerate. Refry them until golden brown just before serving. Once they are done, you can keep them hot and crisp in a 300-degree oven for about 30 minutes or you could reheat them in a 450-degree oven for about 7 minutes.

Cutting

Cut each egg roll into 2 or 3 sections before serving. Do this with a sharp heavy knife, cutting from the side of the roll instead of the top to prevent the pressure from squashing the roll and spilling the filling.

Serve egg rolls with a little hot mustard or plum sauce if you like. They are also good with a side dish of light soy sauce mixed with a little vinegar.

VARIATIONS

You could replace the velveted chicken with slippery-coated shredded pork (*page 342*) or beef (*page 85*). For the bamboo shoots you could use shredded string beans, snow peas, celery, or celery cabbage. You could decrease the meat and add a little diced shrimp or flaked crabmeat. A little finely shredded or diced cooked Smithfield ham (*page 492*) and coriander or scallions could be added for a stronger flavoring.

SHANGHAI WRAPPERS—If you make the egg rolls with these commercial wrappers, you must deep-fry and serve them immediately, since repeated frying will make them too greasy and oven warming will make them too hard and brittle.

Wontons

Even though wontons in broth have been established here as a traditional soup, in China the dish is considered a snack. Filling but not heavy, simple but versatile, and easy to cook and serve, wontons are the mainstay of many food vendors and "small-eats" restaurants in China. There was something very special about having a bowl of wontons from the night vendors who trotted gracefully through the streets of Shanghai, pausing here and there to ladle the small steaming dumplings into bubbling broth with a light touch of soy sauce and sesame oil. And in the narrow, winding back streets of Chungking there were many small stall-like restaurants, where the proprietor scooped wontons from a bubbling pot into a small bowl and seasoned them with dashes of soy sauce, sesame oil, and red chili oil, plus a tasty sprinkling of minced preserved vegetables. Tossed and rolled in this spicy sauce, the wontons were known in the Szechuan dialect as the "tossing hand." In the United States, wontons have also developed into an appetizer when deep-fried. Being neat and compact, they fit in well with the Western idea of an hors d'oeuvre.

雲
吞

WONTONS

The wrappers are available in Chinese markets in a standard thickness or a thinner type, in squares measuring about 3 inches. If you wish to make them at home you can use the egg-roll dough (*page 459*), which is a soft dough, made with eggs, or you can use the following recipe, which employs only flour, water, and a little baking powder. Rolled extremely thin, these wrappers are silky and transparent when boiled and very light and crisp when deep-fried. They also make very good wrappers for egg rolls if cut into 7-inch squares. *Makes about 36 wrappers.*

1 cup all-purpose flour
½ teaspoon salt
¼ teaspoon baking powder

½ cup cold water
Flour for dusting
Cornstarch for dusting

Combine the flour, salt, and baking powder; then add the water little by little, stirring, until the mixture resembles a coarse meal, soft but not too wet. Depending on the flour, you may have to use a little less or more water. Form it into a ball and put it on a floured work surface and knead it about 5 minutes, dusting with flour whenever necessary, until the dough is smooth and no longer sticky. Cover it with a damp cloth and let it rest for 30 minutes.

Divide the dough in half. Cover 1 piece with a damp cloth and roll the other into a thin sheet on a flour-dusted surface so that it is about 9½ inches wide, 18 inches long, and 1⁄16 inch thick. Dust the surface of the dough generously with cornstarch. Trim the edges and then cut the sheet crosswise into six 3-inch strips. Stack the strips and cut crosswise 3 times to make 3-inch squares. (See illustration *page 158*). Repeat with the other piece of dough. You will get about 36 square wrappers from the dough. And don't waste the scraps: shred them or cut them into small pieces and deep-fry them until lightly brown. They are wonderful sprinkled over a creamy soup or just as is—a small munch—sprinkled with a little salt.

Well dusted with cornstarch, stacked, and tightly wrapped in aluminum foil, these wonton wrappers keep in the refrigerator for about 1 week; frozen, they keep for months. In that case, make small stacks. Defrost thoroughly before using.

雲吞湯 WONTON SOUP

Allow 4 to 6 wontons per person for a soup course, 6 to 10 for a snack.

½ pound ground pork

Seasonings:
1½ tablespoons light soy sauce
⅛ teaspoon sugar
1 tablespoon dry sherry
Sprinkling black pepper
1 teaspoon minced peeled ginger
1 teaspoon finely chopped scallions
1 tablespoon cornstarch dissolved
    in 4 tablespoons stock or water
2 teaspoons sesame oil

36 commercial or homemade
    wonton wrappers (*page 463*)
4 to 5 cups chicken stock
2 cups spinach leaves, torn coarsely
Salt or light soy sauce to taste

Preparing the wontons

March-chop the ground meat a few times to loosen its formation. Put it in a bowl and add the seasonings; mix until smooth. Divide roughly into 36 tiny portions and wrap them in the wontons (*page 463*).

Bring 5 to 6 cups water to a boil in a large pot; turn heat to medium high, drop in the wontons, and stir gently. When the water boils again, add 1½ cups cold water; when it comes to a boil again, add another 1½ cups cold water. When it comes to a boil a third time, let it boil for about 2 minutes. The wontons are cooked when they float to the top. Repeatedly adding cold water serves two purposes; it gives the wontons enough time to cook as well as rinsing them, since filled wontons should not be rinsed after cooking as noodles are.

After boiling, the wontons may be covered and stored 2 to 3 days in the refrigerator. Submerge them in cold water to separate them before adding them to soup.

Completing the soup

When ready to complete the soup, bring the stock to a simmer over medium heat and drop the wontons into it. Add the torn spinach, and when the stock comes to a boil, turn heat to medium low and simmer for about 2 minutes. Season to taste with salt or light soy sauce. Serve from a tureen or in individual bowls.

VARIATIONS
The filling may be varied by decreasing the meat and adding a pro-

portionate amount of diced fresh shrimp. Or you could substitute the filling for Crabmeat Wontons. Any leafy green may be used, with additional ingredients such as presoaked dried black Chinese mushrooms and shredded or sliced cooked pork, chicken, or ham.

鴨 CASSEROLE OF DUCK WITH WONTONS
湯
雲 This is a simple long-simmered duck with wontons added for the final
吞 5 to 10 minutes of cooking. Among Chinese, it is considered a "big-affair" snack, often served at the end of a party as a form of "one for the road." *Serves 6 to 8 in small quantities.*

1 duck, about 4½ to 5 pounds

Marinade:
1 teaspoon minced peeled ginger
1 teaspoon salt
¼ teaspoon black pepper

2 tablespoons dry sherry
4 quarter-sized slices peeled ginger

1 large whole scallion
⅓ cup sliced cooked Smithfield
  ham (*page 492*) or substitute
1 one-pound-3-ounce can spring
  bamboo shoots, roll-cut into
  1-inch pieces
18 to 24 boiled wontons (*page 464*)
  or dumplings (*page 454*)
Salt to taste

Remove the fat from the cavity of the duck; discard the tail and trim off excess neck skin. Rinse and drain the duck. Mingle the minced ginger, salt, and pepper, and rub well into the duck, both inside and outside. Let it sit for 1 hour.

Place the duck in a large casserole (earthenware if possible), sprinkle it with the sherry, and add cold water to cover it by 1 inch. Scatter the ginger slices and the whole scallion on top, cover, and bring to a slow boil over moderate heat. Turn heat low, skim off any foam, and adjust heat to maintain a faint simmering. Cover and simmer about 3 hours.

Skim off and discard the fat. Scatter in the ham, the bamboo shoots, and the wontons or dumplings. Cover and simmer another 5 to 10 minutes. Season to taste with salt and place the casserole on a trivet for serving. The duck is tender enough to be pulled apart with chopsticks, but, if you prefer, you could chop it in the kitchen, put the pieces back in the casserole, bring it back to a boil, and serve at the table by ladling into individual soup bowls.

VARIATIONS
You could substitute boiled noodles (*page 432*) or Dough Knots (*next recipe*) for the wontons or dumplings.

Dough Knots

湯
麵
咯
嗒

DOUGH KNOTS IN BROTH

These dough knots in broth are a northern breakfast food. They were frequently served with a cornmeal bun called the O-O bun. The marshmallowish dough is sliced off the rim of the bowl into boiling water, where it curls into "knots." The smooth and fluffy knots are then simmered briefly in chicken or meat stock with some meat and greens. This makes a good dish for brunch or a light supper, *serving 4.*

Dough:
1 cup all-purpose flour
¼ teaspoon salt
1 large egg
¼ cup water

4 cups chicken or meat stock
1 cup spinach leaves, tender
    Chinese or celery cabbage,
    or Swiss chard
½ cup sliced cooked chicken
    breast
Salt to taste

Dough knots

Put the flour in a bowl and sprinkle in the salt. Beat the egg well and combine it with the water. Pour the liquid into the flour gradually, stirring the batter with chopsticks or a spoon until it is a thick batter.

Wash and drain the chosen green. If you use Chinese or celery cabbage or Swiss chard, cut the stalks crosswise into 1-inch pieces, leaving the young heart leaves whole. Tear the spinach leaves coarsely if large. Slice the chicken into pieces about 2 inches long and ⅛ inch thick.

Bring 6 cups water to a boil, turn heat to medium to maintain a gentle but vigorous boil, with rapid bubbles shooting upward. The right heat is important: the dough sinks and sticks if the boiling is too slow and it flakes if too fast.

Tilt the bowl slightly over the pot, and as the dough begins to flow over the edge, shave the rim of the bowl with a knife in rapid succession, cutting dough into thin strips and letting them fall into the water. Stir gently with chopsticks or a wooden spoon to loosen any dough knots that are stuck on the bottom of the pot. Let them boil for about 3 minutes; then drain them into a colander. You may make the dough knots in advance. Cover them with cold water and drain them just before simmering in broth.

Simmering the broth

Bring the 4 cups stock to a boil; add the greens and simmer them over medium heat for 1 minute. Then add the dough knots and chicken, season to taste with salt, cover, and simmer over very low heat for about 3 minutes. Pour into a tureen or individual bowls, arranging the chicken and greens on top.

VARIATIONS

Very thin slices of Smithfield ham (*page 492*), cut in pieces comparable in dimensions to the chicken, may be added for a stronger taste and bright color. Allow 3 pieces for each serving.

The meat may be varied according to what you have on hand. You could use leftover turkey meat, shredded roast duck, or slices of roast pork or Hoisin-sauced Pork. Slices of presoaked dried black Chinese mushrooms could also be added.

DESSERTS

There is no dessert course in the structure of a Chinese meal, at least not as a finale in the Western sense of the word. Sweets are looked upon as interludes; they are eaten as snacks between meals or they are served midway through a banquet as a pause during long hours of elaborate feasting.

Chinese desserts use vegetables as a base in addition to fruit, nuts, rice, and rice and wheat flours. The sweetened paste of red beans is a traditional filling for pastries, cakes, and puddings; a white fungus, simmered in a rock sugar broth, is a prestigious delicacy reserved for formal entertaining; and one of the classic desserts is a creamy stir-fried concoction that uses purée of beans, peas, and yams or lotus seeds. Since ovens are not standard cooking equipment, there is no home baking. There are flaky pastries and tarts available in Chinese bakeries, but these are commercial products that often look better than they taste, and I am not particularly fond of them.

The Chinese desserts that are prepared at home are made very much the same way as the main dishes; at the last minute they are apt to be simmered, steamed, stir-fried, or deep-fried, and usually served still hot. We also have quite a repertoire of sweet soups and I have included two of them. Served in very small cups, they make a delicious ending to a meal.

But, as you will see, I have included recipes for only a very small number of desserts because, to me, Chinese desserts are not at all outstanding. They cannot begin to measure up to those of the Western cuisine in variety, finesse, glamour, and ingenuity. The ones I have selected are those I feel are interestingly different, rather delicious to eat, and simple to make.

One of the nicest ways to conclude a Chinese meal is with a platter of cut pretty fruits on ice—a scattering of canned lichees, kumquats, loquats, served either alone or in combination. Or you can simply serve one of your own favorite desserts; chances are it will go very well with your menu, particularly an ice or a fruit tart.

蓮
子
湯
LOTUS-SEED BROTH

The large white lotus blossoms, veined with red at their tips, are to my mind the most beautiful, and the most useful, of all flowers. It's breathtaking to see those majestic spreading petals above the broad leaves on the water, and their delicate fragrance makes the summer air heady. Besides being a regal ornament in itself, the plant is a gastronomic delight. The roots, linked tubers with hollow tunnels inside, are juicy and crisp when young and fresh. They are eaten raw as a fruit, simmered or stir-fried with meats to make soups and main dishes, stuffed with glutinous rice to make desserts, or ground into powder and mixed with boiling water to make a pudding. The leaves, having a refreshing fragrance, are used as wrappers for steaming meats and poultry. And, finally, the tender yellow-green seeds, shaped like acorns and concealed in the chambered pods that look like round nozzles, are food for the gods.

Even though fresh lotus seeds are not available here, the broth made with dried seeds remains an elegant delicacy. There is something enchanting about winding up a great meal, either Western or Chinese, with a dainty bowl of these lovely fragile seeds. In keeping with their delicate character, each serving shouldn't exceed 10 or 12 seeds. The broth should be accompanied by a solid sweet, such as the Spun-sugared Apples, Cream of Yam with Sugared Walnuts, or a Western cake or tarts.

This serves 4 to 6.

48 dried blanched lotus seeds	2 to 2½ tablespoons crushed rock
4 cups water	sugar or granulated sugar

Soak the seeds in cold water for 4 to 5 hours. Rinse and drain.

Put them in a small saucepan, add the water and rock sugar, and bring to a boil over high heat, stirring until the sugar is dissolved. When the water boils, turn heat low to maintain a gentle simmering, cover, and simmer for 1 to 1½ hours until the seeds are soft and on the verge of bursting into mealy bits. Clear the broth of any floating lotus "hearts"—the tiny green sprouts lodged in the centers of the seeds.

Divide the broth and seeds into small, deep bowls—rice bowls are lovely for this—and serve, to be eaten with a small spoon.

VARIATIONS

You could add miniature glutinous-rice-flour balls to get another texture. To 3 tablespoons glutinous rice flour add 2 tablespoons water, and mix with your fingers until it forms a soft, smooth dough. Pinch it into 16 tiny pieces and roll each in the palms of your hands. Cook the tiny balls for 5 minutes in a small pot of boiling water. Drain and add to the lotus seeds during the last 5 to 10 minutes of cooking time.

A teaspoon of preserved cassia blossoms may be added in either case for a distinctive flowery flavor.

核桃茶 WALNUT TEA

A delicious hot, creamy broth known as a "tea," this is a popular banquet dessert that is also reputed to be a tonic for women who want to keep their dewy complexions. I know little about folk medicine, but my grandmother and mother looked ten years younger than their real ages, and both began their mornings with walnut tea. Beauty aside, walnut tea is delectable. *Serves 6 to 8.*

2 cups walnuts, blanched
4 cups water

¼ cup glutinous rice powder
3 to 4 tablespoons sugar, to taste

Blanch the walnuts for 30 seconds in boiling water. Drain. Then grind them in an electric blender or with a mortar and pestle until puréed and pasty, adding 1 cup water, little by little, as you grind.

Put the rice powder into a saucepan, add the remaining 3 cups water little by little, stirring until the powder dissolves. Add the puréed walnuts and stir to mingle well. Set the saucepan over medium heat, add the sugar, tasting, and bring to a boil, stirring constantly. Turn heat low and let the tea simmer gently for about 10 minutes, stirring now and then. You may do this ahead of time. Reheat when ready to serve.

Pour the hot walnut tea into small bowls or Chinese tea cups if you have them. This is usually served with a solid sweet, and would go beautifully with a Western cake, petits fours, or a fruit tart.

拔絲蘋果 SPUN-SUGARED APPLES

This famous dessert is a specialty of Peking. After the apples are cut, coated with batter, deep-fried, and covered with molten sugar, each wedge is pulled from the serving dish so the caramelized sugar spins into threads. It is then briefly plunged into a bowl of ice water. With the sudden change of temperature, the sugar hardens into a shiny, brittle glaze, making the fruit crackly on the surface while soft in the center. *This recipe serves 4.*

Batter:

3 tablespoons all-purpose flour

3 tablespoons cornstarch

1 large egg, well beaten with

   1 tablespoon water

2 large Delicious apples, or any

   hard eating variety

2 cups oil

½ cup sugar

Ice water

Combine the flour and cornstarch in a bowl. Stir in the beaten egg little by little, until you make a thick, smooth batter—add water if needed.

Peel, quarter, and core the apples; slice each quarter in two lengthwise. Put the fruit into the batter and gently turn to coat pieces evenly.

Heat the oil in a heavy saucepan over high heat until a cube of bread foams snappily, about 350 degrees. Turn heat to medium, drop half the coated apples wedge by wedge into the oil and deep-fry them for about 2 minutes, until lightly brown—turn each wedge once. Remove them with a slotted spoon to a plate and repeat with the other half. This may be done hours in advance; the fried apples will soften and wrinkle but don't worry; they need a second frying just before being coated with the caramelized sugar. Scoop out any batter drippings and set the oil aside.

When ready to serve, start to reheat the oil as you prepare the caramel. Heat a heavy skillet over high heat until hot; add 3 tablespoons oil, swirl, and turn heat to low. Pour in the sugar and stir with the back of a spoon until it melts and begins to foam. Turn heat very low and let the sugar foam and deepen in color to a brown caramel, stirring occasionally. This takes about 3 minutes: the sugar is ready when a drop forms a hard ball in cold water. As you refry the apples, keep the caramel foaming over extremely low heat, not permitting it to burn. Once blackened, it will be bitter and unusable.

Reheat the oil until it foams a cube of bread instantly, about 375 degrees. Refry the apples for about 1 minute, until they are firm and brown. Turn up the heat a little under the caramel and scoop, drain, and transfer the apples directly from the oil to the syrup. Slip a spatula under and around the fruit to coat them well. Then quickly pour them into an oiled serving dish and serve immediately, accompanied by a bowl of ice water. Let everyone pull away one apple wedge at a time to dip into the ice water. The sugar will crackle like thin ice when you bite into it.

VARIATIONS

Use 3 firm bananas instead of apples. Peel and cut them into diagonal slices about ½ inch thick and 2½ inches long. Coat and deep-fry them as you do the apples. For added flavor, add a teaspoon of preserved cassia blossoms or lemon extract to the batter.

The original Peking recipe for this dessert used a root vegetable called *san-yoa* in Chinese. You can substitute yams. Select a well-shaped oblong yam about ¾ pound. Peel and quarter it and then cut each quarter crosswise into 4 pieces. Put them in a small saucepan, cover with water, and bring to a boil. Turn the heat low, cover, and simmer for 15 minutes, until the yam pieces are cooked but still firm. Drain and let them cool; then coat in batter and deep-fry as you do the apples. They are delicious, but heavier than the apples.

桂花蒸梨 STEAMED PEARS WITH CASSIA-BLOSSOM HONEY

These lovely steamed pears are good either hot or chilled. They are soft but still firm and well shaped. As you cut through them with a fork or spoon, the cassia-flavored sauce flows out to sweeten the fruit with an exotic perfume and a faintly salty aftertaste. *Serves 4.*

4 large, firm Bartlett or Anjou pears
4 tablespoons honey

1 teaspoon preserved cassia blossoms

Select pears that will sit up securely. Rinse them and cut off 1 inch from the tops, which will be used as lids. Core the pears with a fruit corer, making sure you don't go through the bottoms. Mix the honey with the cassia blossoms and fill the centers of the pears with this sweet liquid. Cover the pears with their own lids. Place them upright in a heatproof bowl and steam over medium-high heat—30 minutes for Bartletts and 45 minutes for Anjous. Remove them to individual serving dishes and spoon a little of the pan juices over each. You could also refrigerate them until thoroughly chilled.

VARIATION
Soak 4 teaspoons white raisins in 1 tablespoon brandy or any liqueur for 1 hour. Add to the honey mixture.

杏仁豆腐 ALMOND JELLY WITH LICHEES AND LOQUATS

In the old days, before gelatin powder, almond extract, and evaporated milk were introduced to China, this was made with ground almonds and dissolved agar-agar. Known also as almond "bean curd," it is meltingly smooth—one of the very few cold desserts China has to offer besides fresh or preserved fruits on ice.

This jelly is white, and creamier and softer than regular Jell-O. It is not overly sweet, and its almond flavor goes beautifully with the fruit. It's a light, sweet ending to a meal, especially appealing if served in a crystal bowl. *It serves 6 to 8.*

2 envelopes unflavored gelatin powder	2 teaspoons almond extract
3½ cups water	1 twenty-ounce can lichee fruit, chilled
½ cup evaporated milk	1 fifteen-ounce can loquat fruit, chilled
3 tablespoons sugar	

Sprinkle the gelatin over the water in a saucepan, stirring. Then bring to a boil over moderate heat, stirring constantly until the gelatin has dissolved. When the water boils, turn heat very low and add the milk, sugar, and almond extract, stirring until the sugar dissolves.

Pour the liquid into a shallow dish and refrigerate for about 4 hours, or until firm. You may make this 1 to 2 days in advance. It will keep about 4 days refrigerated.

When ready to serve, cut the jelly into squares or diamond shapes and put them in a serving bowl. Add the chilled canned lichees and loquats (either 1 can of either or half of each) plus the juices, and serve.

VARIATIONS

You could use any canned or stewed fruits that strike your fancy, like mandarin oranges, figs, sliced pears, brandied peaches, or sugared or liqueur-marinated strawberries.

八寶飯 CHINESE RICE PUDDING

This is a classic dessert, frequently served at formal dinners. It uses glutinous rice for a soft, creamy consistency, red bean paste for filling, and preserved or candied fruits for decoration. The rice is first boiled and then formed and steamed into a mound. It is rich, and *serves 6 to 8.*

1 cup glutinous rice
1 cup cold water
¾ cup red bean paste
2 tablespoons sugar
2 tablespoons oil
1 cup Chinese or Western pre-
    served or candied mixed fruits

Sauce:
1 cup water
¼ cup sugar, or to taste
2 teaspoons cornstarch dissolved
    in 2 tablespoons water

Rinse and drain the rice. Put it in a saucepan, add the water, and bring to a boil. Turn the heat very low, cover, and let it steam-cook for 30 minutes. In the meantime, soften the red bean paste by putting it into a glass in a pan of hot water for 30 minutes. When the rice has cooked, add the sugar and oil, stirring until well mixed.

Grease a 3- or 4-cup sloping heatproof bowl well with oil or shortening.

Chinese mixed fruits, preserved in syrup, are large, thick, oddly shaped, and colorful. Slice them thinner and arrange them in a pattern on the bottom of the bowl; place some smaller pieces in vertical lines up along the sides. If you use the smaller Western candied fruits, scatter them over the bottom and sides of the bowl in any pattern you like. If the fruits slide, press tiny bits of the rice against the bowl and then adhere fruits to the rice.

Divide the rice into 3 portions. Stir the softened red bean paste and divide it into 2 portions. Spread 1 portion of the rice over the fruits, pressing lightly to form a firm layer. Then fill the bowl with alternate layers of red bean paste and rice, smoothing the final layer of rice with the back of a spoon to pack it down. This can be done up to 3 or 4 days in advance; in fact, the flavor and texture improve with this mellowing time. Cover and refrigerate; bring it out just before the steaming.

When ready to cook, set the bowl in a steamer and steam over medium heat for 1 to 1½ hours, until piping hot and very soft.

Near the end of the cooking time, make the sauce by bringing the water and sugar to a boil in a small saucepan, stirring until the sugar is dissolved. Turn the heat low, add the dissolved cornstarch, and stir in circular motions until smooth. Turn off the heat, cover, and keep warm.

When the rice pudding is ready, remove it from the steamer and invert it over a serving plate. Touch up the fruit pattern if it's askew. Pour the sauce on top of the pudding and serve hot. Cut out a small wedge and spoon a little of the sugary sauce over it for each person.

VARIATIONS

Any number of fruits may be substituted or added, such as sugared lotus seeds, honeyed Peking dates, gingko nuts, canned or peeled and pitted dried lichee fruits, canned loquats, brandied white raisins, peaches, or figs. As an added festive touch, heat 1 ounce cognac or rum, pour it over the pudding, and set it ablaze.

元宵　## NEW YEAR DUMPLINGS

Symbolic of good fortune because they are round, smooth, and full, these small dumplings are a traditional New Year treat as well as a year-round snack or dessert. The dough is smooth and satiny and a little chewy. The filling is sweet and nutty, with the fragrance of the cassia blossoms. *This recipe serves 4.*

Filling:
1 tablespoon sesame paste
1 tablespoon oil
3½ tablespoons red bean paste
1 tablespoon preserved cassia
   blossoms

Dough:
1 cup glutinous rice powder
½ cup cold water, plus a little more

Filling

Scrape the sesame paste into a bowl. Heat 1 tablespoon oil in a small skillet until hot; then pour it over the sesame paste and stir it in until the sesame paste is soft and pasty. Add the red bean paste and cassia blossoms and stir in circular motions until well blended. Put the bowl in the refrigerator and chill for 30 minutes until the filling is firm. Divide it into 16 portions and roll them in the palm of your hand to make small balls. The filling can be made long in advance. Cover and refrigerate.

Making the dumplings

Add the ½ cup cold water to the glutinous rice powder, mixing and squeezing with your hands until a dough forms; add more cold water little by little until the dough holds smoothly, not flaking when you pinch or flatten it. Roll it out into a long sausage about 16 inches long; then cut the sausage into 16 pieces.

Press each piece of dough into a small disk, place a ball of filling in the center, fold over the side, pinch the seam closed, and then roll with your palms to make a small ball. Repeat until all 16 dumplings are formed. The dumplings may be made in advance. Cover and refrigerate.

Boiling the dumplings

Bring 6 cups of water to a rolling boil in a large saucepan; drop in the balls one by one, and let them toss in the vigorously boiling water over medium-high heat for about 5 minutes, until they float and spin to the top of the water. Scoop them into individual bowls and cover with some of the water. Serve immediately, 4 to a bowl.

炒
山
藥　CREAM OF YAM WITH
SUGARED WALNUTS

Simmered with ginger to cut the plain sweetness, the yams are mashed, stir-fried in oil until piping hot and creamy, then served with a generous topping of sugared walnuts. It is a rich but not overly sweet dessert. Deep-fried with the inner skin on, the walnuts are astoundingly light and brittle, and full of that delicious toasted flavor that the Chinese call "charred fragrance." They are almost impossible to stop eating. This would also be delicious as a vegetable accompaniment for roast turkey, ham, or game. *Serves 4 to 6.*

1 pound small yams	*Sugared walnuts:*
1 piece peeled ginger, about	1 cup shelled walnuts, either
½ inch thick, smashed	halves or broken pieces
2 tablespoons sugar	1 cup boiling water
	3 tablespoons sugar
	1 cup oil

Simmering the yams

Select the small oblong-shaped yams without the fibrous pointed ends—they are deeper in color and sweeter than the large ones. Peel, rinse, and cut each in half. Cover them with 3 cups cold water in a small saucepan and bring to a boil with the ginger. Turn heat low, cover, and simmer for 30 minutes. Remove from the water and place them in a bowl. Discard the ginger. Mash yams well with the back of a spoon or in a potato ricer until smooth, picking out and discarding any stringy fibers. Add 2 tablespoons sugar and stir until the sugar disappears. This may be done in advance. Cover and leave at room temperature for a couple of hours or refrigerate for hours or overnight.

Deep-frying the walnuts

While the yams are simmering, place the nuts in a strainer over the sink, and shake to rid them of any powdery residue. Put the nuts into a large bowl and cover with 1 cup boiling water; soak them for 3 minutes. Pour into the strainer and shake until the water is completely drained off.

Wipe the bowl dry, return the nuts, and toss them with 3 tablespoons sugar until the sugar sticks to them. Spread the nuts on a plate to cool for 15 minutes.

Heat a skillet over high heat until very hot; add the oil and heat for about 10 seconds, until it floats a cube of bread but barely foams it, about 240 degrees. Turn heat to medium low, pour in the walnuts, and deep-fry for 3½ to 4 minutes, stirring gently and constantly, until the walnuts are glowingly brown in color and the sugar coating is glistening, about to be caramelized. Do not permit them to be deeply browned; once darkened, they are bitter. Pour the oil and nuts immediately into a strainer over a pot. When the oil has drained off, spread them on a plate or tray, separating all the pieces. Let them cool and harden. This may be done hours in advance. Once cold, the walnuts may be bottled, to stay crisp and delicious for weeks.

Finishing the dessert

Heat a skillet over high heat until hot; add 3 tablespoons of the oil, swirl, and heat for 30 seconds. Add the mashed yams and stir with a spatula in pressing and turning motions for about 3 minutes until the mixture is hot and creamy. Pour into a serving dish, smoothing it into a mound, and cover the top with half or all of the sugared walnuts.

APPENDIX

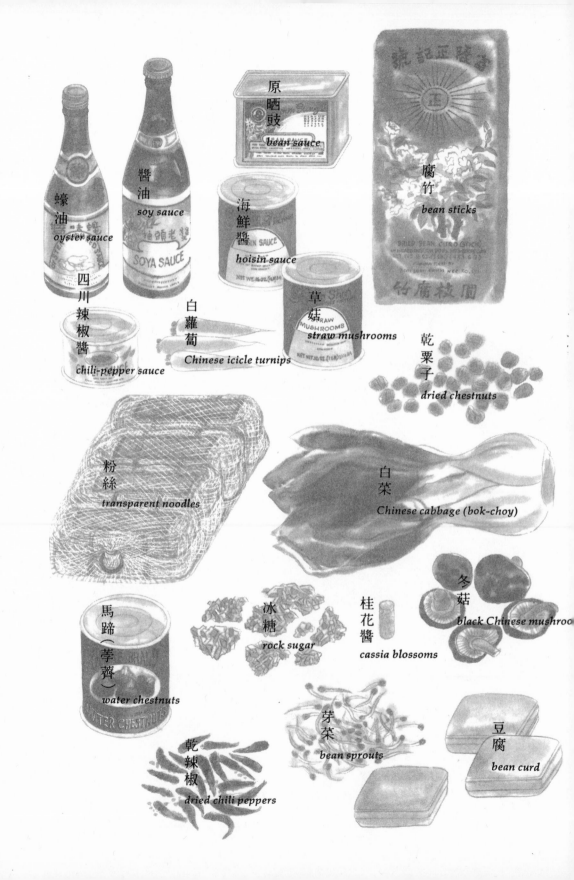

蠔油
oyster sauce

醬油
soy sauce

原晒豉
bean sauce

海鮮醬
hoisin sauce

腐竹
bean sticks

四川辣椒醬
chili-pepper sauce

白蘿葡
Chinese icicle turnips

草菇
straw mushrooms

乾栗子
dried chestnuts

粉絲
transparent noodles

白菜
Chinese cabbage (bok-choy)

冬菇
black Chinese mushroom

馬蹄（荸薺）
water chestnuts

冰糖
rock sugar

桂花醬
cassia blossoms

芽菜
bean sprouts

豆腐
bean curd

乾辣椒
dried chili peppers

腊腸
Chinese sausages

燕窩
birds' nests

東洋菜
agar-agar

豆豉
black beans

醬瓜
pickled cucumbers

紅豆沙
red bean paste

冬筍
bamboo shoots

黃芽白菜
celery cabbage

生薑
ginger

芥菜
Chinese mustard greens

春筍
spring bamboo shoots

花椒
Szechuan peppercorns

金針菜
golden needles

蓮子
lotus seeds

八角
star anise

木耳
cloud ears

芫茜
(coriander) Chinese parsley

雪豆
snow peas

CHINESE
INGREDIENTS

Everything you need for Chinese cooking, from seasonings to fresh produce, is now available in the United States. Browsing through a well-stocked Chinese grocery store in a major Chinatown is like going through the stalls of a market in Taiwan or Hong Kong. But, lest they become relics in the pantry or waste in the trash can, you should make initial purchases in small quantities and limit yourself to essentials, expanding only as you delve deeper into Chinese cooking.

Seasonings are the most crucial. Combined with the food properly prepared and cooked, they will give you dishes that will taste authentically Chinese.

If you don't have a Chinese market in your area, consult the listings on *page 504* for ordering by mail.

鮑
魚　*Abalone*

The meat from an iridescent-shelled mollusk, sold already cooked, in cans. The best kind is imported from Japan; the pieces are small and very silky and tender. Abalone can be eaten directly from the can, sliced thin as a cold appetizer, shredded or sliced for stir-frying with meats and vegetables, or cut into chunks and simmered with meat or poultry. The cooking should be limited to a few minutes, since prolonged cooking will toughen the texture.

東
洋
菜　*Agar-agar*

A processed seaweed, grayish white in color and resembling shredded crinkled cellophane. After being soaked in cold water, it becomes bouncy, resilient, and crunchily crisp. It is used mostly for cold dishes, with chicken, meat, and vegetables. It is sold in 4-ounce packages, and the thin strips measure about 14 inches long. In the old days, before the introduction of gelatin, agar-agar was also used as a thickening agent in making cold jellied dishes. Once soaked in boiling water, it melts into a gelatinous substance.

冬 *Bamboo shoots*
筍

The ivory-colored shoots of bamboo plants are sold in cans—in chunks, slices, or diced. Light and crisp, they are used primarily as a complementary ingredient, to lighten a dish. Some canned bamboo shoots have a faint peculiar odor, which can be eliminated with a good rinsing, brief blanching, or exploding with hot oil. Once the can is opened, the bamboo shoots should be put into a glass jar, covered with water, and refrigerated. Change the water frequently. They will then last for weeks.

春 *Bamboo shoots, spring*
筍

These are small whole shoots, picked and packed during the spring, when new bamboo plants are just beginning to sprout. These are cultivated only for eating. They are tender and crisp, and are wonderful simmered with red-cooked meats and poultry. Like regular bamboo shoots, they must be kept in a glass jar filled with water, which should be changed frequently.

豆 *Bean curd*
腐

Made of soybean powder, fresh bean curd comes in square cakes measuring 2½ or 3 inches to a side. They are white and have the consistency of a firm custard. If you submerge them in water, and frequently change it, they will keep for about a week in the refrigerator.

Of all the vegetarian products, bean curd is the most versatile and important in the Chinese cuisine. Bland but absorbent, soft-textured but strong, it is conducive to all types of cooking. It can be scalded, boiled, simmered, steamed, stir-fried, shallow-fried, and deep-fried with beautiful results. Adding substance without intruding much taste, it combines well with everything. Highly nutritious and very inexpensive, bean curd represents such a good buy that the slang expression in eastern Chinese dialects for taking advantage of a person is "eating bean curd."

豆
腐
乾   *Bean curd, pressed*

When the water is extracted from fresh bean-curd cakes by pressing them with a weight, the bean curd becomes firm and compact. Simmered in water with soy sauce, star anise, and sugar, the pressed bean curd acquires a smooth, resilient texture that is quite unusual. Cut small, it stir-fries beautifully with meat and vegetables; and when cut into chunks it is delicious simmered with red-cooked meats and poultry. In China, pressed bean curd was a vendors' specialty, simmered whole and steeped in a rich flavor-pot brine; you could buy this on the street or at the theater.

原
晒
豉   *Bean paste (sauce)*

This is a thick brown paste made from fermented soybeans, flour, and salt. It comes in two forms: the regular, which contains whole beans and which I prefer, and the ground, which is puréed and more widely available. The latter is slightly saltier, and if you buy it, use it with a little more sugar. A major seasoning agent of the northern and Szechuan schools of cooking, bean paste not only colors the food and thickens the sauce, but also gives the dishes a distinctive flavor.

Bean paste comes in cans. Transferred to a covered jar, it keeps indefinitely in the refrigerator. To prevent the ground bean paste from drying out during long storage, add a little oil or sesame oil, stir well, and then refrigerate. Bean paste is frequently labeled sauce.

紅
豆
沙   *Bean paste, red and/or sweet*

This reddish-brown paste is made of puréed red beans and sugar. It is sold in cans and keeps indefinitely if refrigerated in a covered container. It is used for sweet fillings, as in Chinese Rice Pudding or New Year Dumplings.

辣
椒
豆
瓣
醬   *Bean sauce or paste, hot*

This is a Szechuan specialty; crushed chili peppers are added to the regular bean paste. It is a marvelous spicy agent, giving food a muted hotness. Transferred from the can to a covered jar, it keeps indefinitely in the refrigerator.

芽
菜　*Bean sprouts*

Grown from small pea-like beans known as mung beans, bean sprouts are sold by weight in Chinese markets and in packages by some supermarkets in large cities. They must be soaked in water for storage in the refrigerator. When fresh and at their best, they are white and plump; they become rusty and skinny if kept too long. One week is really their limit in the refrigerator. Bean sprouts are also available in cans, but they don't have the same crisp texture. If you can't find fresh ones, sprout your own.

SPROUTING MUNG BEANS—Wash ½ cup dried mung beans and discard any imperfect ones. Drain the beans and then cover them with lukewarm water; soak them overnight.

Wring out 2 large pieces of double-layered cheesecloth in warm water. Place one over the bottom of a colander; add the beans; then cover them with the other piece of wet cheesecloth. Sprinkle the surface with ½ cup warm water, let it drain, and then set the colander over a shallow pan. Put the pan and colander in a warm, dark place, such as inside a closet. The beans will not sprout below 68 degrees and the sprouts won't be white and plump if exposed to light. Spray the colander with ½ cup lukewarm water at least 4 times a day, draining off the base pan after each spraying.

The sprouting beans will mature and be ready for eating in about 4 to 5 days, depending on the temperature of the sprouting place—the ideal temperature is about 75 degrees.

Remove the cheesecloth and dump the sprouts into a large pot of water. Rinse them gently, drain, leaving green hulls behind, and they're ready for cooking. A half cup of beans will yield about 3 cups of sprouts. The beans are available by the pound in Chinese markets and health-food stores or by mail order.

腐
竹　*Bean sticks*

Made of soybean milk, these come in double-fold curled sticks, measuring about 11 inches long. They are tan in color and glossy and hard. After soaking (*see page 190*) they become soft and white. Simmering makes them very soft and stir-frying makes them chewy with a slight nutty flavor. They keep well tightly wrapped, but after a long time they may acquire a faintly rancid taste.

燕
窩
Birds' nests

No ordinary birds' nests, these are made by the small Asian swifts indigenous to the shore of the South China Sea. They are composed of predigested seaweed from the mouths of the birds. The gelatinous material hardens and forms a small translucent cup. Rare and expensive, they are treasured by the Chinese as a great delicacy. To many people, a banquet, no matter how elaborate, is not a feast without the birds' nests.

Sold in beautifully designed boxes with a window for examining, birds' nests come in three forms: the whole, the broken whole, and the ground. Since the whole or broken ones are expensive and tedious to clean, I prefer using the ground nests, even though they are taboo to classic chefs. Actually, however, the value of the nests is in their light, brittle texture, not their form or flavor. Since the nests are reputed to be youth-giving and are in truth highly nutritious (they are almost pure protein), many Chinese women used to drink a small cup of simmered birds' nest every day. Besides being simmered in stock, birds' nests are sometimes simmered with water and rock sugar for serving as a sweet course at a banquet.

豆
豉
Black beans, fermented

These are a wonderful seasoning agent, particularly when accompanied by garlic. Usually covered with salt, they should be rinsed briefly and chopped before being used. They come in plastic bags, bottles, and cans, and will keep indefinitely in a tightly covered jar, needing no refrigeration.

Bok-choy: see Cabbage, Chinese

黃
芽
白
菜
Cabbage, celery

There are two varieties of this cabbage: the long and the short heads. The long ones, available in most supermarkets and grocery stores, are compact and pale green, with almost all of the vegetable in the stem. This type is especially good for making Spicy Cold Celery Cabbage since it offers more crisp stalk than soft leaves. The short variety is chubby and much leafier; it is sold only in Chinese or Oriental markets. Both are very popular vegetables, used in stir-frying, simmering with meats and poultry, and as moisturizers for fillings.

Both varieties keep well for about 1 week in a closed plastic bag, refrigerated.

白 *Cabbage, Chinese*
菜

This is called "white vegetable" in Chinese—pronounced *bai-tsai* in Mandarin and *bok-choy* in Cantonese. It is a white-stalked and green-leafed vegetable that sometimes sports a flowering center. The taste resembles Swiss chard a little, though Chinese cabbage is sweeter and juicier. It is available only in Chinese or Oriental markets, and is sold by weight (the stalks may vary from ½ to 1 pound). It keeps well for about a week tightly wrapped and refrigerated.

桂 *Cassia blossoms, preserved*
花
醬

These tiny yellow four-petaled blossoms of the cassia tree are marvelously fragrant. They are preserved in salt and sugar and sold in small bottles; they are used to perfume sweet things.

乾 *Chestnuts, dried blanched*
粟
子

Dehydrated chestnuts, shelled and blanched, ready to be used with simmered meats and poultry or for desserts. They must be soaked and simmered (*page 255*) before they're used. They are sold by weight in plastic bags. They keep well, but after a long time they develop a rancid taste. You can, of course, substitute fresh chestnuts: see *page 255* for preparing them to be cooked.

乾 *Chili peppers, dried*
辣
椒

The kind of dried chili pepper used in the book is thin, about 2 inches long, and scarlet red. You can find them, sold by weight, in Chinese, Italian, or Greek stores. They are extremely hot—a few go a long way. They are used to season the oil before the ingredients are added in a stir-fried dish and they are also used for making chili-pepper oil. They keep indefinitely in a tightly covered jar, without refrigeration.

辣 *Chili-pepper oil*
椒
油

This is indispensable to a kitchen where spicy food is favored. It may be used in salads, dip sauces, or added during cooking.

Heat 1 cup oil in a small saucepan until very hot; turn heat low and add ¼ cup crushed chili pepper flakes, or 3 tablespoons powdered chili, or 10 to 12 whole dried chili peppers, and stir for about 1 minute. Turn off heat. When the oil is completely cool, stir well, then strain the oil into a small bottle through cheesecloth or a paper napkin. The oil will keep for a month without losing its flavor.

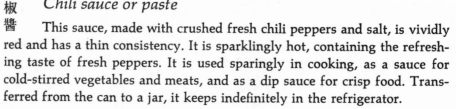

四
川
辣
椒
醬

Chili sauce or paste

This sauce, made with crushed fresh chili peppers and salt, is vividly red and has a thin consistency. It is sparklingly hot, containing the refreshing taste of fresh peppers. It is used sparingly in cooking, as a sauce for cold-stirred vegetables and meats, and as a dip sauce for crisp food. Transferred from the can to a jar, it keeps indefinitely in the refrigerator.

Cloud ears: see Mushrooms, mo-er

芫
茜

Coriander (the Chinese parsley)

This flat-leafed, long-stemmed herb is quite strong in flavor and aroma—almost medicinal. It is used primarily as a seasoning agent or garnish, most often with seafood and poultry. Fresh coriander is available in Chinese, Latin-American, and Italian grocery stores, called *cilantro* in the last. It will remain fresh for a week to 10 days in the refrigerator if you keep the roots in water and the leaves covered by a plastic bag.

Its distinctive fresh flavor is unique, and one I particularly love. If you have a garden, it is a very easy annual to plant, and it thrives in poor soil as well as rich.

If you cannot find it, substitute Italian flat-leaf parsley.

醬
瓜

Cucumbers, pickled

Made from a special type of Chinese cucumber, known as the "flower cucumber," these are very crisp, with that distinctive refreshing smell of cucumbers. They come in small cans, soaked in a soy-sauce brine. If you transfer them to a tightly covered jar, they will keep indefinitely in the refrigerator. The cucumbers are an excellent relish as is, and shredded or diced they add a marvelous taste and texture to other ingredients. Minced, they are very good as a seasoning agent for cold-stirred dishes, such as noodles or vegetable salads. And they are nice in wonton soup.

蘇
梅
醬 *"Duck" sauce*

"Duck" sauce, really plum sauce, is so named because it was served with duck during the early days of Chinese restaurants in America. It is made from plums, apricots, chilies, vinegar, and sugar—a sweet and pungent condiment that has since become a standard dip sauce, particularly popular with egg rolls or roast pork.

五
香
粉 *Five-fragrance powder*

Also sold as "Five Powdered Spices," this is a powerful spice made from ground anise, fennel, cloves, cinnamon, and ginger. It is used sparingly to give food a distinctive aroma and flavor, most noticeably the sweet, pungent flavor of anise.

生
薑 *Ginger, fresh*

This is the ginger root, a knobby affair. In selecting, look for one that is smooth and firm. In almost all dishes it should be peeled first; this is specified in the recipes. Fresh ginger is indispensable to good Chinese cooking. It is used in small quantities as a subtle seasoning agent as well as a subduer of undesirable tastes, such as fishiness, the strong "organ" flavor of meat, and the grassy, raw taste of some vegetables.

Fresh ginger may be stored in a plastic bag in the refrigerator for weeks and keeps fresh in salted water for months.

A standard measurement in this book is 2 quarter-sized slices of ginger, which equals 1 teaspoon chopped. By "quarter-sized" I mean approximately the size of the American coin. Since the main trunk of a ginger root is about the circumference of a quarter, it is easy as you slice off a thin piece to approximate this measure.

Powdered ginger or dried ginger may not be substituted.

白
果 *Gingko nuts*

The beige-colored pits of the gingko fruit are used as a vegetable-fruit garnish in soups or vegetarian dishes. They come in cans, packed in brine. Submerged in water, they keep for 2 to 3 weeks in the refrigerator if you change the water regularly.

金
針 **Golden Needles** (tiger-lily buds)
菜
    Dried tiger-lily buds, Golden Needles have to be soaked and rinsed and the knobby ends picked off. They are wonderful in stir-frying or simmering with other ingredients because they both absorb and lend flavor. These are sold in packages and they keep indefinitely if sealed in a plastic bag or kept in a covered jar.

火 **Ham**
腿
    China produces some of the best hams in the world, particularly those from Che-kiang and Yunnan provinces. They are similar in taste, texture, and color to Smithfield ham. Like dried shrimp, ham is an important seasoning in Chinese cooking.

    Chinese meat markets in the United States sell Smithfield ham by the pound; most other meat markets sell only the entire ham. Since the meat is quite salty, it should be soaked and cooked as follows before you use it.

    Get a 2-pound piece. Scrape and clean off the pepper coating and soak the ham in cold water for an hour, then rinse well and simmer with water to cover for about 40 minutes. Trim off the fat; cut the meat with the grain into 2-inch-wide pieces. Place them in a large jar. Make a sugar solution by dissolving 4 tablespoons sugar in 2 cups boiling water. When cooled, pour over the ham, add 2 tablespoons dry sherry, screw on the cover, and refrigerate. The ham keeps indefinitely and is ready when you need it.

    Once you have the sugar-soaked ham on hand, you might even try it as an appetizer. Cut 1 or 2 pieces against the grain into thin slices. Dip them in cornstarch and deep-fry until the coating is crusty. Place them on a platter and serve with toothpicks with drinks.

    Sliced and steamed for 20 minutes with a little honey and preserved cassia blossoms, this ham makes an exotic appetizer for a formal dinner.

    If you cannot get Smithfield ham by the pound and don't feel like getting a whole one, try smoked knuckles, widely sold in supermarkets, usually in packages of one or two knuckles. They are not as flavorful as Smithfield ham, but they are easy to work with. Steam them over medium heat for 1½ to 2 hours, until the meat and skin shrink from the bone. Slip out the bones and chill the meat until firm before shredding or mincing it for cooking. To store, simply wrap it tightly and refrigerate.

    Another good substitute is the small Westphalian hams. They do not have to be cooked before use. Wrap and refrigerate to store.

海鮮醬 *Hoisin sauce*

This sauce, made from soybeans, flour, sugar, salt, garlic, and chili peppers, is reddish brown and has a creamy consistency. It gives food a glowing hue and seasons to a sweet piquancy. It is used in cooking as well as for a dip sauce. Hoisin sauce is sold in cans. Transferred to a covered jar, it will keep indefinitely in the refrigerator. If it appears a little too dry after long storage, stir in a little oil or sesame oil to soften it.

When using it as a dip sauce for duck or meat, I like to mix it with a little peanut butter and sesame oil. The ratio is 4 parts hoisin sauce to 1 part each peanut butter and sesame oil. This is a great combination—you will love it.

蓮子 *Lotus seeds*

Small pale-yellow seeds from the lotus that are available dried, either with the skin on or blanched. They are used for desserts. Stored in a bottle, they keep indefinitely. They also come in cans. Once opened, they should be soaked in water and refrigerated.

味精 *MSG (monosodium glutamate)*

What we knew as "taste-essence" in China was a seasoning agent made at home primarily from dried fermented wheat gluten and/or soybean protein, often further enriched with powdered dry shrimp or seaweeds. It was used to enhance weak flavors, such as watered-down broths, poorly seasoned foods from unskilled hands, or meager meat dishes, intensifying primarily the natural flavors of meat and poultry. While "taste-essence" is of Chinese heritage, it was never accepted by the elite society of gastronomy where cooking skill and lavish use of natural ingredients are the essence. Today's version is a chemical compound known as monosodium glutamate or MSG and to me it does nothing to enhance flavor. Rather it gives food a peculiar sweetened taste that I find absolutely distasteful, and for some people it has unpleasant side effects.

粉皮 *Mung bean sheets*

Mung bean sheets, made of ground mung beans, just as transparent noodles, come in round sheets, measuring about 8 inches in diameter. They must be soaked in boiling water for about 30 minutes until they are soft and chalk white before they may be used as a salad ingredient or for cooking. Like most dry ingredients, mung bean sheets may be presoaked and kept soft and resilient for a few hours at room temperature, but once chilled in the refrigerator, the texture hardens and the sheets need to be resoaked in boiling water until soft before using.

Mung bean sheets are sold in plastic bags in Chinese food stores and they keep indefinitely.

冬 *Mushrooms, dried black Chinese*
菇

Earthily flavorful, these dried mushrooms range from the size of a quarter to 3 inches in diameter. Their color varies from black to speckled brown or gray. The flavor is better in the medium-sized, thick-capped ones. Dried mushrooms must be soaked in hot water for at least 30 minutes so they will assume their original size and become soft again. Since they always contain a little sand, they must be rinsed briefly before being used, and the stems should always be removed. The soaking water, with its concentrated mushroom flavor, is often reserved for adding to the dish. Dried black mushrooms are sold by weight and keep indefinitely in a covered container.

木 *Mushrooms, mo-er (cloud ears)*
耳

A specialty of Szechuan province, this crinkly tree fungus is also known as "cloud ears." Instead of being spongy like black mushrooms or silky like straw mushrooms, they are thin and brittle. They come in small dry chips, sold in packages. After being soaked in hot water for 30 minutes they expand into resilient clusters of dark brown petals. They should be rinsed well to remove any sand, and the hard "eye" in the center of any large cluster should be discarded. Although mo-er mushrooms have no real flavor or aroma, their texture is incomparable. They combine well with any ingredient as long as the sauce is lightly glazed so that the nonabsorbent mo-er will be flavored by the seasonings.

草 *Mushrooms, straw*
菇

These small yellow mushrooms with pointed black caps are sold in cans. Their texture is wonderfully silky. Once the can is opened, they should be rinsed and transferred to a covered jar and refrigerated. They keep about a week, but you should use them as soon as possible, since storing them in water weakens their delicate taste.

芥
末 *Mustard*

Served as a condiment in all Chinese restaurants, Chinese hot mustard is much hotter than jarred varieties. It is made with English mustard powder diluted with water. Put 3 tablespoons of the mustard in a bowl, gradually stir in 4 to 5 tablespoons cold water, and keep stirring until it forms a thin paste. Transfer to a small bottle and let it mellow for at least 1 hour before using. If used immediately it is harsh and bitter, but with a little time to rest it becomes hot and pungent. The mustard will keep, refrigerated, for a few weeks without losing much of its pungency, but it is always better to make a small amount so you can have it at full potency. The powder is available in tins at specialty shops, better markets, and Chinese grocery stores. Tightly covered, it keeps indefinitely.

芥
菜 *Mustard greens, Chinese*

Short, chubby, and oddly shaped, this green-stalked, green-leafed vegetable has a slightly bitter aftertaste that is much appreciated by the southern Chinese. They are sold by weight and will keep for a week if tightly wrapped and refrigerated.

Mustard stems, Szechuan preserved: see Szechuan preserved mustard stems

麵 *Noodles, Chinese*

The best Chinese noodles are freshly made egg noodles, which can be purchased in Chinatown groceries and noodle factories in most large cities. But you can use commercial substitutes, see page 432.

粉
絲 *Noodles, transparent or cellophane*

Whitish and thin, these are made from powdered mung beans and are sold in packages of a few ounces to 1 pound. Once soaked, they become bouncy and translucent. In spite of being called "noodles," they are considered a vegetable product and are often used in soups and in stir-fried or simmered dishes.

Readily absorbent and bulky, they are marvelous extenders. For instance, if you have some leftover red-cooked meat or poultry, not quite enough to serve alone, add some presoaked transparent noodles and simmer to get a substantial, very tasty dish. Be sure not to overcook them—no more than 10 minutes—or they will become jellylike.

蠔
油 *Oyster sauce*

This is a thick brown sauce made of ground oysters and other ingredients. A Cantonese seasoning, it gives color and a subtle "meaty" flavor to food. A good brand is never fishy. It comes in bottles and large cans, and keeps indefinitely tightly covered.

雪
裏
紅 *Red-in-snow*

Resembling radish tops, this delicious green pickled vegetable is remarkably refreshing and crisp. It is often used as a seasoning in stir-fried pork dishes. It comes in small cans and will keep well in a tightly covered jar.

The name comes from its red roots and the fact that it comes up very early in the spring, often visible in the snow.

糯
米 *Rice, glutinous*

This round-grained rice, which becomes very soft and sticky when cooked, is used for desserts and sweet or savory stuffings. It is sold by weight in bags. Store as you would regular rice.

糯
米
粉 *Rice powder, glutinous*

This flour, made of glutinous rice, is used in dough wrappers for specialty desserts and snacks. After steaming or boiling, the dough becomes chewy and resilient. The powder is sold in 1-pound packages and should be stored as regular flour is.

米
粉 *Rice sticks*

White, thin, and slightly wavy, these sticks (also called rice noodles) are made from ground rice. They are a southern specialty, used in soups and snacks like regular noodles or deep-fried as a garnish for minced dishes. More fragile than wheat noodles, they need only a brief soaking and cooking. They come in ½-pound packages, rolled in tight wads.

Salt-pepper, roasted: see Szechuan salt-pepper, roasted

腊　*Sausages, Chinese*
腸
　　Made with pork, pork liver, or duck liver, the sausages come in hard, compact little links, about 6 inches long, looped in pairs by string or sealed in plastic bags and sold by weight. They are tasty but fatty, and must be steamed until soft and plump before being eaten as is or sliced to cook briefly with other ingredients. They keep well for a month in the refrigerator and indefinitely in the freezer.

紫　*Seaweed, purple*
菜
　　Purple, shiny, and as thin as transparent rice paper, this dried, pressed seaweed is sold in packages. It is used for quick soups. Sealed in a plastic bag, it keeps indefinitely.

蔴　*Sesame oil*
油
　　Thick, light brown in color, and wonderfully aromatic, this oil is made from roasted sesame seeds. The thicker it is, the better the flavor. Sesame oil is used as a seasoning more than for cooking because it burns too easily. It comes in bottles and large cans. The aroma remains indefinitely if the oil is tightly covered at all times.

　　Do not buy the light yellow cold-pressed American sesame oil; it is not the same thing at all.

芝
蔴　*Sesame paste*
醬
　　This comes in a jar covered with oil. The paste is hard and resembles clay in color and consistency, but is extremely aromatic, rich, and tasty. It is used primarily as a dressing for cold vegetables and meats. You must dilute the paste scooped from jar with hot oil or water and then stir it into a creamy paste before using it.

　　If you don't have any sesame paste, a good substitute is peanut butter creamed with a little sesame oil.

蝦
米　*Shrimp, dried*

Highly valued by the Chinese as a seasoning, particularly in vegetable dishes, these small shrimp are salted and dried so that their flavor intensifies during the process. They range in size—the best buy are curled up, about 1 inch from head to tail. They should be bright pink. They turn gray when too old. Dried shrimp must be soaked in hot water for at least 30 minutes before being simmered with other ingredients, and longer if they are going to be stir-fried briefly or used without any cooking. Since they are extremely tasty but have a strong "sea" flavor—no Chinese would ever call them "fishy"—a good way to partially neutralize their strong odor is to soak them in sherry overnight, instead of water. They are sold in ½- to 1-pound packages and keep well as long as they're stored in a sealed plastic bag or a jar.

雪
豆　*Snow peas*

Flat and green, containing the mere outline of the new peas, snow-pea pods are used mainly in Cantonese stir-fried dishes, to give a crisp texture and bright color. They keep well for about 2 weeks sealed in a plastic bag and refrigerated, but they are at their crisp best if eaten soon after buying them. They should be rinsed, stringed, blanched very briefly, and sprayed with cold water before using.

There are frozen snow peas, but they are small, dull-colored, and soggy in comparison. Rather than using this inferior frozen substitute if you can't get fresh ones, use peeled and thinly sliced broccoli stems.

Soybean sticks: see Bean sticks

醬
油　*Soy sauce*

Soy sauces are made from fermented soybeans, wheat, yeast, salt, and sugar. They are the most important of the Chinese seasonings. They are used for cooking, marinating, and as a dip sauce; they enhance the flavor and color of food and they tenderize meat. They are sold as light (sometimes called thin) and dark (sometimes labeled black), and they range in quality, flavor, and degree of saltiness. There are numerous brands; the best are imported from Hongkong, Taiwan, and China. Japanese soy sauce is not a good substitute at all.

The light (or thin) soy sauce: A good one has a clear brown color, not "muddy," and its aroma is beany. It is used for delicate dishes.

The dark (or black) soy sauce: A good one is very dark with a sheen, and it is slightly thicker than the light soy sauce. Its aroma is subtly sweet and the bean aroma muted. It is used whenever a deep glowing color is wanted, and it is indispensable to red-cooked dishes.

Both types of soy sauce come in bottles and large cans. Once opened, the canned sauce must be transferred to tightly covered jars or bottles.

八角 Star anise

A hard, star-shaped spice, made up of the dried seeds plus pod of the anise shrub. It is used in simmering meats and poultry and in making flavor-pot brine. Sold by weight, often in small plastic bags, star anise should be stored as you would any dry spice, in a tightly covered jar.

麥芽糖 Sugar, malt

A very heavy malt sugar that is sold under the name of Genuine Maltose. It is an import from China and comes in a nice crock, 1 pound weight. It is used to coat duck skin so that it browns deeply and beautifully in roasting. Honey may be used as a substitute.

冰糖 Sugar, rock

Made from raw sugar, these chunks of crystallized sugar are indispensable to the red-cooking of meats and poultry. They are sweet but have a subtlety that granulated sugar lacks, and they thicken and glaze beautifully. (In a pinch, however, you may substitute granulated sugar.) To crush them, wrap them in a towel and smash them with a hammer or a mallet.

花
椒 Szechuan peppercorns

These tiny, reddish-brown peppercorns have a strong, pungent smell that distinguishes them from black peppercorns, which are hotter. In taste, they numb rather than burn. They are a regional product of Szechuan province and are used a great deal in its native cuisine, in cooking, marinating, and curing. There are two kinds on the market—the seeded and the whole ones. Always buy the seeded ones, since the flavor and aroma come only from the petal-like husks. Szechuan peppercorns are sold by weight in small packages. If transferred to a tightly covered bottle they will retain their strength and aroma for a long time.

花
椒 Szechuan peppercorns, roasted and crushed
粉
Before adding them to a dish that calls for dry-roasting Szechuan peppercorns, heat in a skillet over low heat about 5 minutes, shaking them occasionally until they are aromatic. When cooled, crush them gently with a mortar, cleaver handle, or rolling pin.

花
椒 Szechuan peppercorn oil
油
This is a seasoned oil that is excellent for cold-stirred dishes or for stir-frying vegetables, such as celery, when you want a very subtle flavor of these exotic peppers. It's also delicious as an oil base for dip sauces to go with white-cut meat and poultry, or poached and steamed fish.

Measure 2 teaspoons Szechuan peppercorns into a small frying pan or saucepan and heat over very low heat for about 3 minutes, shaking the pan occasionally. Add 1 cup oil and heat for about 10 minutes, stirring occasionally with chopsticks. Turn off heat, and when cool, pour the oil and peppercorns into a small bottle. Screw on the top and use when needed.

榨
菜 Szechuan preserved mustard stems

A specialty of Szechuan, this spicy preserved vegetable is made with a particular kind of mustard green that has many knobby growths around each stem. It is these knobs that are preserved in salt and chili powder. They are greenish in color, hot and salty to taste, and very crisp in texture. Sliced, shredded, or diced, they are used for cooking with other ingredients or they are eaten as is with a sprinkling of sesame oil. Finely minced, they are a tasty seasoning for mixed soups, noodles, or salads. They come in cans and keep indefinitely in a covered jar.

椒
鹽 *Szechuan salt-pepper, roasted*

This is a popular national dip sauce that is used all over the country. It is especially good with deep-fried food that needs just a touch of exotic saltiness.

The ratio of salt to pepper is 3 tablespoons table salt to 1 teaspoon Szechuan peppercorns.

Measure the peppercorns into a small frying pan or saucepan and cover them with the salt. Heat the pan over extremely low heat for about 5 minutes, shaking the pan and stirring the contents occasionally with a spatula until the peppers start to smoke faintly and the salt becomes slightly browned. Turn off heat and when cool, crush the salt and pepper together with a mortar, cleaver handle, or rolling pin. Bottle and use when needed.

陳
皮 *Tangerine peels*

Primarily used as a seasoning, like star anise and cinnamon bark, dried tangerine peels, containing a deep citrus flavor, are used for preparing flavor-pot brine, for simmering meats and poultry, and for roasting ducks. Once they've rendered up their flavor they are generally discarded, except in some Szechuan specialties, in which they are shredded or minced and stir-fried in the sauce. They are sold by weight and they will keep indefinitely in a tightly covered jar. You can also make your own: sun-dry tangerine peels until they've completely hardened.

天
津
冬 *Tientsin preserved vegetable*
菜

Chopped celery cabbage preserved with salt, garlic, and spices. It has a deep flavor, and is especially good with simmered meats or poultry. It comes in lovely small crocks, tightly packed and well sealed with paper. It keeps indefinitely in the refrigerator in its own container as long as you tightly cover the opening with aluminum foil or waxed paper.

白
蘿 *Turnips, Chinese icicle*
葡

Called white turnips also. These are as light in texture as the Western white radish, but their flavor is stronger, and they are huge by comparison, measuring from 6 to over 12 inches. They are used in soups, for pickling, simmering with meats and poultry, or stir-frying, either alone or with other ingredients. They are sold by weight and keep for about 2 weeks wrapped and refrigerated.

米
醋   ## Vinegar, Chenkong rice

Black in color with a distinctive mellow flavor, Chenkong rice vinegar comes in bottles, and is used for cooking as well as for a dip sauce. A mild, good red-wine vinegar may be substituted, although its taste is really incomparable.

馬
蹄
（
荸
薺
）   ## Water chestnuts

A walnut-sized bulb covered by a tough russet-colored skin; the meat is white and crisp. In China they are eaten raw, boiled plain in their jackets, peeled and simmered with rock sugar, or candied. Except in the south, they are never used in cooking. Children used to make a game of seeing who could peel them with their teeth the fastest; they looked like squirrels. In the United States, water chestnuts are popular as an ingredient in cooked dishes, and many Americans have come to expect water chestnuts whenever they think of a crisp texture. They are available fresh or in cans, either whole or sliced. The fresh ones, which are coated with mud, can be kept in the refrigerator for about 2 weeks if they are wrapped in foil or plastic. The canned ones will keep for weeks refrigerated if you submerge them in water and change the water frequently.

馬
蹄
粉   ## Water chestnut flour

Made of ground water chestnuts, this extremely fine and light flour is used for coating when you want the crust exceptionally light. It is sold in small cellophane bags and a little goes a long way. Once opened, it should be transferred to a small bottle. It keeps indefinitely.

酒釀 *Wine rice*

This is made of fermented glutinous rice, and is used to create a deeper wine taste in a sauce or in a hot broth laced with miniature glutinous rice-flour balls and mandarin oranges for a dessert or snack. White, whole-grained, and soaked in its winy liquid, it is sold in bottles in Chinese markets. Wine rice keeps a long time if refrigerated.

冬瓜 *Winter melon*

Belonging to the squash family, this round green-skinned melon ranges in weight from 5 pounds to over 20 pounds. The pulp is white, and translucent when cooked. A whole winter melon will keep well for months in a cool place and the wedges keep for about 1 week if wrapped in aluminum foil and refrigerated. You can buy the melon either whole or in wedges. Should the outside of the pulp look a little shriveled, shave off before using.

SOURCES FOR MAIL-ORDER CHINESE FOODSTUFFS AND COOKING AND SERVING UTENSILS

South Eastern Food Supply
6732 N.E. 4th Avenue
Miami, Florida 33138

Asia Trading Company
2581 Piedmont N.E.
Atlanta, Georgia 30324

A. B. Oriental Grocery
3709 Suit Shadeland Avenue
Indianapolis, Indiana 46226

Asia House Grocery
2433 St. Paul Street
Baltimore, Maryland 21218

New England Food
225 Harrison Avenue
Boston, Massachusetts 02111

King's Trading
3736 Broadway
Kansas City, Missouri 64111

Kam Kuo Food Corporation
   (Supermarket)
7 Mott Street
New York, New York 10013

Kam Man Food Products Company
200 Canal Street
New York, New York 10013

Lee's Oriental Gifts & Food
3053 Main Street
Buffalo, New York 14214

Things for Cooking
Suite 400
888 7th Avenue
New York, New York 10019

Crestview Foodtown
200 E. Crestview Road
Columbus, Ohio 43202

Far East Company
247 West McMillian Street
Cincinnati, Ohio 45219

Friendship Enterprises
3415 Payne Avenue
Cleveland, Ohio 44114

Harmony Oriental
247 Atwood Street
Pittsburgh, Pennsylvania 15213

Hon Kee Company
935 Race Street
Philadelphia, Pennsylvania 19107

Da Hua Foods
615 I Street N.W.
Washington, D.C. 20001·

INDEX

About the author

Born into one of the oldest families in China, Irene
Kuo was raised in a home where superb cuisine was
a matter of course. After she came to the United
States, she carried on this tradition of fine Chinese
cooking when she married Major General C. C. Kuo,
military attaché in Washington, and entertained in
diplomatic circles in Washington and in Rome,
Italy. Later she opened her first restaurant in New
York, The Lichee Tree, followed some years later by
The Gingko Tree, whose cuisines she supervised very
closely. She has taught and demonstrated Chinese
cooking in many areas of the United States and
she has been widely interviewed on both the culinary and cultural aspects of China. Mrs. Kuo now
lives in New York City with her husband, who is
also well known for his work in Chinese calligraphy
as exemplified by the seals he designed for the title
pages and chapter headings of this book.

A note about the type

The text of this book was set on the Linotype in
Palatino, a type face designed by the noted German
typographer Hermann Zapf. Named after Giovan-
battista Palatino, a writing master of Renaissance
Italy, Palatino was the first of Zapf's type faces to
be introduced to America. The first designs for the
face were made in 1948, and the fonts for the complete face were issued between 1950 and 1952. Like
all Zapf-designed type faces, Palatino is beautifully
balanced and exceedingly readable.